PART VI Punctuation and Mechani[illegible]

PART VII Research and Writing

PART VIII Documentation

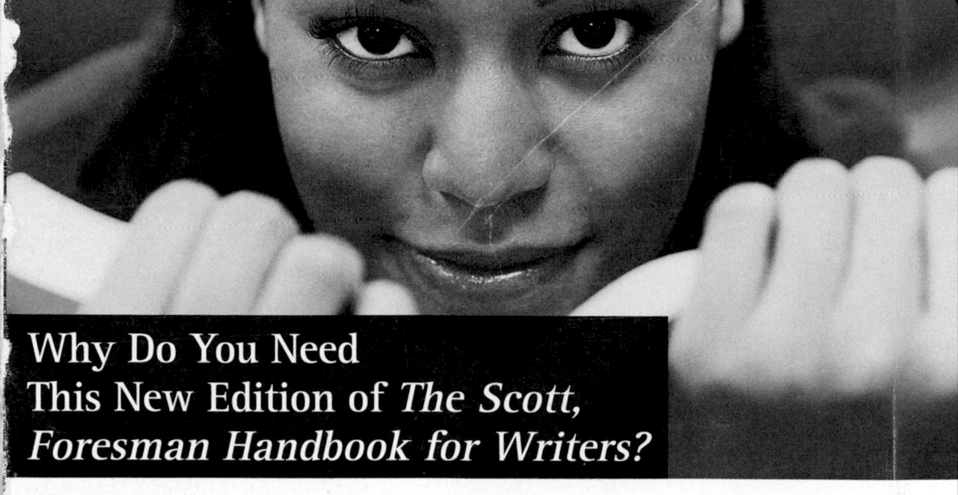

Why Do You Need This New Edition of *The Scott, Foresman Handbook for Writers?*

This new edition of *The Scott, Foresman Handbook for Writers* introduces features designed to give you an insider's view of the writing process so that you can work more efficiently and effectively:

1. More than 25 key issues that can make a significant difference for you as a college writer are highlighted, everything from how to come up with an effective thesis to why you should avoid plagiarism. You can see the complete list of these "Taking Control" items on the inside back cover. Look for the marginal apple icon that identifies these sections in the book.
2. New "Taking Control" boxes throughout the book offer you specific strategies for dealing with intimidating aspects of the writing process (finding reliable sources) or puzzling usage concerns (inserting quotation marks). Going beyond rules and examples, this hands-on advice gives you an insider's perspective on the writing process.
3. A new chapter called "How Do You Write for the Web" (Chapter 21) introduces you to specific academic uses of social media and Web 2.0. It also provides practical advice for composing and responding in these environments, since many instructors now use online course software, blogs, and wikis in their writing courses.
4. Timely new argument examples, ranging from a Pepsi "Joy" ad to a discussion of the Madden curse, help you to master argumentative techniques and to spot logical fallacies. You will find this information in two revised chapters: "How Do Written and Visual Arguments Work?" (Chapter 9), and "How Do You Write Powerful Arguments?" (Chapter 10).
5. The coverage of academic writing has been enhanced to give you more guidance for typical college assignments. For instance, you will find new material on preparing annotated bibliographies (Chapter 6) and literary analyses of films (Chapter 19). And when you need to prepare a personal statement for a scholarship or award application, you can turn to Chapter 19 for advice.
6. A new section on "Avoiding Plagiarism" in Chapter 46, "Using Sources," offers the down-to-earth advice you need to follow academic standards in writing and documentation. No preaching here, just the facts.
7. An expanded glossary and index of *The Scott, Foresman Handbook for Writers* have been reworked to incorporate suggestions from our students. Because you need an intuitive way to find answers, the index now not only lists more items but also helps you with special terms by offering alternative ways to find them. For example, you'll find "&" under either "ampersand" or "*and* sign." Look for ". . ." under "ellipsis mark" or "dot, dot, dot."

NINTH EDITION

THE SCOTT, FORESMAN HANDBOOK FOR WRITERS

JOHN RUSZKIEWICZ
University of Texas at Austin

CHRISTY FRIEND
University of South Carolina

DANIEL E. SEWARD

MAXINE HAIRSTON
Late, University of Texas at Austin

Longman
Boston Columbus Indianapolis New York San Francisco Upper Saddle River
Amsterdam Cape Town Dubai London Madrid Milan Munich Paris Montreal
Toronto Delhi Mexico City São Paulo Sydney Hong Kong Seoul Singapore Taipei Tokyo

Executive Editor: Lynn M. Huddon
Development Editor: Paul Sarkis
Senior Supplements Editor: Donna Campion
Senior Media Producer: Stefanie Liebman
Senior Marketing Manager: Susan E. Stoudt
Production Manager: Bob Ginsberg
Project Coordination, Text Design, and Electronic Page Makeup:
Nesbitt Graphics, Inc.
Cover Designer/Cover Design Manager: Wendy Ann Fredericks
Cover Photo: Philip Rostron/Masterfile
Photo Researcher: Pearson Image Resource Center/Kathy Ringrose
Image Coordinator: Jan Marc Quisumbing
Senior Manufacturing Buyer: Roy L. Pickering, Jr.
Printer and Binder: RR Donnelley & Sons Company/Crawfordsville
Cover Printer: Lehigh Phoenix

Cataloging-in-Publication Data is on file at the Library of Congress

12345678910—-DOC—-13 12 11 10

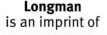

Longman
is an imprint of

www.pearsonhighered.com

ISBN-13: 978-0-205-75198-3
ISBN-10: 0-205-75198-9

Contents

PART III Style 181

PART VI Punctuation and Mechanics 507

Preface

Recent research strongly suggests that college students are more engaged by the audience-driven and networked writing that they do daily—much of it online—than by their more traditional academic work. That's no surprise since out-of-class blogging, texting, and emailing typically demand less reflection and craft than school assignments. Yet if students are to progress as writers and thinkers, they need a serious perspective on what it means to compose. They need to connect the practical insights they gain from writing on their own to the appreciation for evidence, logic, and rhetorical awareness that school assignments foster.

Precisely for those reasons, *The Scott, Foresman Handbook for Writers* has always encouraged students to think about themselves as authentic writers whose work in school can connect to their daily lives and interests. Our previous editions have focused consistently on what writers actually do, highlighting their experiences, showcasing their work, and focusing on contemporary genres and methods. At the same time, we've offered complete and up-to-date material on writing processes, argumentation, style, grammar, mechanics, research and documentation—all presented in a friendly and accessible style. We've shown students that what they learn about composing in the classroom really does matter.

What's New

Taking Control. Our goal in this ninth edition of *The Scott, Foresman Handbook for Writers* is to give students even greater control over their writing processes. To that end, we use visual clues and new "taking control" boxes to identify issues and concerns that we believe will make the greatest difference in improving their work. In one sense, we are drawing upon the heritage of the very first edition of *The Scott, Foresman Handbook for Writers,* which was based on research from Maxine Hairston's ground-breaking essay, "Not All Errors Are Created Equal."

But we have moved beyond lists of errors that can make composing seem like a minefield to novice writers. Instead, we focus on elements throughout the writing process that experienced teachers will recognize as crucial to success in college writing, from *shaping a thesis* and *choosing effective transitions*

130 9b arg How Do Written and Visual Arguments Work?

Following the election of President Barack Obama in 2008, Pepsi created an advertising campaign that capitalized on that candidate's successful theme of *hope*. While the beverage company denied that the ads were political, Pepsi even recast its familiar red, white, and blue logo to resemble more closely Obama's own famous emblem. What argument(s) do you think this advertisement makes, and to what audience? What do you think the redesigned logo adds to the argument? Do you think that the ad's message could be stated as effectively using only words?

different material had been selected, or what portions of film the producer edited out. Because visual texts are the products of human choices, they generally reflect their creators' values, viewpoints, and biases.

- **Be aware that visual arguments come in many genres, each of which operates according to its own conventions.** Think how different your expectations are when you see national news events discussed in an online news site, a late-night talk show, a political cartoon, and a documentary film. These different formats govern how information can be presented.
- **Recognize that many visual arguments are open ended; they may be interpreted differently by different viewers.** Parents often say that they can't make any sense of the music videos their teenage children watch; it's all just noise and disconnected images, they complain. On the other hand, adults who watch the Disney cartoons they loved as kids often catch cultural references or jokes that eluded them when they were younger. Creators of visual arguments rely on these differences when they try to reach several audiences at once.

2 Pay close attention to visual design and layout. As in written arguments, whatever is front and center will get the most attention in a

to *introducing quotations* and, of course, *avoiding comma splices.*

We use marginal apple icons to identify more than twenty such "taking control" items throughout the book. (A full list of these items appears on the inside back cover.) Many of the highlighted sections now include enhanced coverage or additional examples, and all feature new "Taking Control" boxes that offer practical advice for dealing with the particular writing issue. In a sense, we break the fourth wall of handbook formality to speak one-on-one with writers.

Enhanced and updated treatment of MLA and APA documentation. The recently revised MLA and APA documentation standards have been incorporated throughout the new edition. The revised MLA chapter retains its innovative design, but now treats more than a dozen new electronic sources. The chapter also includes a new annotated MLA-style student research paper on "Vegan Diet: The Missing Lesson in Environmental Education."

New chapter on "Web writing." Because more instructors now use online course software, blogs, and wikis in their writing courses, a new chapter introduces students to academic uses of social media, class Web sites, wikis, blogs, and Web 2.0.

Fuller coverage of academic writing. Parts I and II have been substantially reworked to incorporate more detailed guidance on the varied writing assignments that college students encounter in their courses: Among other additions, Chapter 6 features an expanded discussion of annotated bibliographies, including a full-length student sample; and Chapter 11, newly titled "How Do You Write About Literature and Film?" now incorporates terminology and tips for writing about films as well as more traditional literary genres.

Updated chapters on argument. Both Chapter 9 "How Do Written and Visual Arguments Work?" and Chapter 10 "How Do You Write Powerful Arguments?" offer many new examples and exercises illustrating effective persuasion. We've added more timely and varied examples of argumentative techniques and logical fallacies, ranging from a Pepsi "Joy" ad to passages from a speech by Barack Obama.

CHAPTER

10 How Do You Write Powerful Arguments?

10a How do you construct a solid argument?

Take Central

Making a claim and supporting it with reasons and evidence seems like a natural process, since most of us engage in informal arguments nearly every day. But it is not a process to take for granted, especially when you're asked to prepare a formal written argument in school or for a job. In college, you'll be asked to write persuasive papers that include strong theses and carefully chosen support.

Engaging in formal argument is essential because it allows you to demonstrate your knowledge of the topics you study. In fact, formal argument is one of the elements that distinguishes college-level writing from high school essays that merely summarize existing research. Because of the importance of argument in educational and professional settings, you'll want to know how to present your cases effectively and memorably. This chapter walks you through a general process for constructing a formal written argument, using the Toulmin model and terminology outlined in Chapter 9.

1 Clarify your claim. First, figure out what you want readers to take from your piece: Do you want them to look at some issue in a new way? Do you want them to be aware of a problem they hadn't noticed before? To adopt a particular viewpoint? To take action? Your answer is your claim.

Suppose that, after reading in a child development course some studies of the influence of media violence on children, you decide to write a course paper arguing that parents should be cautious about allowing their children to play the video games marketed to young people, since many of them encourage players to participate in realistic portrayals of violent acts. That assertion is your claim, the one set forth in Figure 10.1 (see page 148). In many academic papers, your major claim(s) will be stated early, as part of a thesis statement.

143

Updated coverage of plagiarism. A new section on "Avoiding Plagiarism" in Chapter 46 "How Do You Use Sources?" cites the Council of Writing Program Administrators' definition of plagiarism and then offers common sense advice about adhering to academic standards in writing and documentation.

More helpful guidance on preparing professional and business documents. Chapter 19 now provides not only models and templates of business letters, résumés, memos, personal statements, and other finished documents, but also step-by-step advice that guides students through the process of composing them.

New "Writer at Work" headings. These headings make it easier to identify the numerous student writing samples included throughout the book.

Student review of the manuscript. An undergraduate writer reviewed major sections of the manuscript of *The Scott, Foresman Handbook for Writers* to find and critique any discussions or examples that might raise problems for readers. The comments of this student editor resulted in dozens of changes—large and small—throughout the new edition.

Improved glossary and index. Many new items and clearer definitions have been added to the glossary, including some suggested by the student editor. The index has also been revised, both to include new items and to list some in the ways students might actually search for them. For example, you'll find " . . . " under both "ellipsis mark" and "dot, dot, dot."

Supplements

Accompanying *The Scott, Foresman Handbook for Writers* is an array of supplements for both instructors and students to aid teaching and learning, including book-specific resources such as:

PEARSON mycomplab **MyCompLab.** MyCompLab empowers student writers and facilitates writing instruction by integrating a composing space and assessment tools with pedagogically sound instruction, multimedia tutorials, and exercises for writing, grammar, and research.

Students can use MyCompLab on their own, benefiting from self-paced diagnostics and a personal study plan that recommends the instruction and practice each student needs to improve his or her writing skills. The composing space and its integrated resources, tools, and services (such as online tutoring) are also available to all students as they write.

MyCompLab is a flexible application that instructors can use in ways that complement their course and teaching style. They can recommend it to students for self-study, set up courses to track student progress, or leverage the power of its administrative features to be more effective and save time. The assignment builder and commenting tools, developed specifically for writing instruction, bring instructors closer to their student writers, make managing assignments and evaluating papers more efficient, and put powerful assessment within reach. Students receive feedback within the context of their own writing, which encourages critical thinking and revision and helps them to develop skills based on their individual needs. Learn more at **www.mycomplab.com**.

An Interactive Pearson eText. An e-book version of *The Scott, Foresman Handbook for Writers* is also available in MyCompLab. This dynamic, online version of the text is integrated throughout MyCompLab to create an enriched, interactive learning experience for writing students.

A CourseSmart eTextbook. *The Scott, Foresman Handbook for Writers* is also available as a CourseSmart eTextbook. This is an exciting new choice for students, who can subscribe to the same content online and search the text, make notes online, print out reading assignments that incorporate lecture notes, and bookmark important passages for later review. For more information, or to subscribe to the CourseSmart eTextbook, visit **www.coursesmart.com**.

Creating a Community of Writers: An Instructor's Manual, by Joel Henderson of Chattanooga State Community College, offers guidance to new and experienced teachers for using the *The Scott, Foresman Handbook for Writers* and its ancillary package to the best advantage. An **Answer Key** to the exercises in the handbook is also included for instructors in the Instructor's Manual.

vango notes **VangoNotes.** VangoNotes are study guides in MP3 format that enable students to download handbook information into their own players and then listen to it whenever they wish. The notes include "need to know" tips for each handbook chapter, practice tests, audio flash cards for learning key concepts and terms, and a rapid review for exams. For more information, visit www.VangoNotes.com.

To see a complete listing of the student supplements and instructor support materials available upon adoption of *The Scott, Foresman Handbook for Writers,* please visit the book's online catalog page at www.pearsonhighered.com.

Acknowledgments

With this edition, we are very pleased to welcome Daniel Seward as an author of *The Scott, Foresman Handbook for Writers.* Dr. Seward has consulted on and contributed his remarkable talents to the document design and documentation material in several prior editions of the book; he is also an author of *The Scott, Foresman Writer.*

We are grateful to our editors at Longman who supported this revision and helped us to keep it on track. The revision was begun under the editorial direction of Kevin Molloy and then was handed over to Lynn Huddon, whose connection to *The Scott, Foresman Handbook* traces back to the sixth edition, which she edited. We are delighted to welcome her back. Paul Sarkis provided the editorial advice we needed in preparing the complicated manuscript for turnover to production. He was quietly unflappable and supportive, even when the schedule got hectic. We have worked with Kathy Smith on previous projects, and we once again appreciated her thoroughness and keen eye for detail as production editor. And, finally, we were especially delighted to have Bob Ginsberg once again serving as the production manager of a Scott, Foresman handbook.

We would like to acknowledge the many student writers whose work, from single paragraphs to complete papers, appears in this new edition, and especially Corey Bobco, from the University of Texas, who contributed the MLA research paper. Our student editor on the project was Bryan Cory, also from the University of Texas, whose suggestions were precise, smart, and detailed. We also thank Lisa Bailey, Nicole Fisk, Christian Smith, and Brad Stratton for their research and editing assistance and their helpful suggestions. Your contributions have significantly enriched the book.

Finally, we thank all the instructors who have used *The Scott, Foresman Handbook for Writers* throughout its many editions, especially the following reviewers whose comments enabled us to refine this new edition: Ellesia A. Blaque, Palm Beach Community College; Adam Ellwanger, University of South Carolina; Natalie Grinnell, Wofford College; Jane McClain, University of West Georgia; Tammy Powley, Indian River State College; Christine Rose, Austin Community College; Jenni D. Runte, Metropolitan State University; and Annette Wyandotte, Indiana University Southeast.

We would also like to thank those reviewers who helped us with the eighth edition. Your feedback surely lives on in the ninth edition: Wendy Allman, Baylor University; Susie Berardi-Rogers, Lamar Community College; Clark Draney, College of Southern Idaho; Diana Kaye Campbell, North Carolina Wesleyan College; Deborah Coxwell-Teague, Florida State University; Philip Gaines, Montana State University; Theresa Greenwood, Montana State University; Tim Gustafson, University of Minnesota; Gary Heba, Bowling Green State University; Cheri Hoeckley, Westmont College; Edis Kittrell, Montana State University; Charlotte Laughlin, McLennan Community College; Sandra Marshburn, West Virginia State University; Kelly Martin, Collin County Community College; Theresa McGarry, East Tennessee State University; Brett Millan, South Texas Community College; Paul Miller, Davidson College; Chere Peguesse, Valdosta State University; Amy Phillips, Thompkins Cortland Community College; Melinda Reichelt, University of Toledo; Joyce Sloper, Linn Benton Community College; Jean Sorensen, Grayson County College; Greta Vollmer, Sonoma State University; Eric Waggoner, West Virginia Wesleyan College.

John Ruszkiewicz

Christy Friend

Daniel Seward

PART I

WRITING PROCESSES

CHAPTER

1 What Does Writing Involve?

1a Why write?

Writing is not a mysterious activity at which only a talented few can succeed. Nor is it a purely academic skill that you will leave behind at graduation. On the contrary. In our information-based society, virtually everyone writes.

Through writing, people share what they know, debate issues, accomplish tasks, and advocate change. Whether you are drafting a letter to your senator, making a PowerPoint presentation at work, or reading an original poem at a local coffeehouse, writing gives you a public voice. Writing is also a rich medium for intellectual inquiry. Many people use writing to think through their ideas on an issue or to help organize complex material they learn in school or on the job. In fact, in almost every field, those people who write well are the ones most likely to achieve their goals.

The ability to write has become even more important with the integration of electronic media into our daily lives. People once could get along in school by writing papers that would be seen only by their teachers, or at work by writing an occasional memo to the boss. But now, as text messaging, email, and social networking sites become primary modes of communication, we are all writers who address diverse audiences throughout the course of a typical day.

Years ago, some futurists predicted that computers would make writing obsolete. How wrong they were! Now, more than ever, writing matters.

1b What does it take to write well?

Can writing be intimidating? Yes. But it is a craft that can be learned by almost any literate person willing to invest the time and energy. Don't let the following common myths about writing discourage you:

What activities in your everyday life require writing? What steps or processes do you go through to produce a written document? With whom do you communicate when you write? Do you do most of your writing in or outside school?

- **Myth:** *Good writers are born, not made. Writing takes talent.*
  Fact: People become good writers by working at it, through study and practice.
- **Myth:** *Good writers know what they want to say before they start writing.*
  Fact: Many good writers generate ideas as they work.
- **Myth:** *Good writers get it right the first time.*
  Fact: It's rare for even experienced writers to produce polished work on the first try. Like you, they usually work through several drafts.
- **Myth:** *Good writers work alone.*
  Fact: Even if they do much of the actual composing alone, experienced writers ask editors and friends for help and suggestions.

- **Myth:** *Good writers have to know all the rules of grammar.*
  Fact: Although learning the conventions is important, knowing grammar rules alone won't make anyone a good writer.
- **Myth:** *Writing means putting words on a page—nothing more.*
  Fact: Visual and multimedia elements are integral parts of many documents, such as presentations, proposals, and Web sites. Good writers learn to incorporate these elements when appropriate.
- **Myth:** *Only professional writers publish their work.*
  Fact: Advances in networked computing and publishing software have changed what it means to publish. Today anyone with Internet access can publish his or her writing instantaneously on social networking sites, Web pages, or blogs.

EXERCISE 1.1 When you hear the term *writer,* what kind of person comes to mind? Many people reserve the terms *author* and *journalist* for those who make their living solely by writing. But can you think of other people who write frequently? What kinds of writing do they do? Discuss your answers with your classmates.

1c How does writing work?

It's tempting to believe that there's a secret formula for writing well and that if you could just discover it, your life would be much easier. Unfortunately, there's no foolproof way to turn an initial idea into a polished final text. However, researchers do agree that most people, when they write, follow general thinking patterns similar to those that occur in other creative activities. Chart 1.1 on page 5 lists these stages and describes some of the activities writers engage in during each.

Remember, though, that any formal diagram can only hint at what writers really do. A chart can't show nuances in the process, nor can it differentiate among individual writers and writing situations. Some successful writers shift freely among the preparing, researching, planning, and revising stages as they work. Others delay major revisions until they have a first draft. Still others revise as they go along.

Writers must also adjust their work patterns to their purpose, their audience, and the specific demands of the project. An instant-messaging exchange among friends will require little planning or revision; yet a job application letter or academic research paper may go through several cycles of researching, revising, and editing. So don't think of the writing process as a lockstep march from outlining to proofreading. It's a flexible network of choices and skills.

Chart 1.1 Stages of Writing

- **Preparing:** Read, brainstorm, browse online, and talk to people in order to decide what you want to write about and to generate ideas about it.
- **Researching:** Gather facts or examples from reading, conversations with others, field research, laboratory research, or your own experiences to support your ideas.
- **Planning:** Develop and organize your ideas further, perhaps preparing working lists, outlines, or sketches of visual elements.
- **Drafting:** Begin to put words (and images or other visual elements, if you're using them) onto a page or screen. Compose one or more drafts, rethinking and reshaping your materials as necessary.
- **Incubating:** Take time off to let your ideas simmer. New ideas may come to you after you've taken a break.
- **Revising:** Critically review what you have written and make any large-scale changes you need in topic, organization, content, design, or audience adaptation.
- **Editing:** Critically review your draft to make smaller-scale changes in style, clarity, and readability.
- **Proofreading:** Read carefully to rid your project of mechanical problems such as spelling, punctuation, and formatting errors.

EXERCISE 1.2 Think back to a piece of writing you were proud of—perhaps a letter to the editor that was published, a personal statement that won you a scholarship, or an *A* paper in a difficult class. Write a paragraph describing the preparation you put into the project, how many times you revised it, and why you think it was successful.

EXERCISE 1.3 Write a paragraph or two candidly describing your most hectic writing experience, when you were most pressed to get a project done. What did you have to do to finish the project? Was it successful? Why or why not? What, if anything, would you do differently if you had the chance to do it again?

1d How do you define a rhetorical situation?

Writing is a social activity, a way of interacting with others. Every time you write, you enter into a *rhetorical situation* in which

- *you*
- say *something*
- to *somebody*
- for some *purpose.*

For each writing project you undertake, think carefully about your purpose, your audience, and how you want to come across to your readers. Probably no other single habit will do more to strengthen your writing.

1e How do you define your purpose(s) for writing?

When you begin a project, ask why you are writing in the first place. Do you need to show an instructor that you've mastered a difficult concept or reading assignment, or to document observations or procedures you've performed in a laboratory course? Is there a political debate you wish to enter? Of course, not everything you write must aim at a serious and lofty goal—perhaps you're writing a blog simply to share your opinions about current films. In any case, keeping a purpose in mind will help you to focus and to decide what kinds of supporting materials you will need.

1 Decide what you hope to accomplish. Centuries ago, theorists of *rhetoric*—the art of persuasive communication—identified three basic purposes for writing:

- writing *to inform*, or writing that teaches readers new information;
- writing *to persuade*, or writing that convinces readers to believe or act in new ways;
- writing *to entertain*, writing that diverts and engages readers.

Often you may want to achieve more than one of these goals within a single paper. To review a restaurant for a campus magazine, for example, your primary aim might be to *evaluate* the food and service, but you would also want to *persuade* readers to visit or avoid the restaurant and perhaps to *entertain* them as well. See Section 3c for specific methods of organizing projects to suit particular purposes.

Sometimes you may not be completely sure of your purpose until you've explored the topic by writing a first draft. You may explore several angles on an idea as you figure out what you want to say. Eventually, though, you must articulate a purpose that's clear both to you and to your readers. Use Checklist 1.1 to think about your goals.

Checklist 1.1 Purpose

1. If you are writing a paper for a course, what cues does the assignment provide about purpose? Read the assignment sheet carefully. Target words like *explain, define, argue, evaluate*.
2. What do you want readers to get from your paper? Do you want to inform, persuade, or entertain them? If you have multiple goals, which is the most important?
3. What supporting materials will you draw on to achieve your goals? What research, examples, or personal experiences will you need to discuss?
4. How will you present material in your paper? Will you narrate, describe, compare and contrast, or argue, for example?
5. What form will the project take? Will you write a letter, a report, a Web page, or a research paper, for example? Will you incorporate images, tables, or other visual elements?

2 Consider how other elements in the rhetorical situation shape your purpose(s). Although we discuss each aspect of the rhetorical situation separately in this chapter, in practice it's difficult to consider any single element in isolation. For any project, your purpose(s) will help you define your audience, the form in which you present your ideas, and the impression you want to make. Suppose, for example, that you are angry about a proposal to stop offering evening courses at your college. If you want to convince people that these courses should continue, you have a choice of audiences. Here is where your purpose becomes important.

If you want direct action, you need to write to the person in charge of scheduling courses, perhaps the campus registrar. For this audience, your purpose might be to construct a calm, well-supported letter explaining the harmful effects of cancellation—graduation delays for working students who can attend class only in the evening, shrinking enrollment if evening students transfer to other local colleges, and so on. If, however, you want to get fellow students to join your cause, you might draft a petition and circulate it on a campus electronic mailing list, blog, or social networking site such as Facebook.

1f How do you write for an audience?

Each time you write, think carefully about who your readers might be and how they will respond to your project. Doing this can be a challenge. Writers often have to contend with multiple and possibly conflicting audiences: men and women; young, middle-aged, and older people; liberals and conservatives; teacher and classmates. In some cases, identifying an audience at all seems nearly impossible. When you create a Web page, for example, literally anyone in the world who has access to the Internet might read it.

Learning how to appeal to an audience takes time and practice, but it is a skill that any writer can master. As you begin to think about your readers, consult Checklist 1.2. If within a single project you will reach several potential audiences, run through the checklist for each group.

Checklist 1.2 Audience

1. Who is your primary audience? If you are writing a paper for a class, does the assignment specify a particular audience? What will that audience expect from you?
2. What does your audience need to know? What background information do you need to give them? What details, examples, or information might interest or persuade them?
3. What values and beliefs are important to your readers? To what kinds of examples and arguments are they likely to respond?
4. What kind of approach will they expect? Formal? Informal? Casual? What kind of formats, layouts, or visuals will appeal to them?

How might a paper on sex education in public schools differ if it were written to appeal to each of these three audiences? How might you approach a paper that needed to simultaneously reach all three?

EXERCISE 1.4 Briefly analyze what you think readers would want to know if you were writing

1. a personal statement for a scholarship application.
2. a letter disputing a charge on your credit card account.
3. a description of an experiment you carried out for a chemistry class.
4. a flyer advertising a benefit performance by your best friend's bluegrass band.

EXERCISE 1.5 Working with a classmate, look through a magazine—some possibilities are *Sports Illustrated, Spin, The New Yorker, Maxim, Money, Wired, Newsweek, Source*—and study the advertisements and the kinds of articles it

carries. Then write a paragraph describing the kinds of people you think the editor and publisher of the magazine assume its readers to be. Use Checklist 1.2 to guide your work.

1g How do you present yourself to readers?

Readers respond most favorably when they trust and respect the person sending the message. But presenting an effective image to an audience isn't just about "selling" your ideas. It's also about showing readers that you are a person whose ideas are worth listening to.

1 Show readers that you are credible. Would you take driving lessons from someone whose license has been revoked? Or let someone with no computer expertise replace your hard drive? Of course not. It's a question of credibility. Readers expect you to show that you know what you are talking about before they will give your ideas serious consideration.

One way to achieve credibility is to learn everything you can about a topic before you begin writing. Do your homework. Browse through background sources to get a sense of key terminology, concepts, authorities, and ongoing debates about the subject. Research in detail the particular issues you want to focus on in your project. Once you have this knowledge, you will write with confidence—and you will project this confidence to readers. See Chapters 44 and 45 for more on researching a topic.

Your personal experiences can also build credibility. If you are writing about immigration policy and your family came to the United States from India, for example, don't hesitate to share your story. Even though your experience doesn't make you an authority on every aspect of the subject, it gives you knowledge that is richer and in some ways more powerful than what you can learn from books. Of course, there are forums—such as scientific writing—in which personal expression is generally inappropriate. But when the assignment allows it, readers will respect your close involvement with a topic.

Finally, to win readers' respect, you must come across as a professional. Use an appropriate format, edit carefully, and proofread thoroughly to show

Checklist 1.3 Presenting Yourself to Readers

1. How can you show readers that you are knowledgeable about your subject? What research, reading, or personal experience will you draw upon?
2. How will you show readers that you are trustworthy? What will you do to present information accurately and fully?
3. How will you show readers that you are reasonable and fair? What tone will you adopt, and how will you talk about opposing views?

your audience that you are serious about your work. Checklist 1.3 will help you to credibly present yourself to readers.

2 Present material fairly and honestly. Readers believe writers whom they perceive as trustworthy, so you'll need to present material accurately and fairly in a writing project. Base your arguments on reputable sources, and be truthful about gaps or limitations in what you know.

You will also need to cite the sources of your information, to show that the materials you've consulted are reliable and authoritative. When readers see that you treat your subject honestly, they'll be more open to your ideas. See Chapters 45 through 48 for more about evaluating and documenting sources.

3 Use a civil tone. Being polite to those who disagree with you may seem a bit naive given the hostile tone of much public discussion in our society. But don't be fooled—the loudest voices aren't always the ones that people end up listening to. You will project the most credible image when you treat different viewpoints fairly and generously. It's fine to disagree strongly with another's ideas. But confine your criticism to the issues rather than attack your opponent's worth as a human being. Avoid name-calling, inflammatory language, and ethnic or gender stereotypes. Not only will you sound more professional, but your fairness will lay the groundwork for ongoing conversation with readers who hold different views.

See Section 15d for more on avoiding bias in your language. For advice on addressing opposing views, see Section 10c.

What qualities make musician Sheryl Crow an effective spokesperson for an advertising campaign promoting milk? If you were asked to design a new ad in this campaign, what spokesperson might you choose? Why? Visit <www.whymilk.com> and compare your choice to the celebrities featured in past "Got Milk" ads.

EXERCISE 1.6 Select a subject that you know a lot about, and imagine that you have been asked to write about it for several different venues: a college research paper, a televised public-service announcement, and an editorial for your campus newspaper. Which of these three venues appeals to you the most? How would each element of the writing situation—your purpose, your audience, and the image you want to project as a writer—affect the written product?

CHAPTER

2 How Do You Find and Explore a Topic?

2a How do you find a topic?

Sometimes you will start a writing project knowing exactly what you are going to write about—perhaps an instructor has assigned a specific paper topic, or you're writing in response to a particular issue or situation. When you don't have to find your topic, you can begin immediately to generate ideas, plan, and start a draft.

Occasionally, however, an instructor may ask you to choose your own topic for a paper, believing that students write better when they can investigate subjects that interest them. An interesting topic by itself won't guarantee that a paper is successful. But selecting workable topics is an important skill for any writer.

1 Think beyond broad, traditional topics. Many college students think that they should always write about issues of earthshaking importance. Does this list look familiar?

Abortion	Terrorism	Global Climate Change
School Choice	Capital Punishment	Euthanasia

These subjects *are* important. And if you feel passionately enough about one of them to do the research that will add to the debate, then go for it. But because so much has been written about these issues, you risk bogging down in generalizations and clichés. If you do choose a well-worn topic, look for a new or local angle to investigate. For example, rather than writing a general paper on global climate change, you might explore the effects that recent tropical storms have had on your hometown's economy.

2 Choose a topic in your world. When you write about a subject with authority and passion, your readers will respond. So choose a topic that interests you, preferably one you know well. Brainstorm a list of possibilities: activities you enjoy, interesting experiences you've had, or subjects that have always sparked your curiosity. For example, do you play blues guitar, teach first-aid classes, or volunteer at a local animal shelter? Then decide which topic on your list best fits your assignment. Checklist 2.1 will help you to discover such topics.

You can also make a paper unique by spotlighting issues in your own community. For example, an assignment to research the civil rights movement for a history course could lead you to inquire about local concerns. Was your campus or community ever segregated? How did your city react to civil rights initiatives or legislation? Do contemporary concerns for women's or gay rights have roots in this earlier political movement? Any one of these issues would make a promising paper topic.

Because local topics connect to your everyday life, you're bound to have a strong interest in finding out more about them. You will find it easier to do original research, since expert sources—newspapers, community organizations, and local leaders—are close at hand. And you may discover opportunities to publish your writing on such topics outside the classroom, perhaps as a letter to the editor or to a public official.

Checklist 2.1 Finding a Topic . . .

- **What three subjects do you enjoy reading about or are you curious about?** What magazines do you pick up? What kinds of books do you browse through? Which news headlines catch your eye? When online, what blogs do you check regularly or discussion forums do you participate in?
- **What three subjects do you know the most about?** What topics could you discuss for half an hour without notes? What problems lead people to seek your advice or expertise? What could you teach someone else to do?
- **What three subjects do you enjoy arguing about most?** On what subjects can you hold your own with just about anyone? What opinions do you advocate most strongly?
- **What three issues in your community do you care about the most?** What issues affect you or people you know? For what causes do you volunteer? What opinions or ideas would you like to communicate to government officials or to the community at large?

3 Browse in the library and online. Look in the library catalog or in the directory of the Library of Congress (better known as the *Subject List*). Just the way a broad subject is broken down into headings and subheadings should suggest many topic possibilities. Consult such reference sources as specialized encyclopedias too. If you want to learn about endangered animal species in your state, for example, a glance at the *Encyclopedia of the Environment* might provide several topic ideas.

Even when you don't have a general subject area to direct your library search, try browsing in the new book section or through the op-ed and analysis pages of national publications like *The New York Times, The Wall Street Journal*, or *Slate* for current topics that spark your curiosity. An online search engine such as *Google* or *Yahoo!* will help you identify innumerable subject areas, but you may also find yourself led down stray paths. Consider using a Web directory (see Figure 2.1), which lists Web sites by category and often employs editors who consider the categories a site is best suited for—unlike search engines, which perform automated searches based on keywords. A librarian at your campus library can also help you direct your online research to reliable, manageable sources.

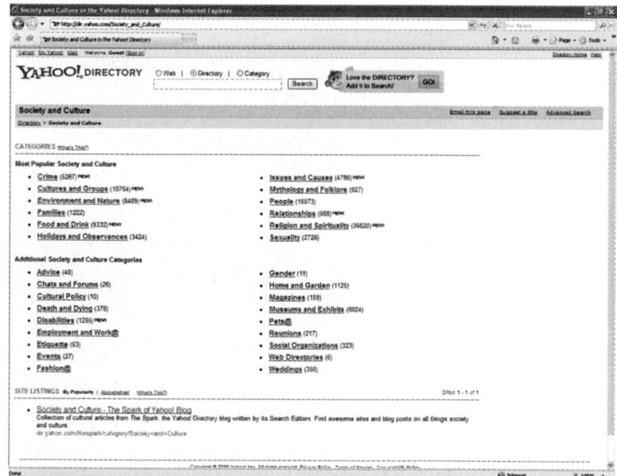

Figure 2.1 *Yahoo!*'s "Issues and Causes" page offers dozens of general topic ideas and thousands of supporting links. You can find it under the "Society and Culture" heading in the *Yahoo!* directory.

4 Talk with others. There's no reason to search for a topic in a vacuum. Discuss possibilities with everyone who has a connection to the project, including your instructor. He or she may be willing not only to suggest interesting areas, but also to steer you away from topics that won't work. Classmates working on the same assignment may also spark your imagination; talk with them outside of class or share ideas via a social networking site or email.

2b How do you refine your topic?

Once you have found a promising topic, you'll probably need to narrow it down. If you don't focus your efforts, you may end up trying to cover more material than you can within the parameters of the project—for example, attempting to present a comprehensive account of the "evolution versus intelligent design" debate in a five-page paper. This kind of overreaching can result in a project long on generalities but short on lively details and thoroughly developed ideas.

1 Don't try to cover everything. Remember that your time to develop a paper is limited. You can't discover all there is to know about a topic in a few weeks. Even if you could, you wouldn't be able to fit all that material into one paper. Narrow your research to something manageable, an aspect of your topic that you will be able to discuss thoroughly. Any paper you write should contain only a portion of what you know about its subject.

If you needed to write a five-page paper about an issue in U.S. high schools, what might you choose as your focus and why? How narrow would your topic need to be? Discuss and compare your choice with a group of classmates, noting the range of possibilities. Then compare your group choices with Tallon Harding's topic proposal, featured on page 25.

2 Make a tree diagram. One way to narrow a topic is to create a tree diagram that divides it into smaller components. Make a chart on which you divide and subdivide your subject into smaller and smaller parts, each of which branches out like an inverted tree. The upside-down tree helps you see many potential areas within each division as well as the relationships among them.

Suppose you've become interested in writing about college student debt after watching your roommate run up several thousand dollars in credit card bills during a single semester. Your tree diagram might look something like this:

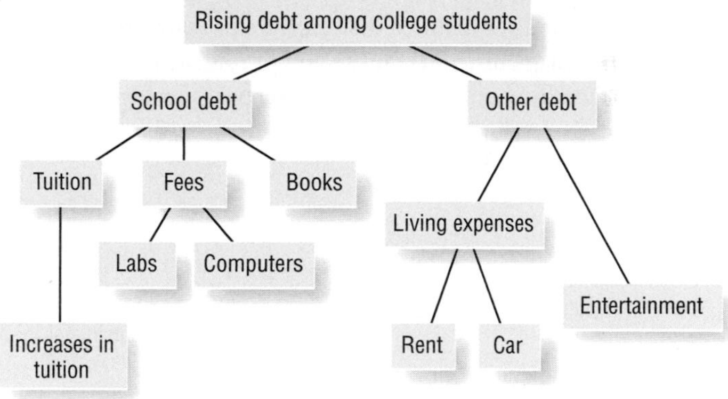

Now select the most promising branch from your first diagram and make a new diagram to refine that idea further.

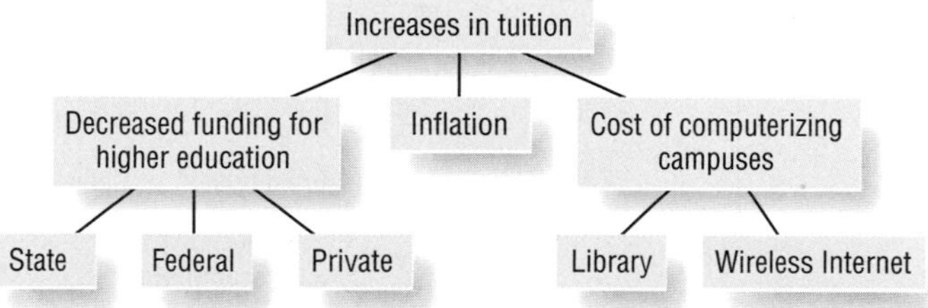

3 Make an idea map. Another way to narrow a topic is to make an idea map that shows patterns of related ideas worth exploring. In the middle of a blank sheet of paper, write down a phrase that describes your general subject. Circle that term—say, *college expenses*—and then, for about ten minutes, attach every word you can think of either to that original term or to others that you have linked to it. Circle all additional words as you write them, and draw lines connecting them to the words that triggered them.

Your finished map might look like the one below. When you're done, examine the map to see whether any clusters of words suggest topics you might develop. For example, one group of ideas (tuition—increases—state funding cuts—fees—student loans) suggests a paper about government funding for higher education. Another (credit cards—"student card" promotions—spring break trip—football weekends—shopping) might lead you to explore the kinds of luxuries that easy credit allows students to purchase. As with tree diagrams, you can use any promising concept from your first idea map as the focal point of a second exercise, starting again with the narrowed subject to develop more ideas.

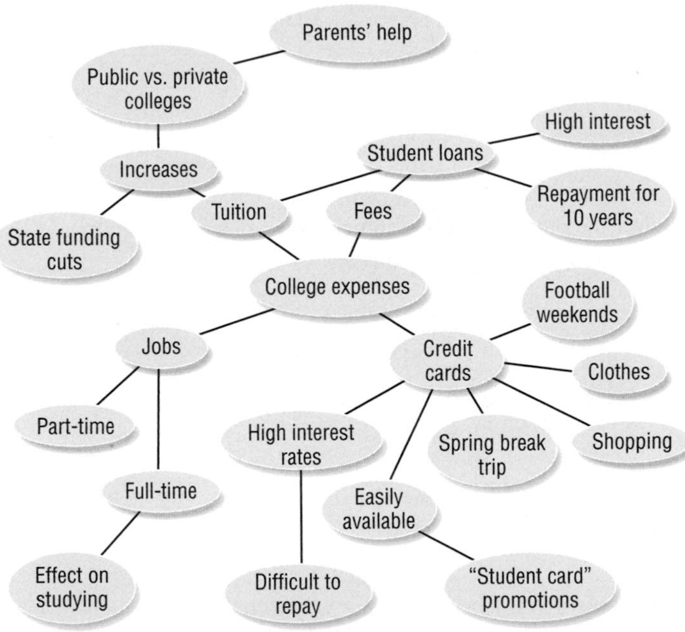

Various types of mind-mapping software are available to help writers and thinkers brainstorm and arrange ideas for their projects. Such programs allow you to generate idea maps that you can easily expand, rearrange, and save as you continue to explore your topic.

4 Investigate an interesting question or hypothesis. Another way to narrow a topic is to pursue an interesting problem involving your topic for which you do not yet have a satisfactory answer—much as investigative reporters look for "leads" that will turn into breaking news stories.

Sometimes a promising issue will take the form of a question. Reading a headline about the scarcity of young women in science-related professions, for example, might spur you to ask this question.

QUESTION Why are young women underrepresented in the scientific professions, despite the fact that they attend and graduate from college in greater numbers than men?

Or you might start a project with a *hypothesis*, a statement that tentatively proposes a claim to be tested. Scientists often begin research projects with these kinds of educated guesses. Here is an initial hypothesis on the topic of women in science.

HYPOTHESIS Many young women are discouraged from taking advanced math and science courses during high school, which may decrease the likelihood that they will pursue science careers in college.

A guiding question or hypothesis will help you focus your topic. But at this stage it is probably too early to commit to a definite position. Until the evidence comes in and you have more information, remain flexible in your thinking and be willing to revise your focus and approach.

How can you find a promising question or hypothesis to focus on? In your preliminary reading and discussion about the topic, look for clues.

- Titles and focal points of published pieces on the topic
- Names of important people, experts, events, or institutions related to the topic
- Issues or questions that come up repeatedly
- Issues about which people disagree

EXERCISE 2.1 Suppose you want to write a short paper for a composition course on one of the following subjects. Write down several promising subtopics that you might focus on; then use a tree diagram or an idea map to generate ideas about the subtopic that you find most interesting.

- Health insurance
- Scandals in professional sports
- The popularity of cosmetic surgery
- Organic foods
- Domestic violence
- Political involvement among college students

2c How do you explore and develop a topic?

You have a topic. What's next? Now you need to explore its implications, find supporting evidence, and fill in specific details. Experts on rhetoric use the term *invention* to describe the techniques writers use to generate subject matter for a paper.

Invention techniques can help you explore and develop a thesis. You can use these techniques at any point in your writing process. Return to them anytime you need to expand and develop your ideas.

1 Freewrite about the topic. Freewriting is writing nonstop for ten to fifteen minutes on a topic to explore what you already know and to discover areas you'd like to learn more about. Don't worry about grammar, spelling, or other niceties while you're freewriting—the point is to generate ideas. Continue to write as long as ideas come, and don't cross out anything. Be alert for phrases and concepts that extend your thinking in promising directions.

WRITER AT WORK **Freewriting**

Here is an excerpt from a freewriting that student writer Tallon Harding did before writing the paper that appears on pages 68–72. Notice that she has not always capitalized, that she doesn't always write complete sentences, and that her style is informal. But also notice how many ideas even this short excerpt articulates.

I definitely want to write about how high schools are pushing students to take too many AP and other college level courses to the point that they don't have time for a lot of the things young people are supposed to do in high school. The move towards college level education in the public high school system is becoming a big problem. Academics have become the main focus, what happened to rounding out the student? Sports and extracurricular activities get sidelined at the expense of the student. Too many AP and IB courses result in stress overload that many high schoolers are not prepared to face. Educators need to focus more on the needs of the students. High school students shouldn't work as hard as college students do, they have less time. . . .

---

2 Use the journalist's questions. Beginning journalists are taught to keep six questions in mind when writing a news story.

Who?	What?	Where?
When?	Why?	How?

Simple as they seem, these questions can help you be sure you have covered all the bases, especially when you are writing an informative paper (though not every question will apply to every topic).

3 Look at your topic from different perspectives. Classical rhetoricians used four broad questions to explore topics: questions of *fact, definition, value*, and *policy*. Originally designed to develop speeches for the law courts, these questions move from simple to more complex ways of examining an issue.

- Questions of **fact** involve things already known about your topic: What has already happened? What factual information is already available? What policies are already in place?
- Questions of **definition** interpret these facts and place them in a larger context: What category does your topic fit into? What laws or approaches apply?
- Questions of **value** ask you to make a judgment: Is the idea you're talking about a good thing or a bad thing? Is it ethical or unethical? Is it workable or unworkable?

- Questions of **policy** allow you to consider specific courses of action: What exactly should be done in response to the issue? Are old solutions working, or is a new approach needed?

You won't be able to answer all these questions in a single paper, but they are useful for comprehensively examining a topic. Below, for example, are ways a writer might use these questions to find material for a paper on whether the fashion industry's use of thin models in advertising indirectly encourages eating disorders among young women. Once you've run through all the questions, decide which one(s) you want to treat most fully in your paper. For example, an editorial on this topic might focus on the definitional question "How does our culture define 'beauty'?" A report, however, might gather information that answers the factual question "How many fashion ads feature unusually thin models?" For more on how these questions can help you construct a thesis statement, see Section 48a.

Highlight Looking at a Topic from Different Perspectives

Fashion and Body Image Among Young Women

- **Questions about the facts:** To what extent do young women draw their beauty ideals from fashion ads? How many fashion ads feature unusually thin models? How many young women have eating disorders?
- **Questions about key definitions:** How does our culture define "beauty"? How preoccupied with thinness must one be to be defined as having an eating disorder?
- **Questions about values:** Is it ethical for fashion designers to display their clothes on models who are much thinner than most women can ever be? Does the artistic value of fashion trends outweigh any harmful social effects they may cause?
- **Questions about policy:** What could the fashion industry do to promote a healthier ideal of beauty? How might young women be discouraged from trying to look like models?

4 Write a zero draft. Just start a draft. The very act of writing will often get the creative juices flowing and help you to organize your thoughts. Think of this first try as a "zero draft," a trial run that doesn't really count. Zero drafts are easy to write, and after they're complete, you can select the best material to use in your next draft. Try writing several zero drafts of a paper to test possible approaches to a topic.

5 Read. Look up your subject in the library or on the Internet and read. Read to find facts. Read to discover how other writers have approached topics like yours. Perhaps you want to write about a bicycle trip you took across the American Northwest. Look up some travel literature. Your eyes may be opened by the sheer variety of approaches available to record your adventures, everything from serious field accounts written by anthropologists to the rollicking narratives in travel magazines. Seeing others' work will suggest possibilities for your own.

You'll find detailed instructions for doing research in Chapters 44 through 46.

6 Talk to others about your topic. From the start, invite others to join in exploring your topic. Look for information about lectures, films, or community meetings where you might meet people interested in your work. And when you find such people, network with them to find more people and organizations tied to your subject.

Social networking Web sites, online discussion forums, and electronic mailing lists offer instant access to an even wider network of contacts. Once you have a good sense of the issues you want to write about, consider posting to one of these forums a short description of your project and a request for input.

Classmates and friends are also useful resources. Utilize a class team, or talk and email with classmates who share an interest in your topic. You'll find that as you start to explain your ideas to others, more ideas will come to you. You may see arguments you hadn't considered and learn about new examples or sources.

7 Visit your campus writing center. Many colleges and universities have writing centers designed to help students with their writing projects. Many students misperceive these facilities as emergency rooms that fix papers in trouble. In fact, the tutors and consultants who staff them are usually eager to help writers at every stage of the writing process—including finding a workable, challenging topic and focusing and narrowing it. Chart 2.1 offers some tips for getting the most out of a writing center session.

Chart 2.1 Getting Help at a Writing Center

- Use a writing center at every stage of the writing process. The consultants there can help you find a topic, formulate a thesis, and evaluate a draft in progress.
- Don't treat a writing center as a one-stop fix-it shop. The consultants are there to help you become a better writer, not to edit your papers for you.
- Bring the assignment sheet with you to a writing-center appointment. The assignment may help a tutor better understand your paper.
- Bring to your session any comments you have received from your instructor or peer editors. Read the comments carefully yourself.
- Be on time for your appointment.
- Decide whether you want a report of the session sent to your instructor. Many writing centers will give you this option.

EXERCISE 2.2 Choose a current controversy in your neighborhood, campus, or city. (If no ideas come to mind, consult a local or campus newspaper.) Use the four categories outlined on pages 21–22 to identify questions about facts, definitions, values, and policies regarding that issue. Which questions generate the most disagreement? Which ones could provide the focus for an interesting paper?

EXERCISE 2.3 Use any two of the techniques described in Section 2c to generate ideas about one of your writing projects in progress. Then discuss your experience with your classmates: Which strategy yielded the best ideas? Which are you likely to use again?

2d How do you write a topic proposal?

Occasionally an instructor may ask you to write a preliminary proposal defining your topic and analyzing the writing situation for a paper. Even when it's not assigned, such a proposal can help you refine your ideas about your topic, audience, purpose, and tone at an early stage, so that your decisions can guide your research and shape your first draft.

A topic proposal typically includes the elements listed in Checklist 2.2. Check with your instructor to find out if he or she has additional requirements.

Checklist 2.2 Writing a Topic Proposal

1. Identify your topic.
2. Articulate a working thesis statement, research question, hypothesis, or key issue that you plan to focus on in the paper (see Section 2b).
3. Indicate what kinds of supporting materials you will use (see Section 6a-3).
4. Briefly analyze your writing situation (see Section 1d).

WRITER AT WORK **A Topic Proposal**

In the following sample proposal, first-year composition student Tallon Harding describes her plan for the paper shown in draft form on pages 68–72. The assignment asked her to write a researched argument on a topic relevant to her and her classmates. Harding begins by describing her topic and purpose, and then she identifies her audience. She ends by considering the kind of impression she wants to make on readers.

Although she has thought carefully about her topic, at this point in the process Harding is still refining and developing her ideas. She hasn't yet developed all the supporting points for her position or located her research materials, and her approach is less formal than her instructor will expect to see in the finished paper.

Harding 1

Tallon Harding

Professor Rollins

English 101

30 October 2009

Today's High Schools Are Failing to Meet Student Needs

School has just let out but the library is packed. Each one of us is studying, working frantically to finish the next day's assignments. The Advanced Placement Tests will be given on Monday; the pressure is almost unbearable. This scene is becoming common in high schools across the nation, as more and more students are encouraged to enroll in college-type courses that are offered in the high school classroom. Do these kinds of courses help students prepare for the demands of college? Or are they robbing students of the well-rounded education that they will need to become mature and well-adjusted adults?

My paper will argue that a good high school education involves more than just academics. It should also include extracurricular activities that help students to mature both physically and socially. However, under the current system, many students have to eliminate extracurricular activities to account for the heavy course loads resulting from a doubled academic burden. I plan to discuss examples showing the sacrifices students make to keep up with heavy academic loads, and I will do research to find statistics to document the size of this problem. I will also briefly explore the reasons why schools are pushing students to overachieve, including the pressures caused by high-stakes testing and federal funding requirements.

My audience will be my classmates, many of whom, I anticipate, experienced a similar environment at their high schools and probably have a strong opinion on this issue. I hope to write a paper that will interest them and give strong support for my position.

CHAPTER

3 How Do You Focus and Organize a Writing Project?

Now you have an interesting, workable topic for your writing project. You've thought carefully about it and gathered information. What's next? It's time to make some decisions about the shape the project will take.

Take Control

3a How do you craft a thesis statement?

Most college instructors expect a *thesis statement* in the papers they assign. A *thesis statement* is a sentence (or sometimes two or three sentences) that explicitly identifies the main idea of a paper. Depending on the project, it may be a conclusion you draw as a result of doing research, your answer to a puzzling question about your topic, or a claim you will spend the rest of the paper explaining or supporting.

You'll find explicit thesis statements most often in reports, arguments, and research papers. But constructing a thesis is a useful exercise for any project. If you are building a Web site or designing a newsletter, you'll benefit from being able to state your purpose in one or two precise sentences—even though that statement may not appear in your final document.

Try to construct a working thesis statement early in your writing process and use it as a framework for developing your first draft. By keeping your thesis in mind, you can be sure of covering all the important points.

1 Make a strong point. A thesis statement is more than just an observation; it is a strong, focused statement that might be questioned or challenged. It should offer a clearly stated analysis, critique, or position on your topic that readers will find new and significant.

INSIGNIFICANT The doughnuts in Jester cafeteria are terrible.
Even if true, few readers will find this observation substantial enough to support an entire paper.

MORE SIGNIFICANT University administrators should investigate the impact a Krispy Kreme franchise might have on revenues for the Student Union.

NOT DEBATABLE Domestic violence harms families. Who's going to argue with this claim?

DEBATABLE The state legislature should pass the current bill mandating harsher penalties for second-offense child abuse and spousal abuse convictions.

TOO GENERAL Environmental groups and landowners disagree over many issues, including land use, species protection, and pollution regulations. You won't be able to research and thoroughly analyze more than one or two specific disagreements in a typical academic paper.

MORE SPECIFIC The debate over whether wolves should still be protected as endangered species, now that wild populations are thriving in the Northwest, raises questions about how to balance individuals' property rights with the long-term viability of the species.

Once you've written a thesis, ask yourself how a member of your audience might react to it. If you can envision a polite yawn ("So what?") or a blank stare ("What's your point?"), revise your thesis, using the "Taking Control: What Makes a Strong Thesis?" guidelines.

Taking Control

What Makes a Strong Thesis?

It should be easy to know when you have a workable thesis, but many writers struggle to write one. Once you've drafted a tentative thesis, check it against the following criteria:

- **A thesis should be a complete sentence (or two).** If all you have is a word or phrase, you may have a topic, but you haven't said anything about it. A thesis, moreover, shouldn't be a question—in most cases, it should *answer* some important question about a topic.
- **A thesis should tell readers what your paper is about.** That means no waffling, vague abstractions, or unspecific pronouns as the subject of the sentence.
- **A thesis should make readers notice your paper.** It should say something substantive, argumentative, and current. It shouldn't restate the obvious.

(Continued)

Taking Control *(Continued)*

- **A thesis should make a claim that you can adequately support with evidence** from your research or personal experience. If your thesis statement is so broad that you would need to write a book in order to do it justice, you need to narrow it.

EXERCISE 3.1 Using the guidelines listed in the Taking Control box on page 28, evaluate the following thesis statements. Revise the statements that don't seem effective to make them stronger.

1. Why are more college students now graduating within four years? Perhaps they are more career oriented and better prepared for college, but the biggest reasons are probably financial.
2. In today's environment of global conflict, should our military restore the draft?
3. Some drivers are so dangerous that they should not be allowed on the road.
4. Movies such as the *X-Men* and *Batman* series show the growing influence of comic books.

2 Preview the direction your paper will take. Write a complete sentence or two that forecasts in some detail the ideas you expect to write about, in roughly the same order in which you plan to address them. Your thesis sentence(s) should be *succinct* yet *comprehensive*—that is, it should be short yet indicate the major points you want to make. Suppose you are writing an article for the business-student newsletter on your campus. This thesis tells readers what to expect:

> When you start looking for a summer internship, think globally: in the past few years, many students on our campus have found lucrative and interesting positions with overseas corporations.

3 Place your thesis effectively. Don't assume that your thesis must be the first sentence of your paper, although it can be. Your decision about where to put your thesis depends on the writing situation: your audience, your purpose, and the position you want to take on the topic.

If you want to present information or arguments in a straightforward, no-nonsense fashion—as you should in an essay examination or a business letter—then state your thesis early. It may even be your first sentence. At other times you'll need to provide a context for your thesis, by defining key terms or giving background information. That's why, in academic papers, the thesis statement often appears at the end of the introductory paragraph.

In other situations, you may delay your thesis even more. If you're writing to explore an issue rather than to present a settled opinion on it, or if your thesis is controversial, you may want to present your evidence first and then lead readers gradually to your point. In the social sciences, writers often begin research reports by describing their methods and data and end with larger conclusions. In such cases, your thesis may not be stated until the last paragraph. Just remember, a delayed thesis doesn't give you license to write an unfocused paper—readers should understand from its very beginning what central ideas your paper will address.

4 Revise your thesis as your project evolves. Don't be surprised if your thesis shifts as you explore, research, and plan your project. Most writers will revise a working thesis statement to make it more precise or to reflect changes in the paper's direction. Don't worry about such changes. This is the right time to test your preliminary ideas so that your final paper will be stronger. Learn from every part of the process, and don't be discouraged easily. Your final thesis may be nothing like what you imagined at the outset—and that's okay.

WRITER AT WORK **An Opening Paragraph with Thesis Statement**

A thesis statement pulled out of context, like the previous examples in this chapter, can seem pretty bland. Fortunately, in a real paper, a thesis isn't solely responsible for shaping a reader's first impression. Notice how Tallon Harding positions her thesis statement in an opening paragraph designed to capture readers' interest. A full draft of this paper appears on pages 68–72.

School let out an hour ago but the library is packed with students. Each of us is working frantically to finish the next day's assignments. The Advanced Placement Tests will be given on Monday and we all need the weekend to study; the pressure is almost unbearable. A couple of years ago this spectacle—an evening not much different from most during my senior year—would have confounded the average high school librarian, who would have been able to leave as soon as school let out. Recently, however, such scenes have become commonplace. Due to a push by school officials looking to receive government grants, students are increasingly being pressured to enroll in college-level courses offered in the high school classroom. As part of the Education and Economic Development Act passed by the South Carolina state legislature in 2005, all high school students in the state will be required to declare a major by 2011 (Smith). What these ambitious administrators forget is that a good high school education should involve more than just academic study. It must also include extracurricular activities that help students to grow socially and physically, to become well-rounded citizens. As schools neglect these qualitative dimensions in their quest to achieve higher and higher academic standards, they leave gaps in students' education and neglect important student needs.

3b How do you avoid plagiarism?

Early in the writing process, you must understand what constitutes plagiarism, particularly if you're writing papers for an instructor who expects you to use outside sources. Doesn't that require you to use someone else's material and ideas? Well, yes it does. The trick is knowing how to incorporate other people's ideas or research into your work while giving them full credit. Chapters 46 and 47 show you several strategies for acknowledging someone else's ideas or arguments in a way that gives the original source its due. The point is always to be up front about where you found the idea, quotation, or conclusion that you're incorporating into your work. You should make it possible for anyone who wants to clarify a point or get more information on your topic to go to the source and check it out.

If in previous years you've attended a school in which teachers expected you to memorize large quantities of material and then demonstrate your mastery of that material, it may seem natural to you to simply repeat information that you've gathered from your reading. You're likely to find, however, that's not what instructors want in most composition courses or in other liberal arts courses for which you write papers or create online documents. Rather, those instructors want you to go beyond mastery of a body of material to synthesize, respond to, and evaluate its ideas and its arguments.

As a Web-savvy student, you know what a wealth of information the Internet can provide on almost any writing topic. You can find anything from a psychological profile of Lady Macbeth, to directions for building a kayak, to an essay about the benefits of Pilates or yoga. Online encyclopedias alone seem to have accurate information on any topic you can think of. You can also find commercial sites that will, for a price, provide you with a finished term paper on just about any topic of your choice. You may have friends who have bought such papers or have done a cut-and-paste job of piecing together a paper from Internet sources. Whatever process they chose, the project they turned in can only be called plagiarism.

When you take a process-centered writing course, you have a special opportunity to master a craft essential for doing well in college and, later on, in most professions—certainly in science, law, engineering, college teaching, public relations, and even in medicine and accounting. A skilled writer has an edge in getting what he or she wants in the everyday transactions of life.You don't want to miss an opportunity to acquire such a powerful tool.

3c How do you organize a writing project?

No matter how good your ideas are, if you don't organize them, readers will get lost and blame you. Coherent organization is the foundation of any writing project. Fortunately, you don't have to invent the structure of a paper, a résumé, a report, or project every time you begin one. Instead, you can study the patterns of organization in existing documents and then apply them to your situation. If you are not sure of how to organize a project, one of the best things you can do is find a successful example of a similar project. If you're writing a college paper, assess the assignment sheet carefully and ask your instructor for sample papers. In writing for a journal or magazine, look at past issues. The document templates included in your word processing or presentation software can also be useful resources. In *Microsoft Word*, for example, look under the Format menu in the "Style Gallery" to find templates for letters, résumés, brochures, newsletters, and more.

Remember that even when you are working with a sample document or organizational template, you are still responsible for the content and effectiveness of your paper: a template can't tell you *what* to write or how to make your arguments persuasive or interesting. Keep your ideas and your rhetorical situation in mind, and when it's necessary, don't hesitate to adapt a pattern to suit your own purpose and audience.

1 Consider an introduction-body-conclusion structure. This basic pattern works for many kinds of projects. Lawyers, scientists, and writers in many academic fields favor this design because it suggests a logical movement from statement to proof.

How might you organize a description of your last summer job differently if you were composing (1) your résumé, (2) a humorous personal narrative for a composition course, or (3) an interview segment for a documentary film on labor conditions in the industry? What would you talk about first? What points would you emphasize? In what order would you present them? What would you discuss in the most detail?

- In the **introduction** you begin by telling your readers clearly and simply what ideas your paper will cover.
- In the **body** of the paper you follow with examples and explanations for each of your main points.
- In your **conclusion** you tie your points together and leave readers with a sense of closure.

In the first section of a paper that uses this basic structure, a writer promises to cover certain issues or address particular questions. For that reason, this structure is sometimes called a commitment-and-response pattern.

Papers that result from the basic introduction-body-conclusion pattern usually take a simple shape.

Basic Introduction-Body-Conclusion Pattern

Introduction *Present thesis . . .*	I.	First-year students need a rep. on the board of the student union.
Body	◆ *First argument* ❐ Support: examples, reasons, evidence, etc.	II. Other years have representation A. All students need a voice B. First-years have special needs
	◆ *Second argument* ❐ Support: examples, reasons, evidence, etc.	III. First-years need to be welcomed A. Student union can be friendlier B. Good to socialize outside dorms
	◆ *Other arguments . . .*	IV. Welcoming campus helps retention
Conclusion *Closing summary . . .*	V.	An inviting student union can help first-years join campus communities.

Such papers can also incorporate significant variations. When you make a point or support an argument, for example, you must usually deal with opposing views; if you don't address them, the paper will seem to evade key questions. Counterarguments—discussions of opposing views—inevitably make the structure of the paper more complex. They can be addressed immediately, near the beginning of the paper, or they can be dealt with as they arise in the body of the piece. Just don't end with a counterargument; it will only weaken your case.

Here's how the basic model might look when counterarguments are added to the mix. (See Section 10c for more on handling different views in a paper.)

Introduction-Body-Conclusion Pattern with Counterarguments

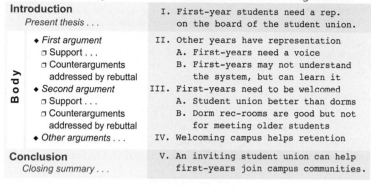

Introduction *Present thesis . . .*	I. First-year students need a rep. on the board of the student union.
Body ◆ *First argument* ❐ Support . . . ❐ Counterarguments addressed by rebuttal ◆ *Second argument* ❐ Support . . . ❐ Counterarguments addressed by rebuttal ◆ *Other arguments . . .*	II. Other years have representation A. First-years need a voice B. First-years may not understand the system, but can learn it III. First-years need to be welcomed A. Student union better than dorms B. Dorm rec-rooms are good but not for meeting older students IV. Welcoming campus helps retention
Conclusion *Closing summary . . .*	V. An inviting student union can help first-years join campus communities.

2 Consider a narrative or a process design. When you narrate a story, you usually describe events in the order they occurred. The structure can be quite straightforward. A narrative can also be more complicated—for instance, by moving back in time as a movie does with flashbacks.

Narrative Pattern

Introduction *Present thesis . . .*	I. Our town's public buildings reflect the architectural styles of several different historical periods.
Body ◆ *First event* ◆ *Second event* ◆ *Third event* ◆ *Other events . . .*	II. Colonial town hall (1793) III. Victorian courthouse (1846) and post office (1888) IV. Art-deco library (1932)
Conclusion *Closing summary . . .*	V. These buildings tell a story about our town's gradual development.

A process pattern is essentially the same as a narrative pattern, but instead of telling a story you are explaining how something works. You list and describe each step in the process.

Process Pattern

Introduction *Present thesis . . .*	I. Winning a reality-TV game show requires patience and cunning.
Body ◆ *First step* ◆ *Second step* ◆ *Third step* ◆ *Other steps . . .*	II. First, display trustworthiness III. Second, form a small coalition IV. Third, lie low for a while V. Last, betray coalition members
Conclusion *Closing summary . . .*	VI. To win the big bucks, you need to remember it is only a game.

Be careful to include all the necessary steps in the proper order. You can find good examples of process patterns in instructional and technical manuals.

3 Consider a comparison-and-contrast structure. In many kinds of papers you will have to examine different objects or ideas in relation to each other, especially when you are evaluating or arguing. In organizing such papers you can use one or two basic plans, either describing the things you are comparing one at a time (*subject by subject*) or describing them in an alternating sequence (*feature by feature*). We show both models below.

Comparison-and-Contrast Pattern: Subject by Subject

Introduction *Present thesis . . .*	I. Sport-utility vehicles, though currently more popular than family sedans, have environmental and safety drawbacks that should make potential buyers beware.
Body ◆ *First subject examined* ❒ First feature ❒ Second feature ❒ Other features . . . ◆ *Second subject* ❒ First feature ❒ Second feature ❒ Other features . . .	II. Pros and cons of SUVs A. Popularity B. Environmental impact C. Safety III. Pros and cons of family sedans A. Popularity B. Environmental impact C. Safety
Conclusion *Closing summary . . .*	IV. Buyers who value safety and the environment over style should bypass sport-utility vehicles in favor of traditional sedans.

The subject-by-subject plan works best in short papers involving only a few comparisons; in such pieces readers don't have to recall a large quantity of information to make the necessary comparisons. When you're writing a longer paper, however, use the feature-by-feature pattern; otherwise, readers may lose track of the features you're comparing.

Comparison-and-Contrast Pattern: Feature by Feature

Introduction *Present thesis . . .*	I. Sport-utility vehicles, though currently more popular than family sedans, have environmental and safety drawbacks that should make potential buyers beware.
Body ◆ *First feature examined* ❐ In first subject ❐ In second subject ◆ *Second feature* ❐ In first subject ❐ In second subject ◆ *Other features . . .* ❐ In first subject ❐ In second subject	II. Popularity A. Of sport-utility vehicles B. Of family sedans III. Environmental impact A. Of sport-utility vehicles B. Of family sedans IV. Safety A. Of sport-utility vehicles B. Of family sedans
Conclusion *Closing summary . . .*	V. Buyers who value safety and the environment over style should bypass sport-utility vehicles in favor of traditional sedans.

4 Consider a division or classification structure. These two ways of organizing a paper are quite different, though both involve creating categories to make material more manageable. A paper organized according to the principle of *division* breaks a topic into its components—its separate parts. A paper on the solar system might devote a section to each planet; a paper on a political candidate might describe her positions on several major issues in an order that seems appropriate.

Division Pattern

Introduction *Present thesis . . .*	I. Candidate Everson's platform is based on four main issues.
Body ◆ *First division* ◆ *Second division* ◆ *Third division* ◆ *Other divisions . . .*	II. Crime prevention III. Local tax rates IV. Traffic control V. Environment
Conclusion *Closing summary . . .*	VI. Everson will devote the most resources to crime prevention.

Classification involves breaking a large subject into categories according to some consistent and useful principle of division. Classification must follow rules that don't apply to division. First, classifications must be *exhaustive*: every member of the class must fit into a category. Any principle of division you use must also be *consistent.* You can't classify by more than one principle at a time—for example, if you group planets according to the number of moons they have *and* whether or not they have rings, you are not really classifying. Finally, classes *must not overlap*. That means you should be able to place an object in only one category.

Classification Pattern

Introduction *Present thesis . . .*		I. This year's most popular bands represent many musical genres.
Body	◆ *First classification*	II. Modern rock
	◆ *Second classification*	III. Reggae and ska
	◆ *Third classification*	IV. Hip-hop and "new soul"
	◆ *Other classifications . . .*	V. Folk, bluegrass, and country
Conclusion *Closing summary . . .*		VI. Young music fans appreciate a variety of musical styles.

Yet most systems of classification break down at one point or another, like the classification of music types shown above. What do you do with performers who play more than one kind of music? Well, you can create yet another class (Latin-pop or folk-rock), or you can classify by the musician's major body of work. But you won't always be able to eliminate every exception.

5 Consider a cause-and-effect design. This design is appropriate when you write a paper explaining why something has happened. The typical cause-and-effect paper moves from an explanation of some existing condition to an examination of its particular causes. In other words, you see what has happened and you want to know why.

Cause-and-Effect Pattern

Introduction *Present thesis . . .*		I. Animated films have succeeded recently due to good writing.
Body	◆ *Effects explained*	II. Animated films have made money and gained critical accolades
	◆ *Least important causes*	
	◆ *More important causes*	III. Because animation is better
	◆ *Most important cause*	IV. Because scripts have broad appeal
Conclusion *Closing summary . . .*		V. Plots and dialogue of new animated films entertain both young & old.

Typically there is more than one explanation for a given event, so a cause-and-effect paper may examine various causes, from the least important to the most important. You can begin your essay by identifying an effect and then go on to hypothesize about the causes, or you can start by listing a number of causes and then show how they contribute to a particular effect.

6 Consider a problem-and-solution pattern. You can use this pattern effectively for papers in which you argue for change or propose an idea to settle a problem.

The first part of this pattern says, "We've got a problem and we've got to solve it—now." This part of the paper provides background information to demonstrate that the problem exists and is urgent.

The second part of the problem-and-solution pattern steers the reader through proposals for solving the problem. Since most of these ideas will be rejected (or furnish only a part of the recommended solution), the advantages and limitations of each are examined carefully. This section of the essay assures readers that no plausible approach has been ignored.

In the third part of this pattern you propose and defend one solution to the problem. You may then want to discuss the disadvantages and advantages of this proposal, highlighting the advantages while allowing readers to feel that no hidden agendas guide your proposal. You can then conclude by explaining how the change can be put into place.

Problem-and-Solution Pattern

Introduction *Present thesis . . .*	I. All business school graduates should be required to take a course on professional ethics.
Body	
◆ *Problem and need for solution established*	II. Public distrust following recent scandals is bad for business
◆ *Rejected solutions*	III. Threat of punishment not enough
❐ First rejected solution	
• Advantages	A. May deter some illegal actions
• Disadvantages	B. But damage is done whether or not crime is punished, and
❐ Other rejects . . .	C. Unethical actions may be legal
◆ *Proposed solution*	VI. Ethics class prevents problems
❐ Feasibility	A. Easy to add a new requirement
❐ Disadvantages	B. Some want fewer requirements
❐ Advantages	C. Focus on ethics not legalities
❐ Implementation	D. Principles addressed via debate
Conclusion *Closing summary . . .*	V. A discussion of principles will help graduates balance obligations to public, customers, & investors.

7 Use formatting and visual elements to reinforce your paper's organization. When the assignment allows it, don't hesitate to use visual devices such as bulleted and numbered lists, headings, color, and images to help readers see at a glance how you've organized your project. For detailed advice on incorporating visual elements into a text, see Chapter 18.

EXERCISE 3.2 Working with your classmates, consider what patterns you might use for writing about two of the topics listed below. Give reasons why you think those patterns would work well in each case.

Where to eat out near campus
The popularity of the Harry Potter series
Safety problems in your community
Home-schooling versus public schooling

3d How do you outline a paper?

An outline can help you keep a writing project on track, whether you are following one of the patterns described in Section 3c or following one of your own. But a blueprint for your essay doesn't have to be a formal, full-sentence outline. Experiment with several techniques until you find out what works best for you.

1 Try a working list. The working list is the most flexible of all outlining devices. Start by jotting down the key points you want to make, leaving plenty of room under each major idea. Then, working from a brainstorming list or perhaps from freewriting on the subject, select subpoints to fit under these major headings. This strategy works best as a preliminary planning technique, because it allows you to add examples and points (under the main ideas they support) as they occur to you.

EXAMPLE 3.1 Working List: Should People Be Allowed to Own Exotic Pets?

Why the issue of owning exotic pets is getting attention

- Internet makes it easy to purchase exotic wildlife
- International animal trade a multibillion-dollar business (recent *Times* article: 5,000-7,000 pet tigers in the US alone)
- More people interested in owning wild animals (quote Juan's roommate)
- Few states have strict laws limiting who can own exotic snakes, big cats, tropical birds, and other wildlife as pets
- Recent safety problems (give examples: neighbor's escaped boa constrictor, North Carolina case of tiger cubs roaming suburban neighborhood)
- Animal welfare agencies are calling for stricter rules

Arguments for owning exotic pets

- Many owners are responsible, take good care of animals
- Some take homeless or rescued animals that no one else wants
- Individual property rights (Florida case)

Why stricter limits on ownership should be imposed nationwide

- Would ensure that people don't buy dangerous animals on a whim, then get tired of them
- Could prevent neglect and abuse of pets by requiring owners to educate themselves (*Animal Finders Guide* site)
- Would still allow reputable wildlife preserves and parks to operate

When you think you have enough material, look over your list and decide which points you want to treat first and how you can arrange the others. Then start writing and, as you work, refer to your list to check that you are staying on track. Add and delete items as you need to—nothing in a working list is untouchable.

2 Make an informal (scratch) outline. Many writers like working from careful plans but dislike the restrictions of formal outlines. For them the informal or scratch outline—which arranges points into categories and subcategories—provides a happy medium.

A scratch outline should begin with a thesis that states your claim or main idea. Then decide what major points you'll use to support that thesis. For each major point you'll need subpoints that support, explain, or illustrate the main point. However, your statement of points and subpoints can be quite loose because the conventions of the full-sentence outline need not be followed. Here's a sample scratch outline, following a cause-and-effect pattern of the sort described in Section 3c-5. Note that the scratch outline is considerably fuller than the working list; thus it provides more organizational guidance.

EXAMPLE 3.2 Scratch Outline Format

Working Title	**Who Should Be Able to Own Exotic Pets?**
Working Thesis Statement	**Thesis:** Lawmakers should pass stricter laws governing who can own exotic wildlife and under what conditions, because the increasing popularity of such pets has created problems with irresponsible owners, neighborhood safety, and unwanted animals.
Main point 1	**1.** Exotic pets have become increasingly popular in the United States during the past few years.
Supporting reasons and evidence for 1	• The Internet makes it easy to buy exotic animals from other nations. • Statistics: international pet trade now a multibillion-dollar business. • Few states strictly limit ownership of these pets. • Ordinary people are increasingly owning such pets: my next-door neighbor, tiger cubs in NC suburbs.
Main point 2	**2.** Many exotic pet owners endorse lax ownership requirements.
Supporting reasons and evidence for 2	• Most owners are responsible and caring.

- Many owners are caring for homeless or rescued animals (*Animal Finders Guide* site).
- Law-abiding citizens should be able to choose their pets.

Main point 3

3. However, stricter ownership requirements are needed to prevent serious problems.

Supporting reasons and evidence for 3

- These can prevent owners from buying exotic wildlife on a whim (give examples of abandoned animals).
- Requirements can ensure that owners are educated enough to properly care for animals.
- Requirements can insist on safety precautions so that animals do not become a neighborhood threat.

3 Make a formal (sentence) outline. A formal outline is a fairly complex structure that compels you to think rigorously about how the ideas in a piece of writing will fit together. (That's why instructors sometimes require them.) If your major points aren't compatible or parallel, a formal outline will expose the problems. When your supporting evidence is thin or inconsistent, those flaws may show up too.

In a formal sentence outline you state every point in a complete sentence, and you make sentences within each grouping parallel, according to the format in Chart 3.1 on page 44. As you read through the chart, imagine how you would convert the preceding scratch outline into the fuller structure of a formal outline.

Chart 3.1 Framework of a Formal Outline

Title: Start by stating the working title of your paper.
Thesis: State your thesis fully as a complete sentence.

I. State the first major point in a complete sentence.
   A. Give the first subpoint for I.
      1. This example, evidence, or subpoint develops subpoint A.
      2. This example, evidence, or subpoint develops subpoint A.
   B. Give the second subpoint for I.
      1. This example, evidence, or subpoint develops subpoint B.
      2. This example, evidence, or subpoint develops subpoint B.
      3. This example, evidence, or subpoint develops subpoint B.
   C. Give the third subpoint for I (and so on).
II. State the second major point in a sentence parallel in structure to the first major point (and so on).

4 Outline using word processing or mind mapping software. What makes outlining on a word processor or using mind mapping software preferable to doing the job on paper is the ease with which an on-screen outline can be expanded, contracted, rearranged, and otherwise altered without waste. Rather than constraining ideas, having a digital outline encourages a writer to be flexible.

EXERCISE 3.3 Make a working list or scratch outline for a paper you're currently working on. When you are done, make a formal outline of the same project. What additions and changes did you make to construct the formal outline? Which outline will you find most helpful when you sit down to begin your first draft? Why?

3e How do you choose a title?

It may seem odd to choose a title while you are still planning and organizing a project. But titles are surprisingly important. Readers want and expect them. In fact, they may be annoyed if they don't find one that helps them anticipate what they will be reading—so craft your title carefully, keeping these tips in mind.

- **Choose a working title early in the process** (one you can change as the work progresses) that will keep you on track as you move through the planning and drafting stages of your project. Check your working title periodically to be sure it still fits the paper and make adjustments if necessary.
- **Be sure your title accurately reflects the content of your paper and uses keywords that are readily searchable online.** No cute titles, please. It's essential that your title let readers know what your paper is really about.
- **Try a two-part title** if you have your heart set on a clever phrase that's not particularly descriptive. Start with the unconventional phrase and follow it with a colon. The second part of the title, after the colon, should clarify exactly what the paper is about, as in "Short Guy, Big Ego: A Psychological Analysis of Napoleon's Military Strategy."

EXERCISE 3.4 Which of these titles are likely to be good predictors of content in a paper? Why?

1. iPods and Identity: How Push Technology Led to a Cultural Revolution
2. The Growing Trend of Hybrid Cars
3. College Students and Religion
4. What's in a Name?
5. Politics in the Hollywood Western

4 How Do You Write a Draft?

4a How do you start a draft?

Even professional writers sometimes feel anxious as they sit and stare at a blank page or computer screen. Beginnings *are* hard, but remember that a first draft doesn't have to be perfect. It's simply a place to start. In this section we offer suggestions to help you through the drafting process—so that you can stop worrying, take the plunge, and *start writing*.

In what writing environments do you produce your best work? What resources and tools help you to write? Make a conscious effort to re-create these conditions each time you begin a draft.

1 Find a place to write and get organized. If you can, find a spot away from friends, family, and noise, where you won't be distracted. Collect your materials—laptop, flash drive, notes, source materials, and a copy of the assignment—and adjust your chair and the light. Try to follow the same routine every time you work on a project.

2 Keep the ideas coming. Try not to agonize over the first few sentences. Treat your first paragraph as a device to get rolling. Write three or four sentences nonstop to build momentum, no matter how imperfect they may be. You may be surprised at how quickly words begin to flow once you've warmed up to your topic.

Remember, too, that you don't have to write the opening paragraph first. You can always begin with whatever section of the paper seems easiest to write and come back to the introduction later. See Section 13a for more on writing opening paragraphs.

3 Don't criticize yourself, or edit prematurely. As you work on a first draft, cut yourself some slack. Good writing develops over time—you can't expect something to be perfectly polished when you first start working on it.

Don't fiddle with problems of mechanics, formatting, or style in your early drafts. You can go back and fix difficulties with spelling, punctuation, parallelism, word choice, and the like *after* you've gotten your ideas down on paper. If you bog down in details of form too early, you may lose your momentum for writing, letting your brightest ideas fade. In a first draft, push yourself to grapple with difficult ideas, try an unfamiliar organizational pattern, or experiment with a more interesting style.

4 Set your own pace. When you're not sure what pace best suits you, try writing quickly at first. If you hit a snag or can't produce the specific phrase or example you need, skip the troublesome spot and move on. Above all, keep writing. A draft in hand, even a sketchy one, will give you a sense of accomplishment and material to develop and refine.

5 Get feedback from other writers. Brainstorm, share ideas, compare findings, and test out arguments with fellow writers. Your classmates and colleagues can serve as important audiences for your first draft and keep you motivated. Many college writers also visit a campus writing center to get feedback as they develop a paper draft.

In Section 4e you'll find tips for approaching collaborative writing projects. See Section 5d for advice on helping another writer revise a draft.

6 Draft on a computer. Even before you begin a draft, use your computer to accumulate and store material for your paper. Start a file that records your initial notes for a project days or weeks before the deadline. Bookmark online sources and download copies of relevant articles and images.

With a computer it's also easy to experiment with major changes without losing the work you've already done. Save alternate versions of your draft until you decide which one you want to use. If you use many different computers, consider using a Web-based office suite such as Google Docs. Such applications allow you to edit and save drafts wherever you have access to a computer and the Internet, even if you forget your flash drive.

You can also try out different formats and visual elements at this stage. See Chapter 18 for more on working with formatting, graphics, and images in your writing.

4b How do you keep a draft on track?

When you begin a draft, you will probably have a thesis and a general organizational plan in mind. You will have gathered the resources you plan to use in the paper (articles, Web sites, statistics) and perhaps developed an outline. But the real work of writing a draft doesn't start until you begin putting words onto a screen or page. Only then can you see precisely how your plan may have to be altered. You will need to be both focused and flexible: focused enough to guide readers through your ideas and flexible enough to shift strategies when necessary.

1 Highlight key ideas. Keep your thesis and main points in mind as you compose the draft. One way to do this is to summarize your thesis up front, in the first paragraph. Beginning with key points gives readers a notion of what to expect; then you can follow with supporting material. Even if you choose to ease your readers into your thesis by opening the paper with background information or an attention-getting anecdote (see Section 13a), you still need to keep your main point in mind so that the opening doesn't wander too far astray.

Continue to highlight main ideas throughout the draft. Use phrases like these to snap readers to attention.

> The main points of disagreement are . . .
>
> The chief issue, however, is . . .
>
> Here is the crucial question:
>
> I propose that . . .

Even cues as simple as *first, second,* and *third* can help readers follow the structure of your paper. For more guidance on using transitional words and phrases, see Section 14b.

2 Keep the amount you write about each point roughly proportionate to its importance in the paper. Be careful not to write a lopsided draft that misleads readers. Your introduction paragraph shouldn't take up half the paper. If your thesis promises to develop a new solution to a problem yet neglects it until the last paragraph, you haven't fulfilled that promise. Should you find yourself writing at length on a minor point, or quoting at length from one source while neglecting others, step back and return to your central argument.

However, although you should respect the principle of proportion, don't be too stingy with words and ideas in a first draft. You'll discover in editing that it is easier to prune material you don't like than it is to fill in where your ideas are thin. Don't stray too far from your thesis, but do capture any fresh thoughts that emerge as you write. The same is true of examples, illustrations, facts, figures, and details: if they don't work, you can always cut them later or find a better place in the draft to use them.

3 Allow yourself enough time to draw conclusions. Conclusions are important, so don't skimp on the final paragraphs. The ending often determines what impression readers will take from your piece.

When you approach the end of a draft, take time to review what you have written. Then consider what remains to be done: What are the larger implications of the ideas you've discussed? What do you want readers to know, believe, or do? What loose ends need to be tied up? Let these concerns shape your concluding paragraph(s). If you have time, try out several endings and choose the one that you think best fits your audience and purpose. See Section 13b for more on closing paragraphs.

WRITER AT WORK **A Drafting Journal**

Student writer Tallon Harding recorded in a writer's journal the steps she went through in drafting "Overwhelmed and Overworked: How Today's High Schools Fail to Meet Students' Needs," which she wrote for a first-year writing course (see the full draft on pages 68–72). In what ways does her process reflect the suggestions made in this chapter? How does her drafting strategy match and differ from your own? Which of her strategies, if any, might you try next time you write a paper?

—When I got the assignment, two weeks before the draft was due, I knew almost right away what topic I wanted to write about—the fact that high schools push students so hard to do college-level work before graduation. I started by freewriting to explore my general argument and my own experiences.
—Next, I made a scratch outline of main points and allotted myself about a week to complete the draft, with the first two days devoted to research. I searched the campus library's online resources and found sources that provided evidence to back up my arguments and new information that helped me to better develop my thesis—I also found sources that disagreed with my viewpoint and had to figure out how to address these in the paper.
—The next day, I began to form my rough draft, using my outline as a guide along with the information that I had gathered in my research. There were several times when I was unable to focus on my paper, and during these instances I would go for a quick run to clear my head. When I returned, I was able to pick up where I had left off.
—In this way, over several days, I wrote most of my paper, working on one or two paragraphs at a time, taking breaks in between each one. Within four or five days I had completed my rough draft, at which point I took a day off, completing the assignments in my other courses.
—After twenty-four hours had passed, I returned to my paper and read it over. With a fresh mind, grammatical and structural mistakes were more obvious, and I was able to edit and proofread. I did this again on the following day, correcting smaller errors and fine-tuning my wording until I was ready to give the draft to my instructor for feedback.

4c When should you take a break?

In the middle of a writing project you may suddenly find yourself stumped. You gaze at your computer screen or look at a blank page, but nothing happens. No ideas come. Such a lull can be stressful, especially when a deadline looms. But don't panic; you may simply need to kick back and let your thoughts *incubate.*

Incubation is an interval during which a writer stops composing for a time to let ideas germinate or develop. You can't force or rush incubation; you can only be ready to grab a new idea when it surfaces. When possible, start a writing project well before its deadline, since you may need several incubation periods. For authors who work consistently, such rest periods are absolutely necessary. When they've written themselves out for the day, they know it's fruitless to sit at the desk any longer.

Don't use incubation as an excuse to procrastinate, however. If you're still having problems with a project after a few hours (or a weekend) of rest, get back to work anyway. Review your notes or outlines; consult your research; reread what you've already written; try focusing on a new section of the paper. Most important, just write!

4d How do you know when you have a solid draft?

Although you'll usually have a chance to revise and polish before the final product is due, don't settle for a first draft that's incomplete or rushed—especially if you plan to ask others to read it. How do you know when you've made a solid effort? Ask yourself the questions in Checklist 4.1.

Checklist 4.1 Knowing When You Have a Solid Draft

1. **Have you made a good-faith effort?** Be sure you've invested substantial time and thought in your paper. If you haven't, it's not ready to pass along to a reader.
2. **Is it a *complete* draft?** Have you stated a thesis, developed it with supporting arguments and examples, and finished with a defensible conclusion? Have you included any charts, tables, or images that will appear in the final project? A few paragraphs don't qualify as a working draft. Nor does a carefully written opening followed by an outline of what the rest of the paper will cover.
3. **Is the draft readable?** You can't expect instructors, classmates, or colleagues to respond carefully to a paper that's hard to read.

(Continued)

Knowing When You Have a Solid Draft *(Continued)*

- Double-space your draft, leaving ample margins all the way around the page for comments.
- Be sure that your printer or photocopier has made dark, legible copies.
- If you must handwrite a draft, *print* in ink on every other line.
- Print or write on one side of the paper only and number your pages.

EXERCISE 4.1 Evaluate a draft you have recently written against the three criteria in Checklist 4.1. Does your paper meet the standards? If not, what changes would you have to make to remedy the problems?

4e How do you work on a draft collaboratively?

Being able to write as part of a group is an important skill in college, in business, and in many community settings. It's always a relief to share the workload, and collaboration often produces better ideas than a single individual could. But pundits joke about the ineffectiveness of committees for good reason. Without a shared focus and careful planning, collaborative writing projects can become frustrating exercises.

The kind of collaborative drafting we discuss in this section is different from the work of peer revision groups that meet to help individual writers improve an already written draft. For more on peer revision, see Section 5d.

1 Decide on shared goals. Suppose your instructor has asked you and several classmates to develop a promotional Web site for a local historical museum as part of a service-learning project. Before you begin work, you'll need to come to a consensus on what you want to accomplish:

- Do you want to construct a primarily informational site where readers can find the museum's address, hours of operation, admission fees, and upcoming exhibits?
- Will your site also try to persuade readers to serve as volunteer tour leaders or to donate funds?
- Will your Web site be technically sophisticated or very basic?

Of course, you may not be able to sharply define a group project in a first meeting. You may need to brainstorm or do background research. If group members have conflicting ideas, you'll need to negotiate these differences.

2 Consider dividing the project into individual sections. You may find it efficient to ask group members to research and compose a section of the project individually, and then schedule a group meeting to combine and edit the sections into a single document. Students working on the museum Web site might ask one writer to take responsibility for constructing an informational home page, another to compose pages on current exhibits, and another to create a list of external links to other Web sites of interest to museum patrons.

When you compose a group project in this way, set aside plenty of time to pull the pieces together. You'll need to eliminate overlap, address gaps in your coverage, and revise for consistency. The finished product shouldn't read like several shorter pieces cobbled together.

Splitting a document into individually authored parts is the quickest way to complete a group writing assignment. However, this approach doesn't work well for texts that aren't easily separated into components or for a document that must represent the shared perspective of a group.

3 Consider writing the document collaboratively. Collaborative drafting—a method in which the entire group writes a document together—can yield impressive results. The advantage of this method is that several ideas and viewpoints are often better than one: you'll have diverse input and ideas at every point in the composing process. There are many online applications that allow you to easily share sources and collaborate on documents. Most Web-based office suites allow multiple users to share and edit the same document; because such tools automatically save multiple versions of the same document, the confusion of having many different writers working on the same document is lessened. The primary disadvantage of this approach is the amount of time required. You'll need to schedule plenty of group meetings or frequent email exchanges to write and discuss the text in progress. If you choose this method, ask one person to be in charge of maintaining the draft in progress and recording new text and ideas.

4 Address disagreements promptly. Some college students resist group projects because they've had bad experiences with classmates who monopolized a project or neglected their responsibilities. To prevent such problems, work out a schedule of meetings and deadlines that everyone can agree on, and distribute copies to each group member. If one writer fails to abide by the agreement, raise the issue in your next meeting. You may need to ask your instructor to help if the problem persists.

Other difficulties arise when group members disagree about the direction a project is taking. Suppose that in a persuasive paper for an English composition course, some members of a group want to create a multimedia presentation on the health risks of body piercing whereas the rest want to write a traditional report. If you can't settle on an approach that satisfies everyone, consult your instructor. He or she may allow you to compose two smaller subprojects or to incorporate a statement of minority views into your document.

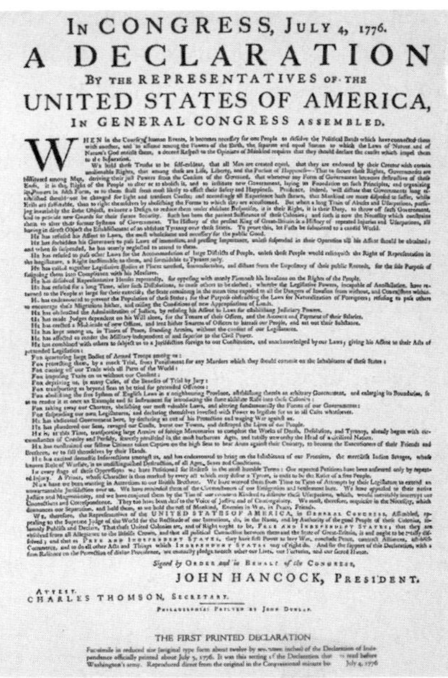

IN CONGRESS, JULY 4, 1776.

A DECLARATION

BY THE REPRESENTATIVES OF THE

UNITED STATES OF AMERICA,

IN GENERAL CONGRESS ASSEMBLED.

Signed by ORDER and in BEHALF of the CONGRESS,

JOHN HANCOCK, PRESIDENT.

ATTEST.

CHARLES THOMSON, SECRETARY.

THE FIRST PRINTED DECLARATION

The Declaration of Independence is one of the most famous and influential collaboratively drafted documents. How do you think the document might have turned out if the signers had split up the work and written different sections individually? What elements of their writing situation might have inspired them to work as a group?

5 How Do You Revise, Edit, and Proofread?

Why make a fuss distinguishing among terms as similar as *revising, editing,* and *proofreading*? Because revising, editing, and proofreading are different phases of the writing process, each of which involves thinking about a different aspect of the paper.

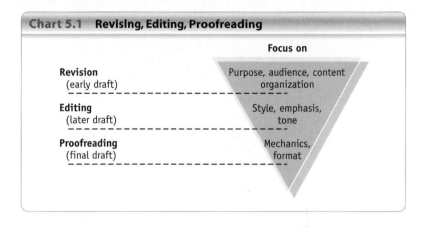

Chart 5.1 Revising, Editing, Proofreading

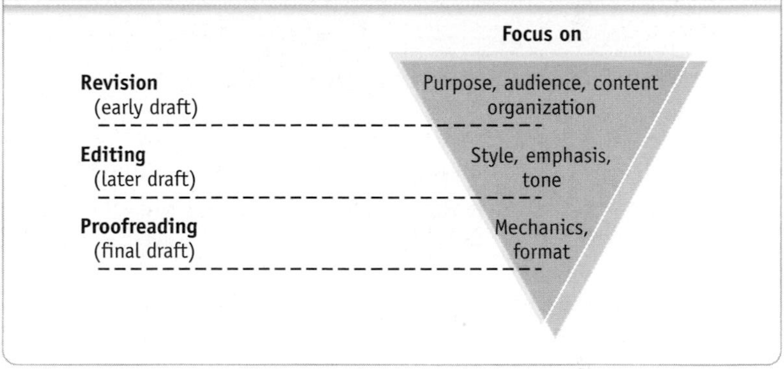

	Focus on
Revision (early draft)	Purpose, audience, content organization
Editing (later draft)	Style, emphasis, tone
Proofreading (final draft)	Mechanics, format

When you **revise** your draft, don't think in terms of *fixing* or *correcting* your writing—that's not really what you are doing. You are *shaping a work in progress,* reviewing what you have written, and looking for ways to improve it. You may get new ideas and shift the focus of the paper; you may cut, expand, and reorganize. At this point you are making large-scale changes.

When you **edit** a paper, you are less concerned with the big issues. Instead, you turn your attention to *clarity, style,* and *tone.* You may rewrite sentences you find awkward or correct problems with parallelism and repetition. Your goal is to create sentences and paragraphs that present your ideas effectively. These are small-scale changes.

When you **proofread** a paper, you go back over it line by line to *correct typographical errors, check for omissions, verify details,* and *eliminate inconsistencies.*

This is the fix-it stage, when you're preparing the paper to appear in public. Postpone proofreading until the end of a project. Otherwise, you may waste time repairing sentences that later are revised or deleted.

Although being able to distinguish among revising, editing, and proofreading is important (especially when your instructor has asked you to do one of these steps), the writing process is often more fluid and complicated than a three-part system. Sometimes, for example, you may not want to wait until the proofreading stage to fix a misspelled word or to insert a comma where you know one is needed, especially if you find that these small problems distract you from the higher-level revisions you're trying to focus on. It's okay to combine revising, editing, and proofreading if that's what works for you.

5a What does revising involve?

When you revise a draft, don't try to work through it line by line, making changes as you go. Large-scale issues of content and rhetorical strategy that affect the entire paper must be addressed before you can polish individual sentences. At this point, reconsider everything you have written. Don't tinker. THINK BIG!

Prototypes of possible future vehicles often appear at auto shows to test consumer reactions. In response, manufacturers then modify the product's design, just as you might revise a draft of a paper after showing it to readers. Think about the last few papers you wrote. Did you make changes in response to readers' suggestions? What kinds of changes did you make? Whose suggestions did you find most useful, and why?

1 Read your draft thoughtfully. Begin by printing out a copy of your draft and reading it from start to finish. Review the assignment and any feedback you have received. Ask yourself how you feel about the draft. What's good that you definitely want to keep? Where does it seem weak? Ideally you should appraise your draft several days (or at least several hours) after you have completed it so that you can read it more objectively.

When you dislike what you've written, readers have found little to praise, or you just need a fresh start, consider writing an entirely new draft. Creating a new draft may seem discouraging, but starting from scratch may be easier than repairing a draft that just won't work. Often an unsuccessful version points a writer toward what he or she really wanted to write.

2 Refine the focus of the paper. Once you've determined that your draft is workable, be sure that it makes and develops a central point. If the draft makes a lot of general statements without supporting and developing them, you have a problem with focus. Check your examples and supporting material. Have you relied mostly on common knowledge? If so, your draft may lack the credibility that comes from specific information.

Check also to see that your draft stays on track. Your introduction and thesis will evoke certain expectations in your readers. As you revise, rein in discussions that wander and tie up loose ends.

Checklist 5.1 Revising for Focus

- Have you taken on a larger topic than you can handle?
- Are you generalizing instead of stating a specific claim or thesis?
- Do you support your main ideas with evidence and examples?
- Does your conclusion agree with your opening?

See Section 2b for more on focusing a topic, and Section 3a for advice on creating and refining a thesis.

EXERCISE 5.1 Using a working draft of one of your papers, try "paragraph mapping" to help you revise for focus. For each paragraph in your paper, write a short paragraph title, a paragraph thesis, and a list of your supporting points. Did you have trouble coming up with a title or a thesis for each paragraph? If so, this section of the paper probably isn't focused enough.

3 Consider your purpose. Ask yourself whether someone reading your draft would understand what you're trying to achieve. Decide exactly what you want to accomplish and be sure that your intentions are evident to yourself and to your readers.

Checklist 5.2 Revising for Purpose

- Do you clearly state in the first paragraph or two what you plan to do?
- Does the draft develop all the main points you intended to make?
- After reading the draft, will most readers be able to summarize your main idea?

See Section 1e for more on refining your purpose.

4 Examine your paper's proportion. *Proportion* means the distribution and balance of ideas. You should develop your ideas in relation to their importance.

Checklist 5.3 Revising for Proportion

- Are the parts of the paper out of balance? For example, have you gone into too much detail at the beginning and then skimped on the rest?
- Can your readers tell what points are most important by the amount of attention you've given to them?
- Does the conclusion do justice to the ideas it summarizes?

5 Check for adaptation to audience. Sometimes a first draft is *writer-centered;* that is, the writer has concentrated on expressing his or her ideas without thinking much about the audience. Such an approach can be productive in a first draft, but a major goal of revising should be to change *writer-centered* writing to *reader-centered* writing. Put yourself in the place of your readers.

Checklist 5.4 Revising for Audience

- Do you spend too much time discussing material that most of your readers already know?
- Do you answer important questions that readers might have about your topic?
- Do you define all the concepts and terms your readers need to know?
- Do you use language your readers will understand?

See Checklist 1.2 on audience (page 8) for more advice.

6 Check the organization. A well-organized project has a plan and a clear direction. Readers can move from the beginning to the end without getting lost. To revise the structure of a draft, you'll need a printed copy because organizational problems can be hard to detect on a screen.

Checklist 5.5 Revising for Organization

- Does your paper state a clear thesis or claim? Does it then develop key points related to that thesis?
- Does the development of your points follow a pattern readers will recognize?
- Do the transitions move readers sensibly from point to point?
- Would the paper work better if you moved some paragraphs around?

See Section 3c for more on organization, and Section 14b for more on making smooth transitions between ideas.

7 Evaluate your design and check images and graphics. Now that you have a complete draft, you can assess how well the document is working visually: Have you used an appropriate format for the writing situation? Are the pages readable? Are sections logically arranged? Check any tables, charts, and images. Are they substantive, accurate, and legible? For more information about revising design elements, consult Chapter 18.

8 Check the content of the paper. When you revise, you may need to add information to give your paper more substance.

Checklist 5.6 Revising for Content

- Do you fully explain and support each main idea?
- Do you need to add specific information and concrete examples that will make your case stronger? Do you need to do more research?
- Do you cite reliable, credible sources to back up your ideas?
- Does the title of your paper reflect its content?

If the content of your draft seems thin, return to the library or to other sources. See Chapters 44 and 45 for more on doing research.

9 Revise from a printed copy. Whether you are revising, editing, or proofreading, you'll probably work best from a hard copy of your paper. Problems that seem all but invisible on a screen (weak organization, sprawling paragraphs, poor transitions, repeated words) show up more clearly in print.

EXERCISE 5.2 Apply the criteria for large-scale revision described in Section 5a to a draft you have written.

5b What does editing involve?

Revision has given you a more focused, better-organized, more interesting draft. Now you're ready to *edit*—that is, to make the small-scale changes that you put on hold while you were revising. Now is the time to use the handbook to check on style (Part III), grammar and usage (Part V), and mechanics (Part VI).

The "deleted scenes" included in DVD versions of most popular movies—such as the scene represented in this still from *Pirates of the Caribbean* (Dir. Gore Verbinski, 2003)—give us clues about how filmmakers approach editing choices in their work. View the deleted scenes from a movie you like. What can you infer about why this material was cut? Do the director's choices suggest strategies that you might apply to your writing?

1 Make your language concrete and specific. Language is *concrete* when it describes things as they are perceived by the senses: colors, textures, sizes, sounds, actions. Language is *specific* when it names particular people, places, and things.

Although generalizations and abstract terms are appropriate in some writing situations, readers usually need vivid descriptions that bring concepts to life. As you edit, add people to your discussions, illustrate generalizations with examples, and supply your readers with facts and images. Give your writing texture. See Chapter 17 for more on adding detail and variety to your writing.

2 Strive for a readable style. Look at your word choices. Do you achieve the right level of formality for the writing situation? Do you balance technical terms with everyday language? Are your subjects specific? Do your verbs express powerful actions? Are your word choices vivid and accurate?

Different writing styles are appropriate in different settings. When in doubt about what kind of language you should use in a piece, take a look at similar pieces others have written. For example, if you are writing a textbook review for an education course, look at similar reviews in education journals to see whether their authors use contractions and first-person pronouns, or whether more formal constructions are the rule. See Chapters 15 through 17 for more advice on style.

3 Be sure that your tone is appropriate. Avoid polarizing or hostile language that will alienate your readers. Replace name-calling stereotypes (such as "traitor" to describe someone who disagrees with the president or "Religious Right fanatic" to describe a member of an evangelical church) with more accurate and objective descriptions.

Nor should a reasoned argument rely on intensely emotional language ("this greedy, evil policy is disgusting . . ."). Although a well-timed expression of feeling can move readers, your personal anger shouldn't become the focus of an argument.

4 Cut wordiness. Many writers produce wordy first drafts. In subsequent drafts, however, it's time to cut. Go after sprawling verb phrases ("make an evaluation" → "evaluate"), redundancies ("initial start-up" → "start"), and strings of prepositional phrases ("in the bottle on the shelf in the refrigerator" → "in the bottle on the refrigerator shelf"). Be ruthless. You can often cut up to a fourth of your prose without losing anything (see Section 17c).

5 Test your transitions. *Transitions* are words and phrases that connect sentences, paragraphs, and whole passages of writing. When transitions are faulty, a paper will seem choppy and disconnected. Read your draft aloud. Improve the places where you pause, stumble, and detect gaps. Often you'll just need to add a word or phrase such as *on the other hand, however,* or *finally*. In some cases you'll have to rearrange whole sections to put ideas in a more coherent order. See Chapters 12 and 14 for additional suggestions.

6 Polish the introduction and the conclusion. The introduction of a draft merits special attention, but don't edit the first paragraph until you know precisely how your paper is going to come out. Then you can make sure that the introduction is accurate and interesting.

The conclusion also warrants special care, but don't fuss with it until you have the main part of the paper under control. Then work out a strong ending that pulls the paper together and leaves your readers satisfied. For more specific suggestions on how to improve introductory and concluding paragraphs, see Chapter 13.

7 Use a computer grammar or style checker very carefully. For all their cleverness, grammar and style checkers identify problems in a draft chiefly by counting items. They can't assess context. And it is usually context that determines, for example, whether expletives or repetitions are appropriate. If you have access to a style checker, use it, but don't assume that it can create a polished paper for you.

8 Refine your layout and design. Now is the time to fine-tune and polish your document's design. For example, would adding color or changing font size make the project more readable? Do you need to adjust the position of images or tables? Do the different parts of your paper look consistent? See Chapter 18 for more detailed advice on design issues.

Checklist 5.7 Editing

- Is your language sharp—concrete and specific?
- Are sentences readable and clear?
- Have you eliminated wordiness?
- Is your tone appropriate for the purpose and audience?
- Are your transitions effective?
- Are your opening and closing paragraphs polished and clear?
- Are format and visual elements appropriate and effective?

EXAMPLE 5.1 Edited Sentences from Student Papers

Here are some sentences from student papers that have been improved by judicious editing. Notice that the changes do not greatly alter the sentences' meaning.

ORIGINAL

wordy — awkward passive construction

At some point ~~or another,~~ the experience of peers pressuring one to engage in binge drinking is a dilemma that most college students ~~will have to~~ face.

EDITED

At some point, most college students face peer pressure to engage in binge drinking.

ORIGINAL

wordy

The companies ~~and products~~ that advertise in ~~women's~~ fashion magazines know that most young women in the United States want to be

awkward — unclear reference — vague

beautiful (and) alluring (and) design their ads to reflect (this).

EDITED

The companies who advertise in fashion magazines know that young women in the United States want to be beautiful and alluring, so they design their ads to reflect these qualities.

EXERCISE 5.3 Apply the criteria for editing listed in Checklist 5.7 to a draft you are working on. Give your paper the attention to detail it deserves, and don't back away from making changes where they are necessary.

5c What does proofreading involve?

Like checking your appearance in the mirror before an important meeting, *proofreading* provides a final measure of quality control. The more you care about the impression a paper makes, the more important it is *not* to neglect this last step.

Use Parts III, V, and VI of the handbook to check punctuation, usage, and the conventions of edited American English.

1 Check your weakest areas. If you are a poor speller, consult a dictionary frequently. If you are inclined to put commas where they're not needed, check to be sure they don't interrupt the flow of ideas. And see that you have chosen the correct words from the troublesome forms *its/it's, your/you're, there/their/they're.*

2 Check for inconsistencies. Have you switched your point of view in ways that might be confusing? For example, have you addressed readers initially as *you* and later referred to them as *we* or *they*? Do you use contractions in some parts of the paper but avoid them in others? Are headings in boldface on some pages and italics on other pages? Is the tone consistent throughout (not casual in some places and formal in others)?

3 Check punctuation. Look for comma splices—places where a pair of independent clauses is mistakenly joined with a comma instead of a semicolon. Take a moment to review all semicolons. See that proper nouns and adjectives (*England, African*) and *I* are capitalized. Check that quotation marks and parentheses are in pairs (see Chapters 38 and 39).

4 Check for typographical errors. Look especially carefully for transposed letters, dropped endings, faulty word division, and omitted apostrophes.

5 Check the format of your paper. Number your pages, italicize or underline titles of sources as needed, and put other titles between quotation marks (see Chapters 38 and 41). Be sure that you've cited outside sources appropriately and listed them in your bibliography (see Chapters 46 and 49 through 52). Set the margins correctly and review the page breaks.

Taking Control

Avoid Common Errors in Grammar, Mechanics, and Punctuation

Ask your instructor which errors in grammar, mechanics, and usage he or she marks most frequently—and then work to avoid these errors. Items such as the following may appear on most instructors' lists:

Comma splices: *Gas prices rose, they were already too high.*	See Section 35c
Fragments: *Gas prices rose. Already too high.*	See Section 35a
Problems with pronoun number: *Everyone took their seat.*	See Section 27a
Confusion of *its* and *it's*.	See Section 28c
Apostrophe problems in possessives: *doctors car; their's*	See Section 25b
Punctuation with quotations: *". . . Nixon lied", Yu claims.*	See Section 47c
Capitalization of proper nouns	See Section 41b
Improperly formatted title pages	See Checklists 50.2 & 51.2
Improperly formatted bibliographies	See Checklists 50.4 & 51.4

EXERCISE 5.4 Proofread a writing project you've recently completed, looking at all five of the areas discussed in Section 5c. Which problems do you spot most often? How do you think you might avoid them in future projects?

5d How do you help another writer revise, edit, and proofread?

Many writing instructors ask students to help each other in the revising, editing, and proofreading phase. (For advice on interpreting your instructor's comments on your paper, see Section 6a-7.) Meeting in small groups, writers read copies of each other's drafts and respond to them. Sometimes called *peer revision*, this method allows each writer in the class to receive feedback from one or more readers. Even if you don't have the chance to participate in a formal peer editing session, try to get several readers' reactions to your work in progress.

It takes skill to respond to another person's writing critically and honestly. When you do so, remember that you aren't taking the place of the writing teacher: you're an editor, not a grader. You can help a fellow writer most by showing an interest in what he or she has written, asking questions, giving encouragement, and making constructive suggestions.

Similarly, use peers' criticism of your own drafts constructively, listening closely and selecting the comments that best suit your goals for the project. This section provides tips to help you get the most out of a revision session.

1 Read the writer's draft straight through once. Get a feel for the big issues before worrying about details of mechanics and usage. Do you understand what the writer is trying to achieve? Could you summarize the point of the paper? Do you find it informative, persuasive, or interesting? First impressions are important; if you don't think the draft works, try to explain why.

2 Read the paper a second time. Use the guidelines in Checklist 5.8 on page 67 to help you formulate specific responses. It's important that you say more than "I really like your paper" or "A few of your points are confusing." Explain *what* you like about it, such as well-researched facts or colorful turns of phrase. Show *where* you believe the paper needs development. At this stage keep your focus on large-scale issues, not on misspellings or editing problems to be dealt with later.

3 Make marginal comments. Jot comments in the margins of the draft as you read it the second time. Editorial comments should be genuine queries or constructive observations, not stinging criticisms. Even when you're pointing out a weakness in a paper, use a supportive tone, not a sarcastic or unkind one. Be as specific as you can about your reaction to the paper, and let the writer know where something is working well.

4 Write a general response to the paper. After you have read and annotated the paper, write a thoughtful note at the end summarizing your reactions. Begin by saying what you think the paper has accomplished. That way the writer knows whether the paper has achieved at least part of what he or she hoped. Conclude your note with suggestions for revision, stressing what you believe the writer's priorities might be.

Checklist 5.8 Responding to a Draft

- What do you like most about the paper?
- How well does the paper achieve its purpose?
- How well does the writer tailor the piece to the audience? What suggestions might you make for better adapting the paper for its intended readers?
- What suggestions can you make about focusing the topic? Does the paper need a sharper thesis?
- Does the writer come across as credible? What suggestions can you make that might add greater authority to the paper?
- What questions does the paper raise? What additional information, discussion, or examples would you like to have?
- How effectively does the writer use language? Are sentences clear and readable? How appropriate is the tone? Do you notice recurring problems with grammar, usage, or mechanics?
- What general comments do you have for the writer?

WRITER AT WORK **Draft with Peer Comments**

Here is a draft of a paper by first-year composition student Tallon Harding. The assignment asked her to write a researched argument on a topic relevant to her and her classmates. It is a fine draft in many respects, focused and thoughtful. It uses personal experience and clearly articulated claims to catch readers' attention, drawing them into the argument. It also incorporates source materials effectively.

However, the draft also has some weaknesses. To summarize them, we've reproduced some marginal comments and a concluding memo that is a composite of comments written by several of Tallon's peers, including undergraduate student writer Todd Lucas. Notice that most of these comments target large issues for revision rather than editing and mechanical problems.

Note, too, that Harding's draft cites and documents sources in MLA Style, the system used for most academic writing in the humanities. You'll find more information about MLA Style in Chapter 50.

Harding 1

Tallon Harding

Professor Rollins

English 101

Paper #2

30 October 2009

Overwhelmed and Overworked: How Today's High Schools Fail to Meet Students' Needs

School let out an hour ago but the library is packed with students. Each of us is working frantically to finish the next day's assignments. The Advanced Placement Tests will be given on Monday and we all need the weekend to study; the pressure is almost unbearable. A couple of years ago this spectacle—an evening not much different from most during my senior year—would have confounded the average high school librarian, who would have been able to leave as soon as school let out. Recently, however, such scenes have become commonplace. Due to a push by school officials looking to receive government grants, students are increasingly being pressured to enroll in college-level courses offered in the high school classroom. As part of the Education and Economic Development Act passed by the South Carolina state legislature in 2005, all high school students in the state will be required to declare a major by 2011 (Smith). What these ambitious administrators forget is that a good, well-rounded high school education should involve more than just academic study. It must also include extracurricular activities that help students to grow socially and physically, to become well-rounded citizens. As schools neglect these qualitative dimensions in their quest to achieve higher and higher

Good point—a lot of high schools are pushing this now.

Can you give more information about this program?

academic standards, they leave gaps in students' education and neglect important student needs.

College-level courses, such as the Advanced Placement (AP) and International Baccalaureate (IB) Programs, were originally developed to give advanced high school students a means to better prepare for the rigorous demands of a postsecondary education. It was hoped that the most gifted, organized students would be able to take classes that would help them bypass introductory college courses and dive into more challenging ones upon entering college. In recent years, however, government grants have been made available to states that have high participation rates in these courses ("Advanced"). As a consequence, many school officials now push as many students as possible to enroll in AP and IB classes, with less regard for the student's qualifications or level of preparedness. This practice has left some students struggling to pass, when they could have done well in a lower-level class. Similarly, the brighter students, for whom the courses were designed, have ended up packing their schedules with many advanced courses and in turn overworking themselves.

Say more about these grants.

The number of high school students taking college-level courses has increased tremendously in the past few years. According to the College Board, sponsor of the Advanced Placement Program, there has been a 50 percent increase in the number of high school students taking the college-level AP exams since 2002; this means that an astonishing 700,000 high school graduates in 2008 took at least one AP exam (Ramírez). The media has greeted these numbers with praise and applause, congratulating the nation's school districts for a job well done. Less attention has been paid to the number of students actually passing the exam, however. According to the College Board's annual *AP Report to the Nation*, the national average for 2008 graduates passing at least one AP exam during high school is only 15.2 percent (de Vise). These numbers show that as the number of students taking college-level courses has increased, the percentage passing the affiliated exams to receive college credit has shrunk.

Is a drop of 5% dramatic?

Unfortunately, as participation in challenging academic programs grows, some high school students are forced to drop extracurricular activities to make time for studying. These students are left with only a narrow portion of a traditional, well-rounded high school education. For example, high school student Jenni Deming, a talented dancer, reported in a personal interview, "I quit ballet training right after the beginning of ninth grade, because I couldn't figure out how to fit in daily dance classes along with the three or four hours of nightly homework I had in my Honors courses." Other students, such as Marisa Astiz, who was featured in a recent news article on high school student stress, find themselves running from one academic activity to another, with little time to make friends and even less sleep (Strauss). In fact, with the use of so many college-level courses and the introduction of high school majors, secondary education is becoming more and more like college. The average college student spends the majority of his or her day studying and is not as involved in the community as one might hope. This pattern increasingly fits the typical high school student. However, the high school student's situation is even more difficult: A college student typically spends a smaller portion of her day in the classroom

Are extra curriculars more important than studying?

and usually enrolls in about five classes per semester, whereas a high school student spends almost eight hours a day in school and may take up to seven classes per semester.

Today's high school students are being cheated. They are no longer free to participate in a wide variety of activities that would help them to grow into well-rounded adults, but are instead skipping that part of their education and basically starting college four years early. The personal cost of focusing too hard, too soon can be tremendous. A recent survey of first-year college students found that rising numbers of students arrive at college already suffering from depression and stress-related disorders (Strauss). An article in the *San Francisco Chronicle* reports that increasing numbers of overachieving students now burn out before they even get to college, deciding to take one or more years off to pursue interests that they did not have time to enjoy in high school (Strauss). Perhaps these students are guilty of being too ambitious, but they are not solely to blame, since many educators and parents are the ones pushing them to overachieve.

If these students are over-achievers, they might be stressed out anyway.

Instead of focusing on grant money and enrollment numbers, school officials need to reevaluate the impact these courses are having on students. Simply studying the recent AP scores would show them that this new form of academics may be doing more harm than good. Instead of packing their schedule with multiple AP and IB classes, students need to take one or two in order to be able to focus their attention on them, and yet still have time for other activities. High school is a critical time in young people's lives, and without both academic and extracurricular activities, they cannot establish the strong and well-developed character that is the goal of any educational system. A good high school education should aim at fostering well-rounded citizens as well as academic achievement, and many high schools today simply do not meet these criteria.

Works Cited

"Advanced Placement Incentive Program Grants." *U.S. Department of Education*. 9 September 2008. Web. 6 July 2009.

Deming, Jenni. Personal Interview. 14 Oct. 2005.

de Vise, Daniel. "Maryland Leads U.S. in Passing Rates on AP Exams." *Washington Post*. Global ed. Washington Post, 5 Feb. 2009. Web. 3 July 2009.

Ramírez, Eddy. "More Students Get Passing Scores on AP Tests." *USnews.com*. U.S. ed. U.S. News and World Report, 13 February 2008. Web. 3 July 2009.

Smith, Gina. "S.C. Public Schools Get Mixed Review." *The State*. Global ed. The State, June 14 2009. Web. June 30 2009.

Strauss, Valerie. "Students Are Taking Time Out Over Stress." *San Francisco Chronicle*. Global ed. San Francisco Chronicle, 23 Oct. 2005. Web. 3 July 2009.

WRITER AT WORK **Peer Comments**

Dear Tallon,

I think your paper is interesting and persuasive. Almost anyone who has graduated from high school in the past few years is familiar with your topic, and they will sympathize with your feeling that students are being pushed so hard academically that they don't have time to do anything else. The examples you give of the students who have had to sacrifice to keep up with their studies are powerful.

Your opening contains good background information to show why schools are pressuring students, especially the statistics about the AP exam. Consider adding more specific facts about the government grant programs. I wasn't familiar with them. I also wasn't sure whether this is the only cause of the problem. Parents sometimes insist that their child be in the best courses regardless of ability, and teachers may want the prestige of teaching advanced courses. Even students can feel competitive with their peers.

I think you also need to say more about why academics shouldn't be the most important priority for schools. I see your point about the importance of maintaining a balance, but that might not sound practical for all readers. Most students know that they have to have good test scores and grades to get into a good college. No one gets admitted to college based on being a "well-rounded" person. Give a little more importance to academics in your argument, because otherwise it might come across as too idealistic.

I marked a couple of confusing places, but overall, I believe that with a little more revision, this will be a good paper.

Sincerely,

Todd

PART II

WRITING FOR ACADEMIC AND PUBLIC FORUMS

CHAPTER

6 How Do You Write in College?

6a How do you write a successful academic paper?

As a college student, you can count on having to write. That's a fact of life, regardless of your major. Academic writing is not necessarily tricky, but it differs from high school writing because college instructors have unique requirements in mind. Although expectations vary from subject to subject, most instructors will expect you to approach topics with a critical eye, to justify your ideas with logical reasons and evidence, and to cite the sources of your information. Once you understand these responsibilities, you can address academic audiences with confidence.

1 Review the assignment. When instructors assign a writing project, they usually have specific expectations in mind.

Before you get too far into a project, ask yourself these practical questions: How much research will you have to do? What special materials will you need? How much time do you have? Some books may not be immediately available, or the library may not carry the periodical you want. If you need to do interviews, allot time to contact people and keep appointments. And if the paper is due in the same week as two papers for other courses, start early. See Section 43c for more on creating a workable schedule for completing a writing project.

2 Don't take on too much. When you make a claim in a paper, you've staked out a piece of territory: you've asserted what you believe and drawn lines around it, and now you have to defend it. You don't want to find out when you're halfway through that your claims are overextended, so stake out a topic that you can manage. Then you'll have a chance to think and write about it in detail. See Section 2b for advice on how to narrow a topic.

Popular and academic publications often report on similar topics, such as diet and health, but they usually support their claims quite differently. How do you think the kinds of information and arguments provided in the two cover articles on the right might differ? Which would you be most likely to consult in writing a paper for a course? Would the kind of course (e.g., an English course versus a biology course) affect your decision? Why or why not?

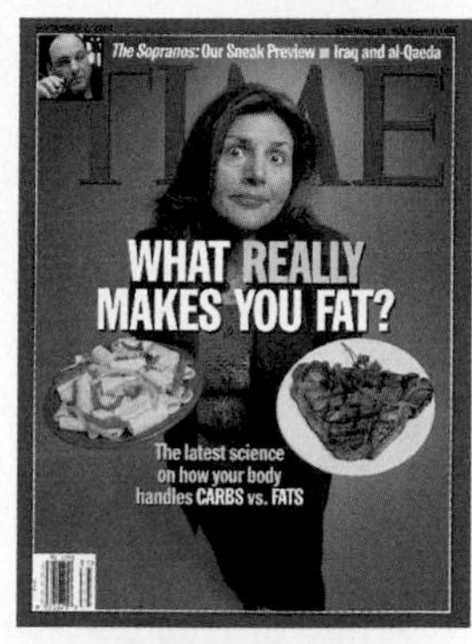

American Family Physician

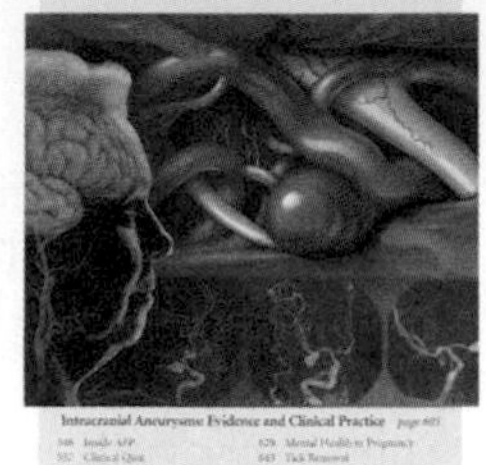

3 Support your claims with logical reasons and sufficient evidence.

Unless you're doing an informal assignment such as a journal entry, it's usually not enough in a college course to claim on the basis of personal feelings or popular opinion that something is true or that something should be done. Instructors want students to support their claims with academic reasons and evidence.

In a paper written for a college course, your supporting materials should come from reliable, recent sources, and you should be able to produce enough of them to show that you know the topic. This means doing research. Depending on the paper you're writing, you might look for the following kinds of data:

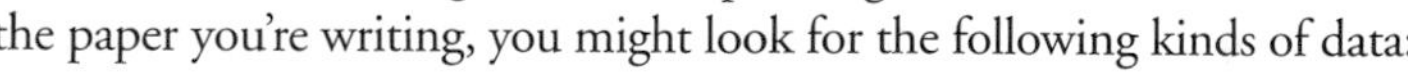

- Historical documents
- Research findings
- Eyewitness accounts
- Analyses written by experts on the subject
- Statistics

You'll find such evidence in reference sources, scholarly books and articles, government archives, and publications produced by professional organizations.

However, be sure your arguments and evidence are appropriate to the writing task. If you are writing a paper for a history class, historical documents and secondary sources written by historians will be the most relevant, whereas a profile article for a journalism course might draw primarily on material collected in personal interviews with your subject. See Sections 44b through 44d for more on finding appropriate sources for an academic writing project.

WRITER AT WORK **Writing an Annotated Bibliography**

An instructor may ask you to turn in an *annotated bibliography* that briefly describes and evaluates the sources you plan to use in a paper. In an annotated bibliography, you should include a full, correctly formatted citation for each source you list, followed by an *annotation* that discusses its relevance to your project. While your annotations should be brief (in most cases, no more than four or five sentences), after reading them, your instructor should have a good idea of not only what the book, article, Web page, or other item is about, but also of whether and how it is useful to your argument.

While instructors' requirements vary, here are some general tips for writing annotations:

- *Describe*—Summarize the source's major arguments and discuss the methods used by the author.
- *Evaluate*—Are the major claims valid? Did the author do a good job of making her point? Here, you will offer your assessment of the argument.
- *Discuss relevance*—How is the source relevant to your paper and how do you plan to incorporate it? Do the arguments in the source help or hurt your own argument?

In the following sample, undergraduate student Irene Elliott from the University of South Carolina assesses materials she discovered while researching the concept of free speech for a paper that she wrote for a composition course. Do you think her annotations meet the above requirements listed above?

Irene Elliott

Dr. Friend

Topics in Writing

17 April 2009

Annotated Bibliography for "The Outer Limits: Defining Free Speech in a Democracy"

De Luca, Tom. "Free Speech, Political Equality, and Campaign Finance Reform: A Paradox for Democracy?" *New Political Science*. 29.2 (2007): 145–166. Print. This scholarly article discusses the importance of political equality and free speech in democracies. Citing many Supreme Court cases and political thinkers, De Luca argues that democracy demands fairness in order to function. Throughout the article, De Luca argues for an amendment to the Constitution that would ensure political equality despite economic circumstance. The article provides convincing quotations and philosophical statements supporting free speech.

Lipschultz, Jeremy Harris. *Broadcast and Internet Indecency: Defining Free Speech*. New York: Routledge, 2008. Print. This book attempts to define free speech and show how it applies to the Internet and other forms of public media. Lipschultz argues that the concept of free speech has always been debated throughout American history. Free speech continues to be questioned today now that radio, television, and the Internet have changed how we think about it. The book is useful in giving different definitions of free speech and explaining different interpretations of the concept.

Liptak, Adam. "Unlike Others, U.S. Defends Freedom to Offend in Speech." *New York Times*. Global ed. New York Times, 12 June 2008. Web. 14 Apr. 2009. This article from the *New York Times* discusses the consequences of offending people through speech in the United States and other countries. Liptak discusses an article in a Canadian magazine that made offensive remarks about the Muslim religion; the magazine was sued as a result. A similar case from France centered on a woman who publicly criticized a Muslim ceremony and was fined $23,000. According to Liptak, if these cases had occurred in the United States, there likely would not have been any apology or fine, due to our different attitude toward free speech. Liptak strongly supports protection of free speech and gives dramatic examples to support this side of the issue.

MacManus, Emily. "Will British Libel Law Kill Net Free Speech?" *OpenDemocracy*. Open Democracy. 27 Mar. 2009. Web. 10 Apr. 2009. This article discusses free speech and libel laws in the United Kingdom, which MacManus characterizes as the defamation capital of the world. This trend she attributes to the Internet, where freedom of expression and the rights to opinion and comment are protected by law but are balanced with the rights of individuals and companies to not have their reputations unfairly harmed by defamatory statements. Traditional media have found this delicate balance, but the Internet's availability to a global audience has created a situation in which, the author argues, any statement published anywhere could conceivably be claimed to lead to damages under UK law. This article argues extreme views but provides a reminder of what happens when control of offensive speech becomes excessive.

Shipley, Robert L. "Why No One Should Be Silenced on Campus." *Boston.com*. The Boston Globe, 9 Apr. 2009. Web. 10 Apr. 2009. Shipley's article asserts that many campuses will allow liberal voices to be heard while attempting to censor conservative ones. The article describes a speech given at U Mass-Amherst in March 2009 by conservative columnist Don Feder. During his speech students became disruptive and continued to heckle Feder until he left the lectern midway through his remarks. The article argues for campuses as "free speech zones" in which anyone's ideas can be expressed, examined, and discussed. This piece is useful because it provides a current example from a college campus.

4 Document your sources. When you cite statistics or research, your instructor will want to know where you got your data. And if you use *any* material that someone else thought of or wrote first, you're obligated to give that source credit. If you don't, you're committing plagiarism. (See Section 46c for more about plagiarism.)

Documenting sources takes time, but it's an essential part of college writing. It's not difficult to do once you know where to look for guidelines. Sections 49a and 49c offer comprehensive information on documenting sources.

5 Follow research and writing conventions appropriate to your subject area. The guidelines we discuss in this chapter apply generally to the writing you'll do in any course, but be aware that some expectations differ from subject area to subject area. Suppose that you want to write a paper on alcoholism. Imagine the various forms it might take in different courses: In a creative writing course you might craft a poem about a character's struggle with recovery. In a sociology course you might write a case study based on interviews with a member of Alcoholics Anonymous. In a biology course you might collect and report on data about the physical effects of alcohol on laboratory rats. All three projects would require critical thought, research, and the ability to construct a clear argument. Their differences grow out of the different goals and approaches valued in each discipline:

- **Goals:** What kinds of topics and questions interest scholars in this discipline? What do they want to find out?
- **Methods:** How do scholars in a particular discipline go about finding out what they want to know? Do they test hypotheses systematically and empirically? Do they critically interpret texts and other artifacts?
- **Evidence:** What kinds of materials do scholars in a subject area typically use to support their arguments—numerical data, historical artifacts, quotations from literary or philosophical texts?
- **Genres:** What kinds of documents do scholars in a field typically produce—lab reports, critical analyses, case studies, personal commentaries? What organizational and stylistic conventions are accepted?
- **Documentation:** What system do scholars in the field use for citing and documenting sources?

The chart on pages 82–83 lists some basic characteristics of research and writing in the humanities, social sciences, and natural sciences. Keep these

Highlight Writing in Different Academic Disciplines

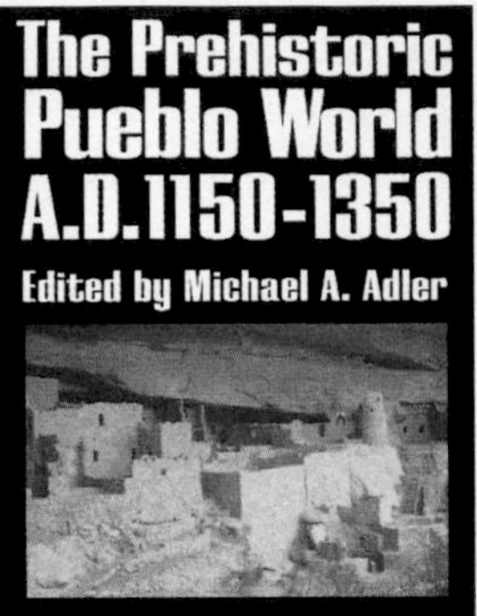

	HUMANITIES	SOCIAL SCIENCES	NATURAL SCIENCES
Subject areas	Literature, philosophy, history, classics	Sociology, psychology, anthropology, social work, education	Astronomy, botany, chemistry, physics, zoology
Purposes	To study how people use language or other symbols to interpret experience	To study how people create and live within social systems	To study the structure and workings of the physical world
Methods	Close reading and analysis of texts	Fieldwork and other observational research; statistical analysis of data	The scientific method, experimental testing of hypotheses
Sources	Literary, philosophical, and historical works and critical commentaries on them	Data collected from interviews, surveys, field observations; previous research by other scholars	Data collected through systematic observation in controlled settings

(Continued)

Writing in Different Academic Disciplines *(Continued)*

HUMANITIES	SOCIAL SCIENCES	NATURAL SCIENCES
Formats		
Critical and interpretive essays, book reviews, personal and reflective pieces, creative writing	Field notes, case studies, research reports, reviews of research	Lab reports, research reports, summaries of research, process analyses
Documentation		
Usually MLA; CMS in certain fields	Usually APA	Often CSE

in mind as you approach writing in various courses, and ask your instructor when you're unsure about what rules apply.

6 Submit professional-looking documents. When you turn in a paper, you send your instructor a message about the kind of student you are. Even if your instructors have been lenient about usage or punctuation errors when they read your drafts or haven't issued special warnings about grammatical correctness, they care about such details in the final product. If your paper looks good, it will make a good first impression.

Before you submit an essay for a grade, proofread for faulty punctuation, agreement errors, and spelling. Get a second opinion from a friend. Consult the grammar and usage portions of this book and run your computer's spell checker. Then make sure that your paper complies with any formatting instructions included in the assignment: Has the instructor specified MLA or APA style? a particular font size? single or double spacing? See Section 5c for advice on proofreading and Chapters 50 through 52 for help with particular formats.

Instructors don't like to get papers they can barely read. Word-process all writing projects, double spaced, with numbered pages. Be sure your printer produces quality output. Fasten pages together with a staple or paper clip.

If the assignment allows it, you may want to experiment with layout, images, and other visual elements to create an even more attractive finished product. Chapter 18 provides comprehensive advice on document design.

7 Understand how your writing will be evaluated. Much of the writing you do in college will be evaluated and graded. Commenting and grading policies differ from institution to institution and from instructor to instructor. But in most courses, you should seek out the following information before you submit a writing project for a grade. Find out

- What are the grading standards in your course and in your school? What specific qualities does *A, B,* or *C* work have? What does *A, B,* or *C* work represent: *Excellent, Superior, Average*?
- How will the grade in the course or the particular assignment be calculated?
- What counts toward the grade? Will outlines, notes, or drafts be evaluated? What role will class participation, quizzes, or peer editing play?
- What will the revision policy—if any—be?

Your instructor will often provide this information in a course syllabus or assignment sheet; if you have questions, ask.

In most college courses, your instructor will also give you periodic feedback, in the form of grades or written comments, to tell you how well your writing matches his or her standards. Not all instructors provide written comments, but most are willing to meet with you to talk about your work.

However, grading is not a one-way street; as a college student, you have the responsibility to

- Recognize that grading standards in college courses are generally more stringent than those in high school courses.
- Assume that your instructor is acting in good faith in evaluating your work.
- Pay attention to instructions, to grading criteria, and to instructor comments on your work.
- Pursue grading inquiries reasonably and responsibly.

Most important, recognize that you can learn from the evaluation process if you approach it as a tool for improving your writing.

Checklist 6.1 Writing for College Assignments

When you write an academic paper, remember to

- Assess the assignment carefully.
- Limit your thesis to one that you can adequately cover and support.
- Support your claims with reasons and evidence.
- Follow conventions appropriate for the subject area.
- Document your sources.
- Hand in only carefully edited, proofread, professional-looking papers.

EXERCISE 6.1 Here are several claims from undergraduate writing assignments. For each claim, suggest specific kinds of supporting evidence you think the writer's instructor would find appropriate and convincing.

1. *From a research project for a social work course:* For children who come from abusive families, high-quality institutional care is a better option than programs that try to reform the parents in an effort to keep the family together.
2. *From a research paper for a first-year writing course:* Professional athletes are poor role models because so many of them engage in unsportsmanlike or illegal behavior, on and off the playing field.
3. *From an essay exam for an ethics course:* Circuses are unethical because they exploit animals purely for entertainment.
4. *From a research review for a human biology course:* A growing body of data suggests that asthma has a strong genetic component.

EXERCISE 6.2 Evaluate a paper you've recently written for a college course against Checklist 6.1 above. Then ask yourself these questions: Does your paper meet the standards? Where does it fall short? If you could write the paper over again, to which item on the list would you pay the most attention? Why?

6b How do you write essay examinations?

If you're like many students, you'll do most of your writing outside the classroom—in your room, the library, or another familiar and relatively comfortable setting. However, every college writer should also know how to compose under pressure. Researchers estimate that up to half the writing you do during college will occur on exams. After you leave school, you'll find that many jobs require the ability to write quickly and efficiently. Unfortunately, many writers resign themselves to failure at this kind of writing, believing, "I freeze under pressure."

Don't give up before you start. You *can* write well in an exam setting if you understand the unique skills involved and work to master them.

1 Know the material. Preparation is half the battle in an essay exam. Lay the foundation for success by attending class regularly, keeping up with required readings, and participating actively in class discussions.

But simply absorbing the material is not enough. You also need to organize and think critically about what you know. Look for clues in course lectures and readings about what ideas and examples are important (*Three basic arguments for . . .; A central figure in . . .*). Summarize important theories and concepts in your own words to be sure that you understand them. Review your notes periodically and ask yourself how new material fits with the old.

If your teacher often asks students to express their views on course material or apply it to new situations, you can bet that he or she will include these kinds of questions on the exam. Prepare yourself by rehearsing your views about key points in the lecture and readings: Do you agree? Do you disagree? What approaches or theories make the most sense to you?

To practice applying your knowledge, imagine how the material you're studying might relate to a current event or controversy. For example, that article you read in your U.S. history course about the debates between the Federalists and the Anti-Federalists in the Revolutionary period might help you understand what's at issue in a contemporary Supreme Court decision about states' rights. See Chapter 8 for detailed advice on getting the most out of your reading.

2 Find out as much as you can about the exam. Because an exam may cover hundreds or even thousands of pages of material, focus your preparation on those portions most likely to appear on the exam. Ask your instructor for details: How many questions will the test include? What kinds of questions? What topics will be emphasized? Will you get to choose from several questions? Knowing some parameters will help guide your study: for instance, if the test consists of four short essays, you won't have time to list many examples or details, so you should concentrate on learning main ideas.

If your instructor provides copies of exams from previous semesters, seize the opportunity. An old exam can help you anticipate what kinds of items will appear, and you can use it for a practice run. If your instructor does not offer sample exams, many schools maintain test files that archive exams from a variety of courses.

3 Use your study time intelligently. This advice may seem obvious, but it's true. An exam requires you to pull together quickly what you know—so you'll need to be in top academic form. Forgo extreme studying techniques, such as cramming or pulling all-nighters, that leave you exhausted at the time of the test. Instead, spend your time practicing the thinking and writing skills that exam essays require. Make scratch outlines of important theories or arguments you think are likely to be covered, along with one or two key examples or details, and use these as the basis for your review.

Classmates can be another valuable resource. If you enjoy working collaboratively, form a study group. Meet before the exam to compare notes, puzzle out gaps in your knowledge, and practice explaining key points to each other. But don't substitute group meetings for individual study. Allow yourself plenty of time to go over group insights and integrate them with your own knowledge.

4 Devise strategies for coping with pressure. Many writers have trouble adapting their writing process to an inflexible test environment. But don't panic. You can anticipate certain difficulties and decide beforehand how you will deal with them.

First, eliminate unnecessary stress. Get a good night's sleep, eat a healthful meal, and keep anxiety-producing cramming to a minimum. Gather all your materials—examination booklets, pens, calculator, and notes or books when the instructor allows them—well in advance. Arrive a few minutes early.

Plan ahead to respond to specific problems that can occur during an exam: If you panic when you see an unfamiliar question, work on the easiest items first, then come back to the more challenging ones. If you fall apart when time runs short, give yourself a safety net by outlining each response before you start writing, so you can attach the outline to any unfinished response. And if you will write the exam on a computer, save frequently so that you don't lose something important.

5 Figure out what the question is asking you to do. Analyze each exam question carefully before you begin writing. Start by locating all the key terms—usually nouns or noun phrases—that *identify* or *limit* the subject: "Discuss the *major components* of *Plato's educational ideal* as elaborated in *The Republic*"; "Explain *four kinds of confounding* that can occur in *observational research*." Next, underline key verbs that tell you what to do with the topic: *analyze, compare, discuss, explain, trace*. Each of these instructions means something a bit different, as Chart 6.1 on pages 89–90 shows.

Cross out any material that does not seem relevant to the question. Instructors sometimes begin an exam with a quotation, an example, or an introductory discussion that serves primarily to clarify the main question. In this example from a British literature course, for instance, the core question is stated only in the last sentence.

> Since the beginning of the semester, we have seen thinkers such as Freud, Marx, and Nietzsche describe the philosophical contradictions that inhabit the twentieth century. *Choose one major text we have read this semester and trace the ways that work describes contradictions in private, public, or intellectual activities.*

Here the references to Freud, Marx, and Nietzsche only introduce the idea of "contradiction," the focus of the main question. To answer this question, you don't need to comment on any of these thinkers; you just have to explain how contradiction shows up in one of the literary texts you studied for the class.

EXERCISE 6.3 Identify key terms in an examination question from a course you are taking or from a standardized test for college admission, job certification, or another purpose. What specific topics does the question stake out? Which verbs tell you what to do with those topics? Make a scratch outline showing how you would address these components of the question in your response.

6 Budget your time. Keep the amount of time you spend on each question roughly proportionate to its importance. If you squander most of your time on a single question, you may jeopardize your success on the remaining items. Here is a simple way to figure out how to allocate your time: Divide the number of points each question is worth by the number of points on the whole exam. The result equals the percentage of time you should devote to that question. For example, suppose you have a fifty-point question on a one-hour test that is worth two hundred total points. You should probably spend about fifteen minutes, or 25 percent of the hour, on that response.

If you run out of time in the middle of a response, resist the temptation to steal time set aside for other questions. Instead, jot a note to your instructor explaining that you ran out of time, and attach your outline. Some instructors will give partial credit for outlined responses.

Chart 6.1 Common Exam Terms

Analyze: Break a text, argument, or concept into parts and explain the relationships among them; evaluate or explain your interpretation or judgment.

> Analyze the effects of ketosis on the digestive system.

Apply: Take a concept, formula, or theory and adapt it to another situation.

> Apply Bernard's elements of sound executive management to President Ronald Reagan's management practices during his first term.

Argue, prove: Take a position on an issue and provide reasons and evidence to support that position.

> Argue whether you believe it is possible to run government agencies like private sector businesses, drawing on the theories and cases we have studied this semester to support your answer.

Compare: Point out similarities between two or more concepts, theories, or situations.

> Compare the educational philosophies of Dewey and Rousseau. How did each conceptualize the learner, the function of education, and the role of the teacher?

(Continued)

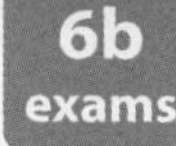

Common Exam Terms *(Continued)*

Contrast: Point out differences between two or more concepts, theories, or situations.

> Contrast the imagery in Yeats's "The Second Coming" and Hardy's "The Darkling Thrush."

Critique, evaluate: Make and support a judgment about the worth of an idea, theory, or proposal, accounting for both strengths and weaknesses.

> Evaluate the effectiveness of medication versus behavioral therapy in the treatment of hyperactivity disorder in children.

Define: State a clear, precise meaning for a concept or object, and perhaps give an illustrative example.

> Define the three measures of central tendency (mean, median, mode); then explain which would provide the most accurate gauge of annual income in a given community.

Discuss, explain: Offer a comprehensive presentation and analysis of important ideas relating to a topic, supported with examples and evidence. These questions usually require detailed responses.

> Discuss the Ebonics controversy, drawing on the research we have studied this semester to clarify key points of difference.

Enumerate, list: Name a series of ideas, elements, or related objects one by one, perhaps giving a brief explanation of each.

> List Jean Piaget's stages of moral development, and give an example of how moral choices are negotiated at each stage.

Review, summarize: Briefly lay out the main points of a larger theory or argument.

> Summarize the definitions of legal discrimination presented in the decisions *Sweatt v. Painter* and *Hopwood v. The University of Texas.*

Trace: Explain chronologically a series of events or the development of a trend or idea.

> Trace the pathway of a nerve impulse from stimulus to response.

7 Make a plan. To pack as much writing as possible into the allocated time, take five minutes or so to map out your answer. If the question asks for independent argument or analysis, brainstorm or freewrite to generate ideas. If the question asks you to synthesize course material, try an idea map that organizes information under key categories. (See Section 2c for more on prewriting techniques.)

Use these initial ideas as the foundation for a list or scratch outline of the full response. Whatever format you choose, it should include your thesis, main supporting ideas, and important examples. Once your outline is in place, you are ready to begin the actual writing. See Sections 3c and 3d for more on organizing and outlining an essay.

8 Understand what a good response looks like. Although no single approach can guarantee you perfect marks on every test you take, most college instructors want a tightly organized response that contains the following elements.

- **A clear thesis statement** in the first paragraph or, better yet, as the first sentence.
- **Logical organization** with a single key idea developed in each paragraph and with clear transitions between points.
- **Adequate support and evidence** for each point, drawn from course readings and lectures.
- **Your own views or analysis** when the question asks for them. Remember, though, to justify your ideas with evidence and support.
- **A conclusion** that ties together main points and summarizes their importance, even if you have time for only a sentence or two.
- **Clear prose** free of major grammatical and mechanical errors.

Finally, before you set aside a lot of time for editing and proofreading, ask your instructor how he or she deals with grammatical and mechanical problems. Many teachers don't penalize minor mistakes unless they hinder the clarity of your argument, but others are sticklers for correctness.

WRITER AT WORK **Framing a Successful Examination Essay**

Undergraduate writer Jena Gentry, a student at the University of Texas, encountered this question on the midterm for a U.S. history course: "Discuss some important causes of the Great Crash of 1929. How did Presidents Hoover and Roosevelt try to deal with the resulting Great Depression? How successful were they?" Note how the opening paragraph of her response, excerpted here, summarizes basic concepts and forecasts the direction of her argument.

> The economic boom of the 1920s had a dramatic impact on the U.S. economy. While corporate profits were large, they weren't being recycled into the consumer market, but rather invested into an inflated stock market whose prices were continually increasing. The terrible result—the Great Crash of 1929—came as a result of four main causes: the saturation of the consumer market, a rigid price structure and speculative market, an unequal distribution of wealth, and Republican public policies that favored the rich. Two presidents, Hoover and Roosevelt, tried to deliver Americans out of the subsequent Great Depression. However, Hoover believed that the government should stay out of the economy, and his modest program of legislation didn't do much. Roosevelt's ambitious New Deal was more successful, bringing many Americans a measure of relief, recovery, and reform.

The rest of Gentry's essay contains eight paragraphs: one devoted to each cause of the Great Crash, one discussing Hoover's efforts to deal with the Depression, two explaining and evaluating Roosevelt's New Deal, and a brief conclusion.

CHAPTER

7 How Do You Write for the Public?

7a How do you write outside the classroom?

Knowing how to write effective academic papers is crucial to your success in college. However, college writers must also adapt their writing to settings outside the classroom. With the advent of texting, instant-messaging, and online social networking sites, college students now do more writing outside school than ever before. Of course, much of the writing you do outside of school is personal and informal—shared only with family or friends. But if you are like most students, you will also compose more formal public writing projects, to wider and less familiar audiences. Instructors at many universities now require students to compose documents for nonprofit groups, to publish pieces in local media, or to post their writing to the Web, in addition to writing traditional papers. On your own, you may write letters to elected officials, post comments to news stories you read online, create publicity materials for campus groups, or even publish your own blog. What do all these tasks have in common? They are all *public* statements of one kind or another.

Yet what impresses readers in one setting may offend them in another, just as the same joke might get a big laugh at a family dinner but raise eyebrows at a church banquet. When you take your writing public, think about your rhetorical situation and what seems appropriate and most effective under the circumstances.

1 Learn to spot opportunities for public writing. Writing can be a powerful way to make your ideas heard and to get things done. But not all situations lend themselves equally well to it. Before you take your writing public, ask yourself these questions.

- **Is writing the most effective response to this situation?** Suppose that your neighbor's dog has just bitten the mail carrier. Would it be more effective to write a letter to your neighbor warning her to keep her dog inside or to simply pry the dog off the mail carrier's ankle? The answer is obvious (at least, we know which answer the mail carrier would prefer). However, if you believe that your neighbor's dog is part of a larger problem caused by lax leash laws in your city, that problem might be addressed by sending an email to the city council members or circulating a citizen petition.

- **Is there an audience who cares (or can be persuaded to care) about your message?** Each year thousands of preteens email declarations of love to pop idols such as Miley Cyrus or Robert Pattison. Are such letters examples of effective public writing? No, because no matter how passionately the writers feel about their statements, neither the stars to whom the letters are directed nor any other audience beyond the individual writer has strong feelings about the emails' topic. On the other hand, a group of students might successfully write to request that Cyrus make an appearance at a school fund-raiser.
- **Is the timing right?** Public writing is most effective if it appears when an issue is relevant to readers. Your boss doesn't want to read your memo calling for longer employee lunch breaks during the busiest workday of the year; nor will many people care to read an online comment on a news story if it's posted two weeks after the story appeared.

Writing is challenging—too much so to waste your effort where it's unlikely to have an impact. When you choose to write, choose the setting and the timing carefully to make sure that every word counts.

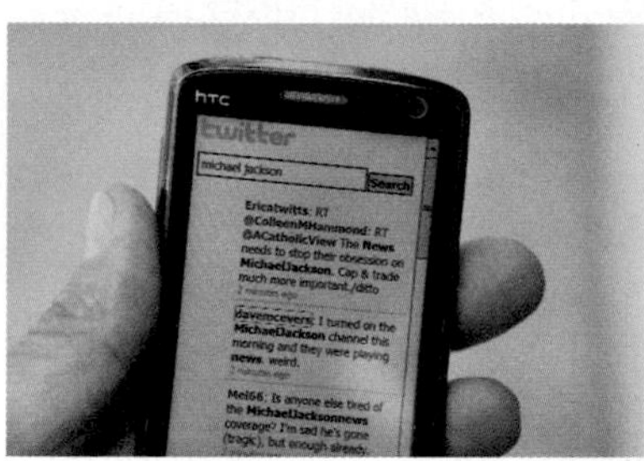

When citizen protests of election results in Iran were met with violence in June 2009, people from all over the world wanted to help document and speak out against the violence. Do some research to learn about reactions to the protests: Did people from your campus or community respond to these events? Which of these efforts involved writing? What purposes and audiences did the writing serve? Can you cite examples of public writing related to this event that were especially effective or ineffective? Discuss your answers with your classmates.

2 Research your readers' expectations. When you write in a public setting—especially a setting new to you—don't automatically fall back on familiar academic conventions. The kind of writing your instructors reward in college will not always be received with enthusiasm in other forums. And different expectations will apply in different situations.

Before you begin any project for an unfamiliar audience or venue, find out what is expected.

- What genres and topics are typical for this forum?
- What are the typical length, style, and tone of documents published in this setting?
- What kinds of arguments and evidence do writers typically draw on?
- What are the expectations for formatting and for citing sources?

Many publications make submission guidelines available to prospective writers. If these are not available, seek out models. If you're entering an essay to win a scholarship, request a copy of the previous year's winning essay. If you hope to publish an article in a local music magazine, skim previous issues to get a feel for the kinds of topics and stories it prints. (Chapter 19 contains models of several kinds of nonacademic writing projects.)

Also call on colleagues, instructors, friends, or the staff of your university writing center for advice and feedback. When you're unsure, it's better to head off a potential mistake than to recover from one that appears in print.

3 Understand the benefits and risks of public writing. Although you may feel anxious when you turn in a course paper, your instructor and classmates are a relatively private audience. Slips in logic or punctuation won't usually damage anything other than your grade, and you can generally experiment with new ideas without fear of offending your instructor. But when you write for larger public audiences, responses may be more direct and less predictable. If you post a note on Facebook complaining about working conditions at your job, co-workers who see it could pass it along to your boss—who may take your complaints personally.

For this reason, any time you make your writing public it's important to consider the various audiences your work might reach and the impression you hope to make. Knowing that your ideas have reached and affected others is precisely what makes writing so rewarding. But be prepared: *Before* you publish, post, or mail your piece, think through the possible responses it might elicit. Once you've anticipated these consequences, you can decide how you want to address them.

For instance, when student writer Jesse Faleris wrote the letter advocating gun control that appears on pages 96–98—a letter he emailed to National Rifle Association (NRA) leadership at their annual convention—he faced a tricky rhetorical situation. As a longtime member of the organization, he understood their entrenched resistance to gun control measures of any kind and knew that such arguments would have to be carefully presented in order to be heard. He solved this problem by prefacing his arguments with a statement of his commitment to gun ownership rights and to the organization's general goals. He recognized that his letter might nonetheless evoke negative responses, but he felt that the argument was important enough to justify the risk. (See Section 1g for more on creating a positive impression on readers.)

4 Be professional. You'll be taken seriously as a writer if you submit attractive, polished, and carefully edited and proofread documents. That rule applies to virtually every writing situation. See Section 5c for more on this topic.

WRITER AT WORK **Shaping an Argument for a Public Audience**

As you read this letter that student writer Jesse Faleris addressed to NRA leaders, note how he carefully tailors his argument to his audience. Consider, too, the ways in which his letter differs from an academic research paper on gun control.

Jesse M. Faleris
3321 Edisto Street
Columbia, SC 29207

January 15, 2009

National Rifle Association of America
11250 Waples Mill Road
Fairfax, VA 22030

To Fellow Members of the National Rifle Association:

I am greatly concerned about the current escalation of gun legislation and how our organization's position may affect the rights of American

(Continued)

citizens to own firearms. Unfortunately, I believe that our organization's current philosophy of "Guns do not kill—people do" is no longer an effective stance, and that if the Second Amendment is to survive future abolition legislation, our organization must transform its image.

Recognizing that NRA leaders receive many letters and requests, Jesse states his claim early.

Before I continue with my suggestions, let me offer a summary of my background. I am a military careerist with ten years' United States armed forces active duty service. I am the son of an accomplished gunsmith who is actively involved in Canadian firearms legislation. I have four years' experience in military public relations, and I am currently a public relations and law philosophy student at the University of South Carolina. I am the coach of the USC ROTC pistol team. Most importantly, I am a gun owner and an advocate of all Americans' right to bear arms.

These personal details build common ground with the audience.

It is this last concern that prompts me to write to you today. The primary mission of our organization is to protect Americans' rights to own and use firearms for sport as well as self-defense. But currently the majority of our literature and activities focus narrowly on opposing all attempts at firearms legislation. I understand why the NRA maintains the firm stance on the Second Amendment that "the right of the people to keep and bear arms, shall not be infringed," but a firm philosophical position does not solve social problems any more than misdirected legislation does. This is because the general public simply no longer accepts our "guns don't kill" logic. In the midst of heightened awareness of hate crimes and random violence, the handgun is quickly becoming the social icon of America's violence problem. Polls from the Gallup Organization, the Associated Press, and others reveal that upwards of 75 percent of Americans favor further gun legislation.

For these reasons, the NRA must drop our current anti-legislation attitude in favor of a "responsible gun owner" platform. We must demand that not only our members, but also the gun owners outside our membership and the firearm manufacturers actively advance responsible gun ownership, even if this means new legislation. As gun owners, we must take responsibility to safeguard our firearms against use by irresponsible persons with the following steps.

A bulleted list highlights the major components of the proposal.

- *We must protect unsupervised minors from access to firearms.* Yes, trigger locks! If used, trigger locks are a responsible means of regulating who uses a firearm. Again, I understand the NRA's fear that any infringement will lead to abolition, but if we look at Canada as an example we may find voluntary compliance unrealistic.

- *The manufacturers must contribute to safeguarding the public from firearm products.* Including trigger locks with the purchase of new firearms is a necessity. Providing additional trigger locks for existing guns at manufacturers' cost is reasonable and would be recognized as a positive and responsible response to consumer America's concerns.
- *Finally, we must work with legislators, particularly those supportive of gun owners, to draft and introduce effective and responsible gun legislation.* This legislation should focus on criminal use of guns. We must find a way to keep criminals from using guns, without limiting law-abiding citizens' right to keep and bear arms.

As a linchpin between gun owners, Congress, and gun manufacturers, the NRA wields the influence to arbitrate these responsible proposals. These are our guns, our streets, our children, and our legislatures—let us take responsible action to safeguard all we hold precious.

I hope that my honest intentions are clear. I do not want to lose my rights, nor my children's, nor my grandchildren's rights to keep and bear arms. I am convinced that the NRA wants to protect our rights in a changing social atmosphere. What I hope is that we can reshape our tactics in order to effect positive changes in the average American's beliefs about gun ownership.

Respectfully,

Jesse M.Faleris

EXERCISE 7.1 Here is a list of four public writing projects completed by undergraduate students. For each project answer these questions: How do you think the piece differs from an academic treatment of the same topic? What kinds of adjustments do you think the writer made for audience, purpose, and setting? Discuss your responses with classmates.

1. An article on aging and nutrition for a nursing-home newsletter.
2. A proposal directed at the city arts commission requesting funding for Diversity Week activities sponsored by a local cultural organization.
3. An informational Web site that rates local landlords and apartment complexes according to the number of renters' complaints filed against them.
4. A review of the latest Harry Potter film for the local paper.

7b How do you write in service-learning courses?

Although much of the writing you do in school will never leave the classroom, an increasing number of college courses now incorporate one or more *service-learning projects*—projects that ask students to engage in community work as part of an academic course. Service learning can take many shapes. Some service-learning courses ask students to draw on their service experiences to write traditional academic papers and assignments. In other courses, students apply what they learn in a course by writing "real" documents for community agencies or groups. For examples, visit the Web site of Campus Compact, a national alliance of colleges and universities committed to community service.

If you're taking a writing class that includes a service-learning component, you'll learn more about organizations in your community and the work they do. You'll gain experience working collaboratively with others, and you'll make contacts that may help you find future volunteer opportunities or a job. Perhaps most important, you'll have a chance to test your research and writing skills on real audiences. However, because they combine several audiences, purposes, and sets of expectations, service-learning projects pose special challenges. This section offers general guidance for dealing with these and introduces you to Ray McManus, a student writer who completed a service-learning project at the University of South Carolina.

1 Understand the dual purpose of service learning. Service-learning projects differ from the volunteer work that you may have done outside school, even if that work has involved writing. Service learning always involves an academic dimension—your instructor asks you to work in the community not just because it's a civic-minded thing to do but so that you can also explore concepts that you're learning in the course. In service-learning projects, both the service and the academic dimensions of the course are equally important; one reinforces the other.

When you begin a service-learning course, ask yourself:

- How does my work in the community reflect, reinforce, or call into question the material I'm learning in class?
- How does the material I'm learning in class help me to effectively approach the work I'm doing in the community?

Ray McManus, the student writer whose work is featured throughout this section, engaged in a service-learning project as part of an English Education course. The project, in which he and other students designed and led poetry workshops for teenagers at the local public library, had both practical and academic components. On the one hand, his experiences with the workshops allowed him and his classmates to test approaches to teaching poetry that they'd studied in class. On the other, the workshops gave Ray, who subsequently graduated and went on to become a teacher of creative writing, valuable practical experience in his major field.

2 Be aware of the different audiences your writing may address. The dual purpose of service learning means that at times, you may find yourself writing for two different audiences—your instructor and the community readers of any document you produce. Sometimes you'll write for both audiences simultaneously. Be aware of their differences and tailor your work accordingly, since the expectations in one setting are likely to differ from those in another. If you have questions about what's expected, don't hesitate to ask.

In Ray McManus's project, for example, he composed some documents to turn in to his professor, some that were seen only by library staff and patrons, and others that were directed to both audiences:

- **Work produced for his instructor** included an annotated bibliography of resources on children's poetry, lesson plans for the poetry workshops, reflective journal entries, and a final research paper.
- **Work produced for the library staff and patrons** included collaboratively written publicity flyers, a newspaper press release, and a thank-you letter to the library director.
- **Work produced for both audiences** included the lesson plans, materials, and activities for the poetry workshops.

3 Find out how your work will be evaluated. The fact that you must write for several audiences sometimes makes it hard to figure out whether you're doing a good job with a service-learning project. For example, what if your instructor expects you to write very detailed lesson plans for tutoring sessions in an adult literacy program, whereas most tutors in the program take a more relaxed approach to planning by jotting down just a sentence or two?

When you encounter different sets of expectations, you'll feel more confident if you know how your work will be evaluated: Which pieces of your writing will your instructor grade? Will he or she evaluate them according to academic criteria? Will the community members you work with judge some or all of your writing? If so, what criteria will they use, and will they determine part of your course grade? Once you know these parameters, you can adjust your work accordingly. See Section 6a-7 for more on how writing is evaluated.

4 Be willing to learn and to collaborate. Certainly a key goal of service-learning programs is to make university students' energy and talents available to others in the community. But remember that anytime you enter a new writing situation, *you're* the novice. Be ready to learn from the people you work with and to collaborate productively with them.

When Ray McManus and his classmates began designing poetry workshops for local teenagers, they had had plenty of experience with writing poetry and had researched ways to engage teenagers in learning about it. But when it was time to craft publicity materials for the sessions, they knew little about how to reach young people likely to attend. Ray and his partners needed the expertise of library staff who had advertised previous youth programs and who had contacts with local teachers. They also needed the library's publication office to translate their ideas into an eye-catching format. The flyer that resulted from this collaboration is featured below.

WRITER AT WORK **Collaboration and Service Learning**

Here's the publicity flyer that resulted from the collaborative efforts of Ray McManus and library staff members. Do you think the flyer is effective? Why or why not?

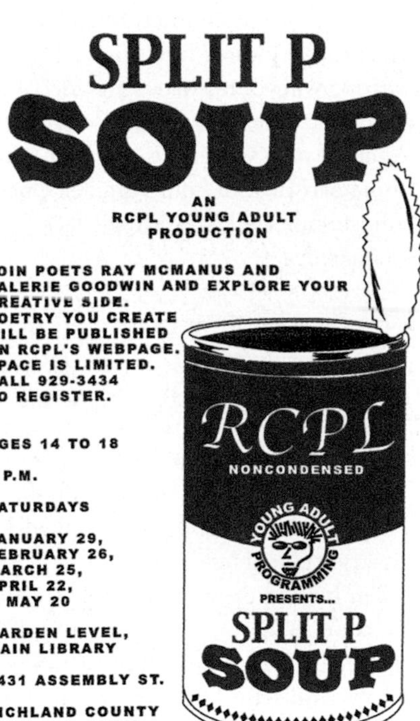

SPLIT P
SOUP
AN
RCPL YOUNG ADULT
PRODUCTION
JOIN POETS RAY MCMANUS AND VALERIE GOODWIN AND EXPLORE YOUR CREATIVE SIDE.
POETRY YOU CREATE WILL BE PUBLISHED ON RCPL'S WEBPAGE.
SPACE IS LIMITED.
CALL 929-3434 TO REGISTER.
AGES 14 TO 18
4 P.M.
SATURDAYS
JANUARY 29,
FEBRUARY 26,
MARCH 25,
APRIL 22,
& MAY 20
GARDEN LEVEL,
MAIN LIBRARY
1431 ASSEMBLY ST.
RICHLAND COUNTY
PUBLIC LIBRARY
COLUMBIA, SC
RCPL
NONCONDENSED
YOUNG ADULT PROGRAMMING
PRESENTS...
SPLIT P
SOUP

CHAPTER

8 How Do You Read and Think Critically?

Each day you are bombarded with messages that try to influence you—that urge you to buy a particular brand of shoes, to support a particular cause, to vote in an upcoming election, and to see the latest blockbuster film. Dealing with these competing messages requires that you examine ideas, ask questions, challenge arguments, and decide which viewpoints are worth accepting—in other words, that you think *critically*. Much of the information you absorb in college will be obsolete in a few years, but the critical and analytical skills you develop will serve you the rest of your life.

In college, a crucial element of critical thinking involves learning to read critically, because much of what you write and think about is in response to what you read.

8a How do you read to understand complex material?

College reading assignments pose special challenges. In high school, teachers may cover a textbook chapter in a few days or a week; in college, instructors often assign several chapters in the same amount of time, along with supplementary readings from scholarly journals, literary texts, and other sources. College assignments may also address more abstract ideas and use more complicated language. Whereas you may be accomplished at reading sources that summarize and analyze issues *for* you—as high school textbooks or popular magazines do—in college you'll often have to weigh issues, interpret data, or negotiate a range of primary and secondary sources on your own.

But the classroom isn't the only place you'll encounter difficult texts. You'll also sift through competing viewpoints and complex material when you research campaign issues before voting, follow news coverage of a local event, participate in online discussions, or draft a report at work. To navigate these texts, you'll need to be an active, engaged reader.

1 Preview the text. Just as you can navigate an unfamiliar city more easily when you have a map, you'll find it easier to read an unfamiliar text if you first scope out its features.

- **Genre.** What kind of document is it? an introductory textbook? a blog post? a literary work? a video clip? a scholarly article? Different genres have different purposes and audiences, which you should keep in mind as you read.
- **Title.** What does the title tell you about the piece's content and purpose?
- **Organization.** If you're reading a printed text, are there headings or subheadings? If you're reading on the Web, are major sections listed in the left-hand frame or on a home page? What do these divisions suggest about the text?
- **Sources.** In a printed source, inspect the bibliography and index. What do the sources listed there tell you about the kinds of information the writer will draw on?
- **Point of view.** Is the author's point of view known and relevant? What are the interests and biases of the publisher or the sponsoring institution? Does the text purport to be objective, or does it present itself as subjective and personal?

Before reading, also determine your goals: Are you skimming to see if a text is relevant to a paper you're writing? Are you interested in general concepts and arguments, or do you need to know details? Do you want to develop your own opinions on the subject? These goals should influence how much time you spend reading and which strategies you use.

2 Look up unfamiliar terms and concepts. Understanding difficult material is easier if you have the relevant background knowledge. When you preview a text, circle key terms, concepts, or topics that sound unfamiliar. For instance, you'll feel completely at sea reading an article about the African diaspora if you don't know what *diaspora* means and your knowledge of the geography of the continent is fuzzy. A look at a dictionary and an encyclopedia entry on Africa will put you on more solid ground.

3 Slow down. Read slowly and reread two or three times to fully grasp a complex argument or explanation. Some experts advise reading everything twice: the first time just to understand what the writer is saying, the second to focus on your own reactions and opinions. If you are reading a literary text for a class in which your instructor will expect you to conduct a close analysis, rereading is especially important; see Chapter 11 for more details.

4 Annotate the text to clarify and respond to its content.

Critical reading involves more than passively absorbing words on a page. It's an active process. One way to read actively is to annotate—that is, attach notes, comments, and questions directly to the text, either by writing on a printed source (or a photocopy of it) or by using the commenting features of your word-processing program.

If you're not accustomed to taking notes on your reading, here are some useful strategies.

- **Content notes.** Many college students highlight key passages in their texts. But if you want to get the most from your reading, don't stop there. When you arrive at an important point or get tangled in a difficult passage, translate it into your own words to clarify its meaning.
- **Context notes.** Notes can also help you follow a text's structure. At crucial transitions, jot down a key word or two that explains where the argument is going or how a new point fits in: "Opposing argument," "Previous theories," "Example 3," for instance.
- **Response notes.** Don't just accept what a text says; talk back. Carrying on a dialogue with your reading develops your own perspective on the issues raised. Does an author's proposal excite or anger you? Write "Yes!" or "Bad logic." If the text raises questions, write them down: "But what about the innocent victims?" or "Does this argument follow?"

The box on page 106 shows how one reader used these three strategies to annotate the opening passage of an opinion piece she read while researching a paper on women in math and science professions. She made response notes in the left-hand margin and content and context notes in the right-hand margin; notice how these notes help her follow a fairly complicated argument.

When you're working on a project that involves research, it's especially important to take notes. Your annotations identify ideas and information worth returning to, highlight passages you want to quote in your paper, and help you to synthesize and engage in dialogue with the authors and texts you are encountering. See Chapters 46 and 47 for more on incorporating material you've read into a research paper.

Highlight Sample Annotations

Caryl Rivers

The Persistence of Gender Myths in Math

By Rosalind Chait Barnett and Caryl Rivers

(*Education Week,* October 13, 2004)

Should we be worried that young girls are not pursuing math-related careers at the same rate as young men? After all, in our technological era, many of tomorrow's well-paying jobs will require competence at mathematics. But today, women make up only 19 percent of the science, engineering, and technology workforce. In 1998, only 16 percent of computer science degrees were awarded to women, down from nearly 40 percent in 1984, and the downward trend continued in 2003.

[Annotation: # of women in science is decreasing—they are asking whether teachers can help reverse this trend]

Can teachers have a role in changing this picture? Or would they just be going up against innate biological differences in a futile attempt at social engineering?

[Annotation: look up]

Some argue that girls don't have the right brain structures to be good at math. Cambridge University Psychologist Simon Baron-Cohen, the author of *The Essential Difference,* goes so far as to say that men have "systematizing brains" well-suited for the hard sciences. Women, in contrast, have "empathizing brains," designed for caretaking and mothering. And the best-selling author Michael Gurian (*The Wonder of Boys*) says that only 20 percent of girls have the right brain structure for performing well at math.

[Annotation: Possible cause #1: girls' brains not suited for math]

[Annotation: fact or his opinion? when published?]

It is indeed the case that men far outnumber women in math-related fields. But is this evidence for innate male superiority? The answer is no. New research finds few sex differences in the math abilities of boys and girls. In 2001, sociologists Erin Leahey and Guang Guo of the University of North Carolina at Chapel Hill looked at some 20,000 math scores of students between the ages of 4 and 18 and found no differences of any magnitude, even in areas that are supposedly male domains, such as reasoning skills and geometry. The finding astonished the researchers, who said, "Based on prior literature . . . we expected large gender differences to emerge as early as junior high school, but our results do not confirm this." And a meta-analysis of SAT scores for some 3 million students found that girls and boys performed virtually identically in math.

[Annotation: new study w/opposite finding]

5 Apply your critical skills when reading online. Although most critical reading strategies apply to both print and online environments, electronic texts pose special challenges. Experts on reading have coined the term *screen literacy* to describe the unique skills readers need to navigate online texts.

Online texts are less stable and more loosely structured than printed texts. Reading a Web site or blog, for example, you may scroll through long passages without page markers, follow complicated series of links, and encounter several media simultaneously. The content or format of the text may change periodically. These features can make it hard to find your place within a text and to return to important material.

The boundaries that separate one online text from another are also blurred. In researching a paper for your American literature class, for example, you may wonder whether a link to biographical information on the poet Walt Whitman that's embedded in an online text of *Leaves of Grass* is a part of that text or a separate text.

These differences mean that you should adjust your reading process when you read online. Here are some strategies that experts recommend:

- Be selective about what you choose to read. Scan to find the most relevant items.
- Approach reading with your own agenda rather than always following the author's preferred path through a text.
- Pay as much attention to visual elements as you do to the words in a text. (See Section 9b for more on this topic.)

You'll also need to develop strategies for keeping track of the material you find online: When you want to read an online text carefully or return to it later, download and save or print it—especially if you find it on a Web site that is likely to change frequently. (Be sure to record the date you found the text; if you use the source in your paper, you'll need the date for the "Works Cited" page.) Use your browser's "bookmark" feature to mark sites that you refer to frequently, so that you don't lose them. You can also bookmark all sites or pages relevant to a project, arranging the items in folders that reflect its overall structure, one folder for each major section or theme.

Finally, online texts support different methods of responding to your reading. You can use the annotation features of many word-processing programs to record your reactions to files you download onto your computer.

(But be careful to clearly separate your comments from the original text.) Web pages can also be marked with comments. It's even possible to annotate bookmarks you've created to remind yourself why a particular site or page is important. (See Section 45b for more advice on organizing research materials and Chapters 46 and 47 for advice on incorporating research into a writing project.)

EXERCISE 8.1 Use the three note-taking strategies described in Section 8a-4 to annotate a reading assignment in one of your courses. How do these strategies compare to your typical approach to reading? Which strategy did you find most helpful, and why?

EXERCISE 8.2 Find and read a text that is published in both print and online versions. Possibilities include magazines (such as *The Nation* and www.thenation.com), informational materials about a nonprofit organization or political candidate, and university documents. Which version do you find more difficult to read? Why? How did your reading process differ for the two media? Discuss your answers with a group of classmates.

8b How do you think critically about your reading?

Critical reading is only an extended and focused version of the kind of thinking we all do every day when we set out to solve problems: we gather evidence, we examine options, we look at advantages and disadvantages, and we weigh others' opinions for possible bias.

1 Read as a believer and as a doubter. You'll get the most from your reading if you approach it with an open mind. Try to learn something, even from perspectives contrary to your own. An excellent way to engage with your reading is to play what the writing expert Peter Elbow calls the "believing and doubting game." This approach asks you to read and respond to a piece twice, each time adopting a dramatically different attitude.

To play the "believing" half of the game, read the piece with as much generosity as you can muster. Try to see what makes the argument so compelling to the writer, and look for claims, examples, or beliefs that seem reasonable or persuasive. Keying in on strengths may keep you from rejecting the writer's arguments prematurely. Write a paragraph exploring whatever seems most worth believing in the piece.

Then read the piece a second time as a "doubter." Scrutinize every statement for gaps, exaggerations, errors, and faulty reasoning. Ferret out any problems you can see in the writer's perspective, even if you agree with it. Again, summarize your conclusions in a paragraph. Finding weaknesses will prevent you from accepting the argument too readily.

Here's how one writer played the "believing and doubting game" with the excerpt from the article on gender myths in math in Section 8a-4.

believing — The study showing that boys and girls have similar math test scores is powerful. If both boys and girls show about the same ability level, but more girls are opting out of math and science, then something cultural must be going on. I do think it's true that parents and teachers tend to assume that smart boys will be good at math and science; gifted girls may not be actively discouraged from these areas, but they usually aren't encouraged as strongly.

doubting — I'm not sure that culture is all to blame. Women have been successful at breaking into so many of the professions historically dominated by men—think of how many lawyers, doctors, and professors are women—despite the stereotypes. If women aren't going into sciences and math in similar numbers, is it realistic to blame it all on the culture? The authors never really refute the idea that maybe girls just don't like math as much as boys do, even if they are very intelligent and have the aptitude for it.

2 Assess the writer's qualifications. Does the writer have expertise in or personal experience with the topic? Does he or she demonstrate adequate knowledge? You might find, in reading a debate about obscene lyrics in hip-hop, that some of the loudest calls for censorship come from writers who admit they have never listened to the music. A lack of expert qualifications doesn't necessarily invalidate a writer's arguments, but it should make you examine them with extra care. See Section 45a-3 for more on evaluating a writer's credentials. Section 45a-4 tells how to evaluate the credibility of different kinds of publications.

3 Look carefully at the evidence presented. A strong argument must back up its claims. When you read an argument, size up its supporting evidence.

- **How much evidence does the writer present?** Does the amount of support seem substantial enough, or does the writer rely on just one or two examples?
- **Where does the evidence come from?** Is it recent, or is it so old that it may no longer be accurate? Does it seem trustworthy, or does the writer rely on dubious sources?
- **Is the evidence fairly and fully presented?** Do you suspect that the writer has manipulated information in order to make his or her case look better?

Guard against the tendency to gravitate toward arguments that confirm your own beliefs and to avoid those that don't. Try to find arguments written by women and men, liberals and conservatives, and supporters as well as opponents of a proposal. See Section 9a for more on evaluating the evidence presented in an argument.

4 Assess whether the writer's claims go beyond what the evidence actually supports. Does the writer draw conclusions that go beyond what his or her support warrants? For instance, safety experts once made claims about the safety of air bags based on crash-test data calculated for crash dummies the size of adult men. These claims didn't hold true for children and small women. Faced with dozens of fatalities attributed to injuries caused by air bags, those experts admitted that their original claims went beyond what the data had established.

Although overstating one's claims doesn't usually result in such tragic consequences, you should question any argument that stretches its conclusions too far.

5 Look for what's *not* there: the unstated assumptions, beliefs, and values that underlie the argument. Does the writer take for granted certain knowledge or beliefs? If what someone takes for granted in an argument can reasonably be disputed, then you should challenge the author's claims.

Consider the assumptions made in this sentence, taken from an article advocating the legalization of drugs.

> The violence brought about by the black market in drugs is attributable in large part to the fact that we have chosen to make criminals out of people who have a disease.

The statement makes two assumptions: (1) People who buy and sell drugs do so primarily because they suffer from a sickness—addiction—beyond their control. (2) It is wrong to criminalize behavior that results from illness. Both assumptions may well be true, but without further explanation and support, a reader might question them on the following grounds: (1) Drug offenders may engage in illegal behavior not because they're sick but for profit, for entertainment, or as a response to peer pressure. (2) Even if drug abuse results from illness, so do many other crimes punishable by law; we don't legalize drunk driving just because many drunk drivers are alcoholics. Also see Section 9a on how to spot and evaluate hidden assumptions in an argument.

6 Note any contradictions. Look for places where pieces of an argument don't fit together. Suppose a political candidate advocates mandatory prison sentences for first-time drug offenders yet dismisses as "immature behavior" her own use of alcohol and other drugs as a young adult. One should question why the candidate excuses for herself behavior that she condemns in others.

7 Examine the writer's word choices to identify underlying biases. Everyone has biases—it's unavoidable. It's only natural that writers who want to convince others use language that favors their own point of view. But critical reading requires that you be sensitive to such biases so that you aren't unwittingly swayed by them.

Being a critical reader doesn't mean you have to distrust everything you read. But you should be alert when writers overload their prose with what rhetoricians call "god terms" (words such as *democratic, responsible, natural, fair*) or "devil terms" (words such as *destructive, fanatic, immoral, selfish*). See Chapter 15 for a more detailed discussion of biased language.

8 Be skeptical of simple solutions to complex problems, and resist black-and-white thinking. Be wary of quick, easy answers to difficult problems. Most serious issues are complex—there is seldom one "right solution."

Consider the complex issue of affirmative action in college admissions and the calls from many sectors that schools judge prospective students on merit rather than taking racial, ethnic, and economic background into account. Here are a few of the questions that complicate this solution.

- What, exactly, constitutes "merit"? Test scores and grades? Special talent in a single area, such as music or sports? Good character? If all these factors count, how should each be weighed?
- Should students who come from educationally disadvantaged backgrounds be judged by the same standards as more privileged students?
- Do some measures of merit favor certain groups of students over others? For example, using high school class rankings as an admissions criterion may work against students who graduate from elite high schools with many high-achieving students.
- Do schools have a responsibility to make up for past discrimination against particular groups? If so, what should this obligation entail?

Any solution to a problem, however perfect it may seem, has consequences. As you read an argument, look for evidence that the writer has neglected to consider the long-term implications of his or her position.

EXERCISE 8.3 Read an editorial in today's news twice, playing the "believing and doubting game" described in Section 8b-1. Which did you find more challenging, reading as a believer or reading as a doubter? Why? Did you notice anything using this method that you might not have noticed if you had read the piece just once?

8c How do you critically interpret charts, tables, and graphs?

When you read texts that present information or make arguments, you'll often encounter visual representations of data, such charts, graphs, and tables. These visual devices help readers grasp a complex body of data that could be hard to absorb through words alone. Imagine, for example, that you wanted to illustrate the cost of student housing in your area. If you could find a fact sheet that used a bar graph to show the prices ranges for two-bedroom apartments in neighborhoods close to your campus, you could quickly determine which areas offer the best rental rates.

Charts, graphs, and tables present information in different ways. This section explains how each works.

1 A pie chart shows how the parts of a whole are distributed.

A pie chart is a simple graphic that shows percentages (the slices) of a total (the whole pie). The example in Figure 8.1 gives basic information about how property tax revenues are spent in Indiana. Using this chart, you could answer various questions: How much of the state's revenue goes to city and county governments? Do schools receive a substantial share? And so on.

But pie charts can't tell readers everything. Since they generally can't include more than six or seven slices without becoming visually confusing, you wouldn't use a pie chart to create fine distinctions. Writers often collapse several smaller categories into a single "slice." For example, you can't tell from Figure 8.1 exactly which county and city services (police, water, roads) are funded by the property tax.

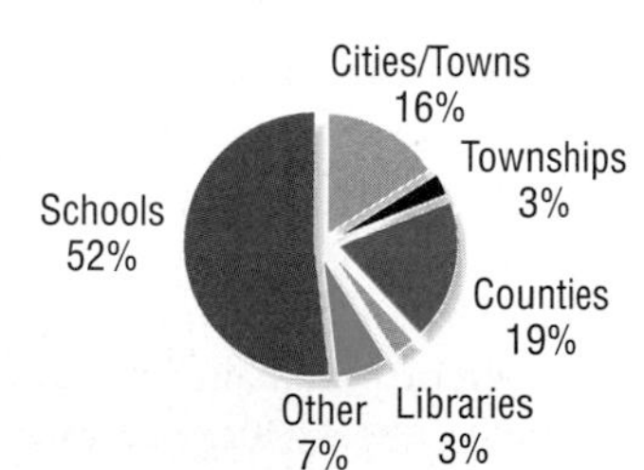

Figure 8.1

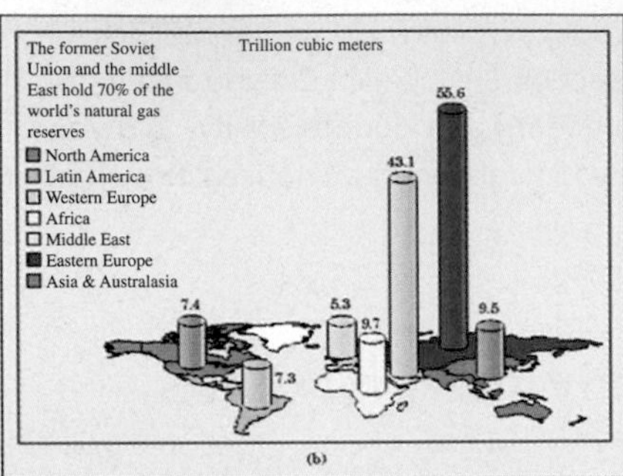

Figure 8.2

2 A bar graph shows the relationship between two variables. It does this by charting the data for one variable along a horizontal scale and the data for the other variable along a vertical scale, using vertical bars to depict data in one or more categories. In Figure 8.2, different parts of the world (Africa, Latin America, etc.) are shown on the horizontal axis; numerical data are represented by the vertical bars. By depicting this information visually, the graph dramatizes how reserves of natural gas compare worldwide.

Bar graphs can give more information than pie charts. They can show not only general trends, but also subtle distinctions within categories of data. For example, each bar in Figure 8.2 could be divided into two or three subcategories, perhaps using different colors for different countries in each region or for urban versus rural areas.

3 Line graphs also show relationships but depict trends more emphatically. Like bar graphs, line graphs chart the relationship between two variables, one depicted along the horizontal axis and one along the vertical axis. The sharply declining line in Figure 8.3 makes a strong impact on readers, who will immediately grasp the sense of what they're seeing—in this case suggesting a steep decline in unemployment between 1992 and 1999.

But you must be careful not to use the impact of a line chart to mislead readers. Figures 8.3 and 8.4 present exactly the same data on unemployment rates in the United States, but Figure 8.3 appears to show a sharp drop in the national rate during the 1990s, whereas Figure 8.4 makes the decrease look insignificant by plotting it on a grid that shows the full range of rates, from 0 to 100 percent of the population. The creators of the graphs may have had different reasons for plotting the charts as they have, either emphasizing or minimalizing the significance of the change in employment rates during the 1990s. But consider also that a reader using Figure 8.3 could more accurately determine the exact unemployment rates from 1990 to 1999 than someone using Figure 8.4.

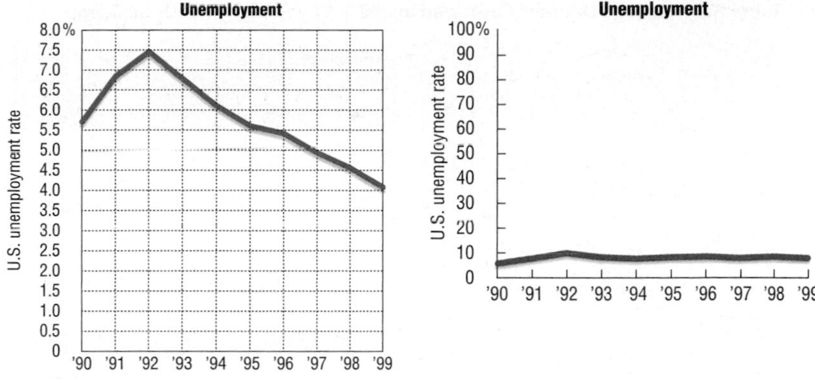

Figure 8.3

Figure 8.4

4 Tables organize categories of information into vertical columns and horizontal rows that show relationships. You can create tables to provide more detailed information than graphs or charts, but they're visually less appealing because readers must look more carefully, analyze data for themselves, and draw their own conclusions.

To create a table, think of how you might array the data most clearly. Provide a heading that identifies the data being given, then break down the data into useful categories. Even word processors typically have a feature to help you to design tables once you know how many columns and rows you need to present—though database programs are far more efficient with large amounts of data. Table 8.1 on page 116 presents information from the U.S. Department of Education about academic degrees earned in the United States in a single year, breaking down the data by gender, race, and ethnicity. Using this table, you could discover which groups are graduating with which number of academic degrees. With a little math, you could also calculate the proportions.

Checklist 8.1 on page 116 will help you detect problems that commonly appear in visual representations of information. For more information on how charts, tables, and graphs are used to make arguments, and for definitions of common statistical terms, visit Robert Niles's Web site *Statistics Every Writer Should Know.*

Table 8.1 College Degrees Conferred in 2001–2 by Racial and Ethnic Group

	U.S. Citizens and Resident Aliens						
	Total	American Indian	Asian	Black	Hispanic	White	Nonresident Aliens
Associate							
Men	238,109	2,306	13,259	22,800	23,963	170,627	5,154
Women	357,024	4,524	17,688	44,537	36,040	247,112	7,123
Total	595,133	6,830	30,947	67,337	60,003	417,739	12,277
Bachelor's							
Men	549,816	3,625	37,666	39,194	32,953	414,885	21,493
Women	742,084	5,540	45,435	77,430	50,016	543,700	19,963
Total	1,291,900	9,165	83,101	116,624	82,969	958,585	41,456
Master's							
Men	199,120	994	11,749	11,796	8,431	128,770	37,380
Women	282,998	1,632	13,665	28,577	13,956	198,865	26,303
Total	482,118	2,626	25,414	40,373	22,387	327,635	63,683
Doctorate							
Men	23,708	67	1,240	921	649	13,334	7,497
Women	20,452	113	1,077	1,476	783	13,571	3,432
Total	44,160	180	2,317	2,397	1,432	26,905	10,929
Professional							
Men	42,507	292	4,613	2,223	2,045	32,224	1,110
Women	38,191	289	4,971	3,588	1,920	26,650	773
Total	80,698	581	9,584	5,811	3,965	58,874	1,883

Source: U.S. Department of Education

Checklist 8.1 Evaluating Charts, Graphs, and Tables

When you interpret a chart, a graph, or a table, ask yourself:

- Are the data up to date?
- Have you labeled all the important elements so that readers can interpret numbers, percentages, and headings? Provide a legend if necessary to explain terms or unfamiliar abbreviations.
- What is the source of your data? Is that source credible?
- Have you argued for no more than the data can actually prove?
- Have you presented the data fairly and without distortion?

EXERCISE 8.4 Imagine that you need to give an oral presentation that uses data on college graduation rates among young men. Read Table 8.1 with this focus in mind. Working with another student, decide what information from the table would be most useful for your talk and how you might supplement the information you find there with other statistics. Share your findings with the class.

EXERCISE 8.5 Browse *USA Today, Time, Newsweek*, or another popular publication that uses charts, graphs, and tables to present information. See if you can find an example that you think presents data in an inaccurate, oversimplified, or misleading way. Bring your example to class for discussion.

8d How do you write a response paper?

When you are enrolled in a small class, particularly in such subjects as history, psychology, government, or literature, your instructor may ask you to react critically to reading assignments by turning in (or posting to a class discussion board) short response papers. Such papers often combine critical reading and argument; you read the material carefully and with a critical eye, and then react to it with an opinion, a question, a challenge, or an expansion of some point. Instructors who assign such papers often set a strict limit of one or two double-spaced pages. Thus it's important to compose responses that are succinct and to the point.

So what's involved in writing such a paper? Well, there are no universal formulas, but we can make some suggestions. First, instructors almost certainly don't want just a summary. They *do* want to know that you've understood the piece and can recount its central points, of course. But they also want to see that you've engaged with the reading: thought critically about what the author said, put the piece into some kind of context, reacted to it, argued with it, or perhaps enlarged on some point in it. Second, your instructor probably doesn't expect you to do research for such a paper, particularly if it's just one assignment of many for the course. If you do bring in an outside opinion, whether from a magazine, book, or Web site, of course you should acknowledge the source. But for the most part you'll want to refer primarily to the reading itself, citing ideas or passages that illustrate the point you're making.

The following sections outline some specific strategies for writing a response paper. These suggestions cover only a few of the possibilities that response papers offer, but they may help you get started if this kind of assignment is new to you. Such assignments give you an opportunity to inject some of your own ideas into a course and set up a productive dialogue with your instructor or with other students if you're posting the response to a class discussion board. They also provide useful practice in focusing and tightening your writing; you have to organize your thinking to develop a cogent response in just one or two pages.

1 Begin with a (brief) summary. Begin your response paper by identifying the author and title of the piece you're responding to and giving a brief overview of its main arguments. In doing so, you'll demonstrate that you read the piece carefully and understood it. Be careful, however, not to devote more than a few sentences to summarizing. Most instructors will want you to spend the majority of your response commenting on the reading—not rehashing it. See Section 46b for more on writing a summary.

2 Challenge an author's assertions. Don't assume that a book or article an instructor assigns is beyond criticism. If you encounter a statement that seems incorrect and you can give your reasons, have the confidence to challenge it. For instance, the book *The Great War and Modern Memory* by Paul Fussell is often required reading in courses on twentieth-century European history. In it, Fussell reflects on the effect that World War I had on the writers and intellectuals of the early twentieth century. In Fussell's view, it was a miserable and ultimately pointless war in which millions of young men on both sides died and European economies were shattered.

But Fussell gets himself out on a limb when he says, "What we call gross dichotomizing (we/them thinking) is traceable, it would seem, to the Great War." At this point, a careful reader might skid to a stop and ask, "What are you saying? That kind of insider/outsider mentality has been around forever. It's the we/them view that made the ancient Greeks call anyone who wasn't a Greek a barbarian. It's also the attitude behind centuries of anti-Semitism that culminated in the Holocaust." You're quite warranted in making this kind of commonsense response even to a distinguished author when you think that he or she has lapsed into careless thinking.

3 Expand on an idea introduced in a book or article that gives you new insights into an important issue. Sometimes you're lucky enough to be assigned a reading that throws new light on a subject about which you already know something or about which you have strong feelings. For example, in an introductory course in child development, you might read "What Makes a Perfect Parent?" an essay from economist Steven D. Levitt and Stephen J. Dubner's 2006 book *Freakonomics*. In it, Levitt and Dubner present statistics suggesting that "what parents *do*" in raising their children may matter less than most people think. For example, reading to one's children, being a stay-home parent, and limiting television viewing—all conventionally thought to increase children's chances of educational success—in fact have no measurable effect. On the other hand, "who parents *are*"—well-educated versus uneducated, affluent versus poor, older versus younger—correlates strongly with a child's later level of success. Given these data, the authors ask whether parenting technique matters as much as previously thought. Their argument shakes up familiar assumptions about how to foster healthy development in young children.

You could respond to this fresh look at the role of parenting in a number of ways. For instance, you could ask whether Levitt and Dubner's findings suggest a parallel to the activities of day-care providers and teachers: Do these caregivers' activities have a similarly negligible effect? Does it really matter whether a preschool teacher reads to her charges or plops them in front of the TV? Or you might consider the policy implications of the findings: If parenting techniques are relatively unimportant, should the resources now spent on parenting education programs be diverted to other efforts? New interpretations like Levitt and Dubner's are rich with possibilities.

4 Analyze and evaluate a writer's argument. Look at the central claim an author makes and how he or she supports it. Do the data seem sound and unbiased? Does the argument seem oversimplified? If so, what's missing? Could there be another, equally useful way to interpret the material being discussed?

WRITER AT WORK **Responding to a Reading**

Sometimes you can grant some of the writer's conclusions but dispute others and show alternative views. That's what student writer Ashley Hamm does in the following sample paper, in which she responds to the editorial on gender myths and math reprinted on page 106.

Ashley L. Hamm

Response Paper #1

Dr. Friend

13 January 2009

Rosalind Chait Barnett and Caryl Rivers's article "The Persistence of Gender Myths in Math" explores theories to explain the difference in mathematical achievement between males and females, questioning the notion of innate male superiority. The authors first discuss biological and psychological theories which suggest that women are not naturally inclined to choose the math or science fields because of their nurturing instinct; this instinct, some experts say, leads girls to pursue people-oriented fields such as history, medicine, or journalism. Cultural influence is examined, and the authors conclude that this is the true reason for the gender differences. The authors contend that the idea of innate male superiority is so deeply ingrained in our society that females assume it to be true, and, therefore, choose to pursue other fields of study; they suggest that even teachers are guilty of perpetuating this stereotype and should undertake special efforts to encourage girls to excel in math.

> It's important to identify the work under review in the response paper. Some writers forget this detail.

> Ashley begins with a brief summary of the piece, demonstrating that she has read carefully.

Barnett and Rivers's argument for cultural influence is both strong and valid, particularly the notion of teachers' own acceptance of the "male = math connection." However, the authors could have included stronger examples to further show the prevalence and transmission of these cultural attitudes. For example, the authors could have explored how men and women are portrayed in the media; it is much more common to see a man portraying a scientist, engineer, or computer specialist, just as it is unsettlingly common to see women portraying fashion experts, housewives, and social workers. Is life imitating art or is art imitating life? Either way, the stereotype is perpetuated.

Now the paper discusses two contributing causes—media and parents' occupations—that the authors did not consider.

It is also important to understand student background, another factor that the authors do not discuss. Because children often emulate their parents (especially the same-sex parent), we should consider the occupation of a gifted student's parents. If a young girl's mother is an engineer, will she accept the stereotype and turn to a career in the humanities—or will she be more likely to see a technical field as a viable option? The same question could be asked about a boy whose father is an artist or a social worker—will his career choice be influenced more by stereotypes or by his father's example? While the authors' arguments are generally valid, they lack specificity and regard for the full range of variables.

Here the paper brings in personal experience to demonstrate the importance of parents' backgrounds.

My experience coincides with these points. My parents both only have a high school education, and, since the curriculum has changed dramatically over the decades, they were unable to help me in math or science after the sixth grade; however, they were able to help me in English and history. Did this affect my decision to major in English? Perhaps. My aptitude for math and science is lacking compared to my peers who grew up with parents in fields requiring advanced knowledge of math or science. In turn, these were also students whose aptitude in the humanities was lacking. My "talent" for literature was not decided by my gender; had I been raised by accountants or engineers, I probably would have excelled in these subjects. The differences are clearly cultural, but all aspects and influences must be thoroughly examined before the stereotype can be fully understood and before it can be expelled.

The paper ends with a general assessment of the arguments made in the article.

CHAPTER

9 How Do Written and Visual Arguments Work?

9a What is an argument?

In college, many of the documents you read and compose will make **arguments**—that is, attempts to persuade an audience to accept a general claim, using **logical reasoning** supported by facts, examples, statistics, or other kinds of **evidence.** Arguments take many different forms and serve different purposes. If you write a paper opposing euthanasia for a composition course, that's an argument. If you email your instructor to convince her that the paper merits a *B* rather than a *C*, that's an argument too. So is a poster urging students to get free flu shots at the campus clinic, or a bumper sticker promoting environmental conservation. This chapter introduces you to some basic structures and strategies for understanding how arguments work, so that you can more critically assess the ones you encounter. For advice on using these strategies to compose your own arguments, see Chapter 10.

1 Know the difference between genuine arguments and other kinds of disagreements. In everyday life, people use the term *argument* to refer to any disagreement. But rhetoricians use the term in a more specialized way, to mean a discussion of an issue with two qualities:

1. People might reasonably disagree about it.
2. There are *reasonable* grounds for supporting one viewpoint over another.

An assertion that no one would dispute is not an argument. Statements such as "A broken leg is painful" and "If you drop that chair, it will hit the ground" can be immediately proved, so there's no need to argue about whether they're true.

Disputes about subjective personal tastes aren't arguments either. It's possible to disagree about whether vanilla ice cream is tastier than chocolate and whether Brad Pitt is more handsome than Johnny Depp, but it's impossible to come up with support that most people would regard as reliable to prove one opinion more valid than the other. One *could* logically argue that vanilla ice cream is more popular than chocolate and that Brad Pitt has a narrower range as an actor than Johnny Depp. Statistics on ice cream sales and flavor preference polls could support the former argument, and examples from particular films and quotations from reviews and experts on acting could build a case for the latter.

Finally, a statement is not an argument when it seeks to persuade with threats, emotional manipulation, or trickery rather than with reasoning. An employer who persuades workers to sign up for weekend shifts by hinting that their annual raises depend on it is using coercion, not argument. A campaign advertisement that depicts a candidate kissing smiling babies is appealing to viewers' emotions, not their intelligence. Although writers who use these techniques may present them as though they were arguments, don't be fooled. Arguments draw on different strategies entirely.

2 Understand an argument as a claim supported by reasons and evidence. British philosopher Stephen Toulmin developed a useful model for understanding how arguments are structured. (Note: We follow the Toulmin model throughout this chapter because it is a commonly used

Though the T-shirt slogans pictured here seem designed to confront and perhaps annoy viewers, each addresses a serious public issue. The "Jesus Loves Me Too" shirt is part of a pro-vegetarianism campaign sponsored by the leftist advocacy group People for the Ethical Treatment of Animals (PETA). The pro–gun rights shirt is available on <*ThoseShirts.com*>, a Web site that caters to politically conservative tastes. Do you think either of these images implies a reasoned argument? If so, what is being argued? If not, what would need to be added for you to consider the slogan an argument?

way of understanding argument, but your instructor or classmates may use different terminology to refer to the basic parts of an argument. Ask your instructor to clarify any confusion you may have about these terms.)

The Toulmin model says that every argument begins by making a general assertion—a *claim*—and then produces one or more grounds for supporting that claim. Support for a claim may include *reasons* (smaller assertions that often begin with the word *because*) and *evidence* (relevant examples, facts, statistics, or experts' statements).

Here's a simple way of outlining how an argument is put together.

Argument = Claim + Reason(s) and Evidence

An editorial in a campus newspaper, for example, might make the following argument proposing a mandatory grade penalty for students who skip classes.

CLAIM Our university should adopt an attendance policy imposing automatic grade penalties on students who miss a substantial number of classes.

REASON (Because) Students who miss class frequently do not truly learn the material, even if they manage to do well on tests and assignments.

EVIDENCE **1.** A recent study found that college students who wrote and talked frequently about course material retained more knowledge after four years than those who did not.

2. My ex-roommate missed so many accounting classes that she had to rely on friends' notes and cramming to pass the final exam. She did not really learn the material and is now struggling in her business courses.

Many written arguments open with a paragraph that leads to a claim stated in a thesis statement, then develop the supporting reason(s) and evidence in subsequent paragraphs. But not all arguments follow this pattern. In some cases, the actual claim doesn't appear until nearly the end of the argument. And in some cases, the claim may be implicit—never directly stated in the piece. Many visual arguments leave it to the audience to give shape to the claim, though the point the author is making is obvious.

VISITOR WARNING
FLORIDA RESIDENTS CAN USE DEADLY FORCE

Florida law now allows people to shoot to kill if they feel threatened.

PLEASE BE CAREFUL

The Brady Campaign to Prevent Gun Violence
www.shootfirstlaw.org

Consider this bumper sticker created by the Brady Campaign to Prevent Gun Violence. What claims does the bumper sticker make? Are the arguments directly stated or implied? What supporting reasons or evidence does the sticker present?

3 Recognize that arguments rest on unstated beliefs, or warrants. Simply laying out a claim and some kind of support isn't enough to make a solid argument. For example, the argument "Mina should do well in college because she's tall" would convince no one. A thinking person would respond, "That's an unwarranted conclusion. Being tall has nothing to do with excelling in school." Obviously some ways of connecting claims with reasons and evidence are more persuasive than others.

Toulmin uses the term *warrant* to describe the justification—the general belief, rule, or principle—that links together the claim and its support in an argument. A persuasive argument must rest on warrants that readers find satisfactory, or readers will reject it.

Sometimes a warrant is so self-evidently true that it's left unstated. The writer assumes that once the claim and its support are presented, readers will supply and accept the warrant on their own: "Mina should do well in college because she made straight *A*'s in high school." The writer doesn't need to state and support the warrant—that making straight *A*'s is a good indicator of success in college—because just about everybody believes this connection is "warranted," or justified.

But sometimes an argument rests on a warrant that not all readers will agree with. Consider this statement: "Mina should do well in college because she has worked at her parents' restaurant for six years." Although the connection may seem reasonable to some readers, others might need convincing. The writer needs to state the warrant and provide some explanation and support for it. Reasons and evidence used to support the warrant in an argument are called *backing*. Figure 9.1 shows how the argument would look with warrant and backing.

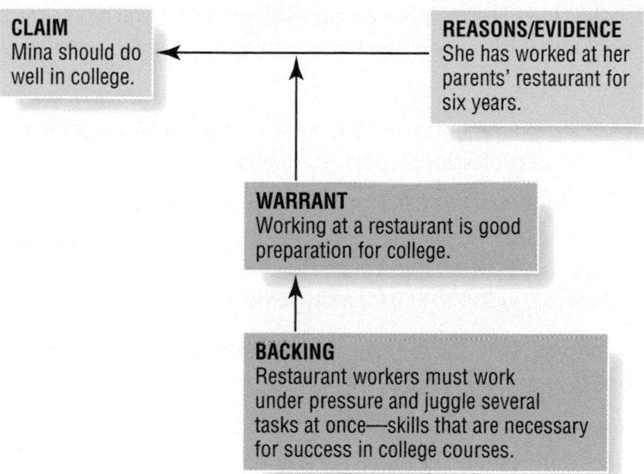

Figure 9.1

EXERCISE 9.1 Each argument below contains a claim and supporting reasons or evidence. Supply the unstated warrant(s) that link each claim to its data, and then evaluate the warrant. Do you find the warrant convincing? Why or why not? We've done the first one for you.

ARGUMENT *Claim:* The federal government should spend more money on cutting-edge cancer research.

Reason/evidence: Studies show that the treatments developed in this kind of research save lives.

RESPONSE *Warrant:* The government should fund programs that save lives.

Analysis: This warrant is fairly convincing. However, it's possible that the government doesn't have enough money to fund *every* program that might save lives. What if a program is very expensive but will save only a few lives? This argument needs some support to show that cancer research is more worthy of funding than other potentially life-saving research.

1. *Claim:* Dr. Olson is an excellent literature professor.

   Reason/evidence: She truly knows her subject matter; she has published nine books on British poetry and is recognized as a leading expert on William Wordsworth.

2. *Claim:* Local governments should not use tax money to subsidize the construction of professional sports stadiums.

   Reason/evidence: Only a small portion of the population attends professional sporting events. Some people simply don't like sports, others don't have the time to attend games regularly, and many simply can't afford to pay $30 to $50 for a single ticket.

3. *Claim:* The push to legislate higher fuel efficiency standards for cars is misguided.

   Reason/evidence: New federal mandates for gas mileage will create a financial hardship for consumers, since the automakers will have to add to the price of new cars the cost of researching and manufacturing more efficient engines.

4 Recognize that many claims include a qualifier that clarifies the limited circumstances in which that claim holds true. Because most claims aren't true in every single case, many arguments include a limiting phrase or statement called a *qualifier*—*probably, in most cases, primarily in suburban areas,* for example. The argument proposing a campus attendance policy laid out in Section 9a-2 would overstate its case if it claimed that *all* students should be penalized for missing classes. Here is a more solid statement of this argument that begins with a qualifier. "*Except in cases of serious illness or emergency,* students absent for a substantial number of classes should incur a mandatory grade penalty."

EXERCISE 9.2 Working with a group of classmates, analyze the following argument taken from a magazine article reviewing recent perspectives on women, welfare, and work. Identify the statements that come after each number as claim, reason, evidence, warrant, backing, or qualifier. You may use some terms more than once and others not at all.

> There are two [. . .] big reasons why [1] the responsible choice for a low-income single mother might be welfare rather than work. [2] Welfare

provides health insurance for her children, and most low-wage jobs don't. [3] And welfare, however miserly, provides security that most jobs don't—at least before [welfare reform laws passed in] 1997. [4] In the jobs available to many low-skilled or unskilled women, such as fast food or home health care, workers can never be sure of getting enough hours to make enough money while they have a job, and they are always subject to firing or layoffs. [5] When insecurity doesn't just mean a little less of something but the possibility of starvation or homelessness, the rational risk-benefit calculation counsels taking the secure but less rewarding option.

—Deborah Stone, "Work and the Moral Woman"

9b How do visual arguments work?

Many of the arguments you encounter every day come through media that consist substantially or almost entirely of visual images. When you watch a music video, scroll through a Web site, or tune in to the evening news, you take in information so quickly that you have little time to critically reflect on it. But it's important to remember that, like written arguments, arguments made in visual media are carefully constructed to appeal to readers, and you should read them as critically as you would any other text.

Increasingly, even traditional types of written documents such as articles, books, and reports assert their claims in conjunction with images. We cannot begin to catalog the many different kinds of visual arguments. However, this section will help you become aware of some basic ways in which visuals persuade, so that you can sharpen your critical viewing skills.

1 Understand that visual arguments are purposefully constructed. The nonprofit Center for Media Literacy suggests the following starting points for critically approaching arguments presented on film, television, or other media that work primarily through images:

- **Remember that, like written arguments, visual and multimedia arguments are created for particular audiences and purposes.** In a single television news story, for example, a team of people filmed footage, interviewed sources, wrote a reporter's script, and combined selections from all that raw material into a carefully produced package. Viewers never see what the film crew *didn't* shoot, what the story would have been like if

Following the election of President Barack Obama in 2008, Pepsi created an advertising campaign that capitalized on that candidate's successful theme of *hope*. While the beverage company denied that the ads were political, Pepsi even recast its familiar red, white, and blue logo to resemble more closely Obama's own famous emblem. What argument(s) do you think this advertisement makes, and to what audience? What do you think the redesigned logo adds to the argument? Do you think that the ad's message could be stated as effectively using only words?

different material had been selected, or what portions of film the producer edited out. Because visual texts are the products of human choices, they generally reflect their creators' values, viewpoints, and biases.

- **Be aware that visual arguments come in many genres, each of which operates according to its own conventions.** Think how different your expectations are when you see national news events discussed in an online news site, a late-night talk show, a political cartoon, and a documentary film. These different formats govern how information can be presented.
- **Recognize that many visual arguments are open ended; they may be interpreted differently by different viewers.** Parents often say that they can't make any sense of the music videos their teenage children watch; it's all just noise and disconnected images, they complain. On the other hand, adults who watch the Disney cartoons they loved as kids often catch cultural references or jokes that eluded them when they were younger. Creators of visual arguments rely on these differences when they try to reach several audiences at once.

2 Pay close attention to visual design and layout. As in written arguments, whatever is front and center will get the most attention in a visual argument. Ask yourself how the arrangement of information directs your attention as you move through a text.

- **What ideas or information is emphasized?** What material takes up the most space? What catches your eye? Many design devices are used to highlight information, from traditional headings and boxes to pull quotes, sidebars, colors, unusual type fonts, shading, pop-ups, animation, and even aural signals in electronic media. Examine the placement of photographs or other images on a page: How do these images shape your perception of the argument? Also examine the layout and placement of graphs, tables, and other visual representations of information. To what data and patterns do these devices draw your attention? (See Section 8c for more on how graphs and tables work.)
- **What ideas or information does the writer downplay?** What information is buried in the middle of the text or set in small print? How does the size or cropping of images influence what you see? What is left out?
- **What formatting and organizational devices are used?** Look for patterns. For example, writers use similarly sized headings to indicate that topics are at comparable levels of importance or generality in an argument. Or they might use recurring colors in a PowerPoint presentation to help viewers understand where they are in an argument. How do such devices affect your perception of the argument?

3 Evaluate images critically. Pictures trigger impressions that are stronger and more immediate than those most writers can convey with words. And because images can be so powerful, it pays to view them with caution. Ask yourself these questions.

- **What emotions, values, or beliefs does the image appeal to?** Is this appeal relevant and fair? For example, a photograph of a soldier holding a child might be an evocative image, but its effectiveness as evidence supporting a claim depends upon how well the argument can move readers beyond their initial emotional reactions (which might be positive or negative, depending on the audience) to consider the significance of the facts displayed by, or left out of, the picture itself.

- **How does the image work in relation with written text or other elements in the argument?** Is the image helpful, or is it only decoration? For example, you've probably seen Web pages that make distracting use of flashy graphics—multicolored backgrounds, blinking lights, animated characters—that don't relate clearly to the content.
- **What does the image reveal about the writer's opinions or biases?** If a televised story on successful local entrepreneurs included only pictures of men, you might wonder whether the story slights women business owners.
- **Does the image exaggerate or distort the information?** This might happen if an advertisement for a summer study abroad program featured only photos showing luxury accommodations, when in fact most participants stay with local residents in modest homes.

EXERCISE 9.3 Examine the posters on the right, which were created by the National Institute on Drug Abuse as part of an anti–steroid-abuse campaign. How does each employ layout, graphics, and images to emphasize and deemphasize certain information or to influence readers? Discuss your findings with a group of classmates. How effective do you believe campaigns such as this one are in changing the behavior of their target audience? If you believe this campaign is ineffective, discuss why.

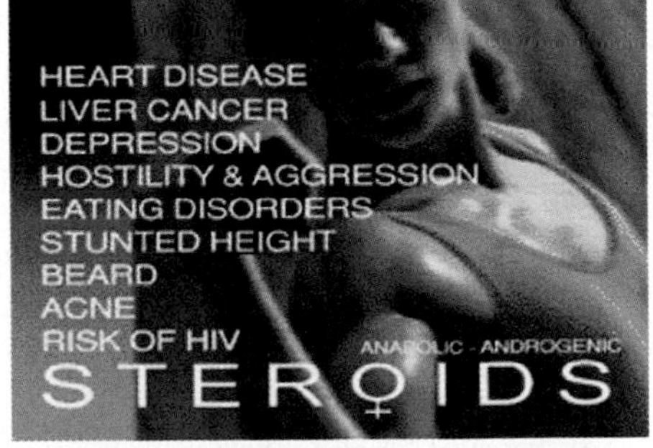

EXERCISE 9.4 Keeping in mind the principles discussed in Section 9b-1, view a television commercial, YouTube video, public service announcement, print advertisement, commercial Web page, or political poster with a critical eye. What features do you notice that you hadn't noticed before? Do you enjoy the text more or less than you would have had you watched it less critically? Why or why not? Bring your answers to class for discussion.

Highlight Analyzing an Advertisement

Writing a critical analysis of an advertisement or other visual argument is a common assignment in composition courses. Here is a professional example of an ad analysis, written by Seth Stevenson for the April 24, 2006 edition of *Slate* magazine. (To see more examples of Stevenson's "Ad Report Card" columns, visit <www.slate.com>.) In this piece, Stevenson critically assesses the effectiveness of a . . . Dunkin' Donuts commercial, looking closely at the visual devices the ad's producers use to create an appealing image for their product. As you read the essay, ask yourself: What specific features of the commercial does Stevenson draw on to support his analysis? Do you agree with his assessment of the commercial and its target audience? In what ways would this piece differ from an academic paper on the same topic?

Coffeeholics A Dunkin' Donuts ad for an addict nation.
By Seth Stevenson
Posted Monday, April 24, 2006, at 6:29 AM ET

The Spot: *In one long take, the camera snakes through the bustling center of a small town, catching various blue-collar types in the midst of busy workdays. House painters, furniture movers, postal workers, tow-truck drivers—all of them are seen bopping around with various Dunkin' Donuts products in hand. Meanwhile, a singer on the soundtrack shouts, "Doing things is what I like to do!" The ad closes with a new slogan flashing on screen: "America Runs on Dunkin'."*

Dunkin' Donuts is spreading its wings. The chain is expanding nationwide and plans to triple in size within the next 10 years. According to a Dunkin' press release, this new ad campaign "marks the most significant repositioning effort in the company's 55-year history." A big part of the goal here is to introduce the brand to Americans not yet familiar with it.

Having grown up in Massachusetts—home to Dunkin' headquarters—I'm plenty familiar with the brand already. Just last week, I got a breakfast sandwich at the Dunkin' . . . around the corner from my mother's house in Brookline. (By the way, that

(Continued)

Analyzing an Advertisement *(Continued)*

particular franchise is completely kosher. Seriously. No sausage on your breakfast sandwich—even if you ask nicely.)

To me, the iconic Dunkin' campaign will always be the one in which that sad-sack fellow with the moustache says, "Time to make the donuts." But donuts are no longer Dunkin's bread and butter (or bread and lard, as the case may be). Coffee is by far the chain's biggest seller now. According to *Business Week*, beverages account for 63 percent of Dunkin' sales, while donuts make up only 17 percent. Which means that Dunkin' is competing less with Krispy Kreme than with Starbucks.

Of course, it's not exactly competing with Starbucks, either. The Starbucks consumer sees his latte as a gourmet indulgence; the Dunkin' guy views his cuppa joe as necessary fuel. The brands' relative price points reflect this, as do their store interiors. John Gilbert, Dunkin' Donuts' vice president of marketing, has been quoted as saying, "We're not about music and WiFi and couches and fireplaces." What they're about is low prices, quick service, and unpretentious reliability.

So, how do you capture those qualities in an ad without creating an image so boring and unsexy that it turns off customers? The gold standard for blue-collar cool of late has been Target, which managed to transform itself from schlocky to hip on the strength of a clever ad campaign. I think the keys to Target's success are twofold. 1) They choose interesting music (they've used songs from Devo, Cornershop, and Sir Mix-a-Lot); and 2) They shy away from showing actual Target stores. Taking us into a store, with its aisles of garbage cans and discount dry goods, would just remind us about the underlying schlockiness. Instead, Target recontextualizes the products it sells inside a colorful, bouncy world of the campaign's own invention.

This flagship "Things I Like To Do" ad from the Dunkin' campaign is pretty straightforward: It suggests that a Dunkin' break helps average Americans power through their busy lives. But it follows Target's lead in not showing an actual Dunkin' franchise. And the music creates an arch sensibility, turning the spot into a sunny ode to caffeine addiction. (Sample lyric: "I'm slightly more productive now than previous because/ I'm slightly more efficient than I previously was.") Nerd rockers . . . They Might Be Giants provide the theme song here and contribute several other songs to the Dunkin' campaign. The band is known for catchy hooks, quirky rhymes, and an often cloying sensibility. Sounds just right for a career in jingle writing!

(Continued)

Analyzing an Advertisement *(Continued)*

Hill Holliday, the ad agency behind the campaign, has been running a blog about the ads and what went into them. . . . Each relies on an oddball They Might Be Giants tune and illustrates an everyday moment. The lyrics inject a bit of whimsy and knowingness into these familiar scenes, lifting the average Joe's workaday existence into a funnier, cooler realm. Some sample lines from the tunes: "Get your 8-year-old out of the tree. He got up there quite a ways" (as we see a mom sip her Latte Lite and then hoist herself up into the branches); "The backs of my legs, sticking to the pleather" (as we watch people drinking Dunkin' iced coffee in an effort to mitigate that post-beach cling to their car seats).

One Hill Holliday blog entry about the jingle from the flagship ad muses: "Doing things is what we like to do. Why do I think millions of people are about to have that line going through their heads on a regular basis?" Funny, I've always wondered how ad execs feel when they inflict some insipid catchphrase or jingle on us. I'm sure there's pride, but is there also a modicum of guilt involved? I hope?

Grade: A. The ads are very watchable, and I think the campaign nails the brand image Dunkin' is striving for. Down-to-earth, value-oriented, but still fun and just a tiny bit hip. As for that new slogan, America Runs on Dunkin'? Given the calorie counts on some of those donuts and flavored coffee items, it might be more accurate to go with America Waddles on Dunkin'. But I guess that doesn't scan quite as well.

9c How can you recognize and avoid fallacies?

Some tactics of persuasion have been branded as *fallacies* because they undermine the goal of serious arguments—to make people better informed and thus better able to make reasoned choices. When a flashy print ad promises you romance on a Caribbean beach just for buying the right deodorant, you should suspect that something illogical is going on. Similarly, you should avoid problems in arguments that rely on tactics described in this section.

1 Avoid *ad hominem* attacks. To take an argument *to the person* means to attack the person making a claim rather than the argument itself.

Such character assassination certainly can work, and name-calling and personal abuse are facts of life in many political environments, but critical readers will see right through the tactic and brand it as the fallacy it is. An argument, idea, or proposal should be offered on its own merits. If you find yourself calling those you disagree with names (greedy corporate lawyers, angry teabaggers), or accusing them of faults unrelated to the issue under discussion, you are guilty of the *ad hominem* fallacy. It's a tempting blunder, especially when your dander is up, as columnist Ralph Peters's probably was when he wrote in defense of an Italian Prime Minister under attack from German politicians:

> Apart from the fact that Italy, the home of grace and beauty, doesn't need any more loud, fat krauts polluting its environment, there's an even more important matter involved: Prime Minister Silvio Berlusconi doesn't take any crap from Eurocrats and the self-righteous sons and daughters of the SS.
>
> —Ralph Peters, "Let 'Em Eat Wurst," *New York Post Online*, July 13, 2003

You can see easily enough why such language is over the top and offensive, but notice, too, that it does not advance any argument. It just makes some people angry and undermines the credibility of the writer.

Of course, character flaws are not always side issues. A chronic gambler might not have much credibility talking about moral discipline nor would a womanizing politician be taken seriously as a champion of the rights of women. It would be appropriate to point out such hypocrisy. But, in most cases, you should avoid making an issue out of the character or behavior of those with whom you take issue.

2 Don't beg the question. This fallacy is also sometimes called circular reasoning because it involves a writer taking for true precisely the claim that needs to be proved. In effect, the disputed claim becomes a part of the evidence. A student who protests that she shouldn't have gotten a *C* on a paper because she's an *A* student is begging the question. She assumes that she should get an *A* because she has done so in the past, but the work on the paper that earned a *C* now argues otherwise.

The claim in a circular argument may, in fact, be true on other grounds, but it gains no authority when it becomes part of circular thinking. When

Chicago Cubs manager Dusty Baker was accused of racism for his remarks about the varying ability of lighter- and darker-skinned athletes to play in the heat, Tony Bernazard, a representative of the player's union, defended Baker this way:

> "It's somebody's opinion," Bernazard said. "I don't think anybody can accuse Dusty Baker of being a racist because Dusty Baker is not a racist."
>
> —Chuck Johnson, "Baker Stands by Heat Comments," *USA Today*, July 7, 2003

Baker may not be a racist, but simply offering that assertion as the *reason* he is not a racist doesn't make an argument.

3 Don't make hasty generalizations. We are all guilty of this fallacy at one time or another, especially in our personal dealings. One bad experience with a retailer, restaurant, or institution may sour us on it for good—even to the extent that we badmouth it to others. In such cases, we take a single piece of data and generalize from it much too broadly. Drawing inferences from limited data in this way is dangerously illogical—the kind of thinking that can lead to stereotyping when we apply it to groups of people.

It is important, then, when drawing inferences from evidence to understand any limits on the data. In a poll, for example, the sample surveyed must be large enough to represent the studied population. The individuals must be chosen at random so that every member of the population has a comparable opportunity of being queried, and the sample must be selected in such a way that it represents the population fairly on the issue being studied. For example, if you surveyed only women at your school in a poll dealing with gender attitudes, you could report results for women only, not for students as a group if the student population also included men. Unless you gather sufficient data with great care, you are in danger of making hasty generalizations.

This principle applies to other kinds of research as well. If you base your conclusions in a research paper on material gathered from a limited number of books and articles, or if you select research materials that reflect your own prejudices, the conclusions you draw won't convince a critical reader.

4 Show care in making causal connections. Whenever you are blamed for something you didn't do, you gain a little insight into "faulty causality." The fallacy involves attributing an event or phenomenon to a force that didn't cause it: for example, believing that seeing an albino squirrel on the way to your next test will earn you an *A*. In many cases, the faulty connection is made simply because one event follows another: you got an *A* the last time you spotted an albino squirrel on your way to an exam. Here's an even more extraordinary example of faulty causality, involving the Madden NFL video game:

> Shaun Alexander became the latest player to fall victim to the so-called Madden Curse a week ago. After playing seven seasons without missing a game, Alexander was injured last week against the New York Giants only a few months after he posed for the cover of Electronic Arts' *Madden NFL 07* video game. Alexander joined Michael Vick, Donovan McNabb, Marshall Faulk and Daunte Culpepper as players who have followed up cover photographs on the most popular sports video game on earth with a prolonged stretch on the injury report that same season.
>
> Other cover stars in Madden have suffered tremendous dropoffs in production (Dorsey Levens), made inexplicable career decisions (Barry Sanders retiring) and continued to do ridiculous dances that resemble Elaine from *Seinfeld* (Ray Lewis). All of these coincidences have conspired to create the sports jinx dubbed "the Madden Curse."
>
> —Clay Travis, "ClayNation: Madden Curse doesn't really exist—yet,"
> *Spin on Sports*, October 2, 2006

Today, controversies over global warming embody many of the potential pitfalls of causal reasoning. Everything from SUVs to flatulent cows are blamed (rightly or wrongly) for changes in the weather, while global warming itself is seen as *causing* phenomena as different as drought and depression. The problem is that thousands of factors influence the climate of the world, interacting in ways difficult to measure and assess. So the temptation to make false or unsupported causal connections is enormous in every political direction.

Sometimes writers simply fail to see causal connections, or interpret them oddly. In August 2000, *New York Times* writer Fox Butterfield wrote with dismay that the number of people in U.S. prisons was still rising, despite a marked decrease in crime rates. His critics pointed out that crime rates were probably dropping *because* of the increased prison population.

5 Avoid either/or thinking. Writers are guilty of the **either/or** fallacy when they try to reduce a complicated situation to just two choices. It's tempting to take a complicated issue like education or global warning and make it seem manageable by offering stark choices: Either we create national standards for public schools, or our educational system will fail. Obviously, many other options should be considered.

The loaded rhetorical question that allows for only one acceptable answer is another form of the either/or argument:

> Are we going to increase funding for the police department, or are we going to let gangs and drugs take over our city?

When a writer presents you with a false dilemma, your best response is to challenge his or her oversimplified view by pointing out alternative possibilities.

6 Question slippery slope arguments. Of course, well-supported causal arguments make perfect sense on their own: *if we do X, then Y might happen.* But such arguments become examples of the slippery slope fallacy when they are pushed too hard: *if we do X, then Y might happen, and then Z, and then a hundred other horrible things.* You can see why such arguments are called slippery slopes: the writer predicts that an avalanche of dire consequences might follow from a single choice, event, or action. Senator Rick Santorum was accused of a slippery slope argument when he suggested the following in anticipation of a Supreme Court decision reviewing sodomy laws:

> If the Supreme Court says that you have the right to consensual [gay] sex within your home, then you have the right to bigamy, you have the right to polygamy, you have the right to incest, you have the right to adultery. You have the right to anything.
>
> —Senator Rick Santorum, April 21, 2003

Similarly, you might imagine someone arguing that if Habitat for Humanity builds one or two low-income homes in a middle-class neighborhood, real estate prices will fall, yards will deteriorate, families will move out, tax revenue will decline, and the local schools will lose their high ratings.

Their intention would be to scare someone into questioning or fearing that first step because of all that *might* follow. Yet many of those alleged consequences would be based on unsupported speculation.

7 Avoid faulty or false analogies. Analogies are useful ways of making arguments because they help readers to understand one idea by comparing it to another. Representative Joe Barton of Texas once succinctly described the NCAA football Bowl Championship Series this way: "It's like Communism—you can't fix it." But analogies become fragile when the comparisons made are sweeping, uninformed, or potentially misleading. Some might suggest that Representative Marcy Kaptur crossed the line into faulty analogy in offering the following argument, as reported in *The Toledo Blade*:

> "When America 'cast off monarchical Britain' in 1776, it involved the help of many religious people who had fled repression in other countries," the 11-term Toledo congressman said. "Among the nontraditional American revolutionaries were the Green Mountain Boys, a patriot militia organized in 1770 in Bennington, Vt., to confront British forces," she said.
>
> **"One could say that Osama bin Laden and these non-nation-state fighters with religious purpose are very similar to those kind of atypical revolutionaries that helped to cast off the British crown,"** Miss Kaptur said.
>
> —David Yonke, "Threat of War Spurs U.S. Soul-searching," *The Toledo Blade*, March 1, 2003

Kaptur complained subsequently that her analogy between American revolutionaries and the head of the al Qaeda terrorist organization was taken out of context by other media. In any case, her risky analogy certainly did more to sensationalize her overall point than to support it.

8 Avoid bandwagon appeals. We can be persuaded to do things just because others have been won over; this is the **bandwagon effect** that plays a role in advertising and politics. It's cool to buy an iPod or vote for Pedro because, well, it's cool.

9 Beware of appeals to authority. Just as bad as the bandwagon appeal is the appeal to **authority** that, in effect, suggests we should agree to a claim or buy a product because it has been endorsed by someone well-known or famous, whatever their expertise might be. Would you take medical advice from a film star or pop singer? Why then take their political ruminations seriously?

Checklist 9.1 Common Fallacies

1. **Argument to the person (*ad hominem*):** attacking the person instead of focusing on the issues.
2. **Begging the question (or circular reasoning):** restating instead of proving a claim.
3. **Hasty generalization:** drawing conclusions from scanty evidence.
4. **False cause:** presuming that if *B* follows *A*, *A* caused *B*.
5. **Either/or:** suggesting that only two choices are possible when in fact there may be several.
6. **Slippery slope:** assuming that one event will set off an unstoppable chain reaction.
7. **False analogy:** making a comparison between things that are too dissimilar for the comparison to be useful.
8. **Bandwagon appeal:** claiming that widespread popularity makes an object or idea valuable.
9. **Appeal to authority:** claiming that an idea or viewpoint is good because someone important has endorsed it.

EXERCISE 9.5 Work with other students in a group to spot the fallacies in these arguments. In some instances you may find more than one.

1. Two kinds of students go to college: the kind who are truly interested in learning and those who simply want to get a diploma with as little effort as possible so that they can graduate and get a job. Our university should only admit the first type.
2. Everyone knows that the next decade will be a poor time to go into medicine because government regulation is ruining the profession.

3. The great peasant rebellions in the Middle Ages happened because the rulers taxed the peasants to the limit to pay for foreign wars and neglected conditions in their own countries; the United States can expect similar uprisings if it doesn't drastically cut its defense budget and invest in domestic social programs.

4. As a legislator, I can't get too upset about the proposed tuition raise when every time I drive by our state university I get caught in a traffic jam of students in their new BMWs and convertibles.

CHAPTER

10 How Do You Write Powerful Arguments?

10a How do you construct a solid argument?

Take Control

Making a claim and supporting it with reasons and evidence seems like a natural process, since most of us engage in informal arguments nearly every day. But it is not a process to take for granted, especially when you're asked to prepare a formal written argument in school or for a job. In college, you'll be asked to write persuasive papers that include strong theses and carefully chosen support.

Engaging in formal argument is essential because it allows you to demonstrate your knowledge of the topics you study. In fact, formal argument is one of the elements that distinguishes college-level writing from high school essays that merely summarize existing research. Because of the importance of argument in educational and professional settings, you'll want to know how to present your cases effectively and memorably. This chapter walks you through a general process for constructing a formal written argument, using the Toulmin model and terminology outlined in Chapter 9.

1 Clarify your claim. First, figure out what you want readers to take from your piece: Do you want them to look at some issue in a new way? Do you want them to be aware of a problem they hadn't noticed before? To adopt a particular viewpoint? To take action? Your answer is your claim.

Suppose that, after reading in a child development course some studies of the influence of media violence on children, you decide to write a course paper arguing that parents should be cautious about allowing their children to play the video games marketed to young people, since many of them encourage players to participate in realistic portrayals of violent acts. That assertion is your claim, the one set forth in Figure 10.1 (see page 148). In many academic papers, your major claim(s) will be stated early, as part of a thesis statement.

(For more detailed advice about discovering and narrowing a topic and developing a thesis statement, see Sections 2a, 2b, and 3a.)

Taking Control

Making a Strong Claim

Sometimes you may find that you have a position you want to support, but don't quite know how to do it. Most writers have a few possible claims in mind when they approach a subject, usually ideas and evidence they have picked up in their reading. But you can miss good arguments that way. So, when you approach a topic, use the four categories of claims outlined in Section 2c-3 to stimulate your thinking: Are you concerned with issues of **fact,** with establishing a trend or that something has happened? Are there issues of **definition** or interpretation at stake? Do questions of **value**—ethics, practicality, or feasibility—come to mind? Do you wish to make a proposal or suggest a change in **policy?** You may be surprised at how many possible claims these questions can generate. Then choose those you think will work best for your project.

2 Generate strong reasons to support your claim. Often these supporting reasons will grow out of the reading and research you do on the topic. However, rhetoricians have also identified general categories of reasons to consider when trying to find serious arguments in favor of your position. When you need help finding good reasons for a paper, use these categories as brainstorming devices:

- **Argue for the greater good; *or* argue for the lesser evil.** More often than not, readers will see merit on both sides of a hot issue; after all, contradictory proposals can offer different yet legitimate benefits. When that's so, you may want your proposals to be perceived as the *greater* good or the *lesser* evil.
- **Argue from fairness and equality.** Perhaps the most dependable line of argument in America today is the appeal to fairness. The argument is hard to challenge because it invokes a key concept of democracy: equal treatment. In almost any situation, if your research shows that people have been treated unfairly, you will find supporters for your case.

- **Argue for the long-term good; *or* argue for the short-term good.** When what you are proposing in your argument will have slow or deferred benefits, urge readers to appreciate the "big picture." A long-term benefit can almost always be portrayed as more substantial and more judicious than an immediate one. On the other hand, your evidence may support immediate action. In such a case you might stress the "critical" status of the current situation and carefully list factors contributing to an imminent crisis.
- **Argue for the benefit of greater numbers; *or* argue the special case.** When your research suggests a course of action that would help a majority of people, you can apply the weight of numbers to your argument, pleading for the common good. It is somewhat harder to argue the case of a smaller group. The key then is to ask individual members of the majority to imagine themselves in the position of those in the minority.
- **Argue from self-interest; *or* argue against self-interest.** Unless readers understand their stake in a case, they aren't likely to act. So explain exactly how readers might benefit from your position and its consequences; be as specific as possible, and cite real advantages when you can. Quite often, however, writers have to urge readers to look beyond self-interest—to act for the good of their institutions, posterity, the nation, or the world community.
- **Argue from the consensus of experts; *or* argue against the consensus of experts.** When your research can show that major authorities in a field support your position, you should have a case worth making. However, there is no reason to be dismayed when your research puts you at odds with most experts in a given field. After all, experts in a field often have a stake in the status quo, and they will resist change. That resistance is worth pointing out, especially when you have hard data to back up your claims.
- **Argue from precedent; *or* argue against precedent.** If something has been done in the past and has been accepted as either legal or traditional, it becomes a defense for similar actions in the present. When the precedents of a given case weigh against your argument, you need information to suggest that they might be outdated or that they do not apply in the current situation.
- **Argue from feasibility.** It's important to show that any proposal you might argue for is workable, not a pie-in-the-sky idea. And the burden

of proof is on you, so gather the figures, furnish the plans, provide examples of comparable projects undertaken elsewhere. Of course, your research may suggest just the opposite—that the project can't be managed or is based on wildly implausible projections. If so, change it.

- **Argue the consequences: where does the argument lead?** Be sure that readers appreciate the implications of your argument. If your findings suggest that a small problem now may only get worse, explain why and how. If necessary, construct a worst-case scenario to show what might reasonably happen if current trends go unchecked.

In planning your argument opposing violent video games for children, for example, you might choose to focus on the *consensus of experts* that exposure to violent media builds violent attitudes and behavior and on promoting the *long-term benefits* of raising children who are empathic and compassionate.

3 Gather supporting evidence. Check the library catalog for books, periodical articles, research reports, and government documents on the topic. Search the Internet. For expert testimony, consider setting up an interview with a professor who specializes in child development, or visit a blog that discusses children's entertainment or video gaming. You should also seek out firsthand evidence by closely examining the games themselves. Borrow or rent several of the most popular—*Grand Theft Auto, Resident Evil,* and *Mortal Kombat*—and take notes on the role-playing elements in each.

Depending on the audience for your paper, you might also explore more personal and anecdotal kinds of support—for example, a description of your shock at seeing your two young nephews engrossed in a game of *Grand Theft Auto* at a recent family gathering. You could also ask friends whether their children or younger siblings play such games.

As you gather evidence, cast a wide net. You may not include everything you find in the finished paper, but new evidence may help you adjust a claim that is overstated or misguided. It can also suggest supporting reasons that hadn't initially occurred to you. For example, you may discover examples of convicted violent offenders who were addicted to video games as teenagers—a point you can then add to your argument. For more information about finding sources, see Chapter 44.

4 Evaluate your evidence. Check that your supporting materials are appropriate to the writing situation. In writing a paper for a course, concentrate on scholarly research and theories. If you're writing an article for a PTA newsletter, you might balance academic sources with real-life anecdotes that will catch busy parents' interest. Wherever your evidence comes from, it should meet several basic requirements.

- **Timeliness.** Are the statistics, information, and examples you use recent, or are they so old that they may no longer be accurate?
- **Comprehensiveness.** Do you have enough support for your claim, or are you making generalizations based on one or two examples?
- **Credibility.** Do you draw your evidence from sources that both you and your readers trust?

For a detailed discussion of how to evaluate source materials, see Chapter 45.

5 Identify the warrants, or beliefs, that underlie your argument and consider whether readers will accept them. If you suspect that readers may doubt or disagree with any of your assumptions, be prepared to explain and support them.

This step is especially important when you're writing for a hostile or unfamiliar audience. In a paper on video games, consider whether some readers might question your warrant that simulating violent acts harms children. Readers who play such games might believe they are cathartic and do no real damage. Here's where the research studies from your child development course fit in: since they establish a causal link between violent media and behavioral problems, you can cite them as *backing* for your warrant.

Figure 10.1 shows how the fully developed argument might look.

EXERCISE 10.1 Review the lines of argument discussed in Section 10a-2, then brainstorm as many reasons as you can think of that could be used in a paper that advocates limiting children and young teenagers' access to video games. Which reasons do you think are the most persuasive? Which, if any, would you recommend that the writer whose argument is featured in Figure 10.1 include in her paper? Explain your answer. Finally, brainstorm a similar list of reasons to support the claim that access to violent video games does *not* harm young people.

Figure 10.1 A Developed Argument

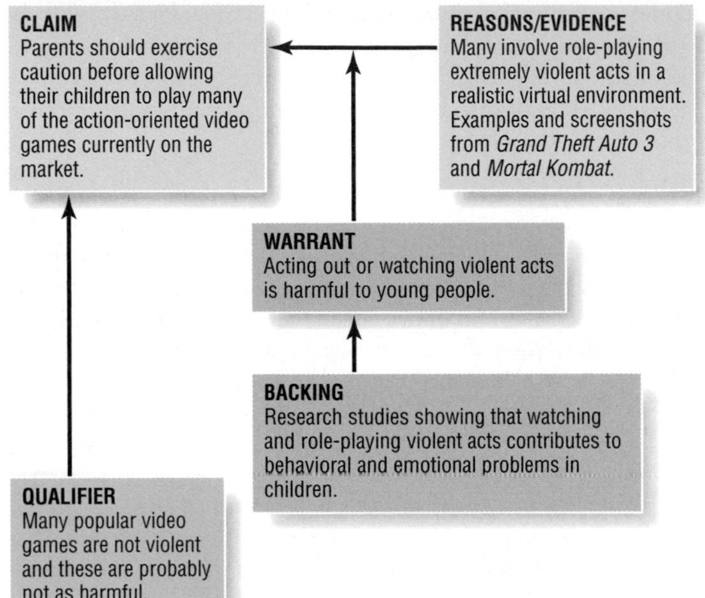

CLAIM
Parents should exercise caution before allowing their children to play many of the action-oriented video games currently on the market.
REASONS/EVIDENCE
Many involve role-playing extremely violent acts in a realistic virtual environment. Examples and screenshots from *Grand Theft Auto 3* and *Mortal Kombat*.
WARRANT
Acting out or watching violent acts is harmful to young people.
BACKING
Research studies showing that watching and role-playing violent acts contributes to behavioral and emotional problems in children.
QUALIFIER
Many popular video games are not violent and these are probably not as harmful.

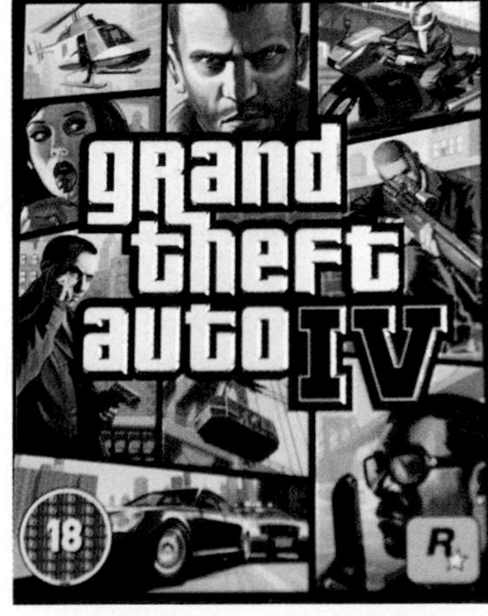

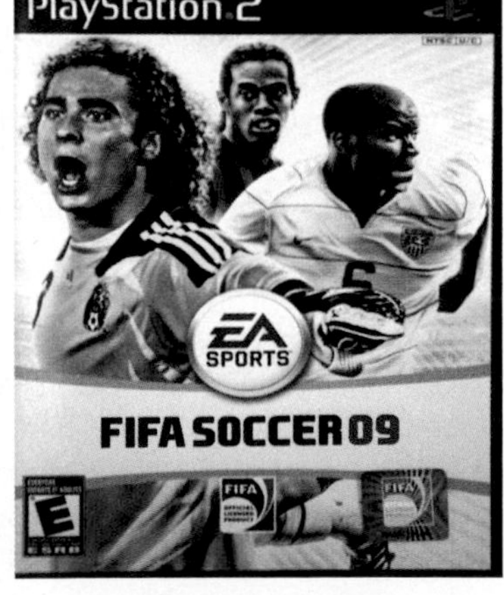

EXERCISE 10.2 Construct a diagram similar to the one presented in Figure 10.1 to outline a claim, reasons, evidence, warrant, backing, and qualifiers for a paper you're working on. Then answer these questions: How helpful did you find these terms in generating persuasive material for your argument? Which portions of the diagram did you find most challenging to complete? Why?

10b How do you write an argument that appeals to readers?

Some people see an argument as a sort of verbal war in which enemies line up on opposing sides of an issue, each with the goal of demolishing the other side. Yet remember that you won't persuade people by making them angry. You'll only make them stick to their positions more stubbornly. For this reason, we suggest that you think of argument not as a battle but as a persuasive dialogue. In a dialogue, both sides exchange ideas as they search for the best stance on an issue. In this section, we offer tips for writing an argument that appeals to and respects readers—even those who may not initially agree with you.

1 Be credible. Be certain that the way you present yourself in your project—your *ethos*—is that of a person readers can respect and trust. People are more likely to listen to what you have to say if you portray yourself as believable, knowledgeable, thoughtful, and fair. If you treat your readers as informed equals who are open to rational persuasion, they'll be more likely to listen sympathetically.

To this end, you'll want to use civil and inclusive language. Slurs, name-calling, and negative stereotyping may impress a small audience that already shares your feelings. But the wider audience of people you don't know will probably think you are simplistic and small-minded if you use terms such as *bleeding-heart liberal* or *conservative wingnut* in an argument.

You'll also need to be sure that your language is directed at your actual audience, not above them or below them. You want readers to identify with you, and they won't do that if you are either too technical for them to understand or too simplistic to be taken seriously.

2 Draw on shared beliefs and values. Even if you're addressing readers whose position is completely opposed to your own, search for common ground. Any shared belief, no matter how general, may serve as a warrant on which you can build an argument those readers will find reasonable. For instance, both proponents and opponents of gun-control legislation value public safety, though they have different ideas about how to achieve it, and both supporters and opponents of school vouchers are concerned about the quality of public education. An argument that begins from these common beliefs may not change anyone's mind immediately. But it probably will get a fair hearing, and it may initiate a civil exchange of ideas. And that's what public argument is all about. (See Section 15c for more on building consensus with readers.)

3 Handle information honestly. It may be tempting to construct an argument by using only sources that favor your argument or to cite information selectively—leaving out data or trends or incidents that don't support your case. In the long run, such an argument won't go down well with critical readers. They'll ask just the sorts of questions about your claims and supporting evidence that may undermine your work:

- Are the claims supported by evidence from reliable and authoritative sources?
- Are the claims supported by evidence from a variety of sources?
- Has evidence been fairly—not selectively—reported?
- Is enough evidence presented to support the claims?
- Has evidence been accurately documented?

You should be able to answer *yes* to every question.

No argument is ever watertight. However, when you are dealing with complex and significant issues, readers want to be informed and enlightened, not bamboozled. Remember, too, that checking out factual claims and assertions is relatively easy these days. A whole generation of bloggers now keep the national media on their toes by constantly assessing their claims and evidence. Critical readers may do the same with your work.

4 Quote fairly from your sources. Citing authorities is a powerful way of supporting an argument. But you must quote responsibly and fairly, presenting the words of any source just as the author intended them, so far as you can tell. You shouldn't trim or embellish a quotation to make it sound more in accord with your positions. Nor should you quote unfairly those who disagree with you, leaving out words or contextual information that might make a difference in the sense. For example, in April 2009, critics of President Barack Obama claimed that he had spoken ill of the United States on foreign soil when he delivered the following lines in a speech in France:

> In America, there is a failure to appreciate Europe's leading role in the world. Instead of celebrating your dynamic union and seeking to partner with you to meet common challenges, there have been times where America has shown arrogance and been dismissive, even derisive.

However, these critics had distorted the President remarks by omitting the context provided by the sentences that immediately followed:

> But in Europe, there is an anti-Americanism that is at once casual, but can also be insidious. Instead of recognizing the good that America so often does in the world, there have been times where Europeans choose to blame America for much of what is bad. On both sides of the Atlantic, these attitudes have become all too common.

5 Use emotional appeals sparingly. Just as your credibility or personal *ethos* plays a role in making an argument work, your ability to generate emotions in your readers can also play a part. In many academic and public forums, overtly emotional arguments don't play well. They are seen as sentimental or manipulative. So you need to deal with emotions carefully, understanding that many arguments do generate feelings such as anger, fear, sympathy, envy, or jealousy. You can raise such feelings with just a few hot-button phrases.

Consider the power of calls to patriotism, for example, in many political arguments, or how easy it is to pit students against administrators or politicians against ordinary citizens simply by contrasting their power. There is a role for feelings to play in arguments, but an emotion should not be evoked as a substitute for reasonable claims or a preponderance of evidence. Rather, emotions should complement a case supported by good reasons and solid evidence.

EXERCISE 10.3 Check all the quotations used in a paper you've written for a course against their original sources. Do you see any problems in how you present information or quoted material? If so, use the guidelines in Section 10b to remedy these problems.

10c How do you effectively address other viewpoints?

If you're going to write about controversial issues, you can't simply pretend that your position is the only one. You'll need to acknowledge that other arguments exist, or readers will think that you haven't done your homework. It is equally important that you learn to describe other positions accurately and respectfully. In doing so you enhance your own credibility.

1 Present opposing arguments fairly. Logicians use the term *straw man fallacy* to describe the misleading practice of summarizing another position in an oversimplified way that makes it easy to knock down. The following statement, from a billboard promoting school vouchers, uses this tactic:

> Care about the children more than the teachers' unions? Put parents in charge of education.

People oppose school vouchers for many reasons, including a desire to put available resources into the public schools attended by most children and the practical difficulties of ensuring that a voucher program would be available to the neediest students. Although many of these concerns are shared by the leadership of teachers' unions, to suggest that opposition to vouchers is solely motivated by a desire to preserve union privileges over children's learning is simplistic. When you compose an argument, summarize opponents' reasoning fully and generously, or readers will perceive you as unfair.

2 Consider refuting an opposing argument. Once you've acknowledged other viewpoints, what do you do with them? Don't just let them sit there; readers want to know how they affect the strength of your argument. One option is to *refute* an opposing position—that is, to disprove the argument by pointing out its weaknesses or fallacies. It's possible to critique an argument on several grounds.

- **Question the claim.** Is it overstated? Is it insufficiently supported? (See Section 8b-5 for more on how to spot a flawed claim.)
- **Question the evidence.** Does the evidence come from reliable sources? Is there enough of it? Is it recent enough to be accurate? (Sections 8b-4 and 45a contain guidelines for evaluating evidence.)
- **Question the warrants and backing.** Does the argument rest on beliefs, values, or assumptions that you think are invalid? Does the writer need to justify and support those assumptions? (See Section 9a for more on warrants and backing.)

When you've identified problems in one or more of these areas, point them out and call on readers to reject the argument.

3 Consider making concessions to another position. Often you won't be able to reject an opposing argument completely; most reasoned arguments do have some merit. In such cases you'll do well to concede that some of your opponent's points are valid, and then argue that under the circumstances you believe yours are stronger. When you do this, you not only seem fair-minded but you avoid backing yourself into an untenable position.

One community organizer successfully used this strategy when she convinced the city council to grant her a permit to locate a homeless shelter across the street from a popular playground.

> I agree with you that safety concerns often make it inappropriate to locate shelters in areas frequented by children. The people served by homeless shelters are often troubled and difficult to monitor. However, the shelter I am proposing is different, because it will serve only mothers with small children who have been recommended by churches and social service agencies as good candidates for job training. These mothers will pose little danger to the neighborhood and their children will make good use of the playground.

By admitting that the city council's concerns are valid in many situations, she established valuable common ground with her audience. In addition, she freed herself from having to argue about the safety of homeless shelters in general, allowing her to focus on the special features of her particular shelter.

WRITER AT WORK **An Annotated Argument Paper**

Lauren Schultz wrote the paper excerpted below in response to a class assignment that asked her to argue a position on an issue she felt strongly about. Her paper is documented using MLA style. As you read, assess how effectively she articulates and supports her position. How does she attempt to create common ground between her position and that of others? Is she fair?

Lauren Schultz

Professor Ruszkiewicz

Rhetoric 368C

18 March 2009

Native American Mascots: Time to Go

For over fifty years, the Native American (Native) community in the United States has fought against the use of sports mascots demeaning to its people. Professional teams that currently have Native mascots include the Washington Redskins, Atlanta Braves, Kansas City Chiefs, and Cleveland Indians. College teams with Native mascots include the Florida State University Seminoles and the University of Illinois Fighting Illini. In October 1991, Native rights activists formed the National Coalition on Racism in Sports and Media in reaction against such mascots. The issue heated up again in August 2005, when the National College Athletic Association (NCAA) published a ruling that will bar college teams from using "hostile and demeaning" mascots in postseason bowl games beginning last year—a ruling that specifically mentioned twelve schools, including Florida State and Illinois ("NCAA Bans"). Officials at Florida State are fighting the ruling, and many sports fans nationwide see the push to get rid of the mascots as misguided. Many non-Native Americans

Term "Native" defined in a special sense for the paper.

(non-Natives) consider such mascots as well-meaning portrayals of Native culture, focusing on positive values such as honor and bravery. However, such non-Native perspectives are often superficial and insensitive. In fact, the misuse of Native imagery in sports mascots is racially offensive because it promotes stereotypes of Native peoples, dehumanizes them, and falsely defines Native cultures. These mascots should be retired by all sports teams, professional, college, and high school alike.

The claim for the argument, stated with three supporting reasons.

Native mascots such as the Cleveland Indians' Chief Wahoo depict Natives stereotypically and disrespectfully. (See fig. 1.) In "The Harm of Native Stereotyping," Native opinion leaders claim that 45% of "anti-Indian sentiment is due to such media stereotypes. The recurring features of these mascots include red skin, scant dress, adornments (feathers, makeup), and weaponry (arrows, hatchets)." Collectively, the features of the Native stereotype reflect the demeaning seventeenth-century term "noble savage," coined by British poet John Dryden. Despite the modifier "noble," the term

The first reason to oppose the mascots, focusing on stereotypes.

The remainder of this paragraph provides evidence of stereotyping.

Fig. 1. Cleveland Indians mascot Chief Wahoo.

"savage" implies inferiority. Native mascots present non-Native cultures as primitive. Modern Native rights activists such as Dr. Cornel Pewewardy of the University of Kansas claim that such stereotypes are not only insulting but harmful because they damage the self-identity, self-concept, and self-esteem of Native peoples.

Citation of an expert to strengthen the argument.

Indian mascots also possess the power to dehumanize Native Americans. Their exaggerated features strip away the uniqueness and civility of individual people and underscore the relationship of non-Native oppressor to Native victim. In "The Harm of Native Stereotyping," Dr. David P. Rider suggests that Native mascots are especially dehumanizing because "negative images and attitudes" serve to assuage the guilt of the white majority while "[justifying] further exploitation."

A second reason to oppose mascots, focusing on dehumanization.

A possible slippery slope fallacy here. (See Section 9c.)

It is true that some mascots focus on the tribal image of the Native warrior, a highly respected figure. The mascot of the Florida State Seminoles depicts a Native warrior in profile who appears with closed eyes and mouth open, as if in mid-chant, thick stripes of paint on his cheeks and nose. (See fig. 2.) Similar Native mascots are also common in American high schools, where values such as honor, good

This paragraph summarizes opposing views.

Fig. 2. The Florida State University Seminoles mascot.

sportsmanship, and pride surround the image. For example, Mirabeau B. Lamar High School in Houston, Texas, my *alma mater,* proudly supports its "Redskin" mascot. Even the Cleveland Indians' brick-red, toothy Chief Wahoo may possess an honorable origin. The name "Indians" supposedly honors player Louis Sockalexis of the Penobscot tribe, the first major league Native player. Sockalexis played from 1897 to 1899 for the former Cleveland Spiders, and Cleveland fans selected the new name "Indians" by a newspaper vote in his honor. However, *CNN Sports Illustrated* suggests that owner Charles W. Somers may have influenced the results of the vote ("What's in a Name?"). Still, it is at least arguable that certain mascots depict the positive attributes of Natives, thus promoting an appreciation for the unity and strength of Native culture.

Yet even if that is so, Native people are still being trivialized for the sake of sporting events. In an article for *Educators Resources,* Dr. Cornel Pewewardy states that the manipulation of any aspect of a culture by an outsider is the ultimate "power and control" that one ethnic group can assert over another. When the predominantly non-Native sports industry presents its distorted images of Natives, it is exerting power over the Native identity. In addition, because foreign cultures cannot understand the full meaning of Native culture, they often make a mockery of deeply meaningful ceremonies, traditions, and dress. Non-Natives who claim to honor Natives through any mascot, crude or not, distort years of tradition and beauty that are inaccessible to outsiders.

This sentence concedes to some points in the previous paragraph, and then offers a rebuttal, which the rest of this paragraph develops.

Because stereotypes harm and dehumanize Native culture, the presence of Native mascots in United States sports is ultimately racially and culturally offensive. In addition, the continuing resistance of schools, the sports industry, and fans to retiring these derogatory mascots shows disrespect for the wishes of Natives. The Civil Rights Movement of the 1970s provided a forum for Natives to voice their disapproval of "Indian" mascots. Yet even when Natives openly spoke out against them, they have been largely ignored. (See fig. 3.)

Fig. 3. Protestor Sonny Hensley holds an anti-mascot button at a 2003 powwow sponsored by Ohio Center for Native American Affairs.

According to *Washington Post* columnist Courtland Milloy, the continued insistence by major sports organizations that it is not harmful to use Native mascots is best characterized as a delusion: "To them, making a mascot out of a people that were nearly exterminated on their homeland is the ultimate show of respect." This lack of response has led Native groups in recent years to file lawsuits against professional baseball franchises and university teams under the 1974 Civil Rights Act. Fear of such lawsuits may have helped to bring about the NCAA's controversial ruling. But even this ruling is a small victory—it applies only to postseason games and only to college teams. In most settings, the mascots still endure. Perhaps Barbara Munson of the Oneida Nation best describes the ethical situation: unintentional harm becomes intentional when people discover their errors and continue in their behavior nevertheless.

Works Cited

Bellecourt, Vernon. "Wahoo-Chant-Chop: Bad Medicine for Cleveland and Atlanta Baseball?" *National Coalition on Racism in Sports and Media.* American Indian Movement. 27 Oct. 1999. Web. 13 Mar. 2009.

"The Harm of Native Stereotyping: Facts and Evidence." *Blue Corn Comics.* Peace Party. 2002. Web. 4 Feb. 2009.

Milloy, Courtland. "Indian Mascots Disrespect Us All." *Washington Post Online.* Washington Post. 14 Nov. 2005. Web. 19 Jan. 2009.

Munson, Barbara. "Not for Sport: A Native American Activist Calls for an End to 'Indian' Team Mascots." *Tolerance.org.* Southern Poverty Law Center. 1 Nov. 1998. Web. 19 Jan. 2009.

"NCAA Bans Postseason Indian Mascots." *Tolerance.org.* Southern Poverty Law Center. 5 Aug. 2005. Web. 19 Jan. 2009.

Pewewardy, Dr. Cornel. "Why Educators Can't Ignore Indian Mascots." *American Indian Sports Team Mascots: Educators' Resources.* N.p. 1998. Web. 4 Feb. 2009.

Simons, Mike. "Protest against Using Symbols of American Indians as Mascots, January 1, 2003, Columbus, Ohio." Photograph. Getty Images. Web. 12 October 2009.

"What's in a Name? Research Leads Indians to Alter History of Nickname." *CNNSI.com.* CNN Sports Illustrated. 18 Jan. 2000. Web. 13 Mar. 2009.

Young, Joanne. "Lincoln Public Schools." *JournalStar.com.* Lincoln Journal Star. 2002. Web. 4 Feb. 2009.

CHAPTER

11 How Do You Write About Literature and Film?

A paper that analyzes literature or film is a common assignment in most English courses, even in composition classes. But requirements and critical approaches range from close readings of individual texts to wide-ranging confrontations with issues of politics, gender, and culture. So how you write about works of literature or popular culture (movies, plays, music, television) may depend as much on how you are taught as on what you read or view. Whatever your instructor's interests or background, you'll likely encounter a few basic types of assignments:

- **A close reading** (also called *close analysis* or *literary analysis*) paper offers a careful, detailed interpretation of one or more texts, grounded in careful observations about specific words, images, characters, or plots. See Sally Shelton's "Queen Jane Approximately" on pages 177–79 for an example of an essay that develops a close reading.
- **A literary research paper** combines close reading with outside research about the work and, depending upon the project, its author, historical period, or other relevant contextual information. Jeremy Corley's "Diomedes as the Hero of *The Iliad*" on pages 779–84 is an example of this kind of paper.
- **A personal response paper or journal** reports your own thoughts, feelings, and reactions to a literary text or film. This type of assignment is typically briefer and less formal than a close reading paper or a literary research paper. See pages 120–22 for a sample response paper written by Ashley Hamm.

What all these types of assignment have in common is that to write them, a simple summary of what happens in the text is not enough. In most cases you'll have to analyze these texts—to take them apart critically and to comment on how the different elements work together.

What is the point of analyzing literature or film? It can be to heighten your appreciation for literary and cultural works, to demonstrate your ability to support a thesis about a literary text, to enhance your skill at interpretation, to expand your knowledge of a particular era or literary movement, or to

Writing a literary or cinematic analysis differs from simply summarizing or reacting to what you see. Look carefully at these two stills from the 2005 film *King Kong*. First, describe your initial reactions: How does the first image, which closely frames Kong and Ann Darrow, make you feel about the two characters? What do you think is happening here? Now, take a more analytical approach to the image. What visual elements can you identify in the frame, and how do they work to elicit the emotions you initially described? What happens in the second image when the camera zooms out?

heighten your sensitivity to other cultures. It can also be a creative activity—a way to explore new ideas through writing.

11a What elements should you look for when you read literature or view film?

There are dozens of ways to read, think about, and analyze literature and pop culture, and all of these approaches begin with a basic assumption: *The work must be read closely, often more than once.* Whether you are studying a short story, a poem, or a movie, you will have to read—or watch—that work carefully to be able to write about it authoritatively.

Many readers, however, initially feel intimidated by literature. Unfamiliar with literary forms and techniques, they may feel unprepared to comment on a text. Or, more commonly, they may worry about "getting it"—about coming away with a poem or short story's "right" meaning. One way to deal with these concerns is to try to see literature as an accessible, if often challenging, form of creative communication. Once you spend some time with the text you are reading, the pressure to "get it" should start to fade. Try to read the text the first time without any goals or expectations—simply enjoy it for the artistic work that it is. On subsequent readings, you can start to study the work, looking carefully at its structure, imagery, or other formal features (see Checklists 11.1 and 11.2 for more on literary elements). Keep a reading journal, a notebook in which you can jot down reactions, questions, and ideas as you read.

Checklist 11.1 summarizes some basic elements that are integral to literary works. (Some of these—diction, tone, and figurative language among them—are not exclusive to literature; they matter in many kinds of writing.) Checklist 11.2 summarizes some basic elements—in addition to plot, setting, and character—that are integral to cinematic works. Recognizing these elements can help you to begin to generate topic ideas, identify potential thesis statements, and find supporting evidence for a paper about either literature or film.

Checklist 11.1 Basic Literary Elements

- **Plot:** Plot refers to the writer's arrangement of events in a story and the reasons behind that arrangement. Plot can be presented in a number of ways, including chronologically and by using flashbacks.
- **Setting:** The setting establishes the world in which the characters live and act, including time, place, and social and cultural contexts.
- **Character:** Writers create characters to make readers care about what is happening or to reinforce symbols or themes in a text. Flat characters are relatively simple and usually static, which means they stay the same throughout the story. Round characters are more complex and usually dynamic, which means they change considerably as the story progresses. Some characters serve as foils, or contrasts, to other characters.
- **Theme:** The theme of the work is, to put it simply, what the work is *about* (its main concept), as opposed to what *happens* in it (see the discussion of plot, above). A writer will often use a theme to pull together several other elements of the work. Some common themes are *jealousy, ambition, hypocrisy*, and *prejudice*.

(Continued)

Basic Literary Elements *(Continued)*

- **Point of view:** Point of view focuses on who is telling the story (the narrator or speaker) and how it is told. Narrators can speak in the first, second (rarely), or third person. Some narrators are *omniscient* (able to tell us what is going on in the minds of characters), whereas others are *objective* (able to tell us only what the characters say and do.) Some are involved in the plot, and others are mere observers.
- **Diction (word choices):** As you read, assume that every word was chosen carefully. Look up any words you don't understand. Dictionaries provide the literal meanings of words, their *denotations*; also be aware of possible *connotations*, or emotional associations and meanings. In addition, look for *ambiguity*, or the possibility of two or more meanings, in a writer's diction.
- **Figurative language:** A figure of speech is a deviation from the literal meaning of a word or phrase. Writers use figurative language to challenge, inspire, or connect with readers, or simply to stretch their creative wings. *Metaphor* and *simile* are probably the most common figures of speech; others include *oxymoron, personification, hyperbole, synecdoche*, and *metonymy*. (Explanations of these terms and other figures of speech usually can be found in the glossaries at the back of literature textbooks.)
- **Imagery:** Writers use concrete language to make readers see what they are seeing, to hear, smell, taste, and feel. As you read, be aware of how the writer uses words to speak to your senses.
- **Symbols:** It can be easy to confuse symbols with metaphors. A metaphor is a comparison of two unlike objects or concepts, whereas a symbol is one thing that stands for another. The dove, for example, can be a symbol for peace, just as the heart is a common symbol for love. A symbol's context will often suggest its meaning.
- **Sound and rhythm:** Because of the musical nature of their work, poets are especially concerned with the sound and rhythm, or *meter*, of words in a text. Common devices that involve sound include *onomatopoeia* (the sound of the word suggesting its meaning) and *alliteration* (the repetition of the same consonant sounds at the start of words near each other in a text).
- **Tone:** Tone is the mood or feeling the writer creates about the subject matter of a text. The tone might be serious or comical, angry or sad, optimistic or pessimistic, for example. Once you have an idea about the tone of a piece, ask yourself how the writer achieves it—through imagery, descriptive details, diction, or symbols, for instance.

Checklist 11.2 Basic Visual and Cinematic Elements

Media such as film and television are primarily visual and thus involve specialized technical elements, a few of which are listed below. When you undertake a writing project that focuses on a visual or multimedia text, ask your instructor which devices he or she expects you to be familiar with.

- **Shots:** A shot is a camera's recorded image. Types of shots include a long shot (which shows the main object at a distance), a medium shot (which shows the main object in relation to immediate surroundings), and a close-up (which shows only the main object).
- **Scenes:** Scenes are segments in films. A group of related scenes is called a sequence.
- **Camera angles/Camera motion:** Camera angles refer to the position of a camera in relation to the subject, and camera motion refers to the movement of the camera during a shot. Examples: a *pan shot* (in which the camera's base remains fixed while the camera swings right or left), a *traveling shot* (in which the camera moves frontward or backward), and a *high- or low-angle* shot (in which a camera is high and looking downward or low and looking upward).
- **Lighting:** Lighting is the supply of light, or lack thereof, that directs our vision. Types of lighting techniques include *background lighting* (which provides a separation between the subject and the background), *cameo lighting* (which illuminates a single subject), and *floodlighting* (which provides even illumination).
- **Editing:** Editing is the process by which film shots are assembled to make a film. Editing techniques include *slow or fast motion* (in which time appears to slow down or speed up), *dissolve* (a transitional device in which one shot dissolves while another appears), *wipe* (a transitional device in which one scene is wiped away to reveal another), and *montage* (in which quick cuts are put together).

11b What approaches can you use to write about literature and film?

When you begin a literary or cinematic analysis, it often helps to have a general strategy in mind. The following approaches are common; you can often choose one or two of these as a framework for your paper. In the section that follows, you'll find brief explanations of each approach, followed by a sample thesis statement grounded in that approach. Remember as you read the samples that a thesis statement is not a fully developed literary analysis: in each case, the writer needed to devote the remainder of the essay to fleshing out the thesis and supporting it with textual evidence.

1 Perform a close reading. A "close reading" of a text carefully explains the meaning and possible interpretations of a selected passage, sometimes line by line (or, in the case of film, shot by shot or scene by scene). In a close reading, you ordinarily consider how the language of a work makes readers entertain specific ideas and images. If a work includes visual images, you may examine how they interact with elements of a written text. Sally Shelton's paper, which appears at the end of this chapter, offers close readings of several passages in a poem. (Also see Section 8a on how to read critically.)

2 Analyze key themes in a work. When reading a work or viewing a film carefully, you might discover certain key themes. In examining a theme, show how the various parts of a work convey their meanings to readers. In this introduction to an essay exam for an American literature course, the student writer identifies a central theme—human selfishness—in Jonathan Swift's *Gulliver's Travels.*

> In *Gulliver's Travels*, Gulliver's sea voyages expose him to the best and worst aspects of human civilization. Through Gulliver's eyes, readers come to share Swift's perception that no matter how good people's intentions, their innate selfishness corrupts the social institutions they construct. All the societies Gulliver visits give evidence of this theme, but we see the problem especially clearly in his descriptions of Lilliput and Brobdingnag.

3 Analyze plot or structure. You may study the way a work of literature or film is put together and consider why a writer chooses a particular arrangement of ideas or plot.

Here is a paragraph that includes the thesis statement of a student's analysis of a subplot of Christopher Marlowe's play *Dr. Faustus.*

> There are two distinct plots in *Dr. Faustus*. The main plot chronicles Faustus's bargain with the devil and fall into damnation, while the subplot shows the humorous adventures of Faustus's servant Wagner during the same period. Although at first the two plots may seem unrelated, the subplot serves three important functions in the play. It serves the practical purpose of creating a break between the main plot's scenes; it provides comic relief from the tragic tone of the play; and finally, the subplot reinforces the play's moral message.

4 Analyze character or setting. You may study the behavior of characters in a novel, poem, play, short story, or film to understand their motivations and the ways in which different characters relate to each other. Or you can explore how a writer creates characters through description, action, reaction, and dialogue and embodies them with specific themes and ideas. The following paragraph comes from an essay by student writer Joshua Michael French that offers a close reading of the central character in Herman Melville's short story "Bartleby the Scrivener":

> By denying his responsibilities and avoiding conflict with the narrator of the story, Bartleby displays his central character trait: alienation. The narrator calls the scrivener into his office to ask him a few simple questions and even offers Bartleby his friendship, but there is no emotional response. Instead, Bartleby stares blankly and refuses the narrator's advances as usual. The narrator notes that Bartleby "[keeps] his glance fixed upon [his] bust of Cicero" (122) instead of looking directly at him. Even when the narrator comments, "I feel friendly towards you" (122), there is no response from Bartleby. His lack of connection with others is absolute.

Similarly, you might study an artist's creation of a setting to figure out how the environment of a work (where things happen in a novel, short story, play, or film) affects what happens in the plot or to the characters. Settings can also be analyzed as the exterior representations of characters' inner being or as manifestations of cultural values.

5 Analyze the text as an example of a particular genre. You can study a particular work by evaluating its form—tragedy, comic novel, sonnet, detective story, epic, situation comedy, film noir, and so on. Compare the work to other literary or cinematic pieces of that genre, looking for similarities and differences, and perhaps comment on the relative quality of the achievement.

The *Lord of the Rings* series, from which this still is taken (*The Return of the King*, 2003), is among the most critically successful fantasy films ever made. If you have seen one or more films in the series, what is your opinion of the films' quality? What features, if any, do you believe set them apart from other films of this genre? If you haven't seen the *Lord of the Rings*, think of another film that you believe is an excellent or interesting example of its genre, and summarize the elements that you believe make it noteworthy.

6 Analyze a work from the perspective of gender. You might examine how a literary or cinematic work portrays women or men and defines their roles in society. Feminist analyses in particular have greatly influenced the reading of literary and cinematic works in the last generation, though such interpretations vary as much as any other form of criticism. Many feminist critics explore the way literary and cinematic works embody relationships of power between men and women. Sally Shelton's paper, which appears on pages 176–79, is an example of this kind of analysis.

7 Explore a historical or cultural analysis. You can study a literary or cinematic work as it reflects the society that produced it or as it was accepted or rejected by that society when it was published or produced. Or you can study the way historical information makes a literary or cinematic work from an earlier time clearer to a reader today.

You can similarly explore how a work of art embodies the culture that produced it. That is, what assumptions about the beliefs and values of a

This etching depicts the famous orphanage scene from Charles Dickens's novel *Oliver Twist*, in which young Oliver pleads for a second helping of gruel. What might a scene such as this one suggest about life in Victorian England? If you are familiar with this novel, what other scenes and details can you recall that reinforce or complicate the impression given in this scene? If you were asked to write a historical analysis of the novel, what might you look for in the text to develop your analysis?

society can be found in the literary or cinematic work? Such analysis may reveal how certain groups gained or maintained power through the manipulation of literary myths or symbols.

8 Examine the biography of the author or the author's creative process. Such analyses may be related to cultural and political studies, but they may also focus on the individual psychology of a writer. Similarly, you might learn all you can about the way a particular work was created. You might examine the sources, notes, influences, manuscripts, and revised texts behind a finished book, poem, or film. Or you might compare different versions of the same work. In the following example, taken from the introduction of a paper written for a composition course, student writer Kathryn R. Samra draws on information about author Langston Hughes's life to interpret "Theme for English B," a poem about being the only black person in a literature class.

Known for his ability to mix popular culture and radical politics with poetry and a few jazzy beats, Langston Hughes became a prominent figure of the Harlem Renaissance. Born in 1902, Hughes lived during a time when African Americans were finally able to express the

> types of music and literature that were a part of their cultural history. And when he died at the age of 65, it was at the pinnacle of the civil rights movement, when African Americans were beginning to be treated as equals. Most of Hughes's poetry reflects this point in his life. Although Hughes did not write it as a protest poem, the images and details in "Theme for English B" reflect his complex feelings about growing up as a black person in Harlem at a time when the country was still segregated, but on the brink of civil rights protest and change.

9 Examine a literary work or film that retells an existing story. For example, you might examine a film adaptation of a novel or other literary work. Once you've sorted out the relationship between the original and the retelling, consider the context of the film adaptation. When was it produced? What were the screenwriter's circumstances? What was going on in the world at that time? In short, why might this particular screenwriter have chosen to retell this particular tale at this particular time in this particular way? A paper using this approach could examine the film *O Brother, Where Art Thou?* (2000) as a response to Homer's *Odyssey* or the 2004 film *A Cinderella Story* as a response to the fairy tale.

Or you might explore how a poem, short story, or novel reinterprets an existing story or event. In the following excerpt, student writer Robin Neumayer introduces the thesis for her paper examining Angela Carter's "The Bloody Chamber" as a retelling of Charles Perrault's "Bluebeard."

> Charles Perrault's "Bluebeard" (1697) is the tale of a girl whose curiosity nearly kills her by means of a psychotic, controlling husband. Nearly 300 years later, Angela Carter published "The Bloody Chamber" (1979), a variation of this dark fable. Much of the plot remains the same, but the noticeable change lies in the portrayal of the female characters. In "The Bloody Chamber," Carter retells the story of "Bluebeard" as a cry for action for women. Written during the fight for the Equal Rights Amendment, Carter's story showcases women's potential through the inclusion of a female hero, but criticizes women's submission through the female protagonist's unwillingness to challenge her husband.

These general approaches can suggest interesting directions to follow in a literary analysis, but that's only a beginning—not a finished paper. To produce a polished paper, you'll need to develop your ideas, gather textual support, and pull them together into a focused interpretation. (See Section 8d.)

EXERCISE 11.1 Use the approaches outlined in Section 11b to generate several possible angles for analyzing a familiar literary text (such as Shakespeare's *Romeo and Juliet* or one of J. K. Rowling's Harry Potter novels) or film (such as *The Wizard of Oz*). Share your ideas with a group of classmates: Which ideas seem most interesting? Most promising to pursue for a literary analysis assignment? What would you need to do to develop the best idea into a full essay?

11c What sources can you use in writing essays about literature and film?

While many instructors won't require outside sources for a literary or cinematic analysis, you may sometimes be asked to do research to contextualize or support your reading of a text. The resources available to you as you begin an analysis can seem overwhelming. But many of them will in fact make your work easier, more authoritative, and more interesting. The sample paper on pages 176–79 of this chapter is a close reading essay, with no outside research. However, there is a sample of a researched literary analysis paper on pages 779–84 in Chapter 52.

1 Understand the primary texts you are reading. In working with literary texts, you may first need to establish certain basic facts about them. Are you reading a first edition of a work or a revised version, an edited version, a translation, or, in the case of a film, a later "director's cut" that differs from the version shown in theaters? Each of these considerations may have a bearing on your subsequent analysis. Evaluate any publication information you find in the prefaces or front matter of works of literature to discover when they were written, by whom they were published, how they might have been transmitted to readers, and how they may have changed over the years. In general, the older a work, the more complicated (and fascinating) its publication history might be. But even relatively recent texts deserve your attention. The techniques of positioning that you apply to research materials (see Section 45b) can be modified to work with literary and cultural texts before you analyze them.

2 Consult secondary sources on literary subjects. To locate secondary sources on literary or cinematic topics, visit your campus library. If you are interested in print sources, you may want to check out an encyclopedia of literature or film. Handbooks, such as the *MLA Handbook for Writers of Research Papers*, are available for reference at your campus library. Use the library catalog, which you can search by subject, or ask a librarian to help you locate print sources.

Many electronic sources may also be available through your campus library. Examples of helpful databases and indexes include the American Film Institute catalog, the International Film Archive Database, the Literature Resource Center, and the Modern Language Association (MLA) International Bibliography. For a list of Web sources that do not require library access, see Checklist 11.4.

Checklist 11.4 Web Sources for Literary and Cinematic Analyses

The English Server. <http://eserver.org>.

Film Studies Resources. <http://www.uiowa.edu/~commstud/resources/film_resources.html>.

Literary Resources on the Net. <http://andromeda.rutgers.edu/~jlynch/Lit>.

MLA on the Web. <http://www.mla.org>.

The On-Line Books Page. <http://digital.library.upenn.edu/books>.

University of Virginia Library Electronic Text Center. <http://etext.lib.virginia.edu>.

11d How do you develop a paper that analyzes literature or film?

How you develop a literary paper or analysis of a film will depend on your course assignment and your own purpose. In some courses you'll be asked to do a close reading of an individual poem, novel, or short story; in others you may be expected to contribute to a class wiki that places artists or works in their historical or political contexts. Here we assume that you are most likely to write a paper with a thesis—but the principles we discuss will apply to other projects as well.

1 Begin by reading carefully. The evidence you'll need to write a thoughtful, well-organized analysis may come from within the literary or cinematic work itself and from outside readings and secondary sources. Your initial goal is to find a point worth making, an assertion you can prove with convincing evidence.

To find your point, begin by **previewing** the work (or works) and then reading and **annotating** them carefully (see Sections 8a and 45b).

Assigned to read Shakespeare's *Macbeth*, you might position the work by doing a little background reading (see Section 11b). You'd quickly learn that *Macbeth* is a tragedy written by the most famous of English playwrights around 1605–06, though not published until 1623. An unusually brief tragedy, *Macbeth* may have been designed expressly to please the English monarch James I, who was fascinated by witches and whose legendary ancestor appears in the play.

Yet you should also read with an open mind, being certain to savor the literary experience. Do, however, annotate texts in some way to record your immediate responses. You might simply ask yourself a series of questions.

- What issues engage me immediately as I read the work?
- What puzzles or surprises me?
- What characters or literary devices seem most striking or original?
- What upsets me or seems most contrary to my own values and traditions?

Make a list of such queries as you read, and reexamine them when you have finished. At this point you might stimulate your thinking both by considering specific ways of approaching a literary text (see Sections 11b and 11c) and by using one of the techniques we describe for finding and focusing ideas, particularly brainstorming and idea mapping (see Sections 2a and 2b).

2 Develop a thesis about the literary or cinematic work(s) you are studying. Begin with questions you are eager to explore in depth, a research query or hypothesis generated perhaps by your reading of secondary sources or by your discussions with classmates. When you've put your question into words, test its energy. Is the answer to your inquiry so obvious that it isn't likely to interest or surprise anyone?

- Is Shakespeare's *Macbeth* a great play?

If so, discard the issue. Try another. Look for a surprising, even startling question—one whose answer you don't necessarily know. Test that question on classmates or your instructor.

- Could Shakespeare's *Macbeth* actually be a comedy?
- What role do the lower classes play in a dynastic struggle like the one depicted in *Macbeth*?
- Are the witches really the physical embodiment of Macbeth's own mind?

When you have found your question, turn it into a claim—your preliminary thesis statement.

- Shakespeare's *Macbeth* is really a comedy.
- The welfare of the lower classes seems to have been ignored in dynastic struggles like those depicted in *Macbeth.*
- The witches in *Macbeth* are a physical representation of the state of Macbeth's mind.

3 Read the work(s) again with your thesis firmly in mind. Look for characters, incidents, descriptions, speeches, dialogue, or images that support or refute your thesis. Take careful notes. If you are using your own text, highlight significant passages in the work. When you are done, evaluate the evidence you have gathered from a close reading. Then modify or qualify your thesis to reflect what you have learned or discovered. In most cases, your thesis will be more specific and more limited after you have gathered and assessed your evidence.

- The many unexpected comic moments in *Macbeth* emphasize how disordered the world becomes for murderers like Macbeth and his wife.

When necessary, return to secondary sources or other literary or cinematic works to supplement and extend your analysis. Play with ideas, relationships, implications, and possibilities. Don't hesitate to question conventional views of a work or to bring your own experiences to bear on the act of reading and interpreting literature or film. Be sure also to keep accurate bibliographic information for your Works Cited page. (See Chapter 43 on planning a research project.)

4 Use scratch outlines to guide the first draft. Try out several organization plans for the paper (see Section 3c), and then choose the one you find most solid or most challenging. Here's how a scratch outline for a paper on comic elements in *Macbeth* might look.

Thesis: Comic moments in Macbeth emphasize how disordered the world becomes for the Macbeths after they murder the king.

I. Comic moments after the murder of King Duncan
II. Comedy at the feast for Banquo
III. Comedy in the sleepwalking scene
IV. Conclusion

When you have a structure, write a complete first draft. Stay open to new ideas and refinements of your original thesis, but try not to wander off into a biography of the author or a discussion of the historical period unless such material relates directly to your thesis. If you do wander, consider whether the digression in your draft might be the topic you *really* want to write about.

Avoid the draft that simply paraphrases the plot of a literary work or film. Equally ineffective is a paper that merely praises its author for a job well done. Avoid extremely impressionistic judgments: "I feel that Hemingway must have been a good American." And don't expect to find a moral in every literary or cinematic work, or turn your analysis into a search for "hidden meanings." Respond honestly to what you are reading or viewing—not the way you think your teacher expects you to. (For full examples of literary papers, see Sally Shelton's essay on pages 176–79 and Jeremy Corley's research paper in Chapter 52, pages 779–84).

5 Follow the conventions of literary analysis. One of those conventions is to introduce most direct quotations. Don't just insert a quotation from a literary work or a critic into your paper without identifying it and explaining its significance. And be sure quotations fit into the grammar of your sentences.

> **The doctor in *Macbeth* warns the gentlewoman,** "You have known what you should not" (5.1.46–47).
>
> **Commenting on the play, Frank Kermode observes that** "*Macbeth* has extraordinary energy; it represents a fierce engagement between the mind and its guilt" (1311).

In shaping the paper, you may want to follow the conventions of the MLA research paper or the *Chicago Manual of Style* paper (see Chapters 50 and 52). Check with your instructor to find out which form he or she prefers.

Checklist 11.5 Conventions in a Literary Paper

- **Use the present tense to refer to events occurring in a literary work:** Hester Prynne *wears* a scarlet letter, Hamlet *kills* Polonius.
- **Identify passages of short poems by line numbers:** (*"Journey of the Magi," lines 21–31*). Avoid the abbreviations *l.* or *ll.* for *line* or *lines* because they are sometimes confused with roman numerals; spell out the words. See Section 40d-4 for advice on punctuating lines of poetry that appear within a paper.
- **Provide act and scene divisions (and line numbers as necessary) for passages from plays.** Act and scene numbers are now usually given in Arabic numerals, although Roman numerals are still common and acceptable: *Ham.* 4.5.179–86 or *Ham.* IV.v.179–86. The titles of Shakespeare's works are commonly abbreviated in citations: *Mac.* 1.2; *Oth.* 2.2. Check to see which form your instructor prefers.
- **Provide a date of publication in parentheses after your first mention of a literary work:** Before publishing *Beloved* (1987), Toni Morrison had written....
- **Use technical terms accurately.** Spell the names of characters correctly. Take special care with matters of grammar and mechanics.

WRITER AT WORK **A Literary Analysis Paper**

In the following literary analysis, "Queen Jane Approximately" (a clever allusion to a song by Bob Dylan), Sally Shelton from the University of South Carolina does a close reading of a poem by Sharon Olds, "The One Girl at the Boys' Party." She approaches the work from a feminist perspective, examining the interplay of gender roles between one young girl and a group of boys. Shelton supports her analysis by carefully citing passages from the poem, which we have reprinted in its entirety.

The One Girl at the Boys' Party
By Sharon Olds

When I take my girl to the swimming party
I set her down among the boys. They tower and
bristle, she stands there smooth and sleek,
her math scores unfolding in the air around her.
They will strip to their suits, her body hard and
indivisible as a prime number,
they'll plunge in the deep end, she'll subtract
her height from ten feet, divide it into
hundreds of gallons of water, the numbers
bouncing in her mind like molecules of chlorine
in the bright blue pool. When they climb out,
her ponytail will hang its pencil lead
down her back, her narrow silk suit
with hamburgers and french fries printed on it
will glisten in the brilliant air, and they will
see her sweet face, solemn and
sealed, a factor of one, and she will
see their eyes, two each,
their legs, two each, and the curves of their sexes,
one each, and in her head she'll be doing her
wild multiplying, as the drops
sparkle and fall to the power of a thousand from her body.

Sally Shelton

Professor Moore

English 102

21 April 2009

Queen Jane Approximately

Sharon Olds's "The One Girl at the Boys' Party" examines the tense competition between the sexes. The poem illustrates the innate vulnerability of men while portraying females as winning attention and respect they rightfully deserve. Olds achieves these insights by examining the isolation of a young girl at a party of boys. She infuses the situation with ironies and repeated images that probe themes of gender, sexuality, and domination.

Imagery and irony are two basic literary elements, ripe for further analysis.

The poem deceives the reader initially by putting the youths in typical gender roles. The speaker takes her daughter (1) to a party where she "set[s] her down among the boys" (2) like a toy or doll for their amusement. She is placed within a situation where she must prove herself. The boys, in turn, "tower and / bristle" (2-3) at the intrusion. While she is being "set down," the boys move like a gang, intimidating and, perhaps, angry. Yet suddenly, the attention of the poem shifts from the girl to the boys as the young woman quickly and nonchalantly asserts her dominance over them.

Remember to use present tense to refer to events occurring in a literary work.

The contrast between the girl and the group of boys is established early in the poem. While the boys "tower and bristle," the lone girl "stands there smooth and sleek" (3), firmly placed, establishing her ground, unabated in her delicate sensuality, and controlling the air about her. It is in this "brilliant air" (15) that her "math scores" (4) begin to unfold. References to mathematics throughout the poem illustrate how the young girl, and perhaps the speaker of the poem, have conquered the situation already. They have figured the boys out through methodical and meticulous calculations.

Remember to use a qualifier, such as "perhaps," when assuming something about the speaker of the poem.

To complete the reversal of gender roles, the boys, who were the first to dominate in the poem, assume a subordinate and effeminate role. As if to expose themselves as sensual and enticing beings, "[t]hey will strip to their suits" (5), leaving themselves vulnerable (she can count the "curves of their sexes" [19]) and hoping that the girl will "strip" to her vulnerability as well. The girl, however, remains in control, "her body hard and / indivisible as a prime number" (5-6). The pool of males will forever attempt to figure her out, but she has solved them. She stands before the boys in the pool, with "the numbers / bouncing in her mind" (9-10), her calculations racing. She, who was initially perceived as an intrusion, has now silently attracted the curiosity of the boys.

Now that the girl's presence has consumed the scene, the boys become enchanted by her sensuality. The infinite "molecules of chlorine" (10) that comprise the girl's intelligence intoxicate the boys, who have by now succumbed to the innocent appeal of "the bright blue pool" (11). Sexual desires come into play: her tomboyish ponytail catches their gaze. Although it "hang[s] its pencil lead" (12), a phallic symbol with piercing connotations, the boys still allow their gaze to follow the ponytail "down her back" (13). Then they notice the girl's figure, more "smooth and sleek" (3) than before, in "her narrow silk suit" (13) with the mouthwatering "hamburgers and french fries printed on it" (14) that "glisten in the brilliant air" (15). Lastly, they notice her face, "sweet," "solemn," and "sealed" (16-17). No longer an

Direct quotations support the writer's claims; note also that she changes one line (indicated by brackets) to make the passage fit into the grammar of her sentence.

object to discard, the girl becomes for the boys an embodiment of a desire that will never be satiated.

Again, the speaker widens the schism between the girl and the youths. It began with the girl doing all the observing and calculating, but soon the boys catch on. Threatened by her ability to strip them, they "plunge in the deep end" (7), hoping to hide their vulnerability while attempting to entice the girl. The act of plunging is risky and the boys nearly drown in their attempts to impress her. Defeated and weakened, they have to "climb out" (11), and they discover how badly they are getting beaten. Then they enter the game, the observed becoming the observers. While the boys "see her sweet face . . . a factor of one", the girl outnumbers them when she "see[s] their eyes, two each, / their legs, two each, and the curves of their sexes, / one each" (21). She sheds some power when she lets her "drops / sparkle and fall" (21), but they will never gain a hold on her because she will forever "be doing her / wild multiplying" (22). The boys cannot enumerate her "to the power of a thousand" (22), so her "power" controls and overwhelms them. She has reduced these once towering and bristling boys to vulnerable, starstruck subordinates by daring them to plunge into the deep end of womanhood.

Through the character of the girl, the speaker offers insight into how women encompass an infinite power and elegance that men miscalculate and misunderstand. The girl triumphs while the boys sink into her deep intelligence, stamina, and sensuality. In the game of relationships, here staged as a pool party, there are those who tower, those who plunge, and those who calculate.

Work Cited

Olds, Sharon. "The One Girl at the Boys' Party." *The Dead and the Living*. New York: Knopf, 1984. Print.

PART III

STYLE

CHAPTER

12 What Makes Paragraphs Work?

Imagine how you'd feel if you opened a newspaper and saw pages filled with a single, unbroken column of print. You'd probably think, "I don't want to read this"—and you'd be right to feel that way. When writers organize material into paragraph form, audiences can follow the material more easily. Paragraphing makes a text look inviting and less intimidating, drawing readers in and encouraging them to work their way through the material. Knowing how to shape effective paragraphs is a key to successful writing.

THE WALL STREET JOURNAL.

Obama to Reappoint Bernanke as Fed Chief

Signs of Economic Recovery, Concern for Continuity Drive President's Decision; Renomination Could Mean Senate Fight

What's News–

New Allegations of Vote Rigging in Afghanistan

GM Balks At Selling Opel Unit

How do the paragraph breaks, images, and headlines help readers to navigate the array of information on this newspaper front page? How would the effect differ if all the text were presented in a single, unbroken stretch?

Take Control

12a How do you construct unified paragraphs?

When we say that a paragraph is **unified,** we mean that it makes a single point and develops it, without detours into irrelevant or tangential information. Such paragraphs help readers understand and follow your thoughts.

1 Anchor a paragraph with a topic sentence. In a unified paragraph, a writer concentrates on a single idea. The first sentence in this paragraph about golf sets the agenda:

> **Here, primarily, is what's wrong with Phil Mickelson, Sergio Garcia, David Duval, Justin Leonard, Jesper Parnevik, Lee Westwood, Darren Clarke, Jim Furyk and a handful of others: They were born at the wrong time.** They were born too close to Tiger Woods, the same way Charles Barkley, Patrick Ewing, Karl Malone and John Stockton were born at the wrong time, too close to Michael Jordan. That's all they were guilty of, being in the wrong place at the wrong time for pretty much the duration of their careers.
>
> —Michael Wilbon, "It's Just Tiger's Time"

Suppose, however, that this writer had written his first sentence and then gone off in another direction, jotting down sentences as they occurred to him. The paragraph might have turned out like this:

> Here, primarily, is what's wrong with Phil Mickelson, Sergio Garcia, David Duval, Justin Leonard, Jesper Parnevik, Lee Westwood, Darren Clarke, Jim Furyk and a handful of others: They were born at the wrong time. Since Tiger Woods has come along, everything in golf has changed. There are more fans watching the game on TV, and Woods is becoming one of the world's best-known people because of all his endorsement deals. Some courses are even changing their layouts to try to "Tiger-proof" them.

Now the paragraph lacks unity because the writer opens with a statement and then, instead of expanding on it or following through with connected examples, jumps into several new subjects.

One way to keep a paragraph focused is to use a **topic sentence** that states your main idea clearly and directly to keep you honest. The topic sentence doesn't have to be the first one in the paragraph, although it often is, particularly in academic writing.

> **Sleep has become another casualty of modern life.** According to sleep researchers, studies point to a "sleep deficit" among Americans, a majority of whom are currently getting between 60 and 90 minutes less a night than they should for optimum health and performance. The number of people showing up at sleep disorder clinics with serious problems has skyrocketed in the last decade. Shift work, long working hours, the growth of a global economy (with its attendant continent-hopping and twenty-four-hour business culture), and the accelerating pace of life have all contributed to sleep

deprivation. If you need an alarm clock, the experts warn, you're probably sleeping too little.

—Juliet Schor, *The Overworked American*

A writer can also lead up to a topic sentence (or topic sentences), first giving readers details that build their interest and then summarizing the content in one sentence.

In 1938, near the end of a decade of monumental turmoil, the year's number-one newsmaker was not Franklin Delano Roosevelt, Hitler, or Mussolini. It wasn't Pope Pius XI, nor was it Lou Gehrig, Howard Hughes, or Clark Gable. **The subject of the most newspaper column inches in 1938 wasn't even a person. It was an undersized, crooked-legged racehorse named Seabiscuit.**

—Laura Hillenbrand, *Seabiscuit: An American Legend*

Not all paragraphs have topic sentences, nor do they need them, since writers can unify paragraphs in a number of ways. But they work especially well to anchor and control the flow of ideas in academic writing. By reading from one topic sentence to the next, you can usually tell if you're developing your thesis as you have planned. For more on organizing a draft around a thesis, see Section 3c.

Taking Control

Identify key points with topic sentences

If you have a problem organizing papers, begin by checking your paragraphs. Does each typically open with a sentence that makes a clear point? And, just as important, do all the subsequent sentences in the paragraph connect to that topic sentence directly, offering support, evidence, or relevant discussion? Revise or delete any sentences that are off target. Writers should always understand exactly how you get from the beginning of a paragraph to its end.

One useful way of testing the clarity of your topic sentences in an academic paper is to read only the first one or two sentences in each paragraph. If the paper still coheres when you browse it this way, chances are good that your topic sentences are doing their job of identifying the key points in paragraphs.

2 Use transitions to unify your paragraphs. Even when you have a clear focus, the connections among sentences or ideas in a paragraph may not always be immediately apparent to readers. In such cases, you'll need to incorporate *internal transitions*—words and phrases that act like traffic signals to move readers from one point in an argument or explanation to another.

Consider this paragraph from a student draft. It is focused on a single issue—the rise of cheating on campus—but the first version seems choppy because it lacks internal transitions.

> **WEAK TRANSITIONS**
>
> Cheating has become frighteningly common. My roommate brought her mother to campus to complain when she failed Spanish for copying her term paper from a Web site. My English professor reported two students in my English literature class to the dean for allowing a high school teacher to write a paper for them. The Academic Affairs office reported that academic misconduct is up by 30 percent over last year. What is happening on our campus? Parents and teachers once instilled in students the value of doing one's own work instead of cheating.
>
> **INTERNAL TRANSITIONS ADDED**
>
> Cheating is becoming frighteningly common **on our campus. Last week** my roommate brought her mother to campus to complain when she failed Spanish for copying her term paper from a Web site. **Earlier this semester,** my English literature professor reported two students to the dean for allowing a high school teacher to write a paper for them. **These cases are not unusual, campus officials say.** The Academic Affairs office reported **last week** that academic dishonesty cases are up by 30 percent over last year. What is happening on our campus? Parents and teachers **used to** instill in students the value of work; **now** many are encouraging cheating instead.

To incorporate internal transitions into a paragraph you've written, try these strategies:

- **Use transition words** such as *first, next, however,* and *in addition* to show the relationships among sentences and ideas. See Section 14b-1 for a list of such words.
- **Repeat key words or phrases** to tie related sentences together. The paragraph above, for example, repeats the term *cheating* to connect the

examples of cheating on campus. The term provides coherence and yet is not tiresome. See Section 14b-2 for more on using repetition.

- **Use parallel phrases**—phrases that begin with the same word or that share the same grammatical structure—to emphasize connections among similar examples or related pieces of information. For more on using parallel structure to unify a paragraph, see Section 14b-5.

See Chapter 14 for a detailed discussion of transitions.

EXERCISE 12.1 Identify the strategies the writer has used to unify the following paragraph: Is there a topic sentence? Do you see transition words, repetition, or parallel structures? Discuss whether and how these devices helped you follow the writer's ideas.

> Day 1 set the tone for our really heavy driving days: We stopped only for gasoline and bathroom breaks, which usually coincided after 350 to 400 miles. We averaged about 70 mph for at least 14 hours. We ate what we had in the car or what we could get from travel plazas and gas stations. We didn't run the air conditioning, though we never talked about why. We didn't listen to the radio much because we had the windows down and could barely hear. We discussed—in shouts—whatever popped into our heads: "What just hit the windshield?" "Did you see what was growing in that bathroom?" "Kansas doesn't look so flat at night." "If there is a hell, do you think I-70 is it?" We slept in cheap motels because we were too tired to pitch a tent by the time we stopped. We thought we would get farther than we did.
>
> —Lee Bauknight, "Two for the Road"

EXERCISE 12.2 Examine critically one or two paragraphs of a draft you're currently working on or have recently completed: Do the paragraphs seem adequately unified? What unifying strategies have you used? Can you think of others that might be useful?

12b How can you organize paragraphs?

Why do specific organizational patterns recur in writing? Perhaps these patterns emerge because they resemble typical ways of thinking. Whatever their origins, the paragraph patterns discussed in this section are common, and writers looking for ways to develop a draft can profit by trying them.

1 Illustration. A paragraph of illustration begins with a general statement or claim and develops it with supporting details, evidence, or examples. In an argument paper, writers often follow a general claim with one or more pieces of supporting evidence.

> For more than 40 states, the days of traditional multiple-choice tests that required teachers to set aside real learning and teach test-taking skills are fading. Today's tests often include open-ended questions, demand writing samples, and require students to show, honestly and accurately, what they know. The new tests ask students to solve complex mathematics problems and explain solutions, to critically examine literary techniques and articulate their thinking in written essays. That's a far cry from drills in information regurgitation. On the recent New York state test for 11th-graders, 92 percent passed the new, tougher test in English language arts. This kind of testing leads to better teaching. It also tells elected officials and educators where they ought to direct resources and efforts.
>
> —Louis V. Gerstner, Jr., "High Marks for Standardized Tests"

2 Question and answer. Asking and answering a question is another way to organize a paragraph.

> How good are graphic novels, really? Are these truly what our great-grandchildren will be reading, instead of books without pictures? Hard to say. Some of them are much better than others, obviously, but this is true of books of any kind. And the form is better suited to certain themes and kinds of expression than others. One thing the graphic novel can do particularly well, for example, is depict the passage of time, slow or fast or both at once—something the traditional novel can approximate only with empty space. The graphic novel can make the familiar look new. The autobiographical hero of Craig Thompson's *Blankets*, a guilt-ridden teenager falling in love for the first time, would be insufferably predictable in a prose narrative; here, he has an innocent sweetness.
>
> —Charles McGrath, "Not Funnies"

3 Narration or process. One way to develop a paragraph is to relate events or the steps of a process in chronological order. This pattern is obviously appropriate for writing personal or historical accounts, but you can also use it effectively to describe a scientific or technical process.

The clanking from within the giant white magnetic resonance imaging (MRI) scanner sounds like somebody banging a wrench on a radiator. "Tommy," a healthy 8-year-old, is halfway inside the machine's round chamber, and his little white-sweat-socked feet keep time with the noise. A mirror on a plastic cage around his head will allow him to see images and video. During the next 45 minutes, Dr. Golijeh Golarai, a researcher at Stanford University, will ask Tommy to hold his feet still as she directs a computer to flash pictures at him, including faces of African American men, landscapes, faces of white men, then scrambled faces in a cubist redux. When the boy thinks he sees the same image twice, he pushes a button. The machine is tracking the blood in his brain as it flows to the neurons he is using to perform the assigned task.

—Joan O'C. Hamilton, "Journey to the Center of the Mind"

4 Definition. Paragraphs of definition often work well in the first part of a report or article that explains or argues. They help to establish the meaning of important terms the author is going to use.

From kids and people my own age I picked up *Pachuco*. *Pachuco* (the language of the zoot suiters) is a language of rebellion, both against Standard Spanish and Standard English. It is a secret language. Adults of the culture and outsiders cannot understand it. It is made up of slang words from both English and Spanish. *Ruca* means girl or woman, *vato* means guy or dude, *chale* means no, *simón* means yes, *churo* is sure, talk is *periquiar*, *pigionear* means petting, *que gacho* means how nerdy, *ponte águila* means watch out, death is called *la pelona*. Through lack of practice and not having others who can speak it, I've lost most of the *Pachuco* tongue.

—Gloria Anzaldúa, "How to Tame a Wild Tongue"

5 Classification. A classification paragraph, which divides a subject into the categories to be discussed, can work particularly well as the opening for a paper. Used this way, it helps to unify the essay by forecasting its organization.

In fact, over the past two decades, there have been essentially two forces contributing new words to the language: rap music and business consultants. One gave us "dis," "props," and "for shizzle"; the other gave us "proactive," "synergy," and "agent of change."

—Adam Sternbergh, "Got Bub All Up in the Hizzle, Yo!"

6 Comparison and contrast. A paragraph can also be built on a comparison-and-contrast pattern. The following example, taken from a report on homeless youth in New York City, sets up a comparison in the first sentence.

> While urban nomads and the city's traditional homeless youth often share a history of physical or sexual abuse, the two groups differ in many respects. Typically, New York's population of runaways and homeless youths is heavily minority and includes both girls and boys. By contrast, urban nomads tend to be white and largely male, with backgrounds that are typically working-class and occasionally middle-class. Many are children from homes where a parent's remarriage has produced family conflicts. Others are simply bored.
>
> — Alison Stateman, "Postcards from the Edge"

7 Cause and effect. Cause-and-effect paragraphs can proceed in two ways: they can mention the effect first and then describe its causes, or they can start by identifying a cause and then describe its effects. We illustrate both patterns here.

EFFECT FOLLOWED BY CAUSES

> Why do so many citizens of the world's oldest democracy not vote when they can, at a time when the struggle for democracy in Europe and throughout the rest of the world has reached its most crucial and inspiring level since 1848? Partly, it's an administrative problem—the disappearance of the old party-machine and ward system, whose last vestige was Mayor Daley. Whatever its abuses, it got people street by street, household by household, to the ballot boxes. Its patronage system did help tie American people, especially blue-collar and lower middle-class ones, to the belief that they as citizens had some role to play in the running of their country from the bottom up, ward by ward. It reinforced the sense of participatory democracy.
>
> —Robert Hughes, *The Culture of Complaint* (From *The Culture of Complaint: The Fraying of America* by Robert Hughes (1993). Reprinted by permission of Oxford University Press, Inc.)

CAUSE TO EFFECTS

> Once overhunted, white-tailed deer have returned in such explosive numbers that they're ravaging forestland and besieging rural and even suburban communities. The animals cause car accidents, carry ticks that can transmit infectious diseases to people, chew up landscaping,

and otherwise make pests of themselves, albeit sometimes strikingly graceful ones.

—Anne Broache, "Oh Deer!"

8 Analogy. An **analogy** is an extended comparison. One especially good use of analogy is to help readers understand a concept by showing a resemblance between a familiar idea and an unfamiliar one.

> Short-order cooking is like driving a car: anyone can do it up to a certain speed. The difference between an amateur and a crack professional isn't so much a matter of specific skills as of consistency and timing. Most diner kitchens are fairly forgiving places. You can break a yolk or two, lose track of an order, or overcook an omelette and start again without getting swamped. But as the pace increases those tolerances disappear. At the Tropical Breeze, a single mistake can throw an entire sequence out of kilter, so that every dish is either cold or overdone. A cook of robotic efficiency, moving steadily from task to task, suddenly slips a cog and becomes Lucy in the chocolate factory, stuffing candies into her mouth as they pile up on the assembly line.
>
> —Burkhard Bilger, "The Egg Men"

EXERCISE 12.3 Use the paragraph patterns discussed and illustrated in Sections 12b-1 through 12b-8 to write paragraphs for two of the following situations.

1. Summarize the arguments on one side of a local controversy you feel strongly about—for example, a new city ordinance, an upcoming election, or a controversial public event or program.

2. Explain how to operate a machine you use regularly—for instance, a cell phone, a jet ski, an iPod, or a coffeemaker.

3. Examine a group of people or things closely and then divide them by some single principle of classification. You might divide your relatives at a family get-together by their sense of style, the students in your major by their rationales for studying that subject, the CDs in your personal collection by their musical genres, and so on.

12c How long should a paragraph be?

The appropriate length for a paragraph isn't a matter of how many sentences it has. Instead, writers need to think about how their work is going to look in print. If readers see a long stretch of text unbroken by paragraphs, white space, or headings, most assume that the material will be difficult to read.

1 Break up long paragraphs that look hard to read. In most situations, readers prefer fairly short paragraphs. How short is that? Probably no more than seven or eight sentences—and in many cases, even fewer. However, don't chop up paragraphs arbitrarily just to make your paper look inviting; typically, a paragraph needs several sentences to develop a complete idea. But whenever you compose an unusually long paragraph, review it carefully from the point of view of readers. If it seems too lengthy, use the items in Checklist 12.1 to spot any places where you might divide the paragraph to make it more readable.

Checklist 12.1 Places to Break Up a Long Paragraph

- **Shifts in time.** Look for spots where you have written words such as *at that time, then,* or *afterward,* or have given other time signals.
- **Shifts in place.** Look for spots where you have written *another place* or *on the other side,* or have used words that point to places.
- **Shifts in direction.** Look for spots where you have written *on the other hand, nevertheless,* or *however,* or have otherwise indicated contrast.
- **Shifts in emphasis or focus.** Look for spots where you have shifted to a new point, perhaps using words such as *another, in addition,* or *not only.*

But don't break an entire paper into one- or two-sentence paragraphs. It's true that long paragraphs intimidate readers; however, too many short ones can distract them or make them feel the material is trivial. Save extremely short paragraphs for narrow newspaper columns or for the special circumstances we describe next.

2 Use short paragraphs for effect. You can use one- or two-sentence paragraphs occasionally, but do so deliberately, to achieve a specific purpose. Sometimes you may want to insert a very short paragraph to make a transition between two longer paragraphs. At other times you can use brevity for dramatic emphasis, as Natalie Angier has done in the passage below.

> Ah, romance. Can any sight be as sweet as a pair of mallard ducks gliding gracefully across a pond, male by female, seemingly inseparable? Or, better yet, two trumpeter swans, the legendary symbols of eternal love, each ivory neck one half of a single heart, souls of a feather staying coupled together for life?
>
> **Coupled for life—with just a bit of adultery, cuckoldry, and gang rape on the side.**
>
> Alas for sentiment and the greeting card industry, it turns out that, in the animal kingdom, there is almost no such thing as monogamy. As a wealth of recent findings makes clear as a crocodile tear, even creatures long assumed to have faithful tendencies and to need a strong pair bond to rear their young are in fact perfidious brutes.
>
> —Natalie Angier, "Mating for Life?"

3 Adapt paragraph length to your writing situation. How long is an ideal paragraph? The answer, as you might expect, depends on your writing situation—your purpose, your audience, and your medium.

Consider long paragraphs when:

- You are developing complex ideas in detail.
- Your audience is experienced and skillful.
- You are writing in a genre, such as the academic essay, in which longer paragraphs are the norm.
- Readers are seeking detailed information.

Consider short paragraphs when:

- Readers are likely to be impatient or skimming for content.
- Readers are inexperienced or unfamiliar with the topic.
- You are writing in a genre, such as a newspaper editorial, in which short paragraphs are the norm.
- You are writing in a digital environment.

EXERCISE 12.4 Analyze the design and paragraphing of the scientific article excerpt pictured below. Who is the intended audience for the article and what might their expectations be? What can you deduce about the writer's purpose just from the shape of this opening page?

Intraguild Predation Among Larval Treehole Mosquitoes, *Aedes albopictus*, *Ae. aegypti*, and *Ae. triseriatus* (Diptera: Culicidae), in Laboratory Microcosms

J. S. EDGERLY,[1] M. S. WILLEY,[2] AND T. LIVDAHL[2]

J. Med. Entomol. 36(3): 394–399 (1999)

ABSTRACT We compared the tendency for 4th-instar larvae to prey on newly hatched larvae, and the vulnerability of those 1st instars to such predation for *Aedes triseriatus* (Say), *Ae. aegypti* (L.), and *Ae. albopictus* (Skuse), all container-breeding mosquitoes. The latter 2 species were introduced to North America and are now sympatric with *Ae. triseriatus*, a native species in eastern North America. The experiment also enabled the assessment of species-specific influences of food supplements and spatial heterogeneity on predatory behavior. *Ae. triseriatus* was substantially more predatory and less susceptible to attack than the other 2 species. These differences were amplified in food-deprived and spatially simple conditions, indicating that *Ae. triseriatus* predatory behavior may have important retarding effects on the colonization of occupied treehole habitats by *Ae. albopictus*. *Ae. aegypti* and *Ae. albopictus* were similar in imposing little (*Ae. aegypti*) or almost no (*Ae. albopictus*) predation on 1st instars and in being susceptible to predation by *Ae. triseriatus*. The general lack of species-specific differences between *Ae. aegypti* and *Ae. albopictus* indicates that interspecific predation is not a likely explanation for the rapid displacement of *Ae. aegypti* by *Ae. albopictus* in domestic containers in the southeastern United States.

KEY WORDS *Aedes albopictus*, *Aedes aegypti*, *Aedes triseriatus*, invasive exotic, cannibalism, mosquitoes

Aedes albopictus (Skuse), a container–inhabiting mosquito recently introduced from Asia, has spread throughout southeastern and midwestern North America. Its range in the United States has expanded quickly from 1985 when it was first recorded (Sprenger and Wuithiranyagool 1986) to include 23 states, including New Jersey (Crans et al. 1996) and Chicago to the north, Texas to the west, and Florida to the south (O'Meara et al. 1992, 1995; Jamieson et al. 1994; Nasci 1995; Richardson et al. 1995). The ongoing colonization by this species has provided an excellent opportunity for ecologists to observe a mosquito invading habitats already occupied by ecologically similar species, particularly its congeners. *Aedes albopictus* has displaced a previously introduced, resident African mosquito, *Aedes aegypti* (L.), in some habitats in Florida (O'Meara et al. 1992) and apparently is in the process of displacing *Ae. aegypti* in South Carolina (Richardson et al. 1995) and Louisiana (Nasci 1995). In contrast, Lounibos et al. (1997) found that *Ae. albopictus* has not displaced the native treehole mosquito, *Aedes triseriatus* (Say), in natural treeholes in Florida.

Temperature extremes may limit the northern extent of the United States population of *Ae. albopictus* (Nawrocki and Hawley 1987, Hanson and Craig 1995), which appears to have originated from a temperate zone population in Japan (Hawley et al. 1987). The biological factors that might promote or restrict range expansion have been less tractable. Numerous biological mechanisms promoting colonization by *Ae. albopictus* have been investigated, including mating interference (Black et al. 1989), competitive displacement by larvae (Barrera 1996, Black et al. 1989, Ho et al. 1989, Livdahl and Willey 1991, Novak et al. 1993, Juliano 1998), oviposition site preferences (Black et al. 1989, Titus 1996), parasitic protozoan parasitism (Fukuda et al. 1997, Juliano 1998), and egg hatch inhibition imposed by larvae (Edgerly et al. 1993).

To further our understanding of potentially significant behavioral interactions in *Aedes*, we investigated the role that intraguild predation might play in successful colonization by *Ae. albopictus*. Facultative predation may occur among *Aedes* larvae, and such predation might contribute to the displacement of *Ae. aegypti* from container habitats by *Ae. albopictus*. Differential predation also might contribute to a slow rate of colonization of natural treeholes by *Ae. albopictus* when they are occupied by *Ae. triseriatus*, despite prevalence of *Ae. albopictus* in nearby domestic habitats. Although their food is predominantly microorganisms and detritus (Merritt et al. 1992), both *Ae. aegypti* (MacGregor 1915) and *Ae. triseriatus* (Koenekoop and Livdahl 1986) are capable of cannibalism; 4th instars consume 1st-instar conspecifics in the laboratory. The ecological significance of canni-

[1] Department of Biology, Santa Clara University, Santa Clara, CA 95053.
[2] Department of Biology, Clark University, Worcester, MA 01610.

EXERCISE 12.5 Review a paper draft you're currently working on, paying attention to paragraph lengths. What patterns do you notice? Do you see places where paragraphs could be combined, divided, or reorganized to better fit the writing situation? If so, make the changes.

CHAPTER

13 How Do You Craft Opening and Closing Paragraphs?

13a What makes an opening paragraph effective?

Like the lead of a front-page newspaper story, the first paragraph of any document you write must do four things:

- Get your readers' attention and interest them in reading more.
- Introduce your main idea.
- Signal to readers what direction your paper will take.
- Set the tone of your project.

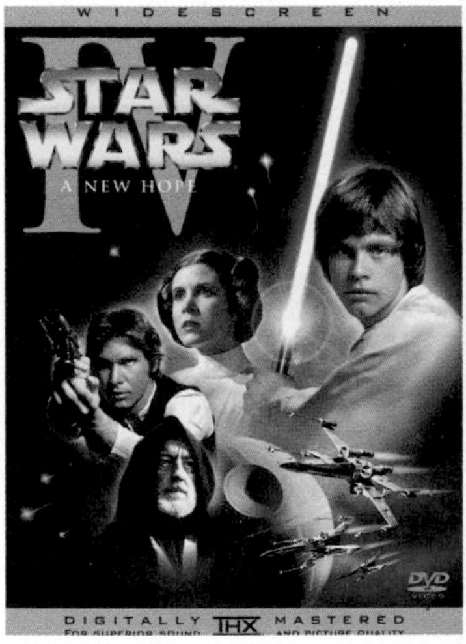

Almost everyone in the United States can recite the opening lines from *Star Wars* ("A long time ago, in a galaxy far, far away ...") and Abraham Lincoln's "Gettysburg Address" ("Four score and seven years ago our fathers brought forth ..."). Why do you think these introductions are so memorable? How does each catch attention, suggest content, and set a particular tone? Which of the strategies used in these opening lines, or in other memorable opening lines, might you try in writing a paper?

These are important functions, and that's why first paragraphs can be difficult to write—but it's also why they're worth your time and attention.

Different kinds of writing call for different opening paragraphs. For certain kinds of writing—laboratory reports, grant proposals, business letters—readers expect specific kinds of opening paragraphs. In such cases, find out what the typical pattern is and use it. In other kinds of writing, such as newspaper articles, critical analyses, personal experience papers, and opinion pieces, you have more freedom and can try various approaches. We list some possibilities below.

1 Begin with a narrative. An attention-getting narrative or anecdote catches readers' attention and sparks their interest in the topic. The following opening paragraph from a magazine article pulls readers into a terrifying experience and makes us want to know more about the situation.

> Like most Peace Corps volunteers, Martin Giannini embarked on his mission full of high hopes and enthusiasm. His assignment in Togo promised to be the adventure of a lifetime. It certainly was—but not the kind he expected. Giannini's African adventure ended in a padded room in a Chicago psych ward. "I was totally loony," admits Giannini. "It felt like I was in some 'X-Files' episode with instructions being planted in my brain. I tried to escape, but couldn't get past the four guards." What led Giannini, a healthy young man with no history of mental illness, to take on a battalion of guards in a psychiatric hospital? A drug, say his doctors. An antimalaria drug the Peace Corps recommended.
>
> —Dennis Lewon, "Malaria's Not-So-Magic Bullet"

You may occasionally want to begin a paper with two or three short anecdotes rather than a single, longer one. This variation works well to show the breadth and significance of a topic.

2 Begin with a description. In this example from an article on exotic Southern cuisine, John T. Edge creates a vivid picture of the region he's writing about and sets a tone of cautious fascination.

> It's just past four on a Thursday afternoon in June at Jesse's Place, a country juke seventeen miles south of the Mississippi line and three miles west of Amite, Louisiana. The air conditioner hacks and spits forth torrents of arctic air, but the heat of summer can't be kept at bay. It seeps around the splintered doorjambs and settles in, transforming the

squat particleboard-plastered roadhouse into a sauna. Slowly, the dank barroom fills with grease-smeared mechanics from the truck stop up the road and farmers straight from the fields, the soles of their brogans thick with dirt clods. A few weary souls make their way over from the nearby sawmill, the kind of place where more than one worker has muscled a log into the chipper and drawn back a nub. I sit alone at the bar, one empty bottle of Bud in front of me, a second bottle in my hand. I drain the beer, order a third, and stare down at the pink juice spreading outward from a crumpled foil pouch and onto the dull, black vinyl bar.

I'm not leaving until I eat this thing, I tell myself.

—John T. Edge, "I'm Not Leaving Until I Eat This Thing"

3 Begin with a question or a series of questions. A provocative question raises readers' expectations about what is to come.

Should we be worried that young girls are not pursuing math-related careers at the same rate as young men? After all, in our technological era, many of tomorrow's well-paying jobs will require competence at mathematics. But today, women make up only 19 percent of the science, engineering, and technology workforce. In 1998, only 16 percent of computer science degrees were awarded to women, down from nearly 40 percent in 1984, and the downward trend continued in 2003.

—Rosalind Chait Barnett and Caryl Rivers, "The Persistence of Gender Myths in Math"

But keep any such question purposeful and simple. Don't begin a paper with a string of broad rhetorical questions.

4 Start with your thesis. Sometimes you will do best to open your essay by simply telling your readers exactly what you are going to write about. Such openings work well for many papers you compose in college courses (especially arguments), for reports you might have to write on the job, and for many other kinds of factual, informative prose. Here's a good example from a student essay that evaluates the effectiveness of spanking.

It is unfortunate that the new spanking advocates get so much attention in the popular press, since their arguments are so poorly supported. These crusaders draw on personal anecdotes and "experts" of dubious credibility to glorify physical punishment and to blame non-spanking parents for everything from school shootings to violent rap lyrics. Yet even a cursory look at the scientific research in this area confirms that kids who are spanked are more—not less—likely to misbehave, turn to criminal behavior, or suffer from mental problems. How we choose to treat our nation's children is a serious matter. We must make these decisions based on the best information available, not on the dire predictions of a few extremists.

See Section 3a for more on constructing a thesis statement and incorporating it into a writing project.

EXERCISE 13.1 Choose from the strategies discussed above and write two versions of an opening paragraph for one of the following essay titles. Then join with classmates who have chosen to write on the same title and read your paragraphs aloud. Discuss which ones seem to work well, and why.

1. The American Medical Establishment as Seen Through *Scrubs, ER,* and *House*
2. What It Means to Live Below the Poverty Level: A Case Study
3. Why You Should Vote in the Next Election
4. Is Steroid Use a Major Problem in Professional Sports?

EXERCISE 13.2 Reread student author Tallon Harding's essay in Chapter 5 (pages 68–72). What strategy does she use in her introductory paragraph? Do you think this was a wise choice? If so, why? What other strategies might Tallon have chosen given the topic of her paper? Once you've settled on another approach that would work well, try your hand at writing this version of the essay's opening paragraph.

13b What makes a closing paragraph effective?

Closing paragraphs can be hard to write because it's often difficult to come to a satisfying conclusion that doesn't fall back on clichés. The only direct advice we can give is that your closing paragraph should make readers feel that you have tied up the loose ends—that you have fulfilled the commitment you made in the opening paragraph. You don't want your readers asking "And so?" when they finish, or looking on the back of the page for something they may have missed.

There are no simple prescriptions for achieving that important goal. However, we suggest five general strategies you can use, alone or in combination, depending upon your rhetorical situation.

1 Summarize the main points you have made. Often you'll want to bring your paper to a close by reemphasizing your main points. (But don't repeat the very same words you have already used, or your ending may sound redundant or artificial.) In this example, student writer Jeremy Christiansen reviews key points about school resegregation.

> America continues to see a growing trend toward public-school resegregation, a problem that was not discovered until recent studies were conducted to test the successes of *Brown v. the Board of Education* after 50 years. The findings were startling, since they suggest that what was once known as the most important court decision of the 20th century may have been a failure. American ideals espouse diversity and equal opportunities for all. School resegregation not only discourages diversity but limits opportunities for minorities and whites alike. We will not have true equality in educational opportunities until we find a way to create racially, ethnically, and economically integrated public schools. Unfortunately, further attempts to desegregate, though necessary, will likely spark even more controversy, which may last 50 more years.

2 Make a recommendation when one is appropriate. Such a recommendation should grow out of the issue you have been discussing. This strategy brings a paper to a positive ending and closes the topic. Here is a conclusion from a piece that explores the cognitive benefits of watching television.

> Kids and grown-ups each can learn from their increasingly shared obsessions. Too often we imagine the blurring of kid and grown-up

cultures as a series of violations: the 9-year-olds who have to have nipple brooches explained to them thanks to Janet Jackson; the middle-aged guy who can't wait to get home to his Xbox. But this demographic blur has a commendable side that we don't acknowledge enough. The kids are forced to think like grown-ups: analyzing complex social networks, managing resources, tracking subtle narrative intertwinings, recognizing long-term patterns. The grown-ups, in turn, get to learn from the kids: decoding each new technological wave, parsing the interfaces and discovering the intellectual rewards of play. Parents should see this as an opportunity, not a crisis. Smart culture is no longer something you force your kids to ingest, like green vegetables. It's something you share.

—Steven Johnson, "Watching TV Makes You Smarter"

3 Link the end to the beginning. One excellent way to end a writing project is to tie your conclusion back to your beginning, framing and unifying your paper. Notice how skillfully Gary Engel uses this strategy in an article analyzing the cultural significance of Superman.

OPENING PARAGRAPH

When I was young I spent a lot of time arguing with myself about who would win in a fight between John Wayne and Superman. On days when I wore my cowboy hat and cap guns, I knew the Duke would win because of his pronounced superiority in the all-important matter of swagger. There were days, though, when a frayed army blanket tied cape-fashion around my neck signaled a young man's need to believe there could be no end to the potency of his being. Then the Man of Steel was the odds-on favorite to knock the Duke for a cosmic loop. My greatest childhood problem was that the question could never be resolved because no such battle could ever take place. I mean, how would a fight start between the only two Americans who never started anything, who always fought only to defend their rights and the American way?

CLOSING PARAGRAPH

In the last analysis, Superman is like nothing so much as an American boy's fantasy of a messiah. He is the male, heroic match for the Statue of Liberty, come like an immigrant from heaven to deliver humankind by sacrificing himself in the service of others. He protects the weak and defends truth and justice and all the other moral virtues inherent in the Judeo-Christian tradition, remaining ever vigilant and ever chaste. What purer or stronger vision could there possibly be for a child? Now that I put my mind to it, I see that John Wayne never had a chance.

Gary Engel, "What Makes Superman So Darned American?"

4 Point to directions for future research or action, or identify unresolved questions. Concluding paragraphs that suggest these sorts of connections are especially common in academic research projects.

> Reading the arguments about assisted suicide reminded me of a line from Bertolt Brecht's *The Three-Penny Opera*: "First feed the face, and then talk right and wrong." As a general rule, that statement itself is wrong, of course, but it can serve as a salutary warning. First, provide decent health care for the living; then, we can have a proper debate about the moral problems of death and dying.
>
> —Michael Walzer, "Feed the Face"

5 Stop when you're finished. Probably the most important thing to remember about closing a paper or essay is not to overdo your conclusion. If you have covered all your points and are reasonably satisfied with what you've said, quit. Don't bore your reader by tacking on a needless recapitulation or adding a paragraph of platitudes.

EXERCISE 13.3 Exchange drafts with two or three other students who are working on the same assignment. Each person should read the closing paragraphs of the other papers. Working in a group, identify the strategies each writer has used to bring his or her paper to a conclusion; discuss how well they work, and suggest alternative possibilities.

EXERCISE 13.4 Look once again at student author Tallon Harding's essay on pages 68–72, this time noting her strategy for concluding the paper. How well do you think she summarizes her main points? Does she link the end of her paper to the beginning, or point to directions for future action? How might you improve her concluding paragraph?

CHAPTER

14 How Do You Manage Transitions?

Skilled writers work hard to help their readers move easily through a piece of writing. They know that readers won't stick around long if they have trouble following an argument or the thread of a narrative. The best unifying device for any piece of writing is *organizational*; that is, it comes from an underlying pattern that moves the reader along smoothly. You'll find examples of such patterns in Sections 3c (for whole papers) and 12b (for paragraphs).

But even when your paper follows a clear pattern, you sometimes need to tighten your writing by using **transitions,** those words and phrases that act like hooks, links, and directional signals to keep readers moving from point to point within a paragraph, and from one paragraph to another.

14a How do you spot problems with transitions?

When you're revising, check for places where your readers might find your writing choppy or abrupt, and revise accordingly. Look for these trouble spots.

1 Check for paragraphs made up of short, simple sentences that seem disconnected. Effective paragraphs follow what writing experts call the "old-new contract"—they advance an argument or idea by linking each piece of new information to something that's gone before, so that the connections are immediately clear to readers. When a writer neglects to link old and new information, a paragraph may read more like a random series of observations than a coherent discussion.

WEAK TRANSITIONS

Some Americans live in affluent suburbs or university communities. It's easy to get the impression that the American population is healthy. Joggers and bicycle riders are everywhere. Many restaurants feature low-fat entrees. Many Americans are unhealthy. Thirty percent are seriously overweight. Alcoholism is a problem and many teenagers smoke. Obesity among children is increasing catastrophically.

Here is a revised version, with some sentences combined and others connected (transitional words are boldfaced).

BETTER

If one lives in an affluent suburb or near a university, it's easy to get the impression that the American population is healthy. In **such** places, joggers **and** bicycle riders are everywhere, and restaurants feature low-fat entrees. The truth is, **however**, that many Americans are not healthy. Thirty percent are seriously overweight, alcoholism is a problem, **and** an increasing number of teenagers smoke. **Moreover**, obesity among children is increasing catastrophically.

2 Check for sentences that begin with vague references such as *it is, there are,* and *there is.* Often sentences that begin with these phrases (called *expletives*) are poorly connected to each other because it's hard to tell who or what the subject is. For example:

WEAK TRANSITIONS

It is a truism that good manners are like skeleton keys. There are few doors they will not open. Some people think that good manners are pretentious. They are a way of condescending to people. That is a misunderstanding. The real purpose of manners is to make social situations comfortable and to put the people you are with at ease. Manners are also practical to have. There are many companies that insist that their executives have good manners. Some business schools include a course on manners in their curricula.

Here is the paragraph reworked with better sentence openings and stronger connections. Transitional terms are boldfaced.

BETTER

Good manners, like skeleton keys, will open almost any door. **Although** some people think that good manners are pretentious and condescending, that's a misunderstanding. **On the contrary**, manners exist to make social situations comfortable by putting everyone at ease. **Moreover**, manners are a practical asset in the job market. Many companies insist on well-mannered executives, **which** has prompted some business schools to include a course on manners in their curricula.

For suggestions on revising to eliminate expletive phrases, see Section 17c-6.

3 Check for gaps between paragraphs. Sometimes major gaps appear between paragraphs, and readers get temporarily lost. Suppose that you encountered the following two paragraphs in a personal essay. You'd probably have trouble figuring out how the second paragraph relates to the first.

> When I arrived here four years ago, I found that the skills I had learned in order to survive in Sudan were useless. I knew how to catch a rabbit, challenge a hyena or climb a coconut palm, but I had never turned on a light, used a telephone or driven a car.
>
> Within a month I understood how to work most modern conveniences and started my first job as a courtesy clerk and stocker at Ralph's grocery store in San Diego. Things like mangoes, chard and yams were familiar, but when customers asked about Cheerios or Ajax, it was as though my years of learning English in the refugee camp were worthless.

Here's the original passage as it appeared in Alephonsion Deng's essay, which appeared in *Newsweek* magazine. The linking sentence is boldfaced.

> When I arrived here four years ago, I found that the skills I had learned in order to survive in Sudan were useless. I knew how to catch a rabbit, challenge a hyena or climb a coconut palm, but I had never turned on a light, used a telephone or driven a car.
>
> **Luckily, the International Rescue Committee provided us with classes and mentors to teach us basics about computers, job interviews and Western social customs.** Within a month I understood how to work most modern conveniences and started my first job as a courtesy clerk and stocker at Ralph's grocery store in San Diego. Things like mangoes, chard and yams were familiar, but when customers asked about Cheerios or Ajax, it was as though my years of learning English in the refugee camp were worthless.
>
> —Alephonsion Deng, "I Have Had to Learn to Live with Peace"
>

Links between paragraphs can take several forms; Section 14b, which follows, explains these in more detail.

Take Control

14b How can you solve problems with transitions?

If you want to use transitions successfully, remember the old-new contract: Each sentence or paragraph should contain a seed out of which the next sentence or paragraph can grow. Always include a hint, a reference, a hook, or a repetition that helps the reader link what you're saying with what has come before and what lies ahead.

1 Use common transition words to connect ideas. You can make your paragraphs tighter and more focused by using transition words to tie sentences together.

- **Pointer words,** such as *first, second, next,* and *last,* set up a path for readers to follow by indicating shifts in time or place.

  One student, a nonsmoker, argued eloquently before the committee that there are many reasons to oppose a campus-wide ban on smoking. **First**, such a policy penalizes an activity that, though obnoxious, is not illegal. **Second**, enforcement of the policy might encourage insidious intrusions on the privacy of students in their dormitory rooms and faculty in their offices. **Last**, a ban on smoking might set an unfortunate precedent, leading to the elimination of other activities certain groups regard as offensive or harmful: drinking alcohol, eating fatty foods, dancing, listening to rock music, or even driving a car.

- **Relationship words,** such as *however, therefore,* and *yet,* show similarity, opposition, addition, or other connections between ideas.

  Opinion at the hearing had generally favored the proposal to abolish smoking on campus. **However**, the student's arguments made some proponents waver as they considered the wider implications of their actions. What would happen, **for example**, if one group on campus, citing statistics on heart disease, demanded a campus-wide ban on fast foods? The ban on smoking would provide a precedent for such a restriction.

As these examples show, transition words are not neutral; each one gives readers a different signal about where your argument is going. When you're in doubt about which term to choose, check Chart 14.1.

Chart 14.1 Common Transition Words and Phrases

TO SHOW SIMILARITY
likewise
like
similarly
in the same way
just as

TO SHOW CONTRAST
however
instead
nevertheless
although
in spite of
on the other hand
not only
but
rather

TO SHOW ACCUMULATION
moreover
in addition to
for example
and
for instance

TO SHOW CONSEQUENCE
hence
consequently
so
therefore
as a result of
thus

TO SHOW CAUSATION
because
since

TO SHOW A SEQUENCE
next
subsequently
after
finally
first, second, third
last

2 Repeat a key term throughout a paragraph to establish a central idea. Using one or two key words or phrases several times in a paragraph can tie it together effectively.

REPEATED WORDS BOLDFACED

The new black middle class came of age in the 1960s during an unprecedented American **economic boom** and in the hub of a thriving **mass culture.** The **economic boom** made luxury goods and convenient services available to large numbers of hard-working Americans for the first time. American **mass culture** presented models of the good life principally in terms of conspicuous consumption and hedonistic indulgence. It is important to note that even the intensely political struggles of the sixties presupposed a perennial **economic boom** and posited models of the good life projected by U.S. **mass culture**. Long-term financial self-denial and sexual asceticism was never at the center of a political agenda in the sixties.

—Cornel West, *Race Matters*

3 Use the demonstrative pronouns *this, that, these, those,* and *such* to tie ideas together. But be very careful that the referent for these pronouns is always clear (see Section 26c). In the following example, each boldfaced word hooks directly and unambiguously into the previous sentence or clause.

DEMONSTRATIVE TERMS BOLDFACED

Making a movie is a collaborative endeavor, and scriptwriters point **this** out frequently. Occasionally a screenplay will survive the transfer from paper to film intact, but **that** is the exception rather than the rule. Typically, producers, directors, actors, and agents all have a say in the final product. Coping with **such** high-handed meddling is often difficult for young writers, and **those** who cannot compromise rarely stay in the business for long.

4 Use relative pronouns to show links between ideas. *Who, which, where,* and *that* are powerful words that link a descriptive or informative statement to something that has preceded it. Relative pronouns can be especially helpful when you need to combine several short, choppy sentences into one. Notice how the boldfaced pronouns in the following paragraph serve as links to previous ideas.

RELATIVE PRONOUNS BOLDFACED

Emma's first few weeks at the conservatory were exhausting but exhilarating. It was a place **that** challenged her, one **where** she could meet talented people **who** shared her passion for dance. The competition among the students was friendly but intense, **which** only increased her determination to practice and learn.

5 Use parallelism to link ideas. You can create tightly focused paragraphs by writing a series of sentences that incorporate parallel phrases.

PARALLEL PHRASES BOLDFACED

I spent my two days at Disneyland taking rides. **I took** a bobsled through the Matterhorn and a submarine under the Polar Ice Cap and a rocket jet to the Cosmic Vapor Curtain. **I took** Peter Pan's Flight, Mr. Toad's Wild Ride, Alice's Scary Adventures, and Pinocchio's Daring Journey. **I took** a steamboat and a jungle boat. **I took** the Big Thunder Mountain Railroad to Coyote Country and the Splash Mountain roller coaster to Critter Country. **I took** a "Pirates of the Caribbean" ride (black cats and buried treasure) and a "Haunted Mansion" ride (creaking hinges and ghostly laughter). **I took** monorails and Skyways and Autopias and People Movers. More precisely, those rides **took** me: up and down and around sudden corners and over rooftops, and all I had to do was sit back and let whatever conveyance I was sitting in do the driving.

—William Zinsser, *American Places*

Zinsser holds the details of his paragraph together by using a parallel pattern that begins every sentence with the phrase "I took"; then, when he reverses the phrase to "More precisely, those rides **took** me," he wraps up his paragraph with a final unifying touch.

6 Use a semicolon to link two closely related statements. The semicolon signals a tight connection that says, "These groups of words go together." Often a semicolon can connect parts of a sentence more effectively than *and* or *also*. For more details about the semicolon, see Section 37a.

CONNECTING SEMICOLONS HIGHLIGHTED

The sculptor Ilya Karensky no longer has to endure his neighbors' contempt for his work**;** now he has to put up with their insincere and inept praise. Ilya knows perfectly well that what his neighbors admire most about his work is the amount of money for which it now sells**;** they like the sculptures themselves no better than they did before.

7 Consider using headings or other visual markers as transitions. In some kinds of documents, writers may use visual signals as well as—or sometimes instead of—words to help readers follow an argument.

Business and technical writers commonly use headings and subheadings to separate sections of a document so that readers can see where one idea ends and another begins. Résumés often use headings such as "Education,"

"Experience," "Awards," and "References" so that readers can locate relevant information. Brochures, flyers, and instructional manuals employ graphics, images, and color to mark divisions or to tie together related material. On the Web, writers create hyperlinks to connect documents.

When you incorporate visual transitions into a writing project, ask yourself whether the particular strategy is appropriate for the situation. Graphics and color fonts aren't always welcome in academic papers, and a flyer or short essay might not need headings. If you're not sure, look at models to see the kinds of visual devices other writers have used in similar situations.

Also be sure that a particular transition gives readers the right signal. For example, a heading indicates a new topic, but it doesn't necessarily show readers how one topic relates to another. You'll often need to supplement visual devices with traditional linking words and phrases.

For more information about integrating visual elements into a text, see Chapter 18. For examples of documents that incorporate visual elements, see the model documents in Chapter 19.

Taking Control

Use transitions for clarity

When you receive a paper back from an instructor, you may see the abbreviation *trans* written in the margin. What that mark usually means is that, for a moment, you have forgotten how tough it can be for readers to follow the sequence of your thoughts. Without a helpful *however*, *therefore*, or *on the other hand*, or more complicated transitional device, readers may have no clue why your paper is taking a turn or introducing a new idea. In editing for continuity, you must try—hard as it may be—to read a draft of your paper the way readers will. If it helps, highlight the transitions you have offered to readers. You may be surprised how few they are. Then fix any problems you detect.

EXERCISE 14.1 Read the following two paragraphs and diagnose the transition problems you find between the paragraphs and within each one. Where do you have trouble following the writer's line of thought? Why? Then revise the paragraphs to improve the transitions, drawing on at least two of the strategies described in this section.

There is nowhere to park on campus. The parking situation is impossible for first-year students. My roommate missed her first college class because she could not find a parking spot. I have received three parking tickets already this semester. Some people say that freshmen should not be allowed to drive to campus. First-year students are required to live in the dorms. The dorm I live in is 15 minutes away from all my classes. I can't walk to them. I have to drive.

There are only a few parking garages and many underutilized grassy areas on campus. There is a large green space on either side of the engineering complex that is not being used. The courtyard in front of the library is always empty. The fountain attracts litter. Why can't the university use some grassy areas for parking garages? The university could use some money from parking tickets to pay for new parking. The shuttle bus system could be used to transport students from remote parking areas onto campus.

EXERCISE 14.2 Use one or more of the transitional devices discussed in this section to strengthen connections between new and old information in a writing project you're currently working on.

CHAPTER

15 What Kinds of Language Can You Use?

Many people assume that *what* we say is more important than *how* we say it. "Just get to the point," we often hear. But even small nuances in the tone, vocabulary, connotation, and formality of your writing can powerfully affect readers and shape the power of your message. These kinds of language choices—often called *stylistic choices*—are the focus of this chapter.

15a How formal should your writing be?

Different writing situations call for different levels of formality. Imagine what would happen if you responded to a casual party invitation with a business memo, or if you began a eulogy with an off-color joke. In either case, you'd likely be using a style inappropriate to the situation—and your audience would quickly let you know it.

How do you strike the right level of formality in a particular writing situation? When you know your readers well or are writing a familiar kind of assignment, these choices may come almost intuitively. When you don't, you will need to analyze your purpose and audience carefully so that you can make good language choices.

Chart 15.1 identifies a range of styles, classifying them as formal, informal, and casual, and listing typical kinds of documents that use each. But you should view these styles as points on a continuum rather than hard-and-fast categories. In practice, different writers approach documents in different ways, and even the same writer may shift between formal and less formal language within a single text.

1 Choose formal language for academic writing. In most college courses, instructors will expect you to write in a relatively formal style (unless the assignment designates a writing situation in which informality is appropriate—for instance, a reading-response journal or a pop quiz). Academic papers require that you discuss serious subject matter in a thoughtful, well-informed manner, and that you maintain some critical distance from

Chart 15.1 Levels of Formality

FORMAL	INFORMAL	CASUAL
Compound and complex sentence structures; longer sentences	Variety of standard sentence types in agent/action style	Shorter sentences; occasional fragments
Abstract and technical language; precise vocabulary: *the diminution of nationalistic sentiment*	Mix of abstract and concrete terms; direct language: *the weakening of patriotic feeling*	Concrete language; slang and colloquial terms: *nixing the flag waving*
Impersonal tone; infrequent use of *I* or *you*	Occasionally and comfortably personal; some use of *I* and *you*	Unapologetically personal; frequent use of *I* and *you*
Few contractions, if any	Use of contractions where easy and natural	Contractions to mimic colloquial speech
Serious and consistent tone and subject matter	Moderate variations of tone and subject	Wide variations in tone and unexpected shifts in topic—sometimes light and satirical
Careful control of imagery and analogy	Conscious and frequent use of figurative language	Deliberate, frequent use of contemporary comparisons and idioms
Standard formats or templates for presentation	Text supported by images and design elements	Aggressive melding of words, images, and graphics
Scholarly books and articles; technical reports; academic papers and projects; job application letters; legal and some business correspondence; some speeches	Newspapers and editorials; general interest magazines; newsletters; popular books; serious blogs; some business letters; professional email; .com and .org Web sites; oral presentations	Special interest magazines; personal email; personal letters; listserv postings; personal Web sites and blogs

your audience. The following excerpt from a book written by a well-known historian effectively demonstrates some key elements of a formal style:

> The women who assembled as delegates at Seneca Falls had demanded equality of opportunity for men and women in affairs of state, church, and family. Elizabeth Cady Stanton, the organizing force and intelligence behind this historic conclave, was an advanced and innovative thinker on women's issues, who understood the complex sources of

> sexual subordination and, in addition to the vote for women, advocated domestic reforms including the right of women to affirm their sexuality if they chose to do so, or contrarily, to refuse sexual relations altogether when necessary to avoid pregnancy. Stanton also supported cooperative child rearing, rights to property, child custody, and divorce. Though venerated within her own small circle, she came to be viewed by more traditional supporters as a source of potential controversy and embarrassment.
>
> —Ellen Chesler, *Women of Valor*

Chesler's tone is authoritative and she uses high-level vocabulary and complex sentences with confidence. She projects the image of a careful, knowledgeable scholar—exactly the kind of persona readers expect in academic writing.

The formal style is also a safe choice when you don't know your audience well enough to risk an informal or casual tone. For example, initial emails between strangers are likely to be much more formal than subsequent messages. The tone may change as correspondents grow more familiar with each other.

2 Choose informal language when you feel comfortable with your audience and want a more relaxed tone. Writers who choose an informal style usually do so because they don't want to sound solemn or impersonal. They want their readers to feel as if they're in a conversation, even when their topics are serious. Writers use informal language in many different kinds of documents. Here's just one example, taken from an article on high school football published in the popular magazine *Texas Monthly.*

> But even if change is afoot, Texas high school football remains one of the few institutions that distinguishes us from the rest of the universe. We have more players, coaches, band members, cheerleaders, and pep squads than anyone else. We send more of our boys to college and the pros than any other state (more than three hundred signed letters of intent to play for Division I schools last year alone). Our fans are more fanatical. Our parents are more passionate. So believe the hype: we're Number One.
>
> —Joe Nick Patoski et al., "Three Cheers for High School Football"

In this vividly descriptive paragraph, Patoski and his co-authors mix high-level and low-level vocabulary: *distinguishes, institution*, and *fanatical* contrast with the colloquial *our boys* and *hype.* They also mix concrete and abstract language, vary the sentence length, and use the first-person *we* to draw readers in.

3 Choose casual language for personal writing and for audiences you know very well. Although it's unlikely you'd choose this style for an academic assignment, you might want to use it if you were posting an entry to your blog or writing for a small group of friends or insiders. Columnists often use casual language because they want their readers to feel like insiders. This example comes from a column in the *Cleveland Free Times*, an alternative weekly published in print and online (the column is about the staff's attempts to stop swearing).

> For years we were the cussingest office it would ever be your misfortune to hear. We turned the air blue, with f-bombs exploding everywhere. Male and female workers alike swore more than a bunch of drunken sailors on shore leave (indeed, a bunch of drunken sailors on shore leave once came by the office and were absolutely appalled).
>
> —Eric Broder, *Cleveland Free Times*

Broder's fast-paced, conversational style—infused with sarcasm and humor—suits the *Free Times*, a publication that deliberately sets itself apart from mainstream media.

Writers also choose casual language for intensely personal writing like autobiographical essays, letters, or journals. The following example comes from a published diary by a first-year teacher.

> October 5, my birthday. Terrible thing. Somebody stole the Columbus comic book. I said, "Whoever did it, just put it back," but nobody did. So after school I took the whole library down and shoved it in the closet and locked it. The kids noticed right away the next morning.
>
> "I told you if you stole from me, I'd take it all back. I'm not a liar."
>
> "That's not fair," one girl complained. "We didn't all steal the book!" . . . I passed out the reading textbooks. The children complained noisily. "You're getting what the rest of the school gets," I reminded them. "I don't see what's the problem."
>
> God, kid! Give me back the stupid book and let me teach you the best way I know how!
>
> —Esme Raji Codell, *Educating Esme*

Codell's choppy sentences, emotional language, and realistic dialogue create a sense of intimacy with her readers. Such a colloquial account wouldn't be appropriate for a research article or an academic paper, but it's effective here.

EXERCISE 15.1 What level of formality do you think would be appropriate for writing in these situations? Give reasons for your choice.

1. A letter to a representative or senator asking to be considered for a summer internship in his or her office.
2. A brochure recruiting volunteers to work on a house being constructed by Habitat for Humanity.
3. A column in your weekly church newsletter that recounts noteworthy activities by members of the church.
4. An email to your calculus instructor.

15b What are denotation and connotation?

Words affect people, and even subtle differences in meaning can have dramatic effects. If they didn't, it would make no difference whether a teacher called your six-year-old "a highly imaginative child" or "a big liar." And we wouldn't see national debates over "hate speech" legislation and "political correctness" on college campuses.

Because language is so powerful, writers must understand both the meanings individual words have (their *denotations*) and the emotional associations that come with them (their *connotations*). Then, the challenge is to use words appropriately. As always, what's appropriate will depend on the rhetorical situation.

1 Understand how denotation and connotation work. **Denotation** is the literal meaning of a word, the object or concept that it refers to. For instance, the denotative meaning of *puppy* is *juvenile dog.* **Connotation** refers to the positive or negative emotional associations that go along with a word. Connotatively, *puppy* suggests cuteness, playfulness, warmth, and affection. Even when words have similar denotative meanings, their connotations may differ greatly. Consider these examples.

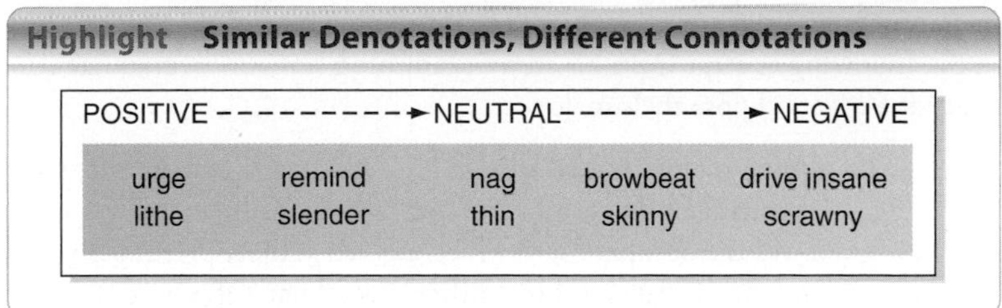

Highlight Similar Denotations, Different Connotations

POSITIVE ----------►		NEUTRAL----------►		NEGATIVE
urge	remind	nag	browbeat	drive insane
lithe	slender	thin	skinny	scrawny

Writers need to be concerned about denotation—that is, you should choose words that precisely convey the idea you're trying to express (don't say *puppy* if you really mean *young wolf*). But choosing words with appropriate connotations is a trickier challenge. Connotative meanings elicit stronger responses from readers. And because they have to do with the contexts in which particular words are used, they also shift more frequently and vary more from audience to audience. For these reasons it's usually not a good idea to simply lift words out of a thesaurus and place them into your writing.

2 Choose mostly neutral language for informative research, academic papers, case studies, and reports. When you're writing a piece that's primarily informative, your readers usually expect you to give

What different words and phrases can be used to denote "homeless person"? Make a list of as many synonyms as you can. Then arrange the words along a continuum moving from the most positive, to neutral, to the most negative connotations. How might readers' impressions of the individual in the photo change depending on which words or phrases you chose to describe him? In which writing situations might each word or phrase on your list be appropriate or inappropriate? Effective or ineffective? Accurate or inaccurate?

them a neutral report on the topic, as anthropologist Michael Moffett does in the following excerpt from his study examining how undergraduate students at Rutgers choose their majors.

> The top ten majors and all the rest . . . fell into a gradient of status in general student opinion, one that was based on three criteria. First, how good was the occupation to which a given subject presumably led? Second, and closely related, how difficult was that subject at Rutgers? And third, much less important, how much social good did the occupation or profession in question accomplish?
>
> —Michael Moffett, "How College Students Choose Their Majors"

Although Moffett probably has opinions about what criteria students should use to pick a major, his purpose here is to report what the students he interviewed for this study thought about the issue. He thus uses neutral, descriptive language, focusing not on his feelings about the topic but on communicating his data.

3 Avoid strongly connotative language when writing newsletters, press releases, or informative brochures. The audience for these documents might expect a writer to put a positive spin on the information he or she is presenting, but they don't want to be showered with emotional language. Consider this paragraph from a brochure describing a student tutoring program called Helping One Student To Succeed (HOSTS). Words and phrases with positive connotations are boldfaced.

> At Zavala Elementary School, teachers select second- and third-grade students to attend the HOSTS program for four half-hour periods each week. Mentors come once a week to meet with students in a **cheerful, book-lined classroom** for 30 minutes. The students and their mentors read together, talk about books, learn study skills, and practice writing. **They also become friends.**

This is not strictly neutral language. But the connotation doesn't distract from the information or give the impression that the writer is selling something.

4 Use connotative language appropriately in arguments, reviews, editorials, and opinion pieces. Connotative language sometimes works well when you want to express strong feelings of approval or disapproval. Here are two examples, one that uses language with moderately strong connotations, and one that's more emotionally charged. The first example is from the conclusion of Roger Ebert's review of the movie classic *Casablanca.* It comes from his Web page. Again, strongly connotative words and phrases are boldfaced.

> Seeing the film over and over again, year after year, I find it **never grows over-familiar.** It plays like a **favorite** musical album; **the more I know it, the more I like it.** The black-and-white cinematography **has not aged** as color would. The dialogue is so spare and cynical it **has not grown old-fashioned.** Much of the emotional effect of *Casablanca* is achieved by indirection; as we leave the theater, we are **absolutely convinced** that the only thing keeping the world from **going crazy** is that the problems of three little people do after all amount to more than **a hill of beans.**
>
> —Roger Ebert, *Casablanca*

Ebert uses connotative language effectively here. His praise is moderate but warm, and he supports his claims with details from the film. Such a review is a suitable model for an evaluative piece you might write for a class or a local paper.

Our second passage, taken from an editorial column in an online political newsletter, uses much stronger language (the column advocates home schooling). Again, strongly connotative terms are boldfaced.

> Why have we put our children into educational **prisons** called public schools? What **crimes** have they committed? Why do we **condemn** almost 45 million **innocent** children to this **punishment?** Do I exaggerate by calling these schools "prisons?" Well, let's compare prisons and public schools. [. . .]
>
> School authorities **force** millions of children to sit in **boxes called classrooms** with 20 other children-**inmates** for six to eight hours a day, five days a week, for up to ten years. The children must **obey** the adult education **wardens** (teachers and principals), who they may **fear** or dislike. They must study subjects they may **hate** or that **bore** them to **death.**
>
> —Joel Turtel, "Public School Prisons"

One encounters this kind of heavy-handed language fairly often on the editorial pages of newspapers, in political campaign literature, in blogs, and on television and radio talk shows. Vehement language is sometimes appropriate in these settings, where writers voice strong positions on important questions.

Yet writers take risks when they choose such charged language. Turtel's piece is so laden with extreme terms ("prisons," "children-inmates," "hate") that it's likely to strike many readers as absurd. Emotionally charged writing is best left for audiences you know well or for settings where readers expect it. This means that it's rarely appropriate for academic writing. (See Section 6a for detailed advice about what instructors expect in academic papers.)

EXERCISE 15.2 Find a syndicated newspaper column such as those written by George Will, Frank Rich, Maureen Dowd, or Thomas Sowell. Underline words and phrases with strong negative or positive connotations. Then find a news story from the same paper. Discuss the differences in how the two pieces use connotative language.

15c How do you improve readability?

Have you ever suffered through an essay that went completely over your head? Or stopped reading an editorial halfway through because the writer made assumptions that seemed wildly implausible? Or fallen asleep while studying a particularly dull textbook? Writers who don't think sufficiently about their audiences sometimes find that their language alienates the readers they want to reach. This is why it's important as you write to consider ways to enhance the reader's experience. Draw readers into your discussion; don't shut them out.

1 Choose words familiar to your readers. When you're drafting or revising a piece of writing, ask yourself whether your readers will be comfortable with the vocabulary you're using. There are times when a difficult or technical term *is* appropriate—when it draws a subtle distinction or describes a complex phenomenon that simpler words can't capture. But writers sometimes wrongly assume that they need to impress readers by choosing formal and highly complicated language. Here's an example from an academic paper.

UNNECESSARILY DIFFICULT LANGUAGE

Scholarly authorities hold a myriad of viewpoints with regard to the ongoing disputation involving the major prescription drug companies' ethical obligation to manufacture minimally profitable pharmaceuticals that ameliorate the world's major diseases.

REVISED

Scholars disagree on whether big drug companies have a moral obligation to manufacture low-profit drugs to treat the world's major diseases.

See how much more readable the second sentence is? Even when you're writing in a relatively formal style, you'll reach more readers by choosing familiar words when you can. (See Section 17c for tips on reworking inflated sentences.)

2 Balance abstract and concrete language.

Abstract words are general; they refer to ideas, concepts, and categories that we can't perceive directly through our five senses—words such as *justice, charm, culture, life.* **Concrete words** do just the opposite; they name specific people and things that we can see, hear, taste, smell, or touch—*Marlon Brando, lopsided grin, turquoise bracelet, my fat schnauzer.* Of course, most words are neither wholly abstract nor concrete. They exist on a continuum between the two extremes, and writers must decide what level of specificity seems most appropriate for their purpose.

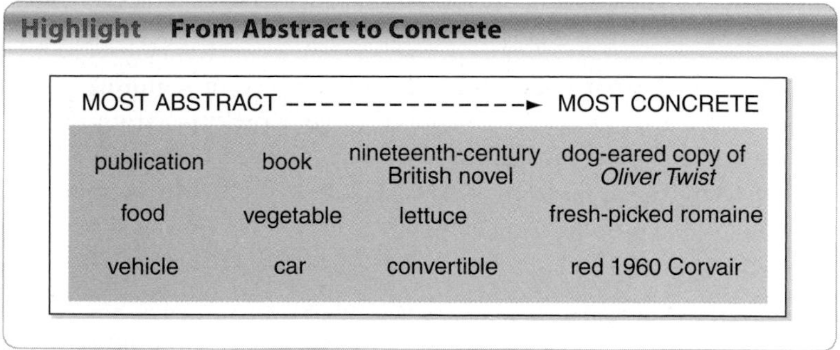

Highlight From Abstract to Concrete

MOST ABSTRACT -----			► MOST CONCRETE
publication	book	nineteenth-century British novel	dog-eared copy of *Oliver Twist*
food	vegetable	lettuce	fresh-picked romaine
vehicle	car	convertible	red 1960 Corvair

Passages with too many abstractions can be intimidating and hard to follow. Yet if writing contains nothing but specifics, readers may not see the larger point amid all the details. That's why skilled writers strive for an effective mix of both. Details help to illustrate abstract concepts that readers might otherwise find difficult, and general statements tie together details that might initially seem unrelated. Here is a writer clarifying a hard-to-grasp, abstract concept by helping us to picture it very specifically.

The distinction between Newton and Einstein's ideas about gravitation has sometimes been illustrated by picturing **a little boy playing marbles**

> **in a city lot. The ground is very uneven, ridged with bumps and hollows. An observer in an office ten stories above the street would not be able to see these irregularities in the ground. Noticing that the marbles appear to avoid some sections of the ground and move toward other sections,** he might assume a "force" is operating which repels the marbles from certain spots and attracts them toward others. But **another observer on the ground would instantly perceive that the path of the marbles is simply governed by the curvature of the field.**
>
> —Lincoln Barnett, *The Universe and Dr. Einstein*

The precise ratio of abstract to concrete language you use in a particular text will depend on your writing situation. For more on balancing concrete and abstract language, see Section 17b-1.

3 Limit your use of jargon. The specialized language of professional groups is called jargon. Physicians, for instance, use terms like *hypertension* and *idiopathic*; graphic artists speak about *pixels* and *color separation.* When you're writing for a group of specialists, these technical terms are a necessary part of your vocabulary, as in the following passage from an article in *Guitar Player Magazine.* Jargon words are boldfaced.

> Your guitar's **passive tone control** is a potent **sound-sculpting** tool—at least when it's correctly matched to your **pickups, stompboxes, amp,** and playing style. But if you find yourself ignoring your guitar's **tone knobs,** it's probably because you hate the **flabby sounds** that result from twisting them counterclockwise.
>
> —Andy Ellis, "Stellartone Tonestyler"

But you'll shut out readers if you use this kind of jargon when you're writing for an audience that includes nonspecialists. When you need to use a specialized term for a general audience, define it the first time you use it and then give an example. For example, an article on guitars for nonspecialists would need to clarify that "stompboxes" are pedals that electric guitar players use to create special sound effects such as echoes and tonal distortion.

4 Avoid clichés. Clichés are expressions that were once fresh and vivid but which have been so overused that they've lost their impact: *dead giveaway, better late than never, powers that be, brought back to reality, back to basics,* and so on. It's easy for phrases such as these to slip into an early draft of a project, but as you edit, replace them with more lively language.

5 Use a civil tone for public writing. Treat your readers—even those who disagree with you—with respect. Most readers will be put off by an author who sounds arrogant and contemptuous. Consider the following passage.

> The existence of a literature presupposes a literate and coherent public that has both the time to read and a need to take seriously the works of the literary imagination. I'm not sure whether the United States ever had such a public; certainly it hasn't had one for the last thirty years. What we have instead is an opening-night crowd, astonished by celebrity and opulent spectacle, tolerating only those authors who present themselves as freaks and wonders and offer the scandal of their lives as proof of their art.
>
> —Lewis Lapham, "Notebook"

Lapham is a longtime social critic who has been writing his grumpy column for *Harper's* for years. Undoubtedly the caustic tone—characterized by name-calling, sarcasm, and sweeping condemnations—appeals to some people, particularly those who already agree with the author. But many readers may feel insulted and quit reading.

If you want readers to pay attention to your concerns, begin with the assumption that your readers are intelligent and that they are able to entertain another point of view. Avoid name-calling and blanket generalizations. Instead of making pronouncements, qualify your claims using words and phrases such as *One solution is . . ., in many cases, often, usually.* (For more on building credibility in your writing, see Section 1g. For advice on handling different viewpoints, consult Section 10c.)

EXERCISE 15.3 Revise one of the passages below to achieve a more effective balance between abstract and concrete language. You may need to add sentences and revise existing sentences. Discuss your revisions with a group of classmates.

1. Never buy a pet from a pet shop without first checking to see where the establishment gets its animals. Many stores buy their stock from unregulated "puppy mills," where large numbers of animals are raised in terrible conditions. Buyers may end up with a sick or mentally damaged pet.

2. During the month of February, twelve students were mugged at knifepoint in the main student parking garage. In April, a woman barricaded herself in the garage elevator to escape an assailant. In June,

two cars parked on the top level of the garage had their windshields smashed. My roommate is even afraid to park her car on campus.

EXERCISE 15.4 Revise the following paragraph to create a more civil tone. Assume that you're writing to readers of your campus newspaper.

> Apparently the university "doesn't have the funds" this year to renovate the dorms on campus. Whatever. It's tough for me to believe that there's a money shortage when every time I pass by the president's mansion he's having another pricey affair for his fat-cat donor cronies. Everyone knows that all the administrators do is go to extravagant parties, mutter a few "inspirational" words every now and then, and draw obscene salaries. What a scam! They don't care about the students; they just care about lining their wallets. If they had to live in our dorms, I bet we'd see some upgrades pretty fast.

15d How do you keep language civil?

Biased language isn't always bad. Slanted but colorful writing regularly enlivens articles in popular books, humorous pieces in magazines, and the editorial pages of any newspaper. When you write papers in college, in business, or in most community settings, however, you have a different kind of audience. You're writing to inform or persuade readers whom you don't know well, and you don't want to offend them by lapsing into language that excludes a part of your audience or suggests that you think in stereotypes.

No matter who their audience may be, responsible writers avoid language that stigmatizes or demeans particular groups. Language that attributes negative associations to individuals based on gender, race or ethnicity, religion, profession, or class is always out of place in public writing.

1 Avoid sexist language. Over the past four decades, women's rights activists have made most of us more aware of how language shapes attitudes and reinforces traditional gender roles. To keep sexist blunders out of your writing, consider these guidelines.

- **Avoid using *he* and *him* as pronouns to refer to people in general.** Instead, you can use *he or she* or *him or her*. Using plurals will often solve the problem of sexist pronouns.

WHY WRITE . . .	WHEN YOU COULD WRITE . . .
Every executive expects *his* bonus.	Every executive expects *a* bonus. Executives expect *their* bonuses. Every executive expects *his or her* bonus.

- **Avoid using the word *man* to refer to all people or all members of a group.**

WHY WRITE . . .	WHEN YOU COULD WRITE . . .
boys who want to be cops	*kids* who want to be cops
men who do their own auto repairs	*car owners* who do their own repairs

- **Avoid implying that professions or roles are primarily for men or for women.**

WHY WRITE . . .	WHEN YOU COULD WRITE . . .
men who hope to become stay-at-home *mothers*	*young people* who hope to become stay-at-home *parents*
police*man*	police officer
business*men*	businesspeople

- **When possible, find out what name a married woman wants to go by and honor that choice.** Here are the possibilities.

woman's first and last names	Olga Perez
woman's first and last names + husband's last name	Olga Perez Marciano
woman's first name + hyphenated last name	Olga Perez-Marciano
woman's first name + husband's last name	Olga Marciano
title + husband's full name	Mrs. Ralph Marciano

Many women, single or married, prefer the title *Ms.* to *Miss* or *Mrs.* When you're not sure, *Ms.* is the best choice.

- **Avoid implying that men and women behave in stereotypical ways.** Don't suggest that women are generally talkative and overly emotional or that most men are sports-minded and sloppy. Avoid sexist descriptions such as "a slim blonde" or "dumb jock." Finally, the generic term *woman* (or *women*) is usually more appropriate than *lady* or *girl*.

EXERCISE 15.5 Rewrite the following sentences to eliminate sexist language or implications.

1. Women in their forties and fifties who want to look their best often consider cosmetic surgery.
2. Today even a high school physics teacher should know his chaos theory, or he'll look out of date to his students.
3. Businesswomen often worry about leaving their children in day care while they work long hours to get ahead.
4. The blonde lady running for Congress in my district has been a county judge for many years.

2 Avoid language that suggests racial or ethnic bias. In most writing situations, you simply don't need to mention race or national origin—it's not relevant. However, when issues of race or nationality are central to your discussion, these guidelines may be helpful.

- **Be specific and accurate in your descriptions.** For example, *Asian* may be too broad to be meaningful; *Filipino, Japanese, Chinese, Korean,* and *East Indian* are more specific. Likewise, rather than use *Hispanic,* use *Cuban, Puerto Rican, Mexican,* and so on, as appropriate. The term *Latino* (or *Latina*), used to refer broadly to people of Latin American descent, is widely accepted.

  When you refer to individuals whose forebears came from another country but who were themselves born in the United States, combine the term with *American:* for example, *Japanese American. Native American* is preferable to *Indian*; *Inuit, Yup'ik,* and *Inupiat* are now preferred by some to *Eskimo.*

  When you're writing about individuals' religious affiliations, be similarly specific; generalizations such as *Eastern sects* and *Christian conservatives* are vague and inaccurate. It's better to specify a particular religion or denomination (*Sunni Muslims, Orthodox Jews, Southern Baptists*) or to name a particular religious group (*Promise Keepers, Campus Crusade for Christ*).

- **Use terminology preferred by the people you're writing about, insofar as you know their preferences.** If you're not sure, adopt the terminology you see in major newspapers and magazines. For example, preferred usage in these media seems to have shifted from *black* to *African American.*
- **Be careful not to allow ethnic, national, or religious stereotypes to sneak into your writing.** Might one infer from your language that you think of Jews as rich financiers? Is there a hint that someone with an Italian surname has underworld connections? Check your writing for such biases.

EXERCISE 15.6 Almost everyone has had some experience with the difficult issue of ethnic labels and names. Working with fellow students, make a list of all the ethnic groups represented in your composition class, writing on the board the terms preferred by members of each definable group. Discuss those preferences.

EXERCISE 15.7 Consider which of these sentences might be inappropriate in an academic paper. Which seem acceptable? Why? Revise those that aren't appropriate.

1. Jewish director-producer Steven Spielberg traces his interest in filmmaking back to his childhood, when he recorded family occasions with his parents' movie camera.
2. Negro baseball players formed their own leagues in the early 1900s.
3. Indians, Eskimos, and other primitive groups are often portrayed sympathetically in the movies.
4. Unlike most American teenagers, Asian students are hardworking, academically oriented, and respectful of authority figures.

3 Avoid stereotypes about age, physical condition, and sexual orientation. A responsible writer strives to treat all groups and individuals fairly and with respect. These guidelines may be helpful.

- **For people in their sixties or older, use specific designations such as *middle sixties* or *early eighties* rather than *elderly, senior citizens,* or *old people.*** Don't slip into patronizing remarks such as "For a 75-year-old man, he's remarkably alert."

- **Reserve the terms *boys, girls, children,* and *kids* for people under age twelve.** *Kids* is appropriate only in casual writing. *Teens* and *youths* are fine for high school students. *College kids* is patronizing as well as inaccurate: almost half of all U.S. college students now are over 25.
- **Be as specific as possible when you refer to people's disabilities or illnesses, and avoid language that implies pity—for example, *crippled* and *victim.*** In general, mention the individual first and his or her handicap or illness second—"a person with AIDS" or "my cousin who is autistic." Terms such as *disabled* and *hearing-impaired* are generally acceptable. Once again, it's useful to know what terms the individuals themselves prefer.
- **Mention a person's sexual orientation only when it is relevant to the issue under discussion, and then use specific, nonjudgmental terminology.** Many people whose sexual orientation is toward their own gender are comfortable with the adjective *homosexual* to refer to both men and women but less comfortable with the noun, *a homosexual.* You may use the terms *gay* and *lesbian* when you want to be more specific. Although some groups of gay rights advocates use the word *queer* in their literature, that term is inappropriate coming from someone outside such a group. The use of the word *gay* as an all-purpose pejorative is also offensive.

EXERCISE 15.8 Working in a group, decide which of these sentences have hints of offensive bias (some of them are certainly arguable). Which might be acceptable in some circumstances? How could you change those that are not?

1. Barney Frank, who is the best-known homosexual in the U.S. Congress, represents a district in Massachusetts.
2. Even in her seventies, Betty Friedan wrote extensively and traveled widely.
3. The hospice is looking for volunteers to help AIDS victims with household tasks and grocery shopping.

4 Avoid language that derides people's professions or implies unflattering class distinctions. In serious writing, don't use *shrink* for psychiatrist or *cop* for police officer. Also avoid terms that have negative class connotations, such as *preppie, soccer mom, welfare mother, redneck,* and *dropout.* Terms such as *ghetto* and *lower class* are often demeaning; instead, use *low income* to describe an economic condition.

5 Use good judgment and keep your sense of humor when you edit for bias. Don't sanitize your writing to the point that it becomes sterile and dishonest. It's unrealistic to say you should never use biased or exaggerated language to convey a mood, create an image, or make sardonic comments. Like a professional writer, however, you should make it your goal to be so attuned to your readers that you can write to them with respect, awareness, and good taste—and still have fun with language.

INFOGRAPHIC

Obama's New Fuel Efficiency Plan

Last week, President Obama announced a plan to lower automobile emissions by requiring new cars to average 35.5 miles per gallon. How can Detroit rise to meet the challenge?

- Launch massive campaign urging drivers to draft a few feet behind one another on the highway to minimize drag
- Will no longer sell or lease to anyone weighing more than 150 pounds
- Remove least fuel-efficient tire from every car
- Gradually decrease the length of a mile
- Slap a sticker that says "35.5" on all new cars
- Bulldoze nation's uphill gradients
- Talk Obama down to 34 miles per gallon by offering to throw in a copy of *The Audacity Of Hope* with each auto purchase
- Copy the Japanese, probably

Humor is not always civil. Satirical items such as this one posted on *The Onion* (<http://www.theonion.com>) push the envelope, hoping to arouse and, sometimes, even offend readers. Do you find this graphic funny? Why or why not? Which, if any, words and phrases would be inappropriate for academic or professional writing? In what situations might you "push the envelope" in your own writing?

6 Check that photos or other visual images in a document don't suggest harmful stereotypes. Because images often affect readers more immediately than words do, select photos and other visuals carefully. Are you writing an illustrated history of jazz for your music history course? Be sure to include photos of African American, white, and Latino musicians. Are you composing a brochure to publicize a campus organization whose members include nontraditional students? Make sure that your cover photo doesn't include only 18-year-olds. Creating a Web page welcoming students to the Writing Center? Be sure to include pictures of both women and men. Visual elements and text should work together to create a fair, accurate picture of the subject at hand.

Taking Control

Use civil language

Use good judgment and keep your sense of humor when you edit for bias. You may watch news commentators (such as Stephen Colbert, Jon Stewart, or Dennis Miller) who use biased language deliberately to spoof, praise, strong-arm, or criticize. But, unlike them, you will want to be restrained with your language choices. Some people seem eager to take offense or are not willing to give others the benefit of the doubt—as many writers and politicians have discovered. So always keep your audience and purpose in mind and, for academic writing especially, err on the side of caution. When you do, you can be candid with language and still be civil and decent. It also makes sense to avoid offensive four-letter words and obscene expressions in most writing.

EXERCISE 15.9 Which of these sentences might alienate a reader sensitive to bias? Should those be changed? Why or why not? What changes would you suggest?

1. The cops used poor judgment about gathering evidence at the crime scene.
2. Welfare mothers have become the target of budget-conscious legislators who believe that hardworking taxpayers shouldn't have to support people who won't work.
3. That organization is known for attracting sorority girls and fraternity guys.
4. It's amazing that Jason became a successful lawyer, since he grew up in the inner-city ghetto, surrounded by poverty and despair.

15e Do you understand dialects?

If you're like most people in the United States, you know several varieties of English, each shaped by your cultural heritage, your region, and your exposure to other languages. Linguists call these varieties of English **dialects.** Dialects of English—which include southern dialect, northeastern dialect, African American Vernacular English (AAVE), and many others—differ from each other in vocabulary, pronunciation, and grammar. They also differ in their prestige, influence, and power.

One dialect of English, sometimes referred to as **edited American English,** or **standard English,** is the language used in most academic, business, and public writing. When you pick up a newspaper, a magazine, a scholarly journal, a business letter, an instruction manual, or a textbook like this one, you'll find yourself reading *standard English.* This version of the language has gained its status and authority because of complex historical, political, and economic circumstances, but it is not inherently superior or more logical than other forms of English. It just seems that way because standard English is the version most widely understood and taught in schools. For good or ill, standard English is the language of power, used by most professional people in their day-to-day work.

If a regional dialect you use in other settings differs from this "standard," you may have difficulties when some of your dialect's features appear in your writing. You can use this handbook and other resources, such as your campus writing center, to edit those features. However, learning to use a standard dialect for certain writing situations doesn't mean that you have to abandon all others. It means only that you have to be adept enough to switch among different ways of speaking as circumstances demand.

In addition to the various dialects of English, many languages are spoken in the United States. If you speak English as your second language (ESL), you'll find information in Chapters 31 through 33, in addition to the information at the end of this chapter, to help you with the challenges of writing in a new language.

The language you hear spoken on national news programs in the United States represents an influential version of Standard English sometimes called "General American." Reporters and commentators typically use this Midwestern accent because it seems less regional than English spoken in, for example, the South or Northeast. Do the TV reporters in your area have discernible accents?

1 Recognize the uses and importance of dialects. Regional and nonstandard dialects are important and useful to the groups that speak them. A dialect helps to hold a group together and to give it a sense of community and identity. Dialects thus should be appreciated and protected for private communication among individuals within a particular community. Usually such communication is spoken rather than written.

However, dialects can also lend color and energy to written narration or description by allowing readers to hear the actual words of speakers, thereby bringing them to life. Here, for example, is an example of a regional dialect from a paper written by a student clinging to her accent and attitudes despite a move to a new school and environment.

> Knowing my love and respect for these people, it is truly no wonder that even in this tiny blue dot in my red state, I found and moved in with a friend who at least once a week comes into my room to ask me, "Jeet yet?" To which I reply, "Naw, ju?"
>
> "Naw. Yawnto?" he asks.

"Aight," I mumble, "whatcha want?"

He'll stare at the ceiling for a minute as though he is thinking, but the answer is always the same. "How bout sumya fried chicken with a nice scald on it?"

—Amy Sue Carter, "Accentuate the Positive"

2 Acknowledge the limitations of dialect and use it appropriately in your writing. When regional or nonstandard dialects show up in *public writing*—and that is what most of the writing you do in college and your profession will be—they can be misinterpreted. Those who don't speak a dialect may not recognize many vocabulary items. They may also regard as nonstandard certain grammatical forms that are completely natural and logical within a dialect community. So letting a private dialect enter your writing, then, is not "wrong"—but it may be inappropriate for reports, arguments, and other forms of academic writing.

When can you use a nonstandard dialect in your writing? First, you can almost always use it in your private life among friends, family, or others who share the dialect, either in conversation or in letters or email. Second, you might use it in a first, discovery draft when you're trying to get your ideas down and don't want to slow your thinking by worrying about conventions. (You can edit out or translate inappropriate dialect features in a future draft.) Finally, you might use dialect in an anecdote you are adding to a paper to illustrate a point, or incorporate it into dialogue that is an essential part of a personal narrative, as Amy Sue Carter does in Section 15e-1. Except for such instances, however, spoken dialect generally doesn't fit into the kind of public writing you'll be doing in college, in business, or in community work.

3 Use languages other than English sparingly. If you speak a language other than English, you might use it in your writing for the same reasons that you'd use a nonstandard dialect of English.

You might also use another language to reproduce a speaker's exact words or to create an authentic atmosphere in a description or narrative. Similarly, it's appropriate to include non-English words that can't easily be translated into English, as the essayist Judith Ortiz Cofer does in the following example.

> Even the home movie cannot fill in the sensory details such a gathering [a family New Year's Eve party] left imprinted in a child's brain. The thick sweetness of women's perfumes mixing with the ever-present smells of food cooking in the kitchen: meat and plantain *pasteles*, as well as the ubiquitous rice dish made special with pigeon peas—*gandules*—and seasoned with previous *sofrito* sent up from the Island by somebody's mother or smuggled in by a recent traveler.
>
> —Judith Ortiz Cofer, "Silent Dancing"

As with dialect, words and phrases from different languages should be used in public writing only to achieve a particular effect—otherwise you'll risk confusing readers. And if the meaning of a word or phrase isn't apparent from the context, it's wise to provide an English translation, as Cofer does above.

CHAPTER

16 How Do You Construct Effective Sentences?

To write well, you need a basic feel for how sentences work. Unfortunately, the traditional terms used to describe the architecture (or *syntax*) of sentences—*clauses, phrases, subordination, coordination, parallelism*—can make composing sentences seem overly complicated. Yet even the most complex sentences are based on a few comprehensible structures and principles you can master easily enough with a little practice. We cover those elements in this chapter.

16a How are sentences structured?

We know, of course, that you'll rarely think about particular sentence structures when you compose. Few writers—if any—work that way. But even while dashing off a draft, you'll be more confident when you've developed a feel for the way sentences function, an instinct for how the parts fit together.

1 Understand sentence patterns. Sentences are tough to define. A **sentence** can be described as a group of words that expresses an idea and that is punctuated as an independent unit. All sentences have a **subject** (the doer of an action) and a **predicate** (the action done). Beginning with this assumption, you'll find that just five patterns can describe the framework of many sentences you write. In recognizing these patterns and their variations, you take a step toward controlling the shape of your sentences.

(SENTENCE TYPE 1) Subject + verb (intransitive). This is the simplest sentence pattern, the one with the fewest parts. Like all sentences, it includes a *subject*, the doer of an action; and a *verb*, the action performed. But in this pattern the verb is *intransitive*—that is, it doesn't need (or take) an object to complete its meaning.

Subject	Verb (intransitive)
The lawyer	fainted.
The floodwaters	receded.
All the children	smiled at once.

EXERCISE 16.1 Compose three sentences that follow the subject–intransitive verb pattern. Underline the intransitive verb in each sentence.

(SENTENCE TYPE 2) Subject + verb (transitive) + direct object. This sentence pattern adds a third element to the subject and verb: an **object,** which identifies to what or to whom an action has been done. Objects can be words, phrases, or clauses. The pattern requires a transitive verb that conveys its action to an object.

Subject	Verb (transitive)	Object
The lawyer	accepted	the case.
The heavy rains	destroyed	the levee.
Some of the children	were reading	magazines.

Note that the subject–verb–object pattern illustrates the *active voice,* in which the subject performs the action described by the transitive verb. But when that action is performed by the object, you have a *passive construction* (see Section 23e).

The case was accepted by the lawyer.

The levee was destroyed by heavy rains.

Magazines were being read by some of the children.

Only transitive verbs can be involved in passive constructions because they require an object that can become a subject. Intransitive verbs don't take objects.

A transitive verb and its object must fit together logically. In the following example, the verb *intimidate* cannot logically convey its action to the object *enthusiasm. Enthusiasm* might be *undermined, dampened,* or *eroded,* but we don't usually speak of it as being *intimidated.*

FAULTY The negative attitudes of the senior staff *intimidated* the **enthusiasm** of the volunteers.

REVISED The negative attitudes of the senior staff *dampened* the **enthusiasm** of the volunteers.

EXERCISE 16.2 Write three sentences that follow the subject–verb–object pattern. Underline the object. Be sure the verb is in the active voice.

EXERCISE 16.3 Revise any of the following sentences in which the boldfaced verb cannot logically convey its action to its object. First try to explain the problem with the original verb; then change the verb, not the object.

1. At her parents' request, Margery **interrogated** her sister Kyla's low grades at college.
2. Kyla **blasphemed** her instructor's methods of teaching history.
3. Her chemistry teacher **obliged** difficult lab reports every week.
4. Worst of all, her English teacher persistently **admonished** the clarity of her writing.

(SENTENCE TYPE 3) Subject + verb (linking) + subject complement. Linking verbs, which are often forms of *to be*, connect a subject to a **subject complement**—that is, to a word or phrase that extends or completes the meaning of a subject or renames it in some way. Among the common linking verbs are *to seem, to appear, to feel,* and *to become.*

Subject	Linking verb	Subject complement
The lawyer	became	a federal judge.
The storms	seemed	endless.
The children	are	happy.

A complement should be compatible with its subject. When it is not, the sentence is illogical, sometimes subtly so.

FAULTY COMPLEMENT **Prejudice** is unacceptable **behavior** in this club.

The problem is that *prejudice* is not behavior; it's an attitude. So the sentence has to be modified to reflect this difference.

REVISED **Prejudiced behavior** is unacceptable in this club.

For the same reason, it's usually wrong to use *when* as a complement, except when you actually are writing about a specific time.

WRONG **Plagiarism** is **when** a writer doesn't credit her source.
RIGHT **Tuesday at 8:00 p.m.** is **when** the film begins.

When is an adverb; *plagiarism* is a noun. *Plagiarism* has to be equated with a concept or an idea, so it cannot be *when.*

RIGHT **Plagiarism** is the **failure** to credit a source.

EXERCISE 16.4 In the following sentences, indicate whether the boldfaced words are objects or complements.

1. Halloween may be the oddest **holiday** of the year.
2. The roots of Halloween are deeply **religious.**
3. But Halloween celebrations today seem quite **secular.**
4. Children and adults wear **costumes** and pull **pranks.**

EXERCISE 16.5 Write three sentences that follow the subject–verb–subject complement pattern. Underline the subject complement. Try to vary your linking verbs.

EXERCISE 16.6 Revise any of the following sentences in which the subject complement cannot work logically with its subject. First explain the problem with the original complement; then change the complement, not the subject. The complement is boldfaced.

1. Photography is an excellent **fun**.
2. Revising every paper in this class four times seems **exorbitant**.
3. Gerald felt **unconscionable** after arriving too late to say farewell.
4. Philosophy is **when** you read Plato and Aristotle.

(SENTENCE TYPE 4) Subject + verb (transitive) + indirect object + direct object. An **indirect object** explains for whom or to what an action is done or directed. As you can see in this pattern, indirect objects ordinarily precede direct objects.

Subject	Verb (transitive)	Indirect object	Direct object
The lawyer	found	the clerk	a job.
The storms	brought	local farmers	needed rain.
The children	told	their parents	stories.

If you have trouble understanding what an indirect object does in a sentence, turn it into the object of a prepositional phrase.

The lawyer found a job **for the clerk.**

The storms brought needed rain **to local farmers.**

The children told stories **to their parents.**

EXERCISE 16.7 In the following sentences, circle the indirect objects and underline the objects.

1. The placement office finds students jobs after college.
2. Did you send Eric, Peg, Lester, and Davida the same email message?
3. Offer Sweetie more dog biscuits.
4. The distinguished senator gives proponents of the National Endowment for the Arts fits.

EXERCISE 16.8 Write three sentences that follow the subject–verb–indirect object–direct object pattern. Circle the indirect object and underline the direct object.

(SENTENCE TYPE 5) Subject + verb (transitive) + direct object + object complement. Just as a subject complement modifies or explains a subject, an **object complement** does the same for the object of a sentence.

Subject	Verb (transitive)	Direct object	Object complement
The lawyer	called	the verdict	surprising.
The flood	caught	the town	napping.
The children	found	their spinach	vile.

EXERCISE 16.9 In the following sentences, underline the direct objects and circle the object complements.

1. Most people find football entertaining.
2. Thoroughbred horses often turn their wealthy owners poor.
3. Our careful preparation makes us lucky.
4. The mayor called the federal court decision against the city ordinance unfortunate.

EXERCISE 16.10 Write three sentences that follow the subject–verb–direct object–object complement pattern. Underline the direct object and circle the subject complement.

2 Understand compound subjects, verbs, and objects. A sentence can include multiple subjects, verbs, or objects to accommodate the ideas you need to express. Such expansions are routine, but some writers do have problems punctuating the resulting sentences.

Compound subjects. Two subjects attached to the same verb are usually connected by the conjunction *and* or *or*. No comma is needed between these compound subjects.

> **Lawyers and judges** attended the seminar.
>
> **Storms or fires** ravage California each year.

When a third subject is added, the items are separated by commas (see Section 36c-2).

> **Storms, fires, and earthquakes** ravage California each year.

Subjects can also be expanded by expressions such as *neither . . . nor* and *either . . . or*, which are called **correlatives.**

Neither the judge nor the lawyer attended the seminar.

Either fires or earthquakes strike California each year.

Compound verbs. Single subjects can perform more than one action. When they do, the verbs attached to them are compound. Like nouns, verbs can be joined by *and, or,* or correlatives such as *either . . . or.* No comma should be used between two verbs that form a compound verb.

The judge **confused and angered** the prosecutor.

The earthquake **damaged or destroyed** many homes.

Children **either like or hate** spinach.

When a third verb is added, as with subjects, the items are separated by commas.

The judge **confused, angered, and embarrassed** the prosecutor.

Compound verbs can each take separate objects, expanding the sentence structure even more.

The judge **confused** *the jury* **and angered** *the prosecutor.*

The earthquake **damaged** *roads* **and destroyed** *homes.*

Compound objects. A verb may also have more than one object. Two objects attached to the same verb are usually connected by the conjunction *and* or *or.* No comma is needed between two objects; commas are required for three or more objects.

Lawyers attended **the seminar and the dinner.**

Forest fires ravage **California, Arizona, New Mexico, or Colorado** every year.

Objects can also be connected with correlatives.

Forest fires ravage **either California or New Mexico** every year.

Many variations of these elements are possible. But don't pile up more compound expressions than readers can handle easily. Sentences should always be readable.

TOO MANY COMPOUNDS

Both lawyers and judges attended the after-lunch seminars and discussion groups; broke for drinks, cocktails, and coffee in the late afternoon;

returned for a film, a professional roundtable, and a business session; and then either went out to dinner or retired to their hotels.

REVISED FOR CLARITY

Both lawyers and judges attended the after-lunch seminars and discussion groups. **They** broke for drinks, cocktails, and coffee in the late afternoon **and then** returned for a film, a professional roundtable, and a business session. **Afterward,** they either went out to dinner or retired to their hotels.

16b What do modifiers do?

Modifiers are words, phrases, or clauses that expand what we know about subjects, verbs, or other sentence elements, including other modifiers and complete sentences. In fact, it would be hard to compose sentences without them. Even simple modifiers change the texture of sentences, while more complex modifiers increase your options for shaping sentences.

1 Use adjectives to modify nouns and pronouns. Adjectives describe and help to explain nouns and pronouns by specifying *how many, which size, what color, what condition, which one,* and so on. Single adjectives are usually placed before the terms they modify.

The **angry** judge scowled at the **nervous** witness.

But adjectives often work in groups. Adjectives in a group are called **coordinate adjectives** when each one works on its own, describing different and unrelated aspects of a noun or pronoun.

the **undistinguished, tired-looking** lawyer

our cat, **shedding and overweight**

Placed before a noun or pronoun, coordinate adjectives can be linked either by conjunctions (usually *and*) or by commas. The order of the adjectives doesn't affect their meaning.

The **angry, perspiring** judge scowled at the **balding and nervous** witness.

The **perspiring and angry** judge scowled at the **nervous and balding** witness.

Coordinate adjectives may also follow the words they modify, giving variety to sentence rhythms.

> The judge, **angry and perspiring,** scowled at the witness, **balding and nervous.**

For a stylish variation, you can also move coordinate adjectives ahead of an article (*the*) at the beginning of a sentence.

> **Tired, angry, and perspiring,** the judge scowled at the nervous witness.

Not all clusters of adjectives are coordinate. Often groups of adjectives must follow a specific sequence to make sense. Changing their sequence produces expressions that are not *idiomatic*; that is, they don't sound right to a native English speaker.

NOT IDIOMATIC	the wooden heavy gavel
IDIOMATIC	the heavy wooden gavel
NOT IDIOMATIC	a woolen green sweater
IDIOMATIC	a green woolen sweater
NOT IDIOMATIC	the American first satellite
IDIOMATIC	the first American satellite

Adjectives in such groupings—which often include numbers—are not separated by commas.

> The judge wielded a **heavy wooden** gavel.
>
> The **first American** satellite was Explorer I.
>
> The police rescued **two lucky** kayakers.

Adjectives (along with adverbs and nouns) can also form *compound* or *unit modifiers*, groups of words linked by hyphens that modify a noun (see Section 40c-5). The individual words in compound modifiers need each other; they often wouldn't make sense standing alone in front of a noun.

> A **well-known** case would provide a **high-impact** precedent.
>
> Are you certain the dinner is a **black-tie** affair?

Finally, adjectives play an important role as subject complements and object complements (see Section 16a-1), modifying words to which they are joined by linking verbs.

The judge's decision seemed **eccentric.**

The children were **sleepy.**

The press called the jury **inept.**

EXERCISE 16.11 Rewrite each of the following sentences so that all the adjectives in parentheses modify an appropriate noun or pronoun. Place the adjectives before or after the word they modify, and punctuate them correctly (for example, be sure to add hyphens to unit modifiers and to separate coordinate adjectives with commas or the conjunction *and* as necessary).

1. The elm trees once common throughout North America have disappeared, victims of disease. (*towering; graceful; Dutch elm*)
2. This infection destroys the vascular system of the elm, causing trees to become husks in a few short weeks. (*fungal; relentless; mature; thriving; leafless*)
3. Few parks in the United States can match the diversity of New York's Central Park, with its zoo, gardens and fields, ponds and lakes, and museum. (*great urban; sizable; pleasant; glistening; world class*)
4. Bankers, show people, and street people alike jostle shoulders and shopping bags in this oasis. (*Wall Street; glittering; down on their luck; refreshing; urban*)

2 Use adverbs to modify verbs, adjectives, and other adverbs.

Adverbs in sentences explain *how, when, where,* and *to what degree* things happen.

ADVERBS THAT MODIFY VERBS

The prosecutor *spoke* **eloquently** to the jury.

Immediately, the defense attorney *replied.*

The jury *tried* **hard** to follow their summaries.

ADVERBS THAT MODIFY ADJECTIVES

Tornadoes seem **freakishly** *unpredictable.*

Tornado chasing remains **quite** *popular.*

ADVERBS THAT MODIFY OTHER ADVERBS

The reading program has improved **very** *considerably.*

Less *easily* appreciated is a new interest in music at the school.

Adverbs increase your options in constructing sentences because they typically can be put in more places than adjectives, enabling you to experiment with sentence structure and rhythm. All three versions of the following sentence convey the same information, but they do so in subtly different ways.

> The news reporter **passionately and repeatedly** defended the integrity of her story.
>
> **Passionately and repeatedly,** the news reporter defended the integrity of her story.
>
> The news reporter defended the integrity of her story **passionately and repeatedly.**

But though versatile, adverbs can't be placed randomly in a sentence. Be sure to review Section 30f on the appropriate placement of adverbs, especially *only*.

EXERCISE 16.12 Rewrite the following sentences so that each adverb in parentheses modifies an appropriate verb, adjective, or adverb. Notice which adverbs work best in one position only and which can be relocated more freely in a sentence.

1. The elm trees once common throughout North America have disappeared, victims of disease. (*sadly*; *quite*; *almost*; *completely*)
2. This lethal infection destroys the vascular system of the elm, causing trees to become husks in a few short weeks. (*nearly*; *always*; *completely*)
3. Annoyed, the senator snapped at the reporter in an angry tone. (*visibly*; *unusually*)
4. We left the camera shop poorer but better equipped for difficult telephoto shots. (*considerably*; *much*; *extremely*)

3 Understand that nouns can operate as modifiers. In some sentences you may find words that look like nouns but act like adjectives, modifying other words. Don't be confused: nouns often work as modifiers.

> We ordered the **sausage** plate and a **vegetable** sampler.
>
> The **instrument** cluster in the BMW glowed red at night.

Proper nouns can serve as modifiers too.

The choir was preparing for the **Christmas** service.

We ordered a **New York** strip steak.

EXERCISE 16.13 In the following sentences, underline any nouns that function as modifiers. Discuss disputed cases with colleagues.

1. The Atlanta Braves, Washington Redskins, and Cleveland Indians are sports teams whose names occasionally stir controversy among Native American political interest groups.
2. Car insurance is getting so expensive in urban areas that many college students have to rely on the city bus.
3. Ike mistakenly signed up for the yoga class because his doctor told him that doing the cobra stretch and the sun salutation would strengthen his injured back muscles.
4. At Martha's Fourth of July party, the Vienna sausage didn't sit well with the Boston cream pie and strawberry ice cream.

4 Understand that verbals can operate as modifiers. Especially common as modifiers are participles—words such as *dazzling, frightening, broken.* Because participles are based on verbs, they give energy and snap to sentences.

The waiter brought a **sizzling** steak on a **steaming** bed of rice.

The margaritas arrived **frozen,** not on the rocks.

The officer, **smiling,** wrote us a $100 ticket.

Trembling, I opened the **creaking** door.

For more about participle and infinitive phrases, see Section 16c-2.

EXERCISE 16.14 In the following sentences, underline any participles that function as modifiers. Discuss disputed cases with colleagues.

1. I. M. Pei is one of America's most inspiring architects.
2. Born in Guangzhou, China, in 1916, Pei came to the United States in 1935 and became a naturalized citizen in 1954.

3. Pei is responsible for some of the most startling and admired buildings of our era.

4. Pei's work includes the glittering and much debated glass pyramid that now serves as the main entrance to the Louvre, one of the leading museums in the world.

5. Yet Pei can also count among his commissions Cleveland's Rock and Roll Hall of Fame, a daring work poised on the shores of Lake Erie.

16c What are phrases?

Technically, a **phrase** is a group of related words without a subject and a finite verb, but this definition is hard to follow. It's probably more helpful to appreciate phrases in terms of their function, doing their part to give shape to sentences.

1 Understand prepositional phrases. Among the more mundane of sentence elements, a *prepositional phrase* consists of a preposition and its object, either a noun or a pronoun. The object can be modified.

Preposition	Modifier (optional)	Object(s)
to		Jeff and me
in	your own	words
beyond	the farthest	mountain

It's easy to generate examples of prepositional phrases: *off the sofa, on the hard drive, across the miles, under the spreading chestnut tree, over the far horizon, from me, for her.* Just try writing a paragraph without using prepositional phrases and you'll appreciate how essential they are to establishing relationships within sentences. Don't, however, mistake prepositional phrases with *to* (*to Starbucks, to Lila*) for infinitives or infinitive phrases, which include a verb form (*to see, to watch the stars, to be happy*). For more on infinitives, see Section 24a-1.

The power of prepositional phrases resides in their flexibility and simplicity. Moving a prepositional phrase into an unexpected slot gets it noticed. Consider what happens to this sentence when its prepositional phrase is repositioned.

ORIGINAL	The power of prepositional phrases resides in their flexibility and simplicity.
PREPOSITIONAL PHRASE MOVED	In their flexibility and simplicity, the power of prepositional phrases resides.

The sentence sounds just different (some might say awkward) enough to cause readers to pause—which may be the effect you wish to achieve. And that's the point: where you position prepositional phrases can influence readers enough to change the way they interpret a sentence. For additional discussion, see Section 17c-7.

EXERCISE 16.15 Study the following passages and discuss the effect of relocating the boldfaced prepositional phrases within the speeches. How would the style of the passage be changed—if at all?

1. **Upon this battle** depends the survival of Christian civilization. **Upon it** depends our own British life, and the long continuity of our institutions and our Empire. The whole fury and might of the enemy must very soon be turned **on us**. Hitler knows he will have to break us in this island or lose the war.

   —Winston Churchill

2. **With malice toward none, with charity for all, with firmness in the right,** let us strive on to finish the work we are in, to bind up the nation's wounds, to care for him who shall have borne the battle and for his widow and his orphan, to do all which may achieve and cherish a just and lasting peace among ourselves and with all nations.

   —Abraham Lincoln

2 Appreciate the versatility of verbals and verbal phrases.

Verbals are verb forms that can act as nouns, adjectives, or adverbs (see Chapter 24). Verbals can stand alone, or they can form phrases by taking objects, complements, or modifiers.

	Verbal	Verbal phrase
Infinitive	to serve	to serve the sick
	to prevent	to prevent forest fires
Gerund	serving	serving the sick [is]
	preventing	preventing forest fires [is]
Participle	serving	serving without complaint
	prevented	prevented from helping

Verbals and verb phrases that act as nouns can serve as subjects or direct objects. As modifiers, verbals can function as adverbs or adjectives. Although verbals may seem complicated, you'll recognize the roles they play in sentences.

Verbals as subjects. Both infinitives and gerunds can act as subjects in sentences. On their own, they don't look much different from other subjects.

INFINITIVE AS SUBJECT

To serve was the doctor's ambition.

GERUND AS SUBJECT

Serving was the doctor's ambition.

But when they expand into phrases, they can be harder to recognize. Yet they remain subjects and can be either simple or compound.

INFINITIVE PHRASES AS SUBJECTS

To serve the sick was the doctor's ambition.

To serve the sick and to comfort the afflicted were the doctor's ambitions.

GERUND PHRASES AS SUBJECTS

Serving the sick was the doctor's ambition.

Serving the sick and comforting the afflicted were the doctor's ambitions.

Verbals as objects. Both infinitives and gerunds can act as objects in sentences. On their own, they don't look much different from other objects.

INFINITIVE AS DIRECT OBJECT

The lawyer loved **to debate.**

GERUND AS DIRECT OBJECT

The lawyer loved **debating.**

As phrases, verbals can seem complicated in their role as direct objects. Yet they play that role like any other noun, simple or compound.

INFINITIVE PHRASES AS DIRECT OBJECTS

The lawyer chose **to object to the motion.**

The lawyer chose **to object to the motion and to move for a mistrial.**

GERUND PHRASES AS DIRECT OBJECTS

The lawyer loved **objecting to the prosecutor's motions.**

The lawyer loved **objecting to the prosecutor's motions and winning concessions from the judge.**

Verbals as complements. Both infinitives and gerunds can act as complements in sentences.

INFINITIVE AS SUBJECT COMPLEMENT

To know Rebecca was **to love her.**

GERUND AS OBJECT COMPLEMENT

The IRS caught Elmo **cheating on his taxes**.

Verbals as adjectives. You'll frequently want to use participles and participle phrases to modify nouns and pronouns in your sentences.

PARTICIPLES AS ADJECTIVES

Frowning, the instructor stopped her lecture.

The **suspended** fraternity appealed to the dean.

PARTICIPLE PHRASES AS ADJECTIVES

Frowning at us, the instructor stopped her lecture.

The fraternity, **suspended for underage drinking,** appealed to the dean.

We kept close to the trail, **not knowing the terrain well.**

Notice the freedom you have in placing participle phrases. You do want to be certain, however, that readers can have no doubt what a particular phrase modifies. (See Section 30a on misplaced and dangling modifiers.)

Infinitives, too, can function as adjectives, although it can be difficult to perceive the infinitive in this role as a modifier.

INFINITIVES AS ADJECTIVES

The manager had many items **to purchase.** modifies *items*

Reasons **to stay** were few. modifies *reasons*

INFINITIVE PHRASES AS ADJECTIVES

The manager had many items **to purchase for the grand opening.** modifies *items*

Reasons **to stay calm** were few. modifies *reasons*

Verbals as adverbs. Infinitives and infinitive phrases can act like adverbs, answering such questions as *why, how, to what degree,* and so on.

INFINITIVES AS ADVERBS

Difficult **to please,** Martha rarely enjoyed movies. modifies *difficult*

The sedan seemed built **to last.** modifies *built*

INFINITIVE PHRASES AS ADVERBS

The gardener dug a trench **to stop the spread of oak wilt.** modifies *dug*

The Senate recessed **to give its members a summer vacation.** modifies *recessed*

The pilot found it impossible **to see the runway in the fog.** modifies *impossible*

EXERCISE 16.16 Underline all verbals in the following sentences and then indicate whether they function as subjects, objects, complements, adjectives, or adverbs.

1. Waving at the crowd, the winner of the marathon collapsed.
2. The waiter certainly seemed eager to please us.
3. The salesperson enjoyed demonstrating the self-closing door on the minivan.
4. Harriet bought an awning to reduce the light streaming through her bay windows.
5. To cherish the weak and the dying was Mother Teresa's mission in life.

3 Understand absolute phrases. **Absolutes** are versatile phrases that modify whole sentences rather than individual words. They are constructed from participles or infinitives. When absolute phrases are based on participles, they always include a subject and may include modifiers and other elements.

> Our representatives will, **time permitting,** read the entire petition to the city council.
>
> **The supply craft having docked,** the astronauts on the *International Space Station* were ready for their space walk.
>
> Our plane arrived early, **the winds having been favorable.**

When the participle is a form of *to be*, it can often be omitted for a more economical or elegant expression.

> **The winds [being] favorable,** our plane arrived early.

Absolutes based on infinitives don't require a noun or pronoun.

> **To speak frankly,** we are facing the gravest crisis in the history of this company.
>
> Your buzz cut, **to be honest,** would look better on a coconut.

Because absolutes are not attached to particular words, you can place them exactly where they work best in a sentence. Absolutes can add sophistication to your sentences.

EXERCISE 16.17 Turn the phrases in parentheses into absolutes and incorporate them into the full sentences preceding them.

EXAMPLE The senator's earmark to the bill would fund a worthless pork barrel project. (*to put it bluntly*)

REVISION The senator's earmark to the bill would, to put it bluntly, fund a worthless pork barrel project.

1. Many newspaper reporters don't know beans about their beats. (*to speak candidly*)
2. We should be able to take the launch to the island. (*the weather having cleared*)

3. Johnson became a viable candidate for governor again. (*the tide of public opinion having turned*)

4. Work in the electronic classrooms had to stop for the day. (*the entire network down*)

4 Appreciate appositive phrases. An **appositive** is a noun or noun phrase that restates or expands the meaning of the words it modifies. Think of appositives as variations on a theme, a second way of naming nouns and giving them more texture. Appositives are placed immediately after the words they modify and are usually surrounded by commas (see Section 36b-2).

Napoleon, the **Emperor of France,** invaded Russia in 1812.

Death Valley, **the largest national park in the continental United States,** blooms with wildflowers in the spring.

Appositives are also routinely introduced by words or phrases such as *or, as, for example, such as,* and *in other words.*

Dachshunds, **or wiener dogs,** are growing in popularity.

Katharine Hepburn's best movies, **including *The African Queen* and *The Philadelphia Story*,** are classics of American cinema.

Most appositives are interchangeable with the words they modify: delete those modified terms and the sentence still makes sense.

APPOSITIVES AS MODIFIERS

Abraham Lincoln, **the first Republican President,** presided over the Civil War.

Halloween, **All Hallows' Eve,** comes two days before All Souls' Day, **also known as the Day of the Dead.**

MODIFIED TERMS REPLACED BY APPOSITIVES

The first Republican President presided over the Civil War.

All Hallows' Eve comes two days before **the Day of the Dead.**

Some appositives—often proper nouns—can't be deleted without blurring the meaning of a sentence. These appositives are not surrounded by commas (see Section 36b-2).

Bob Dylan's masterpiece ***Blonde on Blonde*** is a double album.

Nixon **the diplomat** is more respected by historians than Nixon **the politician.**

EXERCISE 16.18 Turn the phrase(s) in parentheses into appositives and incorporate them into the full sentences preceding them. Be sure to use the right punctuation.

EXAMPLE Sally Ride served on the presidential commission that investigated the 1986 explosion of the space shuttle. (*America's first woman astronaut*; Challenger)

REVISION Sally Ride, America's first woman astronaut, served on the presidential commission that investigated the explosion of the space shuttle *Challenger*.

1. Rudolph Giuliani first gained prominence as a federal prosecutor. (*107th mayor of New York City*)
2. In Anasazi architecture, a prominent feature is the kiva. (*a circular enclosure sunk in the ground and used for ceremonies and meetings*)
3. The technique called pure fresco produces enduring images such as those on the ceiling of the Sistine Chapel. (*painting with plaster stained with pigment; Michelangelo's masterpiece*)
4. The gizzard of a bird is thick with muscles for grinding food. (*a part of the digestive system*)
5. Shakespeare's Scottish play includes three witches. (Macbeth; *the Weird Sisters*)

16d What do clauses do in sentences?

Clauses are groups of related words that have subjects and verbs. As such, they are the framework for most sentences, the parts to which other modifying words and phrases are attached. The four basic sentence types (*simple, compound, complex*, and *compound-complex*) are based on combinations of independent and dependent clauses (see Section 16e).

1 Understand independent clauses. An **independent clause** can stand alone as a complete sentence. Most independent clauses have an identifiable subject and a predicate (that is, a verb plus its auxiliaries and modifiers). Sometimes a subject is understood and is not stated in the clause.

Subject	Predicate
The house	burned.
The dreams we had	came true today.
The children	caught colds.
[You]	Come here at once.

EXERCISE 16.19 Circle the subject and underline the predicate in the following independent clauses. If the subject is understood, write the word *understood* as the subject in parentheses after the sentence.

1. The wood on the deck warped after only one summer.
2. Jeremy has been trying to reach you all day.
3. Attend the rally this afternoon.
4. Keeping focused on schoolwork is hard on weekends.
5. Be careful.

2 Understand dependent clauses. A **dependent clause** is one that cannot stand alone as a complete sentence. Many dependent clauses that have identifiable subjects and predicates are introduced by subordinating conjunctions—words such as *although, because, if, until, when, whenever, while*—that place the dependent clause in relationship to an independent clause.

Subordinating conjunction	Subject	Predicate
When	the house	burned . . .
If	the dreams we had	came true today . . .
Because	the children	caught colds . . .

Dependent clauses can have various functions in a sentence. Easiest to understand are those that act as adjectives or adverbs. Slightly more intricate are dependent clauses that act as nouns (and serve as subjects, objects, or complements). Note that all dependent clauses must work with independent clauses to create complete sentences.

Adjective clauses. Also known as *relative clauses*, adjective clauses attach themselves to nouns or pronouns using one of the relative pronouns: *who, whom, whomever, whose, which*, and *that*.

> Actress Gwyneth Paltrow, **who was born in Los Angeles,** moved to New York when she was 11 years old.
>
> Venus is the planet **that shines brightest in the sky.**

The adverbs *when* and *where* can introduce adjective clauses when the resulting clauses modify nouns, not verbs.

> We enjoy the winter, **when the snow falls.** clause modifies the noun *winter*, not the verb *enjoy*
>
> The immigrants originally settled in those California cities **where jobs were once plentiful.** clause modifies the noun *cities*, not the verb *settled*

Adjective clauses are preceded or surrounded by commas when they are considered nonessential—that is, when they can be removed from a sentence without destroying its coherence. When clauses are essential to the meaning of a sentence, they are not surrounded by commas (see Section 36b-1).

EXERCISE 16.20 Add an adjective clause to each of the following sentences at the point indicated by the ellipses. Remember that adjective clauses are usually introduced by *who, whom, whomever, whose, that*, or *which*. An adjective clause may also begin with *where* or *when* if it modifies a noun instead of a verb.

1. All the students in class who . . . said they supported the Democratic party's proposals.
2. But everyone in the class who . . . opposed the Democrats' policies.
3. Companies that . . . are prospering more today than firms that. . . .
4. The original *Star Wars* trilogy, which . . . , has been joined by a new series of films in the saga.
5. Teens prefer to congregate in places where. . . .

Adverb clauses. **Adverb clauses** work just like adverbs, modifying verbs, adjectives, and other adverbs. They are easy to spot since they are introduced by one of the many subordinating conjunctions, words such as *after, although, as, before, if, since, though, until, when,* and *while.*

Lillian left **before the hail fell.** modifies the verb *left*

The bookcase was not as heavy **as we had expected.** modifies the adjective *heavy*

Rajesh spoke haltingly **whenever Penny looked him in the eye.** modifies the adverb *haltingly*

Sometimes an adverb or subordinate clause modifies an entire sentence or a group of words.

Although the stock market rose slightly, investors had few hopes for a quick recovery.

As subordinate clauses, adverb clauses play a notable role in crafting powerful sentences. For much more about subordination, see Section 16g.

EXERCISE 16.21 Add an adverb clause to each of the following sentences at the point indicated. Remember that adverb clauses are introduced by subordinating conjunctions such as *although, before, since, unless,* and many others.

1. Even though . . . , Americans still vote in low numbers.
2. Many young people put little faith in the social security system because. . . .
3. If . . . the polar ice caps will melt and the level of the oceans will rise.
4. Although they . . . , surprising numbers of children still smoke.

Noun clauses. Whole clauses that behave as nouns are quite common. Such clauses act as subjects or objects, but not as modifiers.

How a computer works is beyond my understanding.
noun clause as subject

The FAA report did not explain **why the jets collided.**
noun clause as direct object

The employment agency gave **whoever applied** a job.
noun clause as indirect object

You may speak to **whomever you wish.**
noun clause as object of a preposition

Because noun clauses are distinctive structures, they can work beautifully in parallel constructions (see Section 16h), as this passage from Abraham Lincoln's Gettysburg Address illustrates.

> The world will little note, nor long remember, **what we say here**; but it can never forget **what they did here**.

EXERCISE 16.22 Underline all the noun clauses in the following sentences. Then identify each clause as either a subject or an object.

1. What politicians say often matters much less than how they say it.
2. Whoever sent a letter of condolence should receive a prompt reply from us.
3. Why so many people care so much about celebrities is beyond my comprehension.
4. Someone had better explain how the dogs got loose.

16e What types of sentences can you write?

Although you'll rarely revise sentences just to make a *simple* sentence *compound* or a *compound* sentence *complex*, recognizing these terms will make it easier for you to diagnose problems in your sentences and to talk about them with peer editors. The most familiar sentence types are all built from just two basic components: independent clauses and dependent (or subordinate) clauses (see Section 16d).

SIMPLE SENTENCE	one independent clause **Windows rattled.**
COMPOUND SENTENCE	independent clause + independent clause **Windows rattled** and **doors shook.**
COMPLEX SENTENCE	dependent clause(s) + one independent clause *As the storm blew,* **windows rattled.**
COMPOUND-COMPLEX SENTENCE	dependent clause(s) + two or more independent clauses *As the storm blew,* **windows rattled** and **doors shook.**

1 Use simple sentences to express ideas clearly and directly.

Simple sentences can attract the attention of readers with the power of their single independent clauses.

> Jesus wept.
>
> I come to bury Caesar, not to praise him.

But don't assume that simple sentences will necessarily be short or without ornament.

> NASA, the federal agency in charge of space exploration, finally has plans for a moon base and eventually for human missions to Mars, the planet most thoroughly explored to date.

As you can see, simple sentences can be expanded by compounding or modifying their subjects, verbs, or objects.

ORIGINAL SENTENCE	Extreme sports worry parents.
VERB EXPANDED	Extreme sports **have captured the attention of a fascinated media but worry many parents.**
OBJECT EXPANDED	Extreme sports worry **police, health-care workers, and many parents.**
EXPANDED SENTENCE	Increasingly popular among teenagers, extreme sports such as BMX biking, bungee jumping, and skateboarding have captured the attention of a fascinated media but worry police, health-care workers, and many parents.

Despite its increased length, the final sentence still has only one independent clause and no dependent clauses, so it remains a simple sentence.

EXERCISE 16.23 Working in small groups, expand the following simple sentences by compounding subjects, objects, and verbs and adding modifying words and phrases as necessary. You may replace a general term (*aircraft*) with particular examples (*helicopters, jets, gliders*). But do not add either full independent or dependent clauses. Make sure the final versions remain simple sentences.

EXAMPLE Bugs scare people.

EXPANDED Tiny spiders, harmless caterpillars, and frail mantises sometimes terrify or even paralyze full-grown adults, from PhDs in physics to NFL linebackers.

1. Pets enrich our lives.
2. The sciences challenge our assumptions.
3. Many activities can damage our health.

2 Use compound and complex sentences to express relationships between clauses. These relationships involve *coordination* when independent clauses are joined to other independent clauses.

The rain fell for days, **but** the city's reservoirs were not filled.

Our fuel pump failed, **so** we were stranded on the expressway.

They involve *subordination* when dependent clauses are joined to independent clauses.

Although the rain fell for days, the city's reservoirs were not filled.

Because our fuel pump failed, we were stranded on the expressway.

To write effective sentences, you need to handle both coordination (see Section 16f) and subordination (see Section 16g) confidently.

16f How does coordination build sentences?

When you coordinate two or more independent clauses, you connect or associate ideas. Independent clauses can stand on their own grammatically, but they grow richer when they enter into coordinate relationships. These relationships can be established in several ways: with *coordinating conjunctions*; with various *correlative constructions*; with semicolons, colons, and dashes; and with *conjunctive adverbs.*

1 Use coordinating conjunctions to join independent clauses. The **coordinating conjunctions** are *and, or, nor, for, but, yet,* and *so.* They express fundamental relationships between ideas: similarity, addition, or sequence (*and*); exception, difference, or contrast (*or, nor, but, yet*); and process or causality (*for, so*). Commas ordinarily precede coordinating conjunctions between clauses (see Section 36c-1).

> The solemn service ended, **and** we went home immediately. sequence
>
> SAT scores in math rose nationally, **but** verbal scores dropped. contrast

Different coordinating conjunctions give readers different signals, so select them carefully. Many writers habitually choose *and* even when another conjunction might express a relationship more precisely.

VAGUE	The statue's hair is carved in early archaic style, **and** its feet show traits of late archaic sculpture.
MORE PRECISE	The statue's hair is carved in early archaic style, **yet** its feet show traits of late archaic sculpture.
VAGUE	Michelangelo's Sistine Chapel ceiling is among the greatest works of Renaissance art, **and** conservators approached the task of cleaning it with great caution.
MORE PRECISE	Michelangelo's Sistine Chapel ceiling is among the greatest works of Renaissance art, **so** conservators approached the task of cleaning it with great caution.

Coordinating conjunctions are also useful for combining sentences that are short, choppy, or repetitive. Linking sentences this way can produce more readable and mature writing.

CHOPPY AND REPETITIVE	We liked the features of the computer. It was too expensive for our budgets. We thought it looked complicated.
COMBINED	We liked the features of the computer, **but** it was too expensive for our budgets **and** it looked complicated.

Relying too much on coordinating conjunctions (especially *and*) to link ideas can be stylistically dangerous. A string of clauses linked by *ands* quickly grows tedious and should be revised, often by making some clauses subordinate (see Section 16g).

TOO MANY *ANDS*	The French physician Nostradamus was active in fighting the plague in the sixteenth century **and** he grew so interested in astrology that he wrote a book of prophecies called *Centuries* **and** it has fascinated readers ever since.

REVISED The French physician Nostradamus, active in fighting the plague in the sixteenth century, grew so interested in astrology that he wrote a book of prophecies called *Centuries,* which has fascinated readers ever since.

EXERCISE 16.24 Use coordinating conjunctions (*and, or, nor, for, but, yet, so*) to create compound sentences by linking the following pairs of independent clauses. Be sure to punctuate the sentences correctly.

1. The housing market finally recovered. Mortgage lenders remained nervous.
2. Citizens' groups invest time and money on get-out-the-vote campaigns. Many voters still skip general elections.
3. Vitamin C is good for colds. Vitamin E keeps the skin in good condition.
4. Most Americans get their news from television. News anchors are powerful people.
5. Tough drunk-driving laws are fair. There is no reason to tolerate inebriated drivers on the roadways.

2 Use correlative constructions to join independent clauses.

Correlatives are conjunctions that work in pairs, expressions such as *if . . . then, either . . . or, just as . . . so,* and *not only . . . but also.* Like coordinating conjunctions, correlatives can be used to form compound sentences that ask readers to examine two ideas side by side.

> **Just as** Napoleon faced defeat in Russia, **so** Hitler saw his dreams of conquest evaporate at the siege of Leningrad.
>
> **Not only** is Captain Janeway a better leader than Kirk, **but** she is **also** a more interesting human being.

EXERCISE 16.25 Create compound sentences by finishing the correlative construction begun for you. Be sure that the sentence you produce is a compound sentence, one with two independent clauses. Punctuate the sentence correctly.

1. If I agree to read *War and Peace* by the end of the summer, then you . . .
2. Either the domestic automakers will find ways to build more economical cars, or . . .

3. Just as eating too much fat contributes to poor physical health, so . . .

4. Not only does the First Amendment protect speech, but it also . . .

3 Use semicolons, colons, and dashes to link independent clauses. Semicolons usually join independent clauses roughly balanced in importance and closely associated in meaning.

> We expected chaos**;** we found catastrophe.
>
> The eyes of the nation were suddenly on the Supreme Court**;** the nine justices could not ignore the weight of public opinion.

Colons are more directive than semicolons: they imply that the second independent clause explains, exemplifies, or expands on the first.

> There was a lesson in the indictment of the mayor**:** even small acts have consequences.

Like colons, dashes can function as conjunctions, connecting clauses with verve and energy. Some writers and editors, however, object to dashes used this way.

> Expect George Ratliff's new film to cause controversy**—**the theme is bold and provocative.
>
> The cathedral of Notre Dame was restored in the nineteenth century**—**its facade had suffered damage during the French Revolution.

See Chapters 37 and 40 for more on semicolons, colons, and dashes.

EXERCISE 16.26 Use a semicolon, a colon, or a dash to link the following independent clauses. Explain why you chose each form of linkage.

1. Don't feel sorry for the sparse and thorny plants you see in a desert. They don't want or need more water.

2. Barren stalks, wicked thorns, and waxy spines are their adaptations to a harsh environment. Such features conserve water or protect the plants from desert animals and birds.

3. Spring rains can create an astonishing desert spectacle. Cacti and other plants explode into colorful bloom.

4. Many animals call the desert home, too, from tiny lizards to scrawny coyotes. They are just as well adapted as the plants.

4 Use conjunctive adverbs with semicolons to join independent clauses. **Conjunctive adverbs** are words such as *consequently, however, moreover, nevertheless, similarly*, and *therefore*. Like any adverb, they can appear at various places in a sentence. But often the adverb follows a semicolon, illuminating the relationship between clauses and holding our attention.

> Members of the zoning board appreciated the developer's position; **however**, they rejected her rezoning request.
>
> The muffler was leaking dangerous fumes; **moreover**, the brake linings were growing thin.

The comma that typically follows a conjunctive adverb in these constructions also gives weight to the word or phrase.

Note that it is the semicolon, not the adverb, that links the independent clauses. That connection becomes more obvious when the conjunctive adverb is moved.

> Members of the zoning board appreciated the developer's arguments; they rejected her rezoning request, **however**.
>
> The muffler was leaking dangerous fumes; the brake linings, **moreover**, were growing thin.

The punctuation surrounding conjunctive adverbs can be confusing. See Section 37a-3 for more details.

EXERCISE 16.27 Use a semicolon and the conjunctive adverb in parentheses to link the following independent clauses. To gain practice punctuating this tricky construction, use the form illustrated in the example—with the semicolon followed immediately by the conjunctive adverb, followed by a comma.

EXAMPLE The aircraft lost an engine in flight. It landed safely. (*however*)

REVISED The aircraft lost an engine in flight; however, it landed safely.

1. Ordinary books are still more convenient than e-books. They employ a technology that doesn't go out of date as quickly—paper. (*moreover*)
2. Most people would save money by using public transportation. They elect to use their private automobiles for daily commuting. (*nevertheless*)

3. American colonists resented England's interference in their political and commercial lives. The thirteen colonies decided to fight for independence. (*therefore*)

4. German and Japanese automakers discovered that they could build quality products cheaper in North America than at home. Foreign computer manufacturers decided to build silicon-chip plants in the United States. (*similarly*)

5. Many cities have been unable to meet air-quality standards. Tougher air-pollution measures have been imposed on their factories and drivers. (*consequently*)

EXERCISE 16.28 Build coordinate sentences by combining the following independent clauses. You may use coordinating conjunctions, correlatives, conjunctive adverbs, semicolons, or colons. Be sure to get the punctuation right.

EXAMPLE	Pencils were invented in the sixteenth century. Erasers were not added to them until 1858.
COORDINATION	Pencils were invented in the sixteenth century; however, erasers were not added to them until 1858.

1. Today, French Impressionist paintings are favorites among art lovers. The public loudly rejected them at their debut in the nineteenth century.

2. Painters such as Renoir and Monet wanted art to depict life. They painted common scenes and ordinary people.

3. Many critics at the time were disturbed by the Impressionists' banal subjects. They thought the Impressionists' paintings themselves looked crude and unfinished.

4. The official Salon refused to hang the Impressionists' works. The painters were forced to exhibit independently.

5. The Impressionists would not abandon their examination of modern life. They would not alter their style to please the critics.

16g How does subordination build sentences?

Use subordination to create complex or compound-complex sentences. Subordinating conjunctions provide the link between main ideas (independent clauses) and secondary ones (dependent or subordinate clauses). Subordination can be achieved with the aid of relative pronouns or subordinating conjunctions. The relative pronouns are *that, what, whatever, which, who, whom, whomever*, and *whose.*

Subordinating conjunctions are more numerous and suggest a wide variety of relationships; see Chart 16.1 below for a partial list. For more on subordinating conjunctions, see Section 16d-2.

Chart 16.1 Some Subordinating Conjunctions

after	in order that	unless
although	now that	until
as	once	when
as if	provided	whenever
as though	rather than	where
because	since	whereas
before	so that	wherever
even if	than	whether
even though	that	which
if	though	while
if only	till	

A subordinating conjunction or a relative pronoun turns an independent clause into a dependent clause that cannot stand alone as a sentence.

INDEPENDENT	I wrote the paper.
DEPENDENT	**While** I wrote the paper . . .
DEPENDENT	The paper **that** I wrote . . .

1 Use subordination to clarify relationships between clauses.

Like most tools for building sentences, subordination provides options for stating and clarifying thoughts. So it's probably misleading to regard the independent clause in a subordinate construction as always more important or more weighty than the dependent clause. In fact, the clauses work together to establish a complex relationship—of time, causality, consequence, contingency, contrast, and so on.

USING SUBORDINATION TO EXPLAIN *WHO* OR *WHAT*

VAGUE The *Morte D'Arthur* includes stories about the Knights of the Round Table. It was the work of Sir Thomas Malory.

CLEARER The *Morte D'Arthur*, **which** was the work of Sir Thomas Malory, includes stories about the Knights of the Round Table.

USING SUBORDINATION TO EXPLAIN *UNDER WHAT CONDITIONS*

VAGUE Many people go into debt. Credit is easy to get.

CLEARER **If** credit is easy to get, many people go into debt.

USING SUBORDINATION TO CLARIFY *CAUSALITY*

VAGUE The film enjoyed a return engagement in theaters. It had won an Academy Award last February.

CLEARER The film enjoyed a return engagement in theaters **because** it won an Academy Award last February.

USING SUBORDINATION TO HIGHLIGHT *CONTRAST*

VAGUE Members of Congress often campaign for a balanced budget. Most of them jealously protect projects in their own districts from cuts in federal spending.

CLEARER **Although** members of Congress often campaign for a balanced budget, most of them jealously protect projects in their own districts from cuts in federal spending.

2 Use subordination to shift the emphasis of sentences.

Generally readers will focus on ideas in your independent clauses. Compare the following sentences, both equally good but with different emphases due to changes in subordination.

> The Supreme Court usually declares efforts to limit the First Amendment unconstitutional, **even though** Congress regularly acts to ban kinds of speech most people find offensive.

Although the Supreme Court usually declares efforts to limit the First Amendment unconstitutional, Congress regularly acts to ban kinds of speech most people find offensive.

The first sentence directs readers' attention to the role of the Supreme Court; the second sentence emphasizes the power of Congress to rein in the First Amendment, despite the Supreme Court. The differences are significant. Notice the same kind of shift in focus in the following pair of sentences.

Jared had never walked a picket line, **even though** he had been a staunch union member for twenty years.

Even though Jared had never walked a picket line, he had been a staunch union member for twenty years.

3 Use subordination to expand sentences. You can often use subordination to combine simple clauses into more graceful or powerful sentences.

CHOPPY	The running back had an ankle injury. He chalked up a hundred-yard afternoon. He had been on the injury list for two months too.
SUBORDINATED	**Although** he had endured an ankle injury and a two-month stay on the injury list, the running back chalked up a hundred-yard afternoon.
CHOPPY	Spectators at the air show were watching in horror. An ultralight aircraft struggled down the runway. It was built of Kevlar and carbon fiber. It hit a stand of trees and disintegrated in a plume of smoke and fire.
SUBORDINATED	**While** spectators at the air show watched in horror, an ultralight aircraft built of Kevlar and carbon fiber struggled down the runway **until** it hit a stand of trees and disintegrated in a plume of smoke and fire.

4 Use subordinate clauses sensibly. If you pile more than two or three subordinate clauses into one sentence, you may confuse readers. Be sure readers can keep up with all the relationships you establish between clauses. If you suspect they can't, simplify those relationships, perhaps by breaking one long complex sentence into several simpler sentences.

TOO MUCH SUBORDINATION	**Although** their book *Chicken Soup for the Soul*, **which** spawned a hugely successful series, **which** has sold millions of copies, was turned down 33 times **while** they tried to find a publisher, Jack Canfield and Mark Victor Hansen did not quit, **which** suggests the importance of persistence.
REVISED	Persistence counts. Jack Canfield and Mark Victor Hansen never gave up, **even though** their book *Chicken Soup for the Soul*, the first in a string of bestsellers, was turned down by 33 publishers.
TOO MUCH SUBORDINATION	An assumption **that** is held by many people in certain cultures, **that** people **who** have college degrees should never have to work with their hands, is often a deterrent to capable young people in those cultures **who** seek nontraditional careers.
REVISED	Many people in certain cultures assume **that** college-educated people should never work with their hands. However, this attitude often deters capable young people from seeking nontraditional careers.

EXERCISE 16.29 Join the following pairs of sentences by making one of the independent clauses subordinate.

1. The original books of Babylonia and Assyria were collections of inscribed clay tablets stored in labeled containers too heavy for one person to move. We think of books as portable, bound volumes.
2. Clay tablets had many drawbacks. They remained the most convenient medium for recording information until the Egyptians developed papyrus around 3000 BC.
3. Egyptian books were lighter than clay tablets but still awkward to carry or read. A single papyrus book comprised several large, unwieldy scrolls.

EXERCISE 16.30 Join the following pairs of sentences by making one of the independent clauses subordinate.

1. Japan was a powerful and thriving nation early in the seventeenth century. Its leaders pursued a policy of isolation from the rest of the world.

2. This policy lasted for more than two centuries. Commodore Matthew Perry of the United States forced Japan to open itself to trade in 1854.

3. Many Japanese resented the presence of Europeans and Americans. They attacked both the foreigners and the rulers (called shoguns) who had yielded to foreign military pressure.

4. A rebellion in 1867 deposed the shogun. The Japanese emperor was restored to power.

16h How does parallelism work?

Sentences are easier to read when closely related ideas within them follow similar language patterns. Subjects, objects, verbs, modifiers, phrases, and clauses can be structured to show such a relationship, called **parallelism.**

PARALLEL WORDS	The venerable principal spoke **clearly, eloquently,** and **honestly**.
PARALLEL PHRASES	**Praised by critics, embraced by common readers,** the novel became a best-seller.
PARALLEL CLAUSES	**It was the best of times, it was the worst of times.**

Items are parallel when they share common grammatical structures.

clearly,
eloquently,
honestly

praised	by	critics,
embraced	by	common readers,

It	was	the	best	of	times,
it	was	the	worst	of	times

The famous opening clauses from Dickens's *A Tale of Two Cities* are exactly parallel. Longer expressions generally show more variation in their parallel terms, especially in the modifiers.

1 Recognize sentence patterns that require parallel construction. When words or phrases come in pairs or triplets, they usually need to be parallel. That is, each element must have the same form: a noun or noun phrase, an adjective or adjective phrase, an adverb or adverb phrase.

The elements of this Navaho rug in the Chinle style are roughly parallel. The rug is by Irene Harvey.

NOUNS/NOUN PHRASES	**Optimism in outlook** and **egotism in behavior**—those are essential qualities for a leader.
ADJECTIVES	The best physicians are **patient, thorough**, and **compassionate**.
ADVERBS	The lawyers presented their case **passionately** and **persuasively.**

Items in a list should also be parallel.

LIST ITEMS	The school board's objectives are clear: **to hire** the best teachers, **to create** successful classrooms, **to serve** the needs of all families, and **to prepare** students for the future.

2 Use parallelism in comparisons and contrasts. Sometimes parallelism adds a stylistic touch, as in the following example. The first version, though acceptable, is not as stylish as the revised and parallel version.

NOT PARALLEL	Pope was a poet of the mind; Byron wrote for the heart.
PARALLEL	Pope was a poet of the mind, Byron a bard for the heart.

Parallelism is required in comparisons following *as* or *than.*

INCORRECT	The city council is *as* likely **to adopt the measure** *as* **vetoing it.**
PARALLEL	The city council is *as* likely **to adopt the measure** *as* **to veto it.**
INCORRECT	**Smiling** takes fewer muscles *than* **to frown.**
PARALLEL	**Smiling** takes fewer muscles *than* **frowning.**

3 Recognize expressions that signal the need for parallel structure. These include the following correlative constructions: *not only . . . but also, either . . . or, neither . . . nor, both . . . and, on the one hand . . . on the other hand.*

As Benjamin Franklin once remarked, *either* **we hang together** *or* **we hang separately.**

A musician's manager sees to it that the performer is *neither* **overworked onstage** *nor* **undervalued in wages.**

We spoke *not only* **to the President** *but also* **to the Speaker of the House.**

On the one hand, **interest rates might be tightened;** *on the other hand,* **prices might be increased.**

4 Use parallelism to show a progression of ideas. You can set up parallel structures within sentences or entire paragraphs. These structures make ideas easier to follow.

Jane Brody, the *New York Times* health writer, says, "Regular exercise comes closer to being a fountain of youth than anything modern medicine can offer." **Exercise halves** the risk of heart disease and stroke, **lowers** the chance of colon cancer, and **reduces** the likelihood of osteoporosis. **It lessens** the chances of developing diabetes and **strengthens** the immune system. **Exercise** even **helps** people overcome depression.

5 Use parallelism for emphasis. Readers really take note when patterns are repeated in longer clauses. By using parallelism of this kind, you will get their attention.

If welfare reform works, **the genuinely needy will** be protected and assisted, **the less conscientious will** be motivated to find work, and **the average taxpayer will** see federal dollars spent more wisely.

You can also use parallelism to express an idea cleverly. Parallelism offers patterns of language perfect for setting up a joke or underscoring sarcasm.

People who serve as their own lawyers in court have *either* **a fool for a client** *or* **a judge for a brother.**

Sentences and paragraphs can be both more economical and more powerful when you set their related ideas in parallel patterns. When revising a passage, look for opportunities to use parallelism.

6 Correct faulty parallelism. It is easy for parallel constructions to go off track. When an item doesn't follow the pattern of language already established in a sentence, it lacks parallelism and disrupts the flow of the sentence. To correct faulty parallelism, first identify the items that ought to be parallel, then choose one of the items as the pattern, and finally revise the remaining items to fit that pattern. Review these examples to see how they have been revised to achieve parallelism.

NOT PARALLEL Criminals are imprisoned for two reasons: **to punish them** and **for the protection of law-abiding citizens.**

PARALLEL Criminals are imprisoned for two reasons:
to punish them and
to protect law-abiding citizens.

NOT PARALLEL When you open a new computer program, it's easy to **feel overwhelmed by the interface, frustrated by the vague documentation,** and **not know what to do next.**

PARALLEL When you open a new computer program, it's easy to
feel overwhelmed by the interface,
frustrated by the vague documentation, and
confused about what to do next.

Sometimes you'll have to decide how much of a parallel structure to repeat. You may want to reproduce a structure in its entirety for emphasis, or you might omit a repeated item for economy.

EMPHASIS We expect you **to** arrive on time, **to** present an ID, **to** have three sharpened pencils, and **to** follow instructions.

ECONOMY We expect you to arrive on time, present an ID, have three sharpened pencils, and follow instructions.

The difference can be striking. Consider what happens when we remove the artful repetition from a famous speech by Winston Churchill that is a model of parallel structure.

EMPHASIS **We shall fight** on the beaches, **we shall fight** on the landing grounds, **we shall fight** in the fields and in the streets, **we shall fight** in the hills; we shall never surrender.

ECONOMY We shall fight on the beaches and landing grounds and in the fields, streets, and hills; we shall never surrender.

No simple style rule can be given for structuring a parallel sentence. But you don't want to be inconsistent within a single sentence, both including and omitting an element that is part of a parallel structure.

WRONG The education bill is expected **to fund** literacy programs for another year, **give** teachers more autonomy in the classroom, **to authorize** a dozen new charter schools, and **make** honors courses more widely available.

The words signaling the parallel structure are inconsistent. Either all the items must be expressed as infinitives (*to fund, to give, to authorize, to make*) or only the first item should include *to.*

REVISED The education bill is expected **to fund** literacy programs for another year, **to give** teachers more autonomy in the classroom, **to authorize** a dozen new charter schools, and **to make** honors courses more widely available.

EXERCISE 16.31 Write a sentence with good parallel structure that incorporates the elements given below. Here is how one example might work.

SUBJECT A football coach: three actions during a game

SAMPLE SENTENCE Controlling his temper as well as he could, the coach paced the sidelines, gnashed his teeth, and tried not to cry during the 66-to-3 drubbing.

1. A shy guy: three actions before asking for a date
2. A senator: two actions in delivering a speech
3. A teacher: three actions in calming a noisy class
4. A schnauzer: three actions to get a cookie

EXERCISE 16.32 Read these sentences and decide which ones have faulty parallel structures. Then revise those in which you find inconsistent or faulty patterns.

1. On opening night at the new Tex-Mex restaurant, the manager called the servers together to be sure they understood all the items on the menu, could pronounce *fajitas*, and that they would remember to ask, "Salt or no salt?" when customers ordered margaritas.
2. Offering the best Southwestern cuisine and to serve the hottest salsa were the restaurant's two goals.
3. But customers soon made it clear that they also expected real barbecue on the menu, so the manager added slow-cooked beef ribs smothered in

sauce, hefty racks of pork ribs dripping with fat, and there was smoked sausage on the menu too that was juicy and hot.

4. Servers had to explain to tourists that one was supposed to eat beef ribs with one's fingers, wrap one's own fajitas, and to bite into jalapeños very carefully.

16i How do you craft balanced sentences?

Effective balanced sentences merge the best attributes of coordination and parallelism (see Sections 16f and 16h). In a **balanced sentence,** a coordinating conjunction links two or more independent clauses that are roughly parallel in structure. The result is a sentence so intentionally designed and rhythmic that it draws special attention to its subject. For that reason, balanced sentences are often memorable and quotable.

> And so, my fellow Americans, ask not what your country can do for you; ask what you can do for your country.
>
> —John F. Kennedy, Inaugural Address

> We live here and they live there. We black and they white. They got things and we ain't. They do things and we can't. It's just like living in jail.
>
> —Richard Wright, *Native Son*

In your writing you might find balanced sentences effective for openings and closings, where you want readers to remember a major point. But they may seem out of place in lighter, more colloquial writing.

In crafting a balanced sentence, you'll almost always begin with two independent clauses joined to make a compound sentence (see Section 16f). Then you can sharpen the relationship between the clauses by making them reasonably parallel. You may need to revise both clauses quite heavily.

COMPOUND New programs to end adult illiteracy may be costly, **but** the alternative is continued support of even more expensive welfare programs.

BALANCED New adult literacy programs may be costly, **but** current welfare programs are costlier still.

COMPOUND Most people involved in education and business take computers for granted, **yet** that doesn't mean these people really understand what computers do.

BALANCED Most people in business and education take computers for granted; few understand what computers do.

EXERCISE 16.33 Complete the following sentences in ways that make them balanced.

1. If Alfred Hitchcock is the master of suspense, then . . .
2. Politics makes strange bedfellows, and . . .
3. If all the world is really a stage, then . . .
4. In theory, college seems the surest pathway to economic security; in practice, . . .
5. When the going gets tough, the tough get going, but when . . .

16j How do you craft cumulative sentences?

The intricate architecture of balanced sentences (see Section 16i) can make them seem formal and even old-fashioned. A structure perhaps better suited to contemporary writing, which tends to be informal, is the **cumulative sentence** in which an independent clause is followed by a series of modifiers, sometimes simple, sometimes quite complex.

> The apprehensive mood was shot through with shafts of gaiety, **as a black sky is streaked with lightning.**
>
> —Maya Angelou, "Champion of the World"

> She is simply hard, **a straight shooter, a woman clean of received wisdom and open to what she sees.**
>
> —Joan Didion, "Georgia O'Keeffe"

In writing a cumulative sentence, you add on to an original thought, expanding and enriching it by attaching modifying words, phrases, and clauses. The effect is artful but also easy and natural. In our daily speech we often state an idea and then explain or embellish it; cumulative sentences can convey the same informality.

> Dusty? Of course, it's dusty—this is Utah. But it's good dust, **good red Utahn dust, rich in iron, rich in irony.**
>
> —Edward Abbey, *Desert Solitaire*

Writing effective cumulative sentences takes practice, but the habit of addition is easy to acquire and especially useful in writing descriptive and narrative passages. Almost any of the modifying phrases and clauses described in Sections 16b through 16d can be attached gracefully to the ends of clauses.

1 Attach adjectives and adverbs. Either as individual words or as complete phrases, these modifiers play an important role in shaping cumulative sentences.

> It was a handsome sedan, **black as shimmering oil, deeply chromed, and sleek as a rocket.**
>
> The storm pounded the coast **so relentlessly that residents wondered whether the skies would ever clear again.**

2 Attach prepositional phrases. You can place prepositional phrases (see Section 16c-1) at the ends of sentences to describe or modify nouns or pronouns within the sentence.

> The church was all white plaster and gilt, **like a wedding cake in the public square.**

When the object of a closing prepositional phrase is artfully compounded, the effect can be memorable. In the following example, dust is described as settling *upon* a rich variety of plants.

> A veil of dust floats above the sneaky, snaky old road from here to the highway, drifting gently downward to settle **upon the blades of the yucca, the mustard-yellow rabbitbrush, the petals of the asters and autumn sunflowers, the umbrella-shaped clumps of blooming buckwheat.**
>
> —Edward Abbey, *Desert Solitaire*

3 Attach appositives and free modifiers. You can conclude cumulative sentences with modifiers that rename someone or something within the body of a sentence. These modifiers act like appositives (see Section 16c-4), but they may be separated in distance from the noun or pronoun they embellish. Here are two such *free modifiers* from Bob Costas's eulogy for baseball legend Mickey Mantle.

> And more than that, he [Mickey Mantle] was a presence in our lives—**a fragile hero to whom we had an emotional attachment so strong and lasting that it defied logic.**
>
> He got love—**love for what he had been; love for what he made us feel; love for the humanity and sweetness that was always there mixed in with the flaws and all the pain that wracked his body and his soul.**
>
> —Bob Costas, *Eulogy for Mickey Mantle*

Notice the way these modifiers are introduced by dashes. Notice, too, that the modifying phrase itself can be quite complex and much longer than the original independent clause.

4 Attach clauses. You can experiment with both relative and subordinate clauses (see Section 16d) at the ends of sentences, compounding them and keeping them roughly parallel.

> Mother Teresa was a woman **who gave her life to the poor and gained the admiration of the world for her service.**
>
> The astronaut argued that Americans need to return to the moon **because our scientific explorations there have only begun and because we need a training ground for more ambitious planetary expeditions.**

EXERCISE 16.34 Combine the following short sentences into one longer cumulative sentence.

EXAMPLE Virginia adopted the dog. It was a friendly pup with skinny legs. It had a silly grin.

COMBINED Virginia adopted the dog, a friendly pup with skinny legs and a silly grin.

1. Caesar was my friend. He had been faithful to me. He had been just to me.

2. Dr. Kalinowski recommended that her patient take up racquetball. It would ease his nerves. It would quicken his reflexes. It would tone his muscles. The muscles had grown flaccid from years of easy living.

3. The members of the jury filed into the courtroom. The members of the jury looked sullen and unhappy. They looked as if they'd eaten cactus for lunch.

4. The reviewer thought the book was a disappointment. It did not summarize the current state of knowledge. It did not advance research in the field.

CHAPTER

17 How Do You Write Stylish Sentences?

Good sentences must be carefully and grammatically constructed, but there's more to writing well than simple correctness. Successful writing uses words much as successful advertisements use color and images—to create powerful effects on an audience. Think about the highly successful advertising campaign for the original Apple iPod. Of course, the iPod needed to be technically and mechanically sound in order for consumers to buy it, but it became the best-selling product of its kind partly because Apple created a hip, modern image with which consumers could identify.

Just as there's more to the iPod than its ability to store and play songs, there's more to effective writing than crafting competent sentences. To affect readers powerfully, you'll want to compose sentences that are varied, rhythmic, rich in detail, and sometimes even memorable. This chapter discusses *some* ways to give your sentences that subtle yet powerful quality called *style*.

Examine closely these still images from a now classic advertisement for the Apple iPod. What words would you use to describe the product's "style"? How do the colors, images, and words in the ad work together to create this style? Would the product have seemed as appealing if the ad had merely listed the iPod's technical features? Now, think about your writing. What words would you use to describe your typical writing style? Straightforward? Ornate? Informal? In what writing situations is your typical writing style most effective? In what situations does it work less well?

17a What are agent/action sentences?

You can build readable sentences by using an agent/action pattern. In agent/action sentences, clear subjects (agents) perform strong actions.

agent /action	agent /action
The **pilot** *ejected.*	My **grandmother** *makes* hand-sewn quilts.

Agent/action sentences are highly readable because they answer these important questions:

- What's happening?
- Who's doing it (and to what or to whom)?

1 Whenever you can, make persons or things the subjects of your sentences and clauses. Readers take more interest in what you're writing if people are involved. And people usually are—most issues touch on human lives, one way or another.

WITHOUT PEOPLE Although the federally funded student loan program has made education accessible to a broader population, the increasing default rate among that group has had a significant effect on the program.

WITH PEOPLE Hundreds of thousands of **young people** have been able to go to college because of federally funded student loans, but **students** who have defaulted on their loans may be jeopardizing the program for **others.**

Whenever you can, start your sentences with references to people.

EXERCISE 17.1 Recast these sentences in agent/action patterns that show more clearly who is doing what to whom. Break the sentences into shorter ones if you like.

1. Raising $3 million to renovate the drama facilities on campus was the goal of Lincoln Brown, the new college president.
2. The experience of having played Horatio in a college production of *Hamlet* had been influential in convincing President Brown of the value of the performing arts.

3. Helping President Brown to convince wealthy donors that restoring and expanding the old theater was a good idea was a small group of actors, all of them alumni of the school.

4. An unexpected donation of $1 million made by a prominent local banker who had once played Hamlet gave the actors and President Brown reason to celebrate.

2 Don't overload the subjects of sentences. Readers will get lost if you bury subjects under abstract words and phrases. When revising, you may have to find the central idea of a particularly difficult or murky sentence. Ask yourself, "What is its key word or concept?" Make that key word your subject or starting point. In the following sentence, the main idea is buried in an opening noun phrase twenty-four words long.

OVERLOADED SUBJECT **The encouragement of total reliance on the federally sponsored student loan program for medical students from low-income families to pay their way through school** causes many young doctors to begin their careers deeply in debt.

What is this sentence about? Many readers would say "young doctors." See what happens when the sentence is revised to focus on them.

REVISED **Many young doctors from low-income families** begin their careers deeply in debt because they have relied totally on federal student loans to pay their way through medical school.

EXERCISE 17.2 Rewrite the following sentences to simplify their convoluted openings.

1. Among those who are unhappy about the lack of morality and standards in the television shows coming from Hollywood today and who would like to see pressure on producers for more responsible programming are activists from remarkably different political groups.

2. The elimination of hurtful gender, racial, and ethnic stereotypes, particularly from situation comedies, where they are sometimes a core element of the humor, is a key demand of political groups on the left.

3. TV's almost complete disregard of the role religion plays in the daily lives of most ordinary people, evident in the fact that so few sitcom characters ever go to church or pray, irritates groups on the political right.

4. Raising the specter of censorship and equating every attack on Hollywood to an assault on the First Amendment has been the quick response of many television producers to criticism of their products.

3 Choose verbs that convey strong actions. Strung-out verb phrases such as *give consideration to* and *make acknowledgment of* slow down your writing. Get rid of them; focus on the action. Ask, "What's happening?" and try to express that action in a single lively verb.

DULL VERBS	Some groups who **are in opposition to** the death penalty **believe that there is an obligation to challenge** its morality.
STRONGER VERBS	Some groups who **oppose** the death penalty **challenge** its morality.

Identifying the action may also help you spot the real agent in a sentence, as in this example.

DULL VERB	American society **has** long **had** a fascination with celebrities.
STRONGER VERB	Celebrities **have** long **fascinated** Americans.

EXERCISE 17.3 Rewrite the following sentences to pinpoint their centers of action and to make their verbs stronger.

1. The fears of many prospective students over age 30 are understandable to college counselors.

2. Many such students are apprehensive about seeing textbooks, syllabi, and assignments for the first time in a decade or more.

3. In many schools, counselors have proceeded to establish special groups or programs for older students so that their feelings of dislocation and discomfort will be relieved.

4. The sobering realization among those responsible for demographic studies of colleges is that older students may hold the key to financial solvency for many institutions.

4 Make sure subjects can do what their verbs demand. Verbs describe actions that subjects perform: *butter melts*; *scholars read.* In most cases, you know when you've written nonsense: *butter reads*; *scholars melt.* But as sentences grow longer, you can sometimes lose the logical connection between subjects and predicates, a problem described as **faulty predication.**

FAULTY PREDICATION The **narrative structure** of Aretha Franklin's song **begins** as a child and continues through her adult life.

Can *narrative structures begin as children*? Unlikely. The writer is probably thinking either of a character in the song or of Aretha Franklin, the singer. The sentence has to be revised.

REVISED In Aretha Franklin's song, the **narrative structure follows** the life of a character from childhood to adulthood.

Notice how heavily the sentence had to be revised to make it work. Just swapping one verb for another won't always solve the problem.

EXERCISE 17.4 Revise any of the following sentences in which the subject cannot logically perform the action described by the verb. Try to explain what is wrong with the original verb choices, which are boldfaced.

1. Hundreds of miles from any city or large airport, Big Bend National Park in Texas **endeavors** an experience of pristine isolation unlike that of busier parks such as Yellowstone.
2. The park **comprehends** mountain, desert, and riparian environments.
3. Although coyotes, road runners, and javelinas are common, a few lucky visitors also **apprehend** mountain lions and bears.
4. Other national parks can **profess** more spectacular landmarks than Big Bend, but few **entertain** a more remarkable outdoor experience.

5 Replace *to be* verbs whenever possible. Though the verbs *is*, *are*, and their variants are often unavoidable, they're not as interesting as verbs that do things. When you use action verbs instead of *to be* verbs, you bring your readers into the action of the sentence immediately.

DULL VERBS It **is** the tendency of adolescents **to be more concerned** about the approval of others in their age group than they **are** about the values parents are trying to instill in them.

ACTION VERBS Adolescents **crave** the approval of their peers and often **resist** their parents' values.

EXERCISE 17.5 Replace the *to be* forms in these sentences with active and more lively verbs. The original verbs are boldfaced. (It may help if you make the agent a person or a concrete object.)

1. There **was** an inclination to protest among restaurateurs when the city decided to increase the number of health inspectors.
2. It **had been** the determination of city officials, however, that many restaurants **were** not in a state of compliance with local health ordinances.
3. The occurrence of rodent droppings in pantries and the storage of meat at incorrect temperatures **were** also matters of concern to several TV reporters.
4. It was the hope of both politicians and restaurateurs that there **would be** a quick solution to this embarrassing problem.

6 Reduce the number of passive verbs. Passive verb constructions (see Section 23e) often make sentences harder to read. It's easy to spot a sentence with a passive verb: the subject doesn't perform the action; rather, the action is *done* to the subject. In effect, the object switches to the subject position, as in the following sentences.

subj. action

Madison **was selected** by Representative Barton for an appointment to the Air Force Academy.

subj. action

The candidate **had been nominated** for the academic honor by several teachers.

Passive verbs are always constructed with some form of *be* plus the past participle. (See Section 23b for an explanation of what a past participle is.)

be + past participle

The controversial sitcom **has been cancelled** by the network.

be + past participle

The cancellation **was caused** by low ratings and bad reviews.

Notice that not every sentence with a form of the verb *to be* is passive, especially when *be* is used as a linking verb.

The producers of the show **were surprised** that audiences seemed unwilling to watch a comedy about organic farmers.

Nor is every sentence with a past participle passive. Perfect tenses, for example, also use the past participle. (See Sections 23a-3 and 32a for an explanation of perfect tenses.) Here's an active verb in the past perfect tense.

Critics too **had balked** at the program's premise.

To identify a passive verb form, look for *both* the past participle and a form of *be*.

The sitcom's pilot episode **had been applauded** by test audiences when it **had been shown** in Portland and Austin.

When you have identified a passive form, locate the word that actually performs the action in the sentence and consider making it the subject.

subj. performer of action

ORIGINAL PASSIVE *Madison* **was selected** by Representative Barton for an appointment to the Air Force Academy.

subj. action

REVISED ACTIVE *Representative Barton* **selected** Madison for an appointment to the Air Force Academy.

In many cases, the revised sentence will be clearer and more succinct. But not every passive verb can or should be made active. Sometimes you simply don't know who or what performs an action.

Hazardous road conditions **have been predicted.**

Our flight **has been canceled.**

EXERCISE 17.6 Identify the passive verbs in the following sentences and then rewrite those that might be improved by changing passive verbs to active verbs.

1. The writing of research papers is traditionally dreaded by students everywhere.
2. The negative attitudes can be changed by writers themselves if the assignments are regarded by them as opportunities to explore and improve their thinking and, potentially, the lives of others.
3. When conventional topics are chosen by researchers, apathy is likely to be experienced by them and their readers alike.
4. But if writers are encouraged to choose topics in their communities that can be explored through books, articles, fieldwork, interviews, and online investigations, a better project will be produced.

17b How can you achieve clarity?

When something is well written, a careful reader can move along steadily without backtracking to puzzle over its meaning. You can work toward this goal by using a number of strategies.

1 Use specific details. Writing that uses a lot of abstract language is often harder to understand and less pleasurable to read than writing that states ideas more specifically. Abstract terms such as *health-care provider system, positive learning environment*, and *two-wheeled vehicle* are usually harder to grasp than concrete terms such as *hospital, classroom*, and *Harley*. Of course you have to use abstract words sometimes; it's impossible to discuss big ideas without them. But the more you use specific details, the clearer and more textured your sentences will be.

An especially effective way to add texture to sentences is to *downshift*—that is, to state a general idea and then provide more and more details. The resulting sentences will be crisp and interesting.

> Toi Soldier was a magnificent black Arabian stallion, **a sculpture in ebony, his eyes large and dark, his graceful head held high on an arched neck.** He was a competitor in any Arabian horse show, **equally poised in equitation classes or under harness.**

Downshifting is the principle behind many cumulative sentences (see Section 16j).

EXERCISE 17.7 Working in a group, develop one of the following sentences into a brief paragraph by downshifting. Each subsequent sentence should add more detail to the original statement.

1. Colleges could do more to get students involved in their communities.
2. It's not surprising that so few Americans speak a foreign language.
3. The commercialization of sports has changed more than just professional athletics.

2 State ideas positively. Negative statements can be surprisingly hard to read. When you can, turn negative statements into positive ones. Your writing will seem more confident and may be more economical.

DIFFICULT Do we have the right **not to be victims** of street crime?

CLEARER Do we have the right **to be safe** from street crime?

DIFFICULT It is **not unlikely** that I will attend the conference.

CLEARER **I will probably** attend the conference.

EXERCISE 17.8 Revise the following sentences to restate negative ideas more positively or clearly where such a change makes for a better sentence. Not all sentences may need revision.

1. It would not be awful if you never turn in a paper late.
2. Would it ever not be inappropriate not to say "Hello" to an ex-spouse?
3. What do I think of your new leopard-skin pillbox hat? Why, I'd say it's not unattractive.

3 "Chunk" your writing. Consider breaking lengthy sentences into more manageable clauses, or creating a list to present unusually complex information. People can comprehend only so much material at one time.

TOO LONG

Citing an instance in which a 16-year-old student was working 48 hours a week at Burger King in order to pay for a new car and simultaneously trying to attend high school full time, New York educators have recently proposed legislation that prohibits high school students from working more than 3 hours on a school night, limits the total time they can work in a week to 17 hours when school is in session, and fines employers who violate these regulations as much as $2,000.

In many respects this long sentence is admirable. It uses parallelism to keep a complex array of information in order. Yet most readers would probably like to see its information broken into more digestible chunks.

REVISED

Educators in New York have recently proposed legislation that prohibits high school students from working more than 3 hours on a school night. In support of the proposal, they cite the example of a 16-year-old student working 48 hours a week at Burger King in order to pay for a new car while simultaneously trying to attend high school full time. The proposed law would limit the total time students can work in a week to 17 hours when school is in session and would fine employers who violate these regulations as much as $2,000.

Another efficient way to cut very specific or technical information to manageable size is to create a list. Lists give readers a sense of order and direction. Which of the following passages do you find more readable?

To get started with your new computer, unpack it, saving the Styrofoam packing; position it away from sources of heat; plug the keyboard, mouse, and printer into the designated ports on the back of the machine; and, finally, attach the power cord to the computer and plug it in.

To get started with your new computer:

1. **Unpack** it, saving the Styrofoam packing.
2. **Position** your computer away from sources of heat.
3. **Plug** the keyboard, mouse, and printer into the designated ports on the back of the machine.
4. **Attach** the power cord to the computer and plug it in.

Notice that all the items in the list are parallel (see Section 16h).

EXERCISE 17.9 Make the following sentences more readable by breaking them into manageable chunks.

1. Parents are often ambivalent about having their high school–aged children work because almost inevitably it causes a conflict between the

demands of schoolwork and extracurricular activities (such as sports, civic clubs, debate teams, band) and the expectations of employers, a balance many high school students are simply not mature enough to handle on their own, often choosing the immediate material goods furnished by a job over the less obvious benefits afforded by a good education.

2. Many parents, however, aware of the limitations of their own education in school, may believe that it is no more important to learn square roots, the capitals of Asian countries, or the metrics of Chaucer's poetry than it is to discover how tough it is to deal with customers, show up on time, manage other workers, or pay taxes, experiences that an after-school job will quickly give most teenagers, whose images of work are badly distorted by films and television.

4 Use charts and graphs to present quantitative information. Readers grasp numbers and statistics much more quickly when they see them presented visually. See Section 18d for more on how charts and graphs work and for advice on incorporating them into your writing.

Take Control

17c How can you reduce wordiness?

For those who aspire to be good writers, the war against "clutter" never ends. Clutter consists of clichés, strung-out phrases, pointless repetitions, and florid descriptions. But wait until you have a first draft before you start trimming your prose. Many writers overstuff a first draft because they want to get all their ideas down. That's fine: it *is* easier to cut material during revision than to create more.

1 Condense sprawling phrases. Some long-winded expressions slow a reader's way into a sentence, especially at the beginning.

WHY WRITE . . .	WHEN YOU COULD WRITE . . .
in the event that	if
in light of the fact that	since
on the grounds that	because
regardless of the fact that	although
on the occasion of	when

in today's society	now
it is clear that	clearly
on an everyday basis	routinely
with regard/respect to	for

We are so accustomed to these familiar but wordy expressions that we don't notice how little they convey.

WORDY **At this point in time,** the committee hasn't convened.

REVISED The committee hasn't convened **yet.**

EXERCISE 17.10 Revise the following sentences to eliminate the sprawling, wordy, or clichéd opening phrase.

1. On the occasion of the newspaper's seventy-fifth anniversary, the governor visited the editorial offices.
2. Regardless of the fact that I have revised the speech three times, I still don't like my conclusion.
3. In the modern American society in which we live today, many people still attend church regularly.
4. By virtue of the fact that flood insurance rates are so high, many people go uninsured, risking their property.

2 Cut nominalizations. **Nominalizations** are nouns made by adding endings to verbs and adjectives. The resulting words tend to be long and abstract. Worse, nominalizations are often grafted onto terms that are themselves recent coinages of dubious merit.

WORD	NOMINALIZATION
connect	connect**ivity**
customize	customi**zation**
historicize	historici**zation**
utilize	utili**zation**
prioritize	prioriti**zation**
victimize	victimi**zation**

Unfortunately, writers in college, business, and government sometimes think that readers will be more impressed by prose laden with these grand abstractions. However, writing full of nominalizations can exhaust readers and often obscures meaning. When possible, replace nominalizations with simpler terms.

WORDY A **falsification** of evidence has occurred.

REVISED Someone falsified evidence.

WORDY An **intensification** of volcanic activity in Alaska is expected.

REVISED Volcanic activity in Alaska will likely intensify.

EXERCISE 17.11 Revise the following sentences to reduce nominalizations that make the prose wordy. You may make other cuts as well.

1. The registrar's note is a clarification of the school's admissions policy.
2. It is a matter of substantial disputation among sociologists whether the gentrification of urban neighborhoods is a beneficial process to inner-city residents.
3. The utilization of creative writing in more and more elementary language arts classes is an indication that many teachers are feeling dissatisfaction with older, more rigid approaches to language instruction.
4. The systems analyst convinced us that the connectivity and interchangeability of our equipment gave our new computer system enhanced potential.

3 Condense long verb phrases to focus on the action. To show tense and mood, verb phrases need auxiliaries and helping verbs: I *could have* gone; she *will be* writing. But many verb phrases are strung out by unnecessary clutter.

WHY WRITE . . .	WHEN YOU COULD WRITE . . .
give consideration to	consider
make acknowledgment of	acknowledge
have doubts about	doubt
is reflective of	reflects
has an understanding of	understands
put the emphasis on	emphasize

Similarly, don't clutter active verbs with expressions such as *start to, manage to,* and *proceed to.* They usually don't add much to a sentence.

CLUTTERED VERBS Malls and supermarkets **always manage to irritate me** when they **start to display** Christmas paraphernalia immediately after Halloween.

REVISED Malls and supermarkets **irritate me** when they **display** Christmas paraphernalia immediately after Halloween.

EXERCISE 17.12 Revise the following sentences to condense long verb phrases into more active expressions.

1. Many people are of the opinion that the federal government has grown too large.
2. An almost equal number of people hold the conviction that many citizens have need of services provided by federal programs.
3. This difference in public opinion is indicative of the dilemma faced by many politicians today.
4. Their constituents often are not in favor of paying for exactly the services that they have expectations of getting.

4 Eliminate doublings and redundancies. *Doublings* are expressions in which two words say exactly the same thing. One word can usually be cut.

trim ~~and slim~~ ~~proper and~~ fitting
ready ~~and able~~ willing ~~and eager~~

Redundancies are expressions in which a concept is repeated unnecessarily.

Our entire society has been corrupted by ~~the evil of~~ greed.

Mother's holiday feast on the table was surrounded by our family ~~sitting around it~~.

One might argue, in some cases, that doublings subtly expand the intended meaning. But they usually don't.

Thanksgiving fosters a sense of belonging ~~and togetherness~~.

I am of two worlds, which are forever at odds ~~with each other~~.

Many habitual expressions are in fact redundant.

WHY WRITE . . .	WHEN YOU COULD WRITE . . .
trading activity was heavy	trading was heavy
of a confidential nature	confidential
her area of specialization	her specialty
red in hue	red

Avoid the repetition of major words in a sentence—unless there are good reasons to emphasize particular terms.

REPETITIOUS When college **friends come** together, you'll inevitably find some **friends** who **come** from the same background.

REVISED When college **friends come** together, you'll inevitably find some who share the same background.

EXERCISE 17.13 Rewrite the following sentences to reduce redundancy and wordiness.

1. I realized that if I were ever to reach law school, I would have to increase my competitiveness in the skill of written prose composition.
2. *Ellen* to me is a daytime talk type of television show.
3. Many traits characterize a truly excellent student adviser, and one of the more important qualities, if not the most important quality, is a lively personality.

5 Eliminate surplus intensifiers. An adverb that functions as an **intensifier** should add weight or power to an expression. You waste its energy when you use it carelessly.

WHY WRITE . . .	WHEN YOU COULD WRITE . . .
We're **completely** finished.	We're finished.
It's an **awful** tragedy.	It's a tragedy.
I'm **totally** exhausted.	I'm exhausted.
That's **absolutely** pointless.	That's pointless.
The work is **basically** done.	The work is done.

EXERCISE 17.14 Review the intensifiers in the following passage and cut any words or phrases you regard as unnecessary.

> The Grand Canyon is a quite unique geological treasure in northwestern Arizona, basically formed by the relentless power of the Colorado River cutting a gorge for many, many eons through solid rock. Standing at the edge of the canyon is a totally awesome experience. The canyon walls drop far into the depths, thousands of feet, a seriously deep drop, exposing very different layers of limestone, sandstone, and volcanic rock. These really magnificent canyons recede into the distance like ancient castles, an absolutely remarkable panorama of color and shadow.

6 Cut down on expletive constructions. **Expletives** are short expressions such as *it was, there are*, and *this is* that function like starting blocks for pushing into a sentence or clause. For example:

It was a dark and stormy night.

There were five of us huddled in the basement.

There are too many gopher holes on this golf course!

It is a proud day for Bluefield State College.

Some expletives are unavoidable. But using them habitually to open your sentences will make your prose tiresome. In many cases, sentences will be stronger without the expletives.

WITH EXPLETIVE	Even though **it is** the oldest manufacturer of automobiles, Mercedes-Benz remains innovative.
EXPLETIVE CUT	The oldest manufacturer of automobiles, Mercedes-Benz remains innovative.

WHY WRITE . . .	WHEN YOU COULD WRITE . . .
There is a desire for	We want
There are reasons for	For several reasons
There was an expectation	They expected
It is clear that	Clearly
It is to be hoped	We hope

EXERCISE 17.15 Revise the following sentences to eliminate unnecessary expletive constructions.

1. There are many different ways to fulfill the science requirement at most colleges.
2. It is usually the case that liberal arts majors are more suited for science courses that are geared to the history of the field.
3. Enrolling in a course in the natural sciences is a challenge, and it should be taken seriously.
4. This is a point that many science teachers make early in a term, but it is a concept that many students don't grasp until after their first examination.

7 Cut the number of prepositional phrases. Stylistically, prepositional phrases are capable of dignity and grandeur, thanks to their clarity and simplicity.

> **In the beginning,** God created heaven and earth.
>
> . . . and that government **of the people, by the people, for the people,** shall not perish from the earth.

But that very simplicity can disappear if you pack too many prepositional phrases of similar length and tempo into one sentence.

TOO MANY PREPOSITIONS — **In** late summer **on** the road **from** our town **into** the country, we expected to find raspberries **in** the fields **near** the highway **by** the recent construction.

REVISED — We expected to find late summer raspberries **on** the country road, **near** the recent construction.

Also avoid strings of prepositional phrases that congeal around abstract nouns, making sentences thick and hard to read. In the example, the abstract nouns are boldfaced and prepositional phrases are underlined.

WORDY — The current **proliferation** of credit cards among college students is the result of extensive **marketing** by banking **institutions** which see college students in terms of their future **affluence**.

Revise a cluttered sentence by looking for the center of action: *who* is doing *what* to *whom*?

> **REVISED** Banks today are marketing credit cards to college students because they see them as affluent future customers.

For more on prepositional phrases, see Section 16c-1.

EXERCISE 17.16 Revise the following sentences to reduce the number of prepositional phrases where they make the sentences awkward or monotonous. Some sentences may require extensive revision.

1. J.R.R. Tolkien was the author of one of the most popular series of fantasy novels about the battle between good and evil forces in the distant past of the fictional world of Middle Earth.
2. Tolkien's series *The Lord of the Rings* focuses on the adventures of a genial hobbit by the name of Frodo Baggins and his sidekick by the name of Sam who, along with Frodo, becomes involved in the race to destroy a ring of magical but evil power.
3. The novels cover a long period of time, focusing on the colossal struggle for the magical ring and for the future of Middle Earth that goes on between Frodo and his allies and the forces of Sauron, the leader of the forces of evil.
4. In his own love of adventure, in his fascination with tales of heroism, and in his faith in the redemptive power of friendship, Tolkien resembled his beloved characters.

8 Cut relative pronouns (*that, which, who, whom*) when you can do it without changing the meaning of a sentence.

Relative pronouns introduce many modifying clauses (see Section 16d-2). You can often cut them for economy.

> **WORDY** The book **that I had quoted** was missing.
>
> **REVISED** The book **I had quoted** was missing.

EXERCISE 17.17 Rewrite these sentences to practice eliminating relative pronouns (*that, which, who, whom*) that might be contributing to wordiness. Retain any such pronouns necessary for clarity.

1. Some of the people who might be willing to endure a little less environmental consciousness are parents of children whom environmental education programs have turned into Green Police.
2. Second graders who used to read Dr. Seuss stories suddenly can't wait to locate "Tips to Save Our Planet" in the daily newspaper, which carries dozens of slick, unrecyclable inserts.
3. Full of moral superiority, youngsters who can barely read are circulating petitions that condemn industries that emit CO2.
4. Shrewd are the parents who steer their children's activist impulses in productive directions by asking them to read supermarket labels and to find the items that are marked "Recyclable."

9 Condense sentences into clauses and clauses into phrases or words. Often a forceful word or two can do the work of several. Say more with less.

ORIGINAL Queen Elizabeth I was a woman of a complex and sensuous nature. She seemed to have great passion for many men, yet she never came close to marrying any of her suitors.

CONDENSED Complex and sensuous, Queen Elizabeth I seemed to love men, yet she never came close to marrying.

ORIGINAL Thanksgiving is a time of holiday celebration for all of us to be together for the simple purpose of enjoying each other's company.

CONDENSED Thanksgiving is a time for enjoying each other's company.

EXERCISE 17.18 Rewrite the following sentences to reduce clutter by substituting single words for wordy phrases. Rearrange the sentences as necessary.

1. In the event that you are in proximity to Greene County this weekend, you should not miss the opportunity to visit the autumn Concours d'Elegance, an annual exhibit of classic cars.
2. There is the possibility that you may have the chance to touch and feel many quite unusual and different vehicles, from dowdy Edsels with gearshift buttons in the middle of their steering wheels to tiny Corvairs with air-cooled engines under louvered deck lids at the back.

3. However, don't expect to make an inspection of the more unique makes and the basically timeless art of such prestigious automakers as Bugatti, Duesenberg, or Hispano-Suiza.

4. Regardless of the fact that Greene County's show is a small show, you can take great satisfaction in examining quite handsome old Hudsons, Nashes, Jaguars, and Corvettes that are tended by owners who are willing and eager to talk about them at great length.

Taking Control

Cut excess verbiage

If an instructor describes your writing as wordy, ponderous, heavy, or slow-moving, you can usually fix the problem by cutting excessive verbiage. Practice on a paper you have already written. Begin by checking the word count on the document (you'll find a function for this under "Tools"), and then aim to reduce it by 10-15% *without losing any content*. Below is a paragraph from the NCAA's "Report on the Sportsmanship and Fan Behavior Summit," which dealt with the problem of fans rioting after athletic events. Below the 96-word original is a second, carefully edited version that is 18 words shorter. Which version is more readable? Why?

Opening is slow and formal.

Not clear *who* should do *what*.

Subject of the second sentence is vague abstraction: *positive relations.*

Conclusion is thick with prepositional phrases and doublings.

Original version: Because celebratory riots are not restricted to sporting events, the aforementioned campus/community communication techniques also should be practiced for non-athletics events. Positive relations between a campus and community can ensure there is a consistent level of enforcement in the campus community, regardless of the context (e.g., athletics events, political rallies, concerts). While the aforementioned policies and practices may cost institutions and communities valuable resources, decisions about whether to employ those techniques should be weighed against the toll taken on campuses and their surrounding communities in terms of property damage, potential lawsuits, and negative public perceptions.

Revised opening clause is more casual.

Action recommended is now much clearer.

Who should do *what* is now evident.

Revised conclusion makes an equivalent point in half the words.

Revised: Because celebrations don't get out of hand at sporting events only, college administrators and coaches should apply the policies we recommend in this report to all campus events, including political rallies and concerts. Campus officials can then use the goodwill they generate with the local community to ensure that policies for maintaining order are enforced consistently. While our recommendations aren't cheap, the property damage, lawsuits, and bad publicity fan riots can trigger will likely cost schools much more.

17d How can you achieve sentence variety?

Your readers will quickly be bored if all your sentences are of the same type and pattern. Your goal is to write sentences that move easily, conveying readers from point to point with appropriate clarity and emphasis; you can't do this without offering some variety.

1 Vary sentence types. The familiar sentence types discussed in Section 16e offer you a range of possibilities. Simple sentences attract the attention of readers with their economy and punch. Compound sentences put ideas of equal weight side by side. Complex sentences give you a means to state ideas subtly and richly. Varying these sentence types will keep your readers engaged.

2 Vary sentence patterns. The five standard sentence patterns in English (see Section 16a) are reliable but can be dull if repeated over and over. Variations can add style. Consider inverting the usual word order.

> **Gone** is the opportunity to win this month's lottery.
>
> **Intelligent, cultured, and politically shrewd** was Eleanor of Aquitaine, a twelfth-century liberated woman.

Or play with the way a sentence opens.

ORIGINAL The punk-rock protest songs of the early 1980s were the musicians' way of criticizing the political establishment.

VARIATION 1 To criticize the political establishment, punk-rock musicians of the early 1980s wrote protest songs.

VARIATION 2 In the early 1980s, punk-rock musicians wrote protest songs as a way of criticizing the political establishment.

The variations are not necessarily better than the original. They're just different, and they demonstrate the options you have in crafting sentences.

Another way to vary the shapes of sentences is to put interesting details into modifying clauses or phrases at different points in a sentence.

AT THE BEGINNING **Convinced that he could not master rhetoric until he knew Greek,** Thomas began studying the language when he was 40.

IN THE MIDDLE Li Po, **one of the greatest of the Chinese poets,** drowned when he fell out of a boat while trying to kiss the reflection of the moon in the water.

AT THE END Sixteenth-century Aztec youths played a complex game called *ollamalitzli,* **which some anthropologists believe to have been the forerunner of modern basketball.**

EXERCISE 17.19 The following sentences all begin approximately in the same way. Rewrite them to vary the pattern. Treat the four sentences as a single paragraph; you may not need to change all the sentences.

EXAMPLE Directors and producers have adapted Shakespeare's plays to contemporary tastes in every age and era.

REVISED In every age and era, directors and producers have adapted Shakespeare's plays to contemporary tastes.

1. Directors and producers were eager to move Shakespeare from the stage to the screen in the early twentieth century.
2. Filmmakers first had to adapt dramas to fit the new medium of film; early Shakespeare movies from the silent era looked much like stage plays performed before a camera.

3. Directors quickly realized that actors on the big screen had to restrain their traditional facial expressions and exaggerated stage gestures.

4. Directors and producers have since produced many Shakespeare films that adopt the dress, music, style, and attitudes of particular decades.

EXERCISE 17.20 To each of the following sentences, add at least one modifying phrase or clause. Vary your placement of the modifiers.

1. Three books stand out in my mind as the ones I would recommend to a friend.

2. Johnny Cash is best known for his song "I Walk the Line."

3. The Super Bowl occurs in late January or early February.

4. Reform of the IRS rarely gets far in Congress.

3 Vary sentence length. Readers like a balance between long and short sentences. If you've produced a cluster of short sentences, your writing may seem choppy. If you write only medium-length sentences, your prose may seem monotonous. Give readers a break; vary the rhythm.

Here is a paragraph that is tedious chiefly because all the sentences are nearly the same moderate length.

> **ORIGINAL**
>
> Our impressions of people are frequently based on our interpretation of their body language. We notice whether or not someone meets our gaze, fidgets constantly, or gestures when speaking. We use our observations to deduce personality traits such as arrogance, submissiveness, or trustworthiness. Most of us are confident of our ability to judge personality by reading body language. We reason that these skills must be highly developed since we rely on them regularly. Recent research confirms that most people can read emotion and gauge social skills from nonverbal signals. However, the same research suggests that they just as consistently fumble or misinterpret cues to more subtle personality traits.

A more lively revised version not only varies the length of sentences but uses varied sentence types.

REVISED FOR VARIETY

Our impressions of people are frequently based on our interpretation of their body language. Does someone meet our gaze or turn away? Does he fidget? Does she gesture? From nonverbal cues such as these we draw our conclusions: this person is arrogant, that one is trustworthy. Most of us are confident of our ability to judge personality from nonverbal cues—after all, we've been doing it all our lives. But how accurate are we really? Not very, it turns out. Recent research reveals that although most people can read emotion and gauge social skills correctly, they consistently fumble or misinterpret nonverbal cues to more subtle personality traits.

An occasional short sentence works well even in academic and professional writing—where the tendency is to avoid the quick jab. The fact is that short sentences catch the attention of readers. Mixed with longer sentences, they can mark a writer as direct and confident, able to make a bold claim or a clear statement.

EXERCISE 17.21 The sentences in the following paragraph are monotonously brief. Combine some of these short sentences and edit as necessary to produce a more readable passage. Compare your version to others written by classmates.

The National Air and Space Museum is in Washington, D.C. It is located on the Mall near the Hirshhorn Museum and Sculpture Garden. The Air and Space Museum is one of the capital's most popular attractions. It presents the artifacts of aviation history. It presents these artifacts in a creative manner. The museum houses a replica of the Wright brothers' first plane. Lindbergh's plane hangs from the ceiling. The plane carried him across the Atlantic to Paris in 1927. It was a solo flight. Also in the museum are planes from World War II and a full-size lunar landing module. Every manner of flying machine is represented in the museum. There are dirigibles and zeppelins. There are fighter planes, passenger planes, and space capsules. There are helicopters and balloons. There is even a remarkable movie projected onto a large screen. The screen towers six stories.

17e How do you use figurative language?

Writers who make an impact on their readers are often those with a gift for finding the image that lasts, the analogy that clarifies, the metaphor that makes a concept come alive. Probably no writer finds it easy to learn to use figurative language. It is a talent developed over time through careful reading and self-conscious experimentation. As you read, stay alert for the way authors use figures of speech such as analogy and metaphor, and have the courage to experiment in your own writing.

1 Look for fresh images that will strike your reader's imagination. Such images are often found by paying close attention to the world you can see and feel, as this writer did.

> I went to high school at J. W. Sexton in Lansing, Michigan, **a Depression-era brick fortress that sat across the street from a Fisher Body auto assembly plant**. The plant was blocks long on each side and wrapped in **a skin of corrugated steel** painted a **shade of green somewhere between the Statue of Liberty and mold.** It loomed so near the high school that on football Fridays, when the Big Reds butted heads in Memorial Stadium, night-shift workers stood on balconies and watched the game.
>
> —Ted Kleine, "Living the Lansing Dream"

To create powerful images, sometimes all you have to do is turn general terms into more particular ones.

GENERAL TERMS	While striking baseball players drove off in **fancy sports cars, newly unemployed laborers** at ballparks struggled to **find work**.
SPECIFIC IMAGES	While striking baseball players drove off in **Porsches and Jaguars, hot dog vendors and ticket takers** at ballparks found themselves **in unemployment lines.**

2 Use similes and metaphors to dramatize ideas. **Similes** are comparisons that use *as* or *like*. Here are two examples.

As another fire season approaches, **anxiety about fires in the West is building as inexorably as piles of dead wood** on the forest floor.
—Ted Williams, "Only You Can Postpone Forest Fires"

Life in China was for millennia **like a lethal board game in which a blind destiny threw the dice, and to land on the wrong square at the wrong moment** could mean sudden ruin and repulsive death.
—Dennis Bloodworth, *The Chinese Looking Glass*

Metaphors are direct comparisons, without the use of *as* or *like*. Here are two examples.

Better watch out or **the pendulum of medical dogma** will bash your head in. **It swings back and forth** far more often than most people realize, and with far more velocity.
—Sherwin B. Nuland, "Medical Fads: Bran, Midwives, and Leeches"

The **geological time scale is a layer cake** of odd names, learned by generations of grumbling students with mnemonics either too insipid or too salacious for publication: Cambrian, Ordovician, Silurian, Devonian.
—Stephen Jay Gould, "The Power of Narrative"

A word of advice: don't mix metaphors. What's a mixed metaphor? It's a comparison that is either inconsistent or illogical because it begins with one image and ends with another.

Don't count your **chickens** until the **tide** comes in.

The Internet marketing **ship has sailed,** and companies that have failed to establish a presence on the Web are already **circling the wagons.**

EXERCISE 17.22 Complete the following clauses by creating metaphors or similes.

1. The kitchen smelled awful, like a ________ that had ________.
2. Like a ________, the senator protested over and over that she was innocent of taking illegal campaign contributions.
3. At the end of summer break, I'm usually a ________.
4. My seat in coach for the six-hour flight felt like a ________.

PART IV

DESIGN AND SHAPE OF WRITING

CHAPTER

18 How Do You Design Documents?

Readers today expect writing to be visually inviting and easy to navigate—otherwise they may not bother to read it at all. Web surfers may skip a page if its graphics load too slowly. Your employer may ignore a long report if all she needs is an executive summary. And your instructor will cringe if you submit a term paper printed in an inappropriately ornate font. You can easily avoid such mistakes by learning the basics of document design. This chapter offers pointers for working with specific design elements and avoiding common pitfalls of poor formatting.

Figure 18.1 With a personal computer and a color printer, writers can publish on their desktops in minutes what historically has taken elaborate equipment and long hours of labor. The lithograph press illustrated here shows how many hands were once involved in producing a professionally printed document.

18a How do you design documents with a computer?

Computers are used for most modern document design. In the past, as Figure 18.1 shows, many laborers and machines were required to produce even the simplest printed sheet. Yet while most people now write and print their own documents with personal computers, few take full advantage of their design capabilities.

1 Explore the design features of your word processor and productivity software. Word-processing programs support a variety of print and electronic formats, and they often have sophisticated options for enhancing visual style. You can easily insert pictures and graphics, add tables, create multiple columns, enhance text with colors and decorations, save texts in online formats (such as HTML), and do much, much more. To explore such features, consult the user manual or help files for your program and try some hands-on experimentation (see Figure 18.2).

Although you can do a lot with word processors alone, other types of software offer additional design options. Explore your options.

SOFTWARE	WHAT IT CAN CREATE OR MODIFY
Spreadsheet software	Complex tables, graphs, statistical reports
Drawing software	Simple images, charts, decorated text
Image, photo editors	Digitized photos, complex images
Presentation software	Slide shows and handouts
HTML editors	Web pages of varying complexity
Sound and video editors	Digitized music and film clips
Publishing software	Posters, brochures, letterheads, pamphlets

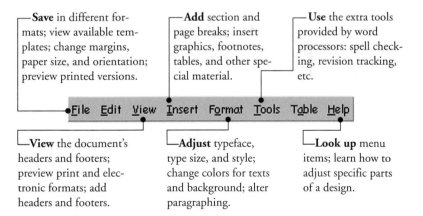

Save in different formats; view available templates; change margins, paper size, and orientation; preview printed versions.

Add section and page breaks; insert graphics, footnotes, tables, and other special material.

Use the extra tools provided by word processors: spell checking, revision tracking, etc.

File Edit View Insert Format Tools Table Help

View the document's headers and footers; preview print and electronic formats; add headers and footers.

Adjust typeface, type size, and style; change colors for texts and background; alter paragraphing.

Look up menu items; learn how to adjust specific parts of a design.

Figure 18.2 Learn the basic features of your word processor through its menu or ribbon. The menu above, while it may not be exactly what you see in your program, shows the typical options for editing a document's formatting and visual style. Which menu items do you use most frequently in designing a project?

2 Choose a suitable document format. Most of us are familiar with the frustration of trying to open computer files incompatible with our viewing software. As writers, besides considering the type of software we use to create documents, we also need to consider how we'll share them with others: as a plain-text email? in an attached PDF? on a Web site? Will your audience have the appropriate software to read what you write? Or perhaps the audience expects printed documents instead. But even printed documents have "compatitibilty" issues: readers expect particular page layouts and visual styles for particular writing situations. To choose the most suitable format, consider how each matches the writing situation:

- **Formats vary in the audiences they reach.** Letters and emails allow you to address your writing reliably to a single person or group. Flyers and Web pages, by contrast, are viewed in public spaces.
- **Formats vary in how they announce purpose.** Book covers and mastheads call out for attention, while subject-lines in emails and memos calmly identify shared issues and pragmatic concerns.
- **Formats vary in how they introduce writers.** Not all formats emphasize the role of the individual writer, as academic papers do. Brochures, for example, put a writer's organization first.
- **Formats vary in how they guide readers through material.** Most print formats allow headers, footers, page numbering, and subsections to help readers navigate the document. Electronic documents also have hyperlinks and keyword searches. Consider how you want readers to move through your writing: from start to finish? as a reference source? one piece at a time?

3 Enhance visual style for readability, impact, and flow. Besides enabling writers to produce a variety of document formats, computers give writers a wide range of control over *visual style*. Unlike *verbal style* (see Part 3), which pertains to word choice, sentence structure, and figurative language (among other things), *visual style* refers to the use of fonts, colors, graphics, and images to present texts more effectively. While your academic papers are usually limited to conventional styles, like MLA (see 50c), APA (see 51c), or CMS (see 52e), when you have more freedom, alter visual style to create deliberate effects (as demonstrated in Figure 18.3):

- **Attract readers' attention.** Sometimes a catchy title isn't enough to reel in readers. Amid a sea of Web pages, for instance, yours may need a distinctive look. Depending on your audience and purpose, that distinction might be flash, fun, or simple readability.
- **Set a tone.** Images, colors, and fonts convey moods and evoke feelings that affect how people receive what you say.
- **Make content more meaningful.** Besides creating a mood, visual style can add meaning. Typefaces, type styles, and colors accentuate contrasts to better emphasize, downplay, or group related material.
- **Help readers follow your ideas.** Frames, rules, and variations in background color can provide useful visual cues, showing readers where one set of ideas ends and another begins.

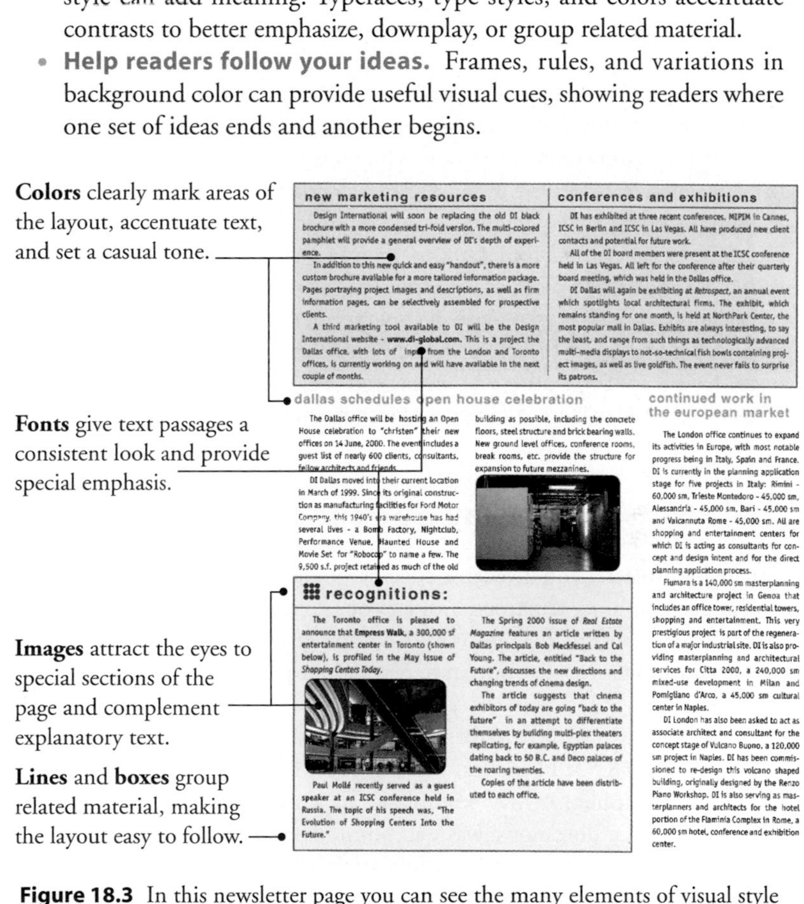
Colors clearly mark areas of the layout, accentuate text, and set a casual tone.
Fonts give text passages a consistent look and provide special emphasis.
Images attract the eyes to special sections of the page and complement explanatory text.
Lines and **boxes** group related material, making the layout easy to follow.

new marketing resources

Design International will soon be replacing the old DI black brochure with a more condensed tri-fold version. The multi-colored pamphlet will provide a general overview of DI's depth of experience.

In addition to this new quick and easy "handout", there is a more custom brochure available for a more tailored information package. Pages portraying project images and descriptions, as well as firm information pages, can be selectively assembled for prospective clients.

A third marketing tool available to DI will be the Design International website - **www.di-global.com.** This is a project the Dallas office, with lots of input from the London and Toronto offices, is currently working on and will have available in the next couple of months.

conferences and exhibitions

DI has exhibited at three recent conferences, MIPIM in Cannes, ICSC in Berlin and ICSC in Las Vegas. All have produced new client contacts and potential for future work.

All of the DI board members were present at the ICSC conference held in Las Vegas. All left for the conference after their quarterly board meeting, which was held in the Dallas office.

DI Dallas will again be exhibiting at *Retrospect*, an annual event which spotlights local architectural firms. The exhibit, which remains standing for one month, is held at NorthPark Center, the most popular mall in Dallas. Exhibits are always interesting, to say the least, and range from such things as technologically advanced multi-media displays to not-so-technical fish bowls containing project images, as well as live goldfish. The event never fails to surprise its patrons.

dallas schedules open house celebration

The Dallas office will be hosting an Open House celebration to "christen" their new offices on 14 June, 2000. The event includes a guest list of nearly 600 clients, consultants, fellow architects and friends.

DI Dallas moved into their current location in March of 1999. Since its original construction as manufacturing facilities for Ford Motor Company, this 1940's era warehouse has had several lives - a Bomb Factory, Nightclub, Performance Venue, Haunted House and Movie Set for "Robocop" to name a few. The 9,500 s.f. project retained as much of the old building as possible, including the concrete floors, steel structure and brick bearing walls. New ground level offices, conference rooms, break rooms, etc. provide the structure for expansion to future mezzanines.

recognitions:

The Toronto office is pleased to announce that **Empress Walk**, a 300,000 sf entertainment center in Toronto (shown below), is profiled in the May issue of *Shopping Centers Today.*

Paul Mollé recently served as a guest speaker at an ICSC conference held in Russia. The topic of his speech was, "The Evolution of Shopping Centers Into the Future."

The Spring 2000 issue of *Real Estate Magazine* features an article written by Dallas principals Bob Meckfessel and Cal Young. The article, entitled "Back to the Future", discusses the new directions and changing trends of cinema design.

The article suggests that cinema exhibitors of today are going "back to the future" in an attempt to differentiate themselves by building multi-plex theaters replicating, for example, Egyptian palaces dating back to 50 B.C. and Deco palaces of the roaring twenties.

Copies of the article have been distributed to each office.

continued work in the european market

The London office continues to expand its activities in Europe, with most notable progress being in Italy, Spain and France. DI is currently in the planning application stage for five projects in Italy: Rimini - 60,000 sm, Trieste Montedoro - 45,000 sm, Alessandria - 45,000 sm, Bari - 45,000 sm and Valcannuta Rome - 45,000 sm. All are shopping and entertainment centers for which DI is acting as consultants for concept and design intent and for the direct planning application process.

Fiumara is a 140,000 sm masterplanning and architecture project in Genoa that includes an office tower, residential towers, shopping and entertainment. This very prestigious project is part of the regeneration of a major industrial site. DI is also providing masterplanning and architectural services for Citta 2000, a 240,000 sm mixed-use development in Milan and Pomigliano d'Arco, a 45,000 sm cultural center in Naples.

DI London has also been asked to act as associate architect and consultant for the concept stage of Vulcano Buono, a 120,000 sm project in Naples. DI has been commissioned to re-design this volcano shaped building, originally designed by the Renzo Piano Workshop. DI is also serving as masterplanners and architects for the hotel portion of the Flaminia Complex in Rome, a 60,000 sm hotel, conference and exhibition center.

Figure 18.3 In this newsletter page you can see the many elements of visual style at work. Which techniques seem most effective to you and why? What audience is this document intended to reach? How would it be altered to reach a different audience?

EXERCISE 18.1 If you have never used the graphic capabilities of your word processor, consult its "Help" features (searching for the boldfaced terms) to learn how to do the following:

- **Insert a picture** into a text file, then **resize** it.
- Place a **horizontal line** on a page.
- Draw an **arrowhead** on a page.
- Create a **text box** on a page and then **color** the **text**.

EXERCISE 18.2 Analyze and evaluate the formats and visual styles of three different types of documents: a local newspaper's editorial page, a gossip magazine's cover, and a government Web site's homepage. Use the guidelines in 18a-2 to break down each document's strategies for reaching an audience, highlighting its purpose, introducing its writers, and leading readers through content. Use the list of strategies in 18a-3 to determine the various effects the creators of each document intended to produce with specific visual design elements. As much as possible, focus on the presentation of content, not the content itself. Which document's design is most successful in achieving its purpose for its intended audience? How might the others be improved? How might the documents be adjusted to reach a different audience? Present your analysis to classmates.

18b How do you lay out pages?

For many projects, you'll receive specific guidelines for page size, margin width, paragraphing, alignment, and so on. Follow them exactly when you must. When you have flexibility, take advantage of it by shaping the layout of your document to suit your audience and purpose.

1 Choose a manageable size and orientation. While the standard page size is 8.5 × 11 inches, you might use larger pages when designing a poster or pamphlet. It may seem easier to work with a wide area, but so much open space does not always accommodate extended verbal passages, because readers must concentrate on a relatively small area within a broad surface. Similarly, large electronic pages may require too much scrolling. Small pages, by contrast, while easier for readers to handle, do not always have enough room for images or large type.

Orientation—the direction material faces on the page—also affects readers. *Portfolio* (or *portrait*) layouts, the most common, are longer than they are wide. In *landscape* layouts, width is greater than length.

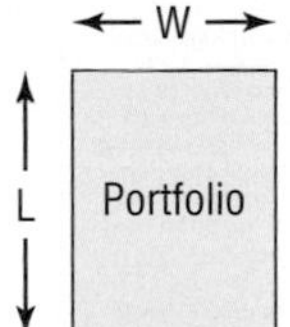

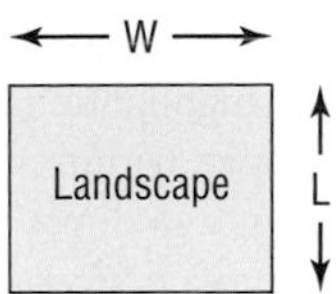

Portfolio orientation works well when presenting lengthy verbal texts, since readers prefer not to follow lines too far across a page.

Landscape orientation is often used for graphic material too wide for portfolio orientation.

2 Break material into readable units and arrange them according to relevance. *Chunking* your writing is especially important with lengthy texts, which readers may find difficult to digest as single, amorphous clumps. Paragraphs offer one option for cutting material into smaller pieces, but you may also benefit from the strategies shown in Chart 18.1.

The key to effective chunking, however, lies in arrangement. Obviously, the most important content occupies the center of the page. Less significant material should nonetheless accentuate this central point of focus. Since readers of English tend to move from the upper left corner of a page to the lower right, put key lead-ins, such as titles and informative images, at the top and left of a page and less crucial, but still necessary, material toward the bottom and right. Here are some general suggestions for the effective arrangement of material on print and electronic pages:

- Move supplementary material, such as comments and brief notes, toward the side margins or the *footer* (i.e., the bottom margin).
- Group related pieces of material (explanatory text and illustrations, for example) near each other, within a frame, for example.
- Distinguish special material by indenting, framing, or "screening" it.
- In *headers*, add navigational details such as current section titles (also called *running heads*) and page numbers.
- In footers, place routine but necessary information such as contact addresses, organizational information, and credits (in cases where the writer's organization is emphasized more than the writer).

Chart 18.1 Common Ways to Break Up Material

Subsections. Subsections, or groups of related paragraphs under a single heading, are just a step up from plain paragraphs. By highlighting and separating specific topics within extended passages, you can direct readers' attentions onto a narrower focus.

Reviews from Center Stage

Lame indeed.

The recent popularity of boy-band parody Wounded Duck isn't all that surprising. What is surprising is the ability of surly fans to endure the tiresome antics for an hour-long set. How many times can you watch the elaborately choreographed dancers flub their moves before it gets old?

Okay, I'll admit to guffawing through the first three songs—but once you get the gist of the show, there isn't much more to see. My advice—should the Duck fly into town opening for another band—show up ten minutes before the headliners, get a few laughs, and then listen to some real music.

How old school is too old school?

Before Friday, I thought I had an answer to this question. DJ Crusty's energetic set showed that digging up musical fossils isn't all about giving rock legends cameos in your music video. There are still treasures to be found—treasures encased in wax. Crusty's ability to synthesize diverse flavors of vinyl into addictive compounds explains why he has crossed over from the club set into the mainstream.

Lists. It's often awkward to form a series of regular, repetitive statements into a paragraph. Try a bulleted list instead. Numbered or lettered lists work better when items need to be in a strict order. In informal writing, stylized bullets (right) can evoke a playful mood.

Festival 2006: Survivor's Guide

The spring rains and crowds can sometimes put a damper on your ability to enjoy the music. Never fear! We've provided a list of suggestions to make the best of your aural outing.

- ♪ Take your own water bottles. You'll have to wait in line for even the basics once inside.
- ♪ A waterproof mat is also a good idea. The ground gets pretty muddy, especially by the final days.
- ♪ Bring plenty of your own toilet tissue. Supplies in the portable facilities run low after just a few hours.
- ♪ If you're planning on attending more than one day, earplugs will keep your hearing from going dull.
- ♪ A hooded raincoat can keep you dry during the early afternoon showers.
- ♪ If you plan on heading for the mosh pit, ignore all of the above and just bring elbow pads.

Tables. Tables work well for presenting structured information, especially (but not exclusively) statistical data. See Section 9b for guidelines on using tables effectively as evidence in academic papers. Tables are also good for categorization and complex lists.

Festival 2006: Daily Venue Schedules

	Center Stage	East Stage	West Stage	Welcome Stage
Wed.	Classic Rock	World Beat	Punk	Polka
Th.	Funk and Soul	Swing	Reggae and Ska	Metal Mania
Fri.	Rock and Pop	Blues	Hip-hop and R & B	Local Grab Bag
Sat.	Rock and Pop	Jazz	Country	DJ Showcase
Sun.	International Folk	Classical	Gospel	Amateur Contest

Frames. When you want to set material apart from the main text, place it in a frame or a box. You can create frames with lines and changes in background color. Manipulate these features by using your software's "Borders" and "Shading" commands.

About the Festival (cont.)

The annual festival began in 1982 as a relatively small, "y'all come" event. There was only one stage in the town square at that time. Those first few years didn't attract much national attention, but the music was rich with a variety of local flavors—from rock to jazz to punk to (we're not ashamed to admit) disco.

> 1987: Going National
> A big break came for the festival in 1987, when national, independent label Snub Pop agreed to host a second stage. Before long, other national labels were seeing the festival as an opportunity to promote otherwise unknown bands.

The menu of bands was interesting enough to attract music lovers from all over the state. Eventually, the small festival grew to include most types of American music, until, last year, we finally added a fourth venue, allowing us to accommodate more and more international genres as well.

3 Indent and space paragraphs and columns for readability. First, choose between block and indented formats. *Block paragraphs* (like those opening each chapter and section in this book) have no first-line indentation, but are preceded by one or more blank lines. By contrast, standard *indented paragraphs* (like the next) need no preceding space. Academic papers generally use all indented paragraphs with no extra spacing between them: see Checklists 50.1 (MLA), 51.1 (APA), and 52.2 (CMS).

In some documents, such as newsletters or brochures (but not most academic papers), you might also be able to lay out material into two or more columns. In doing so, consider carefully how spacing and line length affect reading. Narrower columns, for instance, make smaller typefaces easier to follow. Be aware, however, that columns can be time-consuming to design, especially when you also present images, tables, or charts.

4 Align columns to direct readers' eyes down and across the page. When working with a single column, alignment is fairly straightforward. Left alignment is usually the most readable for extended verbal passages. Images and graphics, however, often call for center or right alignment. If small enough, right-aligned images work well when "wrapped" by left-aligned paragraphs—that is, when the lines of text appear on the same horizontal lines used by the image. Center alignment is better for images not wrapped by paragraphs, since left or right alignment leaves too much white space in the center of the page.

You can also use alignment to make readers pause at important points, as Figure 18.4 illustrates. Page designers will use this technique to make section openings stand out by centering or right-aligning headings within a left-aligned body of text. Use this method of emphasis carefully; too many disruptions can make pages seem choppy.

5 Use white space to avoid clutter. White space reduces clutter by separating material into easy-to-distinguish units. Here are common ways of creating white space.

- Leave ample margins at the top and sides of your pages.
- Pad titles, graphics, and frames with empty surrounding space.
- Double-space between paragraphs and sections.
- Indent special blocks of material, such as long quotations or images.
- Allow adequate space between columns in multicolumn documents.

Rules for Hiking in the Park

Don't go off the trail. The animal habitats in the park are extremely fragile. While we encourage people to enjoy the natural benefits provided inside, in order to maintain the survival of the fauna and flora, visitors must restrict themselves to clearly marked trails.

Don't take anything out of the park. Just as we don't want visitors leaving their marks, we don't want them removing what might be necessary parts of a fragile ecology.

Don't feed the animals. Wild animals can become dependent upon humans, if they expect to be fed. Once in the habit of receiving handouts they can become aggressive when refused—then they must be removed.

Report violations of these rules. It's your park. When other visitors violate these rules, they are destroying public property.

Rules for Hiking in the Park

Don't go off the trail.

The animal habitats in the park are extremely fragile. While we encourage people to enjoy the natural benefits provided inside, in order to maintain the survival of the fauna and flora, visitors must restrict themselves to clearly marked trails.

Don't take anything out of the park.

Just as we don't want visitors leaving their marks, we don't want them removing what might be necessary parts of a fragile ecology.

Don't feed the animals.

Wild animals can become dependent upon humans, if they expect to be fed. Once in the habit of receiving handouts they can become aggressive when refused—then they must be removed.

Report violations of these rules.

It's your park. When other visitors violate these rules, they are destroying public property.

Figure 18.4 Although the subsection headings are clearly emphasized in both pages, the center alignment in the page on the right makes them stand out even more. But this alignment of the headings doesn't lead as smoothly into the main text. Which is more important for this text: emphasis or smoothness?

EXERCISE 18.3 Copy enough text into a word-processing file to fill at least one single-spaced page. (You might use material you have written yourself earlier in the term.) Then use your word-processing software to manipulate it in various ways such as those described below, producing four visually different pages. Then decide for what sorts of documents a page in each of the four styles you have created might be appropriate.

- Double spaced, Courier font, single column, indented paragraphs, portfolio orientation, one-inch margins all around, no images
- Single spaced, New York font, single column, block paragraphs, right justified, portfolio orientation, one-inch margins all around, no images, headings as appropriate
- Single spaced, Times New Roman font, two columns, indented paragraphs (indented just two or three spaces), right justified, portrait orientation, one-inch margins all around, one or more images
- Single spaced, Helvetica font, three or more columns, block paragraphs, landscape orientation, appropriate margins, two or more small images wrapped by text, some material framed or highlighted

18c How do you choose type?

Typefaces (or *fonts*) and *type styles* have their own personalities. A thick, heavy typeface like **Helvetica Black** speaks loudly and commands attention; a script font like *Mistral* conveys a delicate, artistic mood. Type styles, such as **boldface**, *italic*, and SMALL CAPS, serve more practical purposes, enhancing words and phrases to make them stand out. You can also adjust *type size* (usually measured in *points*) to enhance your document's style and readability. As you adjust each facet of the type, weigh carefully how all these qualities work together to affect the readability of each page.

1 Select a suitable typeface. What typeface you choose depends on your purpose and format. Some read better in print than on screen. Others are decorative—not designed for extended passages. Fortunately, fonts have been divided into families that share certain characteristics.

- **Serif fonts.** Serifs are the little lines, or "feet," that appear at the bottom or top of the main strokes in a letter. Two common serif fonts are Courier and Bookman. Serif fonts are highly readable in print.
- **Sans serif fonts.** Sans serif fonts—letters without the little feet—have a clean, contemporary look. Two common sans serif fonts are Arial and Helvetica. This family of fonts is generally the best choice for material to be read on an electronic or low-resolution page.
- **Decorative or ornamental fonts.** Decorative fonts have a lot of personality—they can be elegant, jazzy, authoritative, or comical, but they aren't always easy to read in longer passages. Save these fonts for where you want to create a special effect. Many options will be available on your word processor, from OldTown to *Vivaldi*.
- **Symbol fonts.** Special characters, called *dingbats*, allow you to add simple graphics to your documents. To use these typefaces, select a font with "symbol" or "ding," or use the "Insert Symbol" command.

Stylized bullets
Explanatory diagrams
Business writing
Informative symbols
Technical documentation
Thematic icons
Playful imagery

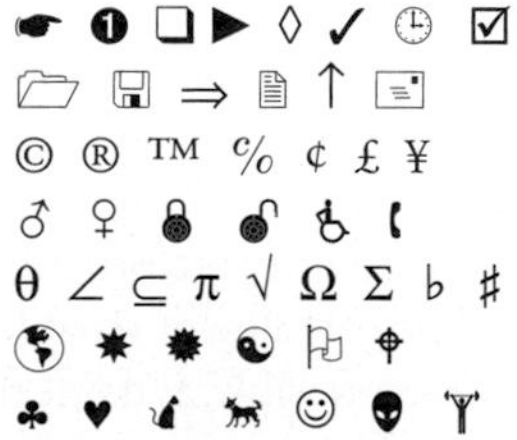

2 Use type styles and colors strategically. Type styles differing from plain text draw readers' attention. Colors, covered in 18e, have similarly striking effects. Both should be used sparingly, so they don't lose their impact. Note that many styles already have conventional uses:

TYPE STYLE	COMMON USES
Boldface	Strong emphasis, headings
Italic	Highlights, special/foreign words, book titles
Underline	Emphasis, headings, hyperlinks, book titles
Superscript and subscript	Footnotes, endnotes, technical notation
~~Strikethrough~~	Revisions in drafts
SMALL CAPS	Subtle emphasis, strong highlights, headings
Shadow, Emboss, Wave	Decorative emphasis, highlights, headings

3 Adjust type size for readability. Medium type sizes (usually 10 to 12 points) work best for the main body of text. Extended passages in large type can be difficult to read. Reserve larger type for headings and titles. "Fine print," on the other hand, isn't always bad. Use smaller type to downplay less important material in margins, headers, and footers. Keep in mind that changing the font face may change the actual size of the type, even though you have not altered the number of points.

18d When do you add graphics and images?

According to the maxim, a picture is worth a thousand words. Used thoughtfully, it can be worth much more; used poorly, much less. Since charts, graphs, and images should always serve a purpose and complement any verbal text, they take a good deal of planning and editing.

1 Present numerical data with graphs. Graphs help readers visualize the significance of statistical information. How better to show a trend in rising prices than a line shooting upward? What more clearly illustrates the allocation of a budget than a simple pie chart? With the help of word-processing or spreadsheet software, you can graph quantitative information clearly and quickly. Chart 18.2 illustrates common types of statistical graphs readily made by many software programs. Keep in mind, however, that you will need to start with a table of reliable data. See Section 9b for how to use graphs and tables responsibly and effectively.

Chart 18.2 Common Forms of Charts and Graphs

Pie charts show portions of a whole.

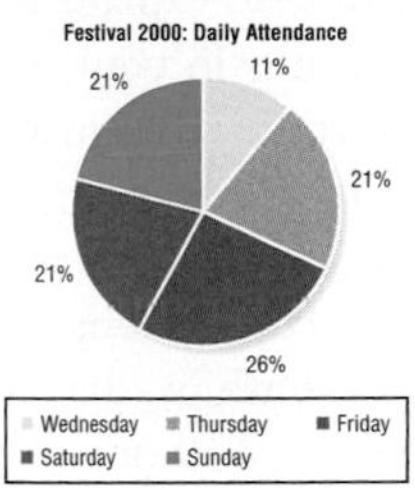

Bar graphs show comparative values.

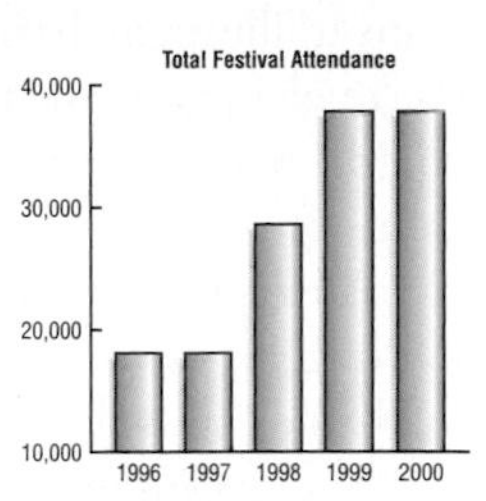

Line graphs show trends and changes across time.

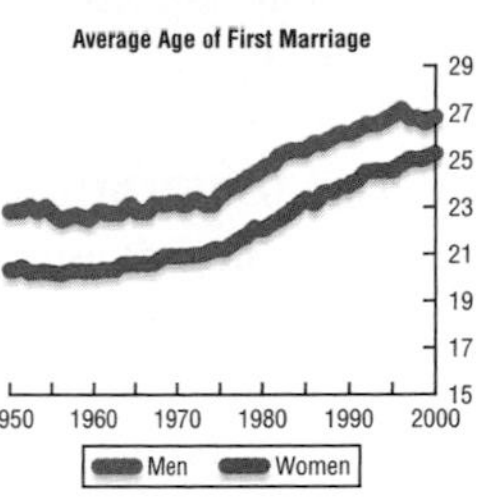

Area graphs show portions of a whole as comparative trends.

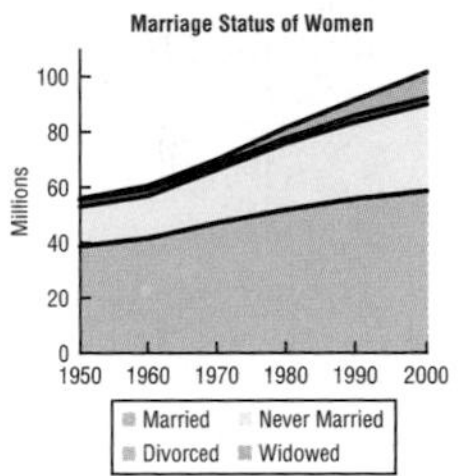

Organizational charts show hierarchical relationships.

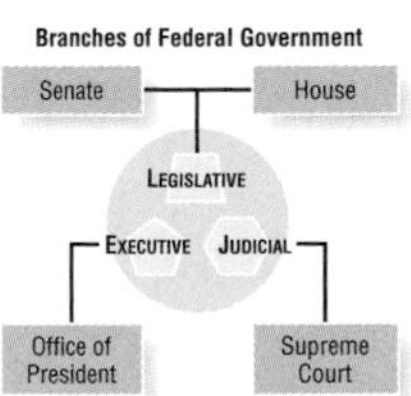

Flow charts show procedural relationships.

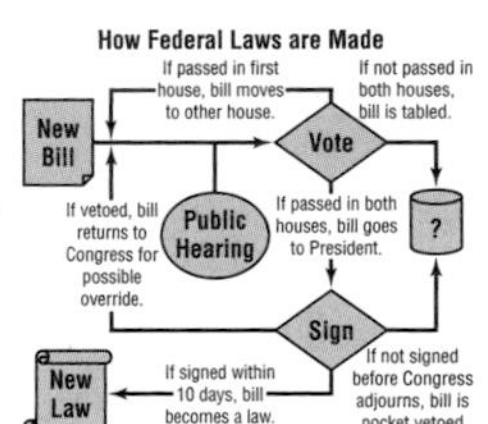

Timelines show sequential relationships.

Project Plan for March

7 14 21 28

Research fund donors

Begin drafting proposal

Meet with fund donors

Give proposal to reviewers

Complete fund application form

Revise final proposal draft

Diagrams illustrate textual descriptions.

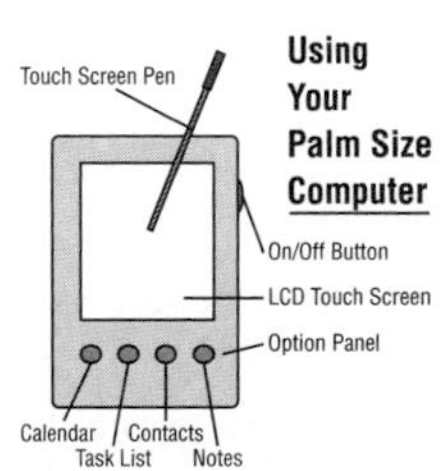

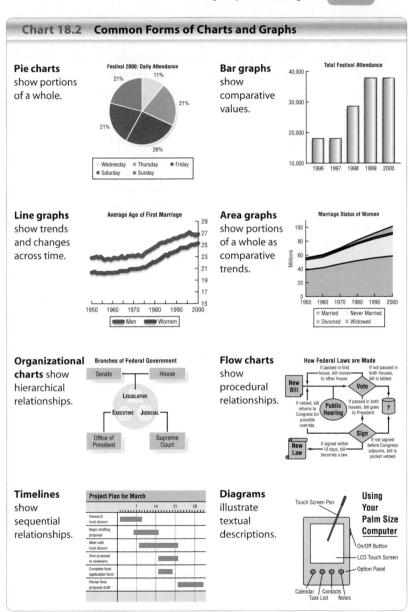

2 Clarify details through charts and diagrams. Statistics aren't the only kind of information you can present visually. Use a chart or a diagram to illustrate details that are cumbersome to explain verbally. Suppose you're giving a presentation on the workgroups in your organization. You could try to describe the complex intergroup relationships with words alone, or you could facilitate your explanation with an organizational chart. This strategy allows you to focus your talk on important policy issues without bogging down your audience in abstract connections.

While charts show connections and relationships, diagrams supplement verbal descriptions with instructive images. Without diagrams, how-to manuals would be a nightmare: "Step 7. Connect four-prong plug A into socket B, above panel C. . . ." Such instructions are easier to follow when accompanied by a diagram of the parts involved.

3 Enliven writing with photos and illustrations. A powerful photo or two may help readers appreciate in an instant aspects of your subject that would otherwise require lengthy descriptions. Just be sure that any images you use—whether photographs, drawings, or cartoons—do not mislead or distract readers, but instead reinforce key points. Snapshots of your pet, for instance, won't really help an argument on animal cruelty.

Many options exist for acquiring photos and illustrations to use in a document. You can purchase digitized photos on the Web (some are even free) or on CDs, usually with certain copyright restrictions. You can create your own with a digital camera, and you can translate existing photos or illustrations into electronic formats with a scanner. Once you have an electronic image file, you can easily modify it and insert it into your document. Tweak the size and positioning of the image on the page to make sure the picture does not interfere with the flow of paragraphs.

One final caution: the power you have to acquire and alter digital images also brings with it the responsibility to use them ethically. To begin with, respect the copyrights of any graphics you don't own or create and get appropriate permissions when required by the owner. Also, you should not modify an image in ways that would alter its original content (for example, cropping people out of a photograph) or make it an inaccurate representation of reality when readers or viewers expect a faithful representation. You would have more license to alter images when creating a parody, for example, than you would when writing a report.

4 Separate material with borders and rules. Borders and rules—horizontal or vertical lines surrounding and separating units of material—provide readers with visual guides for how to read a page. Create borders around frames, photographs, tables, and graphs to more clearly distinguish them from surrounding paragraphs. Select a line width and color that isn't overwhelming, so you don't distract readers from the main point of focus.

Rules often mark the beginnings of new sections; they also distinguish marginal material from the central content of a page. You'll often see horizontal rules separating footnotes or running heads from the main text. Vertical rules can separate marginal comments or graphics at the side.

EXERCISE 18.4 Create a graph from a table of numerical data. (If you do not already have a table of data, go to <http://nces.ed.gov>.) Insert a chart or graph into your word-processing or spreadsheet document. The program will ask you to populate a table with your data, allowing you to label and add rows and columns as needed. Once you have at least three rows and three columns, experiment with various chart styles (see Chart 18.2). Which best portrays the significance of the numerical data?

Spectrum Painters
42002 Research Blvd.
Cambridge, Massachusetts 02141
(617) 555-2349

July 23, 2000

Calhoun Center Law Offices
Attn: Glenn Davis
3820 West 45th Street
Cambridge, Massachusetts 02148

Dear Mr. Davis:

This letter is to confirm the work order to paint each of the five offices in your firm's suite. According to our records, the following colors have been requested:

§ Mr. Davis and Ms. Sievers requested western blue.
§ Ms. Wadhwani requested stoic red.
§ Mr. Lupfer requested thicket green.
§ Ms. Wilder requested winsome beige.

Please confirm the requested colors and the quoted price (on the attached invoice) to initiate painting. We appreciate your business and would like to complete the work you have requested as soon as possible.

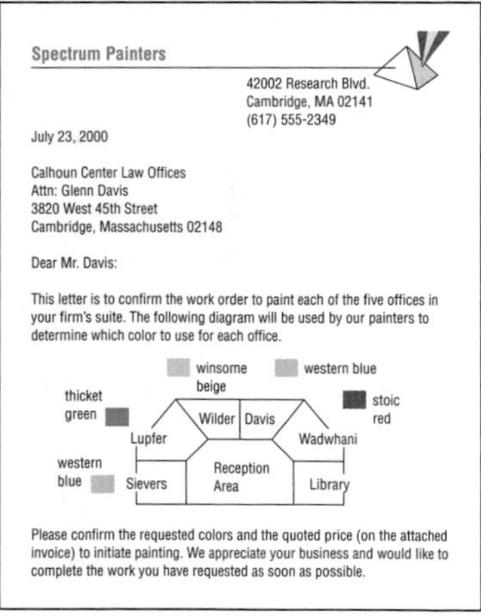

Spectrum Painters

42002 Research Blvd.
Cambridge, MA 02141
(617) 555-2349

July 23, 2000

Calhoun Center Law Offices
Attn: Glenn Davis
3820 West 45th Street
Cambridge, Massachusetts 02148

Dear Mr. Davis:

This letter is to confirm the work order to paint each of the five offices in your firm's suite. The following diagram will be used by our painters to determine which color to use for each office.

Please confirm the requested colors and the quoted price (on the attached invoice) to initiate painting. We appreciate your business and would like to complete the work you have requested as soon as possible.

Figure 18.5 Even a standard business letter (left) can be made more effective with the addition of images (right): (1) A horizontal rule helps distinguish the letterhead from the main content. (2) A graphic logo creates a professional persona. (3) An explanatory diagram helps to clarify written instructions.

18e How do you work with color?

The use of colors to enhance visual style should not be taken lightly, given how much they can raise production costs and affect a document's impact. While not appropriate in most academic papers, color can be necessary to attract readers to brochures, newsletters, and Web pages. Once you've decided to use colors, determine how they can create the best results.

1 Select a readable color scheme. Designers create color schemes to orchestrate the interaction of multiple tones and hues within a layout, all to achieve specific effects, from adding emphasis to setting a mood. They do so by assigning specific colors to various elements on a page (headings, rules, frames, borders, graphics).

The most important decisions in any scheme are what color to use for background and what color for type. To be readable, these colors must contrast but not clash. Bright colors must be used sparingly, since they can tire the eyes. Readable color combinations include dark blue on beige, black on orange, brick red on blue, white on blue-green, and, of course, black on white.

2 Create a mood for your document. Different colors evoke different emotions. Bright ones have a bold effect, even when applied sparingly. Soft colors, on the other hand, may need to cover an entire page to have a noticeable impact. Combinations make a difference too. Some—for example, purple and orange or yellow and black—are vivid; they shout for attention. Others—shades of blue combined with ivory—are subtle. Some colors just seem to clash—pink and bright green, for instance, and purple and yellow. But tastes in color vary greatly, and one can't say flatly that certain colors should never be combined.

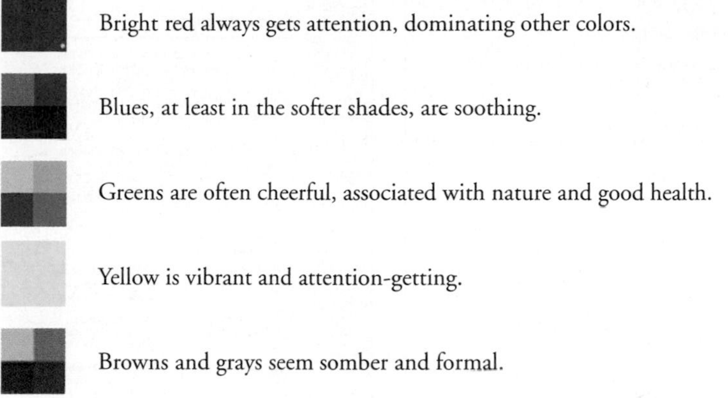

Bright red always gets attention, dominating other colors.
Blues, at least in the softer shades, are soothing.
Greens are often cheerful, associated with nature and good health.
Yellow is vibrant and attention-getting.
Browns and grays seem somber and formal.

3 Use color to highlight or soften elements of your layout. Colors, because of their wide range of effects, give you more control over the impact created by other features of your layout. Once you've decided to go beyond black and white, you'll have many more options for emphasizing or downplaying text and images. A bold heading can be made less striking, for example, by changing the color from black to a softer blue or gray. Plain text in the body of a paragraph can be changed to a striking red. Figure 18.6 demonstrates some of these effects.

QuartoView Support

Our mission is to provide our customers the best service in the electronic book industry; it includes

- giving every customer careful attention, courteous service, and helpful information;
- reducing the down-time for customers to no more than two days; and
- insuring that every customer goes away satisfied after just one call.

The Support Staff

- Jan Davis, Director of Support (5 Years with the company)
- Eliot Porter, Support Manager (Small Business Support Team)
- Matt Galvan, Support Manager (Home Office Support Team)
- Arnie Zimmerman, Support Specialist (Large Client Support)
- Eddy La Follette, Support Associate (Extension 240)
- Carol Macintyr, Support Associate (Extension 239)
- George Miller, Support Associate (Extension 237)
- Denis Ng, Support Associate (Extension 238)

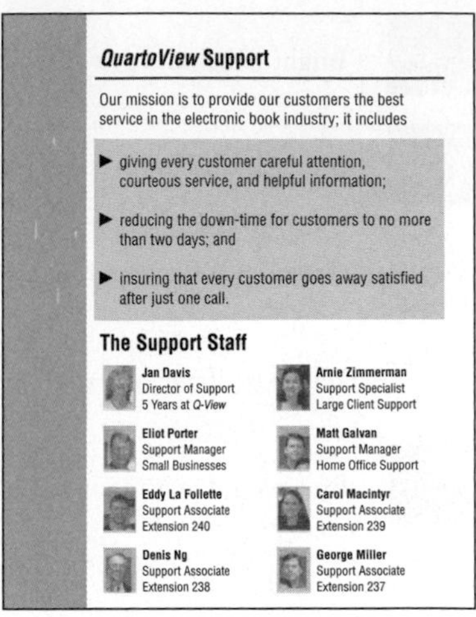

***QuartoView* Support**

Our mission is to provide our customers the best service in the electronic book industry; it includes

► giving every customer careful attention, courteous service, and helpful information;

► reducing the down-time for customers to no more than two days; and

► insuring that every customer goes away satisfied after just one call.

The Support Staff

Jan Davis
Director of Support
5 Years at *Q-View*

Arnie Zimmerman
Support Specialist
Large Client Support

Eliot Porter
Support Manager
Small Businesses

Matt Galvan
Support Manager
Home Office Support

Eddy La Follette
Support Associate
Extension 240

Carol Macintyr
Support Associate
Extension 239

Denis Ng
Support Associate
Extension 238

George Miller
Support Associate
Extension 237

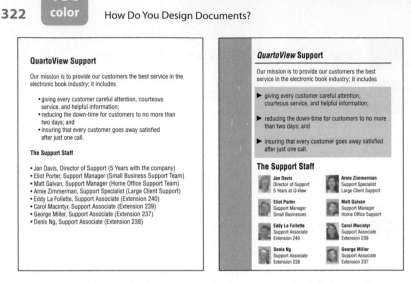

Figure 18.6 Although the formatting in the document on the left is generally effective, the revision on the right enhances the arrangement with colors, images, multiple type styles, and simple graphics. The original would be fine for an internal policy statement; the revision might be suitable for a customer information packet. Note these changes: (1) Display text has been highlighted with color. (2) The first list uses stylized bullets and a background screen for contrast; the second list has portrait photos instead of bullets, is set in two columns, and uses boldface to emphasize each name. (3) The margin has been colored and widened to hem in the main content of the page.

CHAPTER

19 How Do You Write Professional and Business Documents?

If you bristle at the specifications for lab reports and research papers, you might be surprised to learn that institutions and businesses have no less stringent expectations for their documents. In this chapter, we examine some of the formats, both print and electronic, you are likely to encounter today, both in school and out. You'll find model documents illustrating a variety of print and electronic formats. Where possible, we show examples of documents in both media. Each example is accompanied by a discussion of its typical purpose and composition process. Although some of the formats presented here have special formatting, Checklists 19.1 and 19.2 provide general guidelines for presenting typical professional documents.

Checklist 19.1 Typical Print Documents

- Use standard letterhead paper (8.5 × 11″).
- Use portfolio orientation unless you plan to fold the document or you need extra room for graphics and images.
- Leave at least a one-inch margin on all sides. If you plan to bind the document, add more space on the bound edge.
- Single space letters. Double space drafts to allow for comments. The final spacing for some documents will depend on the format used.
- Use headers and/or footers with running titles and page numbers for multi-page documents. Indicate the version for each draft.

Checklist 19.2 Typical Onscreen Documents

- Use short, single-spaced block paragraphs.
- Choose a sans-serif typeface and avoid too much special formatting.
- If you have hypertext links, test them to make sure they work.
- Make sure your audience has the right viewing software.

19a How do you write formal emails?

Over the last decade, instructors and employers have come to expect students and workers to conduct much routine business through email. In classes, you may be asked to submit assignments as file attachments or to collaborate with fellow students through online exchanges. In workplaces, email, an extremely cheap form of communication, has replaced printed, professional memos (see Section 19g) for everyday correspondence.

1 Planning. Precisely because email is so cheap and easy to produce, you need to be especially careful about how and when to use it—just about everyone deeply resents junk email or unnecessary replies:

- **Decide who will be the addressee.** Are you writing to an individual or a group of people? Sending copies to others? Responding to an earlier message sent by another writer? Writing to an email list?
- **Determine what you need to cover in your email.** If you discuss many different items, consider whether all should go in the same message to the same audience. Some administrators and businesses prefer that emails treat one important item at a time.
- **Consider using attachments.** Email isn't the place for displaying long messages or graphical information. Use attachments instead.

2 Drafting. Email messages include four key parts:

- **The subject line.** To make sure your messages don't get passed over in the recipient's inbox, write subject lines that both attract your readers and accurately summarize what the email is about.
- **The salutation.** This may be optional. Use one when addressing an audience you don't know well or to signal a higher level of formality and politeness. See Section 19b-2 for more guidelines.
- **The body.** Divide your message into a series of block paragraphs, lists, even subsections with headings. Most email programs now also have some graphic capabilities and varied options for visual style.
- **The closing.** How you close the message depends on how formal it is. Most professionals close with their title and contact numbers.

3 Polishing. Although you may write emails quickly, when sending them to business or professional audiences, be sure to edit them as carefully as you would any paper letter. You could pay a price for sloppy emails. Errors in business emails tend to be costly in some way, either to the writer's reputation or directly to the bottom line.

- **Make sure the *From* address is correct.** If you have multiple email accounts, make sure you choose one you check regularly.
- **Review the addressees.** Avoid hitting "Reply All" when unnecessary. In the *To* line, list only those from whom you expect responses. In the *Cc* line, list supervisors and others who need to be informed.
- **Don't forget necessary attachments.** Make sure also that your readers have the appropriate viewing software.
- **Adapt your signature to the occasion.** If you use a common signature for all your messages (an automated feature of many email clients), make sure it is suitable for your audience; otherwise, edit it.

Formal email. The message below, illustrating the basic parts of an email, is actually written in a semiformal tone—notice the formality of the salutation and casualness of the closing. The onscreen look of messages will differ according to your addressee's *email client*, the program you use to read and write messages.

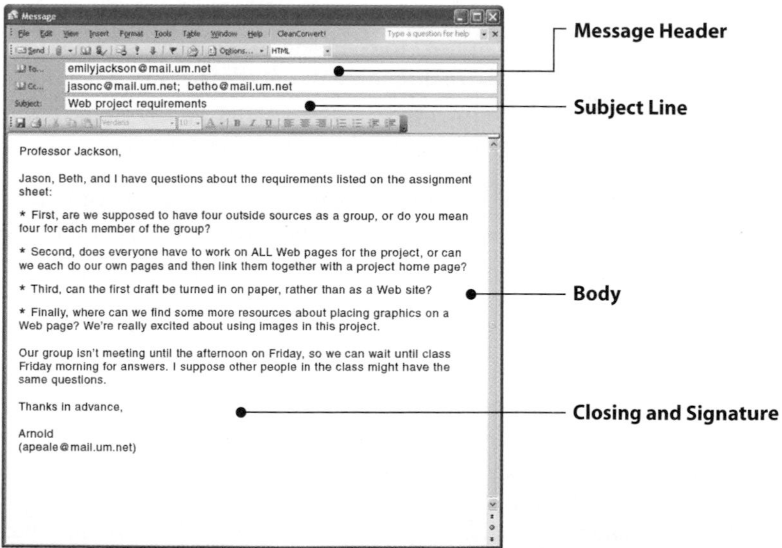

19b How do you write formal letters?

Whenever you write a formal letter, whether to conduct business, present complaints, or establish professional relationships, remember that it may become part of a permanent file documenting your relationship with the recipient. A few extra minutes of planning and polishing can insure that the impression you leave is both positive and rewarding.

1 Planning. Formal letters are often sent to people who aren't expecting your correspondence. The following questions can help you introduce yourself clearly and politely and avoid starting off on a bad foot.

- **How well do you know the recipient?** Are you writing someone you haven't met? A representative of an organization? A possible employer? Use organizational Web sites and professional contacts to learn as much as you can about the recipient. Adjust the length and tone of the letter to fit your likely reader.
- **How much does the recipient know about the topic?** Do you need to explain why you're writing? Describe relevant events? Review previous correspondence to which you're reacting?
- **What action do you want the recipient to take?** Do you want a specific response? Do you want to collaborate in business efforts? What support will the recipient need to complete your action?
- **Should you enclose extra documents?** Don't put large amounts of information (for example, graphs and charts) in the letter itself. Instead, refer readers to enclosed supplemental documents.

2 Drafting. Try to keep your letter to one page, but be certain to include all the formal elements expected in a business or professional letter.

- **Return address and date.** Your reader will obviously need an address to reply to you. The date is also an essential piece of information, particularly if your letter initiates a series of responses and replies.
- **Inside address.** When possible, direct the letter to one person or department in an organization. Find out who in a company or institution can best handle the issue you're raising. Again, the Web has made such investigations much easier than in the past.
- **Salutations.** Set the level of formality by using more or less traditional greetings and titles to address the recipient: *Dear Mr. X, Dear Ms. Y*, etc. By convention, salutations in business letters are followed by colons (:),

at least until you're familiar enough with recipients to address them by first name. Then you might use the less formal comma.

- **Body paragraphs.** Be brief, but give all pertinent facts (names, dates, etc.) so that the recipient(s) can act on your request quickly and effectively. Start with a brief section providing all the details your recipient needs to understand the letter's purpose. Then, state explicitly what you want done in response to the letter. Finally, close the body by mentioning supporting details that might help the addressee more easily perform the action(s) you've requested.
- **Closing and signature.** End the letter by identifying yourself, your titles, and affiliations, just after your closing and signature. Common formal closings include "Respectfully" and "Sincerely."

Checklist 19.1 Formatting Formal Letters

a. Choose a block, modified block, or indented letter format. (See Chart 19.1.)

b. Leave out the return address when using letterhead paper that includes contact information.

c. Follow the salutation with a colon, unless you've established a less formal relationship; then use a comma.

d. Follow your closing with a comma and sign above your name.

e. After your name and title, note enclosures or copies you've sent.

3 Polishing. Beyond the usual editing and proofreading:

- **Make your diction and style fairly formal and polite.** You can grease the wheels for your inquiry or request by showing respect, politeness, and even gratitude. But if you've already established a casual tone with the addressee, maintain it.
- **Be especially careful to get names and dates right.** Not only will inaccurate details confuse readers and make you look careless, but they can also convey disrespect.
- **Send copies to others who may be concerned about this letter.** You can often expedite business by sending copies to people who may be involved (albeit not as directly as the addressee) with the issue at hand. Be certain, however, that everyone copied should be privy to the details you discuss in your letter.

Chart 19.1 Traditional Letter Formats

Traditional formats differ in how pieces of the letter are placed or indented and whether blank lines separate body paragraphs. All paragraphs and sections are single-spaced, except where noted below.

Block format. Align all sections to the left-hand margin and use only block paragraphs.

- Insert three blank lines between the date and inside address.
- Insert one blank line after the inside address, salutation, and each block paragraph, including the last.
- Insert four blank lines between the closing and your name and title.

Indented format. Align the return address, date, closing, and signature to the middle of the page. Align all other sections to the left margin, indenting body paragraphs ½ in.

- Insert three blank lines between the date and inside address.
- Insert a blank line after the inside address, salutation, and final paragraph.
- Insert four blank lines between the closing and your name and title.

Modified block format. Align the return address, date, closing, and signature to the middle of the page. Align all other sections to the left-hand margin.

- Insert three blank lines between the date and inside address.
- Insert one blank line after the inside address, salutation, and each block paragraph, including the last.
- Insert four blank lines between the closing and your name and title.

- **Keep a paper or electronic copy of all important business correspondence.** Whether you are applying for a job or complaining about faulty repairs under a warranty, you'll likely need a record of what you have written for future reference.

Formal letter (in indented format). The letter below was written by a student at Bowling Green State University to the Office of the Registrar asking for action to clear up a bureaucratic mistake. The letter was successful. After receiving the complaint, the registrar sent an email response, promising to watch over the student's loan personally.

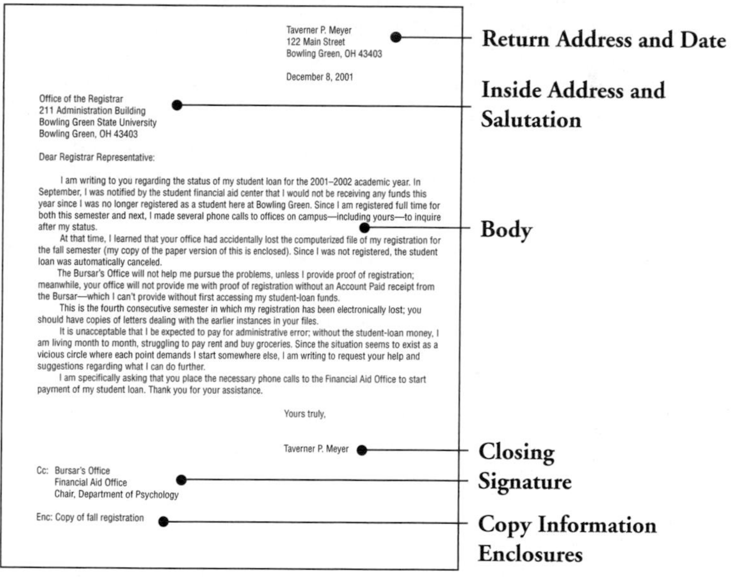

Taverner P. Meyer
122 Main Street
Bowling Green, OH 43403

December 8, 2001

Office of the Registrar
211 Administration Building
Bowling Green State University
Bowling Green, OH 43403

Dear Registrar Representative:

I am writing to you regarding the status of my student loan for the 2001–2002 academic year. In September, I was notified by the student financial aid center that I would not be receiving any funds this year since I was no longer registered as a student here at Bowling Green. Since I am registered full time for both this semester and next, I made several phone calls to offices on campus—including yours—to inquire after my status.

At that time, I learned that your office had accidentally lost the computerized file of my registration for the fall semester (my copy of the paper version of this is enclosed). Since I was not registered, the student loan was automatically canceled.

The Bursar's Office will not help me pursue the problems, unless I provide proof of registration; meanwhile, your office will not provide me with proof of registration without an Account Paid receipt from the Bursar—which I can't provide without first accessing my student-loan funds.

This is the fourth consecutive semester in which my registration has been electronically lost; you should have copies of letters dealing with the earlier instances in your files.

It is unacceptable that I be expected to pay for administrative error; without the student-loan money, I am living month to month, struggling to pay rent and buy groceries. Since the situation seems to exist as a vicious circle where each point demands I start somewhere else, I am writing to request your help and suggestions regarding what I can do further.

I am specifically asking that you place the necessary phone calls to the Financial Aid Office to start payment of my student loan. Thank you for your assistance.

Yours truly,

Taverner P. Meyer

Cc: Bursar's Office
Financial Aid Office
Chair, Department of Psychology

Enc: Copy of fall registration

19c How do you write application letters?

A letter of application—for a job, a scholarship, or admittance to a school or program—is an especially important form of business communication. The same advice and guidelines apply to it as to any formal letter. (See Section 19b.) In a letter of application, however, you have special challenges. You need to present yourself favorably without seeming to brag, persuade a recruiter or administrator to interview you without appearing pushy, and make yourself look confident without being flip.

1 Planning. In application letters, one thing is immediately clear to the recipient—your desire to win a position. Since the purpose is understood, use your planning to explore why this position is good for you. Run through the Taking Control items on page 339; then ask these questions:

- **How does the position fit into your long- and short-term goals?** Recruiters want to know you've thought about the position and where it might take you. Most organizations don't want to spend money dealing with people who are just experimenting with a career.
- **Why have you chosen this organization?** In your letter, show some knowledge about the organization to which you are applying. But offer praise only in order to show your interest in them.

2 Drafting. Letters of application should adopt the standard format of formal letters. Throughout, maintain a respectful—but confident—tone. Avoid self-disparaging remarks, even to look modest. Instead, treat recruiters as competent decision-makers expecting applicants to sell themselves. Be sure also to provide the following in the body of the letter:

- **A statement of application.** Early on, state clearly for which appointment you're applying: a job, a scholarship, an award, etc.
- **A statement of qualifications.** Highlight those academic and employment qualifications that best suit the job in question; the résumé sent with the letter will supply the rest of the details.
- **An explanation of why you're a good match.** Focus on how you might meet the organization's needs, what you could accomplish for them, and why you'd like to work with them.

3 Polishing. Follow the basic formatting guidelines for a formal letter (Section 19b) or email (Section 19a), depending on the medium you use. Most importantly, describe yourself and your accomplishments accurately. Your letter may have a long life. If you're hired, it will become part of your personnel record. Fabrications now may get you fired later. If you're not hired, it may go into a file of applicants for later consideration.

- **Make sure you have the correct addressee.** Position listings will generally identify who to contact. When no specific person is mentioned, direct your letter to the organization's recruitment office.
- **Double check the spelling of names and organizations.** Such mistakes may seem minor, but they are used to weed out candidates.
- **Be sure to include your résumé and other requested enclosures.** Don't assume the recruiter will contact you for missing items.

EXERCISE 19.1 In the classified section of your student or local newspaper, locate an ad for a job for which you might be qualified. Then compose an application letter for that position. Assume that your résumé (see Section 19d) would accompany the cover letter. Present yourself confidently and plausibly in the application.

Letter of application (block letter format). Below is Chad Polatty's letter of application for a Web programming position. You'll also find the same letter in email format. The salutation, the body, and the closing are identical in both. The only major differences are in how Chad reaches the job recruiter and the format of attached résumés and references.

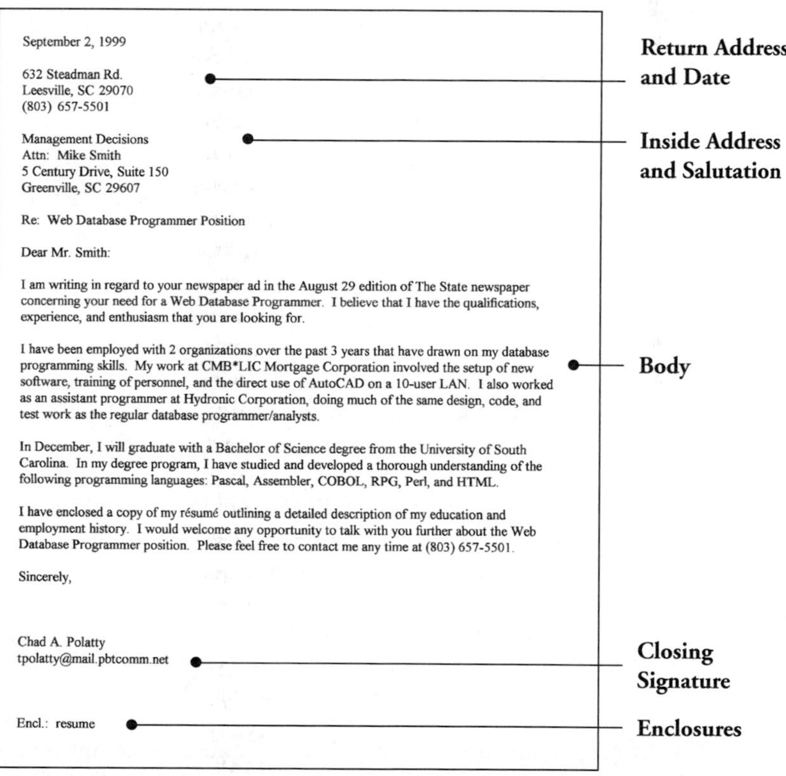
September 2, 1999

632 Steadman Rd.
Leesville, SC 29070
(803) 657-5501

Management Decisions
Attn: Mike Smith
5 Century Drive, Suite 150
Greenville, SC 29607

Re: Web Database Programmer Position

Dear Mr. Smith:

I am writing in regard to your newspaper ad in the August 29 edition of The State newspaper concerning your need for a Web Database Programmer. I believe that I have the qualifications, experience, and enthusiasm that you are looking for.

I have been employed with 2 organizations over the past 3 years that have drawn on my database programming skills. My work at CMB*LIC Mortgage Corporation involved the setup of new software, training of personnel, and the direct use of AutoCAD on a 10-user LAN. I also worked as an assistant programmer at Hydronic Corporation, doing much of the same design, code, and test work as the regular database programmer/analysts.

In December, I will graduate with a Bachelor of Science degree from the University of South Carolina. In my degree program, I have studied and developed a thorough understanding of the following programming languages: Pascal, Assembler, COBOL, RPG, Perl, and HTML.

I have enclosed a copy of my résumé outlining a detailed description of my education and employment history. I would welcome any opportunity to talk with you further about the Web Database Programmer position. Please feel free to contact me any time at (803) 657-5501.

Sincerely,

Chad A. Polatty
tpolatty@mail.pbtcomm.net

Encl.: resume

LETTER OF APPLICATION (EMAIL FORMAT)

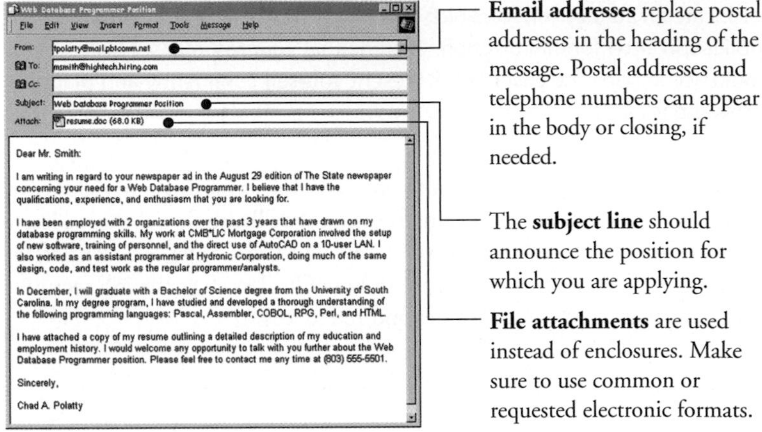

Web Database Programmer Position

File Edit View Insert Format Tools Message Help

From: tpolatty@mail.pbtcomm.net
To: msmith@hightech.hiring.com
Cc:
Subject: Web Database Programmer Position
Attach: resume.doc (68.0 KB)

Dear Mr. Smith:

I am writing in regard to your newspaper ad in the August 29 edition of The State newspaper concerning your need for a Web Database Programmer. I believe that I have the qualifications, experience, and enthusiasm that you are looking for.

I have been employed with 2 organizations over the past 3 years that have drawn on my database programming skills. My work at CMB*LIC Mortgage Corporation involved the setup of new software, training of personnel, and the direct use of AutoCAD on a 10-user LAN. I also worked as an assistant programmer at Hydronic Corporation, doing much of the same design, code, and test work as the regular programmer/analysts.

In December, I will graduate with a Bachelor of Science degree from the University of South Carolina. In my degree program, I have studied and developed a thorough understanding of the following programming languages: Pascal, Assembler, COBOL, RPG, Perl, and HTML.

I have attached a copy of my resume outlining a detailed description of my education and employment history. I would welcome any opportunity to talk with you further about the Web Database Programmer position. Please feel free to contact me any time at (803) 555-5501.

Sincerely,

Chad A. Polatty

Email addresses replace postal addresses in the heading of the message. Postal addresses and telephone numbers can appear in the body or closing, if needed.

The **subject line** should announce the position for which you are applying.

File attachments are used instead of enclosures. Make sure to use common or requested electronic formats.

19d How do you write résumés?

Your résumé is a concise outline of your academic and work history, designed to give prospective employers a quick but thorough overview of your qualifications. Take great care in preparing your résumé. Once in the hands of a recruiter, your list of achievements and skills will be used to decide whether an employer will contact you for an interview.

1 Planning. Good résumés require an understanding of what recruiters look for in job candidates. It might help to run through the Taking Control items on page 339 before proceeding to these steps:

- **Determine your skills and achievements.** What experience do you have in work settings? What academic honors show you can succeed? Which accolades and skills seem most relevant for your field?
- **Identify the buzzwords of the profession.** Recruiters often maintain databases of digitized résumés culled from electronic submissions and scanned paper copies. As a database entry, your résumé will receive a serious look only if it can be found through keyword searches.

2 Drafting. Résumés have no paragraphs and only a few complete sentences. They are effective when organized into smartly headed lists. Some common headings for college graduates include the following:

- **Objective.** Identify the type of position you're seeking, so employers can match you to any and all appropriate openings.
- **Educational achievements.** List years, degrees, and institutions, as well as scholastic honors won. Omit secondary school experiences (unless relevant to the position) once you have a college degree.
- **Work experience.** Mention employers and dates of employment, starting with the most recent; list your most important duties and achievements in succinct but specific (and accurate) terms.
- **Relevant skills.** List only those skills useful to the position sought.
- **References statement.** Résumé footers often include the phrase "References available on request." But if a job listing asks for references, go ahead and provide on an attached document the contact numbers of people who can speak about your work. Be sure to get permission from your referees beforehand.

3 Polishing. For résumés, use standard paper (8.5 × 11 inches) with 1-inch margins on all sides. If you plan on handing out copies at a job fair or interview, consider printing at least a few on high-quality paper. Of course, it is what's on the paper that matters most. Fine-tune your organization, wording, and formatting so those skimming your résumé see at once your strengths and experience.

- **Be sure to provide current addresses, both postal and email.** Student job-seekers often provide both a *local address*, where they live at school, and a *permanent address,* where they reside away from school.
- **Make sure headings stand out clearly.** Recruiters often skim hundreds of résumés, looking only for specific sections.
- **Use parallel grammatical structures for items under each heading.** Such structural patterns (see Section 16h) make lists much easier to read. Participle phrases provide an effective frame for listing work duties.
- **Avoid irrelevant information.** List coursework only to explain how you attained skills outside of official employment. List non-work, non-academic activities only if you think an employer might consider them assets. You cannot be required to mention age, gender, race, religious or sexual preference, political affiliation, or marital status.
- **Edit and proofread scrupulously.** A spelling or mechanical error in a résumé or job application letter can torpedo your hopes.

EXERCISE 19.2 If you don't have a résumé already, follow the guidelines in this section to assemble one of no more than two pages, listing your academic and job experiences, as well as other necessary material, including your contact information. Then experiment with the design of your new or existing résumé by creating two acceptable versions that differ visually. You may also rearrange the content to emphasize different qualifications or job interests.

Résumé emphasizing education and experience. Below is the résumé of Danny Gomez, a student at the University of Texas at Austin.

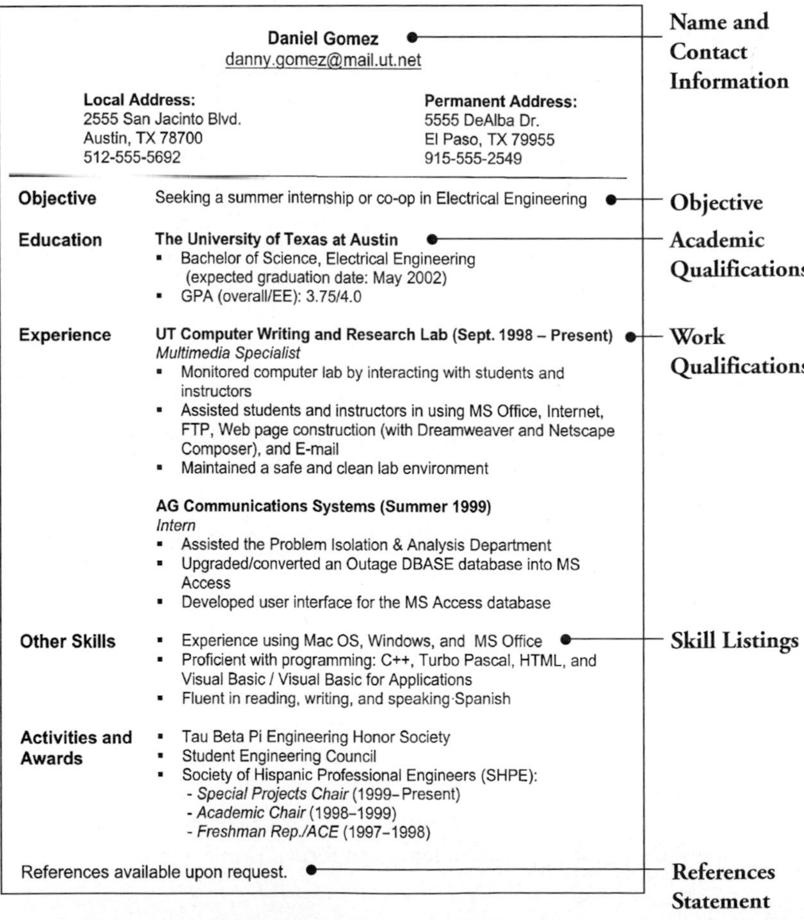

Daniel Gomez
danny.gomez@mail.ut.net

Local Address:
2555 San Jacinto Blvd.
Austin, TX 78700
512-555-5692

Permanent Address:
5555 DeAlba Dr.
El Paso, TX 79955
915-555-2549

Objective Seeking a summer internship or co-op in Electrical Engineering

Education **The University of Texas at Austin**
- Bachelor of Science, Electrical Engineering (expected graduation date: May 2002)
- GPA (overall/EE): 3.75/4.0

Experience **UT Computer Writing and Research Lab (Sept. 1998 – Present)**
Multimedia Specialist
- Monitored computer lab by interacting with students and instructors
- Assisted students and instructors in using MS Office, Internet, FTP, Web page construction (with Dreamweaver and Netscape Composer), and E-mail
- Maintained a safe and clean lab environment

AG Communications Systems (Summer 1999)
Intern
- Assisted the Problem Isolation & Analysis Department
- Upgraded/converted an Outage DBASE database into MS Access
- Developed user interface for the MS Access database

Other Skills
- Experience using Mac OS, Windows, and MS Office
- Proficient with programming: C++, Turbo Pascal, HTML, and Visual Basic / Visual Basic for Applications
- Fluent in reading, writing, and speaking Spanish

Activities and Awards
- Tau Beta Pi Engineering Honor Society
- Student Engineering Council
- Society of Hispanic Professional Engineers (SHPE):
  - *Special Projects Chair* (1999–Present)
  - *Academic Chair* (1998–1999)
  - *Freshman Rep./ACE* (1997–1998)

References available upon request.

19e How do you write a personal statement?

When you apply for a college scholarship, internship, or special program of study, you may be asked to write a personal statement. This kind of essay gives a selection committee a more complete view of your qualifications than an application form or transcript can provide. In it, you can provide a narrative about your interests and goals, as well as additional details about your academic and personal achievements. Such a statement also allows a committee to evaluate your writing skills. In short, it gives readers a sense of you as a person—and as a student.

1 Planning. Because requirements for personal statements vary, it's vital to follow instructions to the letter. In most cases, you will be asked to compose a brief essay (no more than one or two pages, double spaced) that falls into one of two categories:

- A general, comprehensive personal statement is open-ended, allowing you freedom to choose which experiences and qualities you wish to discuss. This type of statement is often required in general medical school and law school applications. For example, the University of Texas at Austin Law School asks applicants to write a brief essay that gives the admissions council "insight into your character and experience."
- A personal statement that responds to specific questions is often required for scholarship applications and for applications for graduate school, internships, or study abroad programs. Questions are typically tailored to the particular nature of the program. For instance, the University of South Carolina Capstone Study Abroad application includes five different essay prompts, including the one that Maria Morozowich responds to in the sample personal statement on page 337.

Before you begin writing a personal statement, review the instructions, then brainstorm a list of your experiences and credentials that fit those parameters. Check the program's Web site or your campus writing center to find samples of successful statements; these can help you decide which approaches and materials to incorporate into your statement.

2 Drafting. Personal statements are often read by committees who have hundreds, maybe even thousands, of applications to review. They'll have little patience for an essay that rambles off-topic or that provides a scattered list of disparate accomplishments. Instead, they'll look for a response that provides a focused, vivid picture of you—one that tells them exactly what makes you an excellent applicant. Here are some tips to consider as you shape your first draft:

- Find a specific "angle," or thesis, and organize your statement around it. You won't be able to tell readers every detail about your qualifications, so focus on one controlling idea that informs the introduction, body, and conclusion of your statement. For example, Maria Morozowich's study abroad application (excerpted below) focuses on how her experiences growing up in a multicultural family have prepared her to undertake the challenge of living and studying overseas.
- Start with a compelling introduction. An opening that gets right to the point and uses precise, vivid language or a specific anecdote will stand out more than a statement that begins with predictable generalities.
- Provide plenty of supporting details. Don't say that you would make an excellent teacher or medical student unless you can back up your claim with specific qualifications or experiences that you develop in your statement. Your stated goal should emerge as the logical, supported conclusion to your argument.
- Be yourself. Your statement should tell readers something about you that they can't learn from your transcripts or standardized application form. Allow your particular background, experiences, and personality to emerge. Your statement should also be reflective, showing that you have thought carefully about your experiences and have developed a clear perspective on what you hope to do in the future.

3 Polishing. Your finished statement should be as professional as you can make it. Ask for suggestions from friends, instructors, or the staff of a campus writing center. Be sure that your response addresses all questions asked and that you adhere carefully to length and formatting requirements. Tighten wordy passages and replace clichés and technical jargon with concrete, vivid prose. Correct any errors in grammar, mechanics, and punctuation—and check for typos one last time before you submit your application.

Finally, if you are applying for several awards or programs, avoid the temptation to use exactly the same statement for every application.

Personal Statement. The following personal statement is one of five required essay responses included in a study abroad application written by Maria Morozowich, a student at the University of South Carolina. She responded to the question, "Describe how you anticipate dealing with adjustments to unfamiliar surroundings, cultural differences, and separation from family and friends."

Having grown up in a family that blends Ukrainian and American traditions, I have long appreciated and valued cultural differences—and this respect and willingness to learn make me a good fit for the Capstone Study Abroad program. My grandmother came to the United States from the Ukraine after World War II, and she never learned to speak English fluently. Despite the language barrier between us, she and I have always had a close relationship that emphasizes family and cultural traditions. From her, I learned how to cook Ukrainian foods, do traditional Ukrainian embroidery, and understand how to speak some basic Ukranian. She also taught several of my cousins these traditional activities, and I remember how proud we all were to show off our sewing and culinary creations (which somehow never turned out quite as well as grandmother's) at family holiday gatherings. Sharing our heritage in this way made our family celebrations special; and feeling connected to both my American and Ukrainian heritage has become a vital part of who I am.

These positive childhood experiences, I believe, have helped to prepare me for the challenges of studying abroad. They will help me to be open and adaptable to—and most importantly, appreciative of—the traditions and practices of my host culture as I study.

Take Control

19f How do you prepare for interviews?

It may seem strange to see job interviews covered in a chapter on professional *documents.* We decided, however, that it would be useful to treat interviews near the documents that usually precede them: letters of application and résumés.

1 Planning. In planning for interviews, you should anticipate what you might be asked. A good starting point might be to review the job application and résumé that won you the interview.

- **What qualifications did you emphasize?** An interviewer will usually give you a chance to sell yourself. For example, you might be asked to explain how you have applied the skills you have listed.
- **What parts of your résumé might raise questions?** Expect to be asked about long gaps in employment and major shifts of interest.
- **What do you know about the job and the organization?** If you go into an interview asking questions about issues already spelled out in the job listing, you'll look underprepared or disinterested.

2 Preparing. Practice for your job interview as you would for any oral presentation (see Chapter 20). Here are some strategies:

- **Read trade journals and books.** You might feel silly, but try reading them aloud so you get used to the technical jargon. You'll feel more comfortable saying the words once in the interview.
- **Join a discussion group and do mock interviews.** Preprofessional organizations allow members to dialogue about current issues and trends in the field. In addition, you can ask someone knowledgeable in the field to interview you. Take any advice seriously.
- **Compose a list of questions about the job and employer.** Interviewers prefer a positive response to their usual closing query: *Do you have any questions?* Good questions show thoughtfulness.

3 Performing. Take a deep breath, speak slowly, and listen attentively, but most of all—be yourself. When employers interview many qualified candidates, it's not always the one with the most honors and highest GPA who wins the position. Part of being qualified is showing that you're a good communicator and a conscientious colleague, qualities that come out more when you're not worried about sounding important or covering up shortcomings. Of course, be sure to dress appropriately.

Taking Control

Search for a job

Students often hear that coursework prepares them for a professional career. The truth is, some graduates end up with jobs having no connection to what they've learned in the classroom. Even so, you can always turn to writing and research skills to make you a more competitive job candidate. After all, you have to sound and write like a professional to be treated like one.

- **Research the trade journals for your field.** Where do people in your field share ideas about best practices and current issues? Use the research techniques covered in Part 7 to locate such periodicals.
- **Practice using the vocabulary current in your profession.** Try writing summaries of articles you read in trade journals. Such explanations will test your fluency in your field's key concepts.
- **Evaluate the field's leading organizations and firms.** Write brief arguments for and against working for each one. Besides helping you determine what kind of employer you'd like to have, some of these points might be recycled in a job application letter.
- **Narrate a prospective career path.** Consider where you would like to be ten years from now. Then, write a plan detailing how you expect to get from where you are now to that place. What hurdles do you face? What type of job gets you started in the right direction?

19g How do you write official memos?

People within organizations usually communicate by memorandums. Memos omit some of the elements used in business letters sent outside the organization: formal salutations and closings, for example, aren't generally required. But memos do maintain a professional tone and retain details for keeping records of business interactions—this is also the case with intra-organizational emails (see 19a), the online cousin of the memo.

1 Planning. The conversations that occur via memos can be relatively quick—especially when delivered electronically—so the exchange can be as dynamic as those that appear in online forums or standard email. Consider how your memo fits into the workflow of ongoing business:

- **Are you planning business activities?** Do you need information to act? Do people need to be notified that they'll be affected? You'll probably write many memos in the process of deciding what to do.
- **Are you in the process of doing business?** Who needs to do what? What steps should take place first, second, third, and so on?
- **Are you announcing completed efforts?** What comes next? Who deserves credit for finishing the job and fulfilling commitments?

2 Drafting. Memos are usually short, direct documents. (Often, however, longer documents are attached, such as reports or proposals.) Since they are part of doing business, each piece of the memo is designed to expedite work and account carefully for important details:

- **Date.** May be used to refer to the memo in future correspondence.
- ***To* section.** The person named here will be the one everyone assumes will take the first action in response to your memo.
- ***From* section.** Lists your name, title, department, and contact information—all that may be necessary for writing a response.
- ***Subject* line.** Be brief and to the point—a subject line can determine whether a memo is acted on quickly or sits in someone's inbox.
- ***Body* paragraphs.** In the body, quickly explain the issue or problem, the options available, and what follow-up actions may be necessary.
- **Cc section.** Include co-workers indirectly involved in the issues.

3 Polishing. When you join an organization, examine carefully how your co-workers format and style their messages, both online and off. Some offices have specific requirements (paper, formatting, etc.) in order to ensure correct delivery of intra-office mail. If your office gives no special guidelines, use standard, letter-sized paper. Other formatting guidelines:

- **Use blocked, single-spaced paragraphs.** Insert a blank line between each section of the memo's header and after each paragraph.
- **Sign the *From* line when required.** Some memos—such as those that involve official expenditures—may require an initial or signature. Place it by your name in the memo's header.

- **Add an opening salutation to email memos.** Though printed memos generally don't have salutations, an email memo sent to more than one person might require that you distinguish the main addressees from those copied on the message.

EXERCISE 19.3 Write a fairly formal business memo (paper or email) to the members of a specific group or local organization to which you belong. In the memo raise a delicate issue in a professional way. You might, for example, request that club members who aren't current on their dues pay up immediately or lose their privileges, or ask that officers in the club no longer abuse the group's travel funds or long-distance accounts. Keep the memo brief—less than one page or screen—but be sure to include enough information for the memo to serve as a record later.

Memos. Below you'll find a memo written by Ryan Starck, a student employee at the University of Texas at Austin. Although the topic of the memo is one you'll rarely use—a farewell message to fellow staff members—the format and tone Starck adopts reflect the professional yet collegial nature of most work environments.

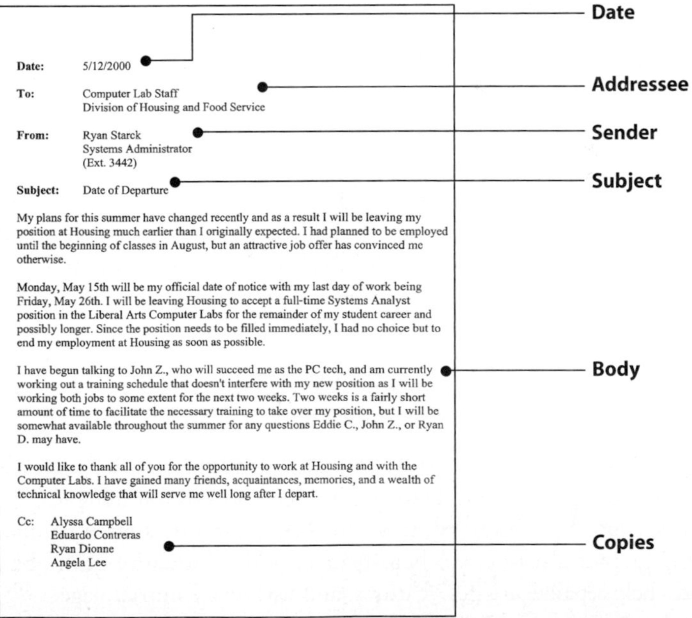

Date: 5/12/2000

To: Computer Lab Staff
Division of Housing and Food Service

From: Ryan Starck
Systems Administrator
(Ext. 3442)

Subject: Date of Departure

My plans for this summer have changed recently and as a result I will be leaving my position at Housing much earlier than I originally expected. I had planned to be employed until the beginning of classes in August, but an attractive job offer has convinced me otherwise.

Monday, May 15th will be my official date of notice with my last day of work being Friday, May 26th. I will be leaving Housing to accept a full-time Systems Analyst position in the Liberal Arts Computer Labs for the remainder of my student career and possibly longer. Since the position needs to be filled immediately, I had no choice but to end my employment at Housing as soon as possible.

I have begun talking to John Z., who will succeed me as the PC tech, and am currently working out a training schedule that doesn't interfere with my new position as I will be working both jobs to some extent for the next two weeks. Two weeks is a fairly short amount of time to facilitate the necessary training to take over my position, but I will be somewhat available throughout the summer for any questions Eddie C., John Z., or Ryan D. may have.

I would like to thank all of you for the opportunity to work at Housing and with the Computer Labs. I have gained many friends, acquaintances, memories, and a wealth of technical knowledge that will serve me well long after I depart.

Cc: Alyssa Campbell
Eduardo Contreras
Ryan Dionne
Angela Lee

19h How do you design newsletters?

A newsletter is an excellent way for organizations to keep in touch with members and patrons. With a desktop publishing program or an up-to-date word processor, newsletters are relatively easy to create. A major concern, however, is cost, especially when the newsletter is printed and distributed to dozens or even hundreds of readers. Online newsletters can, without extra expense, include a more complex visual style than paper brochures, assuming you have the time and skill to create a digital design.

1 Planning. A newsletter appears periodically throughout the year, so consider the events and activities that will interest readers most.

- **What activities and events unify your group?** Plan around these occasions, using the newsletter both to promote and to prepare.
- **How will you format the newsletter for publication?** Select the size of paper and the method of binding. These choices will affect the number of pages you need to design, as well as mail and copy costs.
- **What page layout and visual styles will suit your purpose?** Many of the design options for brochures are available for newsletters as well, so take a look at Section 19i below. Keep in mind, however, that newsletters usually have a narrower audience than brochures.

2 Drafting. In drafting the newsletter you'll need to fit your articles onto a fixed number of pages. Map out each page with two goals in mind: (1) showcasing the most important articles and (2) preventing readers from having to jump from page to page to read any one article. The diagrams on the following pages show typical parts of a newsletter. Your newsletter might include sections such as these: lists of upcoming events, with dates and descriptions; member lists with contact information and the names of officers; editorial pages that publish readers' opinions.

3 Polishing. Much of the final work on newsletters—besides typical proofing and editing—involves fine-tuning the layout and visual style:

- **Adjust headlines and bylines to reflect importance.** Remember bolder headings stand out, lighter ones blend into surrounding text.
- **Frame material with borders and rules.** Newsletters often contain many graphical features to help readers find information: lines and boxes help separate articles, features, and lists on a compact page.

- **Resize images to optimize layouts.** Rather than butcher articles to make things fit, adjust the sizes of images to create more space.

EXERCISE 19.4 Working with several other people, design a one- or two-page newsletter for an invented group—a political, social, or religious organization; a fan club for a local sports team; a techie group; or the like. (Better, create a newsletter for a real group or parody an existing newsletter.) Decide on the stories and features you should cover and then design an appealing newsletter—with at least one illustration or graphic. You may design the newsletter entirely on your own or, with instructor approval, base your newsletter on one of the templates typically offered in word-processing programs.

Newsletter (front page and internal page). The newsletter below, designed by members of an English students' honor society at the Metropolitan State College of Denver, contains six pages, the first and the third of which are shown. The students kept production costs down by limiting the layout to two colors and using black-and-white images—a modest but effective decision for widely circulated print documents.

SIGMA TAU DELTA

INTERNATIONAL ENGLISH HONOR SOCIETY

Spring 2009

CONTENTS

page 2
*President's Corner

page 3
*Do You Have a Mellon Appetite?

page 4
*Sorcerer's Apprentices: How Writers Really Work
*Picturing English: Learning Through ESL

page 5
*Revenge of the Banned
*Submit to Sigma Tau Delta

page 6
*Yahoo-ft, Anyone?
*Great Illustrations From Literature

page 7
*If You Build It, They Will Come

page 8
*Lisa Ross Spaar, "Acatolica Cemetery, Rome"
*2008-09 Journal Award Winners

Storytellers: 2010 Sigma Tau Delta Convention

Carrie Fitzpatrick
Convention Chair
Alvernia University

The Mexican people refer to them as cuentistas. In some parts of Japan, they are called kamishibai. Scéalaí is the name given to them in Ireland. West Africans call them griots. What am I referring to? Storytellers . . . the theme for the International Sigma Tau Delta Convention to be held in St. Louis, Missouri, from March 17–20, 2010.

The state of Missouri, the Show Me State, has given us many fantastic authors: Mark Twain, Kate Chopin, Marianne Moore, Eugene Field, Langston Hughes, and Maya Angelou to name just a few. Just as these writers have contributed to the storytelling tradition, I encourage the members of our English Honor Society to contribute to the narrative thread of our existence, our experiences, our attempts to articulate into words the world around us. As Convention Chair, I invite all of you, and I challenge all of you, to spin a yarn and tell a tale for the 2010 Convention.

All of us are storytellers. We are connected through the power of story. The science fiction writer Ursula K. LeGuin once said, "The story–from 'Rumplestiltskin' to *War and Peace*–is one of the basic tools invented by the human mind, for the purpose of gaining understanding. There have been great societies that did not use the wheel, but there have been no societies that did not tell stories." In other words, storytelling continues to be one of the oldest and most enduring ways to distribute knowledge.

In fact, it's been said that stories are similar to fairy gold. The more you give, the more you have, and the richer you are.

The economic and political upheaval we are currently experiencing will make the next few years difficult ones, and as the poet William Collins stated, "In unsettled times like these, when world cultures, countries, and religions are facing off in violent confrontations, we could benefit from the reminder that storytelling is common to all civilizations. Whether in the form of sprawling epic or a pointed ballad, the story is our most ancient method of making sense out of experience and of preserving the past." Stories are unifying and thought provoking, and they remind us that we are far more similar than different.

[Stories are **unifying** and **thought provoking**, and they remind us that we are **far more similar than different.**]

St. Louis is the perfect location for our storytelling to take place. The city has been the home or the inspiration for many writers and works of literature, and its dynamic intellectual and literary tradition continues today. Furthermore, the 2010 Convention will be held at the newly renovated Hyatt Regency St. Louis Riverfront, situated in the central part of downtown St. Louis and adjacent to the Gateway Arch that stands at the confluence of the Mississippi and Missouri rivers. The view is spectacular.

The hotel is within walking distance of the Gateway Arch Riverboats (for sightseeing cruises) and the MetroLink, the region's light rail system, so that you can visit some of the city's points of interest including the Eugene Field House and Toy Museum, St. Louis Walk of Fame, City Museum, Science Center, Anheuser-Busch Brewery, Old Courthouse, St. Louis Mercantile Library, and many other attractions. Like the famous 1944 musical, I hope you'll "meet me in St. Louis."

The **masthead** identifies a newsletter with a specific organization, often showing logos or catchphrases members recognize immediately. Mastheads also include publication date and issue number.

Lead articles appear on the front pages—they reflect the most important recent events or topics discussed in the issue.

Images are wrapped by text so that the space is used efficiently; related text is closely grouped with the image.

Borders are sometimes used to frame text or decorate the margins.

International English Honor Society 6

Yahoo.fr, Anyone?: The Challenges of an International Service Project

Rebecca Belcher-Rankin
Co-Advisor, Tau Theta Chapter
2008 Sigma Tau Delta Service Award Winner
Olivet Nazarene University

How can I help my former African students gather current research materials in English? That was my question when I came home in 2006 from my Fulbright visiting professor position in Burkina Faso.

Although the dean of my college wanted to help, neither he nor I could solicit anything from my own colleagues. I decided I would have to find some other method to help the students who have nothing but Yahoo.fr as a research tool.

Enter Tau Theta, our small chapter affiliated with Sigma Tau Delta International English Honor Society. My students in Tau Theta at Olivet Nazarene University needed a service project: my former African students needed research materials. For fourth year students at the University of Ougadougou, their memoire projects, which approximate senior honors projects for us, required enough materials to do a paper between 50 to 100 pages. Topics ranging from the impact of the Bush environmental policies on the U.S. economy, to the thematic and stylistic considerations of Toni Morrison's *Paradise*, to Hip Hop as an exploration of Black identity, to Malcolm X's contribution to the civil rights movement meant that we needed to do extensive research.

Dr. Rebecca Belcher-Rankin at the University of Ougadougou, Burkina Faso, Africa, December, 2005. These students were some of those that benefited from the research materials sent to them the following years.

After we had received the topics, but before we began our research, we encountered the problem of copyright. Our librarians reminded us that we would break the law by copying research materials for general consumption. We decided that, if each of our members paired with a particular student who would receive the set of materials, we could solve the problem of copyright infringement. Each of our students was acting as a proxy for a student who could not access databases.

On a cold, snowy night early in 2007, we opened the English computer lab, chose topics that satisfied our curiosity, sat down at the computers, and electronically assaulted our library databases. Our parameters were to find and copy, with correct MLA citation material, at least ten sources for each topic. To make sure that we didn't languish while doing the work, we ate pizza and cookies and drank many sodas. Three hours later we had most of the topics completed. A later research session finished the work.

Then came the tricky part: getting the materials to the students. The only way to ensure that the materials would arrive at the university for distribution was to send packages to the Fulbright professor. Several hours of weighing papers and several postage dollars later, ten packages were on their way. Two weeks later we heard that the Fulbight professor had distributed all the materials. Our work was complete—for that year.

This spring we are again researching, printing copies, and packing envelopes to send to current fourth year students. For the first time, I will not know the students' names. They will have begun university since I was there, but they will need our help to research topics that they can't get from Yahoo.fr sites.

Dr. Rebecca Belcher-Rankin, professor of American literature, is co-sponsor with Prof. David Johnson of the Tau Theta chapter of Sigma Tau Delta at Olivet Nazarene University, located in Bourbonnais, IL. The chapter won the international service award at the 2008 convention for the research partnership with the University of Ouagadougou. The cash award went to the English department library at the university located in Burkina Faso.

Great Illustrations From Literature

The Merry Adventures of Robin Hood (1883)
Author and Illustrator: Howard Pyle

We all know the myth of Robin Hood, the rogue who steals from the rich and gives to the poor. But what you might not know is how Robin Hood has been illustrated through the ages. The most successful of all the Robin Hood illustrations has been that of Howard Pyle. Howard Pyle's revival of Robin Hood in his *The Merry Adventures of Robin Hood* (1883) placed Robin Hood in the foreground of children's adventure literature. Howard Pyle's career ranged from magazine commissions to famous works he both wrote and illustrated. If it weren't for Howard Pyle, the rough wandering rogue wouldn't be such an enthralling figure still today.

Running heads, footers, and side margins often include the same information appearing in the masthead, as well as sometimes page numbering.

Standard articles are introduced with enhanced headlines.

Regular features are columns that appear in each issue; they are often framed or otherwise distinguished from standard articles.

19i How do you design brochures?

Brochures can easily and inexpensively heighten interest in an organization and its activities. They generally use a handsome design and, perhaps, some carefully selected images to answer the basic questions about a group or institution—Who? What? Why? When? Where? Brochures *can* cost a lot to produce. Organizations that want to project a high-profile image, especially for recruiting new members or selling products, may opt for top-end materials and designs. If your organization doesn't have a high production budget, you can still create a simple, handsome document that also points readers to an organizational Web site—which is cheaper to develop than a printed brochure and far easier to update.

1 Planning. Brochures typically demand a balance between laying out necessary information, enhancing visual style, and careful budgeting.

- **What paper format and design features will you use?** Design features—the size and texture of the paper, whether you'll use color and images, and so on—typically depend on your budget. They also affect how much space you'll have to present various kinds of content.
- **What's the purpose of the brochure?** Is it to introduce your organization or to talk about events and activities? How do you want your audience to respond? Choose content accordingly.
- **How will you lay out key information?** Brochures are often divided into *panels* of information. Each panel tends to be a self-contained snapshot of some key aspect of the group or program you're promoting. "Storyboard" panels before drafting, keeping in mind how the finished brochure will lead readers through panels.

2 Drafting. Though each panel will have its own focus, there are three basic layouts in a brochure design: The *front panel* grabs attention, but it also says something about the organization offering the brochure. *Inside panels* are where the main information goes. Try to limit yourself to short paragraphs and lists on these pages; weigh whether it's better to provide lots of details briefly, or to go in depth about one strong point. The *rear panel* is often left mostly blank so that a mailing address can be inserted. It may also include important contact information: the name of the group, address, phone and fax numbers, and email and Web site addresses.

3 Polishing. Costs can be high, so make sure you have everything right before handing your materials over to a print shop. Printers usually don't give refunds for errors you caused by a faulty design.

EXERCISE 19.5 Working with several other people, design a two-sided, three-panel brochure that explains some service or feature of your campus or local community. Decide on the elements you might cover and design appealing pages—with appropriate illustrations and graphics. You may design the brochure entirely on your own or, if your instructor approves, begin with one of the brochure templates typically offered in word-processing or publishing programs.

Brochure (front and inside panels). The brochure below, designed by Brooke Rollins, a student employee at the University of South Carolina's College of Engineering, includes images, colors, stylized fonts, and an unusual square page layout—costly features, but within her budget.

FRONT PANEL OF A BROCHURE

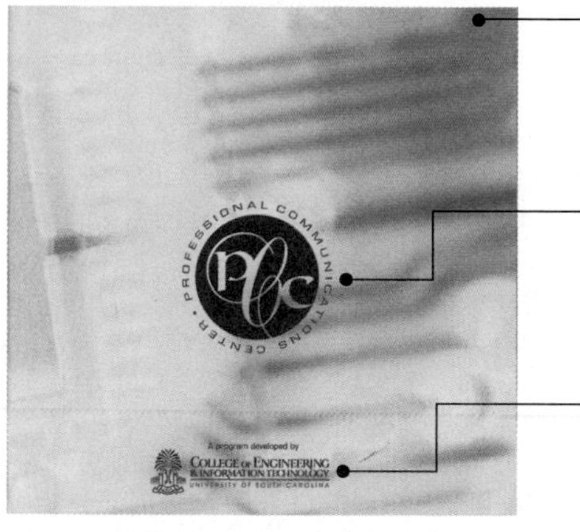

Use **graphics and colors** to attract the eyes of readers. Keep in mind that most brochures must compete for attention.

The **logo** for the organization should appear on the front panel, where you begin building a persona developed by inside panels.

Show **addresses and contact information** so that readers get a clear idea of the organization's affiliations and institutional relationships.

INSIDE PANELS OF A BROCHURE

Each **panel** includes a main heading with related passages of text. Panels have consistent layouts.

Headings are set apart from other text using inverted background and foreground colors. Eye-catching phrases draw readers in.

Contact information and the organizational logo reappear on the end panel, reminding readers where to find more details.

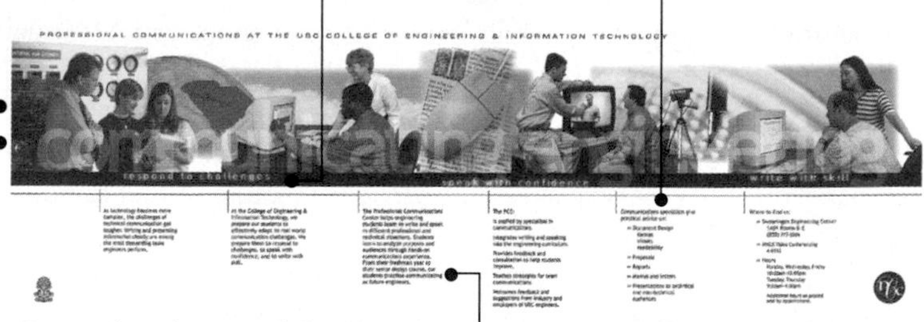

Images have been carefully selected to portray themes and activities related to the organization. Here they form a collage across all panels.

Paragraphs focus on the highlights of the organization, especially those that will seem most intriguing to the target audience.

20 How Do You Design and Deliver an Oral Presentation?

An instructor may ask you to prepare an oral presentation as a way of preparing *you* for a responsibility common in jobs and professions—delivering a speech or leading group discussion. You may feel uncomfortable when talking before crowds (many people are), but public speaking is a valuable skill that can be learned with practice, particularly in the friendly environment a classroom provides. There, listeners are usually familiar, forgiving, and well disposed to what you have to offer.

Effective presentations require many of the same qualities found in good writing—coherent organization, a highly developed sense of audience, an appreciation for audio and visual props, and memorable examples and illustrations. In addition, they often require attention to performance skills such as voice, tone, pacing, and gestures. The sections that follow offer advice on all these elements.

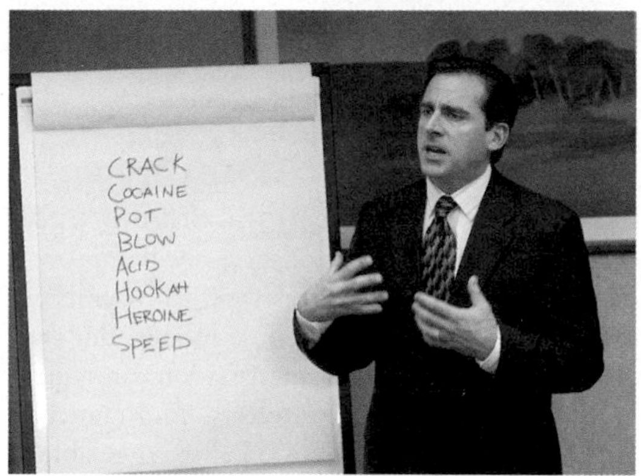

Figure 20.1 Steve Carell, playing Michael Scott in the NBC TV series *The Office*, at least looks good standing in front of his flip chart. Yet Scott's employees regularly point out his gaffes—including the minor error in this particular chart.

20a How do you plan oral presentations?

Whether or not you're comfortable in front of a crowd, your presentation will be more successful if you consider beforehand the conditions under which you'll be speaking: How much time are you allotted? Are you one member of a panel of discussants? Have you been asked to cover specific topics for your audience? Are you expected to use audio-visual aids, to speak from memory, or simply to read a fully written paper? Some of these questions might be answered by the assignment sheet you're given, but others will require deliberate consideration.

1 Choose a topic appropriate to the kind of talk you're giving. Speeches, like other presentation formats, are divided into different genres, each tailored to specific occasions and purposes. *Inaugural addresses*, for example, allow politicians to build support for their agendas and thank voters. *Closing arguments* in the courtroom enable lawyers to sum up their clients' cases. *Graduation speeches* offer inspiration.

The academic forum also has specialized genres of oral presentation, many of which overlap with professional and civic forms of speaking:

- **Research summaries.** Take on the role of instructor and present a subject with some authority. Teach concepts you found in secondary sources. Guide listeners through the results of your experiment.
- **Focused arguments.** Defend your position in an ongoing debate by convincing listeners of your claims and reasoning.
- **Reading responses.** Call attention to parts of a reading that seem especially controversial, interesting, or confusing. Help your audience "work out" the major issues by clarifying troubling passages or providing background information.

2 Assess the background and expectations of your audience. Like anything you compose, your chances of success will improve if you learn about your audience, a task that's relatively easy when your listeners include classmates or members of a group you chose to join. But even when you're familiar with your audience, an oral presentation can require special consideration of their backgrounds and interests. Your choice of wording, for example, must allow for the fact that listeners won't be able to consult a dictionary in the middle of your talk. Your choices of examples will be most effective when they reflect real-world scenarios that the great majority of your audience can relate to. If the subject of your talk requires specialized terminology or introduces less common examples, plan to spend more time explaining such unfamiliar material.

3 Decide how you'll deliver your presentation. Technology has transformed presentations so much that speakers sometimes forget that not every oral presentation must involve *PowerPoint*, an LCD projector, and a screen. Such tools are useful, but they should serve the overall purpose of the presentation, not overwhelm it. Flashy audio-visuals can't save a talk based on scanty knowledge or a poor structure. Not only are technological aids sometimes unavailable, but they can also make you less responsive to your audience, since you may be overly concerned about pressing the right button—or whether the projector works at all.

Traditional methods of presentation also have their pitfalls. Reading from a typed paper, a common academic speaking method, sometimes results in poor eye-contact. Speaking from note cards can make it easier to stumble in transitioning from point to point, leaving listeners confused. Whichever method you choose, you'll avoid mistakes and be most effective with practice. Words you've written will come as second nature, and you'll more easily engage with your audience while speaking.

EXERCISE 20.1 Write a page or two describing an unsuccessful presentation or lecture you have recently attended. Be sure to list specific problems in the presentation and how they might have been fixed.

EXERCISE 20.2 Choose a paper you have written recently for any course—it might be a history report or even a chemistry lab experiment—and imagine how you would adapt it as an oral presentation for a specific audience *other than your classmates*. (You might consider a group of sixth graders or a community group.) What visual or aural components might you use? Describe the presentation in a paragraph or two, highlighting the adaptions you would make for the new audience.

20b How do you script what you'll say?

Know what each part of your presentation is supposed to do. Start by considering what you want your audience to learn from your talk. Should they better understand a key concept? Should they be convinced of a particular claim you make? Then, think of your presentation as meeting a series of smaller goals, each of which will take a specific amount of time to achieve. Begin drafting your talk by scripting a few standard parts:

1 Connect with your audience in the introduction. Ease your audience into the presentation. No matter how good the body of your talk is, it won't succeed if listeners are inattentive or hostile.

- **Introduce yourself.** Your audience will want to know who you are, why you've come to speak to them, and what your qualifications are. Even when your audience knows you, as in a classroom presentation, you can still explain your personal interest in the topic.
- **Set a tone.** If your presentation is light-hearted, start with something humorous—an anecdote often works well. If it's serious, avoid melodramatics, but establish a level of formality that signals to listeners you don't want the topic to be ignored.
- **Draw upon common knowledge.** You can't teach your audience anything new if you don't start with ideas they already understand. A presentation on the economics of extreme sports, for example, might open with popular depictions of the sports on television and in film.

2 Choose an intuitive structure for the body of your talk. When you present ideas in writing, you can hope readers will go back and review earlier paragraphs if they don't understand the direction you've taken (not that you want them to become lost in the first place!). In oral presentations, you don't have such a safety net. You're better off presenting ideas in an order that listeners can easily grasp. A reading response, for example, might trace the key points in the same order adopted by the author; a historical research report might follow a chronological order; an evaluative presentation, a comparison-contrast plan (see Chapter 12). Such commonsense organizational structures invoke a point of familiarity that can make even esoteric subjects easy to understand.

Once you've chosen a suitable structure, plan to forecast it for listeners. Early in the presentation, reveal your organizational scheme, perhaps by way of a simple handout or bulleted slide. This simple summary of what's to come can help you avoid losing people along the way—they'll have an idea of what to look and listen for.

3 Insert clear cues and transitions. Oral presentations rely on verbal cues and physical gestures to help listeners move easily from point to point. In the notes or script for your talk, mark planned pauses and choreographed gestures that can help audience members recognize and recall how you've divided your material. You might, for example, approach your audience when you want to pose challenging questions, or remain silent a moment to let listeners take in an important concept before proceeding.

Visual aids are quite effective for creating less subtle transitional cues. Slides, for example, can display what you've covered, where you are, and where you're headed. The very acts of turning to analyze a projected photo or picking up an object you're going to discuss can quite effectively redirect the attention of your audience.

4 Make a lasting impression in your conclusion. Go beyond recapitulation and summary, but steer clear of grandstanding. Instead, choose a closing strategy that makes it easy for your audience to recall the gist of your talk well after you've stopped speaking.

- **Present an illustrative case in point.** Vivid examples can put a human face or real-world veneer on abstract concepts; they can also make bold or controversial statements seem more credible.
- **Suggest important implications.** Offer a brief interpretation of how the details presented in the body of your talk affect other issues.
- **Ask provocative questions.** Your ending needn't always be neat and tidy, especially if your presentation is exploratory. Go ahead and point out questions left unanswered by your research. Invite your audience to posit some hypotheses.

Try to leave time at the end of your presentation for questions and then handle them with good humor. Occasionally, someone in your audience may ask a "hostile" question. Don't respond in kind. Your audience will respect you more if you respond to the challenge coolly and politely, and then move on.

20c How do you create audio-visual aids?

Audiences today have high expectations for oral presentations because various tools—including computers, LCD projectors, and presentation software such as *PowerPoint* and *Keynote*—have made it easy to create absorbing multimedia events. But bells and whistles alone don't impress people, and they can sometimes overwhelm your key points.

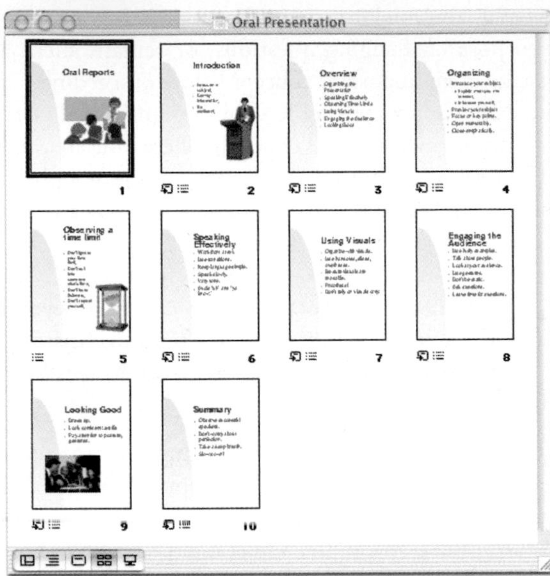

Figure 20.2 Learn your presentation software as you would your word processor. Many programs have special features to help you both design slides and organize your talk—like the Slide Sorter feature of *Microsoft PowerPoint* at left.

1 Choose the appropriate tools, props, and supplements for your report. Don't use more equipment than you require, and never introduce a special effect just because you know how to create it. For many presentations, all the technology you may need is a podium and your lecture notes. But even simple tools must be used well. If you write on a chalkboard or flip chart, do so clearly, boldly, and quickly. Reduce full sentences to key words and phrases, if possible.

Plan ahead for any equipment you require. Do whatever you can to practice with that equipment and, especially, to anticipate problems. LCD projectors, for example, have notoriously difficult controls. Even turning down the lights can be a problem in some rooms. The more details you work through ahead of time, the smoother your presentation will go.

2 Take extra care when designing slides, posters, and transparencies. Chapter 18 features extensive coverage of how to lay out pages in electronic and printed documents—many of these guidelines apply also to presentation slides, posters, and handouts. But a few other guidelines are useful to produce the most effective visual aids:

- **Keep each slide simple.** This applies not only to the concepts you present, but also to the style of presentation. Elaborate ornaments and busy designs can overwhelm the eye, and distract from your words.
- **Present new information one piece at a time.** If you introduce too much at once, listeners will look over your shoulder to see what comes next, rather than focus on what you're saying at the moment.
- **Build upon material you've already presented.** Slides can provide unobtrusive visual reminders of what you've already covered. If you've told your audience that you're comparing four different features of hybrid cars, you can label each slide, "Feature *X* of 4."
- **Be consistent in visual layout and style.** When readers need to adjust their eyes with each successive slide, they become disoriented.
- **Make sure each visual aid is easily seen.** Use large, bold type in your slides, and make images large enough so audience members don't need to move closer to see what you're talking about.

3 Carefully choreograph your use of audio and visual aids.

Everything you show to your audience should at some point be the focus of discussion—otherwise listeners will be led astray from your overall purpose. Plan carefully the words you'll use to introduce each presentation aid, as well as what you'll say about it and how you'll transition to the next idea. With a video clip, for example, tell viewers what they're about to see, how long it will take, and what they should look for. Have the video cued to the exact moment of interest. After playing it, address immediately the parts that are relevant to your presentation, while the images and sounds are still fresh in people's minds.

4 Proof slides and handouts assiduously. Most software programs used to create presentation materials include spelling checkers. Yet these tools cannot catch misspellings of many proper nouns. Spelling *Jane Austen* as *Jean Austin* on a dozen slides will destroy your credibility. Remember that your visual aids will receive full and critical attention from your audience, so you don't want them catching errors in facts, mechanics, or design.

When borrowing material, such as photos, tables, or charts, be sure to identify your sources. You don't need a full MLA citation, but you should make it clear that you did not generate the material yourself.

Chart 20.1 Common Types of Presentation Slides

Title slides introduce the speaker and the subject of the talk. They typically list the title of the talk and the name and affiliation of the presenter. You can follow your title slide with another outlining the structure of your speech and the key points you'll cover.

Illustration and example slides can be used to show text or images you discuss at length. You might present, for example, a picture of an Ibo mask while treating the rituals of African cultures or present a short quote from a play that you're arguing should be appreciated for its comedic dialogue.

Winedale
Costume and Setting
Glendower
(Example 2 of 3)

Concept slides can be used to project a definition or a key idea that you build upon later in your presentation. For example, before you argue a case for "development" of local areas, you might have your audience focus on what this concept means to you and others.

Winedale
Methods (4 of 4)
Performance:
Acting
as
Interpretation

List, diagram, and chart slides present many details together. Keep in mind that it may not be most effective to present listeners with your entire list or chart all at once. In some cases, it may work better to reveal each bullet point or statistic cumulatively, one slide at a time, or to put together your larger diagram piece by piece, like a puzzle you're building with your audience.

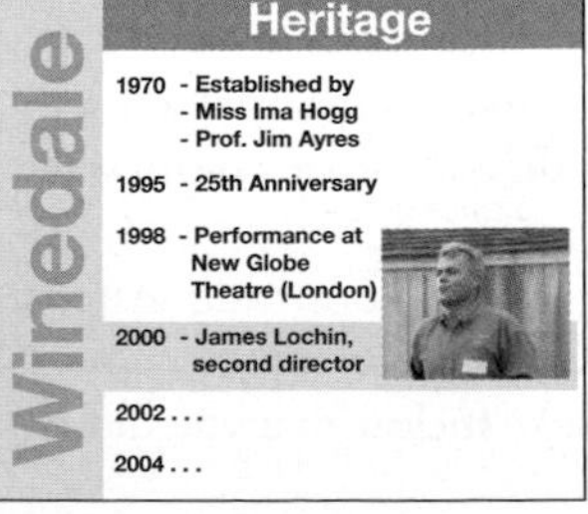

5 Practice the full report aloud several times, complete with the equipment you intend to use. Don't imagine how you'll act—speak the words just as you intend to say them; flip through your slides, overheads, or posters; and be sure to time yourself. As much as possible, get familiar with the podium, lectern, microphone, screen, and other equipment. Practice at least once in the place you will deliver the presentation—ideally with some sort of audience (perhaps a friend who'll give honest feedback). If that's not possible, at least scope out the room or auditorium beforehand, so you know what to expect. A group presentation should be choreographed so that all participants know their parts. Leave nothing to chance, and always anticipate the failure of equipment. Be ready to deliver a professional presentation even if the bulb in the projector burns out or there's no chalk for the board.

EXERCISE 20.3 Working in a group, use presentation software to design a ten-minute explanation of how to use a particular feature of the presentation software effectively. Be creative and imaginative, given that everyone in the class is working on the same assignment, but try earnestly to teach fellow classmates how to make the most of the presentation feature you discuss. Vote on the best presentation, using the guidelines in Section 20b as criteria of evaluation.

20d How do you speak before an audience?

Treat your presentation as a performance. You'll need all your resources to connect with listeners, including your voice, gestures, and physical presence, the last of which is especially important for lively interaction.

1 Engage your audience with voice and gesture. Learn to vary the tone and intensity of your voice: raise or lower it to underscore key points; use pauses to mark shifts in topic. Above all, avoid speaking so swiftly that you garble your words. Inexperienced speakers sometimes start out fine, but begin to speak faster and faster (and softer and softer) until they become almost unintelligible. An oral report is not a race. Take a deep breath every so often and slow down.

Be sure to convey some enthusiasm for your subject. Don't freeze up before an audience; instead, *use* your body. A shrug, a nod, a casual turn, a sweep of the arm, even a scratch of the head can all be used to reinforce a point. If appropriate, move away from the podium and change position during the speech a few times. Compel your listeners to refocus their attention, but don't pace—shifts of position should seem purposeful.

2 Be responsive to your audience. You'll see and hear reactions (*we're bored; we're confused*) immediately in smiles, furrowed brows, coughs, groans, and, maybe, applause. Interpret these expressions carefully and—as much as possible—adapt to the feedback you are receiving: liven up your delivery if the room has lost energy; stop for questions if you perceive some misunderstanding in people's faces.

If you discover you have too much material to cover in the remaining time, edit as you go. Skip some details or examples rather than rush through the presentation. Keep a discreet eye on the clock or keep a wristwatch on the podium. If no length is assigned to your talk, remember the rule of any good performance: leave the audience asking for more.

Taking Control

Speak effectively

Sometimes well-prepared talks are sabotaged by a speaker's poor delivery. While practice is perhaps the most important means of ensuring success, keep in mind four basic tenets of public speaking:

- **Show respect for your audience.** Dress well, for instance. No ripped jeans or baseball caps! Don't belabor points that an audience clearly gets—but be willing to backtrack if people seem confused.
- **Assert your presence.** Maintain eye contact with members of the audience. Smile occasionally. Don't bury your nose in your notes.
- **Own your material.** Study your subject well enough that you can comfortably speak off-script or even without the aid of notes.
- **Maintain composure.** Don't rock back and forth at the podium or punctuate every phrase with "like," "um," or "ya know." These nervous ticks make you look uncomfortable and distract listeners.

CHAPTER

21 How Do You Write for the Web?

Only ten years ago, writers who wanted to publish online generally designed their own Web sites or sent contributions to sites managed by independent editors. Now, not only do popular Web sites like *Wikipedia* and *MySpace* call for content and editorial input from readers, but many business and service Web sites also encourage visitor participation, in order to improve communication between employees and to be more responsive to the public. College instructors and administrators have likewise taken advantage of similar Internet technologies, integrating them into class activities—or even conducting online-only courses. Below we cover some of the most commonly used Web writing environments.

21a When should you use social media at school?

Many college students have become habitual users of popular social networks like *Facebook*, *MySpace*, and *Twitter*. These sites work quite well for sustaining links with friends or for making new connections. Yet, as much as these online communities facilitate networking between people, so also can they create uncomfortable situations when used carelessly.

1 Respect traditional boundaries between instructors and students. As nice a gesture as it may be to "friend" your instructor on *Facebook*, realize that this creates a tremendously awkward situation. Congenial relationships between students and instructors generally make classes more fun, lively, and effective, but there's no getting around the fact that teachers must ultimately evaluate student work. In order to avoid appearances of favoritism, instructors may choose not to respond to electronic correspondence unrelated to coursework, even when they recognize the goodwill behind a student's overture.

There are, however, acceptable ways of using social networking sites to interact with faculty on campus. Many academic interest groups use networking homepages to publicize events of common interest. By participating online (as well as off), you'll no doubt create many rewarding—and less awkward—connections with both teachers and fellow students.

2 Express yourself—but know who's reading. One side effect of social networking that many writing instructors can appreciate is how it encourages people to write on a daily basis, even if the postings do not meet academic or professional standards. In fact, many of these sites offer useful environments for experimenting with verbal and visual style. *Twitter*, for instance, requires that every message be less than 140 characters long. What a great exercise in conciseness! Alternatively, *MySpace* asks members to build online identities through a combination of "blurbs," lists, and images, any of which can evoke commentary from visitors. The result is an instructive lesson on the many different ways writers can alter their self-presentation and evoke varied reactions from readers.

But while social media tend to promote written interaction and experimentation, you should be cautious about what you post. Once you submit something to the Web, you lose control over it—readers can store what you've written permanently or forward it to someone else. You might be surprised how fast a venting remark about your boss travels to coworkers.

21b How do you participate on class Web sites?

A few of your instructors may integrate popular social networking sites into classwork, but most will use more official means for electronic exchanges. Universities now provide Web-based *courseware* (for example, WebCT and Blackboard) for conducting activities traditionally done in classrooms. So don't be surprised if your English syllabus includes a homepage address alongside a reading list.

1 Keep in mind your instructor's purpose for using the site. By navigating to the class Web site soon after your instructor gives you an address, you'll see more clearly how online resources fit into course activities. The site might simply be used to post handouts, supplementary material, or announcements. On the other hand, many instructors use Web sites to extend class discussion and facilitate group writing exercises. Determine your responsibilities for using the class site throughout the term: What features of the site are used in required assignments? Will students turn in formal papers to the site? Discuss readings?

Plan tasks and allocate time according to such expectations. Obviously you'll want to visit the class Web site more often, perhaps daily, if it's used as the primary means for communicating between members outside of face-to-face meetings. Be sure, at least, to avoid using the class Web site for activities your instructor hasn't approved. Don't, for example, turn in papers online, if your instructor wants printed documents.

2 Familiarize yourself with the site's interactive features. As with most computer software, the interactive features of class Web sites can take some getting used to. Fortunately, they tend to use a familiar kind of online interaction called *Web forms* or *online forms.* Web forms consist of one or more editable fields—text boxes, selection lists, checklists, etc.—and a means of saving your entries, often marked by a button labeled "Submit" or something apropos to the activity you are performing, such as "Reply" or "Update." See Figure 21.1 for an example of a Web form used to post a message to an online discussion forum.

Once you learn the technology, however, you still need to use it appropriately. Recognize the typical applications for some of the most common interactive features on class sites:

- **Threaded Discussion Forums.** These online discussion tools offer a flexible means for extending dialogue beyond individual class meetings. Participants can deliberate more about each comment than in an oral debate, because responses to a single line (or *thread*) of debate are posted over an extended period of time. See Figure 21.1.
- **Class Email.** Some courseware provides its own form of messaging. Be aware that these email-like features don't always work with standard Internet email systems, such as *Gmail.* To avoid missing messages you may need to check both your regular email inbox as well as the one on your class site. If in doubt, ask your instructor which email to use.
- **Online Quizzes and Questionnaires.** Your instructor may want to see how prepared students are for discussing assigned material in the classroom. Quizzes help instructors know what to review in class.

WEB MESSAGE FORUM

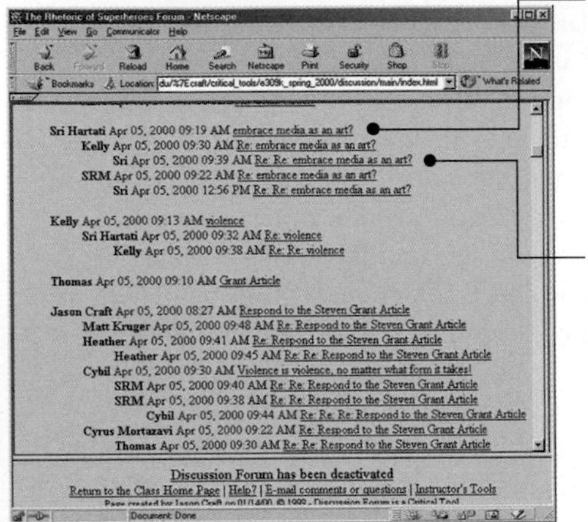

Threads appear as an initial message (starting at the left-hand margin of the page) followed by a series of responses indented below. Each response is listed under the thread to which it replies.

Response postings are listed as linked text, often preceded by "Re:" and followed by the subject line of the initial message in the thread. Click on the link to read the message. Some forums allow respondents to create their own subject lines, rather than maintain the original.

WEB FORUM RESPONSE FORM

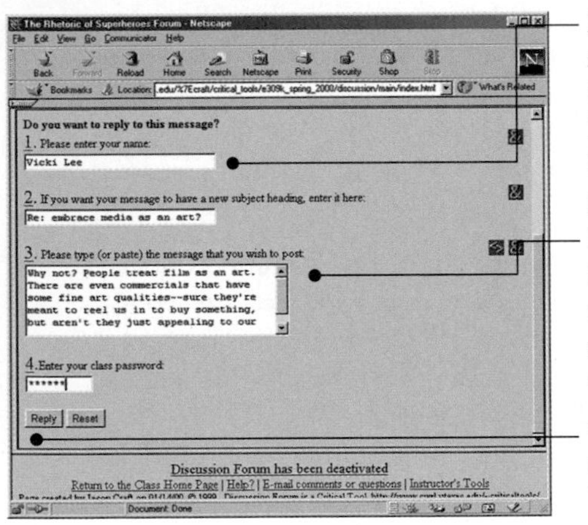

Most forms automatically insert the **name** associated with a user account. Otherwise enter the name you would like to appear with your posting. Some public forums allow anonymous postings.

Enter your **message** in plain-text format. Some forums offer type styles and other visual enhancements; others allow you to use HTML codes to alter the appearance of the message.

Click the **reply** (or "submit") button to add your message to the thread. This forum happens to require a password to participate.

Figure 21.1 The sample Web forum above shows a series of threads about an article read for a University of Texas at Austin composition class. Below the discussion's home page is an image of a Web form used for posting a response. Your courseware will probably show discussions in a slightly different format, but you should be able to identify some of the common elements you see above. If you haven't used other interactive Web sites, online forms may feel strange at first. You'll be more at ease after only a few posts.

3 Don't think of the Web site as a way of avoiding the classroom. Ideally, your online activities should complement your classroom participation in the course and interaction with fellow students. Often, discussions on Web sites are extensions of activities, wherein you need some knowledge of spoken comments in order to add something constructive to the ongoing conversation. Class Web sites can also lead back into classroom activities by providing reading prompts, response forums, and detailed assignment guidelines. These online resources and activities, when used regularly, can spark intriguing questions inside the classroom, or help instructors redirect meeting time to focus on material that has garnered greater attention or caused confusion.

EXERCISE 21.1 Introduce yourself to your classmates with an email. (If you haven't logged into your class Web site, use this as an opportunity to do so. Be sure to acquire appropriate log-in information from your instructor.) Address the email to all the members of the class, including the instructor (see Section 19a for more on how to format emails). In the message, tell everyone the name you prefer to go by, where you're from, and why you came to school where you did. Next, write a paragraph on your interests: What books have you read recently? What did you think about the last movie you saw? Downloaded any new music? You choose your focus. Finally, reveal to classmates your favorite thing about writing, as well as your biggest worry. After receiving others' introductory emails, you may find that classmates share your concerns.

EXERCISE 21.2 Discuss a reading with classmates on a class Web forum. Start a new discussion thread (see Figure 21.1 on the previous page) on a particular issue from the reading, labeling the thread accordingly. Begin your message by directing classmates to a specific passage you'd like to discuss. Provide a short quotation and page reference if possible (see Chapter 47 for guidelines on quotation). Then, write a paragraph explaining why the passage or issue interests you, whether you agree with the author (assuming it is nonfiction), and what might be missing from the author's treatment of the topic. Try to avoid repeating thread topics already posted by classmates. Respond to at least two of your classmates' threads.

21c How do you write for wikis, blogs, and other Web 2.0 environments?

At this moment, you could log on to a site like <blogger.com> and start your own *Weblog* recounting your band's weekly performances. Alternatively, you could add a *knol* page to <knol.google.com>, sharing what you *know* about making ends meet as a student. Or, you could update your school's *Wikipedia* entry to document the creation of a new field hockey club. This relatively new ease and freedom for Web readers to become Web writers is part of a technological trend often dubbed *Web 2.0*, to mark advances many newer sites have made toward greater reader participation.

1 Familiarize yourself with the site's presentation format. Although it's easy to participate on Web 2.0 sites—which provide Web forms of greater or lesser complexity and flexibility (see 21b-2 above)—not all sites display contributed content and updates in the same format. The layout for *blogs* is fairly straightforward: each entry has a timestamp marking when it was posted, creating a journal-like look. *Wikis* work differently. On wikis, multiple writers edit every content page. For example, readers of *Wikipedia* initially see the latest version of the entry on "fuel cells." Yet by clicking on the page's "history" tab, they can also view all changes others have made since the first brief article was posted in 2002. Each successive contribution may be large or small and may take more or less advantage of visual layouts and styles available on the wiki, yet no matter the scope, all contributions are carefully recorded in the page's "history."

Other Web 2.0 sites record and present reader input differently. If you want to participate on a site, first look at some popular pages as models. Then, start an account with the site and read its instructions for posting. Of course, if your instructor or employer asks you to contribute to a wiki or write a blog, they'll no doubt have more specific expectations about the format and length of contributions you should make.

2 Respect the purpose of the site. When you start an account on a Web 2.0 site you become a member of that online community and should expect to adapt all your contributions to community standards. For example, a site like *Wikipedia*, which bills itself as a "free encyclopedia," expects participants to write accurate and informative articles about subjects of common interest. To avoid bias, *Wikipedia* states that account holders should not add entries on themselves. *Blogs*, of course, have quite the opposite aims: users *should* discuss themselves and express personal opinions. By following a site's posting policies, you'll avoid having your account disabled, and others in the online community will view you as a "good citizen." Figure 21.2 below recounts one example of "bad" posting.

When writing on wikis and blogs at school or for work, you need to be doubly cautious about keeping the site's purpose in mind. Your boss will reprimand you (or worse) if you complain about coworkers on a blog intended to publicize the company's community outreach. Your instructor might not give any points for posting music video clips to your research group's wiki, if it's supposed to present an annotated bibliography of newspaper articles treating urban development.

Figure 21.2 In 2006, while live on his show, satirist Stephen Colbert made facetious revisions to some *Wikipedia* entries. As a result, his account was disabled. This incident reveals both the consequences of not following community standards and the reason why *Wikipedia* may not be a good academic source: you never know the credentials and intentions of the last person updating a given entry.

EXERCISE 21.3 As a group, create a wiki-based annotated bibliography treating a topic you'd all like to write more about. (For more on annotated bibliographies, see pages 78–80.) Each member of the group should post at least three entries. Make sure to follow the citation formats discussed in Part 8. Your instructor can tell you which wiki site to use and how to start user accounts. Some schools provide their own versions of wiki sites based, for instance, on *Wikispaces*. Alternatively, some public sites, like *Google Sites* (<sites.google.com/>), allow people to create their own password-protected wikis and blogs.

21d How do you establish your *ethos* online?

One common feature of all the online writing environments mentioned above is participation by means of a password-protected account. Your account's username becomes your identity on the site. On a product rating site, readers may seek out your comments or avoid them depending upon what you've posted before. On a class Web site, your instructor may assign participation credit based on all postings associated with your username. Since your username is your online identity, you should exercise caution with each posting. By posting with care for your own words and consideration for others' opinions, you'll soon be able to establish a trustworthy and respected *ethos* as a contributor to the online community.

1 Assume everything you post will be permanently available. While many sites give you control over what appears in the most recent version of pages to which you contribute, most sites keep copies of what you posted before. Some, like *Wikipedia*, also make past postings publicly available. Avoid putting yourself in the position of having to defend yourself (in a job interview, perhaps) for remarks posted years ago.

2 Maintain composure in online exchanges. The interactive features of these sites can sometimes lead to emotional postings. Avoid expressing anger or ridicule in your postings, even when others vent. Instead, redirect debate to be more constructive—or simply move on.

PART V

GRAMMAR

CHAPTER

22 Questions About Subject-Verb Agreement?

When subjects and verbs don't agree, careful readers notice. Yet the rules for agreement can seem complicated. They merit your attention, especially when you are editing a draft.

22a Agreement: Is the subject singular or plural?

A verb may change its form, depending on whether its subject is singular or plural. The verb is then said to *agree in number* with its subject. Following are guidelines to help you develop confidence about subject-verb agreement.

Subjects and verbs usually agree more readily than politicians.

1 Understand how subject-verb agreement works. With verbs in the present tense, agreement in number is relatively simple: most subjects take the base form of the verb. The base form is the word produced when *to* is removed from the infinitive: to *predict*; to *go*.

First person, singular, present tense:	I predict. I go.
Second person, singular, present tense:	You predict. You go.
First person, plural, present tense:	We predict. We go.
Second person, plural, present tense:	You predict. You go.
Third person, plural, present tense:	They predict. They go.

The single notable exception to this pattern occurs with third person singular subjects (for example, *he, she, it, Irene*). A regular verb in the present tense needs an *-s* or *-es* ending.

Third person, singular, present tense:	She predict**s.** Irene predict**s.** He go**es.**

To choose a correct verb form in the third person (present tense), you must know whether the subject of a sentence is singular or plural. The choice of the verb form can be fairly easy when a subject is clearly either singular or plural.

sing. subj.
The weather channel **predicts** storms today.

plural subj.
Meteorologists **predict** storms today.

sing. subj.
He **goes** to Oklahoma City today.

plural subj.
The teachers **go** to Oklahoma City today.

Agreement is also required with irregular verbs such as *to be* and *to have* in a variety of tenses. (See Section 23b.)

SINGULAR SUBJECTS

The weather **is** stormy today.

The weather **was** stormy today.

The weather **has been** stormy for some time.

PLURAL SUBJECTS

The meteorologists **are** accurate today.

The meteorologists **were** accurate yesterday.

The meteorologists **have been** accurate for several weeks.

EXERCISE 22.1 Decide which verb in boldface is correct.

1. The most violent of all storms, tornadoes (**occur/occurs**) more often in the United States than in any other country.
2. The rotational winds sometimes (**exceed/exceeds**) 500 miles per hour in the vortex of a tornado.
3. Dust devils (**is/are**) less ferocious vortices of warm air.
4. Rising heat currents (**cause/causes**) dust devils.
5. A tornado over water (**has/have**) many of the same characteristics as one over land.

2 In most cases, treat subjects joined by *and* as plural. Joining two subjects this way creates a *compound subject* that takes a verb without an *-s* or *-es* ending (in third person, present).

subj. + subj. verb
Storm chasers and journalists alike **seek** great videos of destructive storms.

subj. + subj. verb
The press and storm chasers **risk** their lives to get close to twisters.

subj. + subj. verb
Meteorologists and the Office of Public Safety **fear** that storm chasers often underestimate the magnitude of tornadoes.

However, some subjects joined by *and* clearly describe a single thing or idea. You should treat such expressions as singular.

subj. verb

Peace and quiet **is** rare in tornado alley during spring months.

subj. verb

Rock and roll **is** usually as noisy as a thunderclap.

Similarly, when a compound subject connected by *and* is modified by *every* or *each*, the verb takes a singular form.

subj. + subj. verb

Every wall cloud and supercell **holds** the potential for a tornado.

subj. + subj. verb

Each spring and each fall **brings** the threat of more storms.

However, when *each* follows a compound subject, you may use either a plural or a singular verb.

The meteorologist and the storm chaser each **have** their reasons for studying the weather.

The meteorologist and the storm chaser each **has** his or her story to tell.

3 Understand that subjects linked to other nouns by phrases such as *along with, as well as,* or *together with* are not considered compound. So the verb agrees only with the subject, which may be either singular or plural.

sing. subj. plural noun verb

The National Weather Service, as well as many *police officers*, **wishes** amateurs wouldn't chase severe storms in their vehicles.

plural subj. sing. noun verb

Many *amateurs*, along with the *press*, **chase** storms in the American heartland.

When singular subjects followed by expressions such as *along with, as well as,* or *together with* sound awkward with singular verbs, use *and* to connect the potential subjects and then modify the verb, as shown in the following example.

SLIGHTLY AWKWARD *The National Weather Service*, as well as *local storm chasers*, **considers** tornadoes unlikely today.

BETTER *The National Weather Service and local storm chasers* **consider** tornadoes unlikely today.

4 When subjects are joined by *or, neither . . . nor,* or *either . . . or,* be sure the verb (or its auxiliary) agrees with the subject closer to it. In these examples the arrows point to the subjects nearer the verbs.

plural / sing.
Neither the local authorities nor the National Weather Service **is** able to prevent people from tracking dangerous storms.

sing. / plural
Either severe lightning or powerful bouts of hail **mark** the development of a supercell.

sing. / plural
Does *the danger or the thrills of chasing storms* attract people to the "sport"?

plural / sing.
Do *the thrills of chasing storms or the danger* attract people to the "sport"?

The rule holds when one or both of the subjects joined by *or, either . . . or*, or *neither . . . nor* are pronouns: the verb agrees with the nearer subject.

Neither *she* nor *we* **admit** to fear of thunder.

Neither *we* nor *she* **admits** to fear of thunder.

If a construction seems especially awkward, it can be revised—usually by making the verb plural or rewriting the sentence.

AWKWARD	Neither *you* nor *I* **am** bothered by lightning.
BETTER	Neither *I* nor *you* **are** bothered by lightning.
BETTER	*We* **are** not bothered by lightning.

5 When the subject of a sentence is a phrase or a clause, examine the subject closely. Many such constructions will be singular, though they may seem plural.

SINGULAR SUBJECTS

Chasing tornadoes **involves** risk.

That George survived the storms that tore through three Oklahoma counties **is** remarkable.

However, phrases and clauses can form compound subjects when joined by the conjunction *and*, requiring appropriate verb forms.

COMPOUND SUBJECTS

Locating a waterspout **and** *taking photographs of it* **are** his chief ambitions.

That the skies are darkening **and** *that the wind is rising* **concern** us.

EXERCISE 22.2 Decide which verb in boldface is correct.

1. Storms of all types (**continue/continues**) to intrigue people.
2. The storm chaser, like other thrill seekers, (**learn/learns**) to minimize the dangers of the hunt.
3. It's unlikely that either the dangers or the boredom of storm chasing (**is/are**) going to discourage the dedicated amateur.
4. The meteorologist and the storm chaser (**know/knows**) that neither ferocious tornadoes nor the less violent waterspout (**is/are**) predictable.
5. That the last ten years have seen an increase in the numbers of storm chasers (**is/are**) troubling.

22b Agreement: Is the subject an indefinite pronoun?

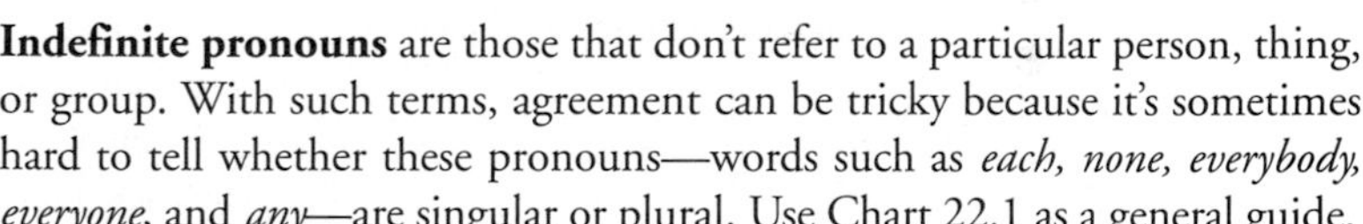

Indefinite pronouns are those that don't refer to a particular person, thing, or group. With such terms, agreement can be tricky because it's sometimes hard to tell whether these pronouns—words such as *each, none, everybody, everyone,* and *any*—are singular or plural. Use Chart 22.1 as a general guide.

1 Determine whether an indefinite pronoun is singular, plural, or variable. Consult Chart 22.1 (or a dictionary) to find out. Then select an appropriate verb form.

2 Be careful when indefinite pronouns are modified. If a pronoun is always singular, it remains singular even if it is modified by a phrase with a plural noun in it. For example, *each* is usually singular in academic usage, even when followed by a prepositional phrase (though this convention is often not observed in speech or casual usage).

subj. verb
Each of the whales **makes** unique sounds.

subj. verb
Each of the animals **has** a personality.

When the indefinite pronoun varies in number (words such as *all, most, none, some*), the noun in the prepositional phrase determines whether the pronoun (and consequently the verb) is singular or plural.

NOUN IN PREPOSITIONAL PHRASE IS SINGULAR

Some of the research **is** contradictory.

NOUN IN PREPOSITIONAL PHRASE IS PLURAL

Some of the younger whales **are** playful.

If the indefinite pronoun is plural, so is the verb.

indef. pron. verb
A *few* in the scientific community **wonder** if the whale will survive.

indef. pron. verb
Many very much **hope** so.

Chart 22.1 Indefinite Pronouns

SINGULAR	VARIABLE (SINGULAR OR PLURAL)	PLURAL
anybody	all	few
anyone	any	many
anything	either	several
each	more	
everybody	most	
everyone	neither	
everything	none	
nobody	some	
no one		
nothing		
somebody		
someone		
something		

Taking Control

Pronouns (indefinite)

Many of the singular indefinite pronouns have a plural feel to them—especially *anybody, anyone, anything, everybody,* and *everything*. When you can't consult a dictionary or the chart in this section, you might simply recall that all indefinite pronouns made up of two words (any-*body*; every-*thing*; no *one*) are singular. This tip is especially useful as these are also among the pronouns most likely to cause you problems in determining the verb.

EXERCISE 22.3 Decide which verb in boldface would be correct in academic writing.

1. Most of New York's immigrants (**is/are**) now non-European.
2. Everybody (**seem/seems**) to have something to contribute.
3. Nobody in the city (**run/runs**) politics anymore.
4. Everybody (**expect/expects**) a piece of the pie.
5. None of the candidates (**is/are**) qualified.
6. All of the groups in the city (**want/wants**) to be heard.

22c Agreement: Is the subject a collective noun?

Nouns that name a group are called **collective**: *team, choir, band, orchestra, jury, committee, faculty, family*. Some collective nouns may be either singular or plural, depending on how you regard them. Here is a sentence with the subject (the collective noun *family*) treated as singular.

> The *Begay family* **expects** that *its* restaurant will benefit from a recent increase in Arizona tourism.

Here's the same sentence with the subject taken as plural.

> The *Begay family* **expect** that *their* restaurant will benefit from a recent increase in Arizona tourism.

Both versions are acceptable.

To be sure verbs and collective nouns agree, decide whether a collective noun used as a subject acts as a single unit (the *jury*) or as separate individuals or parts (the twelve members of the *jury*). Then be consistent with your usage throughout a project, making the verb and any pronouns agree in number with the subject.

SINGULAR The *jury* **expects** its verdict to be controversial.

PLURAL The *jury* **agree** not to discuss their verdict with the press.

SINGULAR The *choir* **expects** to choose a variety of hymns and chants.

PLURAL The *choir* **raise** their voices in song.

Usually you'll do better to treat collective nouns as singular subjects. Making them plural sometimes makes them sound awkward. You can solve this problem simply by referring to "the members" of the group when you want to use a plural verb.

PLURAL *Members of the public* **are** here in great numbers.

PLURAL *The audience members* **are** clapping their hands.

Chart 22.2 should help you manage collective nouns.

EXERCISE 22.4 Decide whether the collective subjects in the following sentences are being treated as singular or plural. Then select the appropriate verb form for academic writing.

1. The research team (**reports/report**) to Captain Picard that its data (**is/are**) not subject to interpretation.
2. The starship crew (**is/are**) eager to resolve their differences.
3. Ten years (**has/have**) passed since the last intergalactic crisis.
4. A number of weapons still (**needs/need**) to be brought online, but the chief engineer reports that the actual number of inoperative systems (**is/are**) small.
5. The jury (**is/are**) still out as to whether a committee of Federation officials (**intends/intend**) to authorize action against the Klingons.

Chart 22.2 Collective Nouns

SUBJECT	GUIDELINE	EXAMPLES
Measurements	Singular as a unit; plural as individual components.	*Five miles* is a long walk. *Five more miles* are ahead. *Six months* is the wait. *Six months* have passed.
Numbers	Singular in expressions of division and subtraction. Singular or plural in expressions of multiplication and addition.	*Four* divided by *two* is two. *Four* minus *two* leaves two. *Two* times *two* is/are four. *Two* plus *two* is/are four.
Words ending in *-ics*	School subjects are usually singular. Other *-ics* words vary; you will need to check a dictionary.	*Physics* is a tough major. *Economics* is a useful minor. *Linguistics* is popular. His *tactics* are shrewd. *Athletics* are expensive. *Ethics* is a noble study. Her *ethics* are questionable. *Politics* is fun. Francie's *politics* are radical.
data	Plural in formal writing; often singular in informal writing.	The *data* are reliable. The *data* is reliable.
number	Singular if preceded by *the*; plural if preceded by *a*.	The *number* has grown. A *number* have left.
public	Singular as a unit; plural as individual people.	The *public* is satisfied. The *public* are here in great numbers.

Taking Control

Noun agreement

As you can see, when the subject in a sentence is a collective noun, agreement with the verb can be tricky, especially with words such as *economics* and *data*. In such cases, a dictionary can always help, especially a college dictionary that provides advice about usage. But consistency can be the tougher problem for many writers. Once you decide to treat a term like *jury, committee, faculty,* or *family* as either singular or plural, you must do so throughout a work, even if you find yourself thinking of the subject as sometimes singular and sometimes plural. So an item like the following won't work:

WRONG The **jury is** deadlocked, but they **are** determined to finish before day's end.

You have various options that enable you to be consistent:

RIGHT The **jury is** deadlocked, but **it is** determined to finish before day's end.

RIGHT The **jury,** though deadlocked, **is** determined to finish before day's end.

RIGHT The **jury is** deadlocked, but **jurors are** determined to finish before day's end.

Then you have to follow this principle in the entire paper, consistently thinking of the jury as a single entity.

22d Agreement: Is the subject separated from its verb?

A verb agrees with its subject only, not with any nouns in modifying phrases or clauses that come between the subject and the verb. So when editing for subject-verb agreement, first identify the subject in a sentence or clause and determine whether it is singular or plural; then choose the appropriate verb form. In the following sentence, for example, a singular subject (*power*) is modified by a prepositional phrase that contains a plural noun (*tornadoes*). But the subject remains singular, and it takes the appropriate verb form (*proves*).

sing. subj. plural noun verb

The *power* of Midwestern tornadoes often **proves** deadly.

The principle is the same for plural subjects modified by phrases or clauses with singular nouns. The subject remains plural.

plural subj. sing. noun verb

Storms that come late in the spring **are** sometimes unusually violent.

Be especially careful with lengthy or complicated modifiers. In the example that follows, the singular subject and verb are separated by ten words. But the plural nouns *mammals* and *humans* in the modifying phrase have no bearing on subject-verb agreement.

subj. modifying phrase

The *killer whale*, the most geographically diverse of all mammals, excepting only humans, verb **demonstrates** highly complex social behavior.

EXERCISE 22.5 Choose the correct verb for academic writing.

1. Most politicians, regardless of their party or ideology, (**embrace/embraces**) the idea that every child should be able to read by the end of third grade.
2. Almost everyone (**agree/agrees**) with this laudable goal.
3. Still, children's ability to learn how to read (**depend/depends**) on a combination of psychological, physical, and social factors.
4. Moreover, many children from low-income families, in both rural and urban environments, (**need/needs**) intensive tutoring because they are not ready to learn when they arrive in kindergarten.
5. The HOSTS tutoring program, which has had great success in helping children to start reading, (**require/requires**) as many as fifty volunteers in a small elementary school, and such volunteers can be hard to find.

22e Agreement: Is the subject hard to identify?

Occasionally you may simply lose track of a subject because the structure of a sentence is complicated or unusual. Just remember the rule: Keep your eye on the subject.

1 Don't lose track of your subject when a sentence or clause begins with *here* or *there*. In such cases, the verb still agrees with the subject—which usually trails after it.

SINGULAR SUBJECTS

Here **is** a surprising *turn* of events.

There **is** a *reason* for the commotion.

PLURAL SUBJECTS

Here **are** my *tickets.*

There **are** already *calls* for the police chief's resignation.

2 Don't be misled by linking verbs. Common linking verbs are *to be, to seem, to appear, to feel, to taste, to look,* and *to become.* They connect subjects to words that extend or complete their meaning.

The mayor's deputy **was** a severe critic of the police chief.

Many citizens **feel** betrayed.

A linking verb agrees with its subject even when a singular subject is linked to a plural noun.

subj. l.v. plural noun

Good *evidence* of the power of television **is** its effects on political careers.

subj. l.v. plural noun

The *key* to a candidate's success **is** television appearances.

The same is true when a linking verb connects a plural subject to a singular noun, but such sentences sound normal and don't ordinarily raise questions of agreement.

plural subj. l.v. sing. noun

The many new *patrol officers* **are** a tribute to Chief Carey's budget ingenuity.

3 Don't be misled by inverted sentence order. A sentence is considered inverted when some portion of the verb precedes the subject. Inverted sentence structures occur most often in questions.

verb subj.

Was their *motive* to gain political advantage?

verb

Among those requesting Chief Carey's resignation **were** many

subj.

political activists.

4 Don't mistake singular expressions for plural ones. Singular terms such as *series, segment, portion, fragment,* and *part* usually remain singular even when modified by plural words.

A *series* of questions **is** posed by a reporter.

A substantial *portion* of many political talk shows **is** devoted to panel discussions.

The word *majority*, however, does not follow this guideline; it can be either singular or plural, depending on its use in a sentence. In this sentence, *majority* is treated as singular.

The *majority* **rules.**

Yet it can also function as a plural noun.

The *majority* of critics **want** Chief Carey's head on a platter.

5 Watch out for subject-verb agreement in the phrase *one of those who.* In college English, the verb in such a clause is plural—even though it looks as if it should be singular.

Carey is one of those people who never **seem** [not **seems**] discouraged.

The verb is plural because its subject is plural. To understand the situation more clearly, rearrange the sentence this way.

Of those people *who* never **seem** discouraged, Carey is one.

Now watch what happens if you add the word *only* to the mix.

Carey is the only one of the city officials who **seems** eternally optimistic.

Why is the verb singular here? The subject of the verb *seems* is still the pronoun *who*, but its antecedent is now the singular pronoun *one*, not the plural *officials*. Again, it helps to rearrange the sentence to see who is doing what to whom.

Of the city officials, Carey is the only one who **seems** eternally optimistic.

EXERCISE 22.6 Choose the correct verb.

1. The mayor of the town (**strides/stride**) to the microphone.
2. Amid grumbles from the reporters, the crowd (**take/takes**) their seats.
3. (**Does/Do**) the mayor's decision to fire Carey surprise anyone after the last election?
4. The city council president claims that she is one of those people who (**objects/object**) most strongly to politics taking precedence over community unity.
5. But she knows she's not the only one who (**wants/want**) a nationally admired park system.

CHAPTER

23 Questions About Verb Tense, Voice, and Mood?

Perhaps the complexity of verbs first dawned on you when you tried to learn a foreign language. Suddenly, you had to pay attention to all the details you had taken for granted when you used verbs in your native tongue. Understanding **tense**, **voice**, and **mood** now mattered. In this chapter, we focus on such general properties of verbs, especially as they affect writers. For more technical descriptions of the ways verbs work, you may want to consult Chapter 32, "Do You Have Questions About Verbs (ESOL)?"—even if you've been speaking and writing English for most of your life.

Photographer Eadweard Muybridge (1830–1904) used stop-action photography to study the motion of people and animals: The horse will gallop; the horse gallops; the horse is galloping; the horse has galloped. For more Muybridge images, look for him at <http://www.masters-of-photography.com>.

23a How do you choose verb tenses?

Tense is the quality of a verb that expresses time. Tense is expressed through changes in verb forms and verb endings (*see, saw, seeing; work, worked*) and through the use of auxiliaries—what you may know as *helping verbs* (*had* seen, *will have* seen; *had* worked, *had been* working). Most native speakers of English handle basic past, present, and future tenses easily. But as a writer, you'll want to be confident about using all the tenses—for example, the more subtle perfect and progressive tenses.

1 Know the tenses and what they do. Tense depends, in part, on *voice*. Verbs that take direct objects—that is, transitive verbs—can be in either **active** or **passive voice**. They are in active voice when the subject in the sentence actually does what the verb describes.

subj. action
Professor Gates **invited** the press to the lecture.

They are in passive voice when the action described by the verb is done *to* the subject.

subj. action
The press **was invited** by Professor Gates to the lecture.

Chart 23.1 outlines the shape and function of English tenses—past, present, and future—in the *active voice.* (See also more detailed treatment of verb tenses in Chart 32.1 "Verb Tenses.")

Chart 23.1 Verb Tenses in the Active Voice

WHAT IT IS CALLED	WHAT IT LOOKS LIKE	WHAT IT DOES
Past	**I answered** quickly.	Shows what happened at a particular time in the past.
Past progressive	**I was answering** the question when the phone rang. **I was waiting** days for the call.	Shows one action in the past interrupted by a second; or shows an action in the past that has continued for some time.
Present perfect	**I have answered** that question often. **I have expected** it for a long time.	Shows something that has happened one or more times in the past; or expresses a condition that extends from the past to the present.
Past perfect	**I had answered** the question twice already when the phone rang.	Shows what had already happened before another event, also in a past tense, occurred.
Present	**I answer** when I must.	Shows what happens or can happen now.
Present progressive	**I am answering** now.	Shows what is happening now.

(Continued)

Verb Tenses in the Active Voice *(Continued)*

Future	**I will answer** tomorrow.	Shows what may happen in the future.
Future progressive	**I will be answering** the phones all day.	Shows something that will continue to happen in the future.
Future perfect	**I will have answered** all the charges before you see me again.	Shows what will have happened by some particular time in the future.
Future perfect progressive	**I will have been answering** the charges for three hours by the time you arrive at noon. **I will have been working** at the company for thirty years on my next birthday.	Shows a continuing future action that precedes some other event also in the future; or expresses a condition that extends from the past to the future.

Verbs usually look even more complicated when they are in the passive voice, as shown in the following chart.

Chart 23.2 Verb Tenses in the Passive Voice

WHAT IT IS CALLED	WHAT IT LOOKS LIKE
Past	**No Chinese cars were exported** to the United States prior to 2010.
Past progressive	**Chinese cars were being exported** to other countries, however.
Present perfect	**Chinese cars have been exported** for years to Asia and Africa.
Past perfect	**Cars had been exported** from China rarely in the past.
Present	**Some cars are exported** today from China to the Middle East.

(Continued)

Verb Tenses in the Passive Voice *(Continued)*

Present progressive	**More cars are being exported** by China today than a decade ago.
Future	**Many more Chinese cars will be exported** in years to come.
Future perfect	**Million of Chinese cars will have been exported** by the next decade.

As you can see, many tenses require **auxiliary verbs** such as *will, do, be,* and *have.* These auxiliary or helping verbs combine with other verbs to show relationships of tense, voice, and mood. Other auxiliary verbs, such as *can, could, may, might, should, ought,* and *must,* help to indicate possibility, necessity, permission, desire, capability, and so on. These verbs are called **modal auxiliaries.** (For much more on modals, see Section 32d.)

Rosalind **can** write well.

Audrey **might** write well.

Marco **should** write well.

2 Use the present tense appropriately. The present tense has several special roles. It may be used to introduce the words of authors you are quoting or citing, whether living or dead.

Lincoln **defines** conservatism as "adherence to the old and tried, against the new and untried."

Clinton **argues** that compromise is necessary for long-term peace in the Middle East.

Use present tense when you are describing the action in literary works or quoting from them.

Hester Prynne **wears** a scarlet letter.

The doctor in *Macbeth* **warns** a gentlewoman, "You have known what you should not" (5.1.46–47).

Use present tense to make a general statement of fact or to express scientific truths.

Oak trees **lose** their leaves in winter.

Einstein **argues** that the principle of relativity **applies** to all physical phenomena.

Use present tense, too, to describe habitual action.

We **get up** at five a.m. every morning.

People today **watch** television more than they **read**.

3 Use perfect tenses appropriately. Because perfect tenses can look intimidating, some writers avoid them. But the result can be sentences a little less precise than they might be.

VAGUE	Audrey **asked** Kyle to the concert when she learned that Ruben wanted to take her. simple past
PRECISE	Audrey **had asked** Kyle to the concert already when she learned that Ruben wanted to take her. past perfect

Perfect tenses enable you to show exactly how one event stands in relationship to another in time. Learn to use these forms; they make a difference. (See Sections 32a-3 and 32a-4.)

SIMPLE PAST	Dr. Roberts **quit** his job even before he learned that he **failed** the polygraph.
PAST PERFECT	Dr. Roberts **had** already **quit** his job even before he learned that he **had failed** the polygraph.

EXERCISE 23.1 For each verb in parentheses, furnish the tense indicated. Use active voice unless passive is specified.

1. In Shakespeare's tragedy *Macbeth*, three witches tell Macbeth that someday he (**rule**—future) Scotland.
2. Macbeth then explains to his wife, the ambitious Lady Macbeth, what the witches (**promise**—past perfect) him earlier that day: the Scottish crown.
3. Lady Macbeth, even more ambitious than her husband, immediately (**devise**—present) a plot to murder King Duncan that very night and then (**convince**—present) her husband to do the horrid deed.

4. But even though the plot succeeds and Macbeth becomes king, the new ruler fears that he (**challenge**—future, passive voice) by other ambitious men.

5. Macbeth is finally slain by Macduff, whose wife and children (**slaughter**—past, passive voice) earlier in the play at Macbeth's orders.

23b How do regular and irregular verbs differ?

All verb tenses are built from these three basic forms, which are called the *principal parts of a verb*:

- **Infinitive** (or **present**)—This is the base or simple form of a verb, what it looks like when preceded by the word *to*: *to walk*; *to choose*; *to go*.
- **Past**—This is the simplest form a verb takes to show action that has already occurred: *walked; chose; went.*
- **Past participle**—This is the form a verb takes when it is accompanied by an auxiliary verb to show a more complicated past tense: *had* **walked**; *will have* **gone**; *would have* **chosen**; *was* **hanged**; *might have* **broken**. It is the form of the verb you will use to create verb phrases.

In English, most verbs are **regular**, which means that they form their past tense and past participles simply by adding *-d* or *-ed* to their infinitive (or present) forms. Here are the three principal parts of some regular verbs.

INFINITIVE	PAST	PAST PARTICIPLE
talk	talk**ed**	talk**ed**
coincide	coincide**d**	coincide**d**
advertise	advertise**d**	advertise**d**

A good many common English verbs, however, are **irregular**. *Irregular* means that they form their past tenses or past participles in nonstandard ways—that is, not by adding a *-d* or *-ed* to the present form. In fact, irregular verbs change their forms in many ways.

INFINITIVE	PAST	PAST PARTICIPLE
choose	chose	chosen
go	went	gone

A few irregular verbs even have the same form for all three principal parts.

INFINITIVE	PAST	PAST PARTICIPLE
burst	burst	burst
set	set	set

Some of the most important and frequently used verbs in English are irregular, for example, *to have* and *to be.*

There are no rules for determining the shape of irregular forms. To be sure you're using the correct verb form, consult a dictionary or check the following chart of irregular verbs, which gives you three forms: (1) the infinitive, (2) the simple past tense, and (3) the past participle.

When in doubt, your safest bet is to check the list, because studies show that errors in verb form irritate readers a great deal.

Chart 23.3 Irregular Verbs

INFINITIVE	PAST	PAST PARTICIPLE
arise	arose	arisen
be	was, were	been
bear (carry)	bore	borne
bear (give birth)	bore	borne, born
become	became	become
begin	began	begun
bite	bit	bitten, bit
blow	blew	blown
break	broke	broken
bring	brought	brought
burst	burst	burst
buy	bought	bought
catch	caught	caught
choose	chose	chosen
cling	clung	clung
come	came	come
creep	crept	crept
dig	dug	dug

(Continued)

Irregular Verbs *(Continued)*

dive	dived, dove	dived
do	did	done
draw	drew	drawn
dream	dreamed, dreamt	dreamed, dreamt
drink	drank	drunk
drive	drove	driven
eat	ate	eaten
fall	fell	fallen
find	found	found
fly	flew	flown
forget	forgot	forgotten
forgive	forgave	forgiven
freeze	froze	frozen
get	got	got, gotten
give	gave	given
go	went	gone
grow	grew	grown
hang (an object)	hung	hung
hang (a person)	hanged, hung	hanged, hung
have	had	had
know	knew	known
lay (to place)	laid	laid
lead	led	led
leave	left	left
lend	lent	lent
lie (to recline)	lay	lain
light	lit, lighted	lit, lighted
lose	lost	lost
pay	paid	paid
plead	pleaded, pled	pleaded, pled
prove	proved	proved, proven
ride	rode	ridden
ring	rang, rung	rung
rise	rose	risen
run	ran	run

(Continued)

Irregular Verbs *(Continued)*

say	said	said
see	saw	seen
set	set	set
shake	shook	shaken
shinc	shone, shined	shone, shined
show	showed	shown, showed
shrink	shrank, shrunk	shrunk
sing	sang, sung	sung
sink	sank, sunk	sunk
sit	sat	sat
speak	spoke	spoken
spring	sprang, sprung	sprung
stand	stood	stood
steal	stole	stolen
sting	stung	stung
swear	swore	sworn
swim	swam	swum
swing	swung	swung
take	took	taken
tear	tore	torn
throw	threw	thrown
wake	woke, waked	woken, waked
wear	wore	worn
wring	wrung	wrung
write	write	written

The glossary at the end of this handbook treats in greater detail various troublesome verbs, including some listed above. Check the entries for *can/may, get/got/gotten, lie/lay, set/sit*, and so on.

EXERCISE 23.2 Replace the verb forms in parentheses with appropriate tenses. You may need to use a variety of verb forms (and auxiliaries), including passive and progressive forms. Treat all five sentences as part of a single paragraph. Consult the chart of irregular verbs on pages 387–89 for help with some of the verb forms.

1. Isambard Brunel (**design**) his ship the *Great Eastern* to be the largest vessel on the seas when it (**launch**) in 1857 in London.

2. Almost 700 feet long, the ship—originally named *Leviathan*—(**weigh**) more than 20,000 tons and (**power**) by a screw propeller, paddle wheels, and sails.

3. Designed originally to be a luxurious passenger ship, the *Great Eastern* (**attain**) its greatest fame only after it (**refit**) to stretch the first transatlantic telegraph cable from England to Newfoundland.

4. In the summer of 1865, the *Great Eastern* (**lay**) cable for many difficult days when the thick line (**snap**) two-thirds of the way to Newfoundland. Nine days (**spend**) trying to recover the cable, but it never (**find**).

5. Many people (**be**) skeptical that the *Great Eastern*, a jinxed ship, (**succeed**) in stretching a cable across the Atlantic, but it finally (**do**) so in 1866.

23c Problems with tense in parallel constructions?

Parallelism is an arrangement that gives related words, clauses, and phrases a similar pattern, making it easier for readers to see relationships between the parallel expressions. For example, the verbs in the following sentence are parallel: The college band *played* out of tune, *marched* out of step, and yet somehow *maintained* its dignity.

But when verbs sharing the same subject don't also show the same tense and form, the result can be **faulty parallelism**. In the following example, the verbs describing a lawyer's action shift from past tense to past progressive tense without a good reason. The verbs lack parallelism.

LACK OF PARALLELISM

subj. verb verb

The *lawyer* **explained** the options to her client and **was recommending** a plea of guilty.

The sentence reads more smoothly when the verbs are revised to show the same tense and form.

REVISED FOR PARALLELISM

subj. verb verb

The *lawyer* **explained** the options to her client and **recommended** a plea of guilty.

Changes in verb tense within a sentence are appropriate, however, when they indicate obvious shifts in time.

Currently, the lawyer **is defending** an accused murderer and soon **will be defending** a bigamist.

For much more on parallelism, see Section 16h.

EXERCISE 23.3 Correct any problems with parallelism that the verbs in boldface are causing. Modify the tenses as needed to achieve parallelism.

1. In the middle of the nineteenth century, young French painters **were rejecting** the stilted traditions of academic art, **found** new methods and new subjects, and **would establish** the school of art one critic derided as "Impressionism."

2. The new artists **outraged** all the establishment critics and also **were challenging** all the expectations of Paris gallery owners.

3. Traditionalists thought that painters should **work** indoors, **depict** traditional subjects, and **be using** a balanced style that hid their brushwork.

4. But the youthful Impressionists, including artists like Monet, Degas, and Renoir, soon **were taking** their easels outdoors to the streets of Paris or to public gardens, **laying** on their colors thick and self-consciously, and **had been choosing** scenes from ordinary life to depict.

5. Now these revolutionary artists and their works **are regarded** as classics on their own and **being studied** and **are collected** by an artistic establishment they **are rocking** from its foundations a century ago.

23d Questions about tense consistency in longer passages?

In paragraphs or longer passages of writing, avoid shifting from tense to tense (for instance, from *past* to *present*) unless clarity and good sense require the moves. Choose a time frame and stick with it. The following paragraph shows what can happen when verb forms shift inappropriately.

> At the dawn of the nuclear era in the 1950s, many horror movies **featured** monsters spawned by atomic explosions or bizarre scientific experiments. For two decades, audiences **flock** to movies with such titles as *Godzilla, Them, Tarantula*, and *The Fly*. Theater screens **come** alive with gigantic lobsters, ants, birds, and lizards, which **spent** their time attacking London, Tokyo, and Washington while scientists **look** for ways to kill them.

The passage sounds confusing because it jumps between two possible time frames. Making the tenses consistent makes the passage more readable. Here it is in past tense.

> At the dawn of the nuclear era in the 1950s, many horror movies **featured** monsters spawned by atomic explosions or bizarre scientific experiments. For two decades, audiences **flocked** to movies with such titles as *Godzilla, Them, Tarantula*, and *The Fly*. Theater screens **came** alive with gigantic lobsters, ants, birds, and lizards, which **spent** their time attacking London, Tokyo, and Washington while scientists **looked** for ways to kill them.

The passage can also be revised to narrate events in the present tense, as they might be in a documentary about the era.

> At the dawn of the nuclear era in the 1950s, many horror movies **feature** monsters spawned by atomic explosions or bizarre scientific experiments. For two decades, audiences **flock** to movies with such titles as *Godzilla, Them, Tarantula*, and *The Fly*. Theater screens **come** alive with gigantic lobsters, ants, birds, and lizards, which **spend** their time attacking London, Tokyo, and Washington while scientists **look** for ways to kill them.

EXERCISE 23.4 Revise the following paragraph to make the tenses of the boldfaced verbs more consistent. You may find it helpful to emphasize the present tense throughout the passage—but not every verb ought to be in the present. (Remember that specific events in a literary work are usually described in present tense: After Macbeth *kills* King Duncan, he *seizes* the throne.)

> (1) *Macbeth*, one of Shakespeare's shortest dramas, **depicts** rebellion, conspiracy, and murder most foul. (2) The smoke of battle **has** barely cleared when Macbeth **encountered** three witches who **promise** him the throne of Scotland. (3) Almost immediately, his wife **persuades** him—against his good conscience—to act, and he quickly **has murdered** King Duncan while the old man **sleeps**. (4) But Macbeth himself **will sleep** no more; his conscience **gives** him no rest for the remainder of the play. (5) Only in the fourth act **did** the pace slow, but then the action **rose** again in the fifth toward a bloody conclusion.

23e Do you understand active and passive voice?

Voice indicates whether the subject acts or is acted upon, although it is a concept easier to illustrate than to define. Only verbs that take objects (called transitive verbs—see Section 32b) can be in either the **active** or the **passive** voice. Verbs are in the active voice when the subject of the sentence actually does what the verb describes.

subj. action
Jamie Duke **managed** the account.

They are in passive voice when the action described by the verb is done *to* the subject.

subj. action
The *account* **was managed** by *Jamie Duke*.

Passive verbs are useful constructions when *who* did an action is either unknown or less important than *to whom it was done*. A passive verb puts the object right up front in the sentence where it gets attention. Passive verbs also work well in scientific writing when you want to focus on the process itself.

Serena Williams **was featured** on ESPN.

Serena Williams **was interviewed** by several reporters.

The beaker **was heated** for three minutes.

The passive is also customary in many expressions where a writer or speaker chooses to be vague about assigning responsibility.

Flight 107 **has been canceled**.

The check **was lost** in the mail.

When you need passives, use them. But most of the time you can make your sentences livelier by changing passive constructions to active ones. In a sentence with an active verb, it is often easier to tell who is doing what to whom. For advice on revising sentences to eliminate weak passive verbs, see Section 17a-6.

EXERCISE 23.5 Identify all the passive verbs in the following sentences; then revise those passive verbs that might be better stated in the active voice. Some sentences may require no revision.

1. Even opponents of chemical pesticides sometimes use poisons after they have been bitten by fire ants, aggressive and vicious insects spreading throughout the southern United States.
2. These tiny creatures have been given by nature a fierce sting, and they usually attack en masse.
3. Gardeners are hampered in their work by the mounds erected by the ants.
4. By the time a careless gardener discovers a mound, a hand or foot has likely been bitten by numerous ants.
5. The injured appendage feels as if it has been attacked by a swarm of bees.

23f What is the subjunctive mood and how do you use it?

As a grammatical term, **mood** indicates how you intend a statement to be taken. Are you making a direct statement of fact? Then the mood of the statement will be **indicative** ("I enjoy reading science fiction"). Are you giving a command or making a request? If so, the mood becomes **imperative** ("Watch out for flying objects!" "Give me that book, please.").

When, however, you express a wish or hope, make a suggestion, or describe a *possible* (rather than actual) situation, you may need to use the **subjunctive** mood. You signal a shift to the subjunctive simply by altering the form of the verb. For example, in *if* clauses that express a wish, hope, or desire, you would use the subjunctive verb form *were* instead of the indicative form *was.*

> *If* George **were** in charge, we'd be in good hands.
>
> *If* she **were** to accept their contract, she would begin work on September 1.
>
> *If* I **were** a rich man, I'd be no happier than I am now.

Rare in English, the subjunctive is still expected in some situations and can be tricky. So you need to understand what the subjunctive looks like and when to employ it.

1 Recognize the subjunctive forms of verbs. For all verbs, the present subjunctive is simply the base form of the verb—that is, the present infinitive form without *to.*

VERB	PRESENT SUBJUNCTIVE
to be	be
to give	give
to send	send
to bless	bless

The base form is used even in the third person singular, where you might ordinarily expect a verb to take another form.

> It is essential that *Jose* **have** [not **has**] his lines memorized by tomorrow.
>
> Albertina insisted that *Travis* **be** [not **is**] on time for their dinner at her mother's.

For all verbs except *be*, the past subjunctive is the same as the simple past tense.

VERB	PAST SUBJUNCTIVE
to give	gave
to send	sent
to bless	blessed

For *be*, the past subjunctive is always *were*. This is true even in the first and third person singular, where you might expect the form to be *was*.

> I wish *I* **were** [not **was**] the director.
>
> Suppose *you* **were** [not **was**] the director.
>
> I wish *she* **were** [not **was**] the director.

2 Recognize occasions for the subjunctive. In addition to appearing in clauses that express wishes and desires, the subjunctive is also used in *that* clauses following verbs that make demands, requests, recommendations, or motions. These forms can seem legalistic and formal, but they are appropriate.

> The presiding officer asked that everyone **be** silent.
>
> I ask only that you **be** courteous to the speaker.
>
> The president asked that everyone **show** courage.

Some common expressions also require the subjunctive.

> **Be** that as it may . . .
>
> **Come** what may . . .
>
> As it **were** . . .
>
> Peace **be** with you.

EXERCISE 23.6 In the following sentences, underline any verbs in the subjunctive mood.

1. It is essential that we be at the airport at 2:00 p.m. today.
2. I wish I were less susceptible to telephone solicitors!
3. Far be it from me to criticize your writing!
4. Come what may, the show must go on.
5. If Madison were to arrive early, what would happen to our plans?
6. It is essential that you take over as the supervisor.

CHAPTER

24 Questions About Verbals?

24a What are verbals?

Verbals lead a double life: they look like verb forms but act like other parts of speech—nouns, adjectives, adverbs. Like verbs, verbals can express time (present, past), take objects, and form phrases. Though you may not recognize the three types of verbals by their names—*infinitives, participles,* and *gerunds*—you use them all the time. (See also Sections 16c-2 and 33a.)

1 Understand infinitives. You can identify an **infinitive** by looking for the word *to* preceding the base form of a verb: *to seek, to find.* Infinitives also take other forms to show time and voice: *to be seeking, to have found, to have been found.* Infinitives sometimes act as nouns, adjectives, and adverbs.

INFINITIVE AS NOUN	**To work** in outer space is not easy. subject of the sentence
INFINITIVE AS ADJECTIVE	Astronauts have many procedures **to learn**. modifies the noun *procedures*
INFINITIVE AS ADVERB	NASA launched STS-125 **to repair** the Hubble Space Telescope. modifies the verb *launched*

An infinitive can also serve as an *absolute*—that is, a stand-alone phrase that modifies an entire sentence.

> **To make** a long story short, the Hubble would not have survived without a Space Shuttle repair mission.

In some sentence constructions, the characteristic marker of the infinitive, *to*, is deleted.

> Crew members on STS-125 practiced various techniques to help them **[to] deal** with unexpected problems when upgrading the Hubble.

2 Understand participles. A **participle** is a verb form that acts as a modifier. The present participle ends with *-ing*. For regular verbs, the past participle ends with *-ed*; for irregular verbs, the form of the past participle varies. Participles take various forms, depending on whether the verb they are derived from is regular or irregular. Chart 24.1 shows the participle forms of two verbs.

Chart 24.1 Forms of the Participle

perform (a regular verb)	PARTICIPLES
Present, active:	performing
Present, passive:	being performed
Past, active:	performed
Past, passive:	having been performed
write (an irregular verb)	PARTICIPLES
Present, active:	writing
Present, passive:	being written
Past, active:	written
Past, passive:	having been written

(For the forms of some irregular past participles, check the list of irregular verbs on pages 387–89.)

As modifiers, participles may be single words. In the following example, the participle *waving* modifies *astronaut.*

> **Waving**, the astronaut turned a cartwheel in the shuttle cabin for the television audience.

But participles often take objects, complements, and modifiers to form verbal phrases. Such phrases play an important role in structuring sentences.

> **Clutching** a camera, the astronaut moved toward a galley window.
>
> The planners of the Hubble repair mission, **knowing** that astronauts had to work in a dangerous orbital environment, took precautions.

Like an infinitive, a participle can also serve as an *absolute*—that is, a stand-alone phrase that modifies an entire sentence.

All things **considered**, the Hubble Space Telescope is probably one of the greatest technological achievements of the space program.

3 Understand gerunds. A **gerund** is a verb form that acts as a noun: *smiling, flying, walking*. Because most gerunds end in *-ing*, they look exactly like the present participle.

GERUND	**Daring** is a quality moviegoers admire in heroes.
PARTICIPLE	Almost all passengers, however, would prefer not to have a **daring** cab driver.

The important difference is that gerunds function as nouns, whereas participles act as modifiers. In the following sentences, for example, *dancing* functions as a noun (and gerund) in the first sentence and a modifier (and participle) in the second.

GERUND	We recognized Marta's **dancing**.
PARTICIPLE	We recognized Marta **dancing**.

Gerunds usually appear in the present tense, but they can take other forms. In the following example, the gerund is in the past tense (and passive voice) and acts as the subject of the sentence.

Having been treated inconsistently by Congress has angered directors of the space program.

Here the gerund is in the present tense and passive voice.

Being asked to fly a mission to Mars is an opportunity NASA anticipates.

Gerunds have many functions.

GERUND AS SUBJECT	**Keeping** within current budget restraints poses a problem for NASA.
GERUND AS OBJECT	Some NASA engineers prefer **launching** space probes without vulnerable human crews.
GERUND AS APPOSITIVE	Others argue that NASA needs to cultivate its great talent, **executing** daring missions.
GERUNDS AS COMPLEMENT	comp. Our future is **exploring** the heavens.

EXERCISE 24.1 Identify the boldfaced words or phrases as infinitives, participles, or gerunds.

1. **Regretting** compromises in the original design, engineers have refined the shuttle after the *Challenger* and *Columbia* disasters.
2. The mainstream media questioned both NASA's **engineering** and its **handling** of the shuttle program.
3. **To be** fair, NASA's safety record in the **challenging** task of space exploration has been defensible.
4. **Costing** even more than the space shuttle, the International Space Station may not prove viable much longer.
5. **To make** budget matters more complicated, NASA is **exploring** the possibility of a return to the moon.

24b How do verbals cause sentence fragments?

A verbal phrase that stands alone can create a **sentence fragment**—that is, a clause without a complete subject or verb. Fragments are considered errors in academic and professional writing.

> The Secretary of Homeland Security declined to be interviewed on CNN. **Having been ambushed in the recent past by an unfriendly reporter.**

Verbals alone cannot act as verbs in sentences. In fact, verbals are even described as **nonfinite** (that is, "unfinished") verbs. A complete sentence requires a **finite** verb, which is a verb that changes form to indicate person, number, and tense.

NONFINITE VERB—INFINITIVE	**To have found** success . . .
FINITE VERB	**I have found** success.
NONFINITE VERB—PARTICIPLE	The comedian **performing** the bit . . .
FINITE VERB	The comedian **performs** the bit.
NONFINITE VERB—GERUND	**Directing** a play . . .
FINITE VERB	She **directed** the play.

Verbal phrases are accepted in much informal writing. You'll see such fragments often in magazine articles and in advertisements.

> Harold loved playing comedy clubs—every bit of it. **Telling political jokes. Making satirical comments.** It made life worthwhile.

But in academic writing, fragments should usually be revised. For help on recasting such fragments, see Section 35a.

24c What is a split infinitive?

An infinitive interrupted by an adverb is considered to be split.

> to **boldly** go   to **really** try   to **actually** see

Some writers believe that constructions such as these are incorrect, a point disputed by grammarians. Split infinitives are such common expressions in English that most writers use them without apology. Here are guidelines to help you through this minor, but still touchy, matter.

1 Check whether any words separate the *to* in an infinitive from its verb. If a sentence sounds awkward or confusing because a word or phrase splits an infinitive, move the interrupter.

SPLIT INFINITIVE Harold, a stand-up comic with a social conscience, hoped **to**, as best he could, **make** people laugh at politicians.

REVISED Harold, a stand-up comic with a social conscience, hoped **to make** people laugh at politicians, as best he could.

2 Revise any split infinitives that cause modification problems. In the following sentence, for example, *only* seems to modify *mock* when it should refer to *the most prominent people.*

CONFUSING Harold intended **to** only **mock** the most prominent people in the news.

CLEARER Harold intended **to mock** only the most prominent people in the news.

Consider, too, whether a word dividing an infinitive is needed at all. Where the interrupting word is a weak intensifier that adds nothing to a sentence (*really, actually, basically*), cut it.

WEAK INTENSIFIER	Harold found it especially easy **to** basically **demolish** the pretensions of politicians.
INTENSIFIER CUT	Harold found it especially easy **to demolish** the pretensions of politicians.

3 Consider whether a split infinitive is acceptable. In most situations, split infinitives are neither awkward nor confusing, so revising them won't improve a sentence.

SPLIT INFINITIVE	Words fail **to** adequately **describe** the cluelessness of some public figures.
REVISED	Words fail **to describe** adequately the cluelessness of some public figures.

In academic and business writing, it's usually best to keep *to* and the verb together because some readers still object strongly to split infinitives.

EXERCISE 24.2 Find the split infinitives in the following sentences and revise them. Decide which revisions are necessary and which are optional. Be prepared to defend your decisions.

1. In his comic monologue, Harold decided to candidly describe his own inept campaign for city council.
2. Harold usually didn't allow his personal life to too much color his comedy routines.
3. But he believed that to really understand how funny modern political campaigns could be, a person had to basically run for office himself.
4. Harold quickly discovered that it was hard to persuade business contributors to only support one candidate.
5. To actually succeed in politics, Harold learned that a candidate had to really understand human nature.

CHAPTER

25 Questions About Nouns: Plurals, Possessives, and Articles?

25a How are nouns made plural?

Plurals can be tricky. Most plurals in English are formed by adding *-s* or *-es* to the singular forms of nouns.

demonstration → demonstration**s**
picture → picture**s**
dish → dish**es**

However, substantial numbers of words have irregular plurals. You could not reliably predict what their plurals would be if you didn't know them.

IRREGULAR
man → m**e**n
ox → ox**en**
mouse → m**ice**
fungus → fung**i** (or fungus**es**)

Plurals may vary, too, according to how a word is used. You might find maple *leaves* on your driveway but several Toronto Maple *Leafs* on the cover of *Sports Illustrated.*

1 Check the dictionary for the plural form of a noun. Most up-to-date college or online dictionaries provide the plurals of all troublesome words. If your dictionary does not give a plural for a particular noun, assume that it forms its plural with *-s* or *-es.*

You may eliminate some trips to the dictionary by referring to the following guidelines for forming plurals. But the list is complicated and full of exceptions, so check the dictionary regularly.

2 Use *-es* when the plural adds a syllable to the pronunciation of the noun. This is usually the case when a word ends in a soft *ch, sh, s, ss, x,* or *zz.* (If the noun already ends in *-e,* you add only *-s.*)

dish → dish**es**
glass → glass**es**
bus → bus**es** or buss**es**
buzz → buzz**es**

3 Add *-s* to form a plural when a noun ends in *-o* and a vowel precedes the *-o;* add *-es* when a noun ends in *-o* and a consonant precedes the *-o*. This guideline has exceptions. A few words ending in *-o* have two acceptable plural forms.

VOWEL BEFORE *-O* (ADD *-S*)	CONSONANT BEFORE *-O* (ADD *-ES*)
studio → studio**s**	hero → hero**es**
rodeo → rodeo**s**	tomato → tomato**es**

4 Add *-s* to form a plural when a noun ends in *-y* and a vowel precedes the *y*. When a consonant precedes the *y*, change the *y* to *i* and add *-es*.

VOWEL PRECEDES *-Y* (ADD *-S*)	CONSONANT PRECEDES *-Y* (CHANGE *-Y* TO *-IES*)
attorney → attorney**s**	foundry → foundr**ies**
Monday → Monday**s**	candy → cand**ies**

An exception to this rule occurs with proper nouns. They usually retain the *-y* and simply add *-s*.

PROPER NAMES ENDING IN *-Y* (ADD *-S*)	EXCEPTIONS TO THE EXCEPTION (CHANGE *-Y* TO *-IES*)
Germany → Germany**s**	Rocky Mountains → Rock**ies**
Nestrosky → Nestrosky**s**	Smoky Mountains → Smok**ies**

5 Check the plurals of nouns ending in *-f* or *-fe*. Some form plurals by adding *-s*, some change *-f* to *-ves*, and some have two acceptable plural forms.

ADD *-S* TO FORM PLURAL	CHANGE *-F* TO *-VES* IN PLURAL
chief → chie**fs**	wife → wi**ves**
belief → belie**fs**	knife → kni**ves**

TWO ACCEPTABLE FORMS

elf → el**fs**/el**ves**
scarf → scar**fs**/scar**ves**

6 Check the plurals of certain nouns that derive from other languages.

analysis → analys**es** medium → medi**a**
criterion → criteri**a** syllabus → syllab**i**

7 Check the plurals of compound words.

In most compounds, pluralize the last word.

dishcloth → dishcloth**s**
grandchild → grandchild**ren**

But pluralize the first word in a compound when it is the most important term, that is, the one modified by other words. This guideline applies especially to hyphenated expressions.

attorney general → attorney**s** general
father-in-law → father**s**-in-law
passerby → passer**s**by

For words that end with *-ful*, add *-s* to the end of the whole word, not to the syllable before *-ful*.

handful**s** [not hand*s*ful]
tablespoonful**s** [not tablespoon*s*ful]

8 Check the plurals of letters, abbreviations, acronyms, and numbers.

These constructions usually form their plurals by adding *-s*.

the SAT**s**
all CEO**s**
the 2000**s**
four PhD**s**

Use *-'s* only where adding *-s* without the apostrophe might cause a misreading.

three e**'s** and two y**'s**

9 Use plurals consistently within a passage. For example, if the subject of a clause is plural, be sure that words related to it are appropriately plural. In the following example, *mind* and *job* should be plural because the subject *leaders* is plural.

INCONSISTENT	**Leaders** able to make up their **mind** usually hold on to their **job**.
REVISED	**Leaders** able to make up their **minds** usually hold on to their **jobs**.

Taking Control

Plural nouns

For possessives, we generally follow the guidelines recommended by the Modern Language Association (see Section 25b). You will find them simple and easy to remember. But, in your reading, don't be surprised if you encounter variations. Some publications will use an apostrophe alone with all proper nouns that end in "s" or an "es" sound: *Jesus' words*; *Katz' menu*; *Lexus' warranty*. Others will use an apostrophe without an "s" to show possession of words that end in a double "s" (*the hostess' job*) or some foreign expressions (*the tableaux' creators*). If you are unsure how to form a particular possessive, or the form you come up with sounds awkward, try writing around it. You can often use "of" to express possession, or find other variations: *the words of Jesus; the menu at Katz; the warranty on a Lexus; the job of the hostess; the creators of the tableaux.*

EXERCISE 25.1 Form the plurals of the following words. Use the guidelines above or a dictionary as necessary.

basis	gas	soliloquy
duo	loaf	zero
tooth	alkali	mongoose
alumnus	datum	heir apparent
moose	Oreo	court-martial

25b Questions about possessives?

A noun or pronoun takes a possessive form to show ownership or some similar relationship: *Rita's, the students', the governor's approval, the day's labor, the city's destruction, hers, his, theirs.* Possession can also be signaled by the preposition *of: the pride of Brooklyn, the flagship of the company, the signature of the author.* Note that there is disagreement about how to form some possessives, especially of words that end with "s." Our guidelines generally follow MLA principles, but you may want to check the style guide used in your own field or major (see Chapter 49). Although you may occasionally see the apostrophe omitted in advertising or on signs—*mens room, Macys*—in academic writing don't omit an apostrophe that shows the possessive.

1 Add an apostrophe + -*s* to singular nouns and to plural nouns that do not end in -*s*.

SINGULAR NOUNS	PLURALS NOT ENDING IN -*S*
dog**'s** life	geese**'s** behavior
that man**'s** opinion	women**'s** attitude
the NCAA**'s** ruling	children**'s** imaginations
the boss**'s** daughter	mice**'s** tails

2 Add an apostrophe + -*s* to singular proper nouns.

SINGULAR NOUNS

America**'s** shores
C. S. Lewis**'s** novels
Katz**'s** restaurant
Zeus**'s** power
Descartes**'s** *Discourse on Method*
Jesus**'s** words

3 Add an apostrophe (but not an *s*) to plural nouns that end in -*s*.

the hostesses' job	the senators' chambers
the students' opinion	the Smiths' home

4 Show possession only at the end of compound or hyphenated words.

president-elect**'s** decision
father-in-law**'s** Cadillac
the United States Post Office**'s** efficiency

5 Show possession only once when two nouns share ownership.

Marge and Homer**'s** family
Smith-Fallows and Luu**'s** project

But when ownership is separate, each noun shows possession.

Marge**'s** and Homer**'s** educations
Smith-Fallow**s'** and Luu**'s** offices

6 Use an apostrophe + -*s* to form the possessive of living things and titled works; use *of* with nonliving things.

Follow this guideline sensibly. Many common expressions violate the convention, and many writers simply ignore it.

TAKE APOSTROPHE + -*S*	TAKE *OF*
the dog**'s** bone	the size **of** the bone
Professor Granchi**'s** taxes	the oppression **of** taxes
*Time***'s** cover	the timeliness **of** the cover

Use *of* whenever an apostrophe + -*s* seems awkward or ridiculous.

RIDICULOUS The **student** sitting next to Peg**'s** opinion was radical.

REVISED The opinion **of the student** sitting next to Peg was radical.

In a few situations, English allows a double possessive, consisting of both -*'s* and *of*.

That tax idea **of** Obama**'s** didn't win much support in Congress.

Another proposal **of** the President's did much better.

7 Do not use an apostrophe with personal pronouns. Personal pronouns don't take an apostrophe to show ownership: *my, your, her, his, our, their, its*. The forms *it's* and *who's* are contractions for *it is* and *who is* and shouldn't be confused with the possessive pronouns *its* and *whose* (see Section 28c).

> **It's** an idea that has **its** opponents alarmed.
>
> **Who's** to say **whose** opinion is right?

Indefinite pronouns—such as *anybody, each one, everybody*—do form their possessives regularly: *anybody's, each one's, everybody's*. For more about possessive pronouns, see Section 28b.

EXERCISE 25.2 Decide whether the forms boldfaced in these sentences are correct. Revise any that you believe are faulty.

1. That claim **of her's** may be right.
2. **James'** belief was that the main concern **of most citizens'** was a thriving economy.
3. **Society's** problems today are not as great as they were in the **1900s'**; each generation benefits from its **parent's** sacrifices while tackling **it's** own problems.
4. **Its** a shame that people forget how much they have benefited from **someone elses** labor.
5. Children are notorious for ignoring their **elders** generosity; ingratitude is even one of the major themes of ***King Lear's*** plot.

25c Should it be *a* or *an*?

Some writers think that they should simply use the article *a* before all words that begin with consonants and *an* before all words that begin with vowels. In fact, usage is just a bit more complicated, as a few examples show: *an* argument, *a* European, *a* house, *an* honorable person. (See also Section 33b.)

Use *a* when the word following it begins with a consonant *sound*; use *an* when the word following it begins with a vowel *sound*. In most cases, it works out that *a* actually comes before words beginning with consonants, *an* before words with vowels.

INITIAL CONSONANTS	**INITIAL VOWELS**
a **b**oat	an **aa**rdvark
a **c**lass	an **E**gyptian monument
a **d**uck	an **i**gloo
a **f**inal opinion	an **o**dd event
a **h**ouse	an **O**edipus complex
a **X**erox product	an **u**tter disaster

But *an* is used before words beginning with a consonant when the consonant is silent, as is sometimes the case with *h*. It is also used when a consonant itself is pronounced with an initial vowel sound (*f* → *ef; n* → *en; s* → *es*), as often happens in acronyms.

SILENT CONSONANT	**CONSONANT WITH A VOWEL SOUND**
an heir	an SAT score
an honest man	an HMO
an hors d'oeuvre	an *X*-ray star
an hour	an *F* in this course

Similarly, *a* is used before words beginning with a vowel when the vowel is pronounced like a consonant. Certain vowels, for example, sound like the consonant *y*, and in a few cases, an initial *o* sounds like the consonant *w*.

VOWEL WITH A CONSONANT SOUND

a European vacation (*eu* sounds like *y*)
a unique painting (*u* sounds like *y*)
a one-sided argument (*o* sounds like *w*)
a U-joint (*u* sounds like *y*)

EXERCISE 25.3 Decide whether *a* or *an* should be used before each of the following words or phrases.

1. L-shaped room
2. hyperthyroid condition
3. zygote

4. *X*-rated movie
5. Euclidean principle
6. evasive answer
7. jalapeño pepper
8. unwritten rule
9. unit of measure
10. veneer of oak

CHAPTER

26 Questions About Pronoun Reference?

Pronouns usually stand in for and act like nouns, but they don't name particular persons, places, or things. As the following examples show, there are many kinds of pronouns, with different functions.

> **Personal:** *I, me, you, he, she, it, they, us, him, her, them*
>
> **Possessive:** *my, your, his, her, its, our, their* (these modify nouns); *mine, yours, his, hers, ours, theirs* (these stand alone)
>
> **Demonstrative:** *this, that, these, those*
>
> **Indefinite:** *any, anybody, someone, no one, none, everyone, each*
>
> **Interrogative:** *who, whose, whom, which, whoever, whomever*
>
> **Relative:** *that, which, who, whom, whoever, whomever*
>
> **Reflexive:** *myself, himself, herself, yourselves, themselves*

Handled well, pronouns help to make writing clear and concise. But you must pay attention to reference (Chapter 26), agreement (Chapter 27), and case (Chapter 28).

26a Do pronouns lack antecedents?

The person, place, or thing a pronoun refers to is called its **antecedent**, the word you'd have to repeat in a sentence if you couldn't use a pronoun.

ant. pron.

> *Jill* demanded that the clerk speak to **her**.

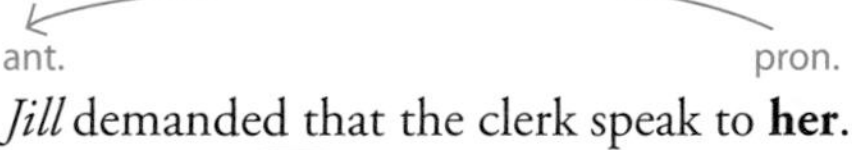

> *Workers* denied that **they** intended to strike.

A pronoun must agree with the antecedent to which it refers in *number* (singular or plural), in *case* (subjective, objective, or possessive), and sometimes in *gender* (masculine or feminine).

You must revise a pronoun reference if readers can't find a specific word in your sentence that could logically serve as an antecedent, the word the pronoun replaces.

When you aren't sure that the pronoun has an antecedent, ask yourself whether another word in the sentence or passage could substitute for the pronoun. If none can, replace the vague pronoun with a word or phrase that explains precisely what it is.

VAGUE The pollsters chose their participants scientifically, but **it** did not prevent a faulty prediction of the mayoral election.

REVISED The pollsters chose their participants scientifically, but **their random sampling** did not prevent a faulty prediction of the mayoral election.

EXERCISE 26.1 Revise or rewrite the following sentences to eliminate vague pronouns. Treat the sentences as a continuous passage.

1. Leah read avidly about gardening, although she had never planted one herself.
2. Her fondness for apartment living left Leah without a place for one.
3. Leah found herself buying garden tools, seeds, and catalogs, but it did not make much sense.
4. Leah's friends suggested building planters on her deck or installing a window garden, but Leah doubted that the landlord would permit it.
5. As for her parents' idea that she invest in a condominium, they overestimated her credit rating.

26b Are pronoun references unclear?

You have a problem with pronoun reference when a pronoun could refer to more than one antecedent.

AMBIGUOUS When Ms. Walker talked to Mrs. Mendoza at noon, **she** did not realize that **she** might be resigning before the end of the day.

AMBIGUOUS As soon as the FDA approves the revolutionary antibiotic, the drug company will begin production in a new plant. **It** will make a major difference when **it** happens.

In the first sentence, who is resigning is not clear; in the second, *it* might be the approval of the drug or the opening of a plant. You can usually eliminate such confusion by replacing the ambiguous pronouns with more specific words or by rewriting the sentence. Sometimes you have to do both.

REVISED When **they** talked to each other at noon, **Ms. Walker** did not realize that **Mrs. Mendoza** might be resigning before the end of the day.

REVISED As soon as the FDA approves the revolutionary antibiotic, the drug company will begin production in a new plant. **The drug** will make a major difference **as soon as it becomes available**.

EXERCISE 26.2 Revise the following sentences to eliminate ambiguous pronoun references. Treat the sentences as a continuous passage. Several versions of each sentence may be possible.

1. Amanda could hardly believe that representatives from Habitat for Humanity would visit wintry Madison, Wisconsin, when it was so bad.
2. When she met them at their hotel, the winds were howling, the visitors were hungry, and it was predicted that they would get worse.
3. But the two women were ready to brave the elements, so she figured this wasn't a problem.
4. Later Amanda learned that one of the visitors, Sarah Severson, had been born in Wisconsin, and she told her she knew a great deal about northern winters.
5. The three of them took off through the blizzard in Amanda's SUV, but it didn't slow them down a bit.

26c Questions about *this, that, which,* and *it*?

Readers may be confused if you use the pronouns *this, that, which,* or *it* to refer to ideas you haven't named specifically in your writing. Vague pronouns of this kind are a problem not just because readers can't locate a clear antecedent, but because writers sometimes resort to vague pronouns when they aren't sure themselves what they mean in a sentence or paragraph. So unpacking a vague *this* or *that* may at times help you get a firmer grip on your ideas.

CONFUSING In Act III, Hamlet has a chance to avenge his dead father by stabbing his murderous uncle while the man is alone at prayer. But **it** bothers him. [What bothers him?]

REVISED In Act III, Hamlet has a chance to avenge his dead father by stabbing his murderous uncle while the man is alone at prayer. But **killing a man in cold blood** bothers Hamlet.

1 Revise a sentence or passage to make it clear what *this, that, which,* or *it* means. Constructions such as the following can be confusing or imprecise.

CONFUSING The minutes of the committee are usually filled with data, charts, and vivid accounts of the debate. I appreciated **this**.

Readers can't tell whether you like data, charts, or debate—or all three. You can usually clear up such confusion by adding a word or phrase that explains what *this* or *that* is.

CONFUSING The minutes of the committee are usually filled with data, charts, and vivid accounts of the dialogue. I appreciated **this** _____?

Now add the noun after *this.*

REVISED I appreciated **this detailed information**.

When the unclear pronoun is *which* or *it,* you ought either to revise the sentence or supply a clear and direct antecedent. Here's an example with *it* as the vague pronoun.

VAGUE Although atomic waste products are hard to dispose of safely, **it** remains a reasonable alternative to burning fossil fuels to produce electricity.

What is the alternative to burning fossil fuels? Surely not *atomic waste products*. The *it* needs to be replaced by a more specific term.

REVISED Although atomic waste products are hard to dispose of safely, **nuclear power** remains a reasonable alternative to burning fossil fuels to produce electricity.

Taking Control

Pronouns: *this, that, which, it*

If you sometimes leave a reader wondering what a *this, that, which,* or *it* might refer to, it may be because you don't know exactly what the pronoun means yourself. Introducing a vague pronoun can seem like a clever way to fudge a complex idea. But if you keep offering ambiguous pronouns, readers just may give up on you. The following passage offers a string of vague pronouns:

> Some new students drop out because they lack study skills; others resort to plagiarism; and many have never experienced so much academic pressure. I had been told that **this** was a major issue on our campus, but I didn't believe **it** until I experienced **it** myself.

That second sentence makes sense—but only *sort of*. Fix lazy writing of this kind by circling all instances of *this, that, which*, and *it* for which you can't find a clear referent—that is, a referent specific enough to underline. Then do whatever thinking is necessary to express those ideas in more descriptive words or phrases. Finally, revise the remainder of the material so that readers know confidently what every *this, that, which*, or *it* means.

> For reasons ranging from poor study skills and plagiarism to high levels of stress, first-year students often experience **a high drop-out rate.** I had been told that **this attrition** was a major issue on our campus, but I didn't believe **it** until I **watched my roommate self-destruct.**

2 Avoid using *they* or *it* without antecedents to describe people or things in general.

VAGUE In Dallas, **they** drive worse than in Houston.

REVISED In Dallas, **people** drive worse than in Houston.

3 Avoid sentences in which a pronoun merely repeats the obvious subject. Such constructions are unacceptable in writing.

INCORRECT The **mayor**, a Democrat, **he** won the election.

REVISED The **mayor**, a Democrat, won the election.

4 Don't let a nonpossessive pronoun refer to a word that is possessive. In the sentence below, *they* seems to refer to *pundits'*, but that word cannot be the antecedent.

VAGUE As for the television **pundits'** coverage, they either mock third-party candidates or ignore them.

Pundits' is a possessive form. Because *they* can't refer to *pundits'* (or to *coverage*), the sentence has to be revised.

REVISED As for the television **pundits**, **they** either mock third-party candidates or ignore them.

EXERCISE 26.3 Decide whether a reader might find the pronouns in boldface unclear. Revise the sentences as necessary.

1. Even tourists just visiting the building soon noticed the aging state capitol's sagging floors, unreliable plumbing, and exposed electrical conduits. **This** was embarrassing.
2. When an electrical fire in the office of the Speaker of the House was soon followed by another in the Senate chamber, it was clear **it** was a problem.
3. Old paintings and sculptures were grimy and cracked, **which** had been donated by citizens over the decades.
4. The governor's proposal for reconstructing the state capitol, the legislators endorsed **it** almost unanimously.
5. **This** was passed by a voice vote.

CHAPTER

27 Questions About Pronoun Agreement?

27a Do antecedents and pronouns agree in number?

Pronouns and nouns are either singular or plural. Singular pronouns (such as *she, it, this, that, her, him, my, his, her, its*) refer to something singular; plural pronouns (such as *they, these, them, their*) refer to plural nouns. This connection is called **agreement in number**.

The soccer **players** gathered **their** equipment.

The **coach** searched for **her** car.

Problems with *pronoun agreement* occur when you use a singular pronoun to stand in for a plural noun or a plural pronoun to substitute for a singular noun.

Like wax figures, pronouns stand in for the nouns they replace. This head is being prepared for the Wax Museum at Fisherman's Wharf in San Francisco.

1 Be sure that singular pronouns refer to singular antecedents and plural pronouns to plural antecedents.

INCORRECT An **investor** (sing.) too often assumes that government agencies will protect **them** (plural) in turbulent economic times.

CORRECT **Investors** (plural) too often assume that government agencies will protect **them** (plural) in turbulent economic times.

CORRECT An **investor** [sing.] too often assumes that government agencies will protect **him or her** [sing.] in turbulent economic times.

Note that words such as *student, individual,* and *person* are singular, not plural. Don't use *they* to refer to these terms.

INCORRECT If a **person** watches too much television, **they** may become a couch potato.

REVISED If a **person** watches too much television, **he or she** may become a couch potato.

2 Keep pronouns consistent in number throughout a passage. Don't switch back and forth from singular to plural forms of pronouns and antecedents. The following paragraph—with pronouns and antecedents boldfaced—shows this common error.

> One reason some **teenagers** [pl.] quit school is to work to support **their** [pl.] families. If **he or she** [sing.] is the eldest child, the **teen** [sing.] may feel an obligation to provide for the family. So **they** [pl.] look for a minimum wage job. Unfortunately, the **student** [sing.] often must work so many hours per week that **they** [pl.] cannot give much attention to schoolwork. As a result, **he or she** [sing.] grows discouraged and drops out.

To correct such a tendency, be consistent. Treat the troublesome key term—in the passage above it is *teenager*—as either singular or plural, but not both. Notice that making such a change may require adjustments throughout the passage.

> One reason some **teenagers** [pl.] quit school is to work to support **their** [pl.] families. If **they** [pl.] are the eldest children, such **teens** [pl.] may feel an obligation to provide for **their** [pl.] families. So **they** [pl.] look for minimum wage jobs. Unfortunately, these **students** [pl.] often must work so many hours per week that **they** [pl.] cannot give much attention to schoolwork. As a result, **they** [pl.] grow discouraged and drop out.

EXERCISE 27.1 Revise the following sentences wherever pronouns and antecedents do not agree in number. You may change either the pronouns or the antecedents.

1. Many a law school class is conducted using the Socratic method, but they aren't always successful.
2. In the Socratic method, a teacher leads a student through a series of questions to conclusions that they believe they've reached without the instructor's prompting.
3. Yet when instructors ask leading questions, the cleverer students sometimes answer it in unexpected ways.
4. However, no instructor can foresee all the questions and answers students might have for them.

EXERCISE 27.2 Revise the entire paragraph in Section 27a-2 to make all the boldfaced nouns or pronouns singular.

Take Control

27b Questions about agreement with indefinite pronouns?

A troublesome and common agreement problem involves references to pronouns described as indefinite—*everyone, anybody, anyone, somebody, all, some, none, each, few,* and *most.* It is not always easy to tell whether one of these indefinite words is singular or plural.

Everyone should keep (**his or her? their?**) temper.

No one has a right to more than (**his or her? their?**) share.

1 Use the following chart or a dictionary to determine whether an indefinite pronoun in your sentence is singular, variable, or plural. Chart 27.1, which is not exhaustive, reflects formal and academic usage.

Chart 27.1 Indefinite Pronouns

SINGULAR	VARIABLE (SINGULAR OR PLURAL)	PLURAL
anybody	all	few
anyone	any	many
anything	either	several
each	more	
everybody	most	
everyone	neither	
everything	none	
nobody	some	
no one		
nothing		
somebody		
someone		
something		

2 If the indefinite word is regarded as singular, make any pronouns that refer to it singular.

sing. sing.
Did **anybody** misplace **her** notes?

sing. sing.
Everyone should keep **his** temper.

sing. sing.
No one has a right to more than **his or her** share.

In speech you'll often hear the plural pronouns *they* and *their* linked to antecedents that are singular indefinite pronouns (*everybody, anyone*). Such mismatches, common as they may be, are considered nonstandard in academic writing.

sing. ant. plural pron.
INCORRECT *Everyone* is entitled to **their** opinion.

sing. ant. sing. pronouns
REVISED *Everyone* is entitled to **his or her** opinion.

INCORRECT *Each* (sing. ant.) of the legislators had **their** (plural pron.) say.

REVISED *Each* (sing. ant.) of the legislators had **his or her** (sing. pronouns) say.

Be careful to avoid sexist language by consciously using both pronouns: *his or her*, not *his* alone or *her* alone. (See Section 29b-1.) If you find *his or her* awkward, choose a plural form.

People (plural ant.) are entitled to **their** (plural pron.) own opinions.

Note that *opinions* needs to be plural as well, since the many *people* referred to in this sentence would have more than one opinion.

In a few situations that strongly imply the presence or activity of a group, however, the singular indefinite pronoun does take a plural referent, even in formal and college writing.

Because **each** (sing.) of the players arrived late, the coach gave **them** (plural) a stern lecture on punctuality.

Nobody (sing.) was late, were **they** (plural)?

Everybody (sing.) has plenty of money, and **they** (plural) are willing to spend it.

Taking Control

Pronoun agreement

In spoken English, most people—even professionals in the media—mistakenly use the plural pronouns *they* and *their* to refer to indefinite pronouns that are technically singular. As this section explains, all of the following sentences would be incorrect, especially in written English:

> ***Everyone*** should cast *their* [should be *his or her*] vote next week.
>
> ***No one*** should ignore *their* [should be *his or her*] civic responsibilities.
>
> ***Each*** of the candidates intends to state *their* [should be *his or her*] position.

(Continued)

Pronoun agreement *(Continued)*

Such mistakes are common because these and other indefinite pronouns certainly feel plural to many readers. Indeed, some grammarians and linguists now support the informal constructions. They point out that indefinite pronouns such as *everyone* and *no one* or expressions like *each of the candidates* do, in fact, describe groups, not individuals. That's why treating such words as singular runs contrary to day-to-day usage; even when explained, the correct answers sound counterintuitive and wrong to many readers and writers.

Can you afford to ignore the rule, hoping it will disappear? It just may, in a few more generations. But in the meantime, you have to get the pronouns correct in any document you write that is going public, whether on paper or screen—which means learning the guidelines in this section. They are complicated, but not actually difficult to use. Moreover, when you finally grasp the principle of agreement, you'll wonder why all those high-paid talking heads on television cannot.

3 If the indefinite word is usually plural, make any pronouns that refer to it plural.

plural — plural

Several of the jet fighters had to have **their** wings stiffened.

plural — plural

Few, however, had given **their** pilots trouble.

4 If the indefinite word is variable, use your judgment to determine which pronoun suits the sentence better. In many cases, words or phrases modifying the pronoun determine its number.

var. — plural — var.

All of the paintings had yellowed in **their** frames. **Some** will be restored

plural

to **their** original condition.

var. — sing. — var.

All of the beer is still in **its** kegs. **Some** of the brew is certain to have

sing.

its quality sampled.

None is considered variable because it is often accepted as a plural form. However, in formal writing, you should usually treat *none* as singular. Think of *none* as meaning *not one.*

> **None** of the women is reluctant to speak **her** mind.
>
> **None** of the churches has **its** doors locked.

EXERCISE 27.3 Select the word or phrase in parentheses that would be correct in formal and college writing.

1. Anybody can learn to drive an automobile with a manual transmission if (**they are/he or she is**) coordinated.
2. But not everyone will risk (**his or her/their**) own (**life/lives**) trying.
3. Few today seem eager to take (**his or her/their**) driver's tests in a five-speed.
4. Everyone learning to drive a manual car expects (**his or her/their**) car to stall at the most inopportune moment.
5. Most of all, nobody wants to stop (**his or her/their**) manual-shift car on a steep hill.

27c Treat collective nouns as singular or plural?

Agreement problems are common when pronouns refer to collective nouns—that is, nouns that describe groups of things: *class, team, band, government, jury, family.* Collective nouns like these can be either singular or plural, depending on how they are used in a sentence.

> The **chorus** sang **its** heart out.
>
> The **chorus** arrived and took **their** seats.

A pronoun that refers to a collective noun should be consistently either singular or plural.

To make sure that's the case, identify each collective noun in a sentence to which a pronoun refers. Choose whether to treat that noun as a single body (*the* jury) or as a group of more than one person or object (the *twelve members* of the jury). Then be consistent. If you decide to treat the word as singular, be sure that subsequent pronouns referring to it are singular. If you decide it is plural, all pronoun references should be plural.

The **jury** rendered **its** decision. [*jury* considered singular]

The **jury** had **their** pictures taken. [*jury* considered plural]

In most cases, your sentences will sound more natural if you regard collective nouns as single objects. Notice how awkward the following sentence seems because the collective noun is treated as plural.

AWKWARD The **band** are unhappy with **their** latest recordings.

BETTER The **band** is unhappy with **its** latest recordings.

You also have the option of adding a clarifying word such as *members* to make the group more clearly plural.

The *band members* are unhappy with **their** latest recordings.

The *citizens* of the jury expressed **their** collective outrage.

EXERCISE 27.4 In the following sentences, select the appropriate words in parentheses. Be prepared to defend your answers.

1. The **class** entered the lecture hall and took (**its/their**) seats, eager to hear from the architect after (**its/their**) field trip to several of his buildings.
2. He belonged to a revitalized **school** of design that had enjoyed (**its/their**) best days four decades ago.
3. The aging architect was accompanied by several **members of his firm**, carrying (**its/their**) designs in huge portfolios.
4. Students hoped that the **board of directors** of the college might give (**its/their**) blessing to a commission by the architect.
5. Any **panel of experts** was likely to cast (**its/their**) vote in favor of such a project.

27d Questions about agreement with conjunctions?

Choosing a pronoun can be puzzling when its antecedents are nouns joined by the conjunctions *and, or, nor, either . . . or*, or *neither . . . nor*. You'll recognize the problem when you see examples.

1 When two nouns joined by *or, nor, either . . . or*, or *neither . . . nor* are singular, be sure any pronoun referring to them is singular.

sing.

Neither Venezuela nor Mexico will raise **its** oil prices today.

2 When two nouns joined by *and* or *or* are both plural, be sure any pronoun referring to them is plural. (See also Section 22a-2.)

plural

Players or managers may file **their** grievances with the commissioner.

3 When a singular noun is joined to a plural noun by *or, nor, either . . . or*, or *neither . . . nor*, be sure any pronoun agrees in number (and gender) with the noun nearer to it. (See also Section 22a-4.)

sing. plural plural

Either poor **diet** or long, stress-filled **hours** in the office will take **their** toll on an executive's health.

plural sing. sing.

Either long, stress-filled **hours** in the office or poor **diet** will take **its** toll on an executive's health.

Pronouns also agree in gender with the nearer antecedent when two nouns are joined by *or*.

masc. fem. fem.

Either a **priest** or a **nun** will escort you to **her** office.

fem. masc. masc.

Either a **nun** or a **priest** will escort you to **his** office.

EXERCISE 27.5 In the sentences below, select the appropriate words in parentheses.

1. Neither the tour guide nor any of his customers had bothered to confirm (**his/their**) flight from Chicago's O'Hare Airport back to Toledo.
2. Either the ticket agents or a flight attendant working the check-in desk had misread (**their/her**) computer terminal and accidentally canceled the group's reservations.
3. Either the tourists or their guide had to make up (**their/his**) (**minds/mind**) quickly about arranging transportation back to Toledo.
4. Neither the guide nor his wife relished the thought of spending (**his/her/their**) hard-earned money on yet another expensive ticket.
5. Wandering about the vast terminal, the guide located a commuter airline willing to fly either the group or its bags to (**its/their**) destination cheaply.

CHAPTER

28 Questions About Pronoun Case?

Some personal pronouns (and *who*) change their form according to their function in a sentence. These different forms are called **case**.

Subjective (or **nominative**) **case** is the form a pronoun takes when it is the subject of a sentence or a clause: *I, you, she, he, it, we, they, who*. A pronoun is also in the subjective case when it follows a linking verb as a **predicate nominative**, a word that renames the subject.

> It is **I**.
>
> It was **they** who cast the deciding votes.

When something is done to a pronoun, it is in the **objective case.**

> Elena broke **them**.
>
> Will loved **her**.

This is also the form a pronoun takes after a preposition: (to) *me, her, him, us, them, whom*. The subjective and objective forms of the pronouns *you* and *it* are identical.

The **possessive case** is the form a pronoun takes when it shows ownership: *my, mine, your, yours, her, hers, his, its, our, ours, their, theirs, whose.*

In most situations, writers are able to select the appropriate case without thinking too much about their choices.

> **Whose** book did she give to **him**?
> **They** were more confident of **their** position than **we** were of **ours**.

But at other times, selecting the right case is no easy matter.

28a Questions about pronouns in subjective and objective case?

Choose subjective forms when pronouns act as subjects, objective forms when pronouns act as objects (especially in prepositional phrases).

Chart 28.1 Pronoun Case

SUBJECTIVE FORMS	OBJECTIVE FORMS
I	me
we	us
you	you
he	him
shc	her
it	it
they	them
who	whom

1 Check pronoun case when pronouns are paired. The second pronoun in a pair is often troublesome. To choose the right pronoun, figure out what the pronoun does in the sentence: Is it a subject or a predicate nominative? Is it an object?

WHICH CASE? You and (**I/me**) don't have the latest designs yet.
These pronouns are subjects, so the subjective form *I* is correct.

CORRECT You and **I** don't have the latest designs yet.

WHICH CASE? The winners are (**he/him**) and (**I/me**).
The pronouns are predicate nominatives and should be in the subjective case.

CORRECT The winners are **he** and **I**.

WHICH CASE? Forward the email to (**he/him**) and (**I/me**).
The pronouns are objects of the preposition *to*; they take the objective case.

CORRECT Forward the email to **him** and **me**.

Alternatively, conduct a simple test by taking out the first pronoun and recasting the sentence with only the troublesome pronoun. You can often tell immediately which choice to make.

WHICH CASE? **You and me** don't have the latest designs yet.

WRONG **Me** don't have the latest designs yet.

CORRECT **You and I** don't have the latest designs yet.

WHICH CASE?	The memo praised **you and she**.
WRONG	The memo praised **she**.
CORRECT	The memo praised **you and her**.

EXERCISE 28.1 Select the correct pronoun from the choices offered in parentheses.

1. The reporter told her colleague in the newsroom that neither (**she/her**) nor (**he/him**) had done a good job in covering the city's financial crisis.
2. It was likely that both political parties would now accuse (**she/her**) and (**he/him**) of media bias.
3. Knowing her colleagues at the competing TV stations, the reporter was convinced that both she and (**they/them**) had rushed their stories.
4. "You and (**I/me**) will just have to accept the criticism," she acknowledged.

2 Check pronoun case when first person plural pronouns are followed by nouns. The pronoun and noun must share the same case.

SUBJECTIVE	subjects **We** *lucky sailors* missed the storm.
OBJECTIVE	objects The storm missed **us** *lucky sailors.*
OBJECTIVE	obj. of preposition For **us** *engineers,* the job market looks promising.

You can test for the correct form by leaving out the noun and recasting the sentence using only the pronoun.

WHICH CASE?	Us *lucky sailors* missed the storm.
WRONG	**Us** missed the storm.
CORRECT	**We** *lucky sailors* missed the storm.

3 Check pronoun case with *who* and *whom*. In informal spoken English, the distinction between the subject form *who* and the object form *whom* (or *whoever/whomever*) is routinely ignored. In written English, however, many readers still expect the convention to be honored. The rule is easier to state than follow: Select the subjective form (*who*) when pronouns act as subjects and the objective form (*whom*) when pronouns act as objects.

The correct choice is especially important in prepositional phrases (see Section 16c-1).

SUBJECTIVE	**Who** wrote this letter?
OBJECTIVE	You addressed **whom**?
OBJECTIVE	To **whom** did you write?

When *who* or *whom* (or *whoever/whomever*) is part of a dependent clause, *who* or *whom* takes the form it should have in the dependent clause only, not in the sentence as a whole. Constructions of this kind are quite common. The words in italics in the following examples are clauses within full sentences.

noun clause

The system rewards ***whoever*** *works hard.*

Whoever is the subject of the noun clause in which it appears. It has its own verb, *works*.

noun clause

Whomever *the party nominates* is likely to be elected.

The pronoun is the object of *nominates*.

adverbial clause

The deficit will increase *no matter* ***whom*** *we elect president.*

The main verb of the subordinate clause is *elect* and its subject is *we*. So the pronoun *whom* is the object of *we elect* and *president* modifies *whom*. Chart 28.1 tells you that *whom*, not *who*, is correct.

EXERCISE 28.2 Decide which of the pronoun forms in parentheses is correct in each of the following sentences.

1. James Carville looks like a man (**whom/who**) wouldn't trust a nun with a prayer.
2. (**Whom/Who**) wouldn't like to win the state lottery?
3. To (**who/whom**) would you go for sound financial advice?
4. Are these the young children (**who/whom**) you took by bus to Santa Fe?
5. Officials couldn't determine (**who/whom**) rigged the state elections.

4 Check pronoun case in comparisons. To determine pronoun case after *than* or *as*, it helps to complete the comparison.

WHICH CASE?	I am taller *than* **(him/he)**.
CORRECT	I am taller *than* **he** (is).

WHICH CASE?	We don't invest as much *as* **(she/her)**.
CORRECT	We don't invest as much *as* **she** (does).

Some comparisons can be expanded two ways.

WHICH CASE?	Football means more to me *than* (**she/her**).
POSSIBLE EXPANSIONS	Football means more to me *than* **she** (does).
	Football means more to me *than* (it means to) **her**.

In such cases, the pronoun you select will determine what the sentence means, so it's probably better to write out the full comparison.

EXERCISE 28.3 Select the correct pronoun from the choices offered in parentheses.

1. Although the Cowardly Lion needed the Wizard's help as much as Dorothy did, the King of the Jungle was less determined than (**she/her**) to hike to Oz.
2. Dorothy probably felt more confident than (**he/him**) that she could deal with the wonderful Wizard.
3. Perhaps Dorothy could relate more easily to (**he/him**) than a lion could.
4. Although more cautious in his appraisal of the Wizard than Dorothy, the Scarecrow was no less eager for guidance than (**she/her**).
5. Perhaps the Scarecrow even feared that Dorothy would like the Wizard more than (**he/him**).

5 Check pronoun case in appositives. *Appositives* are nouns or phrases that add information to a previous noun.

appositive

The teacher gave special help to two of the *students*, **Cheryl and me**.

When an appositive contains a pronoun, the pronoun should be in the same case as the noun it modifies.

The teacher called *two students*, **Cheryl and (I/me)**, to the front of the classroom.

Two students, the noun phrase being modified, is the object of *called*. So the pronoun should also be in the objective case.

The teacher called *two students*, **Cheryl and me**, to the front of the classroom.

6 Check pronoun case after linking verbs. Linking verbs, such as *to be, to seem, to appear, to feel, to become*, connect a subject to a word or phrase that extends or completes its meaning—the **subject complement** (see Section 16a-1). In most cases, use the subjective case of a pronoun when it is the complement of a linking verb.

subj. l.v. subj. comp.
The *culprits are* obviously **they**.

Such constructions are fairly common.

It is **I**.

The next CEO of the corporation will be **she**.

You are **who**?

However, in informal speech, it is acceptable to use the objective case after a linking verb.

It's **me**. That's **her**.

Or work around the problem. Rather than write "The director was he," reverse the order and try "He was the director."

EXERCISE 28.4 Select the correct pronoun from the choices in parentheses below.

1. That is (**he/him**) in the office there.
2. The guilty party certainly was not (**she/her**).
3. Sighting three men in uniform, we assumed that the pilots were (**they/them**).
4. They are (**who/whom**)?
5. We were surprised that the person who had complained was (**she/her**).

Taking Control

Pronouns: Subjective/objective

Most writers recognize when they are struggling to make a choice about pronoun case: Is it supposed to be *Jack and I* or *Jack and me*? Should the card read *From we musicians* or *From us musicians*? Do I use *who* or *whom* after a pronoun? Readers who barely notice pronoun reference blunders (see Chapter 26) will nevertheless spot sentences with pronoun case errors because they can be downright clumsy:

> *Her and me don't really care whom wins the election.*

The point is that you can't afford to guess about pronoun case. If you consistently have problems, you need to be sure you understand the concept of *case* itself (see the opening pages of this chapter), know what a predicate nominative is, recognize possessive pronouns, remember that pronouns that follow prepositions *usually* need to be in the objective case (*from us musicians; to whom*), and so on. As this section demonstrates, choosing the right case for pronouns takes considerable thought and skill:

> *She and I don't really care who wins the election.*

28b Difficulties with possessive pronouns?

The most common way of showing ownership in English is to add an apostrophe + *-s* to a noun: *Akilah's book*, the *dog's owner*. The familiar *-'s* is not, however, used with **personal pronouns** (or *who*): do not add an apostrophe + *-s* with personal pronouns used to show ownership (possession). This is true whether the possessive pronoun comes before or after a noun.

INCORRECT	The coat is **her's**.
CORRECT	The coat is **hers**.
INCORRECT	The TV station made **it's** editorial opinion known.
CORRECT	The TV station made **its** editorial opinion known.

The following examples show the various forms of possessive pronouns. Notice that they don't add apostrophes.

BEFORE THE NOUN	AFTER THE NOUN
That is **my** *book.*	The *book* is **mine**.
That is **your** *book.*	The *book* is **yours**.

That is **her** *book.*	The *book* is **hers**.
That is **his** *book.*	The *book* is **his**.
That is **our** *book.*	The *book* is **ours**.
That is **their** *book.*	The *book* is **theirs**.
Whose *book* is this?	This *book* is **whose**?

Understand, too, that although indefinite pronouns such as *everybody* or *someone* form the possessive by adding *-'s*, others, such as *all, any, each, most, none, some,* and *few,* do not.

INCORRECT	**Some's** opinion
CORRECT	The opinion of **some**

28c Confused by *its/it's* and *whose/who's*?

Don't mistake the possessive pronoun *its* for the contraction *it's* (which means *it is* or *it has*). This error is both very common and easy to fix. Remember that *its* is a possessive form; *it's* is a contraction.

POSSESSIVE FORM	The iron left **its** grim outline on the silk shirt.
CONTRACTION	**It's** a stupid proposal.

Of course, the apostrophe makes the contracted form—*it's*—look suspiciously like a possessive. And the possessive form—*its*—sounds like a contraction. But don't be fooled. The possessive forms of personal pronouns never take an apostrophe, whereas contractions always require one.

WRONG	The school lost **it's** charter because of low test scores.
RIGHT	The school lost **its** charter because of low test scores.
WRONG	**Its** unlikely that the aircraft will lose **it's** way in the dark. **Its** equipped with radar.
RIGHT	**It's** unlikely that the aircraft will lose **its** way in the dark. **It's** equipped with radar.

If you consistently misuse *its/it's,* circle these words whenever they appear in your work and then check them. It may help if you always read *it's* as *it is.* Eventually you will eliminate this error.

A related error is mistaking *whose*, a possessive pronoun, for *who's*, which is the contraction for *who is* or *who has*.

POSSESSIVE FORM **Whose** teammate is on first base?
CONTRACTION **Who's** on first?

EXERCISE 28.5 Circle all occurrences of *its/it's* and *who's/whose* in the following passage and correct any errors.

1. Its taken state governments much too long to recognize that its as dangerous to use a cell phone while driving as it is to drive drunk.
2. "Who's not made a phone call while driving?" one might ask.
3. Yet its not clear if anyone is capable of managing a cell phone, with it's tiny controls, while still keeping an eye on who's in the next lane.
4. If it's permissible for operators of vehicles (including busses and subways) to use cell phones, then whose ultimately responsible for the resulting carnage?
5. Surely its time for legislators across the country to show concern for citizens whose lives are threatened daily by motor vehicle operators who's principle concern is for their own convenience.

EXERCISE 28.6 Review Sections 28b and 28c. Identify and correct any pronoun-related errors in the sentences below.

1. There is usually not much doubt about whose responsible for enormous environmental disasters.
2. Its not hard to spot a capsized oil tanker.
3. Yet anybodys home or yard can contribute to environmental pollution.
4. The earth is our's to protect or despoil.
5. Ecology has to be everyone's responsibility.

CHAPTER

29 Questions About Pronoun Choices?

How you use pronouns can shape how readers respond to your writing. Some issues—such as point of view and sexist pronouns—have a direct impact on the rhetoric and style of what you write. Other matters, such as the proper use of *that/which* and of reflexive and intensive pronouns, are more technical, yet they still matter to many writers concerned with language.

29a When to use *I, we, you,* or *one*?

Pronouns change the distance between writers and readers and establish a point of view ranging from personal to distant. Choosing *I* or *you* puts you closer to readers; using *one* creates distance.

1 Use *I* when you or your opinions belong in what you're writing. In general, avoid the first person *I* in scientific reports and expository essays.

WITH *I* **I learned** through a survey **I did** that students who drive a car on campus are more likely to have jobs than those who do not.

REVISED **A recent survey showed** that students who drive a car on campus are likely to have jobs.

However, when you find that avoiding *I* makes you resort to an awkward passive verb, use *I* instead.

WORDY **It is believed** that procedures for voting in campus elections are too complex.

REVISED **I believe** that procedures for voting in campus elections are too complex.

You can often eliminate an awkward passive without using *I.*

REVISED WITHOUT *I* Procedures for voting in campus elections are too complex.

You should know that some instructors and editors simply will not allow *I* in college, professional, or scientific prose. When writing for them, respect their rules. However, most writers today recognize that using *I* is both natural and sensible even in relatively formal work. Not using *I* or *we* (when more than one author is involved) can even lead to questions about who is taking responsibility for a statement.

2 Use *we* whenever two or more writers are involved in a project or when you are writing to express the opinion of a group.

When **we** compared our surveys, **we** discovered the conflicting evidence.

We believe that the city council has an obligation to reconsider its zoning action.

Or use the first person *we* to indicate a general condition when it is appropriate to comment editorially.

We need better control of our medical care systems in the United States.

Avoid *we* or *us* as a chummy way of addressing your reader. In most college writing, *we* used this way sounds pretentious.

3 Use *you* to address readers personally or to give orders or directions. *You* sounds direct, cordial, and personal. Be sure that you really want your readers included when using the second person in college writing. The following sentence, for example, may be too personal—it seems to implicate readers directly in scholastic dishonesty.

INAPPROPRIATE A recent student government survey suggested that **you** will cheat in two courses during **your** college career.

REVISED A recent student government survey suggested that **most students** will cheat in two courses during **their** college careers.

Because *you* is both vague and potentially personal, it is a pronoun to avoid in most academic writing, especially reports and research projects. *You* may be more appropriate in persuasive writing, however, where your goal is to move people to act. It can also be useful in giving instructions or explaining how to do something.

4 Use *one* to express a general thought. *One* may sometimes be useful for conveying moral sentiments or sweeping claims.

> Consider the anxiety of not knowing where **one's** next meal is coming from.
>
> **One** learns a great deal about prerevolutionary Russia from reading Dostoevsky.

But notice that *one* makes the sentence more formal than it would be if *one* were replaced by *I* or *you*.

EXERCISE 29.1 Revise the sentences below to create a single coherent passage appropriate for a college report. Pay particular attention to the words and phrases in boldface.

1. **I was amazed to learn that** the Chinese speak a variety of dialects of a language they describe as Han.
2. Although there are only eight major varieties of Han, **you would find them** as different from each other as one Romance language is from another.
3. **One finds**, moreover, that each of the eight versions of Han occurs in a great many dialects, adding to **one's** linguistic confusion.
4. **I was surprised**, however, that the Chinese use a common set of ideographs.
5. As **you** might expect, there have been efforts to reform the Chinese language to make it easier **for you** to communicate between one region and another in the vast and populous country.

29b Do your pronouns treat both sexes fairly?

Today members of either sex may belong to almost every profession or group—students, athletes, coal miners, truckers, secretaries, nurses. Let your pronoun usage reflect that diversity. In situations where you cannot assume that members of a group will be all male or all female, be sure your language accommodates both sexes. You can do that in a variety of ways.

1 Use the expressions *he or she, him or her,* or *his or her* instead of the pronoun of either sex alone.

SEXIST Every secretary may invite **her husband**.

REVISED Every secretary may invite **his or her partner**.

Unfortunately, variations of *he or she* grow tiresome when they occur more than once in a sentence. Other expressions have been created to express gender diversity, including *he/she, s/he,* and *(s)he,* but many readers and editors don't like these inventions. So when the widely accepted *he or she* seems clumsy, try the strategies in the remainder of this section to avoid sexist usage.

2 Make singular pronoun references plural. Because plural pronouns do not have a specific gender in English, you can often avoid the choice between *he* and *she* simply by turning singular references into plural ones.

SEXIST **Every** secretary may invite **her husband**.

REVISED **All** secretar**ies** may invite **their partners**.

TIRESOME Before **he or she** leaves, **each** band member should be sure **he or she** has **his or her** sheet music.

REVISED Before leaving, **all** band members should be sure **they** have **their** sheet music.

Notice that these revisions eliminate *he or she* entirely.

3 When possible, cut the troublesome pronouns. Here are more examples.

ORIGINAL	*Anybody* may bring **his or her** favorite CD.
REVISED	*Anybody* may bring **a** favorite CD.
ORIGINAL	*Nobody* should leave until **he or she** has signed the guest book.
REVISED	*Nobody* should leave without **signing** the guest book.

These options are useful, but they are not always available.

4 Switch between *he* and *she*. In most cases in reports and arguments that don't refer to specific individuals, you can vary the pronouns sensibly and naturally within chunks of prose—between paragraphs, for example, or between the examples in a series. Handled skillfully, the shift between general masculine and feminine references need not attract a reader's attention.

> The dean of students knew that any student could purchase term papers through mail-order term paper services. If **he** could afford the scam, a student might construct **his** entire college career around papers **he** had purchased.
>
> Yet the dean also acknowledged that the typical plagiarist was rarely so grossly dishonest and calculating. **She** tended to resort to such highly unethical behavior only when **she** believed an assignment was beyond **her** capabilities or **her** workload was excessive.

Obviously, you should avoid varying pronoun gender within individual sentences.

EXERCISE 29.2 Revise the following sentences to improve the way they handle pronouns—both in terms of gender and number. Treat the sentences as part of one paragraph.

1. Earlier this century, a laborer might have feared that heavy equipment would mangle his limbs or that pollutants might damage his lungs.
2. Today a worker has to be concerned with new threats to her health.

3. Anybody who faces a computer terminal eight hours a day must worry about his exposure to radiation and wonder whether his muscles and joints are being damaged by the repetitive limb motions required by his job.

4. Frankly, the typical worker is often so concerned with her job performance that she may not consider that her workplace poses risks.

5. Naturally, though, every worker wants their job to be safe.

29c Questions about *that*, *which*, and *who*?

Are you puzzled trying to choose between the pronouns *that* and *which*? You may recall a guideline from secondary school that required writers to use *that* as the lead-in for modifying phrases described as *restrictive* or *essential*—that is, for clauses that specify what a noun does or is. If you remove the essential clause, you remove a piece of information that readers need to interpret the meaning of the sentence.

ESSENTIAL CLAUSE — The car **that hit me** rolled into the shallow ditch.

The same rule insists that *which* be used with nonessential or nonrestrictive clauses (that is, with modifiers that add information not crucial to the meaning of a sentence).

NONESSENTIAL CLAUSE — My vehicle, **which is a massive SUV**, sustained little damage.

Yet in reading you may have noticed that some writers use *which* in either situation.

ESSENTIAL CLAUSE — The car **which hit me** rolled into the shallow ditch.

What form is correct? And when is *who* a better alternative to *which* or *that*?

1 Use *that* to introduce essential (restrictive) clauses. A clause introduced by *that* will almost always be essential. No commas are used around such clauses.

The amendment **that** won the city council's approval involved recycling.

Only the amendment **that** I wrote recommended recycling.

2 Use *which* to introduce nonessential (nonrestrictive) clauses.

Such clauses are ordinarily surrounded by commas.

NONESSENTIAL CLAUSE	The Web site, **which** is not on the university's server, contains controversial advice about plagiarism.
NONESSENTIAL CLAUSE	NASA, **which** was created in 1958, oversees the American civilian space program.

But understand that many writers use *which* to introduce essential clauses as well. In these clauses, context and punctuation may determine when a *which* clause is essential or not. If the clause is essential, no commas separate it from the rest of the sentence; if nonessential, commas enclose the clause (for more examples and details, see Section 36b-1).

ESSENTIAL CLAUSE	The business plan **which** intrigued the shareholders was the simpler one.
NONESSENTIAL CLAUSE	The business plan, **which** intrigued the shareholders, was quite simple.

Some readers still prefer to distinguish between *that* and *which*, though the distinction is disappearing in general usage. For more about this issue, see Section 30i.

3 Use *who* rather than *that* or *which* when modifying a person.

INAPPROPRIATE	The woman **that** was promoted is my boss.
BETTER	The woman **who** was promoted is my boss.
INAPPROPRIATE	The delegates, **which** represented all regions of the country, met in Philadelphia for their convention.
BETTER	The delegates, **who** represented all regions of the country, met in Philadelphia for their convention.

EXERCISE 29.3 Decide among *that/which/who* in the following sentences. Add commas where needed.

1. Charlie Chaplin's tramp (**that/which/who**) wore a derby, baggy trousers, and a mustache may still be the most recognized character on film.
2. The popularity (**that/which/who**) Chaplin had in the early days of film may never be equaled either.
3. His graceful gestures and matchless acrobatics (**that/which/who**) some critics likened to ballet were perfectly suited to the silent screen.
4. A flaw (**that/which/who**) weakens many of Chaplin's films is sentimentality.
5. Chaplin's tramp made a last appearance in *The Great Dictator* (1940) (**that/which/who**) satirized Hitler's regime.

29d Questions about reflexive and intensive pronouns?

Reflexive and **intensive pronouns** are created when *-self* is added to singular personal pronouns and *-selves* to plural personal pronouns: *myself, yourself, herself, himself, itself, oneself, ourselves, yourselves, themselves.* These words are *reflexive* in sentences like the following, where both the subject and the object of an action are the same person or thing.

subj. obj.
They took **themselves** too seriously.

They are *intensive* when they modify a noun or another pronoun.

noun pron.
Warren **himself** admitted he was responsible.

noun pron.
I **myself** never vote.

1 Don't use reflexive pronouns to make sentences sound more formal. The basic pronoun form is adequate.

NONSTANDARD	The memo is for Ms. Matthews and **yourself**.
REVISED	The memo is for Ms. Matthews and **you**.

Use the reflexive pronoun only when the subject and object in a sentence refer to the same person or thing.

subj. obj.
Maggie rediscovered **herself** in her paintings.

subj. obj.
Jones had only **himself** to blame.

Similarly, don't use *myself* in place of a more suitable *I* or *me*.

NONSTANDARD	*Jose and myself* wrote the **lab report**.
REVISED	*Jose and I* wrote the **lab report**.

Compare the sentence above to a similar one using *myself* correctly as an intensive pronoun.

I wrote the lab report **myself**.

2 Use intensive pronouns for emphasis.

The gift is for *you* **yourself**.

The *residents* did all the plumbing and wiring **themselves**.

3 Never use *hisself* or *theirselves*. Although you may hear these expressions—especially *theirselves*—in speech, the correct forms in writing are always *himself* and *themselves*.

WRONG	They saw **theirselves** on television.
CORRECT	They saw **themselves** on television.

EXERCISE 29.4 Correct any problems with reflexive or intensive pronouns in the sentences below.

1. "God helps them who help themselves" is an adage credited to Benjamin Franklin.

2. The delegates to the Constitutional Convention in 1787 were not sure they could agree among theirselves on a new form of government.
3. George Washington hisself presided over the convention.
4. Aaron and myself wrote a paper on Madison's contribution to the Constitution.
5. You might want to read more about the topic yourself.

CHAPTER

30 Questions About Modifiers?

Much of the work in sentences is handled by modifiers—especially adjectives and adverbs (see Section 16b). These modifying words and phrases expand what we know about subjects, verbs, and other sentence elements. The most common modifiers are adjectives and adverbs, or the modifying phrases in which they appear. Adjectives modify nouns and pronouns, provide details, and answer questions about qualities: *How many? How big? What color? Which one? What kind?* Adverbs modify verbs, adjectives, other adverbs, and entire sentences.

In this chapter, we examine some issues writers face when dealing with modifiers, including such familiar problems as misplaced modifiers and double negatives. We also help you to determine whether modifying clauses are essential (restrictive) or nonessential (nonrestrictive), an important distinction in some circumstances.

Take Control

30a What's the problem with misplaced or dangling modifiers?

Adjectives and adverbs can cause confusion if they become detached from the words they are intended to modify in a sentence. Two forms of this common problem are **misplaced** and **dangling modifiers**.

A modifier is considered *misplaced* when it connects to the wrong word or phrase, sometimes with comic effect.

MISPLACED MODIFIER	**Carved from solid oak**, the angry mother could not break down the door.
CORRECTED	The angry mother could not break down the door **carved from solid oak**.

A modifier is termed *dangling* when it doesn't have a plausible word or phrase to attach itself to in a sentence. As a result, it doesn't make a logical connection.

DANGLING MODIFIER	**Infuriated by the groom's boorishness**, the wedding was postponed. The boldfaced phrase doesn't describe anything in the main clause of the sentence. The sentence needs a person who might be infuriated.
CORRECTED	**Infuriated by the groom's boorishness**, the bride postponed the wedding.

Following are strategies for avoiding problems with misplaced or dangling modifiers.

1 Be sure that an introductory modifying phrase is followed by the word it modifies. Sometimes you will have to supply a word that the introductory phrase can modify. In other cases, the whole sentence may have to be rearranged.

MISPLACED MODIFIER	**Insulting and predictable**, fewer and fewer television viewers are attracted to the comedian's monologues. The boldfaced phrase doesn't describe *viewers*; it describes *monologues*.
REVISION	**Insulting and predictable**, the comedian's monologues attracted fewer and fewer television viewers.

2 Supply a word for a dangling modifier to modify. This often means rewriting the entire sentence, since you must usually add a word or phrase that the sentence alludes to but doesn't actually include. For example:

DANGLING MODIFIER	**On returning to the office**, the furniture had been rearranged.
ONE POSSIBLE REVISION	**On returning to the office**, the staff found that the furniture had been rearranged.

3 Distinguish between absolute phrases and dangling modifiers. Some modifying phrases may look like dangling modifiers but are actually **absolute phrases**; that is, they are complete in themselves, serving only to give additional information about the sentence of which they are a part.

absolute

Given the fiasco at dinner, the guests weren't surprised when Martha pushed her husband into the pool.

absolute

To be blunt, Axel is a whiny nerd who deserves to be fired.

For more on absolute phrases, see Section 16c-3.

Taking Control

Dangling and misplaced modifiers

Dangling and misplaced modifying phrases can make readers laugh. In most cases, the difference between what a writer intends to write and what he actually puts down on paper is what provokes the humor:

Breaded with peanuts and lightly broiled, Mrs. Dodge served the trout.

Readers often miss the joke because they intuitively make the connection the writer intended—in this case, between the method of cooking and the trout. But writers have exactly the same problem. They know what they *meant* to say and assume they've actually said it—until the error is pointed out. If you are prone to faulty modification of this sort, all you can do is routinely double-check the relationship between any opening modifying phrases and the subjects that follow them. And then make any necessary changes:

Mrs. Dodge served the trout **breaded with peanuts and lightly broiled**.

EXERCISE 30.1 Rewrite or rearrange these sentences, placing modifiers in appropriate positions. You may need to add a noun for the modifier to modify. Not all of the sentences need to be revised.

1. Although they are among the most dangerous of reptiles, biologists have only recently begun to study rattlesnakes.

2. Rattlers belong to the family of pit vipers according to scientists, taking their name from the two characteristic pits on their snouts.

3. Given their lethal capabilities, it is not surprising that pit vipers are universally loathed.

4. Despite their fearful reputation, however, people are seldom bitten by the snakes unless they are provoked.

30b Where should adjectives go?

Adjectives are words that modify nouns or pronouns. They explain how many, which color, which one, and so on. All the words in boldface here function as adjectives.

A **simple** tax return is **rare** these days.

The **darkest** nights are **moonless**.

German beers pour slowly.

The truck, **tall** and **ungainly**, rolled down the hill.

In English, single-word adjectives usually come before the word or phrase they modify: **red** apple, **outstanding** athlete. Phrases and clauses may come before or after the words they refer to.

the woman **in the red dress**

the guy **whom I dated in high school**

Resplendent in his fur hat, the soldier crossed the square.

Whatever kind of modifier you're using, you must position it carefully to avoid ambiguity and awkward pileups. An adjective becomes ambiguous when readers can't tell which word it modifies.

AMBIGUOUS Adam had his **enthusiastic parents' support**.

Enthusiastic could describe *parents* or *support*.

CLARIFIED Adam had his **parents' enthusiastic support**.

Adjectives pile up when writers place one modifier after another until readers get confused or bored.

TEDIOUS **Recent, controversial, divisive** gambling legislation met defeat in the state legislature.

REVISED **Recent** gambling legislation, **controversial and divisive**, met defeat in the state legislature.

1 Relocate any adjectives that are potentially confusing or ambiguous. You may have to read your sentences carefully to appreciate how they might be misread. Better still, ask a friend to review your work and point out where readers might get confused.

AMBIGUOUS	The **long-lost diplomat's memoirs** were revealing. Does *long-lost* go with *diplomat* or *memoirs*?
CLARIFIED	The **diplomat's long-lost memoirs** were revealing.
CLARIFIED	The **memoirs** of the **long-lost diplomat** were revealing
AMBIGUOUS	The **ingenious Web site's designer** resigned. Does *ingenious* go with *Web site* or *designer*?
CLARIFIED	The **ingenious designer of the Web site** resigned.
CLARIFIED	The **designer of the ingenious Web site** resigned.

2 Consider placing adjectives after the words or phrases they modify. You can avoid tedious strings of adjectives this way and make sentences more graceful.

TEDIOUS	A **new, powerful, quick**, and **easy-to-use** database was installed today.
REVISED	A new database program, **powerful, quick**, and **easy to use**, was installed today.

EXERCISE 30.2 Rearrange the adjectives to make each of these sentences clearer or more effective. Several options are possible.

1. Lisa wanted to find a knowledgeable and squeaky-clean neighborhood attorney to help her prepare her rezoning proposal.
2. Lisa viewed the negative council members' attitudes as a challenge to her persuasive abilities.
3. Before explaining her plan, Lisa demanded the undivided city council's attention.
4. Obtaining a hearing was essential if she were to overcome the stubborn city planner's resistance.

30c How do you get predicate adjectives right?

Many people have problems selecting the correct term to follow linking verbs such as *seem, become, look, appear, feel, smell.* An adjective that follows a linking verb is called a **predicate adjective**.

I *feel* **bad**.

He *seems* **uneasy**.

Iris *appears* **calm**.

1 Remember that only adjectives, not adverbs, can modify a noun. So after a linking verb you need an adjective—not an adverb—to modify a noun. In the following example, the first version of the sentence shows the incorrect *adverb* modifier; the second version shows the correct *adjective* form.

INCORRECT The accountant feels **awfully** about underestimating your quarterly taxes.

To describe *accountant* (a noun), the writer should use the adjective form (*awful*) rather than the adverb (*awfully*).

CORRECT The accountant feels **awful** about underestimating your quarterly taxes.

The same principle applies when you modify a noun that acts as the object in a sentence, as in the following example.

INCORRECT The accountant kept the leather in his Lexus **flawlessly**.

To describe *leather* (a noun), the writer should use the adjective form (*flawless*) rather than the adverb (*flawlessly*).

CORRECT The accountant kept the leather in his Lexus **flawless**.

2 Pay special attention to *good/well* and *bad/badly*. *Good* and *bad* are always adjectives. Use *good* (or *bad*) after a linking verb when you are modifying the subject of the sentence.

Tom looks **good** on paper.

His academic record is especially **good**.

But Tom feels **bad** since his arrest for littering.

In academic or formal writing, *good* and *bad* are *not* used as adverbs to describe the action of verbs.

INCORRECT Madeline's children play **good** with other children.

INCORRECT But they usually eat **bad**, like most five-year olds.

That's the job of *well*, which usually is an adverb, or *badly*, which always is an adverb. In the following sentences, for example, *well* and *badly* clearly modify the verbs in the sentences (*play, speak*) by explaining how the actions are performed.

CORRECT Madeline's children play **well** with other children.

CORRECT But they usually eat **badly**, like most five-year olds.

What makes matters tricky is that *well* can also function as an adjective when referring to someone's health.

Madeline hasn't felt **well** since she returned from New York.

Mickey doesn't look **well** either since the trip.

Remember, however, that *badly* is never an adjective. Although you may hear people say, "I feel badly about that," the construction is incorrect.

INCORRECT I feel **badly** because I have a cold.

CORRECT I feel **bad** because I have a cold.

INCORRECT Jackson feels **badly** about hitting my Mustang.

CORRECT Jackson feels **bad** about hitting my Mustang.

EXERCISE 30.3 In these sentences, replace the boldfaced modifier with a better one.

1. In developed countries, most people feel **confidently** that their drinking water is safe.
2. In many parts of the world, however, even water that looks **well** can be full of bacteria and pollution.
3. Some major relief organizations feel **optimistically** that they can bring clean water to the rural areas of underdeveloped nations.

4. They teach villagers how to keep a sanitation system running **good**.

5. But parents who know that their children's drinking water should be boiled feel **badly** because often they cannot afford the fuel to boil it.

30d Questions about absolute adjectives?

Some words called *absolute adjectives* cannot be compared or qualified—at least not logically. For example, since *equal* means "exactly the same," you shouldn't write that something is *more equal* any more than you'd say it is *more empty*. Similarly, either a thing is *perfect* or it's flawed. An object is either *unique* or there are others like it.

In practice, writers and speakers do qualify absolute expressions all the time, often significantly. We know what it means to say something is *almost perfect* or *quite pregnant*. Even the preamble of the Constitution describes "a more perfect union," and the pigs in George Orwell's satire *Animal Farm* are famously *more equal* than other animals. But in most cases you should avoid using qualifiers (such as *less, more, most, least, very*) with the following absolute words: *unique, perfect, singular, empty, equal, full, definite, complete, absolute,* and, of course, *pregnant*.

Consider these examples.

ILLOGICAL We doubted that the new operating system was **absolutely perfect**.

REVISED We doubted that the new operating system was **perfected yet**.

ILLOGICAL Jamie's short story is **more unique** than Jordan's.

REVISED Jamie's short story is **unique**; Jordan's is not.

EXERCISE 30.4 Working with other students in a group, read over these sentences and decide which ones have faulty modifiers and which might be acceptable. Confer to decide how any problems with modifiers might be solved.

1. The technician assured me that the service work on my computer was almost complete.

2. The machine had frozen because my hard drive was totally full of illegal downloads.

3. The repair had required a very complete erasure of my files.

4. Now my drive is mostly empty of music and video files.

30e Questions about adverb form?

Adverbs are versatile. They are words that modify verbs, adjectives, or other adverbs, explaining where, when, and how. Many, but not all, adverbs end in *-ly*.

The Secretary of State spoke **angrily** to the press. modifies verb *spoke*

The water was **extremely** cold. modifies adjective *cold*

The candidate spoke **quite** evasively. modifies adverb *evasively*

Some adverbs have both short and long forms.

slow/slowly	fair/fairly	rough/roughly
quick/quickly	tight/tightly	deep/deeply

The problem for many writers is that the short adverb forms look suspiciously like adjectives. Is it correct then to say "drive slow" or "tie it tight" instead of "drive slowly" and "tie it tightly"? The answer is "Yes"—but you have to consider your audience.

In most cases, the short form of the adverb sounds more casual than the long form. Consequently, in most academic and business situations, you'll do better to use the *-ly* form.

COLLOQUIAL The employees expected to be treated **fair**.

STANDARD The employees expected to be treated **fairly**.

EXERCISE 30.5 If necessary, modify the boldfaced verbs for an academic audience.

1. Max was **real** surprised when he got a response from the IRS to his suggestion.

2. The local IRS director seemed to take his ideas for clearer tax forms very **serious**.

3. She had written back to Max **quick**.

4. But Max reacted **bad** when the IRS rejected his proposals.

30f Where should adverbs go?

Adverbs can take any of several positions in a sentence. For example:

> George daydreamed **endlessly** about his vacation, **thoroughly** reviewing each travel brochure.
>
> **Endlessly** George daydreamed about his vacation, reviewing each travel brochure **thoroughly**.

But because adverbs are so mobile, it's also easy to place them in inappropriate spots, creating confusing or ambiguous sentences.

1 When editing, check to see that you haven't placed adverbs in positions that could cause confusion. In general, locate adverbs as close as possible to the word they modify. In case of confusion, repositioning the modifier will solve the problem.

CONFUSING	Seeing the security officer approach **quickly** James concluded his speech.
CLEAR	Seeing the security officer approach, James **quickly** concluded his speech.
CLEAR	Seeing the security officer **quickly** approaching, James concluded his speech.

As evident in the examples above, punctuation can tell readers how to interpret modifiers.

CLEAR	Seeing the security officer approach **quickly**, James concluded his speech.

And sometimes it's best just to rewrite the sentence to avoid any confusion.

CLEAR	Because the security officer was hurrying toward him, James **quickly** concluded his speech.

2 Place the adverbs *almost, even,* and *only* logically near the words they modify to ensure accurate interpretations. In everyday speech, people usually ignore this convention. But you'll want to be more precise in writing. Notice the ambiguities these words cause in the following sentences because they are misplaced.

ADVERB MISPLACED	Much to his dismay, Connor realized he had **almost** dated every woman at the party. Putting *almost* next to *dated* implies that Connor had dated none of the women—a possibility, but probably not what the writer means.
ADVERB BETTER PLACED	Much to his dismay, Connor realized he had dated **almost** every woman at the party.
CONFUSING	Zoe **even** thought time spent driving to the office could be used productively.
CLEARER	Zoe thought **even** time spent driving to the office could be used productively. **Even** Zoe thought time spent driving to the office could be used productively.
CONFUSING	Javier **only** plays the piano.
CLEARER	Javier plays **only** the piano. **Only** Javier plays the piano.

Taking Control

Adverbs

The correct placement of a word such as *only* may seem like a matter too minor to worry about much. But when you find yourself taking pains to place *only* and other adverbs where they belong in a sentence, you will also be paying more attention to the logic of your prose. Thus, you'll become more precise in what you write and begin to wish that others were too.

EXERCISE 30.6 Rewrite the sentences to clarify them.

1. People who attend the theater often complain that the manners of many audience members are boorish.
2. Sitting next to a woman who spends most of the evening unwrapping candy slowly can provoke even the most tolerant theatergoer to violence.
3. Cellular phones, beepers, and wristwatch alarms even go off routinely.
4. For their part, actors marvel at how audiences today only manage to cough during the quietest moments of a play.

30g What's wrong with double negatives?

Sentences that say *no* in two different ways are emphatic and usually very colloquial.

Can't never remember whatshername's name!

They make their point, but you need to avoid them in academic and professional writing.

1 Check that you don't have two *no* words (a *double negative*) in the same sentence or independent clause. In addition to *no*, look for such words as *not, nothing, nobody*, and *never*. If you've used two of them, you can usually just drop or change a single word.

DOUBLE NEGATIVE	That cell phone will **not** work **no way**.
CORRECTED	That cell phone will **never** work.
DOUBLE NEGATIVE	The child does **not** want **nobody** tying his shoes.
CORRECTED	The child does **not** want **anybody** tying his shoes.

2 Don't mix the adverbs *hardly, scarcely*, or *barely* with another negative word or phrase. Such pairings create double negatives, which should be edited.

DOUBLE NEGATIVE	The morning was so cool and clear that the hikers **couldn't hardly** wait to get started.
CORRECTED	The morning was so cool and clear that the hikers **could hardly** wait to get started.

Double negatives shouldn't be confused with negative statements that express ideas indirectly—and perhaps with ironic twists. Consider the difference in tone between these simple sentences, framed negatively and positively.

NEGATIVE	The proposal was not unintelligent.
POSITIVE	The proposal was intelligent.
NEGATIVE	Chris was hardly unattractive.
POSITIVE	Chris was attractive.

EXERCISE 30.7 Rewrite any sentences that contain double negatives to eliminate the problem.

1. Some critics claim that in this media age, young people barely don't read anymore.
2. Yet many cities haven't never had so many bookstores.
3. Bookstores aren't no longer just places to buy books.
4. They serve as community centers where people can be entertained without ever buying no books.

30h How do comparatives and superlatives differ?

The comparative and superlative forms of most adjectives (and a few adverbs) can be expressed two ways.

ugly (an adjective)		
Comparative	uglier	more ugly
Superlative	ugliest	most ugly

slowly (an adverb)		
Comparative	slower	more slowly
Superlative	slowest	most slowly

As a general rule, use *-er* and *-est* endings with words of one syllable and *more* and *most* (or *less* and *least*) with words of two or more syllables.

Their group is **brighter** than ours.

This group is the **most conservative.**

The candidate talked **faster** than the moderator.

The incumbent spoke **more decisively** than the challenger.

Some modifiers have irregular comparatives and superlatives. Note, too, that some modifiers share the same comparative and superlative forms.

MODIFIER	COMPARATIVE	SUPERLATIVE
good	better	best
well	better	best

bad	worse	worst
badly	worse	worst
little	less	least
many, much	more	most
some	more	most

1 Use the comparative, not the superlative, when you are comparing two items. That means using an adverb or adjective with an *-er* ending or modified by *more* or *less.*

INCORRECT That twin is the **smartest** of the pair.
CORRECT That twin is the **smarter** of the pair.

INCORRECT Of the two orators, Casey speaks **most persuasively**.
CORRECT Of the two orators, Casey speaks **more persuasively**.

2 Use the superlative when comparing more than two items. In most cases in which you compare three or more things or qualities, you must use *-est* adjectives or adverbs or preface the modifiers with *most* or *least.*

INCORRECT Of all New York skyscrapers, the Empire State Building is **taller**.

CORRECT Of all New York skyscrapers, the Empire State Building is **tallest**.

3 Avoid using two comparative or two superlative forms in the same phrase.

INCORRECT McDougal is a **more tougher** boss than Gonzalez is.
CORRECT McDougal is a **tougher** boss than Gonzalez is.

INCORRECT Paula Sung is the **most smartest** lawyer in her firm.
CORRECT Paula Sung is the **smartest** lawyer in her firm.

4 Make sure comparisons are complete enough to be clear. *Incomplete comparisons* come in two common forms. The first kind doesn't provide the second term of the comparison. "My paper is better" is an incomplete comparison. A complete comparison will answer the question "Better than *what*?"

Often the context makes stating the second term unnecessary. When you and a friend have been comparing your writing class papers, you won't need to say "Your paper is better than mine" for the point to be clear. In other cases, leaving off the second term invites confusion.

CONFUSING People who live in rural areas are **healthier**.

Are these people healthier than people everywhere else? Or are they healthier than some specific group of people to whom they are being compared?

CLEARER People who live in rural areas are **healthier than** people who live in heavily industrialized cities, but not **as healthy as** people who reside in suburban areas near major cities.

The second kind of incomplete comparison leaves out important words needed to make the comparison clear.

CONFUSING Sally is **more afraid** of dogs **than** Jerry.

This sentence might be read two ways.

Sally is more afraid of dogs than Jerry is.

Sally is more afraid of dogs than she is of Jerry.

To complete the comparison, supply the words that make your point clear.

EXERCISE 30.8 Choose the appropriate forms of comparison in the following sentences.

1. Today community librarians are constantly trying to decide what is (**more/most**) important: expanding computer facilities or buying more books.
2. These librarians consider who among their clients has the (**greater/greatest**) need—schoolchildren, working adults, or retired people.
3. In general, librarians enjoy the reputation of being among the (**most helpful/helpfullest**) of city employees.
4. In good libraries, librarians are also likely to be among the (**most bright/brightest**) city employees.

5. Well-trained librarians, or information specialists as they are often called today, will find their (**better/best**) job prospects in medium-sized cities with growing populations.

30i Questions about nonessential and essential modifiers?

Writers sometimes puzzle over how to introduce (Section 29c) or how to punctuate (Section 36b) nonessential (or *nonrestrictive*) and essential (or *restrictive*) modifiers. In either case, you first have to understand and reliably identify these structures.

1 Understand nonessential modifiers. A modifier is **nonessential** when it adds information to a sentence but can be cut without a loss of sense. It is typically surrounded by commas.

WITH NONESSENTIAL MODIFIER	The police officers, **who were wearing dress uniforms**, marched in front of the mayor's car.
MODIFIER REMOVED	The police officers marched in front of the mayor's car.

Useful descriptive information can be lost when the nonessential modifier is cut, but the sentence still works.

2 Understand essential modifiers. When you can't remove a modifying expression from a sentence without significantly affecting its meaning, you have an *essential modifier*—which is not surrounded by commas. The sentence may make little sense with the modifier cut.

ESSENTIAL MODIFIER	Diamonds **that are synthetically produced** are less expensive than natural diamonds.
ESSENTIAL MODIFIER REMOVED	Diamonds are less expensive than natural diamonds.
ESSENTIAL MODIFIER	We missed the only speaker **whose work dealt with business ethics**.
ESSENTIAL MODIFIER REMOVED	We missed the only speaker.

Understand, however, that context may sometimes determine whether a modifier is essential. Remember this sentence with a nonessential modifier?

NONESSENTIAL The police officers, **who were wearing dress uniforms**, marched in front of the mayor's car.

We can make its modifier essential simply by pairing the sentence with another that changes its overall meaning by setting up a significant contrast.

ESSENTIAL The police officers **who were wearing dress uniforms** marched in front of the mayor's car. The officers **who were in plain clothes** mingled with the crowd as part of a security detail.

Notice that the punctuation changes, too, with the modifiers no longer surrounded by commas.

Any clause introduced by *that* will be essential (restrictive) and should not be surrounded by commas. (See Section 29c.)

WRONG The committee, that approved the boycott, was abolished.

RIGHT The committee that approved the boycott was abolished.

EXERCISE 30.9 Following the model provided, first write a sentence with a nonessential modifier. Then add a second sentence that would make the modifier in the first sentence essential. Be sure your version shows the same changes in punctuation that occur in the model.

NONESSENTIAL The students, who had stood for hours in line, applauded when the ticket window opened.

ESSENTIAL The students **who had stood for hours in line** applauded when the ticket window opened. Those **who had only just arrived** despaired at ever getting seats for the game.

CHAPTER

31 Is English a Second Language for You (ESOL)?

by Jocelyn Steer and Carol Rhoades

ESOL (English for Speakers of Other Languages) and *ESL* (English as a Second Language) are common terms used to designate language instruction for people whose native tongue may not be English. But these expressions fail to capture the diverse circumstances of many people in college writing classes today. We use ESOL as a familiar term, but we appreciate the diversity of writers for whom more technical instruction in edited American English may be helpful. There is no single type that adequately describes all ESOL writers.

That said, it is obvious that you will face challenges while working to express ideas in a new language. But because you have experienced the grammatical systems and vocabularies of at least two languages, you have already acquired linguistic knowledge that should help you become a proficient writer in English. The next three chapters of this book are designed to help you to further develop your abilities.

- This chapter, **Chapter 31**, reviews common problem areas for ESOL writers. We identify common errors and identify resources to which you can turn for more help. Also look for the boxed **ESOL Tips**, which feature specific advice from successful ESOL writers and instructors.
- **Chapter 32** gives detailed guidelines for choosing the proper verb forms in your writing.
- **Chapter 33** offers detailed advice for using gerunds, articles, count and noncount nouns, and other grammatical elements that ESOL writers often ask questions about.

Of course, even though these three chapters focus specifically on the needs of ESOL writers, you will also find useful material in other chapters. See Chapters 22 to 30 for general discussions of grammar and mechanics. (Chart 31.2 on page 471 lists the most relevant sections of those chapters.)

31a Common problem areas for ESOL writers

It's always a good idea to proofread papers for grammar and punctuation errors before handing in the final copy. (See Section 5c.) Many errors that instructors mark on final drafts could probably have been corrected by more thorough proofreading.

If you know what your most common errors are, check for them first and then look for other problems. In this section, you'll find a list of the most common problems for ESOL writers—and their solutions.

ESOL Tip

State Your Thesis Early **Monika Shehi, Albania**

When I came to America, I found writing papers to be an intimidating task. When I wrote papers in Albania, I would start with an idea and follow wherever my thoughts led, often progressing to several new ideas. My American professors found my papers very chaotic, because in U.S. universities, most papers are about establishing and developing one main point. Once I became aware of that basic structure, writing became much easier. Now I begin a draft by determining my main idea, then supplying evidence to support that idea.

1 Be sure each clause has a subject. Every clause in English must have a subject, except for imperative sentences ("Sit down.").

The subject is missing.

INCORRECT ^Is difficult to write in English. *Subject missing*
CORRECT **It** is difficult to write in English.

2 Be sure a main or an auxiliary verb isn't missing.

The main verb is missing.

INCORRECT The teacher^extremely helpful. *verb missing*
CORRECT The teacher **is** extremely helpful.

The auxiliary verb is missing.

INCORRECT Hurry! The plane ^ leaving right now. verb missing
CORRECT Hurry! The plane **is** leaving right now.

3 Don't forget the *-s* ending on verbs used with third person singular nouns and pronouns (*he, she, it*). If this is a problem for you, check all present tense verbs to make sure you haven't forgotten an *-s*.

INCORRECT The library close at 5:00 today. 3rd person sing. -s
CORRECT The library close**s** at 5:00 today.

When you have the auxiliary *do* or *does* in a sentence, add *-s* to the auxiliary, not to the main verb.

INCORRECT He **don't** knows the answer to the question.
3rd person sing. -s
CORRECT He **doesn't** know the answer to the question.

4 Don't forget *-ed* endings on past participles. Check your papers to be sure that you use the past participle (*-ed* ending) for verbs in the following situations. (See Section 23b for a list of the three parts of a verb.)

In passive voice (see Section 23e).

INCORRECT The amenities were **provide** by the hotel.
CORRECT The amenities were **provided** by the hotel.

INCORRECT The documents were **alter** by the thief.
CORRECT The documents were **altered** by the thief.

In the past perfect tense (see Section 32a).

INCORRECT Juan had **finish** the race before Fred came.
CORRECT Juan had **finished** the race before Fred came.

In participle adjectives (see Section 16c-2).

INCORRECT She was **frighten** by the dark.
CORRECT She was **frightened** by the dark.

Be sure that you *don't* add endings to infinitives.

INCORRECT	George started to **prepared** dinner.
CORRECT	George started to **prepare** dinner.

5 Don't confuse adjective pairs like *bored* and *boring*. The following sentences are very different in meaning, although they look similar.

John is bored.

This means that John is bored by *something*—maybe his class or his homework; it is a feeling he has as a result of something.

John is boring.

This means that John has a personality that is not interesting; he is a boring person.

The ending of the adjective, *-ed* or *-ing*, is what creates a difference in meaning. Adjectives ending in *-ed* have a passive meaning. Adjectives ending in *-ing* have an active meaning. (See Section 23e for an explanation of passive voice.)

The English spelling system often confuses Jorge.

-ED ENDING	Jorge is **confused** by the English spelling system. passive
	The **confused** student looked up words in his spelling dictionary. passive
-ING ENDING	English spelling is **confusing**. active
	It is a **confusing** system. active

Joan's work satisfies her.

-ED ENDING	She is **satisfied** by her work. passive
	She is a **satisfied** employee. passive
-ING ENDING	Her work is **satisfying**. active
	Joan does **satisfying** work. active

Chart 31.1 shows some common pairs of adjectives that confuse students, along with the preposition that is used after the *-ed* adjectives.

Chart 31.1 Adjective Pairs

amusing	amused by	exciting	excited by/about
annoying	annoyed by	frightening	frightened by
boring	bored by	interesting	interested in
confusing	confused by	irritating	irritated by
embarrassing	embarrassed by	satisfying	satisfied with

6 Avoid repeating sentence elements. You may find that you repeat unnecessary words in your sentences. Be on your guard for the three types of repetition shown in these examples.

In adjective clauses.

The store that I told you about ~~**it**~~ closed down.

It is not necessary because *that* replaces *it*.

The man whom I met ~~**him**~~ yesterday was kind.

Whom replaces *him*.

The school where I go ~~**there**~~ is very expensive.

Where replaces *there*.

In the subject of the sentence.

My brother ~~**he**~~ is the director of the hospital.

Because *my brother* and *he* refer to the same person, the *he* is unnecessary repetition.

Multiple connectors.

Although the employee was diligent, ~~**but**~~ she was fired.

Although and *but* both express contrast. You don't need two connectors with the same meaning in one sentence. You must remove one of them.

Because she fell asleep after eating a big lunch, ~~**so**~~ she missed her class.

So and *because* both express cause. Cut one of them.

ESOL Tip

Don't Repeat Points; Develop Them **Mila Tasseva, Bulgaria**

The academic essay model I was accustomed to before I began college in the United States is the one typically taught to students in the countries of the former Soviet bloc. Students are taught to structure their essays so that they spiral around the thesis, repeating the same statement in different words again, and again, and again without actually developing the argument. In contrast, professors in the United States will expect students to support the thesis with details and examples.

If your instructor asks you to work on developing your paper, try the following strategy. When you review a draft, look closely into the argument's development and identify the points that give you evidence in support of the claim. Now review what you just identified and see if you can find the same point repeated in the same or different words. Do you find the spiral? I bet so. It always comes as a surprise; at least it did to me when I received back my first paper written in an American university with the note in the margin, "Why did you repeat this idea so many times?"

7 Place adverbs correctly in the sentence. Adverbs can appear in many different places in a sentence—at the beginning, in the middle, at the end. However, there are a few positions where adverbs *can't* be placed. Here are some guidelines. (For more help with adverb placement, see Section 30f.)

Don't put an adverb between the verb and its object.

verb / adverb / obj.

INCORRECT She answered **slowly** the question.

verb / obj. / adverb

CORRECT She answered the question **slowly**.

Don't place adverbs of frequency before the verb *be*.

INCORRECT Louise **regularly** is late for class.

CORRECT Louise is **regularly** late for class.

Don't place adverbs of frequency after other verbs.

INCORRECT Juan arrives **often** late to class.

CORRECT Juan **often** arrives late to class.

EXERCISE 31.1 Review Section 31a. Then read the following paragraph and proofread it for the mistakes described in the section. In some cases you will need to add something, and in others you will delete an element. (There are seven errors. For answers, see page 473.)

There are long lines at the cashier's office because students signing up for financial aid. Is extremely frustrating to spend the entire day in line. Because some students they have other jobs and classes, so they can't wait very long. Then you very tired when you finally arrive at the desk where you can talk to the clerk there. The clerk usually give you a form to fill out, and then you have to wait in another line!

ESOL Tip

Cite Sources Carefully Carl Jenkinson, England

For me, one of the most significant differences in America is the emphasis placed on full and accurate citation using MLA style. Although citation is required in the UK, and to a lesser extent in France (where it seems more of a courtesy than a necessity), full and accurate citation in the United States is imperative. The solution is straightforward: become as familiar as possible with the MLA handbook, and if in doubt, cite your source.

Take Control

31b Finding other ESOL resources

You may have questions about grammar or punctuation that aren't covered in Chapters 31 through 33, which deal specifically with the concerns of ESOL writers. This section points you to additional resources in this book and in other publications that you can consult.

1 Consult relevant material in other chapters of this book.

Many questions you have about grammar and mechanics are not specific to ESOL writers. Native speakers of English have many of these questions too. Chart 31.2 lists possible questions, each with the chapter or section in this handbook that covers that problem. If you have several areas of difficulty with grammar, focus on one at a time. Study the examples in this chapter and those in the other grammar chapters in this handbook, and work through the practice exercises for rules that you find especially tricky.

Chart 31.2 Where to Look in This Book for Additional Help with Grammar

IF YOU HAVE A QUESTION ABOUT...	EXAMPLES	GO TO THIS CHAPTER/ SECTION
Abbreviations	Dr., APA, Ms.	42a
Adjective clauses	clauses beginning with *who, which, that*	16d, 29c
Capitalization	English, Japanese	41b
Comparatives/ superlatives	more interesting/the most interesting	30h
Dangling modifiers	Reading the paper, the phone rang.	30a
Irregular verbs	*sit, sat, sat*	23b
Parallelism	I like swimming and fishing.	16h, 23c
Passive voice	I was hit by a car.	23e
Plural nouns	child: children	25a
Possessives	the teacher's book	25b
Pronouns	his gain; their loss	26–29
Punctuation	commas, periods	34–40
SENTENCE PROBLEMS		
Run-ons	I am a student I come from Mexico.	35d
Fragments	Because it is my house.	35a–35b
Subject-verb agreement	I comes from Italy.	22

2 Consult reference books and Web sites especially designed for ESOL writers. A general handbook like this one cannot cover all the ESOL information you need. We suggest that you refer regularly to ESOL reference books for help with grammar and usage. ESOL grammar textbooks can give you more detailed grammatical explanations. Some ESOL dictionaries provide useful spelling and usage information. See the following list of ESOL reference books.

Taking Control

Find additional ESOL grammar resources

We suggest the following reference books and Web sites for ESOL students who have questions about grammar and usage.

- Betty S. Azar. *Basic English Grammar: English as a Second Language*. 3rd ed. New York: Pearson, 2005.
- Betty S. Azar. *Understanding and Using English Grammar*. 4th ed. New York: Pearson, 2009.
- Dave's ESL Café at http://www.eslcafe.com.
- ESOL Resources at OWL (the Online Writing Lab at Purdue University) at http://owl.english.purdue.edu.

We also recommend the following dictionary written for the ESOL student.

- *Longman Dictionary of American English*. 4th ed. New York: Pearson Longman, 2004.

3 Look for opportunities to listen to, speak, read, and write English in your everyday activities. Although books can give you thorough explanations of grammatical rules, experts agree that the best way to increase your proficiency in English is to practice. Look for opportunities to use English in everyday contexts: email friends and classmates in English; write letters; chat online in English with friends or classmates; read English novels and magazines; and watch the news in English. Don't hesitate to ask native speakers to explain idioms, terms, or conventions of usage that are unfamiliar to you. Consider, too, using the services of your college writing center, if one is available.

ANSWER KEY

EXERCISE 31.1

There are long lines at the cashier's office because students **are** signing up for financial aid. **It** is extremely frustrating to spend the entire day in line. Because some students ~~**they**~~ have other jobs and classes, ~~**so**~~ they can't wait very long. Then you **are** very tired when you finally arrive at the desk where you can talk to the clerk ~~**there**~~. The clerk usually **gives** you a form to fill out, and then you have to wait in another line!

CHAPTER

32 Do You Have Questions About Verbs (ESOL)?

by Jocelyn Steer and Carol Rhoades

English verbs are complicated. If you are a speaker for whom English is not a native or first language, you will probably still have questions about them, even after many years of studying English. For example, should you write "She is liking the class very much" or "She likes the class very much"? This section addresses some common questions ESOL writers have about verbs. For additional help with verbs, see Chapters 22 and 23.

32a Which verb tense should you use?

A verb's tense expresses time. Chart 32.1 shows the twelve most commonly used verb tenses, along with a list of common adverbs and expressions that accompany them. These words and phrases are the signposts that help you choose the best verb tense. A diagram illustrates the timeline for each tense; in the diagram, an *X* indicates an action, and a curved line indicates an action in progress.

The remainder of this section explains how to use these tenses appropriately. For more information on verb tenses, see Chapter 23.

Chart 32.1 Verb Tenses

WHAT IT IS CALLED	WHAT IT LOOKS LIKE	WHAT IT DESCRIBES	TIME WORDS USED WITH IT
Simple present	• I *sleep* eight hours every day.	Habits, regular activities	• every day • often • regularly • always
——x——	• Water *freezes* at 0°C.	Facts, general truths	• usually • habitually

(Continued)

Verb Tenses *(Continued)*

WHAT IT IS CALLED	WHAT IT LOOKS LIKE	WHAT IT DESCRIBES	TIME WORDS USED WITH IT
Simple past 	• I *slept* only four hours yesterday. • He *went* to sleep three hours ago.	A finished action in the past	• yesterday • last year • ago
Simple future 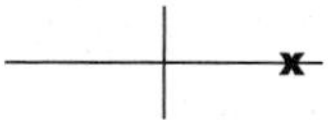	• I *will* try to sleep more. • I *am going to sleep* early tonight. • I *will* improve.	A single action in the future A planned action in the future (use *be going to*) Promises, offers	• tomorrow • in *x* days • next year
Present perfect  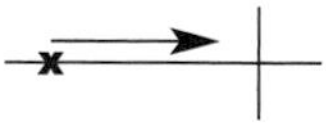	• I *have* already *written* my paper. • I *have lived* here for three months.	A past action that occurred at an unspecified time in the past An action that started in the past and continues to the present	• already • yet • before • recently • so far • for + time period • since + date
Past perfect 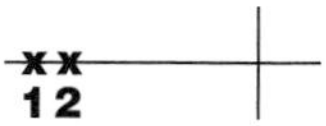 12	• She *had* already *slept* three hours when the burglar broke into the house.	One action in the past that occurs before another action/time in the past	• when • after • before • by the time
Future perfect 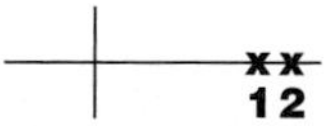 12	• I *will have finished* the paper when you stop by tonight.	One action in the future that will be completed before another action/time in the future	• by the time • when

(Continued)

Verb Tenses *(Continued)*

WHAT IT IS CALLED	WHAT IT LOOKS LIKE	WHAT IT DESCRIBES	TIME WORDS USED WITH IT
Present progressive 	• He *is sleeping* now.	A continuous activity in progress now	• right now • at this time • this week/year
Past progressive 	• While he *was sleeping*, the telephone rang. • He *was sleeping* at 10 A.M.	A continuous activity in progress in the past; often interrupted by another time or action	• while • during that time • between *x* and *y*
Future progressive 	• I *will be sleeping* all day.	A continuous activity happening in the future	• all the while • during that time • between *x* and *y*
Present perfect progressive 	• The woman *has been waiting* for many hours. • He *has been sleeping* since eight o'clock.	A continuous activity that began in the past and continues to the present; emphasis is on the duration	• for + time period • since + exact date
Past perfect progressive  (1 2)	• She *had been waiting* for three hours when he arrived. • He *had been sleeping* for an hour when the train crashed.	A continuous activity in the past that is finished before another action/time in the past	• for • since

(Continued)

Verb Tenses *(Continued)*

WHAT IT IS CALLED	WHAT IT LOOKS LIKE	WHAT IT DESCRIBES	TIME WORDS USED WITH IT
Future perfect progressive	• I *will have been sleeping* for twelve hours by the time you arrive.	A continuing future activity which started before another future event	• by • when

1 Review the difference between the simple present tense and the present progressive tense. You may be confused because the simple present tense doesn't really refer to an action going on in the present; rather, it is used to talk about repeated and habitual actions. You should use the simple present tense when you want to talk about *regular, repeated* activity.

SIMPLE PRESENT — The mail carrier usually **arrives** at 10 A.M.
This is an activity that is repeated daily.

PRESENT PROGRESSIVE — Look! She **is putting** the mail in the box now.
This is an activity occurring at the moment of speaking—now.

PRESENT PROGRESSIVE — She **is delivering** mail for John this month.
This is an activity that is in progress over a period of time. Use the progressive tense with the expression *this + time period.*

2 Review nonaction verbs and the present tense. Some verbs in English can't be used in a progressive form because they express a state and not an activity. Nonaction verbs include verbs of existence, of thought, of emotions, and of sense perceptions. Chart 32.2 lists some of these verbs. To use one of these nonaction verbs, you must use a simple form of the verb even though the time intended is *now.*

INCORRECT — I can't study because I **am hearing** my roommate's singing.

CORRECT — I can't study because I **hear** my roommate's singing.

INCORRECT — Maria **is preferring** Carlos's apartment to her own.

CORRECT — Maria **prefers** Carlos's apartment to her own.

Chart 32.2 Nonaction Verbs*

appear	forget	owe	seem
be	hate	own	smell
belong	have	possess	sound
consist	hear	prefer	surprise
contain	know	recognize	taste
deserve	like	remember	think
desire	love	require	understand
dislike	mean	resemble	want
feel	need	see	wish

*There are exceptions to the nonaction rule ("I **am thinking** about getting a job"; "He **is seeing** a doctor about his insomnia"). These exceptions can usually be paraphrased using other verbs ("He **is seeing** a doctor about his insomnia" means "He **is consulting** a doctor about his insomnia"). You will need to keep a list of these exceptions as you come across them.

3 Review the difference between the simple past tense and the present perfect tense. If an action happened in the past and is finished, you can always use the simple past tense to describe it. (See Chapter 23 on how to form the past tense and for a list of irregular verbs.) Often you will also use a time word such as *ago* or *yesterday* to show the specific time of the past action.

SIMPLE PAST — My brother **saw** that movie three days ago.

We know exactly when the brother saw the movie—three days ago. You *must* use the simple past in this sentence.

Use the **past tense** to show that something is completed, and use the **present perfect tense** to indicate that the action may continue or that it still has the possibility of occurring in the future. Compare these sentences to see how the two tenses express different ideas.

SIMPLE PAST — My grandmother never **used** a computer.

This implies that the grandmother may no longer be alive.

PRESENT PERFECT — My grandmother **has** never **used** a computer.

This sentence indicates that the grandmother is still alive and may use a computer in the future.

When you don't know or you don't want to state the exact time or date of a past action, use the present perfect tense.

PRESENT PERFECT Sarah **has seen** that movie before.

We don't know when Sarah saw the movie; she saw it at an unspecified time in the past.

You must use the present perfect for an action that began in the past and continues up to the present moment, especially when you use the time words *for* and *since.*

PRESENT PERFECT This theater **has shown** the same film for three months! I hope they change it soon.

The action started in the past—three months ago—and continues to the present. The film is still playing.

4 Review the difference between the present perfect tense and the present perfect progressive tense. You can use the **present perfect progressive** tense to show that an action is still in progress.

PRESENT PERFECT PROGRESSIVE Catherine **has been writing** that letter since this morning.

She hasn't finished; she's still writing.

In general, when the statement emphasizes *duration* (length of time), you need to use the present perfect progressive tense.

PRESENT PERFECT PROGRESSIVE My best friend **has been writing** her novel for five years.

This tells us how long the friend has been writing; the emphasis is on duration, or length of time.

However, when the statement emphasizes *quantity* (how much), you will use the **present perfect tense.**

PRESENT PERFECT Toni Morrison **has written** several well-received novels.

This tells us how many books; it talks about quantity.

EXERCISE 32.1 Review Sections 32a-1 and 32a-2. Choose the correct tense—simple present or present progressive. (For answers, see pages 491–492.)

1. Many people have bizarre dreams, but I usually (**dream/am dreaming**) about something that (**happens/is happening**) during the day.

2. I often (**remember/am remembering**) my dreams right after I (**wake/am waking**) up.

3. Sometimes when I (**hear/am hearing**) a noise while I (**dream/am dreaming**), I will incorporate that into my dream.

4. I (**know/am knowing**) a lot about dreams because I (**write/am writing**) a paper about them this semester.

5. To prepare for the paper, I (**research/am researching**) many psychological explanations for various dream symbols, such as snakes, bodies of water, and people.

6. I'm not sure that I (**believe/am believing**) those explanations, but they are very interesting.

EXERCISE 32.2 Review Section 32a-3. Choose the best verb tense—simple past or present perfect. Use the present perfect whenever possible. (For answers, see page 492.)

1. This month the newspapers (**had/have had**) many articles about a phenomenon called the glass ceiling.

2. This refers to an unofficial limitation on promotion for women who (**worked/have worked**) in a corporation for several years and who cannot advance beyond middle management.

3. Last year my mother (**applied/has applied**) for the position of vice president of the company she works for, but they (**did not promote/ have not promoted**) her.

4. She (**had/has had**) the most experience of all the candidates for the job, but a man was chosen instead.

5. She (**was/has been**) with that company for ten years. Now she doesn't know how much longer she will stay there.

EXERCISE 32.3 Review Section 32a. Fill in the blanks with the most precise and appropriate tense of the verb *talk*. Pay special attention to time words. Incorporate the adverbs in parentheses into your answers. (For answers, see page 492.)

1. They __________ about the issue since yesterday.
2. Some employees __________ about the issue when we arrived at work.
3. They __________ (**probably**) about the issue when they leave work.
4. We __________ about it many times in the past.
5. I never __________ about this topic last week.
6. We __________ about this problem for two hours by the time the president visited our office.
7. Workers __________ about this issue quite often these days.
8. They __________ about the subject right now.
9. After they __________ about it for many weeks, they reached a consensus.
10. They __________ (**never**) about this issue again.

ESOL Tip

Punctuate Sentences Carefully **Humberto Castillo, Mexico**

Remember that your native language may form and punctuate sentences differently than English does. For example, many sentences that are grammatically correct in Spanish become run-on sentences if they are translated literally into English. When you translate a sentence from your native language, check the punctuation carefully, and ask a friend or your instructor if you are unsure about where to place commas and periods.

32b How do you use transitive and intransitive verbs?

A **transitive verb** is a verb that has a direct object. This means that the verb has an effect on, or does something to, that object. The verb *raise* in the sentence "She raised her children" is transitive because the subject of the sentence (*she*) is acting on someone else (*her children*). Without the direct object (*her children*), this sentence would be incomplete; it would not make sense.

INCORRECT She raised. This thought is incomplete; we need to know *what* she raised.

CORRECT She raised **her children** on a farm.

There are two types of transitive verbs. (See Chart 32.3 on page 483 for a list of them.) One type—verb + direct object—*must* be followed directly by a noun or pronoun.

VERB + DIRECT OBJECT (trans. v. = transitive verb)

subj. trans. v. noun
This university **needs** more parking lots.

subj. trans. v. pronoun
The trustees **discussed** it at the last meeting.

The second type—verb + (indirect object) + direct object—*can* be followed by an indirect object (a person receiving the action) before the direct object. When you use *to* or *for* in front of the indirect object, the position changes, as you can see in these examples.

VERB + (INDIRECT OBJECT) + DIRECT OBJECT

dir. obj.
Ron bought **a rose**.

indir. obj. dir. obj.
Ron bought *his wife* **a rose**.

or

dir. obj. + *for/to* + indir. obj.
Ron bought **a rose** *for his wife*.

An **intransitive verb** is complete without a direct object. In fact, you cannot put a direct object after an intransitive verb.

INCORRECT She grew up **her children**. *Her children* cannot come after the verb *grew up* because *her children* is an object; objects cannot come after intransitive verbs.

However, other words can come after intransitive verbs.

CORRECT She grew up **quickly.** *Quickly* is an adverb. You can put an adverb after this verb. This sentence means that she matured at a very fast rate.

CORRECT She grew up **on a farm.** *On a farm* is a prepositional phrase, not a direct object.

There are two kinds of intransitive verbs—linking verbs and action verbs. (See Chart 32.3 below for a list of these verbs.)

LINKING VERBS This book **seems** very old. (subj. = This book; l.v. = seems; comp. = very old) l.v. = linking verb

Your professor **is** an expert in law. (subj. = Your professor; l.v. = is; comp. = an expert)

ACTION VERBS Jacqueline **complained.** (subj. = Jacqueline; a.v. = complained) a.v. = action verb

Jacqueline **complained** to me before breakfast. (subj. = Jacqueline; a.v. = complained; prep. phrase = to me before breakfast)

For more information on transitive and intransitive verbs, see Section 23e.

Chart 32.3 Transitive and Intransitive Verbs

TRANSITIVE VERBS*

- **Verb + direct object:** attend, bring up, choose, do, have, hit, hold, keep, lay, need, raise, say, spend, use, want, watch, wear
- **Verb + (indirect object) + direct object:** bring, buy, get, give, make, pay, send, take, tell

INTRANSITIVE VERBS*

- **Linking verbs:** appear, be, become, seem, look
- **Action verbs:** arrive, come, get dressed, go, grow up, laugh, lie, listen, live, rise, run, sit, sleep, walk, work

*These lists are not complete. You can always consult your dictionary to find out whether a verb is transitive or intransitive.

32c How do you use two-word and three-word verbs?

Some verbs in English consist of two or three words, usually a main verb and a preposition. These verbs are idioms because you can't understand the meaning of the verb simply by knowing the separate meaning of each of the two or three words. For example, the verb *put* has a completely different meaning from the verb *put off* ("to postpone"), and the verb *put up with* ("to tolerate") has yet another distinct meaning. There are many two- and three-word verbs in English. Since it would be difficult to memorize all of them, it's best for you to learn them as you hear them and to keep a list for reference. Chart 32.4 lists common two- and three-word verbs. Two-word verbs that are transitive—which means they can have a direct object—are divided into two groups: **separable** and **inseparable**. (See Section 32b for an explanation of transitive verbs.)

Chart 32.4 Common Two-Word and Three-Word Verbs

Here are some common two- and three-word verbs. Such verbs have two parts: the main verb and one (or more) prepositions. This list is not complete; there are many more such verbs. An asterisk (*) indicates an *inseparable* verb: the verb and the preposition cannot be separated by an object. A cross (+) indicates verbs that have additional meanings not given here.

VERB	DEFINITION
break down*	stop functioning
bring on	cause something to happen
call off	cancel
catch up with*+	attain the same position, place
check into*	explore, investigate
come across*	encounter unintentionally
cut down on*	reduce the amount of
do over	repeat
figure out	solve a problem, dilemma
find out	discover
get along with*	have harmonious relations
get in*+	enter a car
get off*+	exit from (a bus, a train, a plane)
get on*	enter (a bus, a train, a plane)
get over*	recover from (a sickness, a relationship)
give up	stop trying
go over*	review
grow up*	mature, become an adult
keep up with*	maintain the same level
look after*	take care of

(Continued)

Common Two-Word and Three-Word Verbs *(Continued)*

look into*	explore, investigate
make up+	invent
pass away*	die
pick out	make a selection
put off	postpone
put up with*	tolerate
run into*+	meet by chance
show up*	appear, arrive
stand up for*	defend, support
sum up	summarize, conclude
take after*	resemble, look alike
touch on*	discuss briefly

1 Separable verbs. You can place the object *before* or *after* the preposition.

CORRECT Lee checked **the book** *out* from the library.

The object *(the book)* is placed *before* the preposition *(out)*.

CORRECT Lee checked *out* **the book** from the library.

The object comes *after* the preposition.

However, whenever the object is a *pronoun* (such as *it* in the following example), the pronoun *must* come *before* the preposition.

INCORRECT Gary checked out **it** from the library.

CORRECT Gary checked **it** out from the library.

2 Inseparable verbs. You cannot separate the verb and the preposition.

INCORRECT My sister **majored** history **in**.

CORRECT My sister **majored in** history.

INCORRECT Please **after** your brother **look**.

CORRECT Please **look after** your brother.

EXERCISE 32.4 Review Sections 32a through 32c. Each of the following sentences contains errors related to verb tense, transitive/intransitive verbs, or two-word verbs. Identify the errors and correct them. (For answers, see page 492.)

1. Before I study psychology, I thought it was an easy subject.
2. Now I am knowing that it isn't easy.
3. It has had a lot of statistics.
4. I am studying psychology since April, and I only begin to learn some of the concepts.
5. I have been tried to learn more of the concepts every day.
6. Last night I have studied from 9:00 to midnight.
7. I went my adviser last Monday.
8. She told to me to see her after class.
9. But when I went to see her after class, she already left.
10. It's January. By the middle of June, I have studied psychology for six months.

32d Which modal should you use?

You already know that a verb's tense expresses time. A *modal*, which is an auxiliary or helping verb, expresses an attitude about a situation. For example, if you want to be polite, you can say, "Open the door, please." To be even more polite, you can add a modal auxiliary verb: "*Would* you open the door, please?" Modals are used to express necessity, obligation, regret, and formality. Modals can be used to express ideas about the past, present, or future.

PAST	I **could** speak Japanese as a child.
PRESENT	My brother **can** speak Japanese now.
FUTURE	I **might** learn another language next semester.

You probably already know the common modals, such as *should, must,* and *have to*. However, you may have questions about others, such as *had better,* or perhaps you are uncertain about the difference between, for example, *have to* and *ought to*. In this section, we list the modals by their uses or functions and provide a list of common modal errors to avoid.

1 Choose the modal that best expresses your idea. Chart 32.5 below summarizes the functions of modals. It also lists the past forms of the modals. Modals in the present are followed by the base form of the verb—for example, "Kim **may** win the prize" (subject + modal + base form of the verb). The forms of modals in the past vary. (See Section 32d-3 for more details.)

Chart 32.5 Modals

WHAT IT MEANS	PRESENT OR FUTURE FORM	PAST FORM
Permission (Informal → Formal)		
can **could** **may** **would you mind***	**Can** I be excused? **Could** I be excused? **May** I be excused? **Would you mind if** I *brought* my dog?	He **could have been** excused, but he didn't ask. **Would you have minded if** I *had brought* my dog?
* *Would you mind* is followed by *if* + the past tense of the verb.		
Ability		
can	Joe **can** drive a car.	He **couldn't** drive a car last year.
be able to	Carl **is able to** study and listen to music at the same time.	Celia **was never able to** play the Mozart concertos.
Advice		
should **ought to** **had better**	You **should** quit. You **ought to** quit. You **had better** quit.	He **should have** quit last year. He didn't quit; this sentence shows regret.

(Continued)

Modals *(Continued)*

WHAT IT MEANS	PRESENT OR FUTURE FORM	PAST FORM
Necessity		
have to	He **has to** pay a fine.	He **had to** pay a fine last week.
must	She **must** pay her taxes.	No past form; use *had to.*
Lack of necessity		
not have to	You **don't have to** attend school in summer.	He **didn't have to** take the final exam last year.
not need to	You **don't need to** pay in advance.	You **didn't need to** pay in advance.
Possibility (*More sure* → *Less sure*)		
can	It **can** get cold in May.	No past form.
may	It **may** get cold in June this year.	I'm not sure, but it **may have** just happened.
could	It **could** get cold in July this year.	It **could have** just happened.
might	It **might** get cold in July this year.	It **might have** just happened.
Conclusion		
must	Your eyes are all red; you **must have** allergies. I'm almost certain that this is true.	You got an *A* on your test. You **must have studied** hard! I'm certain that you did this in the past.
Expectation		
should/ought to	Your keys **should be** on the desk where I left them. I expect them to be there.	John **should have been** elected. He didn't get elected, but I expected him to.

(Continued)

Modals *(Continued)*

WHAT IT MEANS	PRESENT OR FUTURE FORM	PAST FORM
Polite requests (Informal → Formal)		
can	**Can** you give me a hand?	No past forms.
will	**Will** you give me a hand?	
could	**Could** you give me a hand?	
would you mind + present participle	**Would you mind giving** me a hand?	

2 Use the correct form of the modal auxiliary and the main verb that follows it. Modals that express present and future time have this form.

SUBJECT + MODAL + BASE FORM OF VERB

Clarissa **had better** register for classes soon.

Here are specific tips to help you with modal formation.

- Don't use *to* or a present participle (*-ing* form of a verb) after the modal.

INCORRECT	Jacquie **can** ~~to~~ play the guitar very well.
CORRECT	Jacquie **can** play the guitar very well.
INCORRECT	**Must** I ~~to~~ hand in this paper tomorrow?
CORRECT	**Must** I hand in this paper tomorrow?
EXCEPT	We **have to** write a ten-page paper.
INCORRECT	They **should readi~~ng~~** before class.
CORRECT	They **should read** before class.

- There is no *-s* on the third person singular of a modal.

INCORRECT	Kwang **might~~s~~** go to graduate school.
CORRECT	Kwang **might** go to graduate school.

- Don't use two modals together.

INCORRECT	They **might could** drive all night.
CORRECT	They **might** drive all night.

An exception is **be able to**:

EXCEPT	They **might be able to** drive all night.

- *Do, does,* and *did* are not used in questions with modals, except for the modal *have to.*

INCORRECT	**Do** I **must** answer all the questions?
CORRECT	**Must** I answer all the questions?
EXCEPT	**Do** I **have to** answer all the questions?

- *Do, does,* and *did* are not used in negative statements with modals; use *not* instead, placed after the modal.

INCORRECT	They **do not can** enter the test room.
CORRECT	They **cannot** enter the test room.
INCORRECT	Jorge **did not could** have worked any harder.
CORRECT	Jorge **could not have** worked any harder.

3 Use the perfect form to express past time. As you can see from Chart 32.5 (pages 487–89) many modals have a past form. Modals that give advice or express possibility, expectation, and conclusion have a *perfect* verb form for the past (modal + *have* + past participle), as you can see in the following examples.

ADVICE	Gail **should have taken** that marketing job last year. Gail didn't take the job.
POSSIBILITY	Although he chose not to, Bob **could have gone** to Mexico over spring break. Bob didn't go to Mexico.
EXPECTATION	Where is Sue? She **should have been** here by now. Sue hasn't arrived yet.
CONCLUSION	Ted finished the paper; he **must have worked** all night.

EXERCISE 32.5 Review Section 32d-1. Fill in the blanks with a modal from the following list. More than one answer is possible for each blank. Try to use each modal only once. (For answers, see page 492.)

would	must	have to	ought to	should have
should	can	might	had better	must have

1. Can you believe the line waiting to see the movie *Spider-Man 3*? That __________ be a good movie!
2. Where is my purse, Mom? It __________ be on the table where you put it last night.
3. I'm sorry, Professor Lopez, but I __________ take the test tomorrow because I __________ go to Immigration about my visa.
4. Jason, you __________ eat your vegetables or you won't get any dessert.

EXERCISE 32.6 Review Section 32d. Each of the following sentences contains errors related to modal auxiliaries. Identify the errors and correct them. (For answers, see page 492.)

1. Megan's boss told her, "You had better to improve your attitude, or we will have to take disciplinary action."
2. Megan was very distressed by this news; she did not could understand the basis for her boss's complaints.
3. She tried to think of things that she had done wrong. She knew that she should had been more enthusiastic at the last meeting, but she felt she couldn't be hypocritical. She simply didn't agree with her boss.
4. Megan was really worried. Her boss mights send her a "pink slip," which would mean that she had been fired.

ANSWER KEY

EXERCISE 32.1

1. dream; happens
2. remember; wake
3. hear; am dreaming
4. know; am writing
5. am researching
6. believe

EXERCISE 32.2

1. have had
2. have worked
3. applied; did not promote
4. had
5. has been

EXERCISE 32.3

1. have been talking
2. were talking
3. will probably be talking
4. have talked
5. talked
6. had been talking
7. are talking (*or* talk)
8. are talking
9. had talked
10. will never talk

EXERCISE 32.4

1. Before I **studied** psychology, I (**had**) **thought** it was an easy subject.
2. Now I **know** that it isn't easy.
3. It **has** a lot of statistics.
4. I **have been studying** psychology since April, and I **have only begun** to learn some of the concepts.
5. I **have been trying** to learn more of the concepts every day.
6. Last night I **was studying** from 9:00 to midnight.

   or

   Last night I **studied** from 9:00 to midnight.
7. I went **to** my adviser last Monday.
8. She told ~~**to**~~ me to see her after class.
9. But when I went to see her after class, she **had** already **left**.
10. It's January. By the middle of June, I **will have studied** psychology for six months.

EXERCISE 32.5

1. must; has to; should; had better
2. should; ought to; must; had better
3. cannot/might have to; might/should
4. had better; must

EXERCISE 32.6

1. Megan's boss told her, "You had better ~~**to**~~ improve your attitude, or we will have to take disciplinary action."
2. Megan was very distressed by this news; she **could not** (*or* **did not**) understand the basis for her boss's complaints.
3. She tried to think of things that she had done wrong. She knew that she **should have been** more enthusiastic at the last meeting, but she felt she couldn't be hypocritical. She simply didn't agree with her boss.
4. Megan was really worried. Her boss **might~~s~~** send her a "pink slip," which would mean that she had been fired.

CHAPTER

33 Do You Have Questions About Gerunds, Infinitives, Articles, or Number (ESOL)?

by Jocelyn Steer and Carol Rhoades

This chapter offers guidelines for handling grammatical concepts that many ESOL writers find confusing: gerunds, infinitives, articles, and number agreement. If you have learned British English but will now be writing American English, pay special attention to Section 33b on articles and count/noncount nouns.

33a How do you use gerunds and infinitives?

In English, gerunds and infinitives have several functions. (See Section 24a for definitions of *gerund* and *infinitive.*)

A **gerund** can function as a subject, object, complement, and object of a preposition. (See the glossary for a definition of *complement*; see Section 16c-1 for more on the *object of a preposition.*)

subj.
Finding a parking space is impossible here!

obj.
George enjoys **reading** for half an hour before bed.

comp.
His favorite hobby is **cooking**.

obj. prep.
She is afraid of **flying**.

An **infinitive** can be the subject of a sentence, and it can be the object of a verb.

subj.
To find a parking space here is impossible!

obj.
My sister hopes **to be** a marine biologist.

ESOL writers often have difficulty with gerunds and infinitives that act as objects in a sentence. This section will focus on that problem.

1 Review which form—gerund or infinitive—to use. You already know that some verbs in English are followed by gerunds and other verbs are followed by infinitives.

INFINITIVE (*TO* + BASE FORM OF VERB)

I want **to go** with you.

GERUND (BASE FORM OF VERB + *-ING*)

He enjoys **jogging** in the park.

Other verbs, however, can have *either* a gerund or an infinitive after them without a difference in meaning.

GERUND OR INFINITIVE (NO CHANGE IN MEANING)

gerund
The dog began **barking** at midnight.

infinitive
The dog began **to bark** at midnight.

These two sentences have exactly the same meaning.

Finally, some verbs in English (including *forget, regret, remember, stop, try*) can be followed by *either* a gerund or an infinitive, but each has a distinct meaning.

GERUND OR INFINITIVE (DIFFERENCE IN MEANING)

Paul stopped **working** in the cafeteria.

Paul *no longer* works in the cafeteria.

Paul stopped his tennis game early **to work** on his homework.

Paul stopped his game *in order to* work on his homework.

Paul forgot **to visit** his cousin while he was in Mexico.

He did *not* visit his cousin.

Paul will never forget **visiting** Mexico.

Paul visited Mexico and he will always remember the trip.

Native speakers know intuitively whether to use a gerund or an infinitive after a verb, but this is not usually true for ESOL students.

Chart 33.1 on page 495 and Chart 33.2 on page 496 can help you; be sure to keep these charts handy when you write.

2 Review when a verb must be followed by a noun or a pronoun. As we've seen, some verbs in English (called *transitive verbs*) need to have a noun or pronoun after them. For example, when you use *tell*, you need a direct object (*What did you tell?*) or an indirect object (*Whom did you tell?*) to complete the sentence.

Chart 33.1 Verbs Followed by Gerunds or Infinitives

VERB + INFINITIVE

These verbs are followed by **infinitives**.

afford	consent	intend	pretend
agree	decide	learn	promise
appear	deserve	manage	refuse
arrange	expect	mean	seem
ask	fail	need	threaten
beg	hesitate	offer	wait
claim	hope	plan	wish

VERB + GERUND

These verbs are followed by **gerunds**.

admit	deny	mention	recommend
anticipate	discuss	miss	resent
appreciate	dislike	postpone	resist
avoid	enjoy	practice	risk
complete	finish	quit	suggest
consider	can't help	recall	tolerate
delay	keep	recollect	understand

VERB + GERUND OR INFINITIVE

These verbs can be followed by either a **gerund** or an **infinitive**, with no change in meaning.

begin	can't stand	hate	prefer
can't bear	continue	like	start

Chart 33.2 Verbs Followed by Gerunds or Infinitives with a Difference in Meaning

VERB + GERUND OR INFINITIVE

These verbs can be followed by either a **gerund** or an **infinitive**, but the meaning of the sentence will differ depending on which one you use.

VERB	MEANING
try (to be)	make an attempt to be
try (being)	do an experiment
regret (to be)	feel sorry about
regret (being)	feel sorry about *past* action
remember (to be)	not forget
remember (being)	recall, bring to mind
forget (to be)	not remember
(never) forget (being)	always remember
stop (to be)	stop in order to be
stop (being)	interrupt an action

INCORRECT I told ^ to write me a letter.

The object is missing; the sentence is incomplete.

CORRECT I told **my son** to write me a letter.

My son is the indirect object; this sentence is complete.

Remember that an *infinitive verb* comes after transitive verb + noun or pronoun constructions. Chart 33.3 lists the verbs that follow this pattern.

Chart 33.3 Verbs Followed by Nouns, Pronouns, or Infinitives

VERB + (NOUN OR PRONOUN) + INFINITIVE

These verbs must be followed by a **noun** or a **pronoun** + an **infinitive**.

advise	encourage	invite	tell
allow	forbid	order	urge
cause	force	persuade	warn
challenge	hire	remind	
convince	instruct	require	

3 Instead of being followed by an infinitive, the verbs *have, make,* and *let* are followed by a noun or pronoun and the base form of the verb. This means that you omit *to* before the verb.

HAVE I **had** my mother *cut* my hair.

Here *had* means to cause someone to do something.

MAKE The teacher **made** him *leave* the class.

Here *made* means to force someone to do something; it is stronger than *had.*

LET Professor Betts **let** the class *leave* early.

Here *let* means to allow someone to do something.

4 Use a gerund after a preposition. Many verbs are followed by prepositions. Sometimes adjectives are followed by prepositions. Always remember to use a gerund, not an infinitive, after prepositions. Here are two common sentence patterns with prepositions followed by gerunds.

verb adj. prep. gerund

Carla has been very worried **about passing** her statistics class.

verb prep. gerund

Mrs. Short apologized **for interrupting** our conversation.

Chart 33.4 lists common preposition combinations with verbs and adjectives.

Chart 33.4 Common Verb (+ Adjective) + Preposition Constructions

be accustomed to	be divorced from	be interested in
be afraid of	dream of/about	be jealous of
approve of	be envious of	look forward to
be aware of	be excited about	be made of
believe in	be faithful to	be married to
be capable of	be familiar with	object to
be committed to	be fond of	be opposed to
complain about	be good at	be patient with
be composed of	be grateful to	pray for
consist of	be guilty of	prevent from
depend on	hope for	prohibit from
be disappointed in	insist on	protect from

(Continued)

Common Verb (+ Adjective) + Preposition Constructions *(Continued)*

be proud of	be scared of	take care of
rely on	stop from	be tired of
be responsible for	succeed in	be worried about
be satisfied with	take advantage of	

EXERCISE 33.1 Fill in the blanks with the infinitive, gerund, or base forms of the verbs in parentheses. (For answers, see page 505.)

1. Women who have not wanted (**work**) __________ because of health threats can now relax.

2. A recent study completed in California shows that women who work outside the home seem (**have**) __________ fewer health problems than those who work inside the home.

3. Another federal study reports that women employed outside the home do not risk (**have**) __________ more "stress-induced" heart attacks than women working inside the home.

4. In fact, this study appears (**support**) __________ the benefits of working outside the home for women.

5. In general, working women are found (**be**) __________ physically and mentally healthier than women who stay at home.

6. Many working women will appreciate (**hear**) __________ that their chances for depression actually increase if they decide (**drop**) __________ out of the work force.

7. These studies do not pretend (**decide**) __________ for women what is best for them.

8. However, the studies might help some women (**make**) __________ a decision about (**go**) __________ back to work outside the home or about (**quit**) __________ their jobs because they have children.

33b Questions about articles and number agreement?

This section gives you general guidelines about articles (*a, an,* or *the*) and expressions of quantity (such as *a few* or *a little*). For the finer points about articles not covered here, we suggest that you consult one of the additional ESOL grammar references listed on page 472.

1 Decide whether the noun is count or noncount. Before you can know which article to use, you will need to determine whether the noun in question is *count* or *noncount.* A **count noun** refers to something that you can count or that you can divide easily.

COUNT NOUNS There are sixty **seconds** in one **minute**.
Joan bought six **books** for her class.

When there is more than one of the noun (*seconds*), the count noun must be plural. (See Section 25a for a discussion of plural nouns.) If there is only one (*one minute*), the count noun is singular.

A **noncount noun** generally refers to something that cannot usually be counted or divided. Noncount nouns include **mass nouns**, such as materials (*wood, plastic, wool*), food items (*cheese, rice, meat*), liquids (*water, milk*), and **abstract nouns** (*beauty, knowledge, glory*).

NONCOUNT NOUNS Joe drank a lot of **milk** as a teenager.
"Give me **liberty** or give me **death**!"

Some nouns that are noncount in English may seem like things that you can count, such as *money.* Many other noncount nouns in English can confuse ESOL students: *furniture, hair, traffic, information, advice.* Consult an ESOL dictionary or grammar book when you are unsure whether a noun is count or noncount.

Unlike count nouns, which can be singular or plural, noncount nouns have only the singular form. In addition, since you can't count these nouns, you can't use numbers or words that express number (*several, many*) to describe them. You will use other types of expressions to indicate quantity for noncount nouns; these expressions, called *quantifiers,* are discussed in Section 33b-5.

Most nouns are either count or noncount. However, some noncount nouns can change to have a count meaning. Using a noncount noun as a count noun usually limits the noncount noun in some way. For instance, a noncount noun changes to a count noun when you mean *an instance of, a serving of,* or *a type of* the noncount noun.

count noun

His grandmother started a **business.** one instance of business

count noun

I'd like two **coffees** to go, please. two servings of coffee

count noun

There are three new **wines** on the menu. three kinds of wine

2 Decide whether the count noun requires a definite article (*the*) or an indefinite article (*a/an*). When the count noun is singular, you'll need an article, either *a/an* or *the*, in front of it. How do you know which article to use? Generally, when you introduce the noun, without having referred to it before, then you will use the *indefinite* article, *a* or *an.* (See Section 25c for the difference between *a* and *an.*)

INDEFINITE MEANING

Bob: I just signed up for **a** literature class.

Ted: Oh, really? I didn't know you were interested in that.

This is the first time Bob has mentioned the class to Ted.

After that, when both of them know what is being discussed, Bob will use the *definite* article, *the.*

DEFINITE MEANING

Bob: Can you believe **the** class meets on Friday evenings?

Both Bob and Ted now share the same information.

Note how the same guidelines apply to written English in the following sentences on homelessness.

There are several reasons why **a** person may end up homeless. Perhaps **the** person lost his or her job and could not pay for **an** apartment. Or perhaps **the** apartment was sold to **a** new owner who raised the rent. **The** new owner may not realize how expensive the rent is for that person.

Certain other situations also require the definite article, *the*.

- When there is only one of the noun.

  The earth is round. There is only one earth.

- When the noun is superlative.

  This is **the best** brand you can buy.
  There can only be one brand that is the best.

- When the noun is limited. You will usually use *the* before a noun that has been limited in some way to show that you are referring to a *specific* example of the noun.

  The book **that I read** is informative.
  That I read limits the book to a specific one.

  The book **on George W. Bush** is out.
  On George W. Bush limits the book.

If you are making a *generalization*, however, *the* is not always used.

A book **on plants** can make a nice gift.
On plants limits the noun, but the sentence does not refer to a specific book on plants—it refers to *any or all books on plants*. The definite article, *the*, would not be correct here.

3 Choose articles before general nouns carefully. When you want to make generalizations, choosing the correct article can be tricky. As a rule, use *a/an* or *the* with most *singular count nouns* to make generalizations.

A dog can be good company for **a** lonely person.
Use *a/an* to mean any dog, one of many dogs; any lonely person.

The computer has changed the banking industry dramatically.
Use *the* to mean *the computer in general*.

The spotted owl is an endangered species.

The capitalist believes in free enterprise.
Use *the* to make general statements about specific species of animals (*spotted owl*) or groups of people (*capitalists*).

He was ill and went to **the** hospital.
American English uses the definite article with *hospital* even when we do not refer to a specific hospital; British English does not use the article with *hospital*.

Use a *plural count noun* to make general statements, without *the*.

Capitalists believe in free enterprise.

Computers have changed the banking industry dramatically.

Finally, *noncount nouns* in general statements do not have an article in front of them.

Sugar is a major cause of tooth decay.

Many educators question whether **intelligence** can be measured.

Consumed in moderate amounts, **red wine** is thought by some researchers to reduce chances of heart disease.

4 Be aware of two possible article problems with noncount nouns. First, make sure that you don't use *a/an* with noncount nouns.

INCORRECT I need ~~a~~ **work.**

CORRECT I need work.

Second, keep in mind that a noncount noun can never be plural.

INCORRECT Joe needs some information~~s~~ about the class.

CORRECT Joe needs some information about the class.

And remember that sometimes noncount nouns can change to have a count meaning (see Section 33b-1).

5 Pay careful attention to quantifiers. The words that come before nouns and tell you *how much* or *how many* are called **quantifiers**. Quantifiers are not always the same for both count and noncount nouns. See Chart 33.5 below for a list of quantifiers.

A few/a little and few/little It may not seem like a big difference, but the article *a* in front of the quantifiers *few* and *little* changes the meaning. *A few* or *a little* means "not a lot, but some of the item."

There are **a few books** in the library on capital punishment.

Use *a few* with count nouns.

There is **a little information** in the library on capital punishment.

Use *a little* with noncount nouns.

Chart 33.5 Quantifiers

USE THESE WITH COUNT AND NONCOUNT NOUNS	USE THESE WITH COUNT NOUNS ONLY	USE THESE WITH NONCOUNT NOUNS ONLY
some books/money	**several** books	**a good deal of** money
a lot of books/money	**many** books	**a great deal of** money
plenty of books/money	**a couple of** books	(**not**) **much** money*
a lack of books/money	**a few** books	**a little** money
most of the books/money	**few** books	**little** money

**Much* is ordinarily used only in questions and in negative statements: "Do you have *much* milk left?" "No, there isn't *much* milk."

Few or *little* (without *a*) means that there is *not enough* of something. These quantifiers have a negative meaning.

> There are **few** female leaders in the world.
> not enough of them; count noun
>
> My mother has **little** hope that this will change.
> not much hope; noncount noun

Most and most of Using *most of* can be tricky. You can use *most of* before either a count or a noncount noun, but if you do, don't forget to put *the* before the noun.

***MOST OF* + *THE* + SPECIFIC PLURAL NOUN**

Most of the *women* in the class were married. Not: *most of women*

***MOST OF* + *THE* + SPECIFIC NONCOUNT NOUN**

Most of the *jewelry* in the house was stolen. Not: *most of jewelry*

MOST + GENERAL PLURAL NOUN

Most *cars* have seat belts. Not: *most of cars*

EXERCISE 33.2 In the list of nouns below, write *C* after the count nouns and *NC* after the noncount nouns. If you are not sure, consult an ESOL dictionary. Then make a note of the nouns you had to check. (For answers, see page 505.)

1. furniture
2. work
3. dollar
4. job
5. advice
6. people
7. equipment
8. money
9. newspaper
10. traffic

EXERCISE 33.3 Review Section 33b. Each of the following sentences has at least one error in number or in the use of articles or quantifiers. Circle the error and correct it. (For answers, see page 505.)

1. Much people have visited the new restaurant downtown called Rock-and-Roll Hamburger Haven.
2. Most of customers are young people because music in restaurant is very loud.
3. The restaurant serves the usual food—hamburgers, pizza, and pasta. It is not expensive; in fact, most expensive item on the menu is only $8.
4. Food is not very good, but the atmosphere is very appealing to these young men and women.
5. There are much posters on the walls of famous rock star. There is even authentic motorcycle of one star on a platform.
6. Some of regular customers say they have seen some stars eating there.
7. These "regulars" give these advices to anyone who wants to spot a star there: look for dark glasses and a leather coat.

EXERCISE 33.4 Write a descriptive paragraph about ordering and eating a meal at your favorite restaurant. Refer to Chart 33.5 on pages 502–503, which lists quantifiers used with count and noncount nouns, and use at least four words from that list in your paragraph. Underline all the nouns in your paragraph and write *C* (for count nouns) and *NC* (for noncount nouns) above them.

Then check your use of articles. (For help, refer to Sections 33b-2 through 33b-4.) Make sure your subject-verb agreement is correct.

ANSWER KEY

EXERCISE 33.1

1. to work
2. to have
3. having
4. to support
5. to be
6. hearing; to drop
7. to decide
8. to make; going; quitting

EXERCISE 33.2

1. NC
2. NC
3. C
4. C
5. NC
6. C
7. NC
8. NC
9. C
10. NC

EXERCISE 33.3

1. **Many** people have visited the new restaurant downtown called Rock-and-Roll Hamburger Haven.
2. Most of **the** customers are young people because **the** music in **the** restaurant is very loud.
3. The restaurant serves the usual food—hamburgers, pizza, and pasta. It is not expensive; in fact, **the** most expensive item on the menu is only $8.
4. **The** food is not very good, but the atmosphere is very appealing to these young men and women.
5. There are **many** posters on the walls of famous rock star**s**. There is even **an** authentic motorcycle of one star on a platform.
6. Some of **the** regular customers say they have seen some stars eating there.
7. These "regulars" give **this advice** to anyone who wants to spot a star there: look for dark glasses and a leather coat.

EXERCISE 33.4

Answers will vary.

PART VI

PUNCTUATION AND MECHANICS

CHAPTER

34 How Do You Punctuate Sentence Endings?

34a When do you use periods?

Sentences and some abbreviations end with periods. Periods say, "That's all there is." Although periods cause few problems, writers occasionally put them in the wrong place or forget them entirely.

1 Use periods at the ends of statements.

Singer and composer Bob Dylan began his long career in the 1960s as a folksinger**.**

2 Use periods at the ends of indirect questions and mild commands. Indirect questions can sound like questions, but actually make statements (see Section 34b-3).

Musicologists wonder whether any American songwriter in the last fifty years has had more influence than Dylan**.**

Mild commands need a period only, though especially strong commands may be punctuated with exclamation points.

On Wikipedia, look up the date of Dylan's masterpiece *Blonde on Blonde***.**

Find that date now**!**

3 Use periods to punctuate some abbreviations.

Periods generally are used in abbreviations that end in a lowercase letter.

abbr.	anon.
Mr.	Dr.
dept.	Dec.
a.m.	p.m.

Most abbreviations of short, one-word or two-word expressions no longer require periods. Neither do abbreviations for states or the District of Columbia.

US	UN	Washington, DC
FL	TX	CA

For longer terms, abbreviations written in capital letters do not usually require periods. This is especially true for *acronyms,* abbreviations for government agencies, programs, organizations, and other groups that form pronounceable words.

FBI	CIA	DVD	NBA
NOW	MADD	NATO	NAFTA

Abbreviations for academic titles also usually appear without periods.

BS MA PhD

When a sentence ends with an abbreviation that requires a period, don't add another end punctuation mark unless the sentence is a question or an exclamation.

The concert begins on the mall on July 4 at 12:00 a.m**.**

Are you certain the concert begins at 12:00 a.m.**?**

I can't wait until 12:00 p.m.**!**

4 Use periods in conventional ways. Not all periods mark the ends of sentences. They are also used, for example, to indicate decimals, to mark chapter and verse in biblical citations in MLA style, and to separate parts of email addresses and URLs.

0.01 $189.00 75.47

Matthew 3.1
toogie729@mail.utexas.edu
<http://www.google.com>

34b When do you use question marks?

Question marks terminate questions; they can also be used to suggest doubt or uncertainty. Writers sometimes have problems figuring out where to place question marks when they are used with other punctuation, especially with quotation marks.

1 Use question marks to end direct questions.

Who forgot to pay the water bill?

Do you know if the bill is higher this month than last?

Why?

2 Use question marks to indicate that a name, date, or act cannot be established with certainty. But such a question mark should not be used to indicate that a writer is unsure of facts that might be available with more research.

Constantine (272?–337) was the first Christian emperor of Rome.

She survived that terrible crash?

3 Do not use question marks to terminate indirect questions. Indirect questions are statements that seem to have questions within them. Compare these examples to see the difference.

INDIRECT QUESTION	Professor Meade wondered whether Robert would turn in his lab report on time.
DIRECT QUESTION	Will Robert turn in his lab report on time?
QUESTION WITHIN A STATEMENT	Professor Meade wondered, "Will Robert turn in his lab report on time?"

4 Punctuate as questions any compound sentences that begin with statements but end with questions.

The new electric car used cutting-edge battery technologies, but would it be too expensive to succeed in the marketplace?

Don't confuse these constructions with indirect questions, which are, in fact, statements.

5 Place question marks after direct questions that appear in the middle of sentences. Such questions will usually be surrounded by parentheses, quotation marks, or dashes.

Skeptical of their tour guide's recommendation—why would anyone want to eat TexMex food while in Italy?—the group found a restaurant on its own.

6 Place question marks outside quotation marks, except when they are part of the quoted material itself.

Was it Terence who wrote "Fortune helps the brave"?

The teacher asked, "Have you read any Cicero?"

For a more detailed explanation of quotation marks, see Section 38a.

7 Do not allow question marks to bump against other punctuation marks. For instance, you wouldn't place a comma, colon, or semicolon after a question mark.

WRONG	"Where did the battle begin?," the tourist asked.
RIGHT	"Where did the battle begin?" the tourist asked.

Don't multiply question marks to add emphasis. One mark is sufficient.

WRONG	Are you serious???
RIGHT	Are you serious?

34c When should you use exclamation marks?

Exclamations give emphasis to statements. They are vigorous punctuation marks with the subtlety of a Ferrari F430. In academic writing, they should be about as rare too.

1 Use exclamation marks to express surprise, strong feelings or commands.

We are winning!

Come here now!

Oh, no! We're lost again.

Save exclamations for those occasions—infrequent in college and business writing—when your words really deserve special emphasis. Too many exclamations can make a passage seem juvenile.

OVERDONE The Roman army at the Battle of Cannae outnumbered Hannibal's forces roughly two to one**!** Yet Hannibal won**!**

TEMPERED The Roman army at the Battle of Cannae outnumbered Hannibal's forces roughly two to one**.** Yet Hannibal won**.**

2 Do not allow exclamation marks to bump against other punctuation marks. For instance, you wouldn't place a comma, colon, or semicolon after an exclamation mark.

WRONG "Please check your records again**!,**" the caller demanded.

RIGHT "Please check your records again**!**" the caller demanded.

Don't multiply exclamation marks to add emphasis. One mark is sufficient.

WRONG Don't shout**!!!**

RIGHT Don't shout**!**

EXERCISE 34.1 Edit the following passage, adding, replacing, and deleting periods, question marks, exclamation points, and any other marks of punctuation that need to be changed.

1. Hannibal simply outfoxed the Roman general Varro at Cannae!!!
2. Hannibal placed his numerically smaller army where the Aufidius River would protect his flank—could the hotheaded Varro understand such a move—and then deployed his own forces to make the Roman numbers work against themselves!
3. Is it likely that the clueless Roman general noticed how thin the Carthaginian forces were at the center of the battle line?
4. Hannibal expected his troops to outflank the Romans, but would such a strategy work.
5. It did! The Romans found themselves surrounded and defeated!

CHAPTER

35 Problems with Sentence Boundaries: Fragments, Comma Splices, and Run-ons?

Three of the most troublesome and common punctuation problems are the fragment, the comma splice, and the run-on. All these problems arise from confusion about sentence boundaries—that is, where sentences begin and end.

Take Control

35a How do you identify and fix sentence fragments?

Sentence fragments are phrases or clauses that may look like complete sentences, but they lack either a subject, a verb, or both (see Section 16a-1), or they are subordinate constructions (see Section 16g).

NO SUBJECT	Fits perfectly!
NO VERB	The gold ring.
SUBORDINATE	That I found on the subway.
COMPLETE SENTENCE	The gold ring that I found on the subway fits perfectly.

1 Check that all sentences have complete subjects and verbs, either stated or implied. Sometimes subjects may be understood rather than stated—for example, in commands. But complete sentences always need subjects and verbs.

The sun rose. subject is *sun*; verb is *rose*

It was a beautiful morning. subject is *it*; verb is *was*

Keep quiet. subject *you* is understood; verb is *keep*

2 Check that you have not allowed a dependent or subordinate clause to stand alone as a sentence. Subordinate clauses—that is, clauses that begin with words such as *although, because, if, since, unless,* *when, while*—won't work as sentences by themselves even though they have a subject and a verb (see Section 16d-2).

FRAGMENT	It will be a miracle. **If the mail comes on time.**
FRAGMENT	The town decided to ration water. **Since there had been no rain for months.**

Standing alone, these fragments may make sense, but they still need to be attached to a full sentence, one with a complete subject and verb. Such a sentence is usually nearby: the subordinating clause can be joined to it easily and naturally because the fragment ordinarily explains or expands the full sentence in some way. If you attach the subordinate clause to the beginning of a sentence, you usually need a comma between the items.

COMPLETE SENTENCE	It will be a miracle if the mail comes on time.
COMPLETE SENTENCE	Since there had been no rain for months, the town decided to ration water.

3 Check that you have not allowed a relative clause or appositive to stand alone as a sentence. Words such as *who, which, that,* and *where* typically signal the beginning of a relative clause—one that must be connected to a sentence to make a complete thought (see Section 19d-2). If the clause is left unattached, a fragment results. In these examples the fragments are boldfaced.

FRAGMENT	The museum is on Congress Avenue. **Which is the widest street in the city.**
CORRECTED	The museum is on Congress Avenue, which is the widest street in the city.

The appositive, a group of words that gives more information about a noun, is another construction that produces a fragment when left to stand alone (see Section 16c-4).

FRAGMENT	Dr. Anderson resigned her professorship. **The Herstein Chair of Psychology.**
CORRECTED	Dr. Anderson resigned her professorship, the Herstein Chair of Psychology.

4 Check that you have not substituted a verbal for the verb in a sentence. If you have, the result will be a fragment. Verbals look like verbs, but they act as nouns, adjectives, or adverbs (see Sections 24a and 24b). Here are examples of verbals causing sentence fragments.

FRAGMENT The reporter from Reuters asked the senator probing questions. **Frowning all the while.**

ELIMINATED Frowning all the while, the reporter from Reuters asked the senator probing questions

FRAGMENT **To break a story.** That was the reporter's goal.

ELIMINATED To break a story was the reporter's goal.

5 Check that you have not treated a disconnected phrase as a sentence. Turning a disconnected phrase into a full sentence usually requires adding a subject or a verb (sometimes both).

FRAGMENTS David cleaned his glasses. **Absentmindedly. On the sleeve of his lamb's-wool sweater.**

ELIMINATED Absentmindedly, David cleaned his glasses on the sleeve of his lamb's-wool sweater.

6 Check that you have not treated a list as a complete sentence. Sometimes a list gets detached from the sentence that introduces or explains it.

FRAGMENT Bucking a Washington tradition, some politicians have willingly left office to pursue new interests. **Joe Scarborough and J. C. Watts among them.**

ELIMINATED Bucking a Washington tradition, some politicians have willingly left office to pursue new interests, among them Joe Scarborough and J. C. Watts.

Lists are sometimes introduced by words or phrases such as *especially, for example, for instance, such as,* and *namely.*

FRAGMENT People suffer from many peculiar phobias. **For example, ailurophobia (fear of cats), aviophobia (fear of flying), ombrophobia (fear of rain), and vestiphobia (fear of clothes).**

ELIMINATED People suffer from many peculiar phobias—for example, ailurophobia (fear of cats), aviophobia (fear of flying), ombrophobia (fear of rain), and vestiphobia (fear of clothes).

EXERCISE 35.1 Rewrite the following passage to eliminate any sentence fragments.

The news agenda in the United States used to be set by just a few institutions. Chiefly the news arms of the three television networks (CBS, NBC, and ABC). Along with three or four major papers. These media were located mainly on the East and West Coasts. Giving the coastal regions extra clout in political affairs. Especially influential was the *New York Times*. Considered the paper of record in the United States. However, in recent years, 24-hour news channels, radio talk shows, and Internet news outlets have challenged the power of the traditional media. Widening the range of news topics. Creating outlets for regional opinions. Providing places to examine and question mainstream news sources. The *New York Times* has become a favorite target of many critics in the new media outlets. Especially bloggers, who have had a field day finding errors and omissions in its coverage.

Taking Control

Avoid sentence fragments

Sentence fragments are so common in day-to-day speech and writing that it can be hard to steer clear of them, as you must in most academic or formal situations. You can always ask instructors whether fragments might be acceptable in more informal writing assignments or in written dialogue (see Section 35b). But it is probably best to avoid fragments entirely in academic writing, especially with readers who don't know you and who might mistake even an intentional fragment for a sentence error.

35b When are fragments acceptable?

Are sentence fragments considered wrong at some times but not at others? The answer is yes; fragments can be acceptable for some purposes and audiences. In advertising, email communications, and much fiction, phrases without subjects or verbs are routinely punctuated as sentences.

> The classic sports chronometer. Rugged but elegant. Engineered to aviation standards. A cut above.
>
> A Starbucks in a town as small as Muleshoe? Bad idea. Won't get financing. Least not from any local bank.
>
> I spotted a figure sitting in a back pew. A mere child clutching a prayer book—alone and in tears.

Deliberate fragments are not actually puzzling or confusing when audiences expect them—as they might in informal, popular, or creative writing. But such fragments would be considered out of place in academic, professional, or technical writing, where the expression of ideas needs to be explicit and complete.

However, don't be confused by commands—words or phrases in the imperative mood. They may look like sentence fragments because they do not state a subject, but the subject is assumed to be a silent or "understood" *you*. "Don't give an inch in the negotiations!" is a sentence. So is "Vote for Pedro."

EXERCISE 35.2 Bring to class advertisements that use intentional fragments, or locate a Web site or electronic mailing list that routinely includes fragments. Working with other students in a small group, identify the fragments; then join forces to rewrite them and eliminate all incomplete sentences. Assess the difference between the original material and the revised versions.

35c How can you avoid comma splices?

A comma splice occurs when you try to join two independent clauses with a comma only (see Section 16d-1).

COMMA SPLICE	Local store owners were concerned about a recent outbreak of graffiti, they feared that gangs were moving into the neighborhood.
CORRECTED	Local store owners were concerned about a recent outbreak of graffiti. They feared that gangs were moving into the neighborhood.

The error is common and considered serious in academic and professional writing—but it is easy to identify and fix.

1 Remember that commas can't link complete sentences. A comma marks such a brief pause that it doesn't provide the strong boundary needed between two independent clauses. As a result, the reader tends to run right through the gap. A comma between two independent clauses can also confuse the relationship between two sentences.

COMMA SPLICE	Joni Mitchell was an unusually creative songwriter, she had no formal training in music.
CORRECTED	Joni Mitchell was an unusually creative songwriter, **perhaps because** she had no formal training in music.

Very short sentences, usually in threes, may be joined by commas. These constructions are rare.

I came, I saw, I conquered.

He ate, I paid, we left.

2 Correct a comma splice by replacing the faulty comma with a semicolon. Unlike a comma, a semicolon indicates a strong separation—although not as strong as that indicated by a period. (See Section 37a.) Choose a semicolon to correct a comma splice only when the two independent clauses are closely related.

COMMA SPLICE	As the chef set up for the television cameras, he clapped his tongs, tied his apron, and grabbed the huge lobster, he had everything he needed to impress his audience.
CORRECTED	As the chef set up for the television cameras, he clapped his tongs, tied his apron, and grabbed the huge lobster; he had everything he needed to impress his audience.

3 Correct a comma splice by replacing the faulty comma with a period. A period works well when the two independent clauses are *not* closely related.

COMMA SPLICE	Scientists quickly discovered that the Hubble Space Telescope, designed to revolutionize astronomy, had been launched with faulty optics**,** it would need a repair job in space.
CORRECTED	Scientists quickly discovered that the Hubble Space Telescope, designed to revolutionize astronomy, had been launched with faulty optics**.** It would need a repair job in space.

4 Correct a comma splice by inserting a coordinating conjunction after the comma. Add a conjunction when you need a word that clarifies or explains the relationship between the two ideas. The coordinating conjunctions are *and, or, nor, for, but, yet,* and *so.* Notice that the comma is retained.

COMMA SPLICE	The well seemed deep enough**,** the water tasted foul.
CORRECTED	The well seemed deep enough**, yet** the water tasted foul.

5 Correct a comma splice by subordinating one of the independent clauses. You can do that by introducing one of the independent clauses with a subordinating word such as *although, because, since,* or *when.* The subordinating conjunction helps to put the separate ideas in a clear relationship. For more on subordination, see Section 16g.

COMMA SPLICE	Representative Harris left the legislative session after midnight**,** she felt grateful that she still had her voice.
CORRECTED	**When Representative Harris left the legislative session after midnight**, she felt grateful that she still had her voice.

But don't confuse subordinating conjunctions with conjunctive adverbs, which can't turn independent sentences into subordinate clauses. These adverbs include common words such as *consequently, however, moreover, nevertheless, similarly,* and *therefore.* A clause that begins with a conjunctive adverb can be linked to another clause with a semicolon, or they can stand alone. Compare the following examples and be sure you understand the differences.

COMMA SPLICE	Corvettes still come with huge V-8 engines, they get surprisingly good gas mileage.
COMMA SPLICE	Corvettes still come with huge V-8 engines**, however**, they get surprisingly good gas mileage.
CORRECTED	Corvettes still come with huge V-8 engines**; however,** they get surprisingly good gas mileage.
CORRECTED	Corvettes still come with huge V-8 engines**. However,** they get surprisingly good gas mileage.

Taking Control

Avoid comma errors

Comma splices are among the most common errors in academic writing. That may be because they aren't always easy to identify: you have to grasp sophisticated concepts to know when commas can *and cannot* link various phrases and clauses. Eliminating comma splices requires real effort. If this error gives you problems, spend the time it takes to understand the difference between *independent clauses* and *dependent clauses* and *coordination* and *subordination* (see Sections 16f-g). Then be sure you don't confuse *subordinating conjunctions* with *conjunctive adverbs* (see the discussion in Section 35c-5 immediately above). Don't hesitate to ask for help from an instructor or writing center tutor.

EXERCISE 35.3 Identify the sentences with comma splices and correct them.

1. At one time the walls in many Philadelphia neighborhoods were covered with graffiti, however they are covered with murals today.
2. Since 1984 a city-sponsored program has been teaming young graffiti writers with professional artists, the result is the creation of over a thousand works of public art.
3. The murals are large, they are colorful, they are 99 percent graffiti-free.

4. A forty-foot-tall mural of Julius ("Dr. J") Erving has become a local landmark, so that even Dr. J himself brings friends by to see it.

5. The theory behind the program is that graffiti writers, being artists themselves, will not deface a work of art they respect, so far the theory seems to hold true.

35d How can you fix run-on sentences?

A *run-on* occurs when no punctuation at all separates two independent clauses (see Section 16d-1). The reader is left to figure out where one sentence ends and a second begins. Note that run-ons are caused by incorrect punctuation, not by the length of the sentence.

RUN-ON	We hoped for compromise we got nothing.
CORRECTED	We hoped for compromise**.** We got nothing.

1 Correct a run-on by separating two independent clauses with a period.

RUN-ON	Politicians fear reforming social security someday they will scramble to prevent its bankruptcy.
CORRECTED	Politicians fear reforming social security**.** Someday they will scramble to prevent its bankruptcy.

2 Correct a run-on by inserting a semicolon between independent clauses. A semicolon suggests that the ideas in the two sentences are closely related.

RUN-ON	Emily's entire life revolves around ecological problems she can speak of little else.
CORRECTED	Emily's entire life revolves around ecological problems**;** she can speak of little else.

For more on semicolons, see Section 37a.

3 Correct a run-on by joining independent clauses with a comma and a coordinating conjunction. The coordinating conjunctions are *and, or, nor, for, but, yet,* and *so.*

RUN-ON	Poisonous giant toads were introduced to Australia in the 1930s to control beetles they have since become an ecological menace.
CORRECTED	Poisonous giant toads were introduced to Australia in the 1930s to control beetles, but they have since become an ecological menace.

4 Correct a run-on by subordinating one of the independent clauses to the other.

RUN-ON	Albert had to finish the financial report by himself his irresponsible co-author had lost interest in the cause.
RUN-ON ELIMINATED	Albert had to finish the financial report by himself because his irresponsible co-author had lost interest in the cause.

EXERCISE 35.4 Rewrite these sentences to eliminate punctuation problems that create run-on sentences.

1. Centuries of superstition and ignorance have given bats a bad reputation millions of the flying mammals are killed each year in a misguided effort to protect livestock, crops, and people.
2. Entire species of bats are being wiped out at an alarming rate for example, in the 1960s a new species of fruit-eating bat was discovered in the Philippines by the 1980s it was extinct.
3. In truth, bats are industrious and invaluable members of the natural order spreading the seeds of hundreds of species of plants they help to insure diversity in local ecosystems.
4. Strange as it may sound, bats are essential to the economies of many countries they pollinate or seed many cash crops including bananas, figs, dates, vanilla beans, and avocados.
5. Many plants essential to such delicate ecosystems as the African savanna and the South American rain forest rely solely on bats for propagating the entire system could collapse if the bats disappear.

CHAPTER

36 How Do You Use Commas?

Commas are interrupters or signals to pause. As signals, they aren't as strong as semicolons, which typically appear at major intersections between clauses. And they are certainly not as forceful as periods, which mark the ends of sentences. Instead, commas make a reader slow down and pay attention to the words and ideas they set off.

36a When do commas separate items in a sentence?

Some commas keep words, phrases, and clauses apart. But you may have to rely on both some rules and your instincts to place them appropriately. Use too many commas, and your writing will seem plodding and fussy; use too few, and your readers may be confused.

1 Use commas after introductory phrases of more than three or four words. There are many kinds of introductory phrases—adverbial, prepositional, appositive, participial, and so on (see Section 16c).

> **Well before the end of the day,** we were in Amarillo. [adverbial phrase]
>
> **Like a prehistoric monument along I-40,** the Cadillac Ranch outside Amarillo caught our attention. [prepositional phrase]
>
> **A row of rusting cars planted in the ground,** the odd sight surprised many Interstate travelers. [appositive]
>
> **Having driven nonstop most of the afternoon,** we decided to spend the night in Tucumcari. [participial phrase]

A comma isn't needed when an introductory phrase is only a few words long and the sentence is clear without it. You may use a comma in these situations, however, when you believe it makes a sentence easier to read. Commas would be optional, though acceptable, in the following sentences.

On Tuesday, we were in Mesa Verde National Park.

Very carefully, we climbed the ladder at the Balcony House ruin.

Taking Control

Use commas to separate

Writers sometimes worry too much about whether to place a comma after a word or brief phrase that introduces a sentence. While such a comma is sometimes unnecessary, it's usually not wrong—except when following coordinating conjunctions: *and, or, nor, but, yet, so, for*. Although writers today use commas less often than in the past, readers will always be grateful for a comma that eases their entry into a sentence.

2 Use a comma after an introductory dependent clause.

Dependent clauses are signaled by words such as *after, although, as, because, before, if, since, unless, when, while* (see Section 16g).

While the military band played taps, the flag was lowered.

If the CEO can't avert this bankruptcy, she'll likely be fired.

When there is no comma after such an introductory clause, the reader may not understand where the main clause of the sentence begins.

COMMA MISSING	While the crack in the roadway had opened months before the bridge inspector who found it seemed surprised. Does *before* go with the dependent clause or the main clause?
COMMA ADDED	While the crack in the roadway had opened months before**,** the bridge inspector who found it seemed surprised.

3 Use a comma to set off contrasts. The contrast may occur before or after a main clause.

Unlike most women, Jamie despises chocolate.

In most cities, owning a car is a necessity**, not a luxury**.

Do not use a comma, however, when the additional clause or phrase is closely related to the main idea of the sentence. In the following sentence, for example, the phrase in boldface parallels the action of the main clause, despite a contrast between "students" and teachers."

Student test scores increased **along with new incentives for teachers**.

4 Use commas after conjunctive adverbs at the beginning of sentences or clauses. Commas are usually needed because words of this kind—*consequently, nevertheless, however, therefore*—are interrupters that mark a shift or contrast in a sentence.

INCORRECT	The poll was poorly designed. Nevertheless those who commissioned it had faith in its results.
CORRECT	The poll was poorly designed. Nevertheless**,** those who commissioned it had faith in its results.

The comma can be omitted, however, with conjunctive adverbs of only one syllable (*now, then, thus*).

If the second clause in a compound sentence begins with a conjunctive adverb, place a comma after the conjunctive adverb.

The budget cuts are now final; **consequently,** you will have to reduce your staff.

But if a conjunctive adverb occurs in the middle of the second clause, put a comma before and after it.

The budget cuts are now final; you will**, consequently,** have to reduce your staff.

See Section 37a-3 for more on using and punctuating conjunctive adverbs.

5 Use commas to set off absolute phrases. Absolutes are phrases made up of nouns and participles. You are most likely to recognize them through examples. (See Section 16c-3.)

The contract dispute settled, the strikers returned to their jobs.

All things considered, the campus blood drive was a success.

6 Use commas to introduce quotations or to follow them. Commas set off quotations introduced or followed by phrases such as *he said, she repeated, he argued, she insisted.*

> The lawyer kept **declaring,** "My client can't be held responsible for that."
>
> "Don't tell me he can't be held responsible**,"** **retorted** the judge.

A phrase that interrupts a single independent clause is set off by commas.

> "I am sure," she **said,** "you will remember our earlier conversation."

No comma is needed when a quotation fits neatly into a sentence without a separate introductory phrase.

> Oscar Wilde defines experience as "the name we give to our mistakes."

See Section 38a for more on punctuating quotations.

7 Learn other uses of commas that separate. Commas separate words where repetitive phrases have been left out.

> Brad Pitt once worked as a giant chicken; Rod Stewart**,** as a gravedigger; Whoopi Goldberg**,** as a makeup artist for corpses.

Commas separate parts of sentences that might cause confusion.

> The motto of some critics seems to be**,** whatever is**,** is wrong.

Commas separate conversational expressions from the main body of the sentence.

> **No,** I'm sure the inspector wasn't there.

Commas set off direct address in dialogue—when someone is named.

> "**Jane,** bring in the newspaper when you come," I said.

Commas separate mild interjections—short exclamations or expressions of emotion—from the main body of the sentence.

> **Oh,** I'm sure it will be all right.

Commas set off "tag questions." Tag questions turn a statement into a question.

> You can lift the wheel**, can't you?**

EXERCISE 36.1 Insert commas in these sentences where needed, and be prepared to explain your decisions.

1. When Mount St. Helens erupted in 1980 the north slope collapsed sending torrents of mud and rock down into the Toutle River valley.
2. Writing a memoir for NPR.org Howard Berkes remembers the day well.
3. "The precise moment was marked by a sound" he recalls "like a supersonic boom."
4. Yet the explosion had not come as a surprise.
5. "Mount St. Helens had been shaking and gurgling and spitting ash for two months" Berkes notes.
6. Stripped of all vegetation for fifteen miles by a massive explosion the valley was left virtually lifeless; whatever trees there were were dead.
7. In an effort to prevent erosion and speed the valley's recovery ecologists planted grasses and ground covers. However the species they planted were not native but alien or exotic.
8. All in all the scientists probably should have left nature to take its course since the alien plants are now inhibiting the regrowth of native species.

Take Control

36b When should commas enclose words and phrases?

Enclosing some words and phrases with commas makes sentences more readable; the commas chunk information into manageable units.

1 Use commas to set off nonessential (nonrestrictive) modifiers. When you can remove a modifier from a sentence without affecting the primary meaning of the sentence, the modifier is *nonessential.* Such modifiers are surrounded by commas.

NONESSENTIAL MODIFIER	Police officers**, who had practiced for hours,** led the parade.
MODIFIER REMOVED	Police officers led the parade.

When you can't remove the modifier without affecting meaning, the modifier is *essential* (restrictive). Essential modifiers do not take commas.

> The car **that we had received** was not the car **that we had custom-ordered**.

A good rule of thumb: Do not use commas to set off clauses beginning with *that.*

INCORRECT	The bill**,** that was passed by the city council**,** will raise property taxes yet again.
CORRECT	The bill that was passed by the city council will raise property taxes yet again.

For more on essential and nonessential clauses, see Section 30i.

2 Use commas to enclose appositives that are nonessential. An *appositive* is a noun or noun phrase that describes another noun or pronoun more fully. Usually it is nonessential.

> Franklin Delano Roosevelt**, the only President to serve more than two terms,** died in office.

There are, however, essential appositives that follow a noun and give information necessary to the sentence. The following sentence needs the essential appositive to clarify *which* of Green Day's two rock operas is being discussed.

> Green Day's punk rock opera ***American Idiot*** won a Grammy for best rock album in 2005.

But when it's clear from the rest of the sentence which work is meant, the appositive becomes nonessential.

> Green Day's second rock opera**, *21st Century Breakdown*,** was released in 2009.

3 Use commas to enclose various interrupting words, phrases, and clauses. It is important to use commas in pairs when the interruptions come in the middle of sentences.

The president intends, **predictably,** to increase the budget deficit.

The first landmark we recognized, **well before the plane landed,** was the Washington Monument.

The senators, **it seemed,** were eager for a filibuster.

Taking Control

Use commas to enclose for clarity

Enclosing some words and phrases within commas can make sentences more readable when the commas help to break up information into manageable segments. But it's important to place commas only around expressions that really need to be separated for clarity: the fact is that commas are used far less today than they were in the past to mark off brief interruptions. Editors of some magazines and newspapers even allow strong interrupters such as *however, therefore,* and *of course* to be inserted into sentences without punctuation. Remember, though, that it typically takes two commas to bracket material in the middle of sentences. It's very easy to forget that second comma, and many writers do.

WRONG: A radiator**,** if left without service for too long will eventually leave a driver stranded.

RIGHT: A radiator**,** if left without service for too long**,** will eventually leave a driver stranded.

Of course, only one comma is needed before a modifier at the end of a sentence.

RIGHT: A radiator will eventually leave a driver stranded**,** if left without service too long.

EXERCISE 36.2 Discuss the following sentences with your classmates to decide which modifiers are essential and which are not; then fix the sentences that need to be changed.

1. Carter a salesclerk with a passion for Native American art urged Iona his gallery manager to increase her stock of Navajo rugs.
2. On a sales trip, Carter had met with several art dealers who specialized in Native American crafts; the dealer Carter met in Gallup had rugs produced by several well-known artists.

3. The rugs that he showed Carter included examples of all the classic Navajo designs produced from wool which the weavers had shorn, carded, and dyed themselves.

4. Iona who had managed the store for ten years was uncertain that her regular customers would buy the premium rugs which cost as much as $6,000.

5. But because Iona the lover of art was more venturesome than Iona the businesswoman, the gallery soon featured a selection of Navajo rugs which fortunately increased sales traffic.

36c When do commas connect parts of a sentence?

Although commas often mark separations, they can also tell readers that certain ideas belong together.

1 Use commas before the coordinating conjunctions *and, or, nor, for, but, yet,* and *so* when those words link independent clauses to form compound sentences.

Municipal bonds give a more reliable yield than stocks**, and** the interest income is tax free.

Stocks have more long-term growth potential than bonds**, but** the risk is much higher.

A comma is especially important when the two clauses separated by the conjunction are long.

Experts have tried to explain why dogs wag their tails**, but** they have not come up with a satisfactory reason for this attention-grabbing behavior.

Be careful—commas don't *follow* coordinating conjunctions between two independent clauses.

INCORRECT	I lost at tennis **but,** I played a good game.
CORRECT	I lost at tennis**, but** I played a good game.

Remember not to join two independent clauses by a comma. If you do, you'll create a comma splice (see Section 35c).

2 Use commas to link items in a series of three or more. The comma before the conjunction (usually *and*) is described as a serial comma or Oxford comma.

> The mapmaker had omitted the capital cities of Idaho**,** New York**,** and Delaware!

Newspaper and magazine articles follow the conventions of journalism and typically omit the final comma.

> The mapmaker had omitted the capital cities of Idaho**,** New York and Delaware!

No comma is needed between just two items in a series.

> The mapmaker had omitted the capital cities of Idaho and Delaware!

3 Use commas to link coordinate adjectives in series. *Coordinate adjectives* modify the noun they precede, not each other (see Section 16b-1).

> The job calls for a **creative, decisive,** and **intelligent** manager.

When adjectives are coordinate, they can be switched around without affecting the sense of a phrase.

> The job calls for an **intelligent, experienced,** *and* **creative** manager.

A rule of thumb: If you can insert *and* between adjectives, they are *coordinate.*

> The job calls for a **decisive** *and* **intelligent** *and* **creative** manager.

Do not use commas to mark off noncoordinate adjectives in a series. *Noncoordinate adjectives* work together to modify a term. They cannot be switched around or have *and* inserted between them.

> He drives a **shiny blue Mustang** convertible. [not *blue Mustang shiny convertible*]
>
> Tom Cruise has never won the **best supporting actor** Oscar. [not *best and supporting and actor Oscar*]

EXERCISE 36.3 Rewrite the following sentences, adding commas where they are needed to link ideas, moving commas that are misplaced, and correcting comma splices. Some sentences may be correct.

1. Many people freeze when they enter an electronics store cluttered with merchandise shoppers and grinning hyperactive sales staff.
2. Shrewd, and careful shoppers know exactly what they intend to buy when they walk in but, they routinely discover that those gizmos have been discontinued modified or reordered.
3. Fifteen-year-old, sales clerks direct them to twelve, megapixel digital, cameras that cost an arm, and a leg.
4. When a customer explains that she just wants a clock radio, the pimply, faced sales representative will steer her toward a 52-inch plasma-screen TV that has a clock function.
5. Dazed confused and soon-to-be penniless, customers trudge toward gleaming, check-out counters lugging more electronics gear than Agent 007.

36d Where are commas necessary or wrong?

Every comma in a sentence should be placed for a reason: to mark a pause, to set off a unit, to keep words from running together. Cut those that don't serve any purpose.

1 Eliminate commas that interrupt the flow of a sentence.

Sometimes a comma disrupts what would otherwise be a clear statement. In the following example, the second comma raises questions about the meaning of the sentence.

UNNECESSARY COMMA	Five years into graduate school, Frida found herself, without a degree or prospects for a job.
COMMA CUT	Five years into graduate school, Frida found herself without a degree or prospects for a job.

At other times, unneeded commas seem to follow a guideline, but they really don't. In the following example, the writer may recall that commas often follow introductory words, phrases, and clauses. But in this sentence, *however* merely modifies *cold.*

UNNECESSARY COMMA	However, cold it gets, the train arrives on time.
COMMA CUT	However cold it gets, the train arrives on time.

2 Don't let a comma separate a subject from a verb. Such problems usually occur when the subject of a sentence is more complex than usual—perhaps a noun clause or a verb phrase.

UNNECESSARY COMMA	What happened to the team since last season, isn't clear.
COMMA CUT	What happened to the team since last season isn't clear.
WRONG	To keep the team's spirit up, won't be easy.
RIGHT	To keep the team's spirit up won't be easy.

Only in rare cases may a comma be required between subject and verb to ensure clarity.

Those who hope, thrive; those who despair, fail.

Note that when nonessential modifiers or interrupters separate subjects from their verbs, the modifying phrases are set off by *pairs* of commas.

MODIFIER SET OFF BY COMMAS

Frida, who just turned 51, is determined to improve her job qualifications.

See Section 30i for more on nonessential modifiers.

3 Don't let a comma separate a verb from its object.

UNNECESSARY COMMA	During the Cold War, the Pentagon developed and deployed, nuclear submarines, cruise missiles, and MIRV warheads.
COMMA CUT	During the Cold War, the Pentagon developed and deployed nuclear submarines, cruise missiles, and MIRV warheads.

4 Don't use commas to separate compound subjects, predicates, or objects with just two elements.

WRONG The **Mississippi,** and the **Missouri** are two of the United States' great rivers.

RIGHT The **Mississippi** and the **Missouri** are two of the United States' great rivers.

WRONG We **toured** the museum**,** and then **explored** the monument.

RIGHT We **toured** the museum and then **explored** the monument.

Commas are used when a compound has three or more elements

RIGHT Alexander broke his **promise** to his agent**,** his **contract** with his publisher**,** and his **engagement** to Suzanne.

Commas are also used to separate full independent clauses joined by conjunctions. Compare the following sentences, both punctuated correctly.

RIGHT We toured the museum and then explored the monument.

RIGHT We toured the museum**,** and then we explored the monument.

5 Don't use commas to introduce lists.

WRONG States with impressive national parks include**,** California, Utah, Arizona, and New Mexico.

RIGHT States with impressive national parks include California, Utah, Arizona, and New Mexico.

Note, though, how commas works in the following sentences to set off lists introduced by "including" and "such as."

RIGHT Many states have impressive national parks**,** including California, Utah, Arizona, and New Mexico.

RIGHT Many states**,** such as California, Utah, Arizona, and New Mexico**,** have impressive national parks.

Commas may be used to enclose lists that function as nonessential modifiers.

RIGHT Universities with major football programs, Notre Dame, Michigan, and Texas A&M among them, benefit from generous alumni contributions.

In such cases, however, all the commas can be confusing. The modifier might be better enclosed by dashes (see Section 40a).

RIGHT Universities with major football programs—Notre Dame, Michigan, and Texas A&M among them—benefit from generous alumni contributions.

EXERCISE 36.4 Working in a group, analyze these sentences to see if all the commas are needed. Then rewrite the sentences to get rid of commas that cause awkward interruptions.

1. Psychologists, who have studied moods, say that such emotional states are contagious, and describe them as social viruses, which can be passed from person, to person.
2. Moreover, some people are emotionally expressive, and likely to transmit moods; others, seem to be more inclined to "catch" moods.
3. Trying to pinpoint the exact means by which moods are transmitted, is difficult, since the process happens almost instantaneously.
4. One transmission mechanism is *imitation*: by unconsciously aping facial expressions, people produce, in themselves a mood that goes with the expression.
5. People who get along well with others, generally, synchronize their moods, by making a series of changes in their body language.

36e What special uses do commas have?

Aside from the important role commas play within sentences both in linking and separating ideas, commas have many conventional uses you simply have to know to get right.

1 Use commas correctly to separate units of three within numbers. Commas are optional in four-digit numbers.

4,110 or 4110
99,890
1,235,470

Do not use commas in decimals, social security numbers, street addresses, or zip codes.

3.141592653
286-50-0012
14145 Lisa Dr.
78750-8124

2 Use commas correctly in dates. In American usage, commas separate the day from the year. Note that a year is enclosed by commas when it appears in the middle of a sentence.

> World War II began on September 1, 1939.
>
> Germany expanded the war on June 22, 1941, when its armies invaded Russia.

Commas aren't required when only the month and year are given.

> World War II began in September 1939.

Commas are not used when dates are given in British form, with the day preceding the month.

> World War II began on 1 September 1939.

3 Use commas correctly in addresses. Commas set off the parts of addresses, typically separating street addresses or postal box numbers from city/town names, cities from states or provinces, provinces from countries, and so on.

> The Prime Minister's residence is 10 Downing Street, Westminster, London, England.

Commas aren't used between states and zip codes.

Austin, Texas 78712

4 Use commas correctly to separate proper names from titles and degrees that follow.

Tonya Galvin, PhD, has been chosen to replace Howard Brill, MD.

5 Use commas to follow the salutation and closing in personal letters.

Dear Aunt Sue,   Dear Friends,

Sincerely yours,   With regards,

EXERCISE 36.5 Review the following sentences and add commas where necessary.

1. In the autumn of 1863, Abraham Lincoln President of the United States traveled to Gettysburg Pennsylvania to speak at the dedication of a cemetery there.
2. The cemetery was for the soldiers who had fallen at the Battle of Gettysburg, and Lincoln's speech—now known as the Gettysburg Address—opened with the famous words "Fourscore and seven years ago."
3. The Battle of Gettysburg had started on July 1 1863 and had raged for three days.
4. The Civil War would not end until April 1865.
5. The bloodiest battle of the war took place near Sharpsburg Maryland along the banks of Antietam Creek, where a single day of fighting produced over 23000 casualties.

CHAPTER

37 Questions About Semicolons and Colons?

37a When do you use semicolons?

In a sentence, a semicolon (;) marks a stronger pause than a comma, but a weaker pause than a period. Many writers find semicolons confusing. So they avoid them and place commas where semicolons are needed. Or they misuse them, using semicolons where commas or periods work better.

1 Use semicolons to separate items of equal grammatical weight. Semicolons can be used to separate one independent clause from another, one phrase from another, or one item in a list from another.

independent clause; independent clause

> Director John Ford released *Stagecoach* in 1939; a year later, he made *The Grapes of Wrath.*

phrase; phrase

> My film course taught the basics, including how to write treatments, outlines, and scripts; how to direct actors; and how to edit.

item in a list; item in a list; item in a list

> We rented DVDs of *Resident Evil: Apocalypse*; *The Dark Knight*; and *Blade Runner—The Director's Cut.*

Because semicolons work only between comparable items, it would be wrong to place a semicolon between an independent clause and a prepositional phrase, for example, or between a dependent clause and an independent clause. Commas are usually the correct punctuation in such cases.

independent clause, prepositional phrase

WRONG Many young filmmakers regularly exceed their budgets; in the tradition of the finest Hollywood directors.

RIGHT Many young filmmakers regularly exceed their budgets, in the tradition of the finest Hollywood directors.

dependent clause, Independent clause

WRONG Although director Alfred Hitchcock once said that actors should be treated like cattle; he got fine performances from many of them.

RIGHT Although director Alfred Hitchcock once said that actors should be treated like cattle, he got fine performances from many of them.

2 Use semicolons to join independent clauses closely related in thought. Coordinating conjunctions (such as *and, or, nor, for, but, yet, so*) aren't needed when clauses are linked by semicolons.

Italian cinema blossomed after World War II; directors like Fellini and Antonioni won critical acclaim.

Omitting the semicolon in the example above would create a run-on sentence (see Section 35d). Using a comma would produce a comma splice (see Section 35c). Sometimes, however, it can seem like punctuation overkill to place semicolons between independent clauses that are both parallel in structure (see Section 16h) and very short. In these cases, commas are acceptable:

WITH COMMAS For best director, Todd picked Alfred Hitchcock, Ryan nominated François Truffaut, and Jodi chose Agnès Varda.

3 Use semicolons between independent clauses joined by conjunctive adverbs such as *however, therefore, nevertheless, nonetheless, moreover,* and *consequently*. These words by themselves cannot link sentences.

The original *Rocky* was an Oscar-winning movie; **however,** its many sequels exhausted the original idea.

Films about British spy 007 have been declining in popularity for years; **nevertheless,** recent James Bond films starring Daniel Craig have revived the series.

In sentences such as those above, using a comma instead of a semicolon before the conjunctive adverb would produce a comma splice, an error (see Section 35c-2).

But when a word like *however* or *therefore* occurs in the middle of an independent clause, it *is* preceded and followed by commas. In the following pair of sentences, note where the boldfaced words appear and how the shift in location changes the punctuation required.

> *Casablanca* is now a film classic**; however,** its stars regarded it as an average spy thriller.
>
> *Casablanca* is now a film classic; its stars**, however,** regarded it as an average spy thriller.

Chart 37.1 Frequently Used Conjunctive Adverbs

consequently	meanwhile	rather
furthermore	moreover	then
hence	nonetheless	therefore
however	otherwise	thus

4 Use semicolons to join independent clauses connected by words or phrases such as *indeed, in fact, at any rate, for example,* and *on the other hand.* These expressions, like conjunctive adverbs, ordinarily require a semicolon before them and a comma after.

> Box office receipts for *Spider-Man*'s opening week were spectacular**; indeed,** the film unexpectedly broke records for a summer release.
>
> Tobey Maguire had never opened a major film before**; on the other hand,** he was perfectly cast as the boy-next-door superhero.

A period could be used instead of the semicolon in these situations.

> Naturally, *Spider-Man* has spawned several sequels**. In fact,** *Spider-Man 2* was a better film than the original.

5 Use semicolons to separate clauses, phrases, or items in a series that might be confusing if commas alone were used to mark boundaries. Semicolons are especially helpful when complicated phrases or items in a list already contain commas or other punctuation.

The sound track for the film included the Supremes' "Stop in the Name of Love!"; Bob Dylan's "Rainy Day Women #12 & 35"; and Rodgers and Hart's "Glad to Be Unhappy."

Matt Damon's filmography includes *School Ties*, which is set in an upper-class prep school; *Saving Private Ryan*, a Steven Spielberg movie in which Damon plays the title character; and *Good Will Hunting*, the drama that earned him an Oscar for best screenplay.

6 Do not use semicolons to introduce quotations. Direct quotations can be introduced by commas or colons.

WRONG Wasn't it Mae West who said; "When I'm good I'm very good, but when I'm bad, I'm better"?

RIGHT Wasn't it Mae West who said, "When I'm good I'm very good, but when I'm bad, I'm better"?

7 Never use semicolons to introduce lists.

WRONG Paul Robeson performed in several classic films; *Show Boat, Song of Freedom, King Solomon's Mines.*

RIGHT Paul Robeson performed in several classic films: *Show Boat, Song of Freedom, King Solomon's Mines.*

In some cases, semicolons may separate items *within* a list (see Section 37a-1).

8 Use semicolons correctly with quotation marks. Semicolons ordinarily fall outside quotation marks (see Section 38a-6).

The first Edgar Allan Poe work filmed was "The Raven"; movies based on the poem appeared in 1912, 1915, and 1935.

EXERCISE 37.1 Revise the following sentences, adding or deleting semicolons as needed. Not all semicolons below are incorrect. You may have to substitute other punctuation marks for some semicolons.

1. For many years, biblical tales were a staple of the Hollywood film industry, however, in recent years, few such films have been produced.
2. Cecil B. DeMille made the grandest epics; he is even quoted as saying; "Give me any couple of pages of the Bible and I'll give you a picture."

3. He made *The Ten Commandments* twice, the 1923 version was a silent film; while the 1956 was a wide-screen color epic starring Charlton Heston as Moses.

4. The most famous scene in *The Ten Commandments* is the parting of the Red Sea; the waters dividing to enable the Israelites to escape Pharaoh's pursuing chariots.

5. DeMille made many nonbiblical movies, some of them, however, were also epic productions with casts of thousands and spectacular settings.

37b When do you use colons?

Colons (**:**) point to ideas, lists, quotations, and clauses you wish to highlight. They typically follow independent clauses.

1 Use colons to direct readers to examples, explanations, or significant words and phrases.

Orson Welles's greatest problem may also have been his greatest achievement**:** the brilliance of his first film, *Citizen Kane.*

Citizen Kane turns on the meaning of one word uttered by a dying man**:** "Rosebud."

A colon that highlights an item in this way ordinarily follows a complete sentence. In fact, many readers object strongly to colons placed after linking verbs.

WRONG America's most bankable female film star is~~:~~ Angelina Jolie.

RIGHT America's most bankable female film star is Angelina Jolie.

2 Use colons to direct readers to lists.

Besides *Citizen Kane,* Welles directed, produced, or acted in many movies**:** *The Magnificent Ambersons, Journey into Fear, Touch of Evil,* and *Macbeth,* to name a few.

Colons that introduce lists ordinarily follow complete sentences.

The filmmakers the professor admired most were a diverse group**:** Alain Robbe-Grillet, François Truffaut, Spike Lee, and Penny Marshall.

Colons are omitted after expressions such as *like, for example, such as,* and *that is.* In effect, colons are the equivalent of *such as* or *for example.*

WRONG Shoestring budgets have produced many artistically successful films, such as: *Plutonium Circus, Breaking Away,* and *Slackers.*

RIGHT Shoestring budgets have produced many artistically successful films, such as *Plutonium Circus, Breaking Away,* and *Slackers.*

Colons are used, however, after phrases that specifically announce a list, expressions such as *including these, as follows,* and *such as the following.* Review the following sentence to understand the difference.

WITH A COLON The producer trimmed her budget by cutting out frills **such as the following:** special lighting, rental costumes for the cast, and crew lunches.

Never introduce a list with a colon that separates a preposition from its object(s).

WRONG Katharine Hepburn starred in: *Little Women, The Philadelphia Story,* and *The African Queen.*

RIGHT Katharine Hepburn starred in *Little Women, The Philadelphia Story,* and *The African Queen.*

3 Use colons to direct readers to quotations or dialogue.

Orson Welles commented poignantly on his own career**:** "I started at the top and worked down."

Don't introduce short quotations with colons. A comma or no punctuation mark at all will suffice. Compare the following sentences.

Dirty Harry said "Make my day!"

As Dirty Harry said**,** "Make my day!"

We recalled Dirty Harry's memorable phrase**:** "Make my day!"

In the last example, the colon *is* appropriate because it directs attention to a particular comment.

4 Use colons to join two complete sentences when the second sentence illustrates or explains the first.

Making a film is like writing a paper**:** it absorbs all the time you'll give it.

Don't use more than one colon in a sentence. A dash can usually replace one of the colons.

PROBLEM Most critics agree on this point**:** Orson Welles made one of the greatest of films**:** *Citizen Kane.*

SOLUTION Most critics agree on this point**:** Orson Welles made one of the greatest of films—*Citizen Kane.*

Colons and semicolons are not interchangeable, but you can use both marks in the same sentence. A colon, for example, might introduce a list of items separated by semicolons.

The 1950s produced an odd array of science fiction films**:** *It! The Terror from Beyond Space***;** *Earth vs. the Flying Saucers***;** *Forbidden Planet.*

5 Use colons to separate titles from subtitles.

*Nightmare on Elm Street 3***:** *Dream Warriors*

"Darkest Night**:** Conscience in *Macbeth*"

6 Use colons in conventional situations.

Colons separate numbers when indicating time or citing Bible passages—though MLA style uses a period in biblical citations.

12**:**35 p.m. Matthew 3**:**1 (or Matthew 3.1 in MLA style)

Colons traditionally follow salutations in business letters.

Dear Ms. Dowd**:** Dear Mr. Ebert**:**

Colons separate place of publication from publisher and separate date from page numbers in various MLA bibliography entries.

Glenview**:** Scott, 1961 14 Aug. 1991**:** 154–63

Colons appear in Web addresses, with no space left after the mark.

<http://google.com>

EXERCISE 37.2 Revise the following sentences by adding colons or making sure colons are used correctly. Don't assume that every sentence contains an error.

1. No one ever forgets the conclusion of Hitchcock's *Psycho*; the discovery of Norman's mother in the rocking chair.
2. Hitchcock liked to use memorable settings in his films, including: Mt. Rushmore in *North by Northwest*, Radio City Music Hall in *Saboteur*, and the British Museum in *Blackmail*.
3. One actor appears in every Hitchcock film Hitchcock himself.
4. *Rear Window* is a cinematic tour de force: all the action focuses on what Jimmy Stewart sees from the window of his apartment.
5. Hitchcock probably summed up his own technique best, "There is no terror in a bang, only in the anticipation of it."

CHAPTER

38 How Do You Use Quotation Marks and Ellipses?

Take Control

38a When do you use quotation marks?

Quotation marks, which always occur in pairs, highlight what appears between them. Use double marks (" ") around most quoted material and around some titles. Use single quotation marks (' ') when quoted material (or titles) fall within double quotation marks.

1 Use quotation marks around material you are borrowing word for word from sources. Be sure that the material you put inside quotation marks is copied with *perfect accuracy* from the source. Don't rely on your memory, even with well-known expressions.

> According to NASA transcripts of the *Apollo 11* lunar landing, Neil Armstrong actually said, "That's one small step for man; one giant leap for mankind," though he intended to say "one small step for a man."

(See Chapter 47 for guidelines on introducing and framing quotations.)

2 Use quotation marks to set off dialogue. When writing a passage with several speakers, start a new paragraph each time the speaker changes.

> Mrs. Bennet deigned not to make any reply; but unable to contain herself, she began scolding one of her daughters.
>
> "Don't keep coughing so, Kitty, for heaven's sake! Have a little compassion on my nerves. You tear them to pieces."
>
> "Kitty has no discretion in her coughs," said her father; "she times them ill."
>
> "I do not cough for my own amusement," replied Kitty fretfully.
>
> —Jane Austen, *Pride and Prejudice*

When dialogue is provided not for its own sake but to make some other point, the words of several speakers may appear within a single paragraph.

> Professor Norman was confident that his colleagues would eventually see his point. "They'll come around," he predicted. "They always do." And Professor Brown, for one, was beginning to soften. "I've supported many proposals twice as bone-headed."

When the words of a single speaker continue for a second or subsequent paragraphs, omit the closing quotation marks at the end of the those paragraphs, but continue to include a quotation mark at the beginning of each new one, so long as the speech is not interrupted.

> The lawyer arranged the papers on her desk. "Here's what I propose we do about this situation.
>
> "First, we'll contact the opposing party and set up a meeting in our New York offices. Second, we will make a good-faith gesture for a modest financial settlement in this case, based upon the plaintiff's peculiar circumstances.
>
> "And then, gentlemen, we'll just have to wait and see whether the controversy dies down in the newspapers and blogs."

3 Use quotation marks to cite the titles of short works. These include titles of songs, essays, magazine and newspaper articles, TV episodes, unpublished speeches, chapters of books, and short poems. Titles of longer works appear in *italics* (see Section 41a-1).

> "Know Your Enemy" song
>
> "Love Is a Fallacy" title of an essay

4 Use quotation marks to draw attention to specific words. Italics can also be used in these situations (see Section 41a-3).

> Politicians clearly mean different things when they write about "democracy."

You might also use quotation marks to signal that you are using a word ironically, sarcastically, or derisively.

> The clerk at the desk directed the tourists to their "suites"—bare rooms crowded with cots. A bathroom down the hall would serve as the "spa."

But don't overdo it. Highlighting a tired phrase or cliché just makes it seem more fatigued.

Working around electrical fixtures makes me more nervous than "a cat on a hot tin roof."

5 Surround quotation marks with appropriate punctuation. A quotation introduced or followed by *said, remarked, observed,* or a similar expression is preceded by a comma.

Benjamin Disraeli *observed*, "It is much easier to be critical than to be correct."

Commas are used, too, when a single-sentence quotation is broken up by an interrupting expression such as *he asked* or *she noted.*

"If the world were a logical place," Rita Mae Brown *notes*, "men would ride sidesaddle."

When such an expression comes between two successive sentences quoted from a single source, a comma and a period are required.

"There is no such thing as a moral or an immoral book," *says* Oscar Wilde. "Books are well written, or badly written. That is all."

No additional punctuation is required when a quotation runs smoothly into a sentence you have written.

Abraham Lincoln observed that "in giving freedom to the slave we assure freedom to the free."

See Section 47b for guidelines on introducing and framing quotations.

6 Use quotation marks correctly with other pieces of punctuation. In American practice, commas and periods ordinarily go *inside* closing quotation marks; colons and semicolons go *outside* closing quotation marks.

"This must be what the sixties were like," I thought.

Down a dormitory corridor lined with antiwar posters, I heard someone humming "Blowin' in the Wind."

Riley claimed to be "a human calculator": he did quadratic equations in his head.

The young Cassius Clay bragged about being "the greatest"; his opponents in the ring soon learned he wasn't kidding.

Question marks, exclamation points, and dashes can fall either inside or outside quotation marks. They fall *inside* when they apply only to the quotation.

> When Mrs. Rattle saw her hotel room, she muttered, "Good grief!"
>
> She turned to her husband and said, "Do you really expect me to stay here?"

They fall *outside* the closing quotation mark when they apply to the complete sentence.

> Who was it who said, "Truth is always the strongest argument"?

When a sentence ends with a quotation followed by an MLA parenthetical citation, the end punctuation for the sentence follows the parentheses, not the quotation mark.

> Mike Rose argues that we hurt education if we think of it "in limited or limiting ways" (3).

Taking Control

Use quotation marks correctly

Aside from comma splices, problems with quotation marks probably get marked more frequently than any other punctuation error. If you can just remember to place periods and commas inside closing quotation marks, you'll have a leg up on about 90% of your colleagues.

However, the guidelines in this section on quotation marks apply in the United States. Conventions for marking quotations differ significantly from language to language and country to country. French quotation marks, called *guillemets*, look like this: << >>. Guillemets are also employed as quotation marks in Spanish, which uses dashes to indicate dialogue. In books published in Britain, you'll often find single quotation marks **(' ')** where American publishers use double marks **(" ")**, and vice versa.

AMERICAN	Carla said, "I haven't read 'The Raven.'"
BRITISH	Carla said, 'I haven't read "The Raven".'

American and British practices differ, too, on the placement of punctuation marks within quotation marks. In general, British usage tends to locate more punctuation marks (commas especially) outside quotation marks than does American usage.

AMERICAN	To be proper, say "I *shall* go," not "*will*."
BRITISH	To be proper, say 'I *shall* go', not '*will*'.

In the United States, follow American practice.

EXERCISE 38.1 Rework the following passage by adding or deleting quotation marks, moving punctuation as necessary, and creating paragraphs where you think appropriate.

Much to the tourists' surprise, their "uproar" over conditions at their so-called "luxury resort" attracted the attention of a local television station. (In fact, Mrs. Rattle, a member of the tour group, had read "the riot act" to a consumer advocate who worked for the station.) A reporter interviewed Mrs. Rattle, who claimed that she had been promised luxury accommodations. This place smells like old fish she fumed. Even the roaches look disappointed. And the people down the corridor played ¡Viva La Gloria! all night at full blast. Didn't you check out the accommodations before paying? the reporter asked, turning to Mr. Rattle. The sour-faced husband replied that unfortunately he and his wife had prepaid the entire vacation. But Mrs. Rattle interrupted. I knew we should have gone to Paris. You never said that! Mr. Rattle objected. As I was trying to say, Mrs. Rattle continued, I'd even rather be in Philadelphia.

EXERCISE 38.2 Write a passage extending the reporter's interview in Exercise 38.1. Or create a dialogue on a subject of your own.

38b When do you use ellipses?

The three spaced periods that form an ellipsis mark (. . .) signal that words, phrases, or whole sentences have been cut from a passage you are quoting.

1 Place ellipses where material has been omitted from a direct quotation. This material may be a word, a phrase, a complete sentence, or more.

COMPLETE PASSAGE

Abraham Lincoln closed his First Inaugural Address (March 4, 1861) with these words: "We are not enemies, but friends. We must not be enemies. Though passion may have strained it must not break our bonds of affection. The mystic chords of memory, stretching from every battlefield and patriot grave to every living heart and hearthstone all over this broad land, will yet swell the chorus of the Union, when again touched, as surely they will be, by the better angels of our nature."

PASSAGE WITH ELLIPSES

Abraham Lincoln closed his First Inaugural Address (March 4, 1861) with these words: "We are not enemies, but friends. . . . The mystic chords of memory . . . will yet swell the chorus of the Union, when again touched, as surely they will be, by the better angels of our nature."

If you are quoting an author who uses ellipses, put any ellipses you create in brackets [. . .] to distinguish them from the author's original punctuation.

2 Use ellipses to indicate pauses of any kind or to suggest that an action is incomplete or continuing.

We were certain we would finish the report on time . . . until the computer crashed and wouldn't reboot.

The rocket rumbled on its launch pad as the countdown wound down, "six, five, four . . ."

3 Use the correct spacing and punctuation before and after ellipsis marks.

An ellipsis is typed as three spaced periods (. . . not ...). When an ellipsis mark appears in the middle of a quoted sentence, leave a space before the first and after the last period.

mystic chords of memory . . . will yet swell

If punctuation occurs before the ellipsis, include the mark when it makes your sentence easier to read. The punctuation mark is followed by a space, then the ellipsis mark.

The mystic chords of memory, . . . all over this broad land, will yet swell the chorus of the Union.

When an ellipsis occurs at the end of a complete sentence from a quoted passage or when you cut a full sentence or more, place a period at the end of the sentence, followed by a space and then the ellipsis.

We must not be enemies. . . . The mystic chords

When a parenthetical citation follows a sentence that ends with an ellipsis, leave a space between the last word in the sentence and the ellipsis. Then provide the parenthetical reference, followed by the closing punctuation mark.

passion may have strained it . . ." (2001).

4 Keep ellipses to a minimum at the beginning and end of sentences. You don't need ellipses every time you break into a sentence. If your quoted material begins with a capital letter, readers will know you are quoting a complete sentence.

> According to Richard Bernstein, "The plain and inescapable fact is that the derived Western European culture of American life [has] produced the highest degree of prosperity in the conditions of the greatest freedom ever known on planet Earth" (11).

You need ellipses at the beginning of a quotation only when a capital letter in a proper noun (or the pronoun *I*) might lead readers to believe that you are quoting a complete sentence when, in fact, you are not.

> According to Richard Bernstein, " **. . .** American life [has] produced the highest degree of prosperity in the conditions of the greatest freedom ever known on planet Earth" (11).

Whenever you use an ellipsis, be sure your shortened quotation accurately reflects the meaning of the uncut passage.

5 Use a full line of spaced dots when you delete a line or more of verse.

> For Mercy has a human heart,
> Pity a human face,
> . . . .
> And Peace, the human dress.
>
> —William Blake, "The Divine Image" (1789)

EXERCISE 38.3 Abridge the following passage, using at least three ellipses. Be sure the passage is still readable and coherent after you have made your cuts.

> Within a week, the neglected Victorian-style house being repaired by volunteers began to look livable again, its gables repaired, its gutters rehung, its roof reshingled. Even the grand staircase, rickety and worm-eaten, had been rebuilt. The amateur artisans made numerous mistakes during the project, including painting several windows shut, papering over a heating

register, and hanging a door upside down, but no one doubted their commitment to restoring the historic structure. Some spent hours sanding away layers of varnish accumulated over almost six decades to reveal beautiful hardwood floors. Others contributed their organizational talents—many were managers in their day jobs—to keep other workers supplied with raw materials, equipment, and inspiration. The volunteers worked from seven in the morning to seven at night for a solid month, occasionally pausing to talk with neighbors from the area who stopped by with snacks and lunches, but laboring like mules until there was too little light to continue. In the end, they all felt the effort had been worth it, especially when they saw the great house standing on the corner in all its former glory.

CHAPTER

39 How Do Parentheses and Brackets Differ?

39a When do you use parentheses?

Don't use parentheses to explain the obvious.

Parentheses ( ) are common marks of punctuation that allow a writer to add an extra bit of information, a comment, or an aside to a sentence. Precisely because parentheses are so useful, you may find yourself relying on them so often that readers find them intrusive. Keep them to a minimum.

1 Use parentheses to separate material from the main body of a sentence or paragraph, or to insert information. This material may be a word, a phrase, a list—even a complete sentence.

> The helicopter flight to Ouray **(in southwestern Colorado)** was quick and scenic.
>
> The buses arrived early, and by noon the stagehands were working at the stadium. **(One of the vans carried a portable stage.)** Preparations for the concert were on schedule.
>
> If the children get lost, have them call the school **(555-0100)** or the church office **(555-0199)**.

2 Use parentheses to provide source information in MLA and APA documentation.

> Many hikers and environmentalists portray mountain biking negatively **(Coello 148)**.
>
> In the past, acupuncture needles have been made of gold, silver, copper, brass, bone, flint, and stone **(Duke, 1972)**.

See Chapters 50–51 for guidelines on these specific documentation formats.

3 Use parentheses to highlight numbers or letters used in lists.

The labor negotiators realized they faced three alternatives: **(1)** concede on all issues immediately, **(2)** stonewall until the public demanded a settlement, or **(3)** hammer out a compromise.

4 Use parentheses to set off acronyms. The first time you mention a government agency or a civic organization, use its full name, then give the appropriate *acronym* (an abbreviation composed of initials) in parentheses. You can then save space by using the acronym alone in the rest of your paper.

> As law has become a popular professional choice, college graduates flock in increasing numbers to testing sites for the Law School Admission Test **(LSAT)**. The **LSAT** measures logical and analytical reasoning, reading comprehension, and writing.
>
> —Myra and David Sadker, *Failing at Fairness: How Our Schools Cheat Girls*

5 Use the correct punctuation with or around parentheses. When a complete sentence standing alone is surrounded by parentheses, place its end punctuation inside the parentheses.

> The neighborhood was run-down. (Some houses looked as if they hadn't been painted in decades**.)**

However, when a sentence concludes with a parenthesis, the end punctuation for the complete sentence falls outside the final parenthesis mark.

> On the corner was a small church (actually a converted store)**.**

When parentheses enclose a very short sentence within another sentence, the enclosed sentence ordinarily begins without capitalization and ends without punctuation.

> The editor pointed out a misplaced modifier **(the writer glared at her),** crossed out three paragraphs **(the writer grumbled),** and then demanded a complete rewrite.

Punctuation may be used, however, when an enclosed sentence is a question or exclamation.

> The revolution ended **(who would have guessed it?)** almost as quickly as it began.

Don't, however, use punctuation before a parenthesis in the middle of sentences. A comma before a parenthesis is incorrect; if necessary, a parenthesis may be followed by a comma.

WRONG Although the Crusades failed in their announced objective✗ **(Jerusalem still remained in Muslim hands afterward)** the expeditions changed the West dramatically.

RIGHT Although the Crusades failed in their announced objective **(Jerusalem still remained in Muslim hands afterward),** the expeditions changed the West dramatically.

EXERCISE 39.1 Add parentheses as needed to the following sentences.

1. Native Americans inhabited almost every region of North America, from the peoples farthest north the Inuit to those in the Southwest the Hopi, the Zuni.
2. In parts of what are now New Mexico and Colorado, during the thirteenth century, some ancient tribes moved off the mesas no one knows exactly why to live in cliff dwellings.
3. One cliff dwelling at Mesa Verde covers an area of 66 meters 217 feet by 27 meters 89 feet.
4. Spectacular as they are, the cliff dwellings served the tribes known as the Anasazi for only a short time.
5. The Anasazi left their cliff dwellings, possibly because of a prolonged drought A.D. 1276–1299 in the entire region.

39b When do you use brackets?

Like parentheses, brackets [ ] are enclosures. But brackets have fewer and more specialized uses. Brackets and parentheses are usually *not* interchangeable.

1 Use brackets to insert comments or explanations into direct quotations. Although you cannot change the words of a direct quotation, you can add information between brackets.

> "He **[George Lucas]** reminded me a little of Walt Disney's version of a mad scientist."
>
> —Steven Spielberg

In other cases, you can insert bracketed material to make the grammar of a quotation fit smoothly into your own syntax. But use this strategy sparingly, taking care not to change the meaning of the original.

Any change you make in an original text, even if only from an uppercase to a lowercase letter or vice versa, should be signaled with brackets.

> In *The Dinosaur Heresies*, Robert T. Bakker rejects "[o]rthodox theory" that treats the giant reptiles as early creatures of evolution. "By the time they [dinosaurs] appear in the land ecosystem," Bakker notes, "the woodlands and waterways were already full of creatures" (16).

The brackets around the letter *o*, for example, indicate that you have changed Bakker's original capital letter to lowercase; brackets around *dinosaurs* signal that the word was added to clarify the pronoun *they*.

2 Use brackets to avoid one set of parentheses falling within another. Turn the inner pair of parentheses into brackets.

> The Web site included a full text of the resolution (expressing the sense of Congress on the calculation of the consumer price index **[H.RES.99]**).

3 Use brackets to acknowledge or highlight errors that originate in quoted materials. In such cases, the Latin word *sic* ("thus") is enclosed in brackets immediately after the error. See Section 47d-1 for details.

> The sign over the cash register read "We don't except **[sic]** personal checks for payment."

CHAPTER

40 Questions About Dashes, Hyphens, and Slashes?

Dashes, hyphens, and slashes (— - /) have specific and distinct uses in English—some highly rhetorical like the dash, others more technical like the hyphen and slash. We also make a distinction you may have never noticed between dashes of different lengths, the em dash (—) and the slightly shorter en (–) dash.

40a When do you use an em dash?

The em dash is the mark you are most familiar with, the longer dash roughly equal in width to the printed letter *M* (which is where the name comes from). Em dashes can be typed as two connected hyphens (--) with no space left before or after the mark. Or, more elegantly, you can create a dash that appears as a single line (—) by using the appropriate computer keystrokes. On a PC, try Alt + Ctrl + minus sign (on the keypad), or type two hyphens and hit Enter; for a Mac, depress Shift + Option and the hyphen key.

1 Use em dashes to add illustrations, examples, or summaries to the ends of sentences or to emphasize a shift in tone or thought. A dash gives emphasis to any addition.

> Dvorak's *New World* Symphony reflects musical themes the composer heard in the United States — including Native American melodies and black spirituals.
>
> At the podium, Coach Bull said that he was at a loss for words — and then he proved it for more than an hour.

2 Use a pair of em dashes to insert information in the middle of a sentence. Information between dashes gets noticed.

> Many regard Verdi's *Otello* — based on Shakespeare's story of a marriage ruined by jealousy — as the greatest of Italian tragic operas.

Dashes are especially useful for setting off material that already contains its own internal punctuation.

> Marie's writing style — complex, subtle, yet also incisive — earned the admiration of her colleagues.

3 Use an em dash in dialogue to indicate that a speaker has broken off abruptly or has been interrupted.

> "I want some poison," she said.
> "Yes, Miss Emily. What kind? For rats and such? I'd recom— "
> "I want the best you have. I don't care what kind."
>
> —William Faulkner, "A Rose for Emily"

4 When a dash is required, don't mistakenly use a hyphen. Use hyphens to connect items rather than to separate them (see Section 40c).

NOT	Beethoven's music-unlike that of Mozart-uses emphatic rhythms.
BUT	Beethoven's music — unlike that of Mozart — uses emphatic rhythms.

5 Don't use too many dashes. Dashes can clutter a passage; one pair per sentence is the limit.

TOO MANY DASHES	Mozart — recognized as a genius while still a child — produced more than 600 compositions during his life — including symphonies, operas, and concertos.
REVISED	Mozart — recognized as a genius while still a child — produced more than 600 compositions during his life, including symphonies, operas, and concertos.

EXERCISE 40.1 Add and delete em dashes as necessary to improve the sentences below.

1. Legend has it that Beethoven's Third Symphony was dedicated to Napoleon Bonaparte the champion of French revolutionary ideals until he declared himself emperor.

2. Scholars believe—though they can't be sure—that the symphony was initially called *Bonaparte*—testimony to just how much the impressionable Beethoven admired the French leader.

3. The Third Symphony a revolutionary work itself is now known by the title *Eroica*.

4. The Third, the Fifth, the Sixth, the Seventh, the Ninth Symphonies, they all contain musical passages that most people recognize immediately.

5. The opening four notes of Beethoven's Fifth, da, da, da, dum, may be the most famous in all of music.

40b When do you use an en dash?

The en dash is slightly shorter than the em dash, roughly equal in width to the printed letter *N*. Reserve it for the special circumstances listed below. To produce an en dash with word-processing software, hit Ctrl + minus (on the keypad) when using a PC; with a Mac, depress Option and the hyphen key.

1 Use en dashes to connect words and numbers. Think of it as a substitute for the word *to*.

> Richard Nixon (1913–1994) was the thirty-seventh President of the United States.
>
> The meeting is on Thursday, 2:00–4:30 p.m., in the Dobie Room.
>
> We caught the only direct Austin–Santa Fe flight of the day.

You should not use an en dash, however, when the items you are connecting are preceded by *from* or *between*. Use *to* or *and* instead.

> The meeting is on Thursday, **from** 2:00 **to** 4:30 p.m., in the Dobie Room.
>
> We caught the only direct flight that day **between** Austin **and** Santa Fe.

2 Use en dashes to indicate that a period of time is continuing. You'll see this usage most often when the birth date is given for a person still living.

> LeBron James (1984–) won his first NBA MVP award in 2009.

3 Use en dashes to connect complicated compound expressions. When you have to connect compound or hyphenated words or expressions, you may want to use an en dash.

> Our senator presented herself as an odd pro-choice–pro-gun candidate.
>
> We were organizing a college–high school debate team colloquium.

40c When do you use hyphens?

Hyphens either join words together or divide them between syllables. Though a minor sign, the hyphen causes writers many problems because guidelines for its use are complicated. Quite often, the best way to decide whether a word or expression requires hyphenation is to check a dictionary. Hyphens should not be confused with dashes, which look similar but have distinct functions (see Sections 40a and 40b).

1 Learn common hyphenation patterns.

Hyphenate all compounds beginning with the prefixes *all-*, *self-*, and *ex-* or ending with the suffix *-elect*.

all-encompassing	**ex**-hockey player
self-contained	mayor-**elect**

Hyphenate most compounds beginning with *well-*, *ill-*, and *heavy-* when these expressions precede a noun.

well-dressed man **ill**-conceived notion **heavy**-handed tactics

Most, though not all, words beginning with *un-*, *non-*, *anti-*, *pro-*, and *pre-* are not hyphenated.

prenuptial	**anti**slavery	**non**smoker
uncertain	**pre-**existing	**anti-inflammatory**

Unabridged dictionaries and some style manuals provide extensive lists of combinations formed with these troublesome and highly variable prefixes.

2 Follow the conventional uses of hyphens. Use hyphens to write out numbers from twenty-one to ninety-nine. Fractions also take hyphens, but use only one hyphen per fraction.

twenty-nine	one forty-seventh of a mile
one-quarter inch	two hundred forty-six

Use hyphens to indicate double titles, elements, functions, or attributes.

the secretary-treasurer of our club

members of the AFL-CIO

a city-state such as Sparta

in the space-time continuum

Use hyphens in some technical expressions.

uranium-235	A-bomb

Use hyphens to link prefixes to proper nouns and their corresponding adjectives.

pre-Columbian	**anti**-American
mid-Victorian	**neo**-Darwinism

Use hyphens to prevent words from being misread.

a recreation area	the re-creation of an event
a chicken coop	a student co-op

3 Use hyphens to link some compound nouns and verbs. The conventions for hyphenating words are complicated and inconsistent. Here are expressions that take hyphens.

brother-in-law	great-grandmother	cold-shoulder
hocus-pocus	right-hander	double-talk

Here are compounds that aren't hyphenated. Some can be written as either single words or separate words.

cabdriver	best man	sea dog
cab owner	blockhouse	hole in one

When in doubt, check a dictionary or a style manual.

4 Use hyphens to create compound phrases and expressions.

Some classmates resented her **holier-than-thou** attitude.

Product innovation suffered because of a **not-invented-here** bias.

5 Use hyphens to link unit modifiers before a noun. A *unit modifier* is a two-word modifier in which the first word modifies the second. The combination formed by these two words modifies a following noun.

a **bare-chested** warrior

a **no-growth** policy

an **English-speaking** city

a **fifty-dollar** book

When putting a comma between modifying words produces an odd meaning, you probably have a unit modifier that requires a hyphen.

bare, chested warrior (?)

an English, speaking city (?)

But don't use hyphens to link compound modifiers following a noun.

The warrior was **bare chested**.

The book cost **fifty dollars**.

Nor should you use hyphens with *very* or with adverbs that end in *-ly*.

a **very hot** day a **sharply honed** knife

6 Handle suspended modifiers correctly. Sometimes a word or phrase may have more than a single hyphenated modifier. These **suspended modifiers** should look like the following.

Anne planned her vacation wardrobe to accommodate **cold-, cool-,** and **wet-weather** days.

We couldn't determine whether the class should be a **first-** or **second-semester** course.

7 Don't hyphenate words or numbers at the ends of lines.

Most style manuals advise against such divisions when you are typing. If you are using a computer, turning off the hyphenation in your word-processing program will automatically eliminate end-of-line divisions. When you must divide a word, break it only between syllables, and be sure to check a dictionary for the syllable break. Don't guess; your ear and eye will often fool you. Never hyphenate a one-syllable word.

Taking Control

Use hyphens correctly

It may help to separate the rules for hyphenating compound expressions into two categories. First, memorize the two *don't*s:

(1) Don't use a hyphen after an adjective ending in *-ly*.

(2) Don't hyphenate compound adjectives when they *follow* the noun they modify. So you would hyphenate *a souped-up Camaro*, but remove the hyphen if you wrote *a Camaro that is souped up*.

Then remember just how complicated the *do*s are with hyphens, and consult this handbook or a dictionary whenever you have doubts about whether and how to use a hyphen.

EXERCISE 40.2 In the following sentences, indicate which form of the words in parentheses is preferable. Use a dictionary if you are not familiar with the terms.

1. Local citizens have a (**once in a lifetime/once-in-a-lifetime**) opportunity to preserve an (**old-growth/oldgrowth**) forest.
2. A large, wooded parcel of land is about to be turned into a shopping mall by (**real-estate/realestate**) speculators and (**pinstripe suited/ pinstripe-suited**) investors.
3. The forest provides a haven for (**wild-life/wildlife**) of all varieties, from (**great horned/great-horned**) owls to (**ruby throated/ruby-throated**) hummingbirds.

4. Does any community need (**video stores/video-stores**), (**T shirt/ T-shirt**) shops, and (**over priced/overpriced**) boutiques more than acres of natural habitat?

5. This (**recently-proposed/recently proposed**) development can be stopped by petitioning the (**city-council/city council**).

40d When do you use slashes?

Slashes are used to indicate divisions. They should be used rarely, and only for a few specific functions.

1 Use slashes to separate expressions that indicate a choice. In these cases, no space is left before or after the slash.

either/or he/she yes/no pass/fail

Some readers object to these expressions, preferring *he or she*, for example, to *he/she* (sometimes even written as *s/he*).

2 Use slashes to indicate fractions.

2/3 2 2/3 inches 5 3/4 *feet*

3 Use slashes in typing World Wide Web addresses.

<http://www.nps.gov/parks.html>

Note that no spaces precede or follow slashes in Web addresses.

4 Use slashes to divide lines of poetry quoted within sentences. When you punctuate lines of poetry in this way, leave a space on either side of the slash.

> Only then does Lear understand that he has been a failure as a king: "O, I have taken / Too little care of this!"

When you quote more than three lines of verse, set the passage as a block quotation and break the lines as they appear in the poem itself. Do not use slashes.

CHAPTER

41 Questions About Italics and Capitalization?

41a When do you use italics?

Italics, like quotation marks, draw attention to a title, a word, or a phrase. In a printed text, italics appear as *slanted letters.* In typed or handwritten papers, italics are often signaled by underlining the appropriate words.

1 Use italics to set off some titles. Some titles and names are italicized; others appear between quotation marks. Chart 41.1 provides guidance for titles in MLA style.

Neither italics nor quotation marks are used with titles of major religious texts, books of the Bible, or classic legal documents.

the Bible	the Magna Carta
the Qur'an	the Constitution
1 Corinthians	the Declaration of Independence

Neither italics nor quotation marks are used for the names of *types* of trains, ships, aircraft, or spacecraft.

DC-10 Aegis cruiser Mars rover

2 Use italics to set off foreign words or phrases. Italics emphasize scientific names and foreign terms that haven't become accepted into the English vocabulary.

Pierre often described his co-workers as *les bêtes humaines.*

Foreign words absorbed by English over the centuries should not be italicized. To be certain, look them up in a recent dictionary.

crèche gumbo gestalt arroyo

Common abbreviations from Latin appear without italics or underscoring.

etc. et al. i.e. viz.

Chart 41.1 Titles *Italicized* or "In Quotes"

TITLES *ITALICIZED*	
books	*The First Eagle*
magazines	*Time, Car and Driver*
journals	*JAMA, Commentary*
newspapers	*USA Today*
films	*Casablanca*
TV shows	*The No. 1 Ladies' Detective Agency*
radio programs	*Car Talk*
plays	*The Little Foxes*
long poems	*Paradise Lost*
long musical pieces	*The Mikado*
albums	*Dangerously in Love*
works of art	*Adieu*
named ships or spacecraft	USS *Ticonderoga, Apollo 11*
online database	*LexisNexis, Academic OneFile*
web sites	*Google, YouTube*
TITLES "IN QUOTES"	
chapters of books	"Lessons from the Pros"
articles in journals/magazines	"The Monochrome Society"
articles in newspapers	"Inflation Heats Up"
TV episodes	"The Soup Nazi"
short stories	"Araby"
short poems	"The Red Wheelbarrow"
songs	"God Bless America"

3 Use italics (or quotation marks) to emphasize or clarify a letter, a word, or a phrase.

Does that word begin with an *f* or a *ph*?

"That may be how *you* define fascist," she replied.

When some people talk about *school spirit*, they really mean "Let's party."

EXERCISE 41.1 Indicate whether the following titles or names in boldface should be italicized, in quotation marks, or unmarked. If you don't recognize a name below, consult an encyclopedia or another reference work.

1. watching **I Love Lucy**
2. returning **A Farewell to Arms** to the public library
3. discussing the colors of Picasso's **The Old Guitarist**
4. reading Jackson's **The Lottery** one more time
5. whistling **Here Comes the Sun** from the Beatles' **Abbey Road**

41b When do you capitalize?

Capital letters can cause problems simply because you have to remember that their use is guided by conventions—which may vary, depending on what style sheet or institution (newspaper, magazine, federal government) defines the principles. Here, for instance, we follow MLA recommendations for titles.

1 Capitalize the first word in a sentence. Most word processing programs are set to capitalize sentence beginnings automatically.

> **N**aomi picked up the tourists at their hotel.
>
> **W**hat a remarkable city Washington is!

2 Capitalize the first word in a direct quotation that is a full sentence.

> Ira asked, "**W**here's the National Air and Space Museum?"
>
> "**G**ood idea!" Naomi agreed. "**L**et's go there."

Use lowercase for quotations that continue after an interruption.

> "It's on the Mall," Naomi explained, "**n**ear the Hirshhorn gallery."

3 Don't capitalize the first word of a phrase or clause that follows a colon unless you want to emphasize the word. You may also capitalize the first word after a colon if it is part of a student paper title.

NO CAPS AFTER COLON They ignored one item while parking the car: **a** no-parking sign.

CAPS FOR EMPHASIS	The phrase haunted her: **Y**our car has been towed!
CAPS FOR TITLE	*Rebuilt:* ***H****ow Becoming Part Computer Made Me More Human*

4 Don't capitalize the first word of a phrase or sentence enclosed by dashes.

Audrey's first screenplay—**a** thriller about nanotechnology—had been picked up by an agent.

Her work—**s**he couldn't believe it—was now in the hands of a studio executive.

5 Capitalize the major words in the titles of papers, books, articles, poems.

Following are the MLA guidelines for capitalizing titles of works in English.

Capitalize the first word.
Capitalize the last word.
Capitalize the first word of any subtitle.
Capitalize the second word in a hyphenated expression.
Capitalize all other words *except* the following
—articles (*a, an, the*)
—prepositions of any length
—coordinating conjunctions (*and, or, nor, but, yet, for,* so)
—the *to* in infinitives

Here are some sample titles with the capital letters in boldface.

It's Easy Being Green: A Handbook for Earth-Friendly Living [book]

Are You There, Vodka? It's Me, Chelsea [book]

"**T**he **G**enome **I**nitiative: **H**ow to **S**pell '**H**uman'" [journal article]

"**S**topping by **W**oods on a **S**nowy **E**vening" [poem]

When the first line of a poem serves as a title, it is capitalized exactly as it appears in the poem.

E. E. Cummings's "**a**nyone lived in a pretty how town"

Note however that the documentation format for the American Psychological Association (APA) does not follow these guidelines for capitalizing titles. (See Chapter 28.)

6 Capitalize the first word in each line of quoted poetry unless the poet has used lowercase letters.

Sumer is ycomen in,
Loude sing cuckoo!

—"The Cuckoo Song"

anyone lived in a pretty how town
(**w**ith up so floating many bells down)

—E. E. Cummings, "anyone lived in a pretty how town"

7 Capitalize the names of people, and other proper nouns.

People's names are *proper nouns*, which refer to specific people, places, and things, whereas nouns that refer to people, places, and things in general are called *common nouns.*

PROPER NOUNS	COMMON NOUNS
Emily **D**ickinson	poet
John	brother
Ted **K**ennedy	senator

Capitalize the initials in people's names and in titles identified with specific people.

Justice **C**larence **T**homas
J. **H**ector **S**t. **J**ean **C**rèvecoeur
Robert **K**ing, **D**ean of **L**iberal **A**rts
I. **M**. **P**ei
Aunt **J**osephine
Rosa **E**berly, **P**h**D**

But don't capitalize titles used less specifically, or minor titles that stand alone—that is, unattached to a particular proper noun. As a general rule, capitalize titles that precede the noun but do not capitalize titles that follow the noun.

Josephine, my favorite **a**unt
Robert King, a **d**ean at the university
a **c**ommissioner in Cuyahoga County

More prestigious titles may be capitalized even when they stand alone, though style manuals disagree on this point. It is generally acceptable to capitalize a title that is being used in place of a proper name.

the **P**resident *or* the **p**resident
the **S**ecretary of **S**tate *or* the **s**ecretary of **s**tate
the **C**hair of the Classics Department
The **S**enator will be arriving at six o'clock.

Capitalize *God* when you are referring specifically to the God of the Judeo-Christian tradition, but not when you are referring to *gods* in general.

In the Old Testament, **G**od punished those who chose to worship false **g**ods.

8 Capitalize the names of national, political, and ethnic groups. These are proper nouns, since they refer to specific groups.

Kenyans	**C**hicanos	**A**frican **A**mericans
Libertarians	**D**emocrats	**R**epublicans

The names of racial groups, economic groups, and social classes are usually not capitalized—though you will often encounter exceptions.

blacks	whites
the proletariat	the knowledge class

9 Capitalize the names of institutions and specific objects. These include the following.

businesses	**F**ord **M**otor **C**ompany
organizations	**N**ational **R**ifle **A**ssociation
schools	**U**niversity of **M**emphis
religions	**B**uddhism
sacred books	the **B**ible, the **T**orah
place names	**A**sia, **F**rance
geographic features	the **G**ulf of **M**exico
buildings	the **E**mpire **S**tate **B**uilding
ships and planes	**S.S.** *Titanic*, **B**oeing 767
documents	the **D**eclaration of **I**ndependence

cultural movements	**R**omanticism, **V**orticism
historical periods	**P**ax **R**omana, **V**ictorian **A**ge
days and months	**M**onday, **J**uly
holidays	**H**alloween, **F**ourth of **J**uly
course titles	**H**istory 101

Capitalize words such as *river, park, street,* and *road* only when they refer to a specific road, river, or street.

Georgetown **R**oad	a dusty **r**oad
the Mississippi **R**iver	an American **r**iver

Capitalize the days of the week (***M**onday, **F**riday*). Do not capitalize seasons (*winter, spring*) or compass directions (*north, west*) unless they are part of a place name (***N**orth **A**merica*) or unless they are being used as a place name (*the **W**est*). Do not capitalize school subjects unless they are themselves proper nouns (*mathematics, **R**ussian history, **E**nglish*).

10 Capitalize brand names. Many familiar words are really trademarked brand names—proper names that legally refer only to the product of a particular company. Dictionaries will help you decide when to capitalize such names.

Xerox　　**P**ost-**I**t

11 Capitalize adjectives formed from proper nouns.

Elizabethan literature　　**C**hurchillian steadfastness

12 Capitalize abstractions when you want to give them special emphasis. Compare the following examples.

What is this thing called **L**ove?
Adil had fallen in **l**ove again.

13 Capitalize all the letters in most acronyms.

NATO　　**OPEC**　　**SALT** Treaty

Don't capitalize familiar acronyms that seem like ordinary words. When in doubt, check a dictionary.

radar sonar laser

EXERCISE 41.2 Correct the problems in capitalization in the following sentences.

1. The passenger next to me asked,"do you remember when air travel used to be fun?"
2. I couldn't reply immediately: My tray table had just flopped open and hit me on the knees.
3. The plane we were on—A jumbo jet that seated nine or ten across—had been circling Dulles International for hours.
4. "We'll be landing momentarily," the flight attendant mumbled,"If we are lucky."
5. I had seen the film version of this flight: *airplane!*

EXERCISE 41.3 Capitalize in the following sentences as necessary.

1. The constitution and the declaration of independence are on view at the national archives.
2. I heard the concierge at the hilton speaking spanish to the general secretary of the united nations.
3. Visitors to washington, d.c., include people from around the world: russians from moscow, egyptians from cairo, aggies from texas, buckeyes from ohio, farmers from the midwest, lawyers from the east coast, and politicos from everywhere.
4. At the white house, the president will host a conference on socialism and free enterprise in the spring, probably in april.

CHAPTER

42 Questions About Abbreviations and Numbers?

42a How do you handle abbreviations?

Some abbreviations (*a.m., p.m., Mrs., Mr., Dr., BC, BCE, AD*) appear in all kinds of writing. Others (*Jan., ft, no.*) should be limited to forms, applications, technical reports and documents, and similar items.

1 Be consistent in punctuating abbreviations and acronyms.

Abbreviations of single words usually take periods.

abbr. intro. gov. vols. Jan. Mr.

Most abbreviations that are spoken letter by letter are usually written without periods.

HBO IRS WWW AFL-CIO CIA CNN NEH

In fact, periods are disappearing from most abbreviations written in all caps.

USA	BC	AD	PhD
MA	BA	BS	DC (for District of Columbia)

Acronyms spoken as one word (not letter-by-letter) do not require periods.

CARE NATO NOW

Periods are usually omitted after abbreviations in technical writing unless an item might be misread without the period.

ft for *foot* *km* for *kilometer* but *in.* for *inch*

2 Be consistent in capitalizing abbreviations and acronyms.

Capitalize the abbreviations of words that are capitalized when written out in full.

General Motors—GM University of Toledo—UT

U.S. Navy—USN 98° Fahrenheit—98° F

Don't capitalize the abbreviations of words not capitalized when written out in full.

pound—lb. minutes—min.

Always capitalize BCE and CE or BC and AD. You may also see these items set in small caps: BCE and AD.

You may capitalize A.M. and P.M., but they often appear in small letters: a.m. and p.m. You may also see them in small caps: A.M. and P.M.

Don't capitalize acronyms that have become accepted words: *sonar, radar, laser, scuba.*

3 Use the appropriate abbreviations for titles, degrees, and names. Some titles are almost always abbreviated (*Mr., Ms., Mrs., Jr.*). Other titles are normally written out in full, though they may be abbreviated when they precede a first name or initial.

President	President Obama	Pres. Barack H. Obama
Professor	Professor Davis	Prof. Diane Davis
Reverend	Reverend Call	Rev. Ann Call
	the Reverend Dr. Call	Rev. Dr. Call

Never let abbreviated titles of this kind appear alone in a sentence.

WRONG The **gov.** urged the **sen.** to support the bill.

RIGHT The **governor** urged the **senator** to support the bill.

Gov. Martin urged **Sen.** Lu to support the bill.

Give credit for academic degrees either before a name or after—not both. Don't, for example, use both *Dr.* and *Ph.D.* in the same name.

WRONG **Dr.** Katherine Martinich, **PhD**

RIGHT **Dr.** Katherine Martinich

Katherine Martinich, **PhD**

Abbreviations for academic titles often stand by themselves, without names attached.

Professor Kim received her **PhD** from Penn State and her **BS** from St. Vincent College.

4 Use the appropriate technical abbreviations. Abbreviations are often used in professional, governmental, scientific, military, and technical writing.

DNA	UHF	EKG	START
SALT	GNP	LEM	kW

When writing for nontechnical audiences, spell out technical terms in full the first time you use them. Then in parentheses give the specialized abbreviation you will use in the rest of the paper.

> The two congressional candidates debated the effects a tax increase might have on the Gross National Product (GNP).

5 Use the appropriate abbreviations for agencies and organizations. In some cases, the abbreviation or acronym regularly replaces the full name of a company, agency, or organization.

FBI	IBM	MCI	AT&T

6 Use the appropriate abbreviations for dates. Dates are not abbreviated in most writing. Write out in full the days of the week and months of the year.

WRONG They arrived in Washington on a **Wed.** in **Apr.**

RIGHT They arrived in Washington on a **Wednesday** in **April**.

Abbreviations of months and days are used primarily in notes, lists, forms, and reference works.

7 Use the appropriate abbreviations for time and temperatures. Abbreviations that accompany time and temperatures are acceptable in all kinds of writing.

43 BC	AD 144	1:00 a.m.	98° F
143 BCE	1066 CE	4:36 p.m.	13° C

Notice that the abbreviation BC appears after a date, AD always before. You may also see BCE (*Before the Common Era*) used in place of BC and CE (*Common Era*) substituted for AD; both follow the date.

8 Use the appropriate abbreviations for weights, measures, and times. Technical terms or measurements are commonly abbreviated when used with numbers, but they are written out in full when they stand alone in sentences. Even when accompanied by numbers, the terms usually look better in sentences when spelled out completely.

28 mpg	1 tsp.	40 km.	420 lbs.
50 min.	30 kg.	2 hrs.	40 mph

Ella didn't really care how many **miles per gallon** her Escalade got in the city.

The abbreviation for number—*No.* or *no.*—is appropriate in technical writing, but only when immediately followed by a number.

NOT The **no.** on the contaminated dish was **073**.

BUT The contaminated dish was **no. 073**.

No. also appears in footnotes, endnotes, and citations.

9 Use the appropriate abbreviations for places. In most writing, place names are not abbreviated except in addresses and in reference tools and lists. However, certain abbreviations are accepted in academic and business writing.

USA	USSR	UK	Washington, DC

In addresses (but not in written text), use the standard postal abbreviations, without periods, for the states.

Alabama	AL	Idaho	ID
Alaska	AK	Illinois	IL
Arizona	AZ	Indiana	IN
Arkansas	AR	Iowa	IA
California	CA	Kansas	KS
Colorado	CO	Kentucky	KY
Connecticut	CT	Louisiana	LA
Delaware	DE	Maine	ME
Florida	FL	Maryland	MD
Georgia	GA	Massachusetts	MA
Hawaii	HI	Michigan	MI

Minnesota	MN	Oregon	OR
Mississippi	MS	Pennsylvania	PA
Missouri	MO	Rhode Island	RI
Montana	MT	South Carolina	SC
Nebraska	NE	South Dakota	SD
Nevada	NV	Tennessee	TN
New Hampshire	NH	Texas	TX
New Jersey	NJ	Utah	UT
New Mexico	NM	Vermont	VT
New York	NY	Virginia	VA
North Carolina	NC	Washington	WA
North Dakota	ND	West Virginia	WV
Ohio	OH	Wisconsin	WI
Oklahoma	OK	Wyoming	WY

All the various terms for *street* are written out in full, except in addresses.

boulevard	road	avenue	parkway
highway	alley	place	circle

But *Mt.* (for *mount*) and *St.* (for *saint*) are acceptable abbreviations in place names when they precede a proper name.

Mt. Vesuvius **St.** Charles Avenue

10 Use the correct abbreviations for certain expressions preserved from Latin.

i.e. (*id est*—that is)
e.g. (*exempli gratia*—for example)
et al. (*et alii*—and others)
etc. (*et cetera*—and so on)

In most writing, it is better to use English versions of these and other Latin abbreviations. Avoid using the abbreviation *etc.* in formal or academic writing. Never write *and etc.*

11 Use the appropriate abbreviations for divisions of books.

The many abbreviations for parts of books and manuscripts (*p., pp., vols., ch., chpts., bk., sect.*) are fine for use in footnotes or parenthetical citations, but don't use them alone in sentences.

WRONG Richard stuck the **bk.** in his pocket after reading **ch.** 5.

RIGHT Richard stuck the **book** in his pocket after reading **chapter** 5.

12 Use symbols as abbreviations carefully. Symbols such as %, +, =, ≠, <, > make sense in technical and scientific writing, but in other academic papers, spell out the full words. Most likely to cause a problem is % for *percent.*

ACCEPTABLE Mariah was shocked to learn that **80%** of the cars towed belong to tourists.

PREFERRED Mariah was shocked to learn that **80 percent** of the cars towed belong to tourists.

You can use a dollar sign ($) in any writing as long as it is followed by an amount. Don't use both the dollar sign and the word *dollar.*

WRONG The fine for parking in a towing zone is $125 dollars.
WRONG I found a $ bill on the sidewalk.

RIGHT The fine for parking in a towing zone is **$125**.
RIGHT I found a dollar bill on the sidewalk.

The ampersand (&) is an abbreviation for *and.* Do not use it in formal writing except when it appears in a title or name: *Road & Track.*

EXERCISE 42.1 Correct the sentences below, abbreviating where appropriate or expanding abbreviations that would be incorrect in college or professional writing. Check the punctuation for accuracy and consistency. If you insist on periods with acronyms, use them consistently throughout the passage.

1. There's a better than 70% chance of rain today.
2. Irene sent angry ltrs. to a dozen networks, including NBC, A.B.C., ESPN, and CNN.
3. The Emperor Claudius was born in 10 b.c. and died in 54 A.D.
4. Dr. Kovatch, M.D., works for the Federal Department of Agriculture (FDA).
5. I owe the company only $175 dollars, & expect to pay the full amount before the end of the mo.

42b How do you handle numbers?

You can express numbers in writing either through numerals or through words.

1	one
25	twenty-five
100	one hundred
1/4	one-fourth
0.05%	five hundredths of a percent *or* five one-hundredths of a percent

You'll likely use numerals in technical, scientific, and business writing. In other kinds of documents, you may combine words and numerals. (For guidelines on using hyphens with numbers that are spelled out, see Section 40c-2.)

1 Spell out numbers from one to nine; use numerals for numbers larger than nine.

10	15	39
101	115	220
1001	1021	59,000
101,000	10,000,101	50,306,673,432

In most cases, spell out ordinal numbers (that is, numbers that express a sequence): *first, second, third, fourth,* and so on. Spell out numbers that identify centuries.

in the fifteenth century
twentieth-century philosophers

These guidelines have variations and exceptions. The MLA style manual, for example, recommends spelling out any number that can be expressed in one or two words.

thirteen	twenty-one
three hundred	fifteen thousand

The APA style manual suggests using figures for most numbers above ten unless they appear at the beginning of a sentence.

> Thirty-three workers were rescued from an oil platform.

Check the style manual in your field to confirm how numbers ought to be presented in your writing.

2 Combine words and figures when you need to express large round numbers.

> 100 billion $32 million   103 trillion

Avoid shifting between words and figures. When you need numerals to express some numbers in a sentence, use numbers throughout.

> There were over **125,000** people at the protest and **950** police officers, but only **9** arrests.

When one number follows another, alternate words and figures for clarity.

33 fifth graders	12 first-term representatives
2 four-wheel-drive vehicles	five 5-gallon buckets

3 Use numerals when comparing numbers or suggesting a range. Numerals are easier to spot and compare than words.

> A blackboard at the traffic office listed a **$50** fine for jaywalking, **$100** for speeding, and **$125** for parking in a towing zone.

4 Don't begin sentences with numerals. Either spell out the number or rephrase the sentence so that the numeral is not the first word.

WRONG 32 people were standing in line at the parking violation center.

RIGHT Thirty-two people were standing in line at the parking violation center.

5 Use numerals for dates, street numbers, page numbers, sums of money, and various ID and call numbers.

July 4, 1776	1860–1864
115 Texas Oak Dr.	1900 East Blvd.

p. 352	pp. 23–24
$2,749.00	43£
Channel 8	103.5 FM
PR 105.5 R8	SSN 111-00-1111

Don't use an ordinal form in dates.

WRONG May 2nd, 1991

RIGHT May 2, 1991 *or* 2 May 1991

6 Use numerals for measurements, percentages, statistics, and scores.

35 mph	13° C	Austin, TX 78750
75 percent	0.2 liters	5.5 pupils per teacher
2 1/2 miles	15%	Browns 42–Steelers 7

Use numerals for time with *a.m.* and *p.m.*; use words with *o'clock*.

2:15 p.m. **6:00** a.m. **six** o'clock

7 Form the plurals of numbers by adding *-s* or *-'s*.

five **6s** in a row five 98**'s**

See Section 25a for more on plurals.

EXERCISE 42.2 Decide whether numbers used in the following sentences are handled appropriately. Where necessary, change numerals to words and words to numerals. Some expressions may not need revision.

1. 4 people will be honored at the ceremony beginning at nine p.m.
2. The culture contained more than 500,000,000,000 cells.
3. We forgot who won the Nobel Peace Prize in nineteen ninety-one.
4. The examination will include a question about the 1st, the 4th, and the Tenth Amendment.
5. We paid $79.80 for the hotel room and twenty dollars for admission to the park.

RESEARCH AND WRITING

CHAPTER

43 How Do You Plan a Research Project?

Until recently, most college instructors assigned research projects to introduce students to academic standards for research—that is, to the procedures that apply in higher education for gathering, evaluating, and reporting information. Research papers were, and remain, important exercises in handling information responsibly. However, in the past, not many students wrote such papers expecting to publish them or to share them with anyone except teachers and classmates.

But times have changed. As a college student, you now have access to the tools and media needed to support serious research projects and to reach broader audiences interested in your work. You also have access to a much wider variety of source materials. Whereas just a few years ago a research paper was typically a ten-page effort with a dozen sources—six books and six articles—a research project today might also cite a Web site, an email message, a multimedia presentation, a CD-ROM, an article from a full-text database, or any combination of these sources. We can't anticipate all the kinds of research you'll do in college, but we can offer some methods for managing these projects, whether you are preparing a traditional paper, an electronic project, or something else entirely.

You'll find an overview of the research process in this chapter, and more specific advice about finding and using sources in Chapters 44–47.

43a How do you claim a topic?

Think of research as an active process of creating knowledge rather than a passive one of reporting information. College projects can, in fact, start intellectual voyages that last a lifetime; many students find themselves adding majors and redirecting their careers as a result of work they began in a paper or a service project.

1 Size up an assignment carefully. In most cases, you'll receive a set of instructions when you are assigned a major college research project.

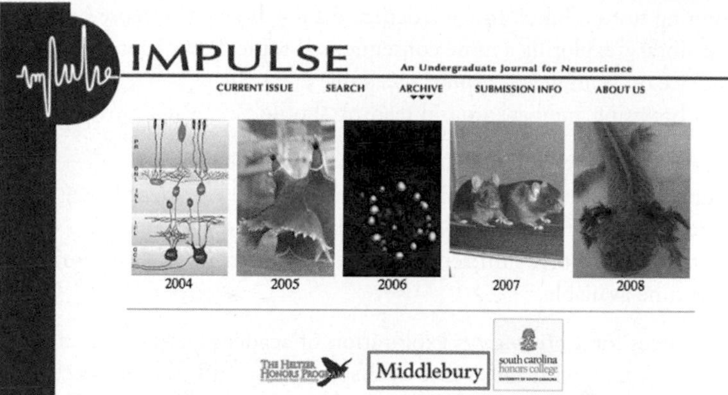

Impulse: An Undergraduate Journal for Neuroscience and *MarSci* are two of the growing number of peer-reviewed research journals that publish only undergraduate student work. Browse online to discover the following: What research publications or conferences exist for students in your major field? Does your college or university sponsor an undergraduate journal? In what classes can you imagine developing a research project that you could present at a professional meeting or submit for publication?

Go over the instructions carefully, as if you were examining a contract, highlighting its key features. Consider issues such as the following:

- **Scope.** Be sure you understand what you must do and at what level of detail. Look for word, page, or time limits at both extremes (*no less than; no more than*).
- **Due dates.** There may be separate due dates for different stages of the project: topic proposal, annotated bibliography, outline, first draft or prototype, final version.
- **Format/Documentation.** Note any specific requirements for the format and style of the paper. If an instructor doesn't give specific instructions, model a paper on one of the professional styles described in Part 8, "Documentation."

2 Browse the library in your topic area. Look for a subject about which you can honestly say you want to learn more. Avoid stale controversies that have long been on the national or local news without resolution—don't be one of a dozen students submitting projects on saving the rainforest or stopping tuition hikes. Instead, dedicate a few hours to intense browsing in your library, exploring a more consequential topic. See Chapter 2 for specific advice on finding and exploring a subject.

Your browsing and background reading should

- confirm whether you are in fact interested in the topic;
- survey the various aspects of your subject so you can identify key issues and perhaps refine the scope of your project; and
- determine whether sufficient resources exist to support your project in the time available.

Good sources for a *preliminary* exploration of academic topics are encyclopedias, beginning with those that deal specifically with your subject. The more specialized the encyclopedia, the better will be its coverage of a subject area. Ask reference librarians for their suggestions.

If no specialized encyclopedia is available, or if the volume you locate proves too technical, use one of the general encyclopedias available in print or electronically. Remember, though, that an encyclopedia is just a starting point for college-level work—a place to go for a topic idea, an overview of a subject, or some basic facts. To do the work of a serious researcher, you must move well beyond what you can learn from an encyclopedia.

3 Browse electronic resources. Studies suggest that many people go immediately to *Google* or *Wikipedia* to find information on the Web. This strategy is not adequate for any but the most basic academic assignments. At the earliest stages of a project, you will want to identify electronic tools and databases designed for serious research. Begin by browsing your library's electronic catalog, using its capacity for searching by subject headings.

Ask a research librarian or your instructor to help you locate electronic tools relevant to your general topic area. General indexes, such as *Academic Search Complete* and *Google Scholar*, do cover a wide range of fields, which may be useful when your topic ideas cross several disciplines. For almost every academic field or subject, however, you'll also find specialized electronic indexes or gateways—for example, *The Voice of the Shuttle* provides coverage of many areas in the humanities. In any index, scan the various subject listings to see how other writers and researchers have approached topics within your subject area. What issues have they examined? What subtopics might you pursue? Some professional indexes (both print and electronic) are listed in Section 44a-4, but don't hesitate to ask a librarian for help at this stage.

If you are having trouble finding *any* topic of interest, Web directories organized by topic (such as *Yahoo!*) can be helpful. For instance, for a lengthy list of potential topics, search "Yahoo! Issues and Causes" on the Web.

Checklist 43.1 Specialized Encyclopedias

FOR A PAPER ON . . .	BEGIN BY CHECKING . . .
American history	*Encyclopedia of American History*
Anthropology	*International Encyclopedia of the Social Sciences*
Communication	*International Encyclopedia of Communication*
Economics	*Encyclopedia of American Economic History*
Film	*International Encyclopedia of Film*
History	*Dictionary of American History*
Law	*The Guide to American Law*
Philosophy	*Encyclopedia of Philosophy*
Political science	*Encyclopedia of American Political History*
Psychology, Psychiatry	*International Encyclopedia of Psychiatry, Psychology, Psychoanalysis and Neurology; Encyclopedia of Psychology*
Social sciences	*International Encyclopedia of the Social Sciences*

43b How do you develop a research project?

Once you have a general subject in mind, review the writing process described in Chapters 1–5 of this book, to help yourself focus on a topic, develop it into a thesis, give it some preliminary structure, and think about potential sources. While a research project is more formal than many other writing projects, it still resembles them in its basic strategies and procedures. In particular, you may wish to review the following sections:

1d How do you define a rhetorical situation?

1f How do you write for an audience?

2a How do you find a topic?

2d How do you write a topic proposal?

3b How do you craft a thesis statement?

You'll also need a plan to deal with the complexities of a task that may draw upon many different technologies and sources.

1 Write a research prospectus. For some research assignments, you may be asked to prepare a proposal that describes your project. Such a prospectus enables an instructor to give you the help and direction you may need. More detailed and formal than a topic proposal (see Section 2d), a prospectus will likely include some of the following elements.

- **Identification of a topic or topic area.**
- **A hypothesis, research question, or thesis.** This item should be stated clearly.
- **Background information or review of literature.** Identify the books, articles, and other materials you expect to read to gain background information on your subject.
- **A review of research resources.** Identify the types of materials you'll need for your project and determine whether they are available locally or online.
- **A description of your research methodology.** Outline the procedures you will follow in your research and justify any choice of particular methodology (interviews, surveys, questionnaires, field work).
- **An assessment of the ethics of your project if it involves experiments with people.** Most universities have strict guidelines for research with human subjects. Your instructor will likely tell you about these rules, especially in fields such as psychology and the social sciences.

2 Decide how you will handle your research materials. If most of your materials will be printed sources, you can still rely on a system of photocopies and note cards to manage much of the project. But most writers now routinely use both printed and electronic sources and depend on their word processors or database research programs (such as *ProCite*) to organize their work. Many projects today also require charts, graphs, and illustrations, some of them generated by software, and some downloaded from Web sources.

Consider other kinds of resources you may need for your project, including any specialized software or electronic equipment such as tape recorders, digital cameras, or color printers. Consider, too, where to store and backup all the materials you accumulate. Keep electronic copies of important projects in two separate locations.

3 Prepare a working and/or an annotated bibliography.

Whether you are using printed or electronic sources, and whether your project will culminate in a paper, a Web site, a slide show, or a brochure, you will eventually need to identify where your information came from. So keep track of the sources you accumulate by listing them in a working bibliography. In that list, be sure to record all the information you will need later when you document your paper and prepare a works cited or references list (see Part 8, "Documentation"). If your instructor asks you to prepare an annotated bibliography (in which you describe and evaluate your sources), see Section 6a, "Writer at Work: Writing an Annotated Bibliography."

Checklist 43.2 Information Included in a Working Bibliography

Listed below are the kinds of information you will need to keep a record of for several common types of sources.

- **For printed books:** author(s), editor(s), or translator(s); full title; edition; place of publication; publisher; date of publication
- **For books online:** all print book information + title of Web site or database; date of access
- **For printed articles:** author; title of article; name of periodical, journal or newspaper; volume and issue numbers (if available); edition (of newspaper); date of publication; page numbers or section/page numbers (for newspaper)
- **For articles online:** all print article information + title of Web site; sponsor of Web site; date of access
- **For articles from databases:** all print article information + name of database or subscription service; date of access
- **For sources in various media (film, TV, music, drama, artwork):** author, artist, or creator; title of work; location (if relevant), publisher, sponsor, institution, or gallery; date of performance or publication

Also be sure to note the medium for each source, as MLA style requires this information for all items in a Works Cited list. Descriptors of media include the following: Print, Web, CD-ROM, E-mail, Film, Television, Radio, Videocassette, Audiocassette, LP (long-playing record), CD, DVD, Laser disc, Slide program, Performance, Address, MS (manuscript), TS (typescript), PDF file, MP3 file, and so on.

4 Make copies of printed sources. Although a case can still be made for taking notes on cards, the fact is that most researchers—both faculty members and students—now either photocopy or download their major source materials, especially any passages that they expect to quote from directly and more extensively. If that's your method too, be sure your photocopies are complete and legible (especially any page numbers). When you are photocopying from a book or magazine, take a moment to duplicate the title page and publication/editorial staff information. Later, you'll be glad that you did. In all cases, attach basic bibliographical information directly to photocopies and printouts so that you know their source, making sure each document is keyed somehow to a full bibliography record (see Checklist 43.2). That way, you'll be able to connect information and source easily. (See Citation Guides on pages 651–655.)

Use highlighter pens to mark passages in photocopies and printouts that you expect to refer to later, and keep all these source materials in a folder. Never highlight material or write comments in the margins of library books.

5 Print or download electronic sources. How you record data from an electronic source will depend on how you expect to use it. Full printouts (with all bibliographic information attached) may be necessary for sources whose content changes from day to day—such as Web sites, newsgroups, blogs, or online conversations. Be sure to record when you made the printout, since you may need a date of access when you document a Web source.

Of course, it is possible to download many electronic sources directly to disk. Clearly label any files and folders you create so that you can easily find this information later. As with printed sources, you will have to document and credit all copyrighted pictures, photographs, and images borrowed from the Web, whether you use the image in a paper or in an electronic project. Because it's so easy to forget where you found an image or video, you may want to make a list of their locations or sources on the Web.

43c How do you schedule a research project?

You may not need to plan simple projects. But you'll need to think more strategically about time management whenever you're assigned a research paper or any project that requires extensive preparation and design. Begin by listing the *hard points* of the assignment—those essential features that you don't control. For instance, when an instructor asks for a ten-page paper on genetic engineering using APA style, due in one month, you have four hard points:

1. Format: ten-page paper
2. Topic: genetic engineering
3. Documentation: APA
4. Due date: one month from today

Then list any activities required to meet those goals, such as doing library or field research, creating images or tables, and so on. Then map these operations on a calendar or timeline. Here's a calendar for a project with three major due dates and a checklist of support activities; you might set a completion date for each of those as well.

Highlight: Sample Calendar for a History Research Paper

______ Choose a topic and define the project
______ Assess campus library resources
______ Generate a working bibliography
______ Prepare the topic proposal
Topic Proposal: Due September 7

______ Gather and evaluate materials/images
______ Outline/design the project
______ Draft the project
______ Prepare the bibliography/works cited list
First Draft: Due October 7

______ Get and respond to feedback
______ Revise and edit
______ Check the documentation
______ Proofread the final version
Final Project: Due November 7

If you are working on a research project with a team of classmates, as is common in many college courses, creating a detailed and realistic schedule is especially vital. Careful management is crucial to the success of any collaborative effort, so be sure to outline a plan that makes clear each group member's roles and responsibilities—and that builds in plenty of time to communicate and coordinate at each stage. See Section 5d for more on collaborative writing.

CHAPTER

44 How Do You Find Information?

As a writer you'll want your research to be accurate and authoritative, so you'll need to gather reliable sources of information. New tools now allow researchers to tap into more information resources, in a wider range of media, than ever before. But not all of these are as well designed as traditional libraries when it comes to locating trustworthy materials. That's why your research skills today have to be more critical and professional than ever. This chapter surveys a range of resources available to support a serious research paper.

44a How do you find library sources?

1 Learn about your library. A first priority for any writer is to learn about the resources of local libraries and research facilities. Be sure you can locate the following places, features, and services:

Online catalog. Learn how to use these terminals to examine your library's collections. Many libraries also have comprehensive Web sites that include links to powerful indexes, databases, and online reference tools.

Card catalog. Not all libraries have electronic catalogs. Even when they do, such catalogs may not include materials acquired before a specific date. Find out if that is the case, and know where the card catalog is located.

Reference room. Study this collection carefully, noting how materials are arranged and where the heavily used items—encyclopedias, almanacs, phone books, databases—are located. Get to know the research or reference room librarians.

Bibliographies and databases. Look for important bibliographies and data terminals in library reference rooms. Print bibliographies will often be large, multivolume collections. Research databases will be arrayed near computer terminals.

Microform collections. Many important materials, including documents, newspapers, and periodicals, are collected (in miniaturized photographic form) on rolls of film called *microfilm* or rectangular sheets of film called *microfiche.*

Periodical collections. You'll need to know both where current journals and other periodicals are located and where older bound or microfilmed materials are housed.

Newspapers. Current newspapers are usually available in a reading room; older newspapers are usually available chiefly on microfilm. Online archives of newspapers are a recent innovation: you won't be able to search more than a few years back.

Audio/video collections. Many libraries now have extensive holdings of audio/video materials as well as facilities for listening to or viewing CDs, DVDs, tapes, and video disks.

Circulation desk/library services. Learn what circulation desk services are available to a researcher. Most libraries participate in interlibrary loan programs that allow you to borrow materials your library may not own.

Photocopiers, computers, and study areas. It's smart to track down two or three copying locations since copiers get heavy use. Also check to see whether certain areas are reserved for study and research.

Study cubicles. Many college and university libraries provide small rooms with desks within the library for persons pursuing serious research. Find out if you are eligible for a cubicle.

2 Use library catalogs efficiently. Almost all libraries now provide access to their resources via computer terminals or the Web. Many libraries also participate in the database called *OCLC WorldCat,* which links the catalogs of libraries around the world, giving you almost unlimited access to materials. In traditional card catalogs, books and other sources could be located by author, title, and key word. Electronic catalogs can be searched by these categories too, but more quickly and with more options. If your library has an electronic catalog, study its screens and learn its basic search techniques and commands. Most basic screens support a variety of author-title-subject-keyword search combinations, as well as more advanced searches that enable you to pick the date, location, format, and language of the research material. Librarians find that most people use online catalogs by performing keyword searches.

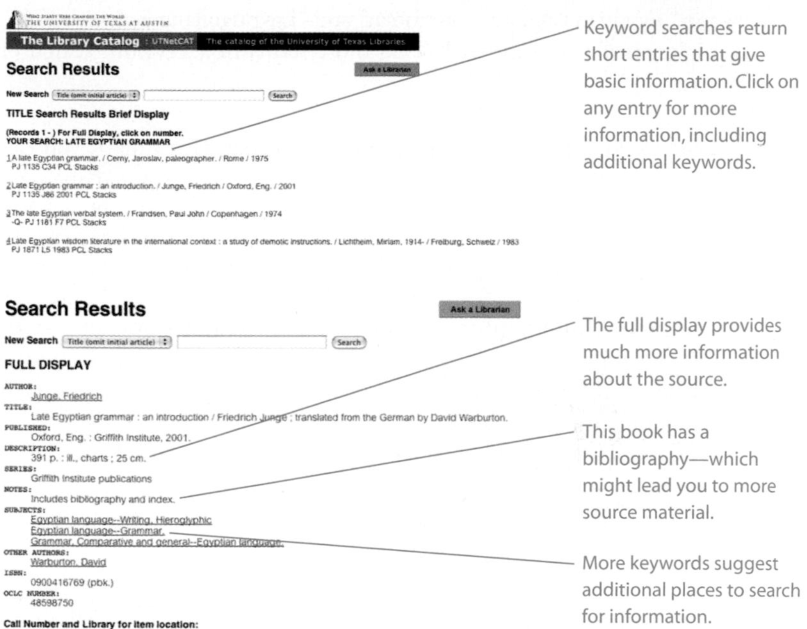

Figure 44.1 Sample brief and full source entries from online library catalog.

An online catalog offers detailed information about most library holdings. As Figure 44.1 illustrates, on screen, you'll often be given a list of brief entries on your subject—typically the author, title, publishing information, date, and call number—with an option to select a full listing. The full listing describes additional features of the item—whether it is illustrated, if it has an index or a bibliography, and so on.

Most card and online catalogs use subject headings determined by the Library of Congress and compiled in the multivolume *Library of Congress Subject Headings*, commonly known by its abbreviation *LCSH*. Be sure to consult this volume (or its electronic equivalent) in the reference room of your library at the start of your research: it will tell you how your topic is described and treated in the library catalog. On any given subject card or screen, pay attention, too, to any additional subject headings offered, because these may offer keywords to use in additional searches. For instance, if you were exploring "hieroglyphics," a listing on that topic might offer the keywords "Egyptian language—grammar" and "Egyptian language—writing." You might not have considered using those terms in a keyword search of your own.

3 Locate suitable bibliographies. You may save time if you can locate an extensive printed bibliography—preferably an annotated one—on your topic. Bibliographies are lists of books, articles, and other documentary materials that deal with particular subjects or subject areas. (See Checklist 44.1.) Bibliographies come in several types.

- **Complete bibliographies** attempt to list all major works in a given field or subject.
- **Selective bibliographies** usually list the best known or most respected books and articles in a subject area.
- **Annotated bibliographies** briefly describe the works they list and may evaluate them.
- **Annual bibliographies** catalog the works produced within a field or discipline in a given year.

Checklist 44.1 Bibliographies

FOR A PAPER ON . . .	CONSULT . . .
American history	*Bibliographies in American History*
Art	*Guide to the Literature of Art History*
Astronomy	*A Guide to the Literature of Astronomy*
Engineering	*Science and Engineering Literature*
Literature	*MLA International Bibliography*
Mathematics	*Using the Mathematical Literature*
Music	*Music Reference and Research Materials*
Psychology	*Harvard List of Books in Psychology*

Another intriguing tool is the "Library of Congress Bibliographies, Research Guides and Finding Aids" at <http://www.loc.gov/rr/program/bib/bibhome.html>. Here you will find materials on a wide range of topics, most of them fairly specialized but still rich and interesting. You can locate other Web bibliographies using a Web search engine: just add the word *bibliography* to your keyword search and see what turns up. For example, to find electronic bibliographies on the Spanish-American War, search "bibliography Spanish American War."

4 Locate suitable indexes to search the periodical literature.

Indexes—in printed form in the past, electronic today—list the journal articles, magazine pieces, and newspaper stories that aren't recorded in a library card catalog. Such material constitutes the *periodical literature* on a subject. You shouldn't undertake any serious research without surveying this extensive body of information in a database or printed index, searching it by subject, article, title, or keyword.

To give you access to a variety of academic databases, both general and specialized, your library likely subscribes to electronic information services. You can use a database to discover who has published materials on a given topic, the titles of such articles, and all the publication information needed to find them. Online databases now routinely provide detailed abstracts of the articles or full texts of the material. The following databases are good places to begin a search:

Academic OneFile

Academic Search Complete

EBSCO

JSTOR

LexisNexis Academic

Then you can move on to more specialized indexes. Here are tips for efficient searching:

- Be sure you are logged on to the right index. A library terminal may provide access to several databases or indexes. Find the one appropriate for your subject.
- Read the description of the index to find out how to access its information. Not all databases and indexes work the same way.
- When searching by keyword, check whether a list of subject headings is available. To save time, match your search terms to those on the list before you begin. (See Section 44b for more on keyword searches.)
- Try synonyms if your initial keyword search turns up too few items or too many.

Checklist 44.2 Computerized and Printed Indexes

FOR A PAPER ON . . .	CONSULT . . .
Anthropology	*Anthropological Literature*
Art	*Art Abstracts*
Biography	*Biography Index*
Business	*Business Periodicals Index; ABI/Inform*
Chemistry	*CAS*
Current affairs	*LexisNexis*
Education	*Education Index; ERIC*
Engineering	*INSPEC*
Film	*Film Index International; Art Index*
History	*Historical Abstracts; America: History and Life*
Humanities	*FRANCIS; Humanities Index*
Literature	*Essay and General Literature Index; MLA Bibliography*
Mathematics	*MathSciNet*
Philosophy	*Philosopher's Index*
Psychology	*Psychological Abstracts; PsycLit; PsycINFO*
Religion	*ATLA Religion Database*
Science	*General Science Index; General Science Abstracts*
Social sciences	*Social Science & Humanities Index*

5 Check the Web. The quality of the information on the Web varies enormously because there are no gatekeepers or referees to edit or evaluate most of what goes online. So you must approach the Web with caution as a resource for research, recognizing the differences in purpose and quality among sites. You may find superb and up-to-date information on your subject, and you might encounter material that is unreliable, speculative, or even malicious. You need to apply all your critical powers when surveying Web sites for information. (See Chapter 45 for more on evaluating sources.)

You probably do most of your Web searching using *Google* or *Yahoo!*, but be careful not to let these resources become your only tool for research. Good as they are, they follow logical pathways that may miss material that you need. At a minimum, try several search tools for any major project. Here are some alternatives:

SEARCH TOOLS
About
AltaVista
Ask
Bing
Dogpile
Excite

Libraries, universities, and government agencies have also created hundreds of reference tools with more scholarly goals. Here are some places to look:

REFERENCE SITES
Infomine
The Internet Public Library
Librarians' Internet Index
Library of Congress Research Centers

6 Consult biographical resources. Quite often you'll need information about famous people, living and dead. Good places to start are the *Biography Index: A Cumulative Index to Biographic Material in Books and Magazines, Bio-Base, LexisNexis, Current Biography*, and *The McGraw-Hill Encyclopedia of World Biography.*

The various *Who's Who* volumes cover living British, American, and world notables, African Americans, and women. Deceased figures may appear in *Who Was Who*. Probably the two most famous dictionaries of biography are the *Dictionary of National Biography* (British) and the *Dictionary of American Biography.* On the Web, you might look at the biography database maintained by the Arts and Entertainment Network (A&E) at <http://www.biography.com>.

Checklist 44.3 Biographical Information

IF YOUR SUBJECT IS . . .	CONSULT . . .
African	*Dictionary of African Biography*
African American	*Dictionary of American Negro Biography*
Asian	*Encyclopedia of Asian History*
Australian	*Australian Dictionary of Biography*
Canadian	*Dictionary of Canadian Biography*
Female	*Index to Women*
Mexican American	*Mexican American Biographies*

7 Locate statistics. Statistics on nearly every imaginable topic are available in library reference rooms and online. Be sure to find up-to-date and reliable figures. Online, check out *iTools* for various reference items and books. Also explore Web resources such as *The Internet Public Library* and *American FactFinder*, a site maintained by the US Census Bureau. For a staggering array of statistics from more than 70 agencies of the federal government, search for *FedStats*.

You'll find material and data on a wide range of subjects—especially on current and pop culture issues—in *Wikipedia*. Note however that this open-source encyclopedia is created and revised by the people who use it. The quality of its entries will vary, like the Web in general, and so you should double-check its factual claims. Many instructors frown on its use in academic papers.

Checklist 44.4

TO FIND . . .	CONSULT . . .
General statistics	*World Almanac; Current Index to Statistics* (electronic)
Statistics about the United States	*Statistical Abstract of the United States; STAT-USA* (electronic); *GPO Access*
World information	*National Intelligence Factbook*
Business facts	*Handbook of Basic Economic Statistics; Survey of Current Business*
Public opinion polls	*Gallup Poll*

8 Check news sources. To find information from newspapers published earlier than the mid-1990s, you'll usually have to rely on printed or microfilm copies. When you know the date of an event, however, you can usually locate the information you want. If your subject isn't an event, you may have to trace it through an index or online archive. Only a few printed papers are fully indexed, notably the *New York Times*. A reference librarian can guide you to other news indexes available in your library—such as *LexisNexis*, *Factiva*, or *InfoTrac Newspapers*.

For very current events, you can search hundreds of online newspapers and news services, which offer immediate information from a wide range of sources around the world. As with any source, exercise caution when using information you find on the Web, making sure that its source is reputable (see Chapter 45). The speed of online journalism seems to have put pressure on fact checkers and editors: don't assume that the facts, quotations, and dates you find will always be correct—even in reputable sources. As a precaution, try to verify what you find in one source with another.

NEWS RESOURCES

C-SPAN Online
National Public Radio
New York Times
Google News
London Times
USA Today News
CNN Interactive
Fox News

9 Check book, film, and product reviews. Sometimes you may need to know how a given book or film was received when it first appeared. To locate reviews of older books, look for *Book Review Digest* (1905–), *Book Review Index* (1965–), or *Current Book Review Citations* (1976–) in the library reference room. *Book Review Digest* lists fewer reviews than the other two collections, but it summarizes those it does include—a useful feature. Many electronic periodical indexes also catalog book reviews. Enter "book reviews" on a search engine or directory, or look for specific sites such as *The New York Times Sunday Book Review* and *The New York Review of Books*.

For film reviews and criticism, see the printed volumes *Film Review Index* (1986–) and *Film Criticism: An Index to Critics' Anthologies* (1975–) as well as the electronic *Film Index International* (a subscription service). Numerous free Web sites—of wildly varying quality—are devoted to films and film reviews.

To locate reviews of other material, try a Web search engine. In the search box, simply type in *review* or *evaluation* after the name of the product: *"21st Century Breakdown" review; Corvette ZR1 road test; Star Trek movie review.*

10 Consult experts and conduct interviews. If you can discuss your subject with an expert, you'll add credibility, authenticity, and immediacy to a research report.

It is now possible to consult with knowledgeable people via email, newsgroups, blogs, and email lists. Although online communications tend to be less formal than face-to-face conversations, they still require appropriate courtesy and preparation. For a directory of experts willing to consult via email, search "ask an expert" online.

To conduct a face-to-face interview with a knowledgeable source, follow these guidelines.

- Write or telephone your subject for an appointment, and make it clear why you want the interview.
- Be on time for your appointment.
- Be prepared: have a list of questions and follow-ups ready.
- Take careful notes, especially if you intend to quote your source.
- Double-check direct quotations, and be sure your source is willing to be cited "on the record."
- If you plan to record the interview, get your subject's approval before turning the machine on.
- Provide your subject with a copy of your completed paper—and don't forget to send a note of thanks.

44b How do you search with keywords?

Writers now routinely find information online by typing names, phrases, or other key terms into *Google* to see what pops up. That habit has largely replaced more refined keyword searches. Yet you still will need keyword search techniques to explore many electronic resources, including the online library catalogs and professional electronic indexes or databases you'll consult while preparing for serious research projects. A **keyword search** is simply a scan of an electronic text or database to find each occurrence of a given word or phrase.

Our best advice for keyword searches is to read the instructions for any tool you are using, whether it is an electronic catalog, a search engine, or a directory. A second tip: Be sure to type keywords carefully, especially proper nouns. A misspelled search term can prevent you from finding available information.

1 Understand how a simple keyword search works. A keyword search finds the items in a catalog or database that contain the keyword(s) you have typed into a box or line on the screen. You might get keyword ideas from the *Library of Congress Subject Headings* (*LCSH*) in the reference room of your library, or ask a reference librarian for help.

When searching a library catalog, always check the screen for cross-listings of your particular subject—that is, other terms under which your subject is categorized. For example, if your project on Civil War ironclad ships leads you to search with the term "Monitor" (the name of a famous Union ship), a particular catalog entry might include the subject cross-listings *Civil War; Merrimac; U.S. Navy, history; Ericsson, John.* You could then probe the catalog using each of these new terms.

You will have to be ingenious at times in choosing keywords for Web searches. Use your preliminary reading on a subject to come up with more specific keywords. If you need to know whether alcohol is legally considered a drug, for example, you could begin with general keywords such as "alcohol" or "drugs." But if you have read that drugs are regulated by the Federal Drug Administration, "FDA" might be a better search term.

So the keywords you choose—whether names, places, titles, concepts, or people—will shape your search. A comparatively small database, such as an online library catalog, may ask you to indicate whether a word you are searching is a title (t), author (a), subject (s), or some other term the system recognizes. But more specialized search techniques may be required when you get more hits from a keyword search than you can reasonably research. One such technique is called Boolean searching.

2 Understand the principles of Boolean searching. A Boolean search uses specific terms (or symbols) to give you more control over the results of your search. Most search engines in online catalogs, databases, or Web sites permit some form of Boolean search.

In a Boolean search, by linking keywords with the term "AND," you will pull up only those database items in which all the linked terms occur. It may help to visualize these constraints in terms of sets: "AND" would mean intersection.

schnauzer AND training

Washington AND Jefferson AND Constitution

Another way to initiate this Boolean search is to select the appropriate built-in command from a search engine menu, such as an "all the words" option. Narrowing your search to look for only those items that contain *all* the words you specify usually prevents an information glut.

Each Boolean operator allows you to direct database searches in a specific way.

OR Using "OR" between two keywords directs the search engine to find any examples of either keyword. Using "OR" might widen a search, but it would also allow you to locate all documents that cover related concepts.

dog OR puppy
Congress OR Senate

NOT Using "NOT" between terms permits you to search for sites that include one term but not another. This may be useful when you want to exclude certain meanings of a term that are irrelevant to your search.

Indians NOT Cleveland
republican NOT party

( ) Putting items in parentheses allows for additional fine tuning of a search. In the first example below, you could locate documents that mention either Senator Boxer or Senator McCain.

Senator AND (Boxer OR McCain)
pickup NOT (Ford OR Toyota)

3 Search by exact phrase. To narrow a search even more, you can search for a specific and distinctive phrase, either by placing it between quotation marks or selecting the "exact phrase" option on a search screen. You can use exact phrase searches creatively in many ways. If you can't recall who is responsible for a particular expression or quotation—for example, "defining deviancy down"—you can make it the subject of an exact phrase search. When you do so, you may find the expression attributed to the late Senator Daniel Patrick Moynihan.

You can also combine exact phrase searches with various Boolean commands to find precisely what you need.

> "Ten Commandments" AND ("Charlton Heston" OR "Yul Brynner")
>
> "pickup truck" NOT (Ford OR Toyota)

To learn more about using Web search engines, search the Web for "Bare Bones 101," a site at the University of South Carolina Beaufort that includes detailed descriptions of important search engines.

45 How Do You Evaluate Sources?

Writers have always had to be careful about the sources they cited in their projects, but in the past they could at least be confident that the library materials they used had been reviewed by publishers, editors, and librarians. Today, however, some materials—pages from the Web, messages from email lists—may come to you directly from their authors, unreviewed and unrefereed. It will fall to you to judge their authority, quality, and credibility. You can learn to make sound judgments if you remember a few basic principles.

45a How do sources differ?

As a critical reader (see Chapter 8), you have to decide what material is suited to your topic and be prepared to defend your choices. Some of the sources you might encounter are discussed in the following pages and summarized in Table 45.1.

Scholarly books and articles. Scholarly works are among the most carefully researched, reviewed, and edited sources. They are rarely current because they take time to prepare and publish. Their authors are recognized authorities, and their assertions are fully documented. Such books and articles are written to share research with a scholarly and professional audience, so they follow the formal structures of research in their fields. Articles, for example, will include abstracts, discussions of methods, formal conclusions, and thorough bibliographies.

Serious trade books and articles. These works are written for well-educated but nonexpert readers who wish to acquire more than general knowledge about a subject. Serious periodicals include *Scientific American, New York Review of Books, The New Yorker, The New Republic, National Review, The Humanist,* and many others.

Popular magazines and books. Works of this kind (print or online) tend to be less demanding and shorter than serious or scholarly materials. Their sources may not be specifically identified, documented, or linked. Some familiar popular magazines include *Wired, Psychology Today, Discover,* and *Smithsonian.*

Newspapers and news organizations. Newspapers (in print and online) and Web news sources (such as *CNN Online* and *Google News*) provide up-to-date and generally reliable information about current events, as well as many features chronicling popular culture and political opinion. Published daily or weekly, newspapers lack the perspective of scholarly works but provide an essential documentary function. Most news sources have political biases that you should take into account.

Sponsored Web sites. Web sites sponsored by well-known institutions, organizations, and companies share in the credibility of their supporting groups. Thus Web sites posted by the U.S. government or by colleges and universities can usually be trusted—though individual student Web sites (on ".edu" sites) are much less reliable.

Individual Web and Internet contacts. These may include individual Web sites, home pages, *Facebook* groups, and email. Individual Web sites are rarely refereed or reviewed by third parties who might take some responsibility for their accuracy. Confirm any hard facts found on such sites using a second, more traditional source. When corresponding with or interviewing an authority on the Web, be sure to record accurately both your questions and the answers you receive.

Email lists and listservs, Usenet newsgroups, and blogs. If you join a group related to your subject, you can quickly learn about current interests and debates. But as in any extended conversation, you have to exercise good judgment: facts and figures may not be reported reliably; the true credentials of participants might be hard to determine. Online discussion groups are often more valuable for what they reveal about the range and depth of feeling on a given subject than for any specific information you may find there. Blogs, which are online forums usually hosted by one or more individuals who provide commentary and links, vary enormously in subject matter, orientation, and credibility—with many being highly serious and professional and others offering more dubious material.

Table 45.1 Assessing Sources

Source	Purpose	Authors	Audience/ Language
Scholarly books	Advance or report new knowledge	Experts	Academic/ Technical
Scholarly articles	Advance or report new knowledge	Experts	Academic/ Technical
Serious books & articles	Report or summarize information	Experts or professional writers	Educated public/ Formal
Popular magazines	Report or summarize information	Professional writers or journalists	General public/ Informal
Newspapers, news services	Report current information	Journalists	General public/ Informal
Sponsored Web sites	Varies from report information to advertise	Varies, usually Web experts	Varies/Usually informal
Blogs and individual Web sites	Varies	Expert to novice	Varies/Casual to slang
Interviews	Consult with experts	Experts	Varies/Technical to colloquial
Email lists, listservs	Discuss specific subjects	Experts to interested amateurs	Varies/Technical to colloquial
Usenet newsgroups	Discuss specific subjects	Open to everyone	Varies/Technical to colloquial

Publisher or Medium	Reviewed/ Documented?	Current/ Stable?	Dialogic/ Interactive?
University Press	Yes/Yes	No/Yes	No/No
Scholarly or professional journal	Yes/Yes	Usually No/ Yes	No/No (unless online)
Commercial publishers	Yes/No	Depends on subject/Yes	No/No (unless online)
Commercial publishers	Yes/No	Yes/Yes	No/No (unless online)
Commercial press or online	Yes/No	Yes/Yes	No/No (unless online)
Web	Sometimes/ Links to other sites	Regularly updated/ Sometimes	Sometimes/ Often
Web	Usually/No	Varies/Varies	Sometimes/ Sometimes
Notes, recordings, email	No/No	Yes/No	Yes/Yes
Web (blogs) or email (lists, listservs)	Sometimes/ Sometimes	Yes/ Sometimes	Yes/Yes
Web, email	No/No	Yes/No	Yes/Yes

45b How do you evaluate source materials?

As you might suspect, sources aren't simply *good* or *bad*. Their value will depend, in part, on how you intend to use them. In writing a report on Abraham Lincoln's positions during the 1860 presidential campaign, you could base the paper on scholarly works on Lincoln or, perhaps, newspaper accounts of his speeches on microfilm. However, in writing about current political campaigns, you'd likely have to use less scholarly materials—campaign literature, articles in daily newspapers and magazines, or maybe even blogs. These sources would lack the meticulousness and authority of scholarly books (which wouldn't be available yet), but they could still provide a valid snapshot of current political attitudes. The following guidelines will help you apply necessary criteria as you evaluate the appropriateness of sources for your project.

1 Consider the authority and reputation of a source. As you accumulate materials for a project, you may find that certain print sources are cited much more often than others. These are likely to be essential materials that most people in the field have as their working knowledge. If you haven't already consulted these books and articles, go to the library and review them. Ask librarians or instructors, too, about the trustworthiness of sources that you expect to use. Take their advice about reputable publishers, journals, and bibliographies.

If you were writing a research paper tracing recent trends in college students' political participation, what kinds of sources would be most useful? What strengths and limitations might you encounter in drawing material from political magazines such as *Utne Reader* (left-of-center) or *The Weekly Standard* (right-of-center)? What about a magazine that focuses on popular culture, such as *Rolling Stone*? Browse these publications' Web sites and discuss your conclusions with a group of classmates.

Do the same with electronic sources: track down the best items as far as you can determine them. Inevitably, the most valuable sites will appear on many "favorites" lists. Sometimes the Web address (URL) can also help you identify the nature (and thus the reliability) of a source. Checking the domain in the address will give you some sense of who is sponsoring the site—though the designation can often be misleading, since some domains are open to anyone.

.edu—a U.S. educational institution

.info—an informative site

.org—an organization

.museum—restricted to museums

.gov—restricted to U.S. government

.travel—restricted to travel

.com—a commercial/business site

.biz—an alternative to .com

.net—may be an Internet service provider; otherwise nonspecific

.fr—country code for France

.jp—country code for Japan

.uk—country code for United Kingdom

For a complete listing of Internet domain names visit the Web site of the Internet Numbers Authority at www.iana.org.

2 Consider timeliness and stability. In general, you want to support your projects with the most current and reputable information in a field, but your instructors and librarians may refer you to classic pieces; that is, older works that have shaped thinking in your topic area. For many college papers you should have a mix of sources, some from the past and some quite recent.

Newer electronic environments can be unstable—that is, they quickly become obsolete or disappear without a trace. But institutionalized sites—such as *The New York Times Online* and other highly regarded sources—are archived and generally dependable. For any Web source, check for dates of the original posting and any updates. Be aware that the Web is full of outdated materials.

3 Consider significance and thoroughness. For academic work, you want source materials that treat subjects seriously and in depth. For many projects, you'll need to use scholarly books and articles that present new research, not that merely rehash what others have written. In such sources, look for formal language, logical structure, full documentation (including a bibliography), and careful handling of quoted materials—in short, the same qualities you are expected to demonstrate in your own work. When evaluating the information presented in a Web site, look for reliability and thoroughness. For example, don't take a quotation from a presidential address from a newspaper when you can locate a more authoritative version—perhaps the full text of the speech—at the White House site or a presidential library site.

4 Consider bias. You'll especially need to consider political, social, cultural, economic, and religious leanings when you are dealing with controversial subjects. In deciding which items to read from a lengthy list, it may help to select opinions from across the spectrum—otherwise, you may write a whole paper unaware that important points of view are being ignored.

Almost all sources have biases and perspectives that shape the information they contain (and also determine what facts and ideas they exclude). Sometimes those biases are apparent. It doesn't take long to realize, for example, that the editorial pages of some newspapers tend to be liberal in their politics and others conservative. It may be harder to detect similar biases in scholarly journals, popular magazines, or news services on the Web, but be assured that they are there. If you are in doubt about the representative range of the sources you have selected, consult with various instructors or librarians—being aware that they, too, have points of view that may influence their advice.

Representatives of two points on the political spectrum offer thought-provoking online assessments of media bias. Check *Fairness & Accuracy in Reporting* for a progressive take on media issues; see the *Media Research Center* for a conservative perspective.

5 Consider the integrity of online information. If you remember that you have to cite sources in your own research project, you have one practical way of judging the trustworthiness of some online materials. A Web site useful for research will state its purpose clearly and provide basic bibliographical information: it will have a comprehensible site name and will identify its authors, participants, sponsors, dates of publication, and sources for data or information.

Checklist 45.1 Evaluating a Web Site

- Is the site sponsored by a reputable group you can identify?
- Do the authors of the site give evidence of their credentials?
- Is the site conveniently searchable?
- Is information in the site logically arranged?
- Is the site easy to navigate?
- Does the site provide an email address for questions?
- Is the site updated regularly or properly maintained?
- Does the site archive older information?
- Is there evidence that the content of the site is affected by commercial sponsorship?

Taking Control

Avoid unreliable sources

As a writer, you might take a chance with the topic of a paper or its organization, but there's no good reason ever to risk using a questionable source. When you have doubts about the merit of a book, the authority of an article, or the credibility of an electronic resource, ask someone more knowledgeable for help—a teacher, a librarian, or an expert in the field. They will quickly recognize when you are about to build a project on outdated, irrelevant, or erroneous materials, or they will at least raise the kinds of questions that might enable you to make better choices. Don't be embarrassed about asking.

CHAPTER

46 How Do You Use Sources Responsibly?

Now that you have found the best sources for your project, you must use the information in them. Your methods for handling these research materials will vary, but three techniques make sense for getting the most from them: annotating, summarizing, and paraphrasing. These methods will also help to assure that you avoid problems with plagiarism and collusion—issues of growing concern, especially now that sources have become more easily copied and shared in electronic form. This chapter offers you guidelines for managing sources successfully and honestly.

46a How do you annotate research materials?

Once you have evaluated a source (see Chapter 45), read it carefully, attaching comments, questions, and reactions directly to the text to mark information worth noting and recalling. Such annotation is difficult when you are reading library books and materials; in these cases, record your reactions in notes, summaries, and paraphrases (see Section 46b). But much research material today is photocopied, downloaded, or read online—and these media support more direct forms of annotation. See Chapter 8 for additional advice on critically assessing and annotating reading material.

Many researchers use highlighter pens to tag important passages in photocopied materials. But be sure to attach a marginal comment to any section you highlight in this way, to explain its importance or record your reaction. For electronic files, you can record your reactions by using both the highlighting and commenting features of word-processing programs. If such annotations are thoughtful and entirely in your own words, you might later incorporate them directly into your paper or project. Following is an example of a source that has been annotated in its margins. (The same article is both summarized and paraphrased in Section 46b.)

This op-ed piece originally appeared in the *New York Times* on June 5, 2002, shortly after the New York State Department of Education admitted that, to avoid offending students, it had been censoring works of literature included in a standard examination.

EDUCATIONAL INSENSITIVITY
By Diane Ravitch

An enterprising parent of a high school senior recently discovered that the literary texts on the New York Regents examinations had been expurgated. Excerpts from the writings of many prominent authors were doctored, without their knowledge or permission, to delete references to religion, profanity, sex, alcohol, or other potentially troublesome topics.

Original audience was readers of the New York Times, America's paper of record

Find out more about NY Regents Exams.

The story was a huge embarrassment to the New York State Education Department, which prepares the examinations, and yesterday Richard P. Mills, the state education commissioner, ordered the practice stopped. From now on, all literary passages used on state tests will be unchanged except for length.

What's the issue now if the policy has been changed?

Mr. Mills is to be commended for this new policy. But the dimensions of this absurd practice reach far beyond the borders of New York, and there are many culprits. Censorship of tests and textbooks is not merely widespread: across the nation, it has become institutionalized.

Ravitch's claim

For decades, American publishers have quietly trimmed sexual and religious allusions from their textbooks and tests. When publishers assemble reading books, they keep a wary eye on states like California, Texas, and Florida, where textbooks are adopted for the entire state and any hint of controversy can prevent a book's placement on the state's list. In Texas, Florida, and other southern states, the religious right objects to any stories that introduce fantasy, witchcraft, the occult, sex or religious practices different from its own. In California, no textbook can win adoption unless it meets the state's strict demands for gender balance, multicultural representation, and avoids mention of unhealthy foods, drugs or alcohol.

Can both right and left be responsible for censorship?

Over the past several decades, the nation's testing industry has embraced censorship. In almost every state, tests are closely scrutinized in an official process known as a bias and sensitivity review. This procedure was created in the late 1960s and early 1970s to scrutinize questions for any hint of racial or gender bias. Over the years, every test development company in the nation has established a bias and sensitivity review process to ensure that test questions do not contain anything that might upset students and prevent them from showing their true abilities on a test. Now these reviews routinely expurgate references to social problems, politics, disobedient children, or any other potentially controversial topic.

Looks like good intentions gone haywire. Shouldn't good literature challenge students?

This is the rationale now used within the testing industry to delete references to any topic that someone might find objectionable. As a top official in one of the major testing companies told me: "If anyone objects to a test question, we delete it. Period."

This self-censorship is hardly a secret. Every major publisher of educational materials uses "bias guidelines," which list hundreds of words and images that are banned or avoided. Words like "brotherhood" and "mankind" have been banished. A story about mountain climbing may be excluded because it favors test-takers who live near mountains over those who don't. Older people may not be portrayed walking with canes or sitting in rocking chairs.

Is Ravitch being dramatic in this or are her examples real?

I serve on the board of a federal testing agency, the National Assessment Governing Board, which is directly responsible for reviewing all test questions on the National Assessment of Educational Progress. We have learned that bias and sensitivity rules are subject to expansive interpretations. Once reviewers proposed to eliminate a reading passage about Mount Rushmore because the monument offends Lakota Indians, who consider the Black Hills of South Dakota a sacred site.

This censorship is now standard practice in the testing industry and in educational publishing. One way to end it is to expose the practice to public scrutiny, forcing officials like Mr. Mills to abandon it. Another way, adopted by the National Assessment Governing Board, is to review every deletion proposed by those applying bias and sensitivity standards to determine whether it passes the test of common sense. I would also recommend that whenever material is deleted from a literary passage in a test, the omission should be indicated with ellipses.

Proposals to solve censorship in schools and textbooks

The bias and sensitivity review process, as it has recently evolved, is an embarrassment to the educational publishing industry. It may satisfy the demands of the religious right (in censoring topics) and of the politically correct left (in censoring language). But it robs our children of their cultural heritage and their right to read—free of censorship.

Ravitch's final claim—and a possible quotation.

Diane Ravitch, a historian of education at New York University, is writing a book about censorship in the educational publishing industry.

What else has she written? What are her politics?

June 5, 2002

46b How do you summarize and paraphrase a source?

Summarizing and paraphrasing represent different ways of restating material you have read.

A **summary** captures the gist of a source or some portion of it, boiling it down to a few words or sentences. Summaries tend to be short. They extract only what is immediately relevant from an article, book chapter, or other source. When summarizing a source, first identify its key facts or ideas, think about their relationships, and then assemble these ideas into a concise, coherent statement about the whole piece. Be sure that what you've written is detailed enough to stand on its own and will make sense several weeks after you examined the material. Of course, any summary should be entirely in your own words.

A **paraphrase** usually treats a complete source in much greater detail than does a summary. When paraphrasing a work, you seek to report its key information or arguments, point by point, in your own words. An effective paraphrase will meet all of the following conditions.

- The paraphrase reflects the structure of the original piece.
- The paraphrase reflects the ideas of the original author, not your reflections on them.
- Each important fact or direct quotation is accompanied by a specific page number from the source when possible.
- The material is entirely in your own words—except for clearly marked quotations.

Practically speaking, the distinction between a summary and a paraphrase is often less important than simply getting the information you need for a project. In taking notes, you'll often find yourself switching between summary and paraphrase, depending on the level of detail you need.

Following are summaries and paraphrases of the article "Educational Insensitivity" by Diane Ravitch reprinted and annotated in Section 46a. To prepare a summary, you would identify the key claim and supporting elements and put them into a concise restatement of the overall argument. The summary should make sense on its own, forming a complete statement you might use later in the project itself. But don't be surprised if you go through several versions of that sentence before you come up with one that satisfies you.

EFFECTIVE SUMMARY #1

Diane Ravitch, a professor at New York University, argues in the *New York Times* (5 June 2002) that educators and textbook authors should not cave in to the demands of the political right or left to censor the topics and the language of literary works because such editing cheats students of their cultural heritage.

EFFECTIVE SUMMARY #2	Diane Ravitch, a professor at New York University, argues in the *New York Times* (5 June 2002) that attempts by educators and textbook publishers to avoid objectionable topics or language are depriving students of their right to read uncensored literature.

How can something as simple as a summary go wrong? There are a number of ways. You might, for example, make the summary too succinct and leave out crucial details. Such a summary scribbled on a note card might be useless when, days later, you try to make sense of it.

INEFFECTIVE SUMMARY	She argues that it's wrong to censor literature. Both the left and right want it.

On the other hand, your summary might fail because it misses the central point of a piece by focusing on details not relevant to the argument. Useful in a different context, these facts are misleading if they don't capture the essence of what the author wrote.

INACCURATE SUMMARY	Diane Ravitch, a professor at New York University, knows about censorship in education because she serves on the National Assessment Governing Board, which reviews questions on tests.

Yet another danger lies in using the actual words of the original author in your summary. If these unacknowledged borrowings make their way into your project itself without both quotation marks and documentation, you are guilty of plagiarism. (See Section 24b.) In the example following, language taken directly and inappropriately from Ravitch's op-ed is underlined.

PLAGIARIZED SUMMARY	Diane Ravitch, a professor at New York University, argues in the *New York Times* (5 June 2002) that the expurgation of literary works by educators and textbook publishers <u>robs our children of their cultural heritage and their right to read—free of censorship</u>.

You can see how you might easily slip these words into the body of a paper, forgetting that you didn't write them yourself. To avoid plagiarism, the safest practice is *always* to use your own words in summaries.

A paraphrase of "Educational Insensitivity" would be substantially longer than a summary because a researcher would expect to use the information differently, probably referring to the source in much greater detail. Here's one possible paraphrase of Ravitch's op-ed article.

EFFECTIVE PARAPHRASE Responding to criticism that it had edited sensitive and controversial passages from literary works on its Regents examinations, the New York State Education Department announced that it would abandon the practice. But Diane Ravitch argues in a *New York Times* op-ed piece (5 June 2002) that the practice of trimming controversial materials from educational materials is so common that it has become institutionalized. Those on the political right demand that morally offensive topics and ideas be cut from exams and textbooks; those on the political left demand gender and ethnic balance. Standardized tests are now routinely subject to reviews for bias and insensitivity, as are other educational materials. Ravitch argues that this embarrassing practice should be ended by letting the public know what is happening and by carefully reviewing any standards applied to educational materials. Censorship robs students of their cultural right to read literature as it was written.

You'll notice that this paraphrase covers all the major points in the editorial in the same order as in the original. It also borrows none of the author's language. With proper documentation, any part of the paraphrase could become part of a final research project without a need for quotation marks.

How can paraphrases go wrong? Various problems can make a paraphrase inaccurate or unusable. A paraphrase should accurately reflect the thinking of the original author. Reserve your own comments and asides for annotations or other separate notes so that you don't confuse your ideas with those of your sources. Consider how the following paraphrase might misreport the views of Diane Ravitch if the researcher later forgets that the underlined comments in the example should have been set out as personal notes or annotations.

INACCURATE PARAPHRASE Responding to criticism that it had edited sensitive and controversial passages from literary works on its Regents examinations, the New York State Education Department announced that it would abandon the practice even though one could argue that many students benefited from the policy. But Diane Ravitch argues in a *New York Times* op-ed piece (5 June 2002) that trimming controversial materials from educational materials is so common that it is institutionalized. Those on the political right, who probably don't want their children exposed to any challenging ideas, demand that morally offensive topics. . . .

Your reactions to the op-ed might be legitimate, but they don't represent an accurate paraphrase of the original article.

A paraphrase also should not reorganize or improve on the structure or argument of the original piece. For example, the following paraphrase doesn't actually add material to Ravitch's editorial, but it rearranges its information radically.

INACCURATE PARAPHRASE Children in school should not be robbed of their cultural heritage by educators and publishers worried that reading what literary authors actually wrote might harm their tender sensitivities. But that's what is happening all across the country according to Diane Ravitch, a member of the National Assessment Governing Board, a group that reviews questions posed on the National Assessment of Educational Progress. Ms. Ravitch reports that the New York State Education Department has quietly gotten into the business of censoring the literary works that appeared on its Regents examinations. This practice has sparked a controversy about how much censorship is occurring in education today as a result of pressure from both the right and the left to advance their political agendas in our nation's schools.

The most dangerous and academically dishonest sort of paraphrase is one in which a researcher borrows the ideas, structure, and details of a source wholesale, changing a few words here and there in order to claim originality. This sort of paraphrase is plagiarism even if the material is documented in the research project; writers can't just tweak a few words in their sources and claim the resulting material as their own work. (See Section 46c.)

PLAGIARIZED PARAPHRASE An inquisitive parent of a high school student figured out recently that the works of literature used on the New York Regents examinations had been cut and edited. Passages from the novels and poems of many famous writers were changed, without their permission or knowledge, to remove all mentions of religion, drugs, sexuality, and other such offensive subjects.

The story embarrassed the New York State Education Department, which creates the tests, and so the state education commissioner ordered a stop to the practice. Henceforth, all literary passages used on New York tests will be unchanged except for length. . . .

You'll see the fault very readily if you compare these plagiarized paragraphs with the opening paragraphs in Ravitch's original editorial.

46c How do you avoid plagiarism?

The Council of Writing Program Administrators (WPA) defines plagiarism as follows: "In an instructional setting, plagiarism occurs when a writer deliberately uses someone else's language, ideas, or other original (not common-knowledge) material without acknowledging its source." Plagiarism is an act of dishonesty that schools punish sternly. But the WPA is very careful to distinguish between writers who knowingly cheat and those who are guilty of no more than using sources carelessly or incorrectly. The former is an ethical failing; the latter an academic problem that can be addressed by better information and instruction.

You may appreciate that taking the words and ideas of others and claiming them as your own is wrong. But if you're accustomed to downloading music or have heard slogans such "Information wants to be free," you may have developed your own questions about the boundaries of intellectual property. You know that electronic technologies have made it remarkably easy to locate (and copy) texts and information. Not infrequently, you are under a lot of pressure to turn in work on time. And so you could also find yourself in circumstances that lead to plagiarism or collusion. Here's how to avoid those thorny situations.

1 Give yourself sufficient time to develop projects. If you wait until the last minute to compose a paper, especially one that requires information from numerous sources, you may find yourself tempted to copy paragraphs rather than to write your own. Sure, you had intended to cite the borrowed material, but under the pressure of a deadline, it's all too easy to ignore details such as notes and quotation marks. Avoid this muddle by creating realistic schedules for your major projects (see Section 43c) and then sticking to them. You'll eliminate a great deal of anxiety, too, if your writing process includes time to get responses from peers, writing center tutors, or instructors. Plagiarism is far less likely when you work with people who care about you and your work.

2 Have confidence in your own abilities. Plagiarism sometimes occurs when writers don't have sufficient faith in their own skills. Using sources responsibly can seem like walking through a minefield. But handling sources well is not really so complicated. With just a little practice, you can learn to paraphrase and summarize reliably (see Section 46b), and then you won't have to worry as much about blurring the lines between another author's words and your own. Similarly, using and formatting quotations is a matter of mastering half a dozen conventions (see Chapter 47). Don't let your anxieties about documentation lead you to consider a quick copy-and-paste fix from an online paper. Errors in documentation are forgivable; cheating is not.

3 Learn what you need to document. Writers sometimes exaggerate the task of documentation because they don't understand the concept of **common knowledge.** If you fall in that camp, review Section 49b, "How Do You Document a Research Paper?" It runs just a few pages. Understand, too, that the standards for plagiarism in academia vary from those in other areas of society. What you see in newspapers or on blogs doesn't apply to school. There are even disparities in how plagiarism is defined in different cultures: in some traditions, quoting material directly is a sign of respect. Resolve any doubts you may have about the definition of plagiarism with your instructor. Writing centers can give you good advice too. It's far better to raise questions about your handling of source materials in a project *before* you turn it in; afterward is too late.

4 Don't take shortcuts with documentation. There are a surprising number of myths about plagiarism. To avoid falling prey to them, follow these guidelines:

- You can't avoid a charge of plagiarism just by altering every tenth or fifth word in a source: you commit plagiarism just as much when you copy ideas as when you take someone else's words.
- You must use *both* quotation marks and an appropriate note when you quote directly. Quotation marks alone would not tell your readers what your source was. A note alone would acknowledge that you are using a source, but it would not indicate that the words in a given portion of your paper are not entirely your own.

If this sounds complicated, it really isn't. Chapters 50–52 provide the full details on how to document papers in three different professional styles: Modern Language Association (MLA); American Psychological Association (APA); and Chicago Manual of Style (CMS).

5 Don't copy and paste without giving credit. You may occasionally feel tempted to copy and paste material from the Web without documenting it, thinking that no one owns or can trace that material. But worthwhile sources on the Web do usually belong to specific authors or institutions that must be cited. Material that you can't attribute to specific authorities or reputable groups probably isn't worth using in a paper. Moreover, instructors can usually tell when the style of your paper changes noticeably at a cut-and-paste insert, or suddenly seems more technically sophisticated than what preceded it. They can also trace most sources that you yourself have located on the Web: they have access to the same tools. So copying and pasting without citation just isn't smart, and it is pointless. If you *have* found worthwhile material on the Web, why not simply summarize or quote it as necessary? That way, you'll get credit for using sources well.

6 Don't get involved in collusion. Very good students with the best of intentions may find themselves editing their friends' papers far too much. It's perfectly fine to offer advice and suggestions about topics, organization, and style (the kinds of issues discussed in Section 4e) to people who request your help. But if you start making substantive changes to a colleague's paper itself, rewriting portions of it or editing it heavily, you may find yourself involved in collusion—that is, helping another student to cheat. Is the peer revision you do in class much the same process since it, too, involves reading another student's paper and making comments? Not at all. The point of peer revision is to offer suggestions for revisions that your classmates must then do on their own. Peer editing is not writing or rewriting someone else's work. See Section 5d for detailed tips on effectively responding to a peer's writing.

7 Don't miss the opportunity to learn. Who gets hurt by plagiarism? You do—*for real.* When taking a writing course, you have an opportunity to develop a craft necessary for college and beyond. Skilled writers have an edge in getting what they want in life. You don't want to miss the chance to acquire such a powerful tool by plagiarizing your way through writing courses.

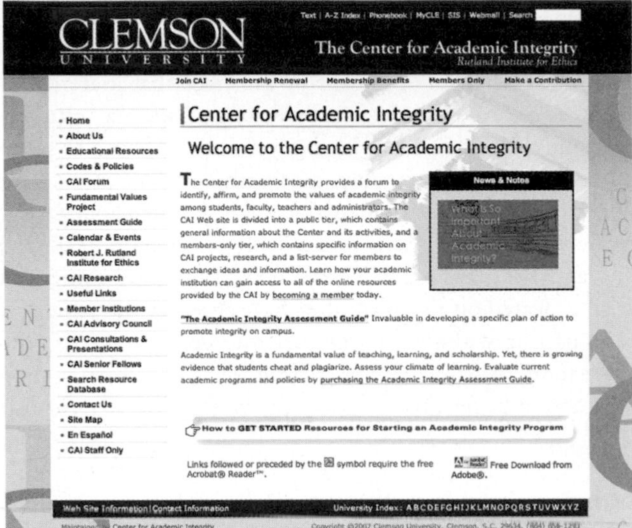

The Center for Academic Integrity at Clemson University is just one of many educational Web sites that discuss the definition and terms of scholastic dishonesty. Spend some time browsing through the resources on this or similar sites. Then discuss your findings with a group of classmates: What new information or ideas did you learn? What questions or issues do you still have about academic honesty in your own work? Don't hesitate to ask an instructor for further advice on this topic.

CHAPTER

47 How Do You Manage Quotations Effectively?

The sources you choose for a project reveal much about the quality of your research and your understanding of a subject. When you begin to write, you'll want to build your project from a variety of these materials, clearly identified and documented, so that readers know who is responsible for which claims and ideas. Much of the source material you present in a paper will be either summarized or paraphrased (see Section 46b); other material will be quoted directly (see Section 47a). Both types of material need to be introduced appropriately so that readers understand their authority and significance and so that the paper reads smoothly.

47a How do you choose quotations?

Every quotation in a paper should contribute something significant to your project. Never use quotations to avoid putting ideas in your own words or to pad your work. Neither should you just string together quotations without significant commentary and analysis of your own to explain the connection to your thesis. Use quotations for reasons such as the following.

- To present an idea that is stated especially well in a source
- To show what others think about a subject
- To emphasize important facts or concepts
- To add color, power, or character to your argument or report
- To show a range of opinion
- To clarify a difficult or contested claim
- To demonstrate the complexity of an issue
- To emphasize a point

Take Control

47b How do you introduce quotations and source materials?

Don't just drop a quotation into a paper and expect it to speak for itself. Instead, introduce readers to any material you borrow word for word from sources by supplying a context or *frame* for the language in quotation marks. Such explanations can be relatively simple—typically, you just identify the author, speaker, or institution responsible for the words. But you may offer more information, as needed, such as the credentials of your source or the title of a work quoted. Note how much information this writer for *Popular Mechanics* provides to explain the credentials of the person he quotes in an essay about running shoes:

> Shoe companies design shoes for the vast majority—the 80 percent of heel-to-toe runners—and their goal is to prevent excessive rolling movement of the foot. "There are people who will pronate a lot but will not get injured," **says Keith Williams, a senior lecturer at the University of California, Davis, who has consulted in the footwear industry for 30 years.** "Then there are those who will pronate a little and get injured." To play it safe, shoe companies bulk up the heel, the arch and extend the sides of shoes, which stabilizes the foot as it rolls from heel to toe.
>
> —Tyghe Trimble, "The Running Shoe Debate"

Introductions or frames can *precede, follow,* or *interrupt* the quoted or borrowed material. The introduction need not even be in the same sentence as the quotation; it may be part of the surrounding paragraph. Here are examples of ways that borrowed material can be introduced or explained.

- *Explanation precedes borrowed material:*

> **In 1896, Woodrow Wilson, who would become Princeton's president in 1902, declared,** "It is not learning but the spirit of service that will give a college a place in the public annals of the nation."
>
> —Ernest L. Boyer

- *Explanation follows borrowed material:*

> "One reason you may have more colds if you hold back tears is that, when you're under stress, your body puts out steroids which affect your

immune system and reduce your resistance to disease," **Dr. Broomfield comments.**

—Barbara Lang Stern

- *Explanation interrupts borrowed material:*

  "Whatever happens," **he [Karl Marx] wrote grimly to Engels,** "I hope the bourgeoisie as long as they exist will have cause to remember my carbuncles."

  —Paul Johnson

- *Surrounding sentences explain borrowed material:*

  In the meantime, [Luis] Jimenez was experimenting with three-dimensional form. "Perhaps because of the experience of working in the sign shop, I realized early on that I wanted to do it all—paint, draw, work with wood, metal, clay." **His images were those of 1960s pop culture, chosen for their familiarity and shock value.**

  —Chiori Santiago

- *Borrowed material integrated within passage:*

  The study concludes that a faulty work ethic is not responsible for the decline in our productivity; quite the contrary, the study identifies "a widespread commitment among U.S. workers to improve productivity" **and suggests that** "there are large reservoirs of potential upon which management can draw to improve performance and increase productivity."

  —Daniel Yankelovich

When you summarize or paraphrase (rather than quote) material from a source, you should also introduce it when you use it in your paper. The frames you provide may vary according to the style of documentation you are using; we show examples in MLA and APA style here.

- *Explanation precedes borrowed material* (MLA):

  In *Freakonomics*, Steven D. Levitt and Stephen J. Dubner observe that there seems to be little correlation between children's success on standardized tests and whether they watch television (168).

- *Explanation follows borrowed material* (APA):

  Contrary to experts who predicted a sterile future, ours is an age of expressive and inventive design, **Postrel (2003) argues.**

- *Explanation interrupts borrowed material* (MLA):

Federal standards for meat processing are so lax, ***Fast Food Nation*** **author Eric Schlosser claims**, that consumers should regard ground beef as a hazardous material (221).

The basic principle for introducing borrowed material is simple: either name (directly or indirectly) the author, the speaker, or the work the passage is from, or explain why the words you are quoting are significant. Many phrases of introduction or *attribution* are available (see Chart 47.1 for some examples; there are many more). Note that the verb of attribution you choose can shape the way readers perceive the quotation that follows. Compare your reactions to the following statements, which differ only in their verb of attribution.

Benson **reports** that high school test scores have dropped again.

Benson **laments** that high school test scores have dropped again.

Benson **complains** that high school test scores have dropped again.

Chart 47.1 Common Verbs of Attribution

accept	allege	demonstrate	insist	say
add	argue	deny	mention	show
admit	believe	disagree	posit	state
affirm	confirm	emphasize	propose	verify

Taking Control

Frame quotations effectively

You do need to introduce sources *smoothly* and *unobtrusively*. The best way to gain that skill is probably to study how scholars and professional writers frame quotations in their work. Take several published pieces of writing that use lots of sources and note every place where the writers introduce words and ideas they attribute to others. You'll likely be surprised by how varied the form and style of introductions can be, and how helpful they are in furnishing information to readers. You'll come to appreciate, too, how frames can strongly influence the way you read borrowed material. Some frames strive for neutrality (in a scholarly article, for example); others may let you know immediately where a writer stands—and, perhaps, how he or she expects you to interpret a passage. In many cases, the lead-in to a quotation can be as influential as the source material itself.

47c How may you modify direct quotations?

You must always quote accurately, and must never omit words or phrases just to make sources seem to support your thesis. You can, however, use the following techniques to make quotations flow naturally with the style of your paper. These techniques preserve the integrity of quotations while giving you some flexibility in their use.

1 Tailor your language so that direct quotations fit into the grammar of your sentences. To create a seamless merger, you may have to modify the words you use to introduce a quotation, or carefully modify the quotation itself with ellipses (see Section 38b-1) or with additions made inside brackets (see Section 39b-1).

CLUMSY As long ago as 2004, David Brooks complained in the *New York Times* that, as the United Nations passed one ineffective resolution after another, "And, meanwhile, 1.2 million people were driven from their homes in Darfur."

REVISED As long ago as 2004, David Brooks complained in the *New York Times* that, as the United Nations passed one ineffective resolution after another, "1.2 million people were driven from their homes in Darfur."

CLUMSY The chemical capsaicin makes chili hot: "it is so hot it is used to make antidog and antimugger sprays" (Bork 184).

REVISED Capsaicin, the chemical that makes chili hot, is so strong that "it is used to make antidog and antimugger sprays" (Bork 184).

2 Use ellipses to show where you have cut material from direct quotations. Sometimes, only part of a long quotation may suit your essay; ellipses (three *spaced* periods: . . .) enable you to present just that appropriate portion and no more. Ellipses in the passage below indicate that the source being cited is not used in its entirety.

> Although working with any part of an original Scripture text is difficult, Barry Hoberman, author of "Translating the Bible," describes the text of the Old Testament as "the stuff of scholarly nightmares." He explains that while "the entire New Testament was written within fifty to a hundred years, the books of the Old Testament were composed and edited over a period of about a thousand years. . . . The oldest portions . . . are probably a group of poems that appear . . . to date from roughly the twelfth and eleventh centuries B.C."

When an ellipsis occurs in the middle of a sentence, leave a space before the first period and after the third one. You don't need ellipses, however, every time you break into a sentence. When readers encounter a quotation that begins with a small letter, they'll assume that introductory phrases or clauses have been cut, so no ellipsis mark is needed. When they see a quotation that begins with a capital letter, they'll assume that you are quoting a complete sentence, and, again, no ellipses are needed. You need an ellipsis mark at the opening of a quotation only when a capital letter in a proper noun (or the pronoun *I*) might lead readers to believe that you're quoting a complete sentence when, in fact, you are not. Compare the following examples.

> According to Richard Bernstein, "The plain and inescapable fact is that the derived Western European culture of American life [has] produced the highest degree of prosperity in the conditions of the greatest freedom ever known on planet Earth" (11).

> According to Richard Bernstein, ". . . American life [has] produced the highest degree of prosperity in the conditions of the greatest freedom ever known on planet Earth" (11).

Whenever you use an ellipsis, be sure your shortened quotation still reflects accurately the meaning of the uncut passage. For more about using ellipses correctly, see Section 38b.

47d What conventions govern direct quotations?

Following are some specific conventions that apply to direct quotations. Quotation marks themselves (" ") do more than set off direct quotations, so you may want to review Section 38a to appreciate all their uses. In that section, you'll also find guidelines that explain where to place quotation marks when they meet up with other punctuation marks in sentences.

1 Use "[sic]" to indicate an obvious error copied faithfully from a source. Quotations must be copied, word by word, from your source—errors and all. To show that you have copied a passage faithfully, place the expression *sic* (the Latin word for "thus" or "so") in brackets one space after any mistake.

> Mr. Vincent's letter went on: "I would have preferred a younger bride, but I decided to marry the old window [sic] anyway."

If *sic* can be placed outside the quotation itself, it appears between parentheses, not brackets.

> Molly's paper was titled "King Leer" (sic).

2 Place prose quotations shorter than four typed lines (MLA) or forty words (APA) between quotation marks.

> In Utilitarianism (1863), John Stuart Mill declares, "It is better to be Socrates dissatisfied than a pig satisfied."

3 Indent more than three lines of poetry (MLA). Up to three lines of poetry may be handled just like a prose passage, with slashes marking the separate lines. Leave a space before and after the slashes. Quotation marks are used.

> As death approaches, Cleopatra grows in both grandeur and dignity: "Husband, I come! / Now to that name my courage prove my title! / I am fire and air" (5.2.287-89).

More than three lines of poetry are set off and indented 10 spaces, and quotation marks are not used. (If the lines of poetry are unusually long, you may indent fewer than 10 spaces.) Be sure to copy the poetry accurately, right down to the punctuation.

> Among the most famous lines in English literature are those that open William Blake's "The Tyger":
>
> Tyger tyger, burning bright,
> In the forests of the night;
> What immortal hand or eye,
> Could frame thy fearful symmetry? (1–4)

4 Indent any prose quotation longer than four typed lines (MLA) or forty words (APA). MLA form recommends an indention of one inch, or 10 spaces if you are using a typewriter; APA form requires 5 spaces. Quotation marks are *not* used around the indented material. If the quotation extends beyond a single paragraph, the first lines of subsequent paragraphs are indented an additional quarter inch, or 3 typed spaces (MLA); or 5 spaces (APA). In typed papers, the indented material—like the rest of the essay—is double spaced.

You may indent passages of fewer than four lines when you want them to have special emphasis. But don't do this with every short quotation or your paper will look choppy. See pages 703–713 (MLA documentation) and 779–784 (CMS documentation) for examples of student papers that incorporate block quotations.

CHAPTER

48 How Do You Produce a Final Draft?

Because academic research projects represent a first level of serious professional work, they must meet exacting standards as you bring them to completion. These requirements vary from discipline to discipline, but the principles and concerns examined in this section apply to most college research papers and projects. (See also Chapter 5.)

48a Is the organization solid?

In many cases, you'll find yourself refining and narrowing the scope of your research project throughout the writing process, as you develop a structure that reinforces clear, though not necessarily simple, points. Your job is to create a framework that will make your project an effective response to the original assignment. See Section 5a-6 for more tips on improving the organization of a paper.

1 Narrow or qualify your claim. The shape you give your project will depend on what your thesis promises. You'll want your thesis to make a distinct and provable claim, and then you will need to follow through with the appropriate support and evidence. Here's an example of such a progression.

ORIGINAL CLAIM

Zoos promote cruelty to animals.

CLAIM SPECIFIED AND LIMITED BY RESEARCH

Confining large marine mammals in sea parks for public amusement is a form of cruelty to animals.

COMMITMENTS

- Find legal/popular definitions for "cruelty to animals."
- Define specific criteria for "cruelty."

- Examine what experts say about the condition of animals in marine parks, or do fieldwork in such a park.
- Find statistics on animal health in marine parks.
- Find expert opinions on both sides of the issue.
- Show that conditions in marine parks meet (or do not meet) criteria for "cruelty to animals."

2 Test your organization. Organizing a sizable paper or project is rarely an easy job. For the draft of a long paper, you may want to check the structure using a method such as the following:

- **Underline the topic idea, or thesis, in your draft.** It should be clearly stated somewhere in the first few paragraphs.
- **Underline just the first sentence in each subsequent paragraph.** If the first sentence is very short or closely tied to the second, underline the first two sentences.
- **Read the underlined sentences straight through as if they formed an essay in themselves.** Ask whether each sentence advances or explains the main point or thesis statement. If the sentences—taken together—read coherently, chances are the paper is well organized.
- **If the underlined sentences don't make sense, examine whether the paragraphs are clearly related to the topic.** If the ideas there really do not develop your thesis in some way, delete the whole paragraph. If the ideas are related, consider how to revise the paragraph to make the connection clearer to readers.
- **Test your conclusion against your introduction.** Sometimes the conclusions of essays contradict their opening paragraphs because of changes that occurred as the paper developed. Revise as necessary.

48b Is the format correct?

Whether you are reporting your research in a conventional paper, on a Web site, or through some other less traditional vehicle, you want the presentation to be effective. Here we focus chiefly on research papers, but you can find advice about crafting other types of projects in Part 4, "Design and Shape of Writing."

1 Pay attention to the format of work you submit. Be sure a paper is submitted on good-quality white paper. Print on only one side of the sheet, double-spacing the body of your essay. Keep fonts simple and use boldface rarely, perhaps to highlight important headings.

Specifications for MLA and APA papers are given in Sections 50c and 51c, respectively. These guidelines, which explain where page numbers go, the widths of margins, and the placement of headings, can be applied even to papers that don't need to follow a specific professional style.

2 Insert tables and figures as needed. Use graphics whenever they help readers understand your ideas better than words alone can.

MLA format requires that you label tables (columns of data) and figures (pictures, illustrations, or maps), number them, and briefly identify what they illustrate. For a table, place the label *Table* followed by an Arabic number above the item and flush left; the title or description of the table follows on a separate line. Any source information is listed under the table.

Table 21.1

First-Year Student Applications by Region

	Fall 2008	Fall 2009	Difference	Percent Change
Texas	12,022	11,590	432	+4
Out-of-state	2,121	2,058	63	+3
Foreign	756	673	83	+11

For a figure or image, the label *Figure* appears (usually abbreviated *Fig.*) flush left beneath the item, followed by an Arabic number and a caption on the same line. To point to an image from within the text of an essay, use the following form: (see fig. 7).

When writing a paper in APA style, check the detailed coverage of figures and tables in the sixth edition of the *Publication Manual of the American Psychological Association*.

Fig. 7 Mountain bike.

3 Be consistent with headings. MLA style (described in detail in Chapter 50) provides fairly open standards for headings. Titles of MLA papers are ordinarily centered on the first page of an essay and headings appear in the text, flush with the left-hand margin. If you descend to a second level, you'll have to distinguish second-level heads by numbering or lettering them or by setting them off typographically (usually by variations in capitalization or underlining). MLA style leaves it to you to decide how you will handle such choices, but in all cases, you must keep the headings clean, unobtrusive, and consistent. Here is one way of handling headings as they might appear in a moderately long MLA-style paper on mountain biking.

Mountain Biking and the Environment	Title
The Mountain Bike	1st level
History of Mountain Biking	1st level
Mountain Bikes and the Environment	1st level
Trail Damage	2nd level
Conflicts with Hikers	2nd level
Mountain Bikes and Responsible Riding	1st level

APA style (described in Chapter 51) is more specific about headings. For major APA papers or articles you submit for publication, consult the sixth edition of the *Publication Manual of the American Psychological Association.*

4 Include all the components your project requires. Before you submit a project, reread the specifications of either the instructor or the professional society whose guidelines you are following. A research paper typically follows a specific order:

- Title page (not recommended in MLA; required in APA)
- Outline (optional; begins on its own page; requires separate title page)
- Abstract (optional, but common in APA; usually on its own page)
- Body of the essay (Arabic pagination begins with body of the essay in MLA; in APA, Arabic pagination begins with title page)
- Content or bibliographic notes (optional)
- Works Cited/References (begins on its own page separate from the body of the essay and any content or bibliographic notes)

5 Submit your project professionally. Whether you've written a paper, designed a brochure, or created a Web site, be sure the work meets appropriate standards. Examine what you've produced to see that everything looks professional: the writing is sharp and correct, the images are crisp and labeled, page numbers are in the right place, any links are operative, and the documentation is solid.

Don't overdo it. For a paper, bind the pages modestly with a paper clip. Nothing more elaborate is needed, unless an instructor asks you to place the essay (still clipped) in a folder along with all the materials you used in developing it. As a general rule, keep the bells and whistles (and gaudy colors) to a functional minimum.

Checklist 48.1 Research Project Requirements

- Have you placed your name, your instructor's name, the date, and the course name on the first or title page?
- Is the title centered? Are its major words (see Section 41b-5) capitalized? Your title should not be underlined or appear between quotation marks.
- Did you number the pages? Are they in the right order?
- Have you used quotation marks and parentheses correctly and in pairs? (The closing quotation mark or parenthesis is often forgotten.)

(Continued)

Research Project Requirements *(Continued)*

- Have you placed quotation marks around all direct quotations that are shorter than four lines?
- Have you indented all direct quotations of four or more typed lines (MLA) or of forty words or more (APA)?
- Have you remembered that indented quotations are *not* placed between quotation marks?
- Did you introduce all direct quotations with some identification of their author, source, or significance?
- Did you use the correct form for parenthetical notes?
- Have you handled titles correctly, italicizing the titles of books and putting the titles of articles between quotation marks?
- Did you include a Works Cited or References list? Is your list of works cited alphabetized? Did you indent the entries correctly?

PART VIII

DOCUMENTATION

CHAPTER

49 How Do You Document a Research Paper?

In writing a research project you will create a dialogue among the many sources you have read, summarized, and paraphrased (see Chapter 46). But readers will need to know which ideas and claims are your own and which should be credited to those sources. They may also want to assess the quality of your research and pursue it further, beginning with the materials you have examined. For these reasons, you need to acknowledge the sources you have used in academic or professional projects conscientiously, honestly, and gracefully, using an appropriate system of documentation. Presented in subsequent chapters are documentation systems of the Modern Language Association (MLA), the American Psychological Association (APA), and *The Chicago Manual of Style* (CMS). This chapter examines the general principles for acknowledging and using sources.

49a What are documentation styles?

Documentation refers to the forms devised to keep track of sources used in a project—typically some type of notes (endnotes, footnotes, parenthetical notes) and a full bibliography. Systems of documentation offer detailed models for handling a variety of sources, from traditional books and articles to newer electronic media. In high school and college, most student writers learn the documentation procedures established by the Modern Language Association (MLA), but different fields and majors observe their own rules about documentation and style. We list various style guides in Chart 49.1.

Style here refers to guidelines for handling the myriad details of printed or online texts. Major newspapers and publishers, for example, will often have in-house "style sheets" describing the conventions to be followed by writers working for those companies. Such style sheets are designed to answer questions such as the following: Which words in a title are capitalized? How are words hyphenated or spelled? How are dates expressed? How are figures and illustrations treated? A published example of such a style sheet is *The New York Times Manual of Style and Usage,* advertised as "the Official Style Guide Used by the Writers and Editors of the World's Most Authoritative Newspaper."

Systems of documentation like MLA reflect the professional needs of various academic disciplines. Researchers in the humanities typically use MLA style because it is well adapted to working with authors and their texts. But a system of documentation created for scholars who deal with language and literature might not suit professionals whose occupation involves numbers, equations, charts, and experiments. So the scientific fields have their own documentation guidelines, the most familiar to college students likely to be those of the American Psychological Association (APA) or the Council of Science Editors (CSE).

And there are many more professions and groups that publish rules for writers in their areas. For more than a hundred years, the Government Printing Office (GPO) has offered a style manual to assist people preparing federal documents. Even more famous and almost as old is the widely cited *Chicago Manual of Style* (CMS), a compilation of guidelines that has been adopted by many publishers, journals, and writers. (For more on Chicago style and a sample paper, see Chapter 52.) The point is that there are many systems of documentation and style, each serving different professions, audiences, and purposes. The more serious your own academic work becomes, the more you'll need to know what your field expects from a writer. So find out what stylebooks are used in your major or profession.

Chart 49.1 Style Guides in Various Fields

- **Chemistry:** *The ACS Style Guide: Effective Communication of Scientific Information* (3rd ed., 2006) by Anne M. Coghill and Lorrin R. Garson
- **Earth science:** *Geowriting: A Guide to Writing, Editing, and Printing in Earth Science* (5th ed., 1995) by Robert Bates
- **English language and literature/humanities:** *MLA Handbook for Writers of Research Papers* (7th ed., 2009)
- **Federal government:** *United States Government Printing Office Manual* (30th ed., 2008) by the United States Government Printing Office (GPO)
- **Journalism:** *The Associated Press Stylebook and Briefing on Media Law* (2008)
- **Law:** *Uniform System of Citation: The Bluebook* (18th ed., 2005) by the Harvard Law Review Association

(Continued)

Style Guides in Various Fields *(Continued)*

- **Mathematics:** *A Manual for Writers of Mathematical Papers* (8th ed., 1990) by the American Mathematical Society
- **Music:** *Writing About Music: An Introductory Guide* (3rd ed., 2001) by Richard J. Wingell
- **Nursing:** *Writing for Nursing Publications* (1981) by Andrea B. O'Connor
- **Physics:** *AIP Style Manual* (4th ed., 1990) by the American Institute of Physics
- **Political science:** *Style Manual for Political Science* (2006) by the APSA Committee on Publications (available online)
- **Psychology and social sciences:** *Publication Manual of the American Psychological Association* (6th ed., 2010)
- **Science:** *Scientific Style and Format: The CSE Manual for Authors, Editors, and Publishers* (7th ed., 2006) by the Council of Science Editors

49b How do you document a research project?

Knowing what to document in a research paper can be as complicated as the documentation styles themselves. Here are some guidelines.

1 Provide a source for every direct quotation. A *direct quotation* is any material repeated word for word from a source. Direct quotations in college papers typically require some form of parenthetical documentation—that is, a citation of author and page number (MLA) or author, date, and page number (APA).

MLA It is possible to define literature as simply "that text which the community insists on having repeated from time to time intact" (Joos 51–52).

APA Hashimoto (1986) questions the value of attention-getting essay openings that "presuppose passive, uninterested (probably uninteresting) readers" (p. 126).

You are similarly expected to identify the sources for any diagrams, statistics, charts, or pictures in your paper. You need not document famous sayings, proverbs, or biblical citations drawn from your own memory.

In less formal writing, you should still identify the author, speaker, or work from which you borrow any passage and indicate why the words you are quoting are significant. Many phrases of introduction or attribution are available (see Section 25b). Here are just a few.

One noted astronomer **reported** that . . .

Secretary of State Clinton **asserts** that . . .

According to the Government Accounting Office (GAO), the figures . . .

2 Document all ideas, opinions, facts, and information that cannot be considered common knowledge. *Common knowledge* includes the facts, dates, events, information, and concepts that a person in your *intended* audience can be assumed to know or that would be uncontroversial if they had to look them up. Writing a history paper, you might need an encyclopedia to find out that the Battle of Waterloo was fought on June 18, 1815, but such an important date would be considered common knowledge because it is well established and undisputed. You would not have to give credit to a particular source to use such a fact in a paper. Similarly, you would not have to document the claim that nine planets orbit our sun, but you would likely have to cite sources were you to examine the controversy over whether Pluto ought to be classified as a planet—which astronomers now dispute. The particular claims and arguments made by scientists questioning and defending Pluto's planetary status would not be considered common knowledge.

Similarly, when you find that a given piece of information or an idea is shared among several of the sources you are using within an academic field or discipline, you usually need not document it. For example, if in writing a paper on anorexia nervosa you discover that most authorities define it in the same way, you probably don't have to document that definition. What experts know collectively constitutes the common knowledge within a field; what they claim individually—their opinions, studies, theories, research projects, and hypotheses—is the material you *must* document in a paper.

3 Document materials that readers might question or wish to explore further. If your subject is controversial, you may want to document even those facts or ideas considered common knowledge in the field. Suppose that in writing about witchcraft you make a historical assertion well known by scholars within a field but liable to surprise nonspecialists. If you are writing for nonspecialists, you should certainly document the assertion. Writing for experts, you might skip the note. But when in doubt, document. A note enables any reader to follow up on your claims by checking the sources you have used. A note also means that you will include that item on your Works Cited or References page.

4 Furnish dates, credentials, and other information to assist readers. Provide dates for important events, major figures, and works of literature and art you mention in your paper. Identify anything readers might not recognize.

> After the great fire of London (1666), the city was . . .
>
> Henry Highland Garnet (1815–1882), American abolitionist and radical, . . .
>
> *Pearl* (c. 1400), an elegy about . . .

2 WALTER ISAACSON

Benjamin Franklin is the founding father who winks at us. George Washington's colleagues found it hard to imagine touching the austere general on the shoulder, and we would find it even more so today. Jefferson and Adams are just as intimidating. But Ben Franklin, that ambitious urban entrepreneur, seems made of flesh rather than marble, addressable by nickname, and he turns to us from history's stage with eyes that twinkle from behind those newfangled spectacles. He speaks to us, through his letters and hoaxes and autobiography, not with orotund rhetoric but with a chattiness and clever irony that is very contemporary, sometimes unnervingly so. We see his reflection in our own time.

He was, during his eighty-four-year-long life, America's best scientist, inventor, diplomat, writer, and business strategist, and he was also one of its most practical, though not most profound, political thinkers. He proved by flying a kite that lightning was electricity, and he invented a rod to tame it. He devised bifocal glasses and clean-burning stoves, charts of the Gulf Stream and theories about the contagious nature of the common cold. He launched various civic improvement schemes, such as a lending library, college, volunteer fire corps, insurance association, and matching grant fund-raiser. He helped invent America's unique style of homespun humor and philosophical pragmatism. In foreign policy, he created an approach that wove together idealism with balance-of-power realism. And in politics, he proposed seminal plans for uniting the colonies and creating a federal model for a national government.

But the most interesting thing that Franklin invented, and contin-

Isaacson's memorable description of Franklin would be a good passage to quote directly (and document properly).

Franklin's kite flying is common knowledge even to the general public. You could mention it without citing this source—assuming you do not also use Isaacson's words to describe the event.

The information here is not common knowledge. In a paper, the idea should be paraphrased and credited to Isaacson so readers could check your sources and his.

Figure 49.1 In this selection from Walter Isaacson's *Ben Franklin: An American Life* (2003) you can see how a single source might offer different kinds of information for a paper.

In the last example, the *c.* before the date stands for *circa,* which means "about."

When quoting from literary works, help readers locate the passages you are citing. For novels, identify page numbers; for plays, give act/scene/line information; for long poems, provide line numbers and, when appropriate, division numbers (book, canto, or other divisions).

5 Use links to cite sources in electronic sources. Links in Web pages can function as a type of documentation: they should take readers directly to supporting material or sources. But it's important that readers of hypertexts understand where a highlighted passage is leading them. Hyperlinks should be used judiciously to provide real information. Don't overwhelm a Web page with links; they can seem as fussy as a page with too many footnotes. Check to make sure the links work, because Web addresses change with distressing frequency.

6 Use computer programs to document your project. Software programs such as Noodlebib are available to help you document a paper or create a bibliography. If you choose to use such a program, be sure it supports the documentation style—for example, MLA, APA, CMS—required for your project and that it is up to date. Read the instructions for such software carefully and proofread the output to be sure you have entered your data accurately.

49c Finding Documentation Information (Source Maps)

When working with research materials, you'll encounter many unfamiliar terms and concepts. An instructor may assume, for example, that you know what an *edition* is, where the publication information for a book can be found, or why some magazines have volume numbers and others do not. We'll cover some basics of documenting books, articles, and electronic sources here, but don't hesitate to ask an instructor or librarian questions.

1 For books, check the title and copyright pages for documentation information. You'll usually find the title page just inside the front cover. Most title pages will include a full title (including any subtitle);

the names of the author(s), editors, or translators; the number of the edition; and the publisher. For the year and place of publication, check the copyright page, which immediately follows the title page. The copyright page may also offer details about previous editions of the book, as well as the current Library of Congress call number and International Standard Book Number (ISBN). If information you need is not in the book—a place of publication, a date, or even an author's name—just omit that information from your citation. Don't guess or make it up.

Large books may comprise several *volumes* either because a single volume would be too large or because the book was produced over a long period of time, with different volumes appearing in different years. A book in a *series* is a separate work that is part of a collection of books by different authors on a common theme. If a book is published in several volumes or is part of a series, you'll need to mention the fact in your citation.

2 For scholarly journals, check the cover or contents page for documentation information. Any additional information will be in its table of contents, though you'll need to check the article itself to get its closing page number. Most scholarly journals use *volume* numbers to identify the work produced in a particular year because they rarely come out monthly or on a particular date. For easy reference, all the issues of a journal produced during a single year constitute one *continuously paginated* volume. (For example, the "winter" issue of a journal may begin on page 389.) When citing a journal article, you will always need the volume and issue number, the year of publication, and the page numbers of the article you are using.

It is likely that you will locate and read many scholarly articles, magazine pieces, and newspaper stories online, finding them via library databases supplied by services such as EBSCO and JSTOR. Such materials usually appear with full bibliographical information attached—author, title, journal, date, page numbers, etc. Sometimes the information is even offered in citation form. Be sure, however, that any provided citation conforms to the documentation system you are using. You can find more about documenting sources taken from library subscription services on page 686 (MLA) and page 736 (APA).

Some online journal articles and other materials may now also include a digital object identifier (DOI) designed to give that source a single dependable location on the Web. All DOIs begin with 10, followed by additional groups of numbers (see source map "How Do You Cite Scholarly Articles?"

on pagc 652). APA documentation now uses DOIs whenever possible to locate source material. For each scholarly journal or book you use in an APA paper, look for a DOI. If you cannot find one on the site or database housing the source, check the following site allowing free DOI searches: <http://www.crossref.org/guestquery>.

3 Check magazine articles for documentation information. Although you will find most of the information you need to cite an article from a popular magazine (name of periodical, date, author, title of article) in its table of contents, be especially careful with titles and page numbers. Titles may be shortened on a contents page. To get an exact title, go to the article itself. Page numbers can be tricky too. Although articles in scholarly journals run uninterrupted from beginning to end, those in magazines are often broken up by ads and other stories. If you are using MLA style, you give the first page of an interrupted story followed by a plus sign: 60+. In APA style, you list all the pages on which the interrupted story appears: 60–65, 96, 98–99.

Quite often, you'll be citing a magazine article not from an original copy, but from a printed version provided by a library subscription service, perhaps emailed to you. The piece will ordinarily provide all the bibliographical information you need for a citation, including page numbers, but it may not include images or other textual features of the original article.

4 For newspapers, check the masthead and credits column for documentation information. A masthead is the distinctive banner that runs across the front page identifying the paper. If the masthead indicates that you are using a particular edition of the paper—*morning, evening, suburban*—be sure to note it. Copy the headline of any article you cite from the first page of the story; the continuation of a story on a later page might have an altered title. When stories appear across a series of pages, follow the same procedure for newspapers as for magazines, but note that newspapers are paginated by sections as well as numbers. In MLA style, you simply give the first section and page of the story, followed by a plus sign: B60+. In APA style, list all the pages on which the story appears: B60–65, B96, B98–99.

A copy of the article provided by a library news service such as *LexisNexis* will also provide full bibliographical information, usually before the body of the article.

5 Expect full documentation from the Web sites you use. The Web page for a site you use for a research paper should give you enough information to provide adequate documentation—at a minimum the name of the site, an institutional sponsor, and a date for the most recent material. (Sometimes you may have to go back to the home page of the site for information.) For online books, articles, and newspapers, look for the same bibliographical date that you would gather for printed versions of these materials, with the possible exception of page numbers. When a Web site provides virtually no documentation information, aside from the title of the page and the URL, you should question its worth as a source for an academic project.

How Do You Cite a Book?

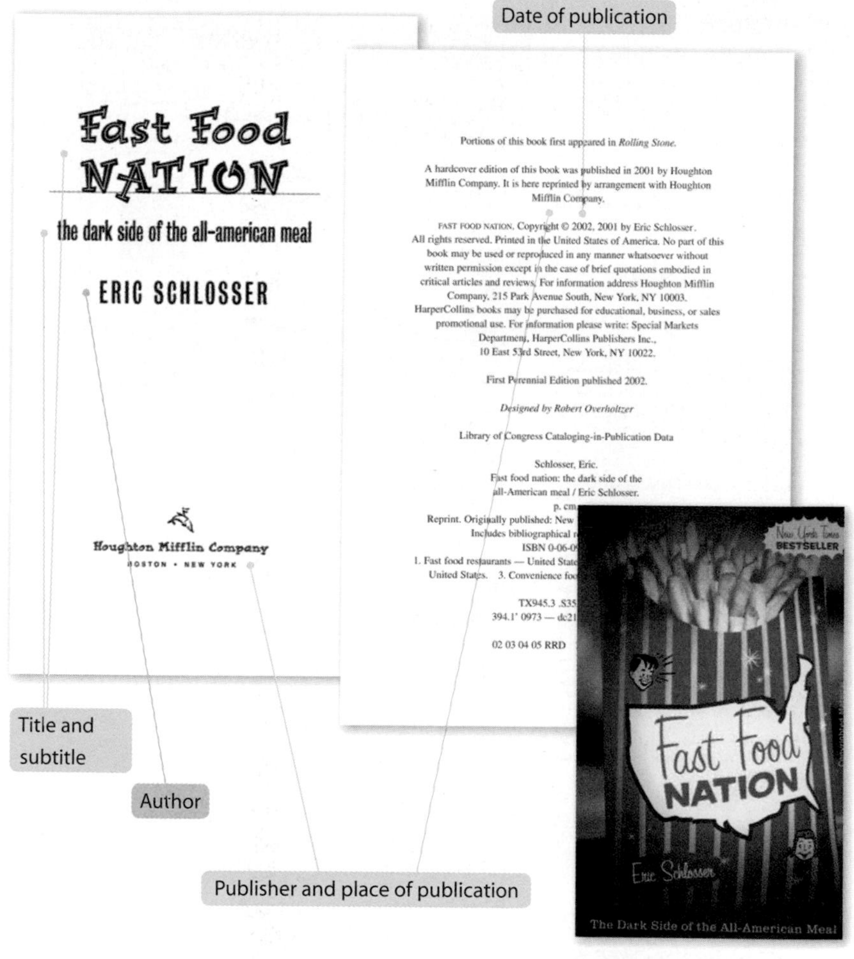

Date of publication
Fast Food NATION
the dark side of the all-american meal
ERIC SCHLOSSER
Houghton Mifflin Company
BOSTON • NEW YORK
Portions of this book first appeared in Rolling Stone.
A hardcover edition of this book was published in 2001 by Houghton Mifflin Company. It is here reprinted by arrangement with Houghton Mifflin Company.
FAST FOOD NATION. Copyright © 2002, 2001 by Eric Schlosser. All rights reserved. Printed in the United States of America. No part of this book may be used or reproduced in any manner whatsoever without written permission except in the case of brief quotations embodied in critical articles and reviews. For information address Houghton Mifflin Company, 215 Park Avenue South, New York, NY 10003. HarperCollins books may be purchased for educational, business, or sales promotional use. For information please write: Special Markets Department, HarperCollins Publishers Inc., 10 East 53rd Street, New York, NY 10022.
First Perennial Edition published 2002.
Designed by Robert Overholtzer
Library of Congress Cataloging-in-Publication Data
Schlosser, Eric.
Fast food nation: the dark side of the all-American meal / Eric Schlosser.
p. cm.
TX945.3 .S35
02 03 04 05 RRD
New York Times BESTSELLER
Fast Food NATION
Eric Schlosser
The Dark Side of the All-American Meal
Title and subtitle
Author
Publisher and place of publication

MLA: Schlosser, Eric. *Fast Food Nation: The Dark Side of the All-American Meal.* 2001. New York: Houghton, 2002. Print.

APA: Schlosser, E. (2002). *Fast food nation: The dark side of the all-American meal.* New York, NY: Houghton Mifflin.

How Do You Cite Scholarly Articles?

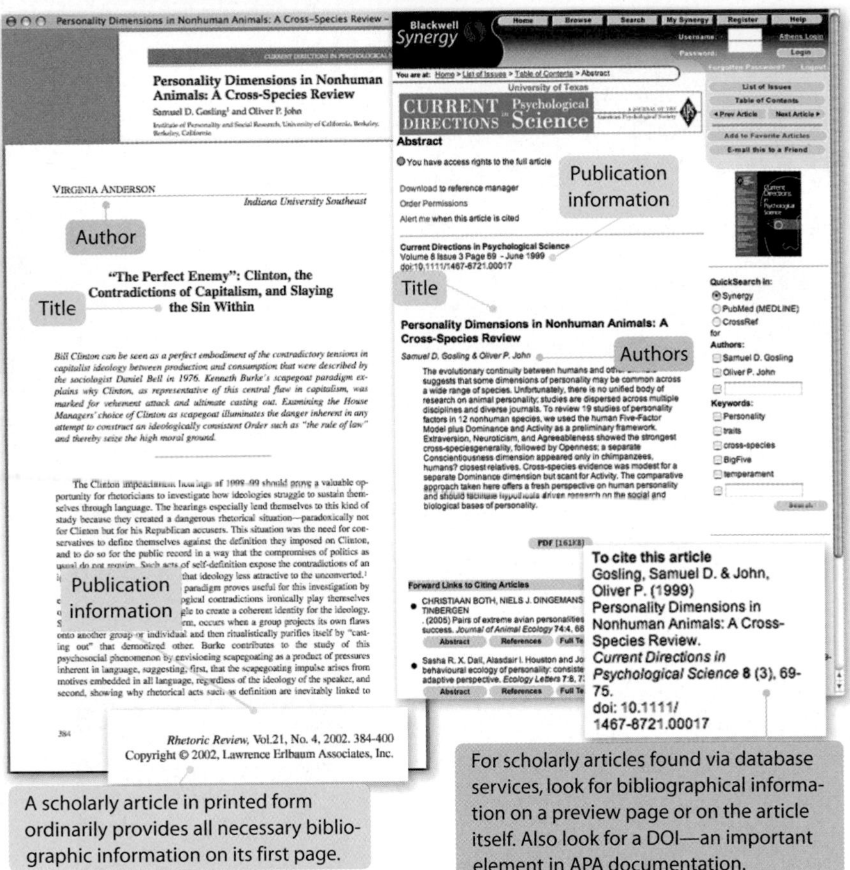

A scholarly article in printed form ordinarily provides all necessary bibliographic information on its first page.

For scholarly articles found via database services, look for bibliographical information on a preview page or on the article itself. Also look for a DOI—an important element in APA documentation.

MLA: Anderson, Virginia. "'The Perfect Enemy': Clinton, the Contradictions of Capitalism, and Slaying the Sin Within." *Rhetoric Review* 21.4 (2002): 384-400. Print.

APA: Gosling, S.D., & John, O.P. (1999). Personality dimensions in nonhuman animals: A cross-species review. *Current Dimensions in Psychological Science, 8*(3), 69-75. doi:10.1111/1467-8721.00017.

How Do You Cite a Magazine Article?

Record: 1
Title: Tyler Hollansworth.
Authors: Hollandsworth, Skip
Source: Texas Monthly; Sep2003, Vol. 31 Issue 9, p64-64, 1p, 2c
Document Type: Article
Subject Terms: *CHEERLEADING
*CITIES & towns
*GIRLS
*LIFE style
*STEREOTYPE (Psychology)
Geographic Terms: TEXAS
UNITED States
Abstract: Characterizes the growth of a six-year old girl born in Dallas, Texas. Lifestyle similarities and differences between Dallas and Austin; Stereotype of a Dallas baby; Popularity of cheerleading in Dallas; Appeal of cheerleading to children.
Full Text Word Count: 806
ISSN: 0148-7736
Accession Number: 10664624
Database: Academic Search Premier

Section: reporter

ERE ARE THEY NOW?

Tyler Hollansworth

years ago I wrote that my new daughter was a stereotypical Dallas baby. But she idn't seem to be a stereotypical Dallas girl until she broke out the pom-poms.

. 1997 I WROTE A STORY FOR THIS magazine about the birth of my daughter Tyler and how it compared with the birth, just a couple of weeks earlier, of Carson Smith,

Full bibliographical information attached to library service printout of the *Texas Monthly* article entitled "Tyler Hollandsworth"

MLA: Hollandsworth, Skip. "Tyler Hollandsworth." *Texas Monthly* Sept. 2003: 64. Print.

APA: Hollandsworth, S. (2003, September). Tyler Hollandsworth. *Texas Monthly, 31*(9), 64.

How Do You Cite a Newspaper?

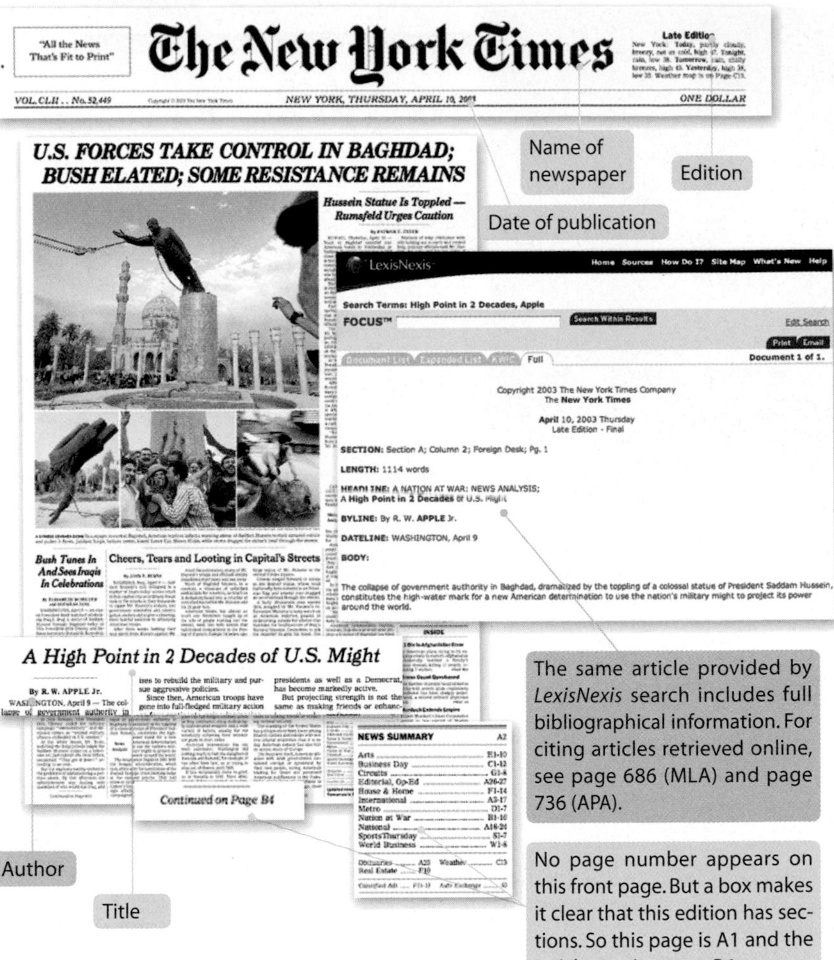

MLA: Apple, R.W., Jr. "A High Point in 2 Decades of U.S. Might." *New York Times* 10 Apr. 2003, late ed.: A1+. Print.

APA: Apple, R.W., Jr. (2003, April 10). A high point in 2 decades of U.S. might. *The New York Times*, pp. A1, B4.

How Do You Cite a Web Site?

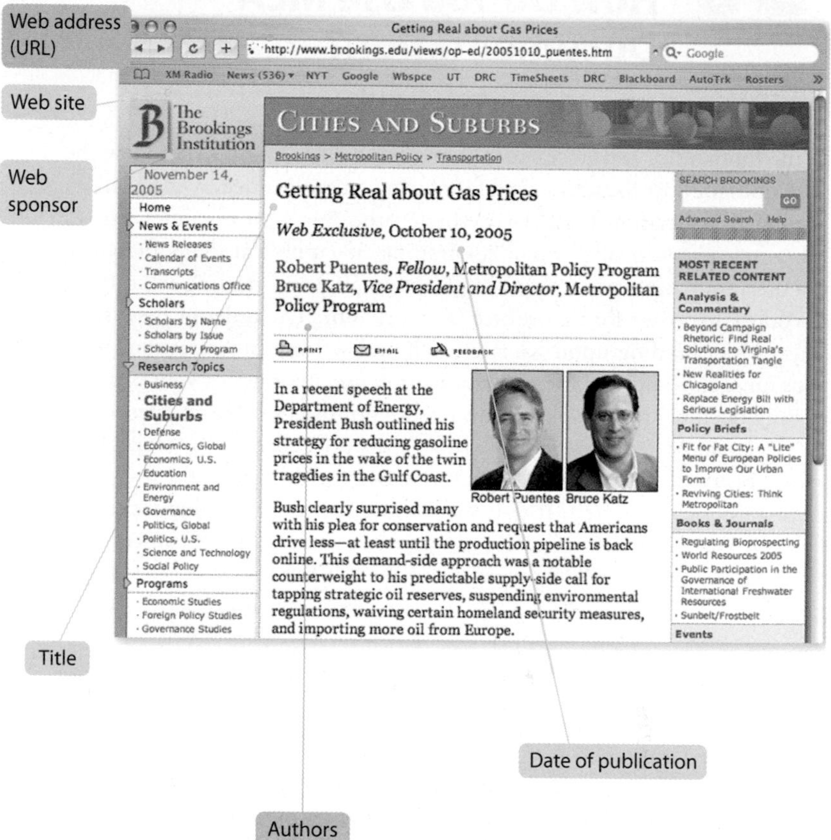

MLA: Puentes, Robert, and Bruce Katz. "Getting Real About Gas Prices." *Brookings*. The Brookings Institution, 10 Oct. 2005. Web. 24 May 2009.

APA: Puentes, R., & Katz B. (2005, October 10). Getting real about gas prices. Retrieved from Brookings website: http://www.brookings.edu/

CHAPTER

50 How Do You Use MLA Documentation?

In the humanities and liberal arts, many writers and publishers follow the guidelines for documentation and formatting recommended by the Modern Language Association (MLA). The basic procedures for documenting an MLA-style paper involve two basic steps: placing a note at the point where you use a source in a paper or project (Section 50a) and creating an entry on a Works Cited page for that source (Section 50b). The order of these steps may vary depending upon your research and writing processes, but both steps must be completed for every source you use, in order for your paper to be fully documented. If you run into issues not discussed here, refer to the *MLA Handbook for Writers of Research Papers* (7th ed., 2009), available at your library's reference desk or at the MLA Web site: <http://www.mlahandbook.org/style>. If you want more information about citation styles in general or are uncertain about what you should document in a paper, see Chapter 49, "Documenting a Research Paper."

50a Insert in-text notes wherever you use sources in the body of your paper.

Each time you quote, paraphrase, or in some way use ideas from outside sources, you must acknowledge that you've done so with a note. You can create in-text notes several ways. One is to use *parenthetical citations*, which present information about a source between parentheses, usually at the end of a sentence: **(Prosek 246-47)**. Or you may use *signal phrases*, which identify sources within the normal flow of the sentence: **According to Eric Foner** in *The Story of American Freedom* . . . . Often you will combine these basic forms, using both a signal phrase and a page number in parentheses: **Anderson claims** that the TV show *South Park* "spares no sensitivity" **(76)**.

Parenthetical notes tend to be the easiest form of citation to create, but they can interrupt the flow of your writing. Consequently, MLA guidelines suggest that you use them sparingly and make them as concise as possible. Signal phrases, on the other hand, allow you to mention details about your

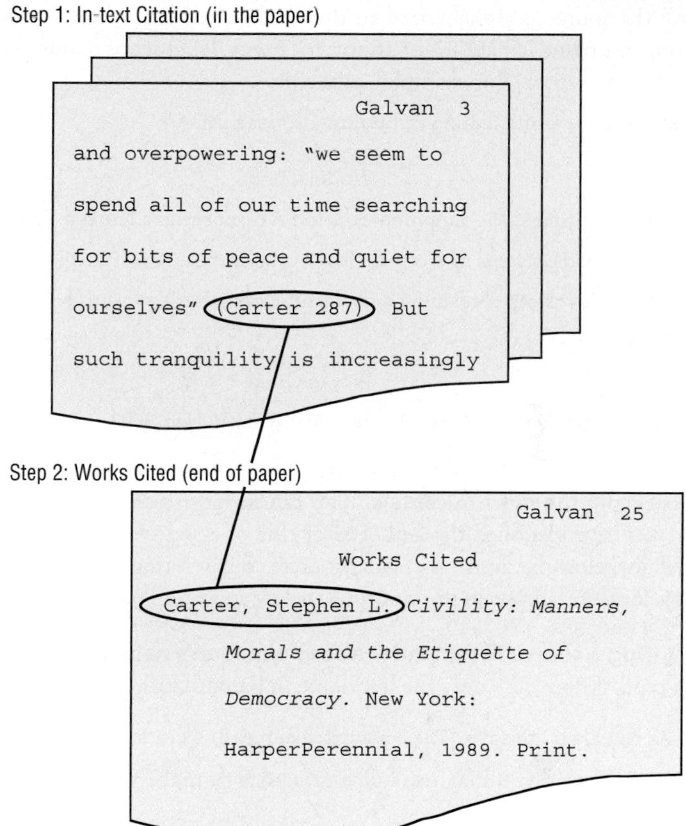

Step 1: In-text Citation (in the paper)
Galvan 3
and overpowering: "we seem to
spend all of our time searching
for bits of peace and quiet for
ourselves" (Carter 287). But
such tranquility is increasingly
Step 2: Works Cited (end of paper)
Galvan 25
Works Cited
Carter, Stephen L. Civility: Manners,
Morals and the Etiquette of
Democracy. New York:
HarperPerennial, 1989. Print.

source in order to establish its credibility, explain its relevance, or clarify its positions. (Review Section 46b for more on how to introduce borrowed material effectively.)

1 Identify outside sources clearly each time you use them. Whether you introduce sources with parenthetical notes or signal phrases, your readers will always need to know precisely which source on the works-cited list you are using. Make sure that the note clearly refers to the word by which the source is alphabetized in the works-cited list, whether that is a person's last name (an author or editor, for example), a set of names (groups of authors or editors, for example), or a title.

IN-TEXT NOTE: . . . while fishing in England (**Prosek** 246-47).

Works Cited

Prosek, James. *The Complete Angler: A Connecticut Yankee Follows in the Footsteps of Walton*. New York: Harper, 1999. Print.

IN-TEXT NOTE: A variety of resources for "daily poetry" are available at ***Poets.org***. . . .

Works Cited

Poets.org. Acad. of Amer. Poets, 2008. Web. 12 Dec. 2008.

As you can see, you will need to know how a source will appear on your works-cited list in order to create a note. But in most cases, that will be easy once you have identified the author(s) or title of a source. Simply apply the guidelines below that fit the particular sources you are citing. (The works-cited entries for the examples in the guidelines below appear on pages 661–662.)

1.1 Citing a source listed under a single person's name. This is a common type of note. Use only the last name in parenthetical notes:

> As one historian says, "The scientist, like the artist, is one of us" (**Jardine** 5).

In signal phrases, you may use full first names to make your passage more readable.

> "Today's secular disruption between the creative aspect of art and that of science," anthropologist **Loren Eiseley** contends, "is a barbarism that would have brought lifted eyebrows in a Cro-Magnon cave" (271).

When your works-cited listing contains sources by different people having the same last name, use initials or full first names to refer to their works without confusion.

> Dr. Frankenstein assumes "[a] new species would bless [him] as its creator" (**M. Shelley** 51; vol. 1, ch. 4)—perhaps, *if* he were driven by the "purest and truest motives" of his literary counterpart, Prometheus (**P. Shelley**, pref.).

1.2 Citing a source listed under a group of people's names. Give the *last names of all individuals* in the same order they appear at the beginning of the corresponding works-cited entry. When a source is listed under four or more persons' names, you have the option of using the Latin abbreviation *et al.* (*et alia*, "and others") after the first person's name. If you choose the shortened form *et al.* for your works-cited entries, then use it also for all in-text notes.

> **Varela, Thompson, and Rosch** ask, "What challenges does human experience face as a result of the scientific study of the mind?" (xvii).
>
> The Royal Society was chartered in 1662 to further scientific enquiry and advance the study of natural philosophy (**Abrams et al.** 1: 1571).

1.3 Citing a source listed under a corporate or group author. In this case, a signal phrase is often more readable than a parenthetical note. When you do use a parenthetical note to identify the source, abbreviate the name of the author.

> Technological patents are awarded for "novelty" and "non-obviousness" (**USPTO**)—roughly the same criteria we use to praise "creative" work.

1.4 Citing a source listed by title. Put the *title* in your in-text citation when a work doesn't have an author or creator. Shorten the title as much as possible: the shortened title, however, should always include its first word (excluding *A, An,* and *The*), so readers can easily find the entry on the alphabetized Works Cited page. Also, use the same formatting (italics or quotation marks) as that used in the works-cited entry.

> Scientific creativity relies on expensive technology and tends to be limited more by money than ideas (**"Art"**).

1.5 Citing a source that is one of many listed under the same person's name. Mention *both* the *last name* of the author and the *title* of the particular source. When using parenthetical citation, follow the person's last name with a comma and a shortened version of the title (see the preceding section).

> Even the most cultivated "habit of thought" can be questioned when we acknowledge that "conviction of the 'truth' . . . is founded exclusively on rather incomplete experience" (**Einstein**, *Relativity* 3-4).

A readable way of handling such a citation is to mention the person's name in a signal phrase and then use a parenthetical citation to clarify which work you are referring to in the particular passage.

> **Spielberg**'s films have explored how science and technology shape our views of morality (***Minority Report***), as well as how they challenge our ideas of humanity (***A.I.***)—traditional concerns of humanist scholars.

1.6 Citing material from sacred texts, classical literary works, and legal documents. These works are often identified by standard abbreviations, especially when parenthetical notes are used. For classical literary works, look for a standard shortened title in the textual notes of the edition you're using or in a scholarly reference on the subject or author; if none is available, follow the guidelines presented in Section 50a-1.1–5 above.

> **Shakespeare**'s Caliban values his education in the language arts only because it helps him "know how to curse" (***Tmp***. 1.2.364).

For sacred texts, standard abbreviations are often used to identify the work in both signal phrases and parenthetical notes. When you use the generic name of a sacred work—including terms such as the Bible, Torah, Qur'an, as well as sections and chapters within them—do *not* italicize the title of the version in your in-text notes.

> The spiritual and emotional value of pursuing truth is articulated well in the **King James Version** of the **Bible**: "He that hath knowledge spareth his words: *and* a man of understanding is of an excellent spirit" (**Prov.** 17.27).

Do, however, italicize titles of particular published *editions* of such works.

> It is not clear how the works that comprise the Torah came to be seen as one book (***New Oxford Annotated Bible***, HB 6).

Similar rules apply to historic legal documents (for example, the Declaration of Independence and the Treaty of Versailles), and also to specific government acts and laws (for example, the Selective Service Act). You would not ordinarily italicize such titles.

1.7 Citing multiple sources in a single parenthetical note. Separate each citation by a semicolon, following the other guidelines listed above. Do this sparingly, however, since such long notes can be distracting.

> Newer editions of literary anthologies include scientific texts of historical significance (**Abrams et al.** xxiii; **Henderson and Sharpe** vii, xii).

1.8 Citing material repeatedly from the same source. Readers can assume that any parenthetical notes that don't identify a source refer to the last works-cited entry mentioned in the body of the paper. Omit the source identifier in notes referring repeatedly to different locations in the same work when no other work is mentioned.

> Dr. Frankenstein, whose "sole occupation" is "natural philosophy" (**M. Shelley** 49; vol. 1, ch. 4), studies the human animal through biological experiments. His creation, a so-called "monster" (60; vol. 1, ch. 5), *learns to be human* by reading poetry and history (124-27; vol. 2, ch. 7).

The following Works Cited list shows the works-cited entries for sample citations 1.1 to 1.8.

Works Cited

Abrams, M. H., et al., eds. *The Norton Anthology of English Literature*. 6th ed. 2 vols. New York: Norton, 1993. Print.

"The Art of Science—Big or Small." Editorial. *Los Angeles Times* 13 Dec. 1993: B6. *LexisNexis Academic*. Web. 13 May 2003.

Einstein, Albert. *Letters to Solovine*. Trans. Wade Baskin. Intro. Maurice Solovine. New York: Philosophical Lib., 1987. Print.

---. *Relativity: The Special and General Theory*. Trans. Robert W. Lawson. New York: Bonanza, 1961. Print.

Eiseley, Loren. *The Star Thrower*. Intro. W. H. Auden. San Diego: Harcourt, 1978. Print.

Henderson, Heather, and William Sharpe, eds. *The Longman Anthology of British Literature*. 2nd ed. Vol. 2B. New York: Longman, 2003. Print.

The Interpreter's Bible. Ed. John W. Bailey, et al. 12 vols. New York: Abington, 1952. Print.

Jardine, Lisa. *Ingenious Pursuits: Building the Scientific Revolution*. New York: Anchor-Random, 2000. Print.

Shakespeare, William. *The Riverside Shakespeare*. Ed. G. Blakemore Evans. Boston: Houghton, 1974. Print.

Shelley, Mary. *Frankenstein: The Modern Prometheus*. 1818. Ed. and intro. Maurice Hindle. London: Penguin, 1992. Print.

Shelley, Percy Bysshe. *Prometheus Unbound*. 1820. *LiteratureClassics.com*. Classics Network, 2003. Web. 15 May 2003.

Spielberg, Stephen, dir. *A.I.* Warner, 2001. DVD.

---. *Minority Report*. Fox, 2002. Film.

United States. Patent and Trademark Office. "Novelty and Non-Obviousness, Conditions for Obtaining a Patent." *United States Patent and Trademark Office*. USPTO, 2003. Web. 12 May 2003.

Varela, Francisco J., Evan Thompson, and Eleanor Rosch. *The Embodied Mind: Cognitive Science and Human Experience*. Cambridge: MIT P, 1991. Print.

2 Locate referenced material as precisely as possible. Besides identifying a source, in-text notes also tell readers exactly where to find the material you are borrowing or citing. Typically, you would simply provide page numbers, but many electronic sources don't give you that choice. The guidelines below present your options.

2.1 Locating passages in sources with standard pagination. In a parenthetical note, give the page number(s) after naming the source, separating the two with a space only. If the author or source is not named, you can just enclose the page numbers. Use whatever page-numbering scheme the source itself uses—roman numerals, letter-number combination, etc.

SINGLE PAGE You may omit the page reference when the source is only one page long.

According to Jones . . . (**142**)
(Jones **142**)
("Blame" **21**)

RANGE OF PAGES Separate the first and last pages in the range with a hyphen.

(Dyson, *Disturbing* **11-13**)
(Savlov **E4-E5**)

NONCONSECUTIVE PAGES Separate by a comma and space each page where the idea is referenced.

(**151, 156, 198**)
(Gilbert and Gubar **xxix, xxxiv**)

PAGES IN MULTI-VOLUME SOURCES Insert the volume number, a colon, and a space before page references.

(**2: 132**)
(Churchill **4: 3461-62**)

2.2 Locating passages in sources using alternative numbering schemes. Works in newer media often have numbered paragraphs or screens, rather than pages, and most classical works have traditional numbering mechanisms: chapters and sections for novels and treatises; acts and scenes for dramatic works; cantos and line numbers for poetry. Traditional schemes help readers find material no matter which edition they use.

SOURCES WITH NO PAGINATION
After the source identifier (if given in the note), insert a comma, an abbreviation for the numbering scheme, and a reference number.

(Neruda, **lines 2-9**)
(USPTO, "Intellectual," **par. 4**)
(UNFAO, "Education," **sec. 2**)
(**screen 3**)

LITERARY WORKS WITH PAGINATION
Follow the page reference with a semicolon and reference to the chapter, section, etc.

(Eliot, *Middlemarch* **273; ch. 28**)
(**75-76; ch. 4, sec. 1.5**)
(Stoppard **58-59; act 2**)

WORKS WITH TRADITIONAL NUMBERING
Classic works that are divided into precise hierarchical sections need no page references. Instead, list each section from largest to smallest with periods in between. Use hyphens to indicate a range.

(Aristotle, *Prior* **68b.9-15**)
(*Ham*. **3.6.4-5**)
(*Interpreter's Bible*, **Mark 10.25**)

2.3 Quoting or paraphrasing a statement that your source itself quotes. Start a note with *qtd. in* to indicate that the author of the work did not make these statements, but rather someone named within the source:

> According to eminent scientist Albert Einstein, "Imagination is more important than knowledge" (**qtd. in** Thomas **1**).

3 Place and punctuate parenthetical citations correctly. Place parenthetical citations just before the first natural pause that follows the cited material: after closing quotation marks but before ending or connecting punctuation marks.

AFTER BORROWED IDEA OR QUOTE, BEFORE END PERIOD	As Carter notes, "we seem to spend all of our time searching for bits of peace and quiet" (287).
TWO PARENTHETICAL NOTES IN ONE SENTENCE	The seclusion of the Lake District would often result in "the deepest melancholy" (D. Wordsworth 19), but the lakes themselves could be "soft . . . and beautiful" (36).
AFTER FINAL PUNCTUATION FOR BLOCK QUOTATIONS (SEE CHECKLIST 50.3)	Fixed ideas of permanence And transience, Finitude and infinity, Have no place when all is well. (Nagarjuna, lines 28-31)

50b List all cited sources on a separate "Works Cited" page.

The Works Cited page, which appears after the body of the essay, provides readers with full bibliographical information on each source mentioned in your in-text notes: when it was published, by whom, in what format, and so on. List only sources you actually reference in your in-text notes, even if you examined many others in the course of developing your project. The format of each works-cited entry will vary, depending on the type of source you are citing. To help you manage these variations, we've provided numerous model citations in sections 50b-1–13. The directory on pages 666–667 lists the models according to type; the directory on the inside back cover lists them alphabetically.

As you create entries, you'll note that some sources are the work of many people: movies and plays have directors and scriptwriters; books may have editors and translators, as well as authors. So whom do you credit? You can usually name all the major contributors—but you may need to decide whose contribution will receive **primary acknowledgment** and whose **secondary**. This choice will depend both on the genre of the source and which contributor's work is most important to your project. If you discuss the films of a particular director, give her primary acknowledgment for each film you cite. If you intend to analyze the work of an editor, list his name first, rather than the author's.

Besides attending to the acknowledgments of each work cited, you'll also need to look carefully at how each was published, especially the **medium** of production, whether in *Print*, on the *Web*, as a *CD* recording, etc. Different media have different standards of production that determine how you'll list the source's **publication details**. Remember that you ultimately want to give your readers enough information to find the source themselves, in particular, the version you used. This process has become a little trickier since many printed and recorded sources have been digitized and reproduced on the Web. You'll avoid many complications, however, if you simply read what your source says about its own production.

Pages 668–673 describe the basic parts of a works-cited entry in detail. Then, on pages 674–699, you'll find model works-cited entries (with their accompanying in-text notes) for more than a hundred kinds of sources in various media. Note that all entries follow these rules:

- **Each part of an entry begins with a capitalized word and ends with a period.** Look at the models carefully for other punctuation.
- **A space follows each comma, semicolon, and period**–*except* when the mark is followed by other punctuation, when it is part of certain standard abbreviations (see Chart 50.1 on page 673), or when it is part of a title that omits such spacing intentionally.

DIRECTORY TO MLA MODELS—BY TYPE

Print Media

50b-1 Books and pamphlets

50b-2 Books with editors, translators, etc.

50b-3 Book parts, chapters, etc.

50b-4 Articles in periodicals

Web Media

50b-5 The basics

50b-6 Online articles and blogs

50b-7 Databases and library subscription services

50b-8 Online postings, streaming content, etc.

Other Media

50b-9 Recorded media

50b-10 Broadcast and live media

50b-11 Other media

Special Genres

50b-12 Editorials, reviews and special visual content

50b-13 Sacred texts, musical compositions, and government documents

MLA Guidelines for Formatting Specific Parts of Works-Cited Entries

For examples of full MLA "Works Cited" pages, see 159, 661–662, 712–713

BASIC PARTS OF MLA WORKS-CITED ENTRIES

Works-cited entries are composed of five basic parts, each of which is listed below, then marked and color-coded in the sample entries at the bottom of the page. In addition to these five parts, there are occasions where you have an opportunity to add supplemental information, such as a full URL address for Web entries. Consult Checklist 50.5 at the end of the chapter for guidelines on further informing readers of extra details.

Primary Acknowledgment (Author). Each entry usually begins with the name(s) of the author(s) or artist(s). In some cases you'll have the option of focusing on other contributors—for example, a book's editor, a CD's producer, a Web site's compiler, or a movie's director.

Title. Usually the entry's second item, a title sometimes appears first—for instance, with unsigned sources. You might also list two titles within your entry—for example, the title of a book and that of a chapter inside.

Secondary Acknowledgments. Some works are created by many hands. After the title, list the names of other people (aside from the primary acknowledgment) who are given credit for creating the source.

Publication or Production Information. This part often seems very technical, but you're simply offering readers three key details: *where the source was published* (city, periodical, etc.), *who published it,* and *when.* Pay close attention to the models to see how these details are separated by various punctuation marks.

Medium Accessed. The last item in a works-cited entry is always a description of the media format of the material you're citing, for instance, *Print, Web, DVD-ROM, Speech, Radio,* etc. The models in sections 50b-1–11 are arranged according to the medium used to access the source.

Works Cited

Achebe, Chinua. *Things Fall Apart*. 1954. New York: Anchor-Doubleday, 1994. Print.

Schoolnik, Skip, dir. "Slouching towards Bethlehem." Writ. Jeffrey Bell. Perf. David Boreanaz and Charisma Carpenter. *Angel*. WB. KTLA, Los Angeles, 27 Oct. 2002. Television.

"W. B. Yeats." *Poets.org*. Acad. of Amer. Poets, 2009. Web. 2 July 2009.

Primary Acknowledgments (Author)

Identify the author of a source in last-name-first order, spelling names as they appear in the source, even if those given are known pseudonyms.

- *Omit* titles and degrees, such as *M.D., S.J., Ph.D., President.*
- *Include* identifying suffixes such as *Jr.* or *III.* Suffixes should be listed immediately after an individual's name, preceded by a comma.
- *Include* traditional identifying modifiers (*de Medici*, for example) for a person with no last name (a common case for pre-modern authors), placing them immediately after the first name.

One author or artist. List the last name first, followed by a comma, and first names and initials as they appear on the title page of the source. Add essential suffixes (e.g., *Jr.*) after the first name. When no last name is given, simply list the name by which the individual is recognized in the source.	Bloom, Amy. — Christine de Pisan. — King, Martin Luther, Jr. — O'Keefe, Georgia. — Shakira. —
Two or three authors or artists. List their names in the same order they appear on the title page or byline. The first person appears last-name-first, followed by all others in normal order. Separate each with a comma (even when only two persons are listed), preceding the last person's name with the word *and.*	Armstrong, Lance, and Sally Jenkins. — Black, Francis, and Kim Deal. — Harrison, Maureen A., Ian F. Rae, and Ann Harris. — See Models 3, 5, 10, 17, 26, 27, 38, 64, 77
Four or more authors or artists. You may use a shortened form, listing only the Latin abbreviation *et al.* ("and others") after the first author's name (last-name-first).	Page, Jimmy, et al. — Roberts, Henry M., III, et al. — See Model 49
Corporate or group authors or artists. List them as they appear on the title page or byline of the source, omitting initial articles (*A, An,* or *The*) when the name stands for a company or institution.	Blue Man Group. — The Who. — World Health Organization. — See Models 35, 60, 63, 92, 100, 101, 102
Editors, translators, compilers, etc. When they are given primary acknowledgment, these individuals are listed first in place of authors. Before the period, however, insert a comma and an abbreviation that identifies the form of contribution (see Chart 50.1). When listing multiple persons, place the abbreviation (pluralized by inserting *s* before the period) after the last individual's name.	Cash, Johnny, and June Carter, perfs. — Heaney, Seamus, trans. — Lee, Spike, dir. — Selfe, Cynthia L., and Susan Hilligoss, eds. — See Models 10, 14, 15, 39, 60, 64, 66

Titles

Capitalize the first word of each title and all other words, except articles (*a*, *an*, and *the*), prepositions (also *to* when part of an infinitive), and coordinating conjunctions. Most titles have other formatting as well. Note that these formatting rules apply also to titles appearing in the body of the paper—although you'll use shortened titles in parenthetical notes.

Italicized titles. Italicize the titles of major works, including books, plays, operas, musicals, TV programs, radio programs, artworks, CDs, movies, long poems, and periodicals. (See also Section 43a.) *Do not* italicize the period after the title, but *do* italicize exclamation points and question marks that are part of the title. Underline when italics are not available.	*Revolutionary Road*. *Lost*. *Bullet in a Bible*. *Mamma Mia!* *Omeros*. *Spin*. *Starry Night*.
Titles in quotation marks. Enclose in quotation marks the titles of short works, such as periodical articles, essays, speeches, short poems, short stories, individual TV episodes, radio segments, and songs. End punctuation goes *within* the closing quotation mark.	"Hitchin' a Ride." "Tabula Rasa." "Redwoods Go Wireless." "Self-Reliance." "The Tyger."
Subtitles. Place subtitles after the main title, inserting a colon and a space between the two. Capitalize letters in the subtitle like any other title; be sure to make the first letter uppercase.	*Seeing Voices: A Journey into the World of the Deaf*. See Models 1, 6, 8, 10, 13, 17, 19, 27-9, 43, 51, 61, 96
Descriptive titles. Some works are identified by generic descriptive phrases, rather than (or in addition to) original titles. Capitalize the first letter of the first word only. *Do not* italicize the phrase or place it in quotation marks—but do format titles within the descriptive phrase.	Interview with Toni Morrison. Online posting. 17 Aug. 2009. Review of *Clueless*. See Models 17-8, 30, 35-6, 55-8, 60, 67, 71-2, 83-4, 87-95
Titles within titles. Many works refer to other works within their titles. Refrain from italicizing a title when it appears within another italicized title. For titles ordinarily enclosed in double quotation marks, use single quotes when they appear within another title enclosed by double quotes. Otherwise, follow the standard rules for formatting titles.	"*Four Weddings* Director Eyes *Potter IV*." *The* Apocalypse Now *Book*. "Jagger Not Impressed with Spears' 'Satisfaction.'" See Models 14, 18, 25, 30

Secondary Acknowledgments

List any secondary contributors after the title of the work they helped create and before publication details. Present their names in normal order, preceding each with an abbreviation indicating the form of contribution (see Chart 50.1 on page 673). You may list more than one secondary contributor— simply group into a single acknowledgment the names of those who contribute in the same way. Note that sometimes authors and artists are not listed before the title, but instead after (following the word *By*).

—. By William Shakespeare. Dir. Laurence Olivier. —

—. Ed. Andrea Lunsford and John Ruszkiewicz. —

—. Writ. and dir. Andy Wachowski and Larry Wachowski. Perf. Keanu Reeves, Laurence Fishburne, and Carrie-Anne Moss. —

See Models 9, 11-15, 18-20, 22, 38, 46, 52, 56, 60, 62, 64-6, 74-6, 96-9

Publication and Production Information

These details vary greatly depending on the type of source you're documenting. The models in Sections 50b-1 through 50b-13 cover most of the sources you'll encounter. As you look at the models, notice how the following details are formatted and punctuated:

Places. Omit state and nation specifications, even from obscure cities. When no place of publication is available for books, use the abbreviation *N.p.* For some sources, such as performances, identify a specific venue before the city.	Englewood Cliffs London Odyssey Theatre, Los Angeles
Names of publishers. You can abbreviate publishers' names by omitting articles and indistinctive words (*Inc., Co.*, etc.) and by using standard abbreviations (see Chart 50.1). When no publisher is given where expected, use the abbreviation *n.p.*	Amer. Medical Assn. Norton U of Texas P
Dates. MLA works-cited entries include one or more dates depending on the type of source. All dates should be presented in day-month-year order. Abbreviate all months except *May, June,* and *July.* If no date is given where expected, put *n.d.*	4 July 1776 Oct. 1929 2001
Pages, etc. For page ranges, list the first and last with a hyphen between. For nonconsecutive pages, list only the first page followed by a plus sign. Use the same format (roman numerals, letters, etc.) as the source. Use the abbreviation *N. pag.* when the source is not paginated, unless a different scheme is used (paragraphing, etc.); indicate the type of numbering with an abbreviation.	9-16, 145-49, 501-615 E1+ iii-xi pars. 4-10 screen 3

Medium Accessed

The final piece of an MLA works-cited entry tells readers how you accessed the source, whether in print, through the Web, on a DVD, in an art gallery, and so on (see also Checklist 43.2.). Such information is especially important now that some sources, like books and newspapers, are digitized and made available online. Sections 50b-1 through 50b-11 give you guidelines for listing sources in different media formats, some of which may require extra informative details, such as the date of last access for online sources or the current museum where an artwork is held.

Some examples of medium descriptions:	—. Print. —. Web. 22 June 2008. —. Speech. —. Oil on canvas. Museum of Modern Art, New York.

Chart 50.1 Useful MLA Abbreviations

SECONDARY ACKNOWLEDGMENTS			
Adapted by	adapt.	Introduced by	introd.
Compiler	comp.	Narrator	narr.
Conductor	cond.	Performer	perf.
Director	dir.	Preface by	pref.
Editor	ed.	Producer	prod.
Foreword by	fwd.	Translator	trans.
Illustrator	illus.	Written by	writ.
PUBLICATION INFORMATION			
Book	bk.	Press	P
Chapter	ch. or chap.	Scene	sc.
Edition	ed.	Section	sec. or sect.
Line	line	Series	ser.
Lines	lines	University	U
Page	p.	University Press	UP
Pages	pp.	Volume	vol.
Paragraph	par.	Volumes	vols.

50B-1 Print sources—books and pamphlets

1. Book—basic entry

Author — Title

Balliett, Whitney. *New York Notes: A Journal of Jazz, 1972-1975.* Boston: Houghton, 1976. Print.

Publication information (Place: Publisher, Year.) — Medium

IN-TEXT NOTE: (Balliett 5)

For many books, pamphlets, and brochures, you need only list author(s), title, and basic publication details (place, publisher, and year), followed by the word *Print.* Be sure also to address the following questions to avoid omitting details relevant to many kinds of books used for academic research:

- **Is an editor, translator, or other contributor listed on the title page?** List secondary acknowledgments after the title. See 50b-2.
- **Is an original publication date given on the book's copyright page or in an introduction?** Insert the original year of publication (no italics) after the title and before both secondary contributions (if any) and publication details for the edition used. See Models 2, 3, 9
- **Does the title page list a name or number for the cited edition?** Insert the name or number of the edition (no italics) after the title and secondary contributors (if any). See Models 3, 4
- **Is the book part of a multi-volume set?** After the title and names of secondary contributors or the edition (if any), list the volume number you are using (no italics). But if you use more than one volume, give the total number of volumes, citing specific volume numbers in your in-text notes (see 50a-2.1). See Models 4, 5
- **Is the book, pamphlet, or brochure part of a series?** If the title page lists a publication series, provide the series title (neither italicized nor in quotes) and the series number (if any) as supplementary information, following the *Print* medium (see Checklist 50.5). See Model 6
- **Are you using a digitized version of the book posted to a Web site or database?** For books appearing on *Google Books, Bartleby.com,* or any other Web site, begin your entry with original print publication details, which will either be given by the site or appear at the beginning of facsimile editions. Instead of closing with the *Print* medium, list the Web site or database housing the book and standard Web access details as discussed in 50b-5–8. See Models 8, 51, 97

2. Book—with original publication date

Angelou, Maya. *I Know Why the Caged Bird Sings.* 1969. New York: Bantam, 1997. Print.

IN-TEXT NOTE: (Angelou 45)

3. Book—subsequent edition

Holiday, Billie, and William Dufty. *Lady Sings the Blues.* 1956. Revised discography ed. London: Penguin, 1992. Print.

IN-TEXT NOTE: (Holiday and Dufty 113-14)

4. Book—multi-volume set, referring to one volume

Rampersad, Arnold. *The Life of Langston Hughes.* 2nd ed. Vol. 2. New York: Oxford UP, 2002. Print.

IN-TEXT NOTE: (Rampersad 14, 21)

5. Book—multi-volume set, referring to many volumes

Titon, Jeff Todd, and Bob Carlin. *American Musical Traditions.* 5 vols. New York: Schirmer-Gale, 2002. Print.

IN-TEXT NOTE: (Titon and Carlin 4: 36)

6. Book—one that is part of a series of books

Tuso, Joseph F. *Singing the Vietnam Blues: Songs of the Air Force in Southeast Asia.* College Station: Texas A&M UP, 1990. Print. Texas A&M U Military History Ser. 19.

IN-TEXT NOTE: (Tuso 78)

7. Pamphlet—unsigned

Women in Music and Art. Pittsburgh: Carnegie Lib., 1981. Print.

IN-TEXT NOTE: (*Women* 2)

8. Brochure—reproduced on Web site

Got Talent? Young Artist Talent Search 2009. Newark: New Jersey Performing Arts Center, 2008. *New Jersey Performing Arts Center.* Web. 20 May 2009.

IN-TEXT NOTE: (*Got* 8)

50B-2 Print sources—books with editors, translators, illustrators, etc.

9. Book—edited

Weems, Mason L. *The Life of Washington*. 1800. Ed. Marcus Cunliffe.
Cambridge: Harvard UP, 1962. Print.

IN-TEXT NOTE: (Weems 202)

Scholarly editions, translations, and anthologies rely on individuals besides the author(s). When editors, translators, or other contributors appear on the title page of a book, list their names and contributions after the title in the works-cited entry. The following questions should also be asked of other kinds of sources that list secondary efforts under the title:

- **Are you citing a reader, compilation, or anthology not focused on a single author?** List the editors or compilers first, unless citing a specific selection (see 50b-3). See Models 10, 19
- **Are multiple secondary contributors listed on the title page?** A book might be both edited and translated, for example. List each contributor shown on the title page as either the primary acknowledgment or a secondary one. See Models 11, 12, 15
- **Is someone listed as contributing in two ways?** List both contributions before the person's name; after, if the person is given primary acknowledgment. See Models 13, 15
- **Does it make sense to focus on someone other than the author?** If your paper focuses on an editor or translator, for example, present that person first in the entry, before the title. Then list the author of the source (preceded with the word *By*) after the title, where you would normally provide secondary acknowledgments. See Models 10, 14, 15
- **Are you citing a graphic novel or illustrated work?** Often the illustrator(s) are also the author(s). Yet sometimes multiple contributors appear on the cover. Determine who should be listed as the primary acknowledgment based on how you intend to discuss the source in your paper. Give others as secondary credits. See Model 15

10. Anthology or reader

Crane, Diana, Nobuko Kawashima, and Ken'ichi Kawasaki, eds. *Global Culture: Media, Arts, Policy, and Globalization*. New York: Routledge, 2002. Print.

IN-TEXT NOTE: (Crane, Kawashima, and Kawasaki iv-v)

11. Book— translated (with help of author)

Fuentes, Carlos. *A New Time for Mexico*. Trans. Marina Gutman Castañeda and Fuentes. Berkeley: U of California P, 1997. Print.

IN-TEXT NOTE: (Fuentes 89)

12. Book— multiple secondary contributors

Gandhi, M. K. *The India of My Dreams*. Comp. R. K. Prabhu. Fore. Rajendra Prasad. Bombay: Hind Kitabs, 1947. Print.

IN-TEXT NOTE: (Gandhi 131)

13. Book— one person contributing in two ways

Nagarjuna. *Verses from the Center: A Buddhist Vision of the Sublime*. Ed. and trans. Stephen Batchelor. New York: Riverhead, 2000. Print.

IN-TEXT NOTE: (Nagarjuna 91)

14. Book— focus on editor

Rice, Julian, ed. *Ella Deloria's* The Buffalo People. By Ella Deloria. Albuquerque: U of New Mexico P, 1994. Print.

IN-TEXT NOTE: (Rice 45)

15. Book— graphic novel, adapted from book

Porcellino, John, adapt. and illus. *Thoreau at Walden*. By Henry David Thoreau. Intro. D. B. Johnson. New York: Hyperion, 2008. Print.

IN-TEXT NOTE: (Porcellino 11-12)

50B-3 Print sources—book parts, chapters, and selections

16. Book part—story by author of collection

Author | **Title of book part** | **Title of book**

Mason, Bobbie Ann. "Detroit Skyline, 1949." *"Shiloh" and Other Stories.* New York: Colophon-Harper, 1982. 34-52. Print.

Publication information (Place: Publisher, Year. Pages.) | **Medium**

IN-TEXT NOTE: (Mason 36)

When using only part of a book, create an entry for the book itself, inserting the title of the selection used just before the title of the book. After the book's publication information, provide the pages where the selection appears, just before the *Print* medium. Some book parts are cited differently, especially those not written by the book's main author(s).

- **Is the selection an introduction, preface, foreword, or afterword?** Describe the type of selection after the name of the selection's author(s) or title (if any). See Models 17, 18
- **Is the selection an interview, letter, map, diagram, or other special genre?** Consult 50b-12 for other special information to include before the book's publication details and medium. See Model 22
- **Is the selection by someone other than the book's author?** List the *selection's* author(s) first, then its title, the book's title, and the book's author(s) as a secondary acknowledgment (see 50b-2), all before the publication details and pages. See Model 18
- **Is the selection from an anthology?** List the selection's author(s) first, then the title of the selection. Name editors or compilers after the title of the book (see 50b-2). See Model 19
- **Is the selection an article from a reference work?** For well-known reference works, omit page numbers, secondary acknowledgments, volume information, place, and publisher. But provide this information for less familiar, more specialized reference works. Always list edition and year. See Models 20, 21

17. Book part—untitled preface by authors of book

Alfrey, Judith, and Catherine Clark. Preface. *The Landscape of Industry: Patterns of Change in the Ironbridge Gorge*. London: Routledge, 1993. xi-xii. Print.

IN-TEXT NOTE: (Alfrey and Clark xi)

18. Book part—by secondary contributor

Surtz, Edward. "*Utopia* Past and Present." Introduction. *Utopia*. By Thomas More. Ed. Surtz. New Haven: Yale UP, 1964. vii-xxx. Print.

IN-TEXT NOTE: (Surtz xii)

19. Book part—from reader, anthology, or compilation

Tschumi, Bernard. "Architecture and the City." *The Unknown City: Contesting Architecture and Social Space*. Ed. Iain Borden, et al. Cambridge: MIT P, 2001. 370-85. Print.

IN-TEXT NOTE: (Tschumi 382)

20. Reference article—less-known reference

"Polixenes." *The Oxford Companion to English Literature*. Ed. M. Drabble. Oxford: Oxford UP, 1998. Print.

IN-TEXT NOTE: ("Polixenes")

21. Reference article—well-known reference

"Ypsilanti." *The New Encyclopædia Britannica: Micropædia*. 15th ed. 1987. Print.

IN-TEXT NOTE: ("Ypsilanti")

22. Letter—published in edited book

Steinbeck, John. "To Lyndon B. Johnson." 24 Nov. 1963. *Steinbeck: A Life in Letters*. Ed. Elaine Steinbeck and Robert Wallsten. New York: Viking, 1975. 787-88. Print.

IN-TEXT NOTE: (Steinbeck 788)

50B-4 Print sources—articles in newspapers, magazines, journals, and other periodicals

23. Newspaper article

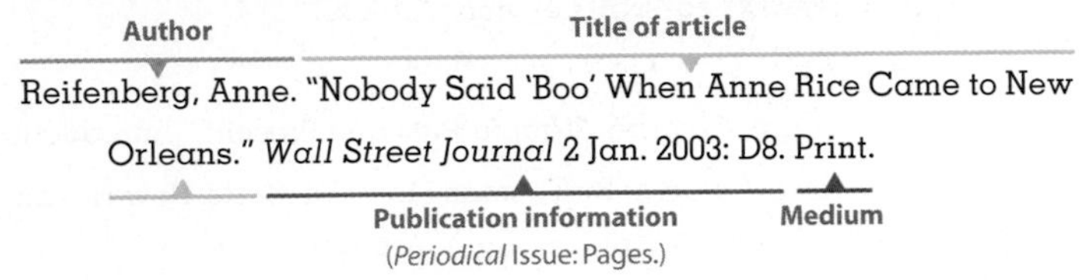

Author
Title of article
Reifenberg, Anne. "Nobody Said 'Boo' When Anne Rice Came to New
Orleans." Wall Street Journal 2 Jan. 2003: D8. Print.
Publication information
(Periodical Issue: Pages.)
Medium

IN-TEXT NOTE: (Reifenberg)

Begin with the author(s) and title of the article (in quotation marks). Then list the periodical (italicized), the issue, and pages where the article can be found. If you accessed the article through a printed copy, end your entry with the word *Print.* If you used the Web to access a digitized version of the article, consult also 50b-6 (for articles read on newspaper, magazine, or journal Web sites) or 50b-7 (for articles acquired from online research databases or library subscription services).

Whether you accessed the article in print or on the Web, note the different ways of identifying the issue, depending on the type of periodical being used:

- **Are you citing a newspaper article?** Identify the issue by the date that appears on its masthead. After the date, provide information about the edition you used and the section where the article appeared. *Do not* list volume or issue numbers, but *do,* when not clear from the title, list the publication city (in square brackets). See Models 23, 24
- **Are you citing a magazine article?** Identify the issue of the magazine by the date that appears on the cover—*do not* list volume or issue numbers. See Models 25, 26, 30
- **Are you citing a journal article?** Identify the issue of the journal by the combined volume (if any) and issue numbers (separated by a period) and year (in parentheses). *Do not* insert *vol., volume,* or *issue* before the volume and/or issue numbers. In the rare case that the journal has restarted its numbering sequence, tell readers which series you are using just before the volume and issue numbers—use *ns* for "new series." See Models 27–29
- **Are you citing an editorial, review, letter to the editor, interview, cartoon, comic strip, or advertisement?** Insert a description of the type of article after the title. See 50b-12.

24. Newspaper article—with edition

"Despite Recent Appeals, Blood Supplies Are Low." *New York Times* 3 Aug. 1998, late ed.: B4. Print.

IN-TEXT NOTE: ("Despite")

25. Magazine article—weekly

Klein, David. "Emmy-Worthy *Buffy* Musical Slays This Critic." *Television Weekly* 8 July 2002: 6. Print.

IN-TEXT NOTE: (Klein)

26. Magazine—monthly

Olders, Henry G., and Anthony D. Del Genio. "What Causes Insomnia?" *Scientific American* Oct. 2003: 103. Print.

IN-TEXT NOTE: (Olders and Del Genio)

27. Journal article

Ratcliffe, John M., Brock M. Fenton, and Bennett G. Galef. "An Exception to the Rule: Common Vampire Bats Do Not Learn Taste Aversions." *Animal Behavior* 65.4 (2003): 385-89. Print.

IN-TEXT NOTE: (Ratcliffe, Fenton, and Galef 386-87)

28. Journal article

Whalen, Tom. "Romancing Film: Images of Dracula." *Literature-Film Quarterly* 23.2 (1995): 99-101. Print.

IN-TEXT NOTE: (Whalen 99)

29. Journal article—in journal with multiple series

Johnson, Judith E. "Women and Vampires: Nightmare or Utopia?" *Kenyon Review* ns 15.1 (1993): 72-80. Print.

IN-TEXT NOTE: (Johnson 77)

30. Magazine article—interview printed in weekly

Stewart, Kristen. "*Twilight*'s Rising Star." Interview. *People* 1 Dec. 2008: 40+. Print.

IN-TEXT NOTE: (Stewart 40)

50B-5 Web sources—the basics

31. Web page

Author — Title of page

Mendonca, Tami. "Commute-Altering Epiphany." *Rails-to-Trails Conservancy*. RTC, 2007. Web. 20 Apr. 2009.

Publication information (*Site*. Sponsor, Date.) — **Medium** with access date

IN-TEXT NOTE: (Mendonca)

Begin by listing primary credits for the source and the title of the specific page or section used. Then, list the title of the containing site (in italics), the sponsor or publisher of the site, and the date the source was posted to the site. Finally, identify the medium as *Web* and give the date you last accessed the source. A Web address (or URL) is not required for MLA style, but may be provided as supplementary information after the access date (see Checklist 50.5 on page 715). Ask your instructor if a URL is required.

- **Are you citing an entire Web site?** First list authorial credits for the full site (if any). Then give the site's title, its publisher, the last update or copyright date, and Web access details. See Model 32
- **Are you citing a home page for a site or person?** After or in place of the title of a specific page, put *Home page.* See Models 35, 36
- **Is a posting date missing for the specific page(s) cited?** When no dates are provided for the pages used (check headers and footers), give the last copyright date for the full site. If no dates are found at all, put *n.d.* in place of the publication date. See Models 32, 38, 39
- **Is it unclear who sponsors the site?** A publisher's name usually appears somewhere on a site: check page footers, the home page, or "about" pages. The publisher is often listed alongside a copyright date. Put *N.p.* for sites listing no publisher. See Models 36, 56
- **Are secondary contributors listed for the source?** When emphasized by the source, list them after the title of the specific page or overall site, depending upon their contributions. List a secondary contributor first if it better suits your purpose. See Models 38, 46, 56, 60
- **Does the site containing the source provide different editions or versions of content?** Some sites vary content according to language, membership, or interactivity (e.g., *Flash version*). Some number subsequent editions. Indicate the version or edition you used after the site's title and secondary contributors. See Models 33, 34, 37

32. Web site

Active Living by Design. North Carolina Inst. for Pub. Health, n.d. Web. 24 Apr. 2009.

IN-TEXT NOTE: (*Active*)

33. Web page—online reference undated article

"Extreme Sports." *Encyclopaedia Britannica Online*. Premium ed. Encyclopaedia Britannica, 2009. Web. 24 Apr. 2009.

IN-TEXT NOTE: ("Extreme")

34. Web page—online reference

"Mountain Bike." *Wikipedia*. English ed. Wikimedia Foundation, 16 May 2009. Web. 18 May 2009.

IN-TEXT NOTE: ("Mountain")

35. Home page—organizational

Natl. Recreation Trails Prog. Home page. *National Recreation Trails Program*. American Trails, 2008. Web. 24 Apr. 2009.

IN-TEXT NOTE: As National Recreation Trails notes . . .

36. Home page—personal

Overend, Ned. Home page. *Facebook*. N.p., 2009. Web. 24 Apr. 2009.

IN-TEXT NOTE: (Overend)

37. Web page—on multi-version site

"Provo River Parkway." *TrailLink.com*. Members vers. Rails-to-Trails Conservancy, 2009. Web. 27 Apr. 2009.

IN-TEXT NOTE: ("Provo")

38. Web page—with secondary contributors

Riter, Jan, and Mike Riter. "Rolling Crown Switchbacks—The Basics." Illus. Tommy Reagh. Blueprint Rick Knoke. *IMBA.com*. Intl. Mountain Biking Assn., n.d. Web. 29 Apr. 2009.

IN-TEXT NOTE: (Riter and Riter)

39. Web page—signed by compiler

Weir, Don, comp. "A Bibliography of Trail and Recreation Issues." *IMBA.com*. Intl. Mountain Biking Assn., n.d. Web. 29 Apr. 2009.

IN-TEXT NOTE: (Weir)

50B-6 Web sources—online articles and blogs

40. Online article—Web magazine

Author | **Title of article**

Gross, Daniel. "Bubble, Bubble, Toil and Trouble." *Slate*. Washington Post; Newsweek Interactive, 2 Mar. 2007. Web. 10 Jul. 2009.

Publication information (*Site*. Sponsor, Date) | **Medium** with access date

IN-TEXT NOTE: (Gross)

Some Web sites are similar to print periodicals: they feature regularly contributed articles from many different writers, all edited and approved (more or less) by the site's sponsor or chief editor. These sources are cited like other Web pages, albeit with minor variations.

- **Are you citing an article on a Web magazine or news site?** Begin with author and title (in quotation marks), as you would for a printed article (see 50b-4), but use the site name in place of the periodical title. Next list the site's publisher(s) and the date the article was posted. Close with *Web* access information. See Models 40, 41
- **Are you citing an article on a print periodical's Web site?** Cite it like articles in Web magazines, even though the site stands for a print source. Don't forget to list the site's sponsor (no italics)—even when the sponsor's name is the same as the site's title. See Models 42, 43
- **Are you citing an article published in a regularly issued Web journal?** Follow the same guidelines you would for articles in print journals (50b-4), but put *Web* access information in place of *Print*. Note that some Web-only journals won't have page numbering. If no other numbering exists (e.g., paragraphs), put *n. pag.* See Model 44
- **Are you citing a blog entry?** Cite it as you would an online magazine article, but use the blog's title (italicized) as the site name. Be sure to list the author, title, and date of the *specific blog entry used.* When the entry's author is different than the blog's primary author, list the blog's primary author after the blog's title. For content posted by *readers of the blog,* use the guidelines in 50b-8. See Models 45, 46, 90
- **Was the article originally published in print?** If the Web site provides details about an earlier printing, insert periodical publication details (50b-4) before the title of the Web site. (For articles from library research databases, see 50b-7.)

41. Online article—cable news Web site

Brennan, Tom. "Analyst: Housing Bubble Fears behind Us." *CNBC*. CNBC, 27 Dec. 2006. Web. 1 May 2009.

IN-TEXT NOTE: (Brennan)

42. Online article—print magazine's Web site

Shilling, A. Gary. "The Pin That Bursts the Housing Bubble." *Forbes.com*. US ed. Forbes.com, 21 Jul. 2005. Web. 17 May 2009.

IN-TEXT NOTE: (Shilling)

43. Online article—newspaper's Web site

Leonhardt, David. "Be Warned: Mr. Bubble's Worried Again." *New York Times*. Global ed. New York Times, 21 Aug. 2005. Web. 17 May 2009.

IN-TEXT NOTE: (Leonhardt 2)

44. Online article—Web-only journal

Lazonick, William. "Evolution of the New Economy Business Model." *Business and Economic History On-line* 3 (2005): 1-60. Web. 1 May 2009.

IN-TEXT NOTE: (Lazonick 34)

45. Blog posting

Glick, Alexis. "Housing Bubble Caused Bigger Burst than Expected." *Glick Report*. Fox News Network, 26 Sep. 2008. Web. 11 May 2009.

IN-TEXT NOTE: (Glick)

46. Blog posting—not by blog's primary authors

Hirsh, Michael. "The Dotcom Bubble Revisited." *Wealth of Nations*. By Rana Foroohar, et al. Newsweek, 8 Apr. 2009. Web. 1 Jun. 2009.

IN-TEXT NOTE: (Hirsh)

50B-7 Web sources—online databases and library subscription services

47. Newspaper article—republished in library database

Author | Title of article

Ceccarossi, Kristi. "He Delivers, from Farm to Doorstep." *Boston Globe* 7 Sep. 2008, 3rd ed.: Reg3. *LexisNexis*. Web. 2 May 2009.

Publication information (Print details from 50b-4 and *Database*) **Medium** with access date

IN-TEXT NOTE: (Ceccarossi)

One of the most common and reliable ways to find sources is through your library's research databases, which may include *LexisNexis*, *Academic Search Premiere*, or more specialized indexes. Many of them provide the full text of articles and books originally appearing as print sources, or even audio and video recordings originally produced as CDs or DVDs. If you access the content of the source directly from the Web database (rather than by finding a copy of the original printed or recorded source), provide both original publication details *and* those for the Web.

- **Are you citing a journal, newspaper, or magazine article originally appearing in print?** Start with the print details outlined in 50b-4, but replace the original *Print* medium with the name of the database (italicized) and Web access details. See Models 47–49
- **Are you citing a printed book or book part digitized and republished on the Web?** Start your entry with the print information outlined in 50b-1–3—use the details provided by the database. Replace *Print* with Web database and access details. See Models 50, 51, 97
- **Are you citing an image, video clip, or audio track found in a database?** If the database lists earlier production information (in a book, on a CD, as an LP, etc.), create an entry for the original publication, but replace the original medium description (*Print*, *CD*, etc.) with Web database and access details. See Models 52, 54
- **Does the database omit earlier publication details?** List primary credit(s), title, and secondary acknowledgments like a source of similar genre. Then give database and Web access details. See Model 53
- **Does the database link you to an independent Web site housing the source?** Cite the source as you would any other Web content found without using the database. You don't need to list the database or search engine if all it did was help you find another Web site.

48. Magazine article—in database

Erney, Diana. "Farm-Fresh Food Comes to Cities." *Organic Gardening* May 2009: 42. *Academic Search Complete*. Web. 15 May 2009.

IN-TEXT NOTE: (Erney)

49. Journal article—in database

Burcher, Chris L., et al. "Fish Assemblage Responses to Forest Cover." *Environmental Management* 41.3 (2008): 336-46. *Agricola*. Web. 22 May 2009.

IN-TEXT NOTE: (Burcher et al. 339, 345)

50. Book part—in database

Taylor, Henry C. "The Choice of Crops." *Agricultural Economics*. New York: MacMillan, 1919. 43-53. *Google Book Search*. Web. 11 May 2009.

IN-TEXT NOTE: (Taylor 52)

51. Book—in database

Dean, Virgil W. *Opportunity Lost: The Truman Administration and the Farm Policy Debate*. Columbia: U of Missouri P, 2006. *Ebrary*. Web. 25 May 2009.

IN-TEXT NOTE: (Dean 202-03)

52. Audio track—CD digitized to database

Tchaikovsky, Pyotr Ilyich. "August: The Harvest." Perf. Rosson Popov. *Les Saisons*. Bella Musica, n.d. *Naxos Music Library*. Web. 29 Apr. 2009.

IN-TEXT NOTE: In Tchaikovsky's "Harvest," . . .

53. Photo—in database, no earlier version

Talbot, Toby. *Vegetable Farmer Joe Buley*. 14 Oct. 2008. *AP Images*. Web. 29 Apr. 2009.

IN-TEXT NOTE: Toby Talbot captures . . .

54. Painting—image of museum piece in database

Walker, Horatio. *The Harrower*. 1890-5? Metropolitan Museum, New York. *Oxford Art Online*. Web. 15 May 2006.

IN-TEXT NOTE: Walker's *Harrower* depicts . . .

50B-8 Web sources—online postings, streaming multimedia content, and downloaded files

55. Online posting—discussion forum

Puzzled. "World Music." Online posting. *Salon TableTalk: Music and Performing Arts*. Salon Media, 15 Apr. 2006. Web. 13 Feb. 2009.

IN-TEXT NOTE: (Puzzled)

Below we discuss some special Web genres. While the citation guidelines for these sources are essentially the same as those already discussed for Web sources, there are some variations to note, especially when the cited material (whether content or comments) has been posted by a reader or user of a Web site, rather than by a site's own authors or editors.

- **Are you citing a posting to a discussion forum?** Start your entry with the author of the posting (often a username), its title (if any), and the words *Online posting*. Then list the forum's title (in italics), the site's sponsor, and the posting date. Close with *Web* access details. See Model 55
- **Are you citing reader comments posted to a specific Web page or article?** Follow the guidelines above for forum postings, but, in place of the forum title, list the title and authorial credits for the page receiving comments just before the site, sponsor, and date. See Model 56
- **Are you citing reader-posted content?** Cite the source like a discussion forum posting, replacing the forum title with the name of the user-generated site or blog. See Models 57, 60
- **Are you citing streaming audio or video content?** Cite streaming content like Web pages, but list appropriate secondary credits after the title of the source, just as you would for similar material on broadcast or recorded media (see 50b-10–11). See Models 58, 60
- **Are you citing audio or video previously broadcast or produced as CD, DVD, etc.?** If listed on the Web site, insert the original production details just before the title of the site. See Models 52, 58
- **Are you citing a file downloaded from the Web?** No matter the file format (*MPEG, PDF, JPEG, Word*, etc.), treat the source as you would any other Web source with similar content (i.e., articles, videos, images, interviews, etc.). For digital files acquired through other means (podcasts, etc.) see 50b-11. See Models 59, 61

56. Online posting— reader comment to page

Friedman, Richard S. [Kinky]. Online posting. "Gillian Welch." Home page. By Welch. *MySpace.com*. N.p., 21 May 2009. Web. 1 Jun. 2009.

IN-TEXT NOTE: (Friedman)

57. Online posting— reader-contributed article

Indiananews. "Folksinger, Storyteller, Railroad Tramp Utah Phillips Dead at 73." Online posting. *iReport*. Cable News Network, May 2008. Web. 15 Feb. 2009.

IN-TEXT NOTE: (Indiananews)

58. Streaming audio—radio interview reproduced on Web

Mellencamp, John. "The Modern Mortal." Interview with Terry Gross. *Fresh Air*. Natl. Public Radio. WHYY, n.p., 31 Mar. 2009. *NPR Music*. Web. 23 Apr. 2009.

IN-TEXT NOTE: (Mellencamp)

59. Photo series— downloaded from Web site, many sponsors

Viri, Denis. *Dancers and Musicians*. 1996. *The Pascua Yaqui Connection*. Pascua Yaqui Tribe, Pima CC, and U of Arizona, n.d. Web. 15 Feb. 2009.

IN-TEXT NOTE: (Viri)

60. Streaming video—user-posted content

Sampradaya School of Dance, perfs. "Kolata—An Indian Folk Dance." Online posting. By Psamak. *YouTube.com*. YouTube, 20 Mar. 2008. Web. 6 Feb. 2009.

IN-TEXT NOTE: (Sampradaya)

61. Newsletter article—PDF file downloaded from Web site

Massari, Nashma Carrera. "Nuestra Musica: Latino Chicago at the Folk and Roots Festival." *Talk Story* Fall 2008: 11-12. *Smithsonian Center for Folklife and Cultural Heritage*. Web. 12 Feb. 2009.

IN-TEXT NOTE: (Massari 12)

50B-9 Recorded media—films, CDs, DVDs, etc.

62. CD—musical recording

Artist | Title of recording | Secondary credits

Mayer, John. *Heavier Things*. Prod. Jack Joseph Puig. Sony, 2003. CD.

Production information (Vendor, Year.) | Medium

IN-TEXT NOTE: (Mayer)

List the vendor and year of the recording just before the media format used (*Film, CD, DVD, Cassette, VHS, DVD-ROM,* etc.). What precedes the production details and medium depends on the type of source:

- **Is the source an audio recording?** Begin with the artist(s) or composer(s), unless it makes sense to focus on a different contributor (a producer, for example). Next list the title and other contributors. If you want to focus on a single selection, a song or other kind of track, list its title before that of the recording. See Models 62, 63
- **Is the source a film or video recording?** Begin with the title, unless you wish to foreground a particular contributor (the director, scriptwriters, etc.). See Models 64–66
- **Are you referring to supplementary or "bonus" material?** List the author(s) of the supplement first; then describe the material (*Libretto, Liner notes, Booklet, Interview with director*, etc.). Finally, provide basic production details for the recording. See Models 67, 68, 99
- **Is the source a recording of a live performance?** List information about the performance before the production details for the audio or video recording. See 50b-10. See Model 77
- **Are you using a source published on a CD-ROM or DVD-ROM?** Recorded media can, like the Web, provide a variety of kinds of content, from encyclopedia articles to interactive maps. Entries begin with typical acknowledgments and titles for a source of similar genre (article, drawing, painting, etc.). If the source lists information about an earlier publication, provide these details just before the vendor, date, and media format (*CD-ROM* or *DVD-ROM*). See Model 69
- **Are you using a Web reproduction of a recording?** Create an entry for the recording, including original production information (if available), but alter the medium description to reflect the version used. For files downloaded from a Web site or database, see 50b-7–8. For files acquired through other means (podcasts, etc.), see 50b–11.

63. CD audio track—song

Funkadelic. "Biological Speculation." *America Eats Its Young*. Westbound, 1972. LP.

IN-TEXT NOTE: (Funkadelic)

64. DVD—movie adaptation of book

Haas, Philip, and Belinda Haas, adapt. *Angels and Insects*. By A. S. Byatt. Dir. P. Haas. Samuel Goldwyn, 1996. DVD.

IN-TEXT NOTE: (Haas and Haas)

65. Film—viewed in theater

Species. Dir. Roger Donaldson. Perf. Ben Kingsley, Forest Whitaker, and Natasha Henstridge. MGM, 1995. Film.

IN-TEXT NOTE: (*Species*)

66. Film—focus on director

Spielberg, Stephen, dir. *Jurassic Park*. Perf. Jeff Goldblum, Wayne Knight, and Sam Neill. Universal, 1993. Film.

IN-TEXT NOTE: (Spielberg)

67. DVD bonus material

Maguire, Tobey. Actor's audio commentary. *Spider-Man 2*. Columbia, 2004. DVD.

IN-TEXT NOTE: (Maguire)

68. CD booklet

Terrell, Tom. Booklet. *Evolution (and Flashback): The Very Best of Gil Scott-Heron*. BMG, 1999. CD.

IN-TEXT NOTE: (Terrell)

69. CD-ROM article—from electronic reference

"Galápagos Islands." *Encarta Reference Library*. Microsoft, 2004. CD-ROM.

IN-TEXT NOTE: ("Galápagos")

50B-10 Broadcast and live media—TV, radio, speeches, dramatic performances, etc.

70. Speech

Speaker — Title of speech

Kelly, Randy. "The Future of Saint Paul: Progress through Partnerships." U of Minnesota Student Center, St. Paul. 10 Apr. 2003. Speech.

Production information (Venue, City. Date.) — Medium

IN-TEXT NOTE: (Kelly)

Performances, speeches, and broadcasts occur at specific times and places. Their citation formats reflect these conditions.

- **Are you citing a speaker you heard as a live audience member?** List the speaker(s) and title of the talk or a description (*Reading of*. . ., etc.). Then list the event and its sponsoring group (if applicable), the venue, the city, and the date. For the medium, describe the presentation format (*Lecture, Keynote address*, etc.). See Models 70, 71
- **Is the source an interview you conducted?** List the interviewee, the medium (e.g., *Telephone interview*), and the date(s). See Model 72
- **Are you citing a television or radio broadcast?** Begin with the title of the program, unless you wish to foreground a particular contributor (a narrator or an actor, for example). After the program title, list secondary contributors, the broadcasting network, the station, the city, and the date. Close with *Television* or *Radio*. See Model 73
- **Are you citing a specific episode or segment of a TV or radio program?** Insert the episode or segment title (in quotation marks) before the program title. (Note that secondary acknowledgments may apply to the episode or segment, but not the entire program—place contributors' names after the appropriate title.) See Model 74
- **Are you citing a live performance?** Begin with the title of the work being performed, unless you wish to foreground a particular contributor (a scriptwriter or the director, for example). After the title, list secondary contributors, the performance venue, the city, and the date of the show. The medium is listed as *Performance*. See Model 75
- **Is the source reproduced as a recording or transcript?** Begin with standard details, noted above. For recordings, insert the abbreviation *Rec.* before the original production information. Replace the original medium with publication and medium details for the source used. For transcripts insert *Transcript* after the medium. See Models 76, 77

71. Reading of book— sponsored group event

Alter, Beth. "Reading of Robert D. Putnam's *Bowling Alone*." New Book Forum. Sociology Book Club. Library Cafe, Atlanta. 21 Feb. 2002. Reading.

IN-TEXT NOTE: (Alter)

72. Interview— by researcher

Halsam, Gerald. Personal interview. 24 Apr. 2003.

IN-TEXT NOTE: (Halsam)

73. TV program— miniseries

Eyes on the Prize. 14 episodes. PBS. WOSU, Columbus, 2 Oct.-18 Dec. 2006. Television.

IN-TEXT NOTE: In *Eyes on the Prize*, . . .

74. Radio segment

"L.A. Votes to Break Up Its Landmark—Hollywood." *Which Way L.A.?* Host Warren Olney. Natl. Public Radio. KCRW, Santa Monica, 5 June 2002. Radio.

IN-TEXT NOTE: ("L.A.")

75. Dramatic performance

Our Town. By Thornton Wilder. Perf. Paul Newman. Dir. James Naughton. Westport Country Playhouse, Williamstown. 26 Sep. 2002. Performance.

IN-TEXT NOTE: In the production of *Our Town*, . . .

76. Speech— recorded audio on Web site

King, Martin Luther, Jr. "I Have a Dream." Rec. Lincoln Memorial, Washington. 28 Aug. 1963. *American Rhetoric*. By Michael E. Eidenmuller. N.p., 2009. Web. Apr. 26 2009.

IN-TEXT NOTE: (King)

77. Live musical performance on CD

Simon, Paul, and Art Garfunkel. *The Concert in Central Park*. Rec. 19 Sep. 1981. 2 discs. Warner Bros., 1990. CD.

IN-TEXT NOTE: (Simon and Garfunkel)

50B-11 Other media—gallery art, unpublished documents, e-mails, podcasts, digital files, etc.

78. Sculpture—viewed as public installation

Artist / Title of work / Medium

Rodia, Simon. *Watts Towers*. 1954. Mixed media on steel. Watts Towers Art Center, Los Angeles.

Collection information (Venue, City)

IN-TEXT NOTE: (Rodia)

For sources not accessed via any of the previously listed media, use the guidelines presented below. Some of these details may also be relevant for citing sources republished or reproduced in the forms already listed.

- **Are you citing artwork viewed in a gallery, museum, or public installation?** After the artist and the title of the work (italicized), describe the medium with as much detail as available. Then, identify the current holder of the work (a person or institution) and the city where it is housed. Use *Private collection* for works held by anonymous or unknown collectors. Cite images of the work in like manner, but replace the medium with Web or print details. See Models 78–80
- **Are you citing an unpublished letter, memo, or other non-digital document?** List the author(s), the subject line in quotation marks (for emails, memos), a description of the format and recipient (*Letter to* . . . , *Message to the author*, etc.), and the date sent. End the entry by describing the medium. Use *MS* for handwritten (manuscript) sources and *TS* for typed documents. If the document is held in an archive, give a reference number, collection, and city. See Models 82–84
- **Are you citing an e-mail?** Cite it like an unpublished memo (see above), but use *E-mail* as the medium. See Model 81
- **Are you citing a podcast?** Begin with primary credits and the title for the podcast. Then give the podcast program, its provider, and the date of the cast. For the medium, list the digital file format (*PDF file, JPEG file,* etc.); when unclear, put *Digital file*. See Models 85, 86
- **Are you citing a digital file not acquired from a Web site or podcast?** Begin the entry with the same details you would provide for a source of similar genre (book, memo, song, etc.). To find publication details, check the file's "info" or "properties." As with podcasts, close with a description of the digital file format.

79. Photo—in museum

Lange, Dorothy. *The Road West, New Mexico*. 1938. Gelatin silver print. Museum of Modern Art, New York.

IN-TEXT NOTE: (Lange)

80. Painting—in gallery

Cassatt, Mary. *In the Omnibus*. 1891. Drypoint and aquatint on laid paper. Chester Dale Collection. Natl. Gallery of Art, Washington.

IN-TEXT NOTE: (Cassatt)

81. E-mail—unpublished

Schwarz, Sigmar. "Who's Going to Sacramento?" Message to the author. 8 Oct. 2003. E-mail.

IN-TEXT NOTE: (Schwarz)

82. Memo—unpublished

Seward, Daniel. "Forum on Richard Rodriguez's *Hunger of Memory*." Memo to English Dept., California Lutheran U. 1 May 2003. TS.

IN-TEXT NOTE: (Seward)

83. Letter—unpublished

Galvan, Jill. Letter to the author. 1 July. 2001. MS.

IN-TEXT NOTE: (Galvan)

84. Archived document—speaker's notes

Sadler, Ralph. Speech to English House of Commons. N.d. MS Additional 33591. British Lib., London.

IN-TEXT NOTE: (Sadler)

85. Podcast—song

Yuill, James. "You Always Do." *Second Stage from* All Songs Considered. Natl. Public Radio, 23 May 2009. MP3 file.

IN-TEXT NOTE: (Yuill)

86. Podcast—video segment

"Sea Ice 2008." *NASACast: Earth Video*. Natl. Aeronautic and Space Assoc., 2 Oct. 2008. MP4 file.

IN-TEXT NOTE: ("Sea")

50B-12 Special genres—editorials, interviews, reviews, advertisements, cartoons, maps, and diagrams

87. Editorial article—in journal

Author | Title of piece and description

Goett, Pamela. "Houston, We Have a Problem." Editorial. *Journal of Business Strategy* 23.1 (2002): 2. Print.

Publication information (depends on medium used) **Medium**

IN-TEXT NOTE: (Goett)

Some special genres of writing or graphic content should be identified by inserting a descriptive word or phrase into the entry immediately after or in place of the title. The publication and medium information following the descriptor will depend upon how you accessed the source—use the guidelines for the appropriate media format presented in the preceding sections.

- **Is the source an editorial?** If the material appears on an editorial page or section, after the title, insert *Editorial.* See Models 87, 88
- **Is the source a letter to the editor or a reply to a letter?** After the title (if any), insert *Letter* or *Reply to letter.* See Model 89
- **Is the source an interview?** Begin with the interviewee, the title (if any) and a descriptor (*Interview with . . .*). For interviews you conduct yourself see 50b-10. See Models 30, 58
- **Is the source a critical review of another source?** After the title (if any), insert *Rev. of* followed by the title of what's being reviewed. You may list contributors for the work being reviewed after its title, separated by commas (not periods in this case). See Models 90, 91
- **Are you citing a map, chart, cartoon, or comic strip?** When the item is published separately, list the artist (if known), the title (italicized), a description (*Diagram, Map, Chart,* etc.), and standard publication details for the medium used. When the item appears inside another source, place the title in quotation marks instead of italics and provide standard publication and medium details for the containing source (book, Web, CD-ROM, etc.). See Models 93–95, 102
- **Is the source an advertisement?** Begin with the name of the product or the company (if no product is mentioned). Then insert *Advertisement* before publication and medium details. See Model 92
- **Is the source published correspondence?** Cite as you would memos or letters (see 50b-11), replacing the original medium with appropriate publication details for the source used. See Model 22

88. Editorial article—unsigned

"Houston, You Have a Problem." Editorial. *Scientific American* Aug. 2003: 10. Print.

IN-TEXT NOTE: ("Houston")

89. Letter to the editor—signed

Ceniceros, Claudia. Letter. *New York Times* 20 Aug. 2002, late ed.: A18. Print.

IN-TEXT NOTE: (Ceniceros)

90. Review of film—on Weblog

Johanson, Mary Ann. "Sounds of Silence." Rev. of *Apollo 13*, dir. Ron Howard. *The Flick Filosopher*. N.p., 10 Apr. 2002. Web. 8 Mar. 2008.

IN-TEXT NOTE: (Johanson)

91. Review of book—in printed journal

Bauman, Zygmunt. Rev. of *Risk and Blame: Essays in Cultural Theory*, by Mary Douglas. *British Journal of Sociology* 45.1 (1994): 143. Print.

IN-TEXT NOTE: (Bauman)

92. Ad—in magazine

PeopleSoft's Real-Time Enterprise. Advertisement. *Business Week* 9 June 2003: 17. Print.

IN-TEXT NOTE: (PeopleSoft)

93. Cartoon—in newspaper

Matson, R. J. "The Smartest Guys in the Room." Cartoon. *St. Louis Post-Dispatch* 26 May 2006: E1. Print.

IN-TEXT NOTE: (Matson)

94. Map—printed as govt. brochure

United States. Natl. Park Service. *Arches National Park*. Map. Natl. Park Service, 2001. Print.

IN-TEXT NOTE: (US Natl. Park Service)

95. Diagram—on a Web site

"How Small Wind Turbines Work." Diagram. 2002. *American Wind Energy Association*. Am. Wind Energy Assoc., 2003. Web. 2 Sept. 2003.

IN-TEXT NOTE: ("How")

50B-13 Special genres—sacred texts, musical compositions, and government documents

96. Sacred text—printed book

Title of edition — Editors, translators, etc.

The Bible: Authorized King James Version. 1611. Ed. Robert Carroll and Stephen Pricket. Oxford: Oxford UP, 1997. Print.

Publication information (depends on medium used) — Medium

IN-TEXT NOTE: (Matt. 19.24)

Although these works have traditionally appeared in print, they now are regularly accessed online. Provide standard publication information for the edition you are using, as you would with other kinds of sources.

- **Are you citing a sacred text?** Begin with the title of the edition (italicized); then list the date the particular edition was originally published (if available), secondary acknowledgments from the edition's title page, and publication and medium details. See Models 96, 97
- **Are you citing a musical composition?** If citing a published score, libretto, or lyrics, begin with the composer. Then give the title: italicize major works; put songs in quotation marks. Format the rest of the entry like other sources in the same medium. See Models 98, 99
- **Are you citing a government document?** Begin with the government entity (nation, state, etc.) and specific agency or department (if any). Then list the title (usually in italics, but in quotes for Web pages or parts of documents), secondary contributors (if any), and available publication information. See Models 100–102
- **Are you citing congressional documents?** If citing the *Congressional Record*, simply begin with *Cong. Rec.*; then list the date, page numbers, and medium consulted. For other congressional documents, start the entry like other government sources; after the title, list the session, the type and number of the document (see below), and publication and medium details for the version used. See Models 101, 103

Govt. Printing Off.	GPO	Senate	S
House of Representatives	HR	Senate Misc. Document	S. Doc.
House Misc. Document	H. Doc.	Senate Report	S. Rept.
House Report	H. Rept.	Senate Resolution	S. Res.
House Resolution	H. Res.	Session	sess.

97. Sacred text—Web version of printing

Rig Veda. Trans. Ralph T. H. Griffith. 1896. *Internet Sacred Text Archive*. Web. 29 Aug. 2003.

IN-TEXT NOTE: (Rig Veda 7.32)

98. Musical composition—book of classical scores

Vivaldi, Antonio. The Four Seasons *and Other Violin Concertos*. Ed. Eleanor Selfridge-Field. New York: Dover, 1995. Print.

IN-TEXT NOTE: Vivaldi's *Four Seasons* is . . .

99. Song lyrics—in CD booklet

White, Jack. "Seven Nation Army." Booklet. *Elephant*. By The White Stripes. Third Man Records, 2003. CD.

IN-TEXT NOTE: (White)

100. Govt. publication—brochure from local govt.

City of Columbus, OH. Public Services Dept. *Columbus Snow and Ice Plan*. N.p., n.d. Print.

IN-TEXT NOTE: (City of Columbus)

101. Govt. publication—printed official document of U.S. Congress

United States. Cong. Joint Committee on Printing. *1985-86 Official Congressional Directory*. 99th Cong., 1st sess. Washington: GPO, 1985. Print.

IN-TEXT NOTE: (US Cong. Joint Committee on Printing)

102. Govt. publication—map on state agency's Web site

Vermont. Agency of Natural Resources. "Environmental Interest Locator." Map. *Vermont Agency of Natural Resources*. VTANR, 2009. Web. 25 Apr. 2009.

IN-TEXT NOTE: (Vermont)

103. Congressional Record

Cong. Rec. 8 Feb. 1974: 3942-43. Print.

IN-TEXT NOTE: (*Cong. Rec*. 8 Feb. 1974)

50c Sample Research Paper—MLA

Corey Bobco, a student at the University of Texas at Austin, wrote the following research paper exploring and evaluating the environmental arguments of vegetarian and vegan advocates. Some modifications to Bobco's original paper have been made to highlight specific features of MLA style, but the paper still represents a typical example of what an extended academic research paper might look like. The paper is accompanied by annotations and checklists designed to help you set up a paper correctly.

Checklist 50.1 Formatting the Paper—MLA

Use the following settings in your word processor for most MLA papers, but adjust them to match special preferences set by your instructor. Subsequent checklists provide details for the title page, special items (quotations, tables, and figures), and the Works Cited page.

- **a. Use white, 8½-by-11-inch paper.** For a traditional academic assignment, never use colored or lined paper. Handwrite a paper only with an instructor's permission.
- **b. Insert your last name and page number one-half inch from the top of *every* page, aligned with the right-hand margin.** Insert a running *page header* into your document with your word processor's *Page Format* or *Insert* commands. (For more guidance, see also Section 13a.) Your options for page headers will usually allow you also to insert an automatically incremented page number.
- **c. Use the same readable font face throughout your paper.** Use a black typeface and avoid fonts with too much decoration, since they can be hard on the eyes. Also be sure to use a moderate text size, 10 to 12 points depending on the font face. (See also Section 18c.)
- **d. Double-space the entire document.** This includes the Works Cited page and title page. Use your word processor's *Format* or *Paragraph* options to select line spacing.
- **e. Left-align the body of the paper and do not hyphenate words at the end of the line.** You may need to turn off your word processor's automatic hyphenation tool. Do not right-justify the paper.
- **f. Indent the first word of each paragraph one-half inch.** Most word processors already set an indent for the first line of paragraphs. But insert a tab if necessary. Use your word processor's *Format* or *Paragraph* options to change indentation.

Checklist 50.2 Formatting Title Pages—MLA

MLA does not require a separate cover sheet or title page—instead, at the *top of the first page* list each of the following items on a *separate* line. All these items are double-spaced. Make sure not to add extra spaces before the title.

a. **List your full name on the first line of the first page, aligned to the left.**

b. **List your instructor's name with appropriate title, aligned to the left.** When uncertain about academic rank, use *Mr., Ms.*, or *Prof.* Better yet, look up the title in a campus directory—or simply ask.

c. **List the course for which you're writing the paper, aligned to the left.** You need only give the course prefix and number.

d. **List the date you submit the assignment, aligned to the left.** If submitting multiple drafts, make sure your final one has the correct date, so your instructor won't think you're turning in an older version.

e. **Give the title of your paper, capitalized and centered.** Follow the usual capitalization rules for titles—see Section 43b. Do not end the title with a period, but use a question mark when appropriate. Do not bold, underline, italicize, or specially format your title *except* specific words and phrases that typically require special formatting, such as titles of works being discussed and foreign language phrases.

Note: If your instructor does ask for a title page, center the title of your paper and your name in the upper third of the paper. Center the course title, your instructor's name, and the date on the lower third of the sheet, double-spacing each item. (See sample to the right.)

Vegan Diet: The Missing

Lesson in Environmental Education

Corey Bobco

Prof. Ruszkiewicz

Rhetoric 368C

25 May 2009

Checklist 50.3 Quotations, Tables, and Figures—MLA

a. **Format quotations correctly.** MLA requires that you present long quotations—more than four lines—in block format. *Block quotations* are *not* enclosed by quotation marks. The entire quotation is indented one inch from the left margin. Parenthetical citations go at the end of the full quotation, *after* end punctuation (unlike other parenthetical citations). Use the same double-spacing as the rest of the document. See Chapter 47 for more guidelines.

b. **Label and number tables, placing them as close as possible to related text.** Above the table, provide the label *Table*, an identifying number, and a caption, capitalized according to the standard rules for titles (see Section 43b). Double-space the table (assuming you're not using a borrowed image of a table), citing any source(s) used in a caption at the bottom. See also Sections 8c, 18b-2, 48b-2.

c. **Label and number illustrations and other visual material.** Place the item as close as possible to the related text, providing underneath the label *Fig.* (or *Figure*), an identifying number, the title (or a descriptive label or caption), and a source (if you did not create it yourself). For more on figures, see Sections 18d and 48b-2.

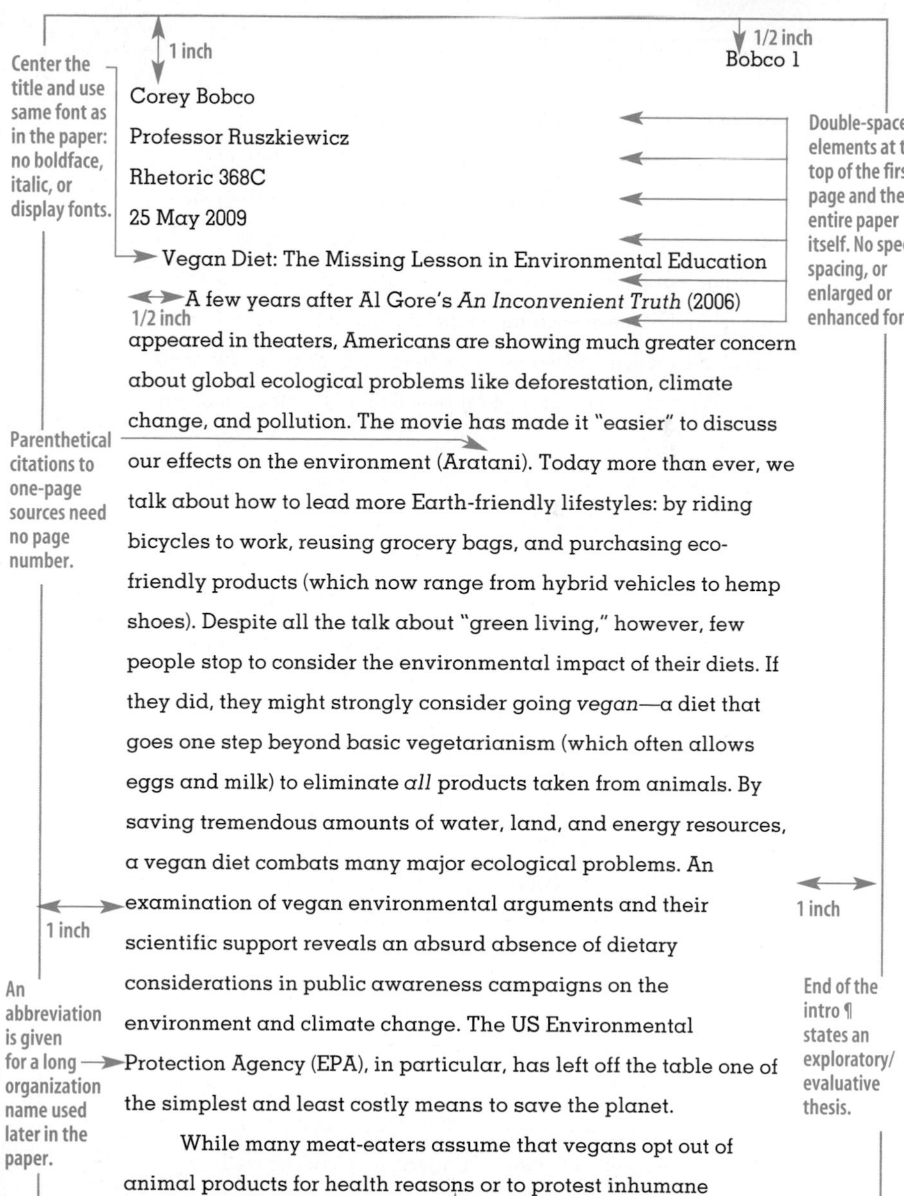
1 inch
1/2 inch
Center the title and use same font as in the paper: no boldface, italic, or display fonts.
Double-space all elements at the top of the first page and the entire paper itself. No special spacing, or enlarged or enhanced fonts.
1/2 inch
Parenthetical citations to one-page sources need no page number.
1 inch
1 inch
An abbreviation is given for a long organization name used later in the paper.
End of the intro ¶ states an exploratory/evaluative thesis.
1 inch

Bobco 1

Corey Bobco

Professor Ruszkiewicz

Rhetoric 368C

25 May 2009

Vegan Diet: The Missing Lesson in Environmental Education

A few years after Al Gore's *An Inconvenient Truth* (2006) appeared in theaters, Americans are showing much greater concern about global ecological problems like deforestation, climate change, and pollution. The movie has made it "easier" to discuss our effects on the environment (Aratani). Today more than ever, we talk about how to lead more Earth-friendly lifestyles: by riding bicycles to work, reusing grocery bags, and purchasing eco-friendly products (which now range from hybrid vehicles to hemp shoes). Despite all the talk about "green living," however, few people stop to consider the environmental impact of their diets. If they did, they might strongly consider going *vegan*—a diet that goes one step beyond basic vegetarianism (which often allows eggs and milk) to eliminate *all* products taken from animals. By saving tremendous amounts of water, land, and energy resources, a vegan diet combats many major ecological problems. An examination of vegan environmental arguments and their scientific support reveals an absurd absence of dietary considerations in public awareness campaigns on the environment and climate change. The US Environmental Protection Agency (EPA), in particular, has left off the table one of the simplest and least costly means to save the planet.

While many meat-eaters assume that vegans opt out of animal products for health reasons or to protest inhumane

Author's last name appears on every page

Bobco 2

treatment of animals, environmental concerns underscore the choice of many to eat a plant-based diet. The Vegan Society's Web site, for instance, dedicates a full section to revealing the environmental impacts of large-scale livestock production, observing, "Farmers used to be seen as 'custodian's [sic] of the countryside,' but the overriding image of modern industrial farming is one of destruction and waste." Likewise, on *EarthSave*, a site that "promotes a shift to a healthy plant-based diet," Dr. Stephen Boyan even more vividly presents the ecological case against cattle:

> Livestock now produces 130 times the amount of waste that people do. This waste is untreated and unsanitary. It bubbles with chemicals and disease-bearing organisms. It overpowers nature's ability to clean it up. It's poisoning rivers, killing fish and getting into human drinking water. . . . Even the oceans are polluted: 7,000 square miles of the Gulf of Mexico are a dead zone.

Boyan's picture of the toxic footprint left by livestock appears alongside other points presented at greater length in earlier writings of vegan advocates, including John Robbins, author of *Diet for a New America* (1987), and Peter Singer, author of *Animal Liberation* (1990). Robbins's book begins by presenting his "dream of a people . . . cherishing and caring for the natural environment, conserving nature instead of destroying it" (xiii), and he provides an entire chapter on "America the Poisoned" (308-49). Singer also highlights the pollution of industrial livestock farming (166-70). While Singer and Robbins both call attention to the ethics of caring for animals, many of their arguments are directed toward caring for the planet as well.

1 inch

EarthSave is italicized because it refers to the title of a Web site. Vegan Society above is not because it refers to a corporate author.

Introduce sources to show their credibility and relevance to your points.

1 inch

Indent block quote 1 inch from left-hand margin and double-space it. Omit " " around quotation.

If this source required a parenthetical page reference, it would go after the punctuation at the end of a block quote.

Tell readers when a source was published if it helps you show relevance or explain context.

Ellipsis show where material has been cut from the original quotation.

Bobco 3

To that end, Robbins, Singer, and other vegan activists go on to critique the meat diet's heavy consumption of water and land resources. The claims of the activists might at first sound exaggerated. Singer says, "more than half of all water consumed in the United States goes to livestock" (167). Robbins asserts, "It takes less water to produce a *year's* food for a pure vegetarian than to produce a *month's* food for a meat-eater" (367). But these statements become more believable when we consider that, aside from the drinking water required to sustain livestock, tremendous quantities are needed as well to irrigate the crops used to feed livestock. The Vegan Society's "Water" page lists various authorities for support. One is the United Nations Food and Agriculture Organization (FAO), which seeks to make sure people across the globe have healthy food and water, regardless the nature of their diets. The FAO's educational brochures point out that a kilo of beef requires 15,000 liters of water, while a kilo of wheat requires only 1,500 liters (*World*). (For the results of another study, see Table 1.) In terms of real meals, a hamburger requires 2,400 liters, an egg 130, an apple 70, a piece of bread 40, and a potato 25 (*Producing*). A meat-eater's hamburger needs almost a hundred times more water to produce than the potato used to make the accompanying French fries.

The UN FAO has multiple works-cited entries, so the title of the specific source referenced in each sentence is listed in the parenthetical note.

Raising livestock requires similarly disproportionate amounts of land. The Vegan Society's "Land" page refers to a 2002 study by scientists trying to determine the ecological "footprint" left by a typical diet in an industrialized country (Gerbens-Leenes, Nonhebel, and Ivens 55). As Table 1 below illustrates, the land requirements for meat drastically surpass those for plant-based foods.

It may seem cumbersome, but list all the last names for sources having two or three authors.

Make sure to explain the significance of figures and tables to readers.

Bobco 4

Label, number, and provide a caption for tables above the item.

Table 1

Water, Land, and Energy Inputs for Food Production

	(a) Water: liters/kg	(b) Land: meters²/kg	(c) Energy: input/output
Beef	43,000	20.9	20:1
Pork	n/a	8.9	14:1
Poultry	3,500	n/a	4:1
Eggs	n/a	3.5	39:1
Fruit (avg.)	n/a	.5	.91:1 (apple)
Vegetables (avg.)	n/a	.3	.24:1 (soybean)
Wheat	900	1.6 (flour)	.46:1
Potato	500	.2	.81:1

Sources: Column (a) from Pimentel and Pimentel 72; (b) from Gerbens-Leenes, Nonhebel, and Ivens 53; and (c) from Pimentel and Pimentel 69, 118, 132-5. Note that these columns come from separate studies giving results for different food items, so some values are not available (n/a) or substituted with a similar item (in parentheses).

List source information beneath the table.

Beef production requires 20.9 square meters per kilogram yielded, pork 8.9, and eggs 3.5. On the other hand, fruits and vegetables (the staples of a vegan diet) require, respectively, only .3 and .2 square meters per kilo of food yielded (53)—a tiny fraction compared to the massive demands of animal products. Again, the obvious explanation for the differences is simply that livestock require significant amounts of grain or forage land to build protein: 21 kilograms of grain yield only one kilo of beef (Pimentel and Pimentel 69). According to one article in the livestock trade journal *Feedstuffs*, adult cows are maintained with about 25 pounds per day of dry grain

Sources with four or more authors may include just the first author's name with *et al.*, as long as you followed the same format on the Works Cited page.

Bobco 5

(Linn et al. 12). Such masses of feed lead Robbins to point out that American livestock eat over "80% of the corn we grow, and over 95% of the oats," while the meat produced carries less than a fifth of the original grain's nutritional value (351). Ironically, *more* individuals eating *more* vegetables in place of meats requires *less* cropland and *less* water for irrigation, in order to feed the *same* number of people.

While people living in industrialized countries may take water and agricultural land for granted, usable quantities of these natural resources are becoming scarcer across the globe, a scary fact in itself and one that may contribute further to the even more catastrophic prospect of global warming. The FAO estimates that over one billion people currently have no access to clean water (*Water*). As for land, the huge appetites of livestock have consequences in a world with limited farmable acreage. To increase production, livestock producers often cut down long-standing forests. As Figure 1 below illustrates, in the Earth's "carbon cycle," forests act as "pools" collecting carbon-dioxide and draining it from the atmosphere (US EPA, "Local"). The arrows in the diagram show how the vital element carbon circulates between the atmosphere (as carbon-dioxide), the ground (in soil and fossil deposits), and living plants and animals. But as most people now know, carbon contributes to global warming when it accumulates in the atmosphere, where it adds to the greenhouse effect. The arrows pointing into the tree represent the ability of vegetation to absorb carbon-dioxide from the atmosphere and "sequester" carbon in living plants and under the soil (US EPA, "Local"). While all plants collect carbon as they grow, trees help

The EPA is a corporate author with multiple works-cited entries, so the title of the specific source used here is needed also.

store it for longer periods of time than feed crops, because the animals who eat the crops speed the return of carbon-dioxide back to the atmosphere. The more old trees we fell to grow feed for livestock, the more carbon migrates from the soil to the atmosphere.

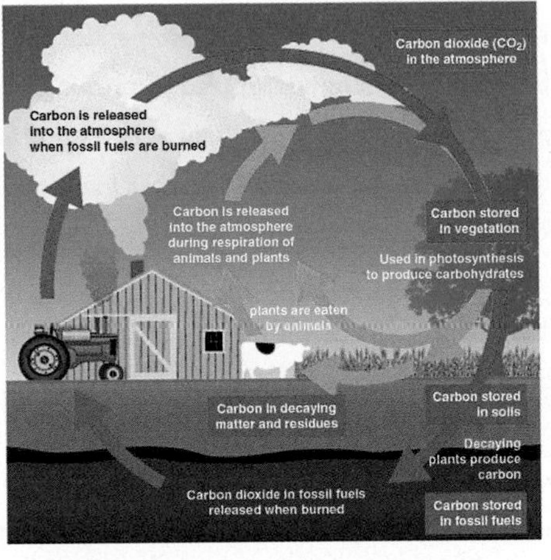

Label, number, and provide a caption for figures below the item, using "Fig." or "Figure."

Fig. 1. "The Carbon Cycle of a Farm," *Farming Futures* (Farming Futures, 2009), accessed on the Web. 10 May 2009.

Provide the source for the figure after the label. If the source is not referenced elsewhere in the paper, put full citation details here instead of on the Works Cited page.

Given our greater concern about greenhouse gas emissions, energy conservation has become the most vibrant aspect of contemporary environmental agendas, since the burning of fossil fuels, our primary source of energy, also accelerates the movement of carbon from the ground to the atmosphere (see fig. 1 above). Here again, vegan activists have been ahead of the curve in critiquing the inefficiency of livestock farming. Robbins observes, "If we kicked the meat habit . . . dependence on foreign oil would be greatly reduced" (376). This claim again has scientific bases.

Bobco 7

David and Marcia Pimentel, in the third edition of *Food, Energy, and Society* (2007), trace the cumulative fossil fuel energy requirements for the production of various foods. Column (c) in Table 1 above demonstrates the excessive energy requirements for producing meat in comparison to the energy it yields as food protein. Pimentel and Pimentel sum up their findings succinctly by noting, "energy input [for animal protein] is more than 10 times greater than the average input to output ratios for grain protein production" (70). The ratios for fruit and vegetables show that most provide more energy than used. Based on these figures, it is no wonder that the WorldWatch Institute has proclaimed, "American feed (for livestock) takes so much energy to grow that it might as well be a petroleum byproduct" (qtd. in Vegan Society, "Energy" sect.).

Brackets indicate that the quotation has been modified for readability—here a pronoun was replaced to clarify meaning.

The quotation from the World Watch Institute was quoted from the Vegan Society site, not directly from its original source—do this sparingly.

But carbon-dioxide is not the only greenhouse gas emitted by livestock production. Methane comes both from livestock manure and "enteric fermentation"—that is, the natural digestive process of cattle. As EarthSave's Boyan aptly summarizes (with a dash of humor), "cattle produce almost one fifth of global methane emissions. Cattle fart. Big time." The EPA lists methane as the second most abundant greenhouse gas, in terms of how it affects the atmosphere ("U.S. Greenhouse"). The EPA's calculations also show that the combined outputs of livestock manure and enteric fermentation represent the largest source of methane in the atmosphere ("Greenhouse," "Methane" sect.).

"Greenhouse Gas Emissions" is a multi-page source on the EPA Web site—here the title of the section referenced is given, almost like a page number for print sources.

Although the statements of vegan advocates about the environmental impacts of diet at first sound over-the-top, readers looking into the bases for vegan claims will find current scientific support, enough that the truly surprising fact is how diet has been

Bobco 8

omitted from taxpayer funded public-awareness campaigns about global warming. On one hand, the EPA has finally created a full *Climate Change* Web site to educate Americans about global warming, explaining the phenomenon, as well as giving tips for how individuals and organizations can help slow it down. On the other hand, the site's fairly limited "What You Can Do" section mentions nothing about choosing a plant-based diet, nor does it even suggest the simple solution of eating less meat. Instead the EPA offers a range of advice, from suggesting the exceedingly simple (if costly) task of replacing incandescent bulbs with compact fluorescent ones, to repeating the overly general mantra of "reduce, reuse, recycle" ("At Home" sect.). The EPA's advice seems surprisingly limited, given that the findings discussed above show eating plants instead of meat would seem to be one of the most simple *and* broadly effective means to conserve all types of resources. So why is it not mentioned?

There seems to be an inexplicable bias toward meat when it comes to taxpayer-sponsored environmental education in America. Have the vegan advocates missed something? Popular writer and journalist Michael Pollan thinks so. In a 2002 *New York Times* Web article, Pollan notes that many areas of the world, including his own hilly New England, suit grazing animals quite well, but not many crops. Thus he argues that a "vegetarian utopia" would be forced to import plant-based food, making such a region "even more dependent than [it] already [is] on an industrialized national food chain," and consequently, "even more dependent than it already is on fossil fuels and chemical fertilizer, since food would need to travel farther and manure would be in short supply" (10).

Some Web sources actually do have page numbers—cite them when available.

Bobco 9

Pollan, an advocate of *local* food production (to cut down the burning of transportation fuel), raises some valid concerns about possible unwanted side effects of mass veganism. His arguments, however, presume that people in such areas would primarily eat locally produced animal products. In other words, he envisions a local food utopia, which belies the true production method of the vast majority of meat Americans consume.

Concluding ¶ reconnects to opening thesis and expands upon its implications.

Whether or not Pollan's dire projections about mass veganism are accurate, the seeming resistance to recognizing veganism as a possible means for *individuals* to conserve resources seems incompatible with the urgency of our collective situation, both as popularized in Gore's film, but also as conveyed by those we charge with protecting our environment. If the EPA can advocate energy-saving compact fluorescent bulbs, which have been critiqued for increasing the danger of mercury poisoning (Matthiessen; Scelfo; Sheridan), then shouldn't the EPA present Americans with the vegan, or even vegetarian, option as another way of helping the environment? As people increasingly search for ways to reduce their negative impacts on the environment, it seems reasonable that the potential benefits of plant-based diets be made more public, perhaps in a manner similar to the FAO's educational brochures about water usage. It may be a touchy subject for many of us with cultural traditions or moral teachings that uphold the consumption of meat and other animal products, but the capacity of a vegan diet to save tremendous quantities of precious resources demands our attention as the threat of environmental devastation looms. After all, going vegan is a much more affordable option than a hybrid car for most of us . . . and does quite a bit more for our health and that of our planet.

Multiple references in one note are separated by semicolons—these sources are all one page, so need no page ref.

1/2 inch

1 inch

Bobco 10

Works Cited

Aratani, Lori. "Environmentalists Find Being Green Is Getting Easier: Al Gore's Film Has Raised Awareness of Energy Conservation, Officials Say." *Washington Post* 13 July 2007, suburban ed.: B03. *LexisNexis Academic*. Web. 12 May 2009.

Boyan, Steve. "How Our Food Choices Can Help Save the Environment." *EarthSave*. EarthSave International, n.d. Web. 7 May 2009.

Gerbens-Leenes, P. W., S. Nonhebel, and W. P. M. F. Ivens. "A Method to Determine Land Requirements Related to Food Consumption Patterns." *Agriculture, Ecosystems and Environment* 90.1 (2002): 47-58. Print.

Gore, Al, narr. *An Inconvenient Truth*. Dir. Davis Guggenheim. Paramount, 2006. Film.

Linn, J., et al. "Monitoring Feed Efficiency May Help Lactating Cows." *Feedstuffs* 11 Oct. 2004: 11-14. Print.

Matthiessen, Alex. "The Dark Side of Green Light." *New York Times* 29 July 2007, late ed.: CY9. *LexisNexis Academic*. Web. 22 May 2009.

Pimentel, David, and Marcia H. Pimentel. *Food, Energy, and Society*. 3rd ed. Boca Raton: CRC Press-Taylor and Francis, 2007. Print.

Pollan, Michael. "An Animal's Place." *New York Times*. New York Times, 10 Nov. 2002. Web. 3 May 2009.

Robbins, John. *Diet for a New America*. Walpole: Stillpoint, 1987. Print.

Scelfo, Julie. "Worrying about the Impact of Mercury in Fluorescents." *New York Times* 10 Jan. 2008, late ed.: F6. *LexisNexis Academic*. Web. 12 May 2009.

1/2 inch

1 inch

1 inch

Source comes from a library subscription service: LexisNexis.

An Inconvenient Truth is listed under Gore's name, since that is how it is referred to in the paper. Secondary acknowledgments give credit to its director.

Articles published on a newspaper's Web site are not cited the same way as those originally published in the printed newspaper itself.

Bobco 11

Sheridan, Michael. "'Green' Light Bulbs Poison Workers." *Sunday Times* [London] 3 May 2009, 3rd ed.: 25. *LexisNexis Academic*. Web. 12 May 2009.

Singer, Peter. "Becoming a Vegetarian." *Animal Liberation*. 1975. 2nd ed. New York: New York Review of Books, 1990. 159-84. Print.

United Nations. Food and Agriculture Organization. *Producing Food*. Chart. *FAO Water*. FAO, 2009. Web. 13 May 2009.

---. *Water Scarcity*. Chart. *FAO Water*. FAO, 2009. Web. 13 May 2009.

---. *The World Is Thirsty Because It Is Hungry*. Chart. *FAO Water*. FAO, 2009. Web. 13 May 2009.

United States. Environmental Protection Agency. "Greenhouse Gas Emissions." *Climate Change*. EPA, 12 May 2009. Web. 13 May 2009.

---. "Local Scale: Carbon Pools in Forestry and Agriculture." *Climate Change*. EPA, 19 Oct. 2006. Web. 13 May 2009.

---. "U.S. Greenhouse Gas Inventory." *Climate Change*. EPA, 20 Apr. 2009. Web. 11 May 2009.

---. "What You Can Do." *Climate Change*. EPA, 2009. Web. 11 May 2009.

Vegan Society. "Environment." *The Vegan Society*. N.p., 2008. Web. 9 May 2009.

The Vegan Society is not italicized when referring to the corporate author, but the corresponding Web site title is.

Checklist 50.4 Formatting the Works Cited Page—MLA

Works Cited pages use the same double-spacing, one-inch margins, and running headers (including your last name and page number) as all other sections of an MLA document, so you can easily insert this page at the end of your electronic file for your paper. But use these additional guidelines:

a. **Insert a page break before your Works Cited page.** Begin the works-cited list at the top of the first full page after the body.

b. **Center the title "Works Cited" on the first line.** *Do not* repeat this title on subsequent pages if the entries require more than one page.

c. **Provide works-cited entries for every source you use in the paper.** Do *not* list materials you examined, but did not cite. (If you do include such items, the list should be re-titled *Works Consulted*.)

d. **Arrange the entries alphabetically.** Use the first words of each entry—a last name or title (excluding *A*, *An*, and *The*)— to order the list. When more than one entry begins with the same person's name, replace the repeated information with three hyphens followed by a period. This helps readers see easily that the same person is responsible for more than one source on your list:

van der Plas, Rob. *The Mountain Bike Book*. 3rd ed. San Francisco: Bicycle, 1993. Print.

---. *Mountain Bike Magic*. Mill Valley: Bicycle, 1991. Print.

e. **Use a hanging indentation of one-half inch for each entry.** Unlike paragraphs in the body of the paper, the first line of each works-cited entry is not indented, but all subsequent lines are. To adjust the indentation, use your word processor's paragraph formatting feature or, if provided, the word processor's indentation and tabbing ruler.

f. **Use cross-references to shorten entries.** If citing multiple selections from the same book, you don't need to repeat all information for each works-cited entry. Instead, create a separate entry for the book itself. Insert cross-references to that entry after each selection's title, where you would normally put the book's title and publication details. Use the same format to reference the containing book as you would for locating a source in a parenthetical citation.

(Continued)

Formatting the Works Cited Page—MLA *(Continued)*

Behrens, Laurence, and Leonard J. Rosen. *Writing and Reading across the Curriculum*. 8th ed. New York: Longman, 2003. Print.

Koplan, Jeffrey P., and William H. Dietz. "Caloric Imbalance and Public Health Policy." Behrens and Rosen 440-47.

Morrison, Toni. "Cinderella's Stepsisters." Behrens and Rosen 590–92.

Checklist 50.5 Optional Details for Works-Cited Entries

It can help readers sometimes to provide supplemental information in works cited entries. Ask your instructor if you should follow any of the optional MLA guidelines explained below.

a. **Give a full URL (or online address) for a Web source.** If your instructor requires URLs or you have reason to believe that the information you list in the entry won't be enough to allow readers to easily locate the page through a search engine, then provide the full Web address. After the date you last accessed the source, give its network address (within angle brackets <> and preceded by a space). When the address extends beyond the end of the line, insert a space after a slash to allow a line break. Repeat if necessary.

   Selzer, Jack. "Message from the President of RSA." *Rhetoric Society of America*. RSA, 2009. Web. 5 May 2009. <http://associationdatabase.com/aws/RSA/pt/sp/ presmessage>.

b. **Use brackets to insert known details not recorded on the source itself.** Sometimes historical research has clarified the authorship of unsigned, pseudonymous, or misattributed sources or discovered previously unclear publication details of older sources. If you think it would help readers to know these details, use square brackets to insert them where omitted information should be.

   Tudor, Elizabeth [Elizabeth I]. "The Golden Speech." . . .

(Continued)

Optional Details for Works-Cited Entries *(Continued)*

c. **Tell readers if a source is part of an ongoing series on the same subject.** After the medium, give the name of the series (no italics or quotation marks) and a series number.

Dowling, Neil. "Ascent to the Dizzy Heights of Italy's Roof." *The Daily Telegraph* [Australia] 20 Dec. 2008: 60. Print. Pt. 2 of a series, Europe's Best Roads, begun 22 Nov. 2008.

d. **Tell readers if the source was originally published under a different title.** After the medium of the version you used, begin with the abbreviation *Rpt. of* followed by the original title and publication details for the source.

Didion, Joan. "Goodbye to All That." *Slouching Towards Bethlehem.* 1968. New York: Farrar, Straus and Giroux, 1990. 225-38. Print. Rpt. of "Farewell to the Enchanted City." *Saturday Evening Post* 14 Jan. 1967: 62-67.

51 How Do You Use APA Documentation?

In the social sciences, articles published in professional journals often follow a form designed to connect new findings to previous research. The *Publication Manual of the American Psychological Association* (6th edition, 2010) describes five basic genres of research papers, each adding in its own way to the collective study of a topic:

- **Reports of empirical research** present results of experiments or surveys. Besides describing the results of new studies, these reports offer a short review of previous studies, explain the methods used to collect data, and show how new data adds to knowledge of the topic.
- **Literature reviews** don't present the results of new studies, but rather analyze the results of previous ones, attempting to instruct readers about the major issues and questions surrounding a topic. In many ways, these papers resemble research papers in nonscientific fields (see, for example, the sample paper in the previous chapter).
- **Theoretical papers** go a step beyond literature reviews by arguing for new theories to explain existing research better. They also argue against existing theories that fail to explain common phenomena.
- **Methodological papers** explain, critique, or advocate new and existing practices for conducting research in a particular field. They usually present new research only in order to demonstrate the method.
- **Case studies** present empirical data collected from studying individual persons or groups. Unlike reports of experiments and surveys, these papers go into more detail about the qualities of the research participants (albeit without compromising privacy), focusing less on proving cause-effect relationships.

In preparing such papers for social science and related courses (anthropology, education, economics, linguistics, political science, psychology, sociology), writers are expected to document their sources using the APA *Manual*'s citation guidelines. The basic procedures for producing an APA style paper are spelled out in this chapter. APA documentation involves two basic steps: inserting an in-text note at each point where a paper or project needs documentation (Section 51a) and recording all sources used in these notes on a separate References list (Section 51b), appearing after the body of the paper. For further explanation, see <http://www.apastyle.org> or find a copy of the manual in your library.

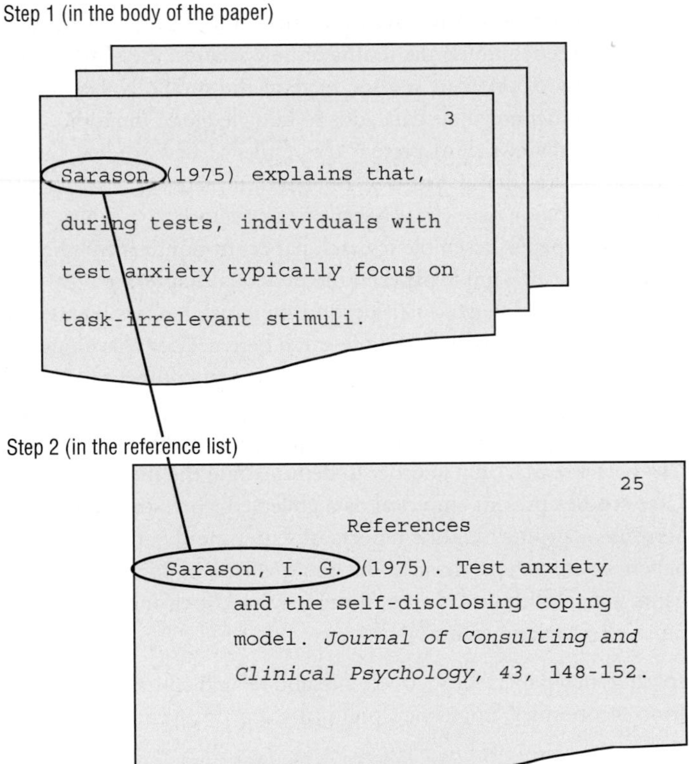

Step 1 (in the body of the paper)

3

Sarason (1975) explains that, during tests, individuals with test anxiety typically focus on task-irrelevant stimuli.

Step 2 (in the reference list)

25

References

Sarason, I. G. (1975). Test anxiety and the self-disclosing coping model. *Journal of Consulting and Clinical Psychology, 43,* 148-152.

DIRECTORY TO APA NOTES—BY TYPE

Print Sources

51b-1 Books, book parts, pamphlets, reports,

51b-2 Periodical articles

Web Media

51b-3 The basics

51b-4 Research databases, library subscription services, print periodical Web sites

Special Formats and Genres

51b-5 Recordings, broadcasts, Web multimedia

51b-6 Special academic genres

APA Rules for Formatting Specific Parts of Reference-list entries

Listing **authors'** names: see 727
Formatting publication **dates**: see 728
Formatting **titles**: see 728
Formatting **publication** details: see 729
Listing **online retrieval** information: see 729
For an example of a full APA "References" page, see 756–757

51a In the body of your paper, place a note for each source you use.

Each time you introduce material from an outside source into an APA paper, insert a note to tell readers what your source is and when it was published. You create such notes by using a combination of *parenthetical citations*, which put information about a source between parentheses, and *signal phrases*, which name sources within the normal flow of the sentence. The following example shows how you can combine the two devices when quoting a source in APA documentation style:

Identifies outside source — Locates source material

Zuboff (1988) notes, "While . . . computer-based automation continues to displace the human body and its know-how (a process . . . known as deskilling), the information power of the technology simultaneously creates pressure for a profound reskilling" **(p. 57).**

In APA style, you need a page number only when you're quoting directly or citing material you have paraphrased. As you read the following guidelines, you'll see other patterns for citing sources in your paper.

1 Identify sources clearly each time you use them. Whether you introduce sources with parenthetical notes or signal phrases, your readers will need to know which source you're using from the paper's References page. You establish that connection by making sure that the note itself clearly refers to the word by which the source is alphabetized in that reference list, whether that is a person's last name (an author or editor, for example), a corporate author's name, or a title.

To help better identify and indicate the timeliness of sources, APA style also requires that you give the year the source was published, which is always the second item in the reference-list entry.

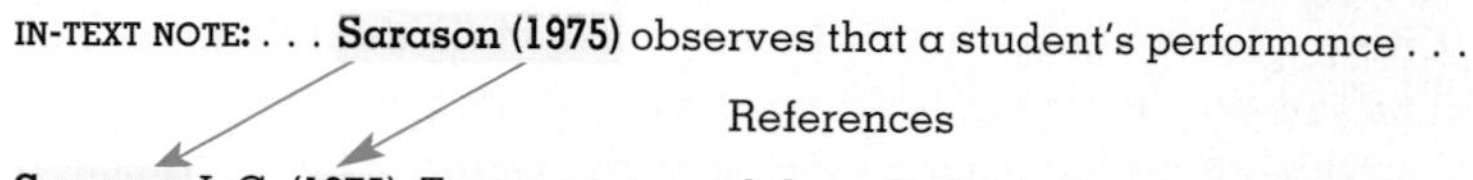

IN-TEXT NOTE: . . . **Sarason (1975)** observes that a student's performance . . .

References

Sarason, I. G. (**1975**). Test anxiety and the self-disclosing coping model. *Journal of Consulting and Clinical Psychology, 43*, 148–152.

IN-TEXT NOTE: . . . proves the need for more attention to national parks ("**Deferred repairs**," **2003**).

References

Deferred repairs take toll on parks. (**2003**, June 15). *The Los Angeles Times*. Retrieved from http://pqasb.pqarchiver.com /latimes

1.1 Citing a source listed under one person's name. Mention the individual's *last name*, in either the signal phrase or the parenthetical note. Provide first and middle initials before the last name when another entry on your reference list begins with an individual having the same last name.

> "Any institution that is going to keep its shape needs to gain legitimacy by distinctive grounding in nature and in reason" (**Douglas, 1986**, p. 112).

> **Nightingale (1858)** reveals that a major cause of deaths in the Crimean War was unsanitary living conditions, not conflict on the battlefield.

1.2 Citing a source listed under two individuals' names. Give the *last names of both individuals*, separated by *and* (or *&* in parenthetical notes).

> **Tarr and Pinker (1990)** define *object constancy* as "the ability to recognize an object despite changes in its retinal image" (p. 253).

> Previous research (**Hazelhurst & Hutchins, 1998**) has shown that logical propositions are not so much the product of an innate ability to reason, but rather the result of trying to communicate in a shared world.

1.3 Citing a source listed under three to five individuals' names. The first time you cite the source, list the *last name of every person*, separated by commas. Precede the last name in the list with *and* (or & for parenthetical notes). Shorten subsequent notes by naming only the first author followed by the abbreviation *et al.* (Latin for "and others").

> Human experience is a conundrum: "Minds awaken in a world. We did not design our world. We simply found ourselves with it; we awoke both to ourselves and the world we inhabit" (**Varela, Thompson, & Rosch, 1991**, p. 3). . . . [*later in paper*] . . . **Varela et al. (1991)** reconcile Eastern and Western views of human experience in order to . . .

1.4 Citing a source listed under six or more individuals' names. Mention only the *last name of the first person*, followed by *et al.*

> Youth who are unsatisfied with their outside obligations have a greater tendency towards risky behavior (**Donohue et al., 2003**).

1.5 Citing a source listed under the name of a corporation or group. Give the full name of the organization. If you need to mention the source again, you may use a well-known abbreviation or acronym, providing it in parentheses (or brackets if the citation is already in parentheses) after the first citation; use only this short version in subsequent notes.

> In 1999 over 350,000 were home-schooled for religious reasons, 38.4% of all home-schooled students (**National Center for Education Statistics [NCES], 2001**). . . . [*later in paper*] . . . According to the **NCES (2001)** . . .

1.6 Citing a source listed by title. For unsigned sources, the title will appear first in the reference-list entry—so in corresponding in-text citations, give a shortened version of the title (including always the first alphabetized word). Italicize titles that are italicized on the References page (see Section 51b); place others in quotation marks when used in in-text notes.

> A tight labor market does not necessarily result in greater job satisfaction for those who are already employed (**"Job Satisfaction," 2003**).

1.7 Citing a source that is one of many listed under an author or title. Do nothing special for most sources, because the year can be used to distinguish the entries. But when two sources are listed under the same name(s) in the same year, distinguish between them by attaching an identifying lowercase letter to the year (*1991a, 1991b*, etc.). The same letter should appear in the date of the corresponding reference-list entry.

> The charge is made by **Rosner (2004a)**, quickly answered by **Anderson (2004)**, and then raised again by **Rosner (2004b)**.

1.8 Citing multiple sources in one in-text note. For multiple works all by one author, provide the years for each source after the name, separating each by a comma. When listing multiple sources by different authors, separate the references by a semicolon when using a parenthetical note; separate them by commas when using a signal phrase. Notice that authors who work with different co-authors are listed separately for each group of collaborators, even when their names appear first in all entries.

> Earlier studies have found similar support for the therapeutic effects of music on children with special developmental needs (**Goldstein, 1964; Goldstein, Lingas, & Sheafor, 1965; Murphy, 1957, 1958**).

1.9 Citing sacred texts, classical works, entire Web sites, home pages, and unpublished correspondence. None of these sources needs to be listed on your References page, but they do need to be cited in the body of your paper. For sacred texts and classical works (those that are widely available in commonly accepted versions), simply identify the source, naming the version in parentheses after the first reference.

> **Exodus** 22:33–37 (**King James Bible**) provides a basis for assessing and compensating damages in private torts. **Deuteronomy** 25:1–4 further . . .

When referring to an entire Web site or home page (rather than an individual posting, internal page, or section), give the name of the site in your signal phrase followed by its Internet address in parentheses (for the first reference only).

> The **U.S. Census Bureau** regularly publishes statistics on home purchases (http://www.census.gov), along with other demographic data.

For unpublished correspondence, name the person who wrote the letter or email in the signal phrase, followed in parentheses by the words *personal communication*, a comma, and the date the piece was written.

According to **Rice (personal communication, August 28, 2002)**, . . .

2 Provide page numbers to locate quotations and paraphrased passages. When you reference a specific passage from a source, you need to provide page numbers—or another kind of specific reference—in addition to identifying the source and its publication year. Page numbers appear in parentheses just after quoted or paraphrased material. If presented in a parenthetical note with author and year, the page reference follows a comma.

SOURCES WITH STANDARD PAGINATION Use *p.* or *pp.* (two or more pages) before the reference. Use an en-dash to separate page ranges—for example, when a quote runs onto the next page.	**(p. 42)** (Tannen, 1990, **pp. 130–131**) (Man, Tam, & Li, 2003, **p. 778**)
SOURCES WITH NO PAGINATION Indicate the numbering scheme used (*para.* for paragraphs), and provide a reference number. If no numbering is available, state the heading of the nearest subsection, and identify the paragraph within the section.	(TEA, 1998, **chapter 110.c–d**) (**para. 4**) (Green Day, 2004, **track 2**) (Cheadle, 2001, **"Methods," ¶2–3**)
WORKS WITH TRADITIONAL NUMBERING Classic works that are divided into precise hierarchical sections need no page references. Instead, identify the relevant sections using the standard numbering.	(Aristotle, *Prior Analytics*, **68b.9–15**) (Mark **10:25**)

3 Place and punctuate parenthetical notes appropriately.

Insert citations immediately after the relevant quoted or paraphrased material.

> Predictions that the future would be uniform and sterile are proving to be wrong **(Postrel, 2003)**.

If the citation occurs in the middle of a sentence, add no extra punctuation after the closing parenthesis, except what may be needed to resume the normal flow of the sentence.

> Statistical analyses **(Levitt & Dubner, 2005)** suggest that what candidates spend on political campaigns matters much less than who they are and how much the public likes them.

When the citation occurs at the end of the sentence, place the parenthetical note before the ending period and after the end quotation mark.

> Schlosser **(2001)** claims that fast food is a "revolutionary force in American life" **(p. 3)**.

51b On a separate page at the end of your project, list alphabetically every source you have cited.

An APA References page, which appears after the body of the paper and before any appendixes, provides readers with full bibliographical information on all the sources that you mention in the body of your paper—except sacred texts, Web sites (when referring to the entire site), Web home pages, and unpublished correspondence. The following pages outline the basic formatting of those APA reference-list entries and show how specific kinds of sources might appear using these guidelines. If no model is given for the kind of source you are citing, use the details you know about a source to fill in the different parts of a similar kind of entry. You can also consult the official APA *Publication Manual* (6th ed., 2010) or look for similar entries cited on the References pages of articles published in journals using *APA* style.

APA reference-list citations begin with **author** and **date** followed by **title** and **publication information**. Readers familiar with past editions of APA publication standards will be at ease citing traditional types of sources, such as books and periodical articles. For electronic sources, however, the new APA guidelines are quite different. In particular, they ask for Digital Object Identifiers (DOIs) when available to replace traditional Web addresses (see more in Sections 49c-2, 51b-3, and 51b-4). Of course, the constantly changing forms of electronic sources tend to make them more difficult to cite in any documentation style. If the models provided in Section 51b do not meet your needs, consider consulting the APA Style Blog at <http://blog.apastyle.org/> for the most current citation recommendations.

BASIC PARTS OF APA REFERENCE-LIST ENTRIES

Reference-list entries are composed of four or five basic parts, each of which is explained below and marked with color-coding in the sample entries. Notice that each part begins with a capital letter and ends with a period (although there are exceptions when listing online retrieval information). As you'll see from the models, other formatting is also used.

Author. APA defines authors as the "primary contributors" for a specific source. In most entries, the author(s) will be the researcher(s) who wrote the study. But in some cases, you'll list others types of contributors—for example, a book's editor, a CD's producer, or a movie's director.

Date. The date of publication appears in parentheses as the second item in an entry. The year will appear in any in-text note that refers to the entry. Spell out fully the names of months when listed (unlike MLA style).

Title. Usually the third item of a reference-list entry, a title will appear first when a source lists no author. When a title is listed first, the date comes next. Sometimes, you'll need two titles within an entry, for example, both the title of an anthology and that of a selection it contains.

Publication or Production Information. Tell readers where the source was published and by whom—details that depend on the type of source you're referencing. The guidelines in Sections 51b-1–6 tell you what information to include and how to format that information.

Online Retrieval Information. For online sources, state the date you last viewed the source (unless the source is unlikely to change), and the source's online address (the URL and in some cases the site name) or Digital Object Identifier (DOI). Don't place a period after this item unless more details come after it.

References

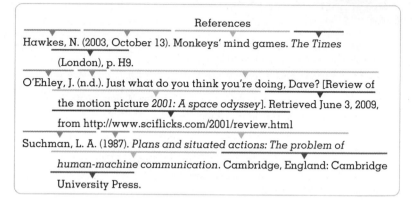

Hawkes, N. (2003, October 13). Monkeys' mind games. *The Times* (London), p. H9.

O'Ehley, J. (n.d.). Just what do you think you're doing, Dave? [Review of the motion picture *2001: A space odyssey*]. Retrieved June 3, 2009, from http://www.sciflicks.com/2001/review.html

Suchman, L. A. (1987). *Plans and situated actions: The problem of human-machine communication*. Cambridge, England: Cambridge University Press.

Authors

List all authors last-name-first, using initials instead of full first names. Omit titles (*M.D., S.J.,* etc.), but provide identifying suffixes (*Jr., III,* etc.) after the name. Always put a period after the last author listed.

One author. List the last name first, a comma, and then the initials of first and middle names appearing on the title page of the source.	Ruffin, M. T., IV. Tannen, D.
Two to seven authors. List their names in the order they appear on the title page or byline. Present all names last-name-first, separating them by commas (even when only two are listed). Precede the final name with an ampersand (&).	Crowley, B. J., Hayslip, B., Jr., & Hobdy, J. Tarr, M., & Pinker, S. See Models 7, 17, 26, 33, 41-42
Eight or more authors. List the first six, a comma, and the Latin abbreviation *et al.*	See Model 10
Corporate or group authors. Provide the full name of the organization or corporation.	Veterans of Foreign Wars. See Models 6, 8, 16, 32, 35
Editors, directors, etc. When the main authors credited for a work are listed as contributing in a special way, describe the contribution in parentheses after each name. When several people contribute in the same way, place a pluralized description after the last person's name: for example, *(Eds.).*	Alda, A. (Writer/Director). Coyne, J. (Ed.). Sherman-Palladino, A. (Writer), & Glatter, L. L. (Director). See Models 2, 31, 34-37
Consulting authors. An author listed on the title page preceded by *with* appears in parentheses after the primary author(s) in a reference-list entry; *omit* consulting authors from in-text notes.	Armstrong, L., & Carmichael, C. (with Nye, P. J.). Symonds, M. (with Ellison, L.).

Dates

Listing year only. List the year of publication in parentheses after the author(s), followed by a period.	Jones, A. (1975).
Providing months and dates. When listing more than year alone, insert a comma before the month (unabbreviated) and date. (Note: Dates in other parts of an entry appear in month/day/year order.)	Garza, J. (1971, May 15). Smith, C. (1975, January). See Models 12-13, 15, 19, 22, 24-25, 28, 35-38
Multiple sources with same year. When more than one source is listed under the same author for a given year, place a small lowercase letter after the year to distinguish the sources.	Doe, J. (1972a). Doe, J. (1972b, July 20).

Titles

For *all* titles, capitalize the first word and all proper nouns within the title. Some titles have other formatting as well.

Italicized titles. Italicize complete works and publications, including books, brochures, reports, TV and radio programs, CDs, and movies. *Do not italicize* titles of articles, chapters, individual TV episodes, radio segments, songs, etc.	*Civilization and its discontents.* *A dictionary of sociology.* *Every second counts.* *Report on medical services.*
Subtitles. Place a subtitle after the main title, inserting a colon between the two. Handle subtitles like any other title—capitalize the first word and all proper nouns.	*Seeing voices: A journey into the world of the deaf.* See Models 1, 3, 4, 8, 16, 19
Supplementary details. For some sources, you'll list supplementary details or indicate the media format bracketed after the title. Do not italicize these details.	*Interpretation of dreams* (3rd ed., A. A. Brill, Trans.). *The ring* (Widescreen ed.) [DVD]. See Models 2, 3, 5, 8, 14-15, 31-39

Publication and Production Information

Format these publication and production details as follows:

Places. List US cities with their state's postal code (omitted if the publisher is the state's university). List foreign cities with their country.	Englewood Cliffs, NJ London, England Cambridge, England
Publishers and organizations. Give the full name of the organization, but omit designations such as *Inc.*, *Co.*, and *Ltd.*	Norton Oxford University Press
Periodical names. Italicize the name and capitalize all words, except articles, conjunctions, and prepositions fewer than four letters.	*Monitor on Psychology* *USA Today*
Pages. Separate page ranges by en-dashes and nonconsecutive pages by commas. For newspaper articles, put the abbreviation *p.* or *pp.* before the reference.	103–140 pp. A3, A7

Online Retrieval Information

After an online source's publication information, tell readers when you last accessed the source (beginning with the word *Retrieved* . . .) and where the source is located. The location of the source may be identified by an online address (a URL), a database name, or a Digital Object Identifier (DOI), depending upon the source. See more in Sections 51b-3 and 51b-4.

51B-1 Books, book parts, pamphlets, and reports

1. Book

Author — Date — Title

Stone, C. N. (1989). *Regime politics: Governing Atlanta 1946–1988.* Lawrence: University Press of Kansas.

Publication information (Place: Publisher.)

IN-TEXT NOTE: (Stone, 1989, p. 78)

Above, note the basic parts of book citations. Check also for these details:

- **Are editors listed as the primary authors?** List them first in the entry; note their contributions in parentheses. See Model 2
- **Is the book or report a revised edition, a translation, part of a multi-volume set, or a numbered item in a series?** Insert edition names, volume numbers, and report IDs in parentheses after the title. Here you would list translators, as well. See Models 3, 5, 8
- **Are you citing only part of a book or reference work?** List the author(s) of the part first, then the book's date, and the selection's title. Next, list standard book details (preceded by *In*): start with the book's editors (if any) in normal order, followed by (*Ed.*). Insert pages for the selection in parentheses after the book's title. See Models 4, 5, 7
- **Are you citing a brochure or pamphlet?** Describe the work in brackets following the title. Such items may lack authors or publication details; provide any listed in the document. See Model 6
- **Are you citing a report prepared by a group or agency?** When no individual authors are given, list the agency or institution as the author. If the report is part of a series, identify the series within parentheses (no italics) after the title. If the agency, group, or organization responsible for writing the report also published it, put the word *Author* where you would list a publisher. See Model 8
- **Are you using an online version of a book, brochure, or report?** If it's only available in electronic format, not widely circulated in print, or the print publication details are unavailable, provide online retrieval information as explained in Section 51b-3.

2. Book— edited multi-volume set

Eldredge, H. W. (Ed.). (1967). *Taming megalopolis* (Vol. 2). New York, NY: Doubleday.

IN-TEXT NOTE: Eldredge (1967) includes . . .

3. Book— subsequent edition

Philips, E. B. (1996). *City light: Urban-suburban life in the global society* (2nd ed.). New York, NY: Oxford University Press.

IN-TEXT NOTE: Philips (1996) claims, ". . ." (p. 132).

4. Book chapter—by author

Putnam, R. D. (2000). Mobility and sprawl. In *Bowling alone: The collapse and revival of American community* (pp. 204–215). New York, NY: Simon & Schuster.

IN-TEXT NOTE: Putnam (2000) concludes . . .

5. Reference work—article

Rapid transit. (2002). In *Encyclopædia Britannica* (15th ed., Vol. 9, p. 943). Chicago, IL: Encyclopædia Britannica.

IN-TEXT NOTE: ("Rapid transit," 2002)

6. Brochure

Apple Computer. (2002). *Welcome to Mac OS X* [Brochure].

IN-TEXT NOTE: (Apple Computer, 2002, pp. 3–4)

7. Anthology, collection— selection in edited book

Williams, O. P., Herman, H., Liebman, C. S., & Dye, T. R. (1988). Suburban differences and metropolitan policies. In R. L. Warren & L. Lyon (Eds.), *New perspectives on the American community* (pp. 214–219). Chicago, IL: Dorsey.

IN-TEXT NOTE: (Williams, Herman, Liebman, & Dye, 1988)

8. Report— published by group author

National Endowment for the Arts. (2004). *Reading at risk: A survey of literary reading in America* (Research Division Report #46). Washington, DC: Author.

IN-TEXT NOTE: (National Endowment for the Arts, 2004)

51B-2 Periodical articles

9. Journal article

Author — Date — Title of article

Matthews, J. (2003). The Philadelphia experiment. *Education Next, 3*(1), 51–56.

Publication information (*Periodical Name, Volume* (issue), Pages.)

IN-TEXT NOTE: (Matthews, 2003, p. 52)

List the author(s), date of the issue, title of the article, periodical name, volume (with issue in parentheses), and page numbers where the article appears. Italicize both the periodical's name and volume number and capitalize all words in the name, except grammatical articles (*a, an,* and *the*), conjunctions, and prepositions fewer than four letters. Some details might vary, however, depending on the type of periodical being used:

- **Is the article from a journal?** List only the year for the date. Omit the issue if page numbering does not restart at 1 with each subsequent issue. Do *not* precede the pages with *pp.* See Models 9–11, 14
- **Is the article from a magazine or newsletter?** Always give the same date appearing on the cover; begin with the year, a comma, then the month and date. Do *not* precede the page references with *pp.* Omit the volume number if not on the cover. See Model 15
- **Is the article from a newspaper?** Give the year, month, and day, as you would for magazine articles, but for both dailies and weeklies, omit volume information. Provide the abbreviation *p.* or *pp.* before page references. See Models 12, 13
- **Is the article unsigned?** List the title before the date and provide publication information as usual. See Model 13
- **Is the source a review, abstract, or letter to the editor?** Indicate the special genre in brackets after the title, or in place of the title when none exists. For reviews, you can also tell readers what was reviewed. See Models 14, 15
- **Are you using an online version of an article that originally appeared in a print periodical?** Provide online retrieval information after the page numbers, as explained in Sections 51b-3 and 51b-4.

10. Journal article—paged by volume, eight or more authors

Allie, S., Buffler, A., Campbell, B., Lubben, F., Evangelinos, D., Psillos, D., . . . Smith, J. (2003). Teaching measurement in the introductory physics laboratory. *Physics Teacher, 41*, 394–401.

IN-TEXT NOTE: (Allie et al., 2003)

11. Journal article—paged by issue

Kennedy, M. (2003). Building better schools. *American School & University, 75*(5), 30–35.

IN-TEXT NOTE: Kennedy (2003) shows . . . (p. 33)

12. Newspaper article

Brown, L. (2002, September 28). Funding formula broken, panel told. *The Toronto Star*, p. A08.

IN-TEXT NOTE: Brown (2002) suggests . . .

13. Newspaper article — unsigned

Costs mar science training plan. (2003, January 17). *Times Educational Supplement* (London), p. 4.

IN-TEXT NOTE: ("Costs mar science," 2003)

14. Journal article—book review

Egan, B. (2003). [Review of the book *Teaching and learning design and technology* by J. Eggleston (ed.)]. *Education Review, 55*, 82–83.

IN-TEXT NOTE: (Egan, 2003, pp. 82–83)

15. Letter to editor—monthly magazine

Sullivan, K. (2003, August). [Letter to the editor]. *Building Design and Construction*, 10.

IN-TEXT NOTE: (Sullivan, 2003)

51B-3 Web sources—the basics

16. Web page—on an organizational site

Author | Date | Title

The Royal Society. (n.d.). *Science issues: Humans in research.* Retrieved May 1, 2009, from http://royalsociety.org/landing.asp?id=1257

Online retrieval information

IN-TEXT NOTE: (The Royal Society, n.d.)

List the author(s), date of publication or posting (if available), the title of the source (italicized, unless an article), and online retrieval information, including the Web address (or URL) of the source. These retrieval details may be altered for some kinds of sources:

- **Is the source from an online database, library subscription service, or print periodical's Web site?** See Section 51b-4.
- **Is the publication date unclear?** Put *n.d.* where you would list the posting date and be sure to provide a retrieval date. See Model 16
- **Is the source considered fixed or unlikely to change?** For these sources, you can omit the retrieval date. See Models 17-19, 21-30
- **Do you need to clarify the name of the site housing the source?** If the site is not apparent from the source's author, title, or URL, name the site (no italics) before the URL. See Models 17, 19, 39
- **Is the source an online report, book, or book part?** Begin the entry as you would for a similar print source, but list online retrieval details (see above) instead of place and publisher. See Models 17, 18, 27
- **Is the source a dated article?** Begin as you would for a print article, but in place of the periodical and issue number give a full URL for the article (and also a site name, if unclear). If the site requires a login, the URL should point to the home page. See Models 19, 28
- **Are you citing an article from an online reference?** Begin the entry as you would an article from a print reference (see Section 51b-1). But instead of place, publisher, and volume, supply the address of the article in the retrieval statement. See Model 20
- **Are you citing a message to a discussion forum or reader-posted content?** List the poster's name (a login-name may be all that's available), the title of the posting, and a bracketed description: *[Online forum comment]*, *[Web log comment]*, etc. See Model 21
- **Is the source a blog entry?** Cite those by a blog's official author as dated articles; cite others as reader postings. See Model 22

17. Online report— published on organizational Web site

Lenhart, A., Arafeh, S., Smith, A., & MacGill, A. (2008, April 24). *Writing, technology, and teens.* Retrieved from Pew Internet and American Life Project website: http://www.pewinternet.org/Reports/2008/Writing-Technology-and-Teens.aspx

IN-TEXT NOTE: (Lenhart, Arafeh, Smith, & MacGill, 2008)

18. Online book—fixed source on the Web

Darwin, C. (1872/1898). *The expression of the emotions in man and animals.* Retrieved from http://www.gutenberg.org/dirs/etext98/eemaa10.txt

IN-TEXT NOTE: (Darwin, 1872/1898)

19. Online article—news Web site

Miller, D. (2009, April 1). Holy hormones! What to expect when puberty hits. Retrieved from CNNHealth.com website: http://www.cnn.com/2009/HEALTH/04/01/parenting.when.puberty.hits

IN-TEXT NOTE: Miller (2009) advises . . .

20. Online reference article

Emotion. (2009). In *Encyclopædia Britannica.* Retrieved from http://www.britannica.com/EBchecked/topic/185972/emotion

IN-TEXT NOTE: ("Emotion," 2009)

21. Posted message

Safelight. (2009, June 8). Raising sons [Online Forum Comment; Msg. 2645]. Retrieved from http://tabletalk.salon.com/webx/.773b365f

IN-TEXT NOTE: (Safelight, 2009)

22. Blog entry— by blog's author

Postrel, V. (2006, March 26). Protection or education? Retrieved from http://www.dynamist.com/weblog/archives/001087.html

IN-TEXT NOTE: (Postrel, 2006)

51B-4 Online research databases, library subscription services, and print periodical Web sites

23. Journal article—in database

Author | Date | Title of article | Publication details

Huntley, M. I. (2009). Take time for laughter. *Creative Nursing, 15*, 39–42.
doi:10.1891/1078-4535.15.1.39

Online retrieval information

IN-TEXT NOTE: (Huntley, 2009, p. 41)

Many college writers now gain access to materials from information services to which their school libraries subscribe, such as *LexisNexis* or *Academic Search Complete.* Writers also read articles on periodical Web sites providing online archives of past issues. How you cite these sources will depend upon the type of source archived and whether it has a Digital Object Identifier (DOI).

- **Does the source have a DOI?** Some publishers are turning to DOI numbers as a standard means for referencing online content. If the site housing the source provides a DOI, list it instead of retrieval date and URL or database. If the site lists no DOI, search for one at <http://www.crossref.org/guestquery/>. When giving a DOI, omit all other online retrieval information and preface the DOI with *doi:*. See Models 23, 26
- **Are you citing a journal, newspaper, or magazine article from a library research database?** Treat the article as you would a print item from a similar kind of periodical. If you use the database record to find a print version of the source, no other details are needed. But if you access the text of the article directly from the database, provide *one* of the following pieces of retrieval information (listed in order of preference): a DOI; the URL of the periodical's Web site (often locatable through a search engine); or the URL of the database's home page. See Models 23-25, 29, 30
- **Are you citing a book or book part in a library research database?** Cite the item like a similar print source, but replace the print publication information with either a DOI or the address of the home page for the database from which the book or book part was retrieved. See Model 27
- **Are you citing an article on a print periodical's Web site?** Cite the article as you would a print article, but also give the home page of the periodical's Web site or a DOI (if available). See Models 28-30
- **Is the source an article from a Web-only journal?** Treat such articles as you would those retrieved from a print journal's Web site, listing volume, issue, and pagination as provided.

24. Magazine article—in database, no DOI

Buckley, W. F. (2001, July 23). The laughter of Archie Bunker. *National Review*, 58. Retrieved from http://www.nationalreview.com.

IN-TEXT NOTE: Buckley (2001) claims . . .

25. Newspaper article—unsigned, in database, no DOI

Former king of comedy out on his own. (2002, August 15). *St. Petersburg Times*, p. 37W. Retrieved from http://www.tampabay.com/publication

IN-TEXT NOTE: ("Former king," 2002)

26. Journal article—identified by DOI

Romero, E., & Pescosolido, A. (2008). Humor and group effectiveness. *Human Relations*, *61*, 395–418. doi: 10.1177/0018726708088999

IN-TEXT NOTE: Romero and Pescosolido (2008) note . . .

27. Book—in database, no DOI

Burton, R. (1621). *The anatomy of melancholy*. Retrieved from http://eebo.chadwyck.com/home

IN-TEXT NOTE: Burton (1621) describes . . . (pp. 223–224)

28. Online article—newspaper Web site

Garcia, Lily. (2009, April 30). Keeping a sense of humor in check. *Washington Post*. Retrieved from http://www.washingtonpost.com

IN-TEXT NOTE: (Garcia, 2009)

29. Magazine article—from unrestricted magazine site

Winerman, L. (2006). The anatomy of funny. *Monitor on Psychology, 37*(6), 66. Retrieved from http://www.apa.org/monitor/

IN-TEXT NOTE: Winerman (2006) points out . . .

30. Journal article—from restricted journal site, no DOI

Bowen, B.C. (2003). A neglected Renaissance art of joking. *Rhetorica*, *21*, 137–148. Retrieved from http://caliber.ucpress.net/loi/rh

IN-TEXT NOTE: Bowen (2003) refers to . . . (pp. 145–146)

51B-5 Recordings, broadcasts, and Web multimedia

31. Video recording—documentary film

Author — **Date** — **Title and format (in brackets)**

Pennebaker, D. A. (Director). (1997). *Monterey pop* [Videotape]. United States: Rhino. (Original date, 1967)

Production information (Place: Production company)

IN-TEXT NOTE: Pennebaker (1967/1997) documents . . .

Recorded media, broadcast programs, podcasts, and multimedia content downloaded or streamed from the Web all require extra information to tell readers about the source's special format. Note that many of these formats also have special kinds of authors:

- **Are you citing a video recording?** Give scriptwriters, directors, and producers primary credit, listing their contributions in parentheses after each name. After the title, list the media format (*DVD*, *Videocassette*, etc.—*Motion picture* for films viewed in a theater). Close the entry by listing the production city and studio. See Models 31, 34
- **Are you citing an audio recording?** Begin with the name on the byline of the recording. After the production date and title (with the media format in brackets), list the city and company. See Models 32, 33
- **Are you citing a specific song from a music recording?** List the songwriter first, the song's copyright date, its title, and the person recording the song (if not the songwriter) in brackets, all before giving the production details for the full recording. See Model 33
- **Are you citing a broadcast radio or television program?** List producers, directors, and scriptwriters first, before the date and main title of the program. If applicable, name a specific episode (indicated with bracketed comment) before the title of the program (preceded by *In*). Close the entry with city of broadcast and station. See Models 35, 36
- **Are you citing a podcast or multimedia content downloaded or streamed from the Web?** Begin entries for these sources as you would similar kinds of work on recorded media, listing producers, directors, etc. After the date, give the title of the source, followed by a bracketed description of the electronic format (e.g., *[Audio podcast]*, *[MP3 file]*). End with a retrieval statement including the URL. See Models 37–39
- **Is the downloaded or streamed content user-posted?** Treat like other postings (Section 51b-3), but also describe the format. See Model 38

32. Audio recording

Big Brother and the Holding Company. (2002). *Live in San Francisco 1966* [CD]. Studio City, CA: Verèse Sarabande.

IN-TEXT NOTE: (Big Brother and the Holding Company, 1966/2002)

33. Audio recording— emphasis on songwriters

Cropper, S., & Redding, O. (1967). (Sittin' on) the dock of the bay [Recorded by M. Bolton]. On *The hunger* [CD]. United States: Sony. (1987)

IN-TEXT NOTE: Cropper and Redding (1967) wrote . . .

34. Film— theatrical release

Crowe, C. (Writer/Director/Producer), & Bryce, I. (Producer). (2000). *Almost famous* [Motion picture]. United States: Dreamworks.

IN-TEXT NOTE: (Crowe & Bryce, 2000)

35. Radio broadcast

King Biscuit Entertainment (Producer). (2003, July 6). *King Biscuit flower hour* [Radio program]. Santa Rosa, CA: KMGG.

IN-TEXT NOTE: (King Biscuit Entertainment, 2003)

36. Television show—specific episode

Kuhn, R. L. (Creator/Host), & Fefernan, L. (Director/Producer). (2003, May 13). What makes music so significant? [Television series episode]. In L. Fefernan, *Closer to the truth*. Los Angeles, CA: KCET.

IN-TEXT NOTE: (Kuhn & Fefernan, 2003)

37. Podcast

Bragg, B. (Performer). (2006, April 7). KEXP at SXSW: Billy Bragg [Audio podcast]. Retrieved from http://www.kexp.org/podcast_instudio.xml

IN-TEXT NOTE: (Bragg, 2006)

38. Web video—user posted

Educationalmaterials. (2008, October 13). 'Let it be' acoustic guitar lesson [Video file]. Retrieved from http://www.youtube.com/watch?v=TenrIDHGinI

IN-TEXT NOTE: (Educationalmaterials, 2008)

51B-6 Special academic genres

39. Presentation slides—distributed online

Hines, M. A. (2004). *Scientific presentation skills* [PDF file]. Retrieved from Cornell Center for Nanoscale Systems website: http://www.cns.cornell.edu/documents/CAPES04_Presentation_Skills.pdf

IN-TEXT NOTE: (Hines, 2004)

Academic sources, such as conference papers and dissertations, may have special features when listed on a References page.

- **Are you citing lecture notes or presentation slides published on the Web?** List the source as you would any other Web download, putting a description of the media format (*PowerPoint slides*, etc.) in brackets after the title. End with typical retrieval details. See Model 39
- **Are you citing a paper delivered at an academic conference?** Unpublished academic papers read at conferences may be cited simply by identifying the meeting and location after the title. Papers appearing as part of the published proceedings of a conference are treated as selections in anthologies (see Section 51b-1). See Models 40, 41
- **Is the source an online abstract from an online database or library subscription service?** Cite an online abstract as you would cite the document described in the abstract, but for printed abstracts, place [*Abstract*] after the title; for online abstracts, begin the retrieval details with the phrase *Abstract retrieved from*, listing the DOI, database, or URL as available. See Model 42
- **Are you citing a dissertation or thesis?** Begin the entry as you would a book: list author, date, and title (italicized). For those sources accessed from a university or personal Web site, describe the source (*Doctoral dissertation*, etc.) and list the university, all in parentheses after the title. For those accessed from an official distributor of dissertations and theses, provide standard online retrieval or publication details. For dissertations listed in *Dissertation Abstracts International* (DAI), provide the DAI listing numbers and the UMI order number after the title (no italics). See Models 43, 44

40. Conference paper— unpublished

Tebeaux, E. (2005, March). *The evolution of technical writing: From text to visual text in applied discourse.* Paper presented at the annual meeting of the Conference on College Composition and Communication, San Francisco, CA.

IN-TEXT NOTE: Tebeaux (2005) explains . . .

41. Conference paper— published in proceedings

Matthews, T., Fong, J., & Mankoff, J. (2005). Visualizing non-speech sounds for the deaf. In *Assets 2005. The seventh international ACM SIGACCESS conference on computers and accessibility* (pp. 52–59). New York, NY: ACM Press.

IN-TEXT NOTE: (Matthews, Fong, & Mankoff, 2005)

42. Online abstract—for article, from database

Cox, B. S., Cox, A. B., & Cox, D. J. (2000). Motivating signage prompts safety belt use. *Journal of Applied Behavior Analysis, 33*, 635–638. Abstract retrieved from Social Science Abstracts database.

IN-TEXT NOTE: (Cox, Cox, & Cox, 2000)

43. Dissertation— unpublished

Kinkade, J. (2005). *Samuel Johnson's Rambler and the invention of self-help literature* (Unpublished doctoral dissertation). University of Texas, Austin.

IN-TEXT NOTE: (Kinkade, 2005)

44. Dissertation— published

Anderson, V. (1997). Unpersuasive truths: Critical theory, pedagogy, and democratic education. *Dissertation Abstracts International* 59(01), 154. (UMI No. 9822533)

IN-TEXT NOTE: Anderson (1997) argues . . .

51c Sample Empirical Research Paper—APA

The following APA-style research report was written by Jessica Carfolite at the University of South Carolina. In structure and language, it represents the kind of essay routinely prepared in psychology courses: it includes a title page, an abstract, a statement of hypothesis, sections explaining method and results, a formal discussion section, references, and two tables. Carfolite's paper assumes that readers will be familiar with many technical terms and statistical procedures, as well as various research conventions in the field. Not every part of the paper will be easily accessible to every reader, but that is often the case with research in various scientific disciplines.

Checklist 51.1 Document Formatting—APA

While some sections (see Checklist 51.2) require minor adjustments, the guidelines below should work for the paper as a whole.

a. **Use white, 8½-by-11-inch paper with at least 1-inch margins.** Set margins by adjusting the document's Page Setup.

b. **Use 12-point Times New Roman.** Some instructors may allow other fonts. (Note: Our example uses a smaller typeface and margins to allow us to show the paper in a condensed space.)

c. **Double-space the entire document.** This includes the References page and title page. In certain circumstances you may use single spacing to improve readability—for example, with tables and captions.

d. **Indent the first word of each paragraph one-half inch.** Note that the Abstract and the References pages do not follow this standard indentation, see Checklists 51.4 and 51.5.

e. **Left-align the body of the paper and do not hyphenate words at line breaks.** Make sure also that the right side is not "justified" by your word processor.

f. **Use two spaces after the end punctuation of every sentence.** This rule is recommended by the latest *APA Publication Manual*, but some instructors may prefer one space; when in doubt, ask your instructor.

g. **Insert a shortened title for your paper (all in capital letters) and consecutive page numbers one-half inch from the top of *every* page.** Use your word processor's *header* tool. The title should be aligned to the left and the page number tabbed to the right margin.

Checklist 51.2 Parts of a Research Report—APA

When presenting the results of an empirical study, divide your paper into the following sections. Provide a heading at the beginning of each section. Each major section heading should be bold (except the Abstract and References sections), centered, and on a separate line. You can also create subsections (see, for example, the Method section in the sample paper), which should have bold headings aligned to the left-hand margin on a separate line. Note below that some sections should start on a new page.

a. **Title page.** This page presents the title of the study and identifies the researchers and their affiliations. (See also Checklist 51.3.)

b. **Abstract.** The abstract is a concise summary of the paper. Start the abstract on a separate page. (See also Checklist 51.4.)

c. **Introduction.** The introduction is the first section of the main text of the paper. In this section you present your hypothesis and a review of literature related to your study. Unlike the other sections, don't begin the introduction with a heading—instead, repeat the title of the paper you placed on the title page. Start this section on a new page.

d. **Method.** This section provides a detailed description of the procedures used in the research. Because the validity of the research depends on how the data were gathered, this is a critical section for readers assessing the report. Don't start this section on a new page—start this section on the line immediately following the Introduction section.

e. **Results.** This section reports the data, often given through figures, charts, graphs, and so on—some of which will be presented fully in later appendixes. The reliability of the data is explained here, but little comment is made on the study's implications. Don't start this section on a new page—start this section on the line immediately following the Method section.

f. **Discussion/Conclusions.** Here you analyze and interpret the data presented in the Results section. Don't start this section on a new page—start this section on the line immediately following the Results section.

g. **References.** As covered in Section 51b, this section is an alphabetized list of research materials cited in the report. Begin this section on a new page. (See also Checklist 51.5.)

h. **Appendixes.** Provide, in consecutively lettered appendixes, materials germane to the study but too lengthy to include in the body of the paper. You might, for example, provide a copy of a questionnaire you presented to participants in Appendix A, provide a copy of your consent form in Appendix B, and so on.

Checklist 51.3 Formatting the Title Page—APA

APA style requires a separate title page; use the facing page as a model and apply the following guidelines:

a. **Choose an effective title.** Don't state the obvious, that you're presenting the results of a study. Instead, state the key variables you're researching. Try to make the title twelve words or fewer.

b. **Present the title of your paper, centered, on the upper half of the page.** Capitalize the first word and all others *except* articles (*a, an*, and *the*), prepositions, and conjunctions that are shorter than four letters.

c. **List your first name, middle initial, and last name, centered under the title.**

d. **List your institutional affiliation under your name, centered on the page.**

e. **Make sure the title page is numbered like the rest of your paper.** The page header should include (aligned to the left) a shortened title of the paper (less than fifty characters) and the page number *1* tabbed to the header's right-hand margin.

f. **For an article that will be published,** indicate at the top of the page what the running head for the essay should be in all caps. Running heads should not exceed fifty characters. Put the same running head in the upper margin of all subsequent pages, albeit without the preceding "Running head:" label.

g. **Repeat the title at the top of the first page of the body of the paper.** Center the title on the top line(s) of the first page of the body of the paper.

1/2 inch

Running head: ASSESSING SOCIAL SKILLS MEASUREMENTS 1

Assessing Social Skills Measurements in

Middle School Students

Jessica Carfolite

University of South Carolina

ASSESSING SOCIAL SKILLS MEASUREMENTS 2

Abstract

This study investigates the validity of the newly developed Social Activities Questionnaire (SAQ) for measuring children's social skills relative to an established measure, the Social Skills Rating System (SSRS). Based on data from 34 middle-school students and their parents, both of which were participating in an after-school program for children with learning or behavioral problems, the SAQ was found to have small-to-moderate correlations with the widely used SSRS. However, unlike the SSRS, the SAQ showed moderate correlations with children's grade point average in school, which research finds to be an important predictor of children's social success. This study suggests the SAQ is a promising measurement tool that should be further developed and validated through studies having larger and more diverse samples.

Checklist 51.4 Creating an Abstract—APA

Abstracts are common in papers using APA style and are required for articles submitted for publication.

a. **Place the abstract on a separate page after the title page.** Use the same spacing and margins as the rest of the document.

b. **Make sure the manuscript head and correct page number (2) appear at the top of the page.**

c. **Insert the heading "Abstract" on the first line of the body of the page and center it.** Begin the abstract on the following line.

d. **Do not indent the first line of the abstract.** Present the paragraph containing the abstract in block form, not indented like paragraphs in the body of the paper.

e. **Summarize the paper accurately and concisely (120 or fewer words).** To be accurate, avoid discussing material not treated in the body of the paper. Also, avoid using abbreviations or references that aren't clear within the abstract itself—which is usually intended to be read as a stand-alone description of the paper. Describe in the abstract the problem or issue treated, the type of research used, and conclusions drawn from the study.

1/2 inch

1 inch ASSESSING SOCIAL SKILLS MEASUREMENTS 3

Assessing Social Skills Measurements

in Middle School Students

Effective social functioning can be a protective factor for students struggling to adjust to middle school. Social Skills Training (SST) intervention is often employed to improve a child's functioning, but it repeatedly fails to attain general application (Gresham, 1998). One limitation of prior research on SST programs is the lack of empirically valid tools to measure social functioning. To address this issue, this study investigates the validity of the newly developed Social Activities Questionnaire (SAQ). This paper begins by addressing the complex and often ambiguous definition of social skills. It then explains the importance of social competence to children in the middle school age group. It also describes problems with past measurement tools and the recently proposed development of a Social Activities Questionnaire (SAQ). Finally, the introduction states the hypotheses for this study.

Importance of Social Functioning

Repeatedly, researchers have found evidence that poor peer adjustment can put children at risk for later difficulties in life. Peer interactions affect the development of social competence. If children are not accepted by peers, they are more likely to lack key social competencies (Parker & Asher, 1987). Conversely, positive peer relations may buffer other vulnerabilities children experience. Nagle and Erdley (2001) have shown that peer acceptance, as well as the number and quality of friendships, correlates to loneliness and depression in children. Research on social competence in schools has found lower substance abuse

1 inch

1 inch

1 inch

This abbreviation will now be used in place of "Social Skills Training" throughout the essay.

For standard APA style, use two spaces after the end of each sentence.

A second abbreviation (SAQ) is introduced in parentheses.

Headings at this level are bold and flush left.

Note the ampersand (&) to separate the authors' last names.

and a decrease in aggression and emotional distress among socially skilled students (Hartup, 1996).

Because social skills lessen the day-to-day frustrations adolescents face in schools, it is not surprising that they might also enhance academic performance. Social skills create a "social context" for learning by providing rules and role expectations for students. As a result, social skills can facilitate academic success by working in tandem with learning goals (Maleki & Elliott, 2002). But it is not necessarily social competence that leads to academic competence. The relationship may also go in the opposite direction. Welsh, Parke, Widaman, and O'Neil (2001) found that academic competence in first grade influenced second grade social competence. Thus there is probably a reciprocal relationship between social competence and academic performance. Success in one arena likely promotes success in the other. Conversely, problems with teachers and peers can obstruct learning, and difficulties in academics lead to social stigmas.

When multiple authors are named outside parentheses, "and" is used instead of &.

Defining Social Skills

Despite the hundreds of published studies on the topic, there is no general consensus on what constitutes "social skills" and how they should be measured in children. Several studies have defined social skills in terms of peer acceptance or popularity (Asher, Oden, & Gottman, 1977). These definitions do not actually target the social skills themselves, but the outcome of using them. Other studies define social skills by actual behavior, such as the ability to start a conversation, make a joke, or resist the urge to interrupt mid-conversation (Foster & Ritchey, 1979). Still others look at a combination of behaviors and levels of acceptance (Asher, 1978).

Problems defining "social skills," a key term, are examined.

Another key term is defined.

"Social validity," a term coined by Gresham (1998), defines social skills as socially significant behaviors exhibited in specific situations that predict important social outcomes. These outcomes might include friendships, teacher and parent acceptance, and even school adjustment. Gresham's emphasis on establishing the social validity of interpersonal behaviors helps to focus skills measurement and intervention on specific behaviors and outcomes important for current and future functioning.

Development of the SAQ

The SAQ was designed to measure outcomes of social skills training. The SAQ questions are direct, short, and easy to answer. A parent completes a report of 12 items about the social activities of his or her child. Items were selected based primarily on practical experiences from outcome-related treatment goals coming out of the Challenging Horizons Program (CHP), an after-school program for students with AD/HD at Hand Middle School and Crayton Middle School in Columbia, South Carolina. The final version of the SAQ was refined by suggestions made by the research staff of faculty advisors, graduate students, CHP counselors, and parents at James Madison University. This study is one of the first empirical tests of the SAQ.

Statement of Hypotheses

The purpose of this study is to explore the predictive validity of the Social Activities Questionnaire (SAQ). It is expected that the SAQ and the SSRS should moderately correlate, and these scales should also predict a child's grade point average (GPA) and disciplinary referrals.

Headings at this level are centered.

Method

Headings at this level are flush left and bold.

Participants

The sample from the CHP included 34 middle school students and 34 parents who completed and returned survey packets. Approximately 47% of the students in the study had screened positive for AD/HD, based on rating scales completed by parents or due to a parent's report that the student had previously been clinically diagnosed with AD/HD.

This section supplies important data about participants.

Crayton Middle School has approximately 936 students in grades 6–8. The racial distribution is 45% black, 50% white, and 6% other, with 46% of the students living at or below the poverty level. Hand Middle School has approximately 958 students in grades 6–8. The racial distribution is 50% black, 47% white, and 3% other. Nearly half live at or below the poverty level. The gender distribution for the study was 70.5% male and 29.5% female. For the study, the grade distribution was 50% sixth grade, 44% seventh grade, and 6% eighth grade.

Measures

The measures in this study consisted of (1) the Social Activities Questionnaire, (2) the Social Skills Rating System for Parents, (3) the Social Skills Rating System for Students, (4) Grade Point Averages for the 2004–2005 school year, and (5) disciplinary referrals for the 2004–2005 school year.

SAQ. The Social Activities Questionnaire (SAQ) is designed to be an objective measure of adolescent social activities with peers. Question 1 asks the actual number of friends matching these criteria: "within 2 years of the child's age, not related to the child and that they spend time with the child outside of school, at least

Details about the SAQ are provided, including sample questions.

once a month." Question 2 inquires how many children live within walking distance of the child's home; it is used for interpretive value. The subsequent 9 questions ask about specific activities and the frequency of those activities, for example: "My child invites friends over ______ times in a typical month," or "My child participated in ______ organized activities over the past year."

Other SAQ questions describe the quality of interactions during these activities, for example: "The time my child spends with friends often ends with one or both children angry" or "Some of my child's friends use alcohol, tobacco, or other prohibited substances." The final item asks about the percentage of time the child spends alone, with friends, and with family. The SAQ is an experimental measure with no published reliability or validity studies.

The SSRS questionnaire is explained.

SSRS. The Social Skills Rating System (Gresham & Elliott, 1990) provides components for teachers, parents, and students to evaluate student social behaviors. These components can be used separately or together. For practical reasons related to the challenges of getting teacher data, this study used only the parent and student versions, which are broken into five subscales that make up the total social skills score. Both the SSRS-Parent and SSRS-Student measure cooperation, assertion, and self-control. The SSRS-Parent version also measures responsibility; the SSRS-Student version also measures empathy. Research supports the reliability (.77 to .84 for parents; .52 to .66 of students) and validity for the SSRS (Gresham & Elliott, 1990).

Procedures

Permission was granted through Richland One School District to administer the SSRS-Student version to the student participants. After completing the SSRS-Student version, they were given a packet to be taken home and filled out by a parent or guardian. Each packet included a self-addressed stamped envelope, the SAQ, the Social Skills Rating System, and a letter explaining the forms within the packet. The parent participants were asked to mail the two forms back in the stamped envelope provided or to send it back with their children. Each child who filled out an SSRS-Student version received a small candy, and each child that returned a completed packet received a large candy bar of his or her choice.

Data Analysis

This section presents statistical details requiring technical expertise.

The hypothesis, which asks whether there might be correlations between the social skills scores, GPA, and the number of disciplinary referrals, was tested with bivariate correlations with a statistical significance level of $p = .05$ (see Tables 1 and 2). It is noteworthy that this study had low statistical power. Specifically, the power to find a small to moderate size correlation (i.e., $r = 0.20$; according to Cohen's conventions) was only .30 (with a directional alpha of .05). Given this low power, these non-significant statistical findings might be a series of Type II errors. Therefore, it is worthwhile to examine effect sizes.

Tables appear at the end of the paper.

Results

While it was hypothesized that GPA and disciplinary records would correlate with both social skills scales, none were statistically significant. However, because correlations with an absolute value greater than .20 are considered large enough to be interesting, they are highlighted in Tables 1 and 2. When

Note that the results do not support the initial hypothesis.

examining the predictive power of the SSRS and SAQ for Grade Point Average and Disciplinary Referrals, it appears that the SAQ items 9 and 10 were correlated with Grade Point Average (see Table 1). In addition, the SAQ detects a positive correlation between question 10 (about the use of prohibited substances) and the number of disciplinary referrals (see Table 1). Table 2 shows that the SSRS does not have those same predictive powers for GPA and disciplinary referrals.

Discussion

This is a preliminary investigation into the construct validity of the Social Activities Questionnaire (SAQ), which is designed to measure important social behaviors of middle school children. While it was hypothesized that the SAQ and the SSRS rating scales would be moderately correlated, at first glance, the data support little to no convergent validity between these scales. In addition, the failure to find statistically significant correlations between these scales, GPA, and disciplinary referrals raises questions about the concurrent validity of the SAQ and the SSRS.

It is important to note that, as stated in the data analysis plan, this study was limited by low statistical power and, therefore, it may be appropriate to examine effect sizes. Indeed, examining the effect size does show some interesting results. Most notable were the positive correlations between the GPA scores and the scores on the SAQ, especially since the SSRS did not show correlations between the two. This suggests that the SAQ may be more ecologically valid than the SSRS because it is a better predictive tool for a critically important variable, GPA.

This study was limited by a small sample size, and future research should have a larger sample and a much larger and more diverse population. Despite these weaknesses, the study does provide unique information about a new social skills assessment tool. Although the results of this study are modest, there are indications this SAQ might be an even better tool for predictor variables like GPA than are scales like the SSRS.

In future studies, it is recommended that the users of the SAQ consider some modifications. For instance, it would be helpful to have the parents indicate their level of confidence in each question. This type of question, and other questions, might be used to create an index of parental monitoring, which has been shown to be an important predictor of outcomes in middle school students. It would also improve the questionnaire to inquire about the availability of activities for the student and to create indices that look at the ratio of engagement in available activities. These recommended additions might improve the overall assessment of the SAQ.

The article concludes by suggesting future research needs and opportunities.

1 inch

1/2 inch

References

Asher, S. (1978). Children's peer relations. In M. Lamb (Ed.), *Social and personality development*. New York, NY: Holt, Rinehart, & Winston.

Asher, S. R., Oden, S. L., & Gottman, J. M. (1977). Children's friendship in school settings. In L. G. Katz (Ed.), *Current topics in early childhood education* (Vol. 1, pp. 32–61). Norwood, NJ: Ablex.

Cohen, J. (1992). A power primer. *Psychological Bulletin, 112,* 155–159.

Foster, S. L., & Ritchey, W. L. (1979). Issues in the assessment of social competence in children. *Journal of Applied Behavior Analysis, 12,* 625–638.

Gresham, F. (1998). Social skills training: Should we raze, remodel, or rebuild? *Behavioral Disorders, 24,* 19–25.

Gresham, F., & Elliott, S. (1990). *Social skills rating system manual*. Circle Pines, MN: American Guidance Service.

Gresham, F., Sugai, G., & Horner, R. (2001). Interpreting outcomes of social skills training for students with high-incidence disabilities. *Exceptional Children, 67,* 331–344.

Hartup, W. W. (1996). The company they keep: Friendships and their developmental significance. *Child Development, 67,* 1–13.

Maleki, C., & Elliott, S. (2002). Children's social behaviors as predictors of academic achievement: A longitudinal analysis. *School Psychology Quarterly, 17,* 1–23.

Nagle, D., & Erdley, C. (Eds.). (2001). The role of friendship in psychological adjustment [Special issue]. *New Directions for Child and Adolescent Development, 2001*(91).

double space

1/2 inch

1 inch

1 inch

Note that volume numbers of journals are italicized, as are the surrounding commas. Page numbers are not italicized.

This item refers to the entire issue of a journal paginated issue-by-issue. No page numbers are given but an issue number is included within parentheses.

1 inch

Parker, J., & Asher, S. (1987). Peer relations and later personal adjustment: Are low-accepted children at risk? *Psychological Bulletin, 102,* 357–389.

Welsh, M., Parke, R., Widaman, K., & O'Neil, R. (2001). Linkages between children's social and academic competence: A longitudinal analysis. *Journal of School Psychology, 39,* 463–481. doi: 10.1016/50022-4405(01)00084-x

This source can be found online by looking up the DOI provided.

Checklist 51.5 Formatting Reference Pages—APA

Begin the References list on a separate page. Use the same formatting you used for the rest of the document, including double-spaced paragraphs, headers at the top of the page (with numbers and a shortened version of the paper's title), and 1-inch margins. But make the following adjustments:

a. **Center the title "References" at the top of the page.** If the list of entries runs over to a new page, *do not* repeat this title at the top.

b. **Create a one-half-inch hanging indentation for each entry.** In other words, the first line should be aligned with the left margin, and subsequent lines in an individual entry should be indented. (You can create hanging indentations easily by adjusting the paragraph settings.)

c. **List all sources referenced in the body of the paper.** See Section 51a-1.9 for a list of sources that don't need to appear on the References page. Don't list sources you viewed but do not use in the paper.

d. **Alphabetize the list according to the first word in each entry—** excluding articles (*A, An,* and *The*). When an author appears more than once, order entries from earliest to latest year; for sources from the same year, order by title and append lowercase letters to the year. When an individual appears first for entries as both single author and co-author, place the single-author entries first, alphabetizing subsequent entries by the second (or third, or fourth, if necessary) co-author.

e. **Proof carefully your punctuation and capitalization for each entry.** Pay close attention to the punctuation and capitalization used in the models in Section 51b-1–6. (For long URLs, insert a space *before* one or more punctuation marks, to allow for line breaks.)

Table 1

Grade Point Average and Disciplinary Referrals and Social Activities Questionnaire

SAQ questions	GPA	Disciplinary referrals
1. Friends not related, within 2 years, spends time once a month	**0.20**	-0.06
2. # of children within 2 years of age, within walking distance	0.03	-0.06
3. Invites friends over X times in a month	-0.08	0.12
4. Spends time with friends X times in a month	0.11	0.10
5. Participates in X activities in the past year	**0.30**	-0.02
6. Number of leadership roles in these activities	0.11	0.08
7. Amount of time on the phone	**-0.23**	0.15
8. Amount of time instant messaging (ICQ, AOL)	-0.10	0.12
9. Frequency of time spent with friends with one or both children angry	**-0.25**	0.01
10. Frequency of friends who use alcohol, tobacco, or like substances	**-0.34**	**0.27**
11. Frequency of friends who are in trouble with authority	-0.32	0.16
Free Time Alone	**0.38**	**-0.34**
Free Time Friends	-0.08	0.11
Free Time Family	-0.16	-0.03

Note. Values are Pearson Product Moment Correlation Coefficients. All p values were greater than .05 (df = 33). Correlations with an absolute value greater than .20 are printed in boldface type.

Table 2

Parent and Student Social Skills Rating System and GPA and Disciplinary Referrals

	Parent cooperation	Parent assertion	Parent self-control	Parent responsi-bility	Parent standard score
DR	0.16	0.00	0.13	-0.15	0.01
GPA	0.14	**0.20**	0.07	0.17	0.12
	Student cooperation	Student assertion	Student empathy	Student self-control	Student standard score
DR	0.14	0.04	0.10	**0.25**	0.01
GPA	0.15	**0.24**	0.17	0.04	0.18

Note. Values are Pearson Product Moment Correlation Coefficients. All *p* values were greater than .05 (*df* = 33). Correlations with an absolute value greater than .20 are printed in boldface type.

CHAPTER

52 How Do You Use CMS Documentation?

Writers who prefer full footnotes or endnotes for their projects (rather than in-text notes) often use the humanities style of documentation recommended in *The Chicago Manual of Style* (15th ed., 2003), now also available in a searchable online version. Basic procedures for the CMS documentary-note system are spelled out in the following sections. If you encounter documentation or formatting problems not discussed here, consult the full CMS manual or *A Manual for Writers of Research Papers, Theses, and Dissertations* (7th ed., 2007) by Kate L. Turabian, a long-standing, though recently updated, guide for students using CMS style.

If you have questions about Chicago style or general queries about editing, check out the splendid Q&A page at the University of Chicago Press. Go to the Press's main site <http://www.press.uchicago.edu/> and then look up the *Chicago Manual of Style* site.

52a How does CMS documentation work?

Whereas MLA and APA styles use *in-text notes* together with *works-cited* or *references* lists to document outside sources (see Chapters 50 and 51), CMS style uses *footnotes* or *endnotes*. Footnotes offer a fairly simple and traditional method of citation. A raised, or *superscript*, reference number (like this[2]) appears in the body of the paper where a writer quotes from, borrows from, or refers to another's work. These superscript numbers in the body of the paper then correspond to numbered notes that appear at the bottom of a page. The notes include all bibliographic information necessary to identify outside sources, as well as page numbers to direct readers to specific locations in these items. No separate bibliography page is necessary—although one may be included (see Section 52d). The directory on the following page is arranged according to medium and genre. Use it to locate model CMS footnotes and endnotes in the pages that follow.

DIRECTORY TO CMS NOTE MODELS

Print Sources

52c-1 Books and book parts

52c-2 Periodical articles

Web Sources

52c-3 Web pages, online articles, etc.

Special Formats and Genres

52c-4 Other Media and Special Genres

CMS Rules for Formatting Specific Parts of Notes and Bibliographies

General guidelines for formatting different parts of notes: see 765

General guidelines for formatting bibliographies: see 774

For an example of a full CMS "Bibliography" page, see 784

See more in Sections 52b-3 and 52b-4.

Writers using CMS may have the option of using *endnotes*. Endnotes work like footnotes except the notes appear at the end of the paper rather than in the footer of each page. Footnotes tend to work better for longer papers because endnotes require readers to flip to the end of the document for source details. We provide guidelines that apply to both endnotes and footnotes, but Chicago style discourages endnotes. Consult with your instructor to determine whether one type of note is preferred.

52b How do you use CMS footnotes and endnotes?

There are two kinds of notes: *reference notes*, which cite the use of outside sources, and *content notes*, which add details you regard as important, but that may seem digressive if inserted into the main text. This chapter focuses on *reference notes*, which are necessary for proper citation. Whether using reference notes, content notes, or both, number them all consecutively according to their order of appearance in the body of the paper.

1 Insert a raised note number after each cited passage. To insert the number, use your word processor's footnote or endnote feature, which will not only format the raised number correctly (in *superscript* typestyle), but will also automatically number and renumber notes to ensure that they are ordered consecutively throughout the paper. Place the note number after the material being documented, either at the end of the sentence or at the first natural pause after the borrowed material. As you can see in this example, note numbers appear outside end quotation marks:

> Ralph Bunche never wavered in his belief that the races in America had to learn to live together: "In all of his experience of racial discrimination Bunche never allowed himself to become bitter."[3]

You may also mention sources in the course of introducing quotations, paraphrasing passages, or borrowing ideas. Readers will appreciate the smooth transitions between your own words and those of other writers. Consult Section 25a for more on quoting sources effectively.

2 Document a source fully in the first note mentioning it. After the full citation, give a page reference (preceded by a comma) to the passage in the source referenced in that particular note:

3. Brian Urquhart, *Ralph Bunche: An American Life* (New York: Norton, 1993), 435.

Note: You don't always need a page reference in your note—for example, when you simply mention a source, rather than a specific passage within it. But *always* provide specific location references (as specific as possible) when quoting or paraphrasing another person's writing.

3 Shorten subsequent notes for sources you've already fully documented. You don't need to provide all the publication details for a source already introduced to readers. Instead, simply list the last name of the author, a shortened title (four or fewer words), and a page reference.

4. Helen Wilkinson, "It's Just a Matter of Time," *Utne Reader*, May/June 1995, 67.

5. Urquhart, *Ralph Bunche*, 177.

6. Wilkinson, "Matter of Time," 66.

This shortened format is sometimes used when a full bibliography is provided at the end of the paper. (See Section 52d.) Readers can use the last name and title to look up the full citation details for a source on the bibliography. Consult the requirements of your paper to determine whether a bibliography is required and whether shortened notes are accepted.

Finally, you can shorten references to the same source in consecutive notes by using the Latin abbreviation *Ibid.* ("from the same place"):

7. Simon Singh, *The Code Book* (New York: Anchor, 1999), 293.

8. Ibid., 303–304.

4 Use in-text parenthetical notes for numerous citations of one source. To cite multiple passages from one source, you may use a string of *Ibid.* notes. But consider using in-text parenthetical notes instead, especially when repeatedly citing well-known works (sacred texts, etc.) that are identified by standard abbreviations and numbering schemes. Simply provide full bibliographic details for the edition you're using in the first note, along with the abbreviation you will use in-text.

9. William Shakespeare, *Measure for Measure*, in *The Complete Works of Shakespeare*, 4th ed., ed. David Bevington (New York: Longman, 1997), act 1, sc. 3, ll. 39–43 (hereafter cited in-text as *MM* by act, scene, and line).

A subsequent parenthetical citation would look like this: The Duke exclaims, "O heavens, what stuff is here?" (*MM* 3.2.4).

52c How do you format CMS footnotes and endnotes?

Both footnotes and endnotes are indented, single-spaced, and double-spaced between notes. Each begins with the number of the note in regular typestyle (*not* superscript). Endnotes begin on a separate page titled *Notes*. Footnotes appear at the bottom of pages preceded by a 1½-inch horizontal rule (usually inserted automatically by your word processor). The following guidelines explain the basic parts of each reference note.

BASIC PARTS OF CMS FOOTNOTES AND ENDNOTES

CMS notes have five basic parts, each of which is discussed here and marked and color-coded in the sample entries that follow. Notice that all items within a note are separated by commas and that the entire citation ends with a period. Review the models for other required punctuation.

Primary Acknowledgment (Author). Each note usually begins with the names of the author(s) or artist(s), but some begin with the names of other contributors (a book's editor, a movie's director, etc.). List all names in normal order: first name/last name. When four or more individuals are given for the source, list only the first person and the phrase *and others.*

Title. Capitalize the first word and all other words in the title, except articles (*a, an,* and *the*), prepositions, and coordinating conjunctions. Place the titles of longer works in italics and enclose the titles of shorter works in quotation marks. All titles within titles are in quotation marks.

Secondary Acknowledgments. Some works are the result of many types of contributors: authors, editors, and translators for books; directors, performers, and scriptwriters for films; and so on. After the title of the source, list the names (in normal order) of those given secondary credits.

Publication or Production Information. This part of a footnote can be the most complicated, but you're always providing three key details: who published the source, where, and when. The models show the variations.

Location Reference. List the page number (or other reference marker) where the cited material appears in the source. This reference should be as specific as possible when citing quotations or paraphrased passages.

1. Sandra Cisneros, *The House on Mango Street* (Houston: Arte Público Press, 1983), 89.

2. Kathy Lowry, "The Purple Passion of Sandra Cisneros," *Texas Monthly,* October 1997, 148–49.

3. Gregory Nava, prod., "La Casa," *American Family,* perf. Raquel Welch and others, PBS, November 23, 2003.

52C-1 Books and book parts

1. Book

Author / Title

1. Andrew Feffer, *The Chicago Pragmatists and American Progressivism* (Ithaca: Cornell University Press, 1993).

Publication information (Place: Publisher, Year)

A reference note for a book includes the name of the author, the title of the book (italicized, preceded by a comma), and publication information (in parentheses). To refer to specific pages in the book, insert page numbers after the publication information, preceded by a comma: See Models 2, 4, 5, 6, and 7. In addition to these basic parts of a book citation, consider these requirements:

- **Is the book or report a revised edition or a volume in a set or series?** Insert edition names, volume numbers, and series titles (no italics) after the book title, preceded by a comma. See Models 2, 4
- **Is the book edited or translated?** List editors and translators after the title and before volume and edition details, preceded by a comma and an abbreviation (*ed.* or *trans.*) indicating their contribution(s). See Model 5
- **Are editors listed first on the book's title page?** For citing entire anthologies and readers, list the editors first followed by an abbreviation (*ed.* or *eds.*) to indicate their contribution(s). See Model 3
- **Are you citing only part of a book?** List the author(s) of the part first, then the selection's title. Next, list the title of the book (preceded by *in*), acknowledgments for those named on the book's title page, the pages where the selection appears, and standard publication details for the book. For untitled parts, use a descriptive title (*preface to* . . . , etc.), omitting the word *in*. See Models 6-8
- **Are you citing a sacred text, reference work, or government document?** See Section 52c-4 for guidelines for these special genres.
- **Are you using an online, digitized version of the book?** Begin with the full citation for the original print edition, but before the note's closing period, insert the Web address of the version used and the access date, as explained in Section 52c-4.

2. Book— subsequent edition

2. Ralph L. Pounds and James R. Bryner, *The School in American Society*, 2nd ed. (New York: Macmillan, 1967), 503.

3. Book— anthology

3. Tiffany M. Field and others, eds., *Review of Human Development* (New York: John Wiley, 1982).

4. Book—one of a series

4. Ella Flagg Young, *Ethics in the Schools*, Contributions to Education, no. 4 (Chicago: University of Chicago Press, 1902), 31–32.

5. Book—with editor

5. George Herbert Mead, *Play, School, and Society*, ed. Mary Jo Deegan (New York: Peter Lang, 1999), 59.

6. Book part— by author of book

6. John Dewey, "Education as Conservative and Progressive," in *Democracy and Education*, 81–93 (New York: Macmillan, 1922), 82.

7. Book part— selection from an anthology

7. Jane Addams, "The Arts at Hull House," in *The Work of Teachers in America: A Social History through Stories*, ed. Rosetta Maranz Cohen and Samuel Scheer, 173–80 (Mahwah, NJ: Lawrence Erlbaum, 1997), 179.

8. Book part— not by book's author

8. Norman Angell, introduction to *Approaches to the Great Settlement*, by Emily Greene Balch (New York: B. W. Huebsch, 1918).

52C-2 Periodical articles

9. Newspaper article

Author | Title

9. Ashley Hassebroek, "Public Art Will Have a Place at Omaha Convention Center," *Omaha World Herald*, April 23, 2001, sunrise edition.

Publication information (*Periodical*, Issue)

List the author(s) of the article, its title, the periodical name (italicized), and the issue (not italicized, preceded by a comma). List specific page references just before the closing period, preceded by a colon: See Models, 12, 13, 14, and 15. Make the following adjustments depending on the type of periodical:

- **Is the article from a newspaper or magazine?** Identify the issue by the date on the cover or masthead. If the article is part of a regular column, such as "The Talk of the Town" in *New Yorker* or "My Turn" in *Newsweek*, list the title of the column (no quotation marks or italics) in place of or after the article title (if each issue has a new title for the column). Page references are usually omitted for newspapers, but you may list the section containing the article (before the issue date) and identify the edition used (after the date). See Models 9-11, 15
- **Is the article from a journal?** Immediately after the periodical name, list the volume number and year in parentheses. If the journal restarts pagination with each issue, list the issue number (preceded by a comma and the abbreviation *no.*) before the year. See Models 12, 13
- **Is the source a review, editorial, or letter to the editor?** Describe the type of article (*editorial, letter to editor, review of*. . ., etc.) immediately after the title (if any). See Models 14, 15
- **Are you accessing the article from an online, digitized version?** Begin with the full citation for the original print article, but before the note's closing period, insert the Web address of the version used, as explained in Section 52c-4. You may also need to list an access date.

10. Newspaper article— unsigned

10. "Officials Solicit Proposals for City Public Arts Projects," *St. Petersburg Times*, sec. 5, October 29, 2003, late Tampa edition.

11. Magazine article

11. Ramiro Burr, "Los Tigres Del Norte 30th Anniversary: The Writing's on the Wall—An L.A. Mural and Los Tigres Del Norte CD Cover Depict a Vision of Struggle and Ambition," *Billboard*, November 11, 2001.

12. Journal article— volume pagination

12. Kerri N. Boutelle and others, "Using Signs, Artwork, and Music to Promote Stair Use in a Public Building," *American Journal of Public Health* 91 (2001): 2005–6.

13. Journal article—issue pagination

13. Gerald C. Cupchik, Andrew S. Winston, and Rachel S. Herz, "Judgments of Similarity and Difference between Paintings," *Visual Arts Research* 18, no. 2 (1992): 49.

14. Journal article —movie review

14. Joan M. West and Dennis West, review of *Frida*, dir. Julie Taymor, perf. Salma Hayek, *Cineaste* 28, no. 2 (2003): 39.

15. Letter to editor— magazine

15. Lance Cantor, letter to the editor, *Spectator*, October 26, 2002, 40.

50C-3 Web pages, online articles, etc.

16. Web page

16. Sondra A. O'Neale, "Phillis Wheatley," The Poetry Foundation, http://www.poetryfoundation.org/archive/poet.html?id=81619 (accessed June 9, 2009).

List the author (or site's sponsor if unsigned), the title of the page (in quotation marks), the site name (no italics, unless an online *periodical*), the site's sponsor (if not already mentioned), the address of the page, and the date you last viewed the source (in parentheses after the address). Some online sources require slight variations:

- **Is the source an article from an online periodical, news service, or database?** Cite like print periodical articles, using the name of the Web site when no other periodical is named. Insert location references (for instance, page, paragraph, or section numbering) before the address. If the address of the article is long and cryptic, list the address of a search page for the site. See Models 18, 19
- **Is the source a digitized version of a book, book part, recording, or broadcast?** Cite typical publication or production details for the original source (see Sections 52c-1 and 52c-4), then list the address of the online version. For multimedia sources, identify the Web site and the format as well, just before the address. See Models 20-22
- **Is the source a Weblog posting or reader-contributed comment?** Begin with the name of the author (which may be just a login name), the title of the post (if any), the title of the blog, discussion forum, or reader-generated Web site, and a description of the source (*entry posted*, *comment posted*, etc.) followed by the date of posting. End with the Web address of the source and an access date, as described above. See Models 23, 24

17. Web page— unsigned

17. Boston Public Library, "Hyde Park Branch," Neighborhood Branches, http://www.bpl.org/branches/hyde.htm (accessed June 2, 2009).

18. Online article— review of a book in Web magazine

18. Melanie Rehak, "One a Day, Plus Irony," review of *The Daily Mirror*, by David Lehman, *Salon.com*, January 14, 2001, http://archive.salon.com/books/feature/2000/01/14/rehak_lehman (accessed June 2, 2009).

19. Online article— from journal, in library database

19. Mary Loeffelholz, "The Religion of Art in a City at War: Boston's Public Poetry and the Great Organ, 1863," *American Literary History* 13 (2001): 221, http://muse.jhu.edu/search/search.pl (accessed June 6, 2009).

20. Online book— with section reference

20. Emily Dickinson, *The Complete Poems of Emily Dickinson* (Boston: Little, Brown, 1924), pt. 1, poem 89, http://www.bartleby.com/113 (accessed June 3, 2009).

21. Online book part

21. Ralph Waldo Emerson, "The Poet," in *Essays: The Second Series* (1844), http://etext.lib.virginia.edu/toc/modeng/public/EmeEssS.html (accessed June 2, 2009).

22. Online video— recording of speech

22. Derek Walcott, reading of poems (Sackler Lecture Hall, Harvard University, Cambridge, MA, April 14, 2003), WGBH Web site, RAM file, http://forum.wgbh.org/node/1147 (accessed May 9, 2009).

23. Blog entry

23. Boston Poetry Collective, "Peter Gizzi & David Larsen Reading," Boston Poetry Blog, entry posted May 4, 2009, http://bostonpoetry.blogspot.com/2009/05/peter-gizzi-david-larsen-reading.html (accessed May 19, 2009).

24. Reader-posted comment

24. María [pseud.], comment on "Infobox," Wikipedia: Talk: Emily Dickinson, Wikimedia Foundation, comment posted February 17, 2008, http://en.wikipedia.org/wiki?title=Talk:Emily_Dickinson (accessed May 19, 2009).

52C-4 Other Media and Special Genres

25. Speech

Speaker — Title of speech

25. Vera Katz, "Let's Get Portland Back to Work," (mayoral address, Governor Hotel, Portland, OR, October 28, 2002).

Publication information (depends on the genre)

Some genres and media formats have different means of publication and production than traditional print or newer Web sources. Notes citing such sources are adjusted to accommodate these differences:

- **Are you citing a speech?** List the speaker, a comma, and the title of the talk (in quotation marks). After title, describe the type of talk, the venue, city, and date, all in parentheses. See Model 25
- **Are you citing a government document?** Name the government agency, the title of the document, and basic publication information (in parentheses). For congressional documents, begin by identifying the house, committee, and session; then list the type of document, an identifying number, and other publication details. See Models 26, 27
- **Are you citing a sacred text?** Identify the book (abbreviated, no italics) and verse. In the first note, also mention the version used (not italicized). In later notes cite specific sections only. See Model 28
- **Are you citing a reference work?** Begin with the title, listing also other typical book details. Reference a specific entry, with the abbreviation *s.v.* (*sub verbo*, Latin for "under the word") and the phrase under which the article appears. See Model 29
- **Is the source an audio or video recording?** List the writer or artist, the title of the recording, the media format used (*CD, DVD,* etc.), and production details (in parentheses), including the place of production, the production company, and the year released. If citing a specific track (CDs, cassettes, etc.) or chapter (DVDs), list its title in quotes, before the title of the full recording. List secondary acknowledgments where appropriate. See Models 30, 31

26. Government publication— print, with table reference

26. U.S. Census Bureau, *Statistical Abstracts of the United States: The National Data Book*, 120th ed. (Washington, DC: GPO, 2000), table no. 643.

27. Government publication— online, with section reference

27. U.S. Department of Labor, "Minimum Wage and Overtime Pay," *Employment Law Guide*, "Who is covered," http://www.labor.gov/asp/programs/guide/minwage.htm (accessed May 2, 2006).

28. Biblical reference

28. Ps 104:23 (Revised Standard Version).

29. Reference article

29. *Dictionary of American History*, 3rd ed., 10 vol., ed. Stanley I. Kutler (New York: Charles Scribner, 2003), s.v. "Labor Day" (by Irving Dilliard).

30. Video recording

30. Nunnally Johnson, dir. and adapt., *The Man in the Gray Flannel Suit*, VHS, prod. Darryl F. Zanuck, perf. Gregory Peck and others (1956; US: 20th Century Fox, 1997).

31. Audio recording— specific track

31. Sting [Gordon Sumner], "Synchronicity II," perf. The Police, *Synchronicity*, CD (1983; US: A&M SP-3735, 2003).

52d How do you format CMS bibliographies?

As noted earlier in the chapter, bibliographies are not always required for CMS projects. If you need to create one, use Checklist 52.3 later in this chapter to format the page and follow the guidelines below to produce individual entries. We don't offer an extensive list of models for CMS bibliographic entries because the models and guidelines for MLA works-cited entries (Section 50b) can be used with a few minor adjustments. Compare the parts of a CMS entry with those of an MLA entry (pages 672–699):

- **Primary Acknowledgments (Author).** CMS uses the same basic format as outlined in the guidelines for MLA entries.
- **Titles.** Format titles as you would in MLA, except for titles within titles, which should always appear within quotation marks.
- **Secondary Acknowledgments.** CMS generally uses full phrases rather than abbreviations to introduce secondary contributors. For example, replace *Trans.* with *Translated by*, *Ed.* with *Edited by*, and so on. As in MLA, list the names of these contributors in normal order.
- **Publication and Production Information.** Present most details just like you would in MLA, but do not use abbreviations for most items: for instance, spell out *University Press*. Also, give *dates* in month-day-year order, with a comma after the day: *July 1, 2001*; *November 27, 2000*; but *May 1999*, *December 1998*, and so forth.
- **Medium Access Information.** Unlike MLA, give no medium description. But for Web sources, do provide an address at the end of the entry, along with the access date (in parentheses). For example: http://www.dailycandy.com/everywhere (accessed May 1, 2009).

Besides the minor differences just listed, make the following adjustments for entries citing these special kinds of source:

- **For book parts, insert the word *In* before the title of the book.** And list untitled parts immediately before the title of the book, replacing MLA's stand-alone descriptive title with a full phrase: *Introduction to . . .* instead of *Introduction*; and so on.
- **For periodicals, insert a comma after the periodical name, before the issue date or number.** Also, omit issue numbers for journals with pagination that does not restart with each issue. When listing a journal issue, however, precede it with *no.*, rather than just a period.

- **For unsigned periodical articles and Web pages, list the periodical name or site sponsor first.** In MLA, you would normally list the title of the article or Web page first. In CMS, list the periodical name or site sponsor as the primary acknowledgment.

52e Sample literary analysis—CMS

The sample CMS pages that follow are taken from "Diomedes as Hero of *The Iliad*," a paper written by Jeremy A. Corley, a student in Joi Chevalier's course "The Rhetoric of Epic Narratives." Jeremy wrote a short analysis of the characters Diomedes and Achilles in Homer's *Iliad*. Notice how Jeremy merges his analysis with those of his secondary sources, mostly literary critics. He uses what previous scholars have said about the epic as building blocks for presenting his own claims (supported by plenty of textual evidence and explication) about characters in Homer's *Iliad*. For more on writing a literary analysis, see Chapter 11.

Although Jeremy's paper is fairly short, the style (CMS) used for documentation is often recommended for longer papers you'll write in college, especially senior theses and graduate-level term papers. The style typically divides such long documents into three parts: the *front matter* (title page, table of contents, preface, etc.), the *main text*, and the *back matter* (endnotes, bibliography, appendixes, etc.). We don't show all the parts required for long, formal thesis papers, but we do show the basic CMS formats for presenting a title page, the main text, footnotes and endnotes, and a bibliography. For more on using CMS paper formatting, see Kate L. Turabian, *A Manual for Writers of Research Papers, Theses, and Dissertations* (7th ed., 2007).

Checklist 52.1 Document Formatting—CMS

For the paper, use the following settings in your word processor, but adjust them to match preferences voiced by your instructor or set by your school.

a. **Use white, 8½-by-11-inch paper with at least 1-inch margins.** For a bound manuscript, use a 1½-inch left margin.

b. **Use a 10- to 12-point readable font face throughout.** But use a slightly smaller size for footnotes.

c. **Double-space the body of the paper.** Single-space block quotations (used for material extending beyond seven lines of prose or three lines of verse). Don't enclose block quotes within quotation marks, but indent them one-half inch from the left.

d. **Indent the first word of each paragraph one-half inch.** Insert a tab each time or set a standard indentation in your document.

e. **Left-align the body of the paper.** You may also need to turn off your word processor's automatic hyphenation and justification tools.

f. **Insert a page number at the upper right corner of every page.** The first page of the body of the main text should begin with *1*.

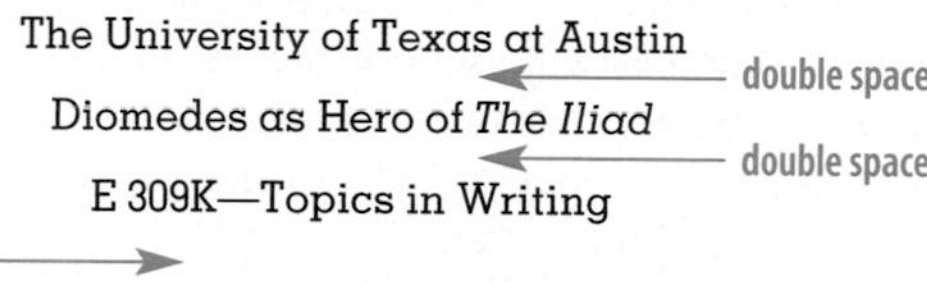

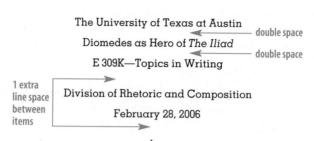

The University of Texas at Austin

Diomedes as Hero of *The Iliad*

E 309K—Topics in Writing

1 extra line space between items

Division of Rhetoric and Composition

February 28, 2006

by

Jeremy A. Corley

Checklist 52.2 Formatting Front Matter—CMS

Short term papers usually need only a title page. Here we offer common guidelines for formatting all pages of front matter—though schools can set standards for formally submitted projects:

a. **Begin with a title page that includes basic information.** Centered, at the top of the page, list your school, the title of the paper, the course, the date, and your name. Insert blank lines to separate items clearly. Don't number this page. Repeat the title of the paper at the top of the first page of the body of the paper.

b. **Insert copyright, dedication, and epigraph pages when appropriate.** These pages usually only appear in formal theses. Pages are centered in alignment with no title or page number.

c. **Create a table of contents for long papers.** Place it after the title page and label it *Contents* (centered at top). List labeled pages and sections, noting the corresponding page number on the same row.

d. **Number all front matter with lowercase roman numerals.** The copyright page (if any) would be *ii*; and so forth.

1 inch

1/2 inch

1

Diomedes as Hero of *The Iliad*

1/2 inch

double space

Achilles is the central character of *The Iliad*, but is his prominence alone enough to make him the story's hero? There are many episodes in the epic that indicate otherwise. One of the most interesting aspects of the narrative is its use of a lesser character, rather than the technical protagonist, as the tale's benchmark for heroism. This lesser character is Diomedes, and his leadership skills and maturity prove to be far superior to those of Achilles. Book V of *The Iliad* is devoted almost entirely to Diomedes' feats, and there are many scenes in which he is presented as a leader and hero throughout the rest of the text. While Diomedes is singled out for his gallantry, Achilles is, by contrast, noted for his immaturity and selfishness. Homer depicts Diomedes in a much more positive light than Achilles, despite the latter's obvious natural superiority as a soldier. It seems evident that Homer is emphasizing the total use of one's abilities—rather than just the presence of those abilities—as the basis of heroism. Diomedes, therefore, is the actual hero of *The Iliad*.

1 inch

1 inch

The paper offers a challenging thesis.

Achilles is immediately placed at the focal point of the story, and his pride and immaturity surface almost instantaneously. In Book I, Agamemnon embarrasses Achilles publicly, prompting Achilles to challenge the power of the Achaians' commander: "Khryseis / being required of me by Phoibos Appollo /. . . I myself / will call for Briseis at your hut . . .to show you here and now who is the stronger."[1] Achilles can hardly be faulted for taking offense at this

The first note identifies the edition of the classic.

1-1/2 inch rule

1/2 inch

1. Homer, *The Iliad*, trans. Robert Fitzgerald (New York: Anchor Press, 1974), bk. 1, lines 211–17 (hereafter cited in-text by book and line number).

1 inch

2

incident. As critic R. M. Frazer points out, it "threatened to invalidate . . . the whole meaning of his life."[2] But Achilles' refusal to fight afterward must be looked at from another perspective. This is the first example of Achilles acting according to his pride, as demonstrated by his regard for himself as "peerless among Akhaians" (1.475). While it is understandable for a soldier such as Achilles, who "towers above all the other characters of *The Iliad*," to be hesitant to fight for and under the man who embarrassed him, Agamemnon,[3] it is also folly for a soldier to stop fighting because of anything as relatively unimportant as an insult, even a public one. A soldier's duty is to defend the homeland and fight in its wars, and Achilles misses this greater duty for his own selfishness. This refusal to fight is compounded by his request to his mother, Thetis, to "tell [Zeus] your good pleasure / if he will take the Trojan side / and roll the Akhaians back to the water's edge" (1.469–471). This is wholly selfish. Achilles is willing to put the fate of the entire Greek army in peril to feed his own wounded ego. Achilles is acting nothing like the leader that his divine gifts give him the power to be. Homer clearly leaves his central character open for some significant personal and psychological development.

Subsequent references to *The Iliad* are to book and line number. See the first footnote.

Note 3 is both a reference and content note.

For clarity, the word "Zeus" has been added in brackets.

In contrast to Achilles' infantile behavior, which is consistent throughout most of the story, Diomedes is cast in a different light. Athena makes Diomedes "bold" (5.2), and "impelled him to the center where / the greatest number fought" (5.8–9). While not

Transitional sentence emphasizes the contrast between Achilles and Diomedes.

1-1/2 inch rule

1/2 inch

2. R. M. Frazer, *A Reading of "The Iliad"* (Lanham, MD: University Press of America, 1993), 12.

3. Ibid., 11. Frazer discusses Achilles' reaction at length.

3

Achilles' equal as a soldier, "Diomedes was extremely fierce" and proved to be a terrific leader for the Achaians.[4] Diomedes defeats a great number of Trojan warriors in Book V, acting as many hoped Achilles would, and even fighting through an injury suffered from the bow of Pandaros. Rather than back down, Diomedes prays to Athena for aid and joins the battle even more fiercely than before, assailing Trojan soldiers as well as any Greek hero (5.111–37). At this point, as W. Thomas MacCary explains it, Diomedes is "obviously a paradigm of heroic behavior in Achilles' absence."[5] But is Diomedes merely a surrogate for Achilles, as MacCary suggests, or is he the genuine heroic figure advocated by Homer? Diomedes represents a well-behaved, properly subservient soldier in the Akhaian army who uses his courage and his honor to accomplish feats that are beyond his natural abilities.

Quotation is nicely introduced by identifying its author.

Diomedes exhibits self-control above all else, which is the element critics note is most wanting in Achilles.[6] Diomedes' courage is further proven when he speaks against Agamemnon at the beginning of Book IX, when the Achaian commander is advocating a Greek retreat: "Sthenelos and I will fight alone / until we see the destined end of Ilion" (9.56–57). In contrast to Achilles' childish retort to Agamemnon in Book 1, this is the moment when Diomedes is

A space is left before and after a slash used to divide lines of poetry.

---

4. Scott Richardson, *The Homeric Narrator* (Nashville: Vanderbilt University Press, 1990), 159.

5. W. Thomas MacCary, *Childlike Achilles: Ontogeny and Philogeny in "The Iliad"* (New York: Columbia University Press, 1982), 95.

6. G. S. Kirk, *"The Iliad": A Commentary*, vol. 2 (New York: Cambridge University Press, 1990), 34.

4

confirmed as one of the Greeks' greatest leaders, as even in a time when the army is "shaken by . . . fear" (9.4), we see that "a cry went up from all Akhaians / in wonder at his words" (9.59–60). The scene underscores Diomedes' rise to greatness in the Achaian army.

Achilles and Diomedes finally come into direct conflict with one another in Book IX, after Agamemnon has decided to make a peace offering to Achilles in hopes of the latter's return to battle. Agamemnon makes an offer to Achilles that is outrageously generous in exchange for Achilles' return to battle. Achilles' response is far from heroic, presenting a dilemma that is characteristically self-centered on both points:

1 inch

> if on the one hand I remain to fight
> around Troy town, I lose all hope of home
> but gain unfading glory; on the other,
> if I sail back to my own land my glory
> fails—but a long life lies ahead of me. (9.502– 6)

Block quotation makes the selection easier to read.

These words show utter selfishness on the part of the man who is supposedly the greatest warrior in Greek history, and Achilles is certainly not, at this point, living up to his reputation or his potential. Observing that Achilles will "fight again /. . . whenever his blood is up / or the god rouses him" (9.853–55), Diomedes speaks against Achilles for the first time, effectively casting himself as something of an adversary to Achilles in the hopes of bringing him back into the battle, an action that serves the overall good of the Achaians. Once more, Diomedes is doing what is best for his people and his army while Achilles thinks only of himself. Peter Toohey observes that

Ellipses indicate that some lines have been omitted.

"Homer likes to juxtapose"[7]—here he uses that device to highlight the stark contrast between the protagonist of the story (Achilles) and the true hero of the story (Diomedes).

Homer centers *The Iliad* on Achilles, whose actions are notably selfish and immature. Homer then uses Diomedes, at first a lesser character, as a dramatic foil. Diomedes comes across as an example of the ideal young Greek soldier. Achilles' capacities as a warrior are far superior to those of any man alive, yet Diomedes betters him in both words and actions throughout most of the story. Achilles is finally brought to realize his supreme military prowess, but it is the death of his friend Patroclos that spurs his fighting spirit, still another example of Achilles' penchant for acting on emotion rather than judgment (18.88–106). Achilles is finally reconciled to Diomedes' example when he meets Priam at the end of the story and responds honorably: "I have intended . . . / to yield up Hektor to you" (24.671–72), agreeing to return the corpse of Priam's son for a proper burial. Achilles at last achieves a measure of respect that his abilities could have earned him long before. It is in that time, however, when Achilles was still selfish and immature, that Diomedes' less temperamental nature shines through as a firm example of leadership and valor, and consequently the true hero of *The Iliad*.

Conclusion brings the lines of argument together.

---

7. Peter Toohey, "Epic and Rhetoric: Speech-Making and Persuasion in Homer and Apollonius," *Arachnion: A Journal of Ancient Literature and History on the Web* 1 (1995): sec. 2, http://www.cisi.unito.it/arachne/num1/toohey.html (accessed February 21, 2006).

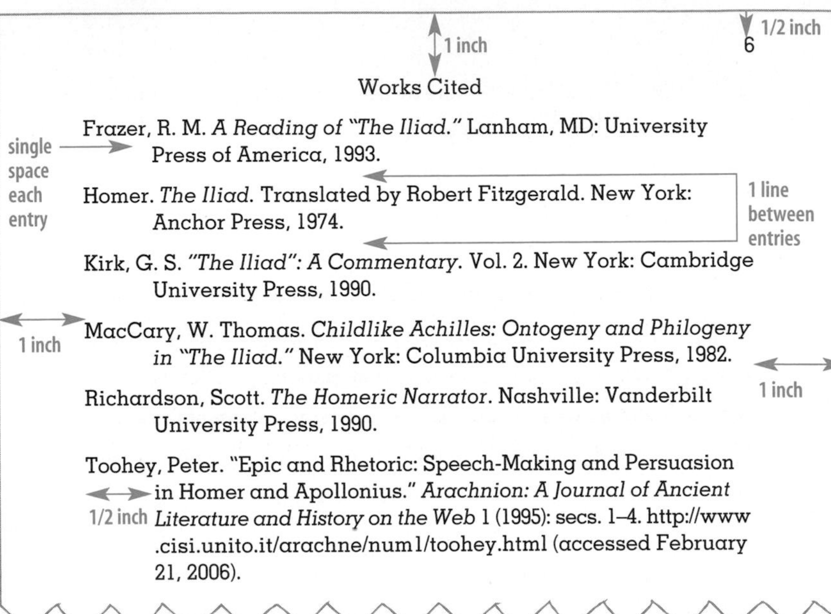

1 inch
1/2 inch
6
Works Cited
Frazer, R. M. *A Reading of "The Iliad."* Lanham, MD: University Press of America, 1993.
Homer. *The Iliad*. Translated by Robert Fitzgerald. New York: Anchor Press, 1974.
Kirk, G. S. *"The Iliad": A Commentary*. Vol. 2. New York: Cambridge University Press, 1990.
MacCary, W. Thomas. *Childlike Achilles: Ontogeny and Philogeny in "The Iliad."* New York: Columbia University Press, 1982.
Richardson, Scott. *The Homeric Narrator*. Nashville: Vanderbilt University Press, 1990.
Toohey, Peter. "Epic and Rhetoric: Speech-Making and Persuasion in Homer and Apollonius." *Arachnion: A Journal of Ancient Literature and History on the Web* 1 (1995): secs. 1–4. http://www.cisi.unito.it/arachne/num1/toohey.html (accessed February 21, 2006).
single space each entry
1 line between entries
1 inch
1 inch
1/2 inch

Checklist 52.3 Formatting Bibliography Pages—CMS

Use the same font face and size used in the body of the paper, but make the following other adjustments to the page layout:

a. **Center the title "Works Cited" or "Bibliography" at the top of the page.** Use the title "Works Cited" for reference lists including only those works mentioned in the body of the paper or its notes. Do not repeat the title when the list of entries runs over to another page.

b. **Single-space each entry, inserting a blank line between them.**

c. **Create a one-half inch hanging indentation for each entry.** In other words, the first line of each entry should be aligned with the left margin and subsequent lines of the entry should be indented.

d. **Alphabetize the list according to the first word in each entry.** Ignore initial articles (*A*, *An*, and *The*) when alphabetizing by title. When the same author appears at the beginning of multiple entries, you can replace the author's name with three hyphens (---).

e. **Proof carefully your punctuation and capitalization for each entry.** Review the guidelines in Section 52d.

Checklist 52.4 Formatting Endnotes and Footnotes—CMS

The following guidelines apply to both footnote and endnote entries:

a. **Indent each note the same space (usually one-half inch) as paragraphs in the body of the paper.**

b. **Begin each note with the number corresponding to that which appears in the body of the paper.** Do *not* use superscript typestyle for the number preceding the text of the note.

c. **Single-space each entry and insert a blank line between entries.** Alternatively, you can set the paragraph options in your word processor to allow space following each note.

d. **Separate multiple references in a note by semicolons.** You can also add commentary after the references, giving readers more details about each source's significance to your paper. Example of multiple references:

4. Mary Carruthers, *The Book of Memory: A Study of Memory in Medieval Culture* (Cambridge, England: Cambridge University Press, 1990), 86; Marjorie Curry Woods, "The Teaching of Poetic Composition in the Later Middle Ages," in *A Short History of Writing Instruction: From Ancient Greece to Modern America*, 2nd ed., ed. James J. Murphy, 123–44 (Mahwah, NJ: Hermagoras Press, 2001), 143.

Glossary of Terms and Usage

This glossary covers grammatical terms and matters of usage. Whether you require the definition of a key term (*verbals, noun*), or advice about correct usage (What's the difference between *eminent* and *imminent*?), you'll find the information in this single, comprehensive list. For convenient review, key grammatical terms are marked by the * symbol.

* **absolute.** A phrase that modifies an entire sentence. Absolutes are often infinitive or participial phrases. Unlike other modifying phrases, absolutes need not modify a word or phrase standing near them.

> **To put it politely**, the president's press secretary is disingenuous.
>
> The witness intends to recount the entire story, **time permitting**.
>
> **Scripts stored, props disassembled, costumes locked away in trunks**, the annual Shakespeare festival concluded.

accept/except. Very commonly confused. **Accept** means "to take, receive, or approve." **Except** means "to exclude, or not including."

> I **accepted** all the apologies **except** George's.

* **adjective.** A word that modifies a noun or pronoun (see Section 30b). Some adjectives describe the words they modify, explaining how many, which color, which one, and so on.

> an **unsuccessful** coach   a **blue** Challenger R/T
> the **lucky** one   a **sacred** text

Such adjectives frequently have comparative and superlative forms (see Section 30h).

> the **fatter** cat   the **happiest** people

Other adjectives limit or specify the words they modify.

> **this** adventure   **every** penny
> **each** participant   **neither** video

Nouns (including proper nouns) can also serve as adjectives.

> **typewriter** keyboard   **Eisenhower** era

* **adverb.** A word that modifies a verb, an adjective, or another adverb (see Section 30e). Adverbs explain where, when, and how.

> adverb (immediately)   verb (suspected)
> Bud **immediately** *suspected* foul play at the Hutton mansion.

adverb adjective

It seemed **extremely** *odd* to him that Mrs. Hutton should load a large burlap sack into the trunk of her Mercedes.

adverb adverb

Mrs. Hutton replied **rather** *evasively* when Bernardo questioned her about where she had been at 8:00 a.m. that day.

Some adverbs modify complete sentences.

adverb

Evidently, Mr. Hutton had been murdered.

adverse/averse. Often confused. **Adverse** describes something hostile, unfavorable, or difficult. **Averse** indicates opposition; it is ordinarily followed by *to*.

Travis was **averse to** playing soccer under **adverse** field conditions.

advice/advise. These words aren't interchangeable. **Advice** is a noun meaning "an opinion" or "counsel." **Advise** is a verb meaning to "to give counsel or advice."

I'd **advise** you not to give Margo **advice** about running her business.

affect/effect. A troublesome pair! Each word can be either a noun or a verb, although **affect** is ordinarily a verb and **effect** a noun. In its usual sense, **affect** is a verb meaning "to influence" or "to give the appearance of."

How will the stormy weather **affect** the plans for the outdoor concert?

The meteorologist **affected** surprise at the sudden drop in barometric pressure.

Only rarely is **affect** a noun—as a term in psychology meaning "feeling" or "emotion." On the other hand, **effect** is usually a noun, meaning "consequence" or "result."

The **effect** of the weather may be serious.

As a verb, however, **effect** means "to cause" or "to bring about."

The funnel cloud **effected** a change in our plans.
Compare with: The funnel cloud **affected** our plans.

aggravate/irritate. Many people use both of these verbs to mean "to annoy" or "to make angry." But formal English preserves a fine—and useful—distinction between them. **Irritate** means "to annoy" while **aggravate** means "to make worse."

It **irritated** Shea when Ahmed **aggravated** his cough by smoking.

* **agreement, pronoun and antecedent.** A grammatical principle which requires that singular pronouns stand in for singular nouns (*his* surfboard

= *Richard's* surfboard) and plural pronouns stand in for plural nouns (*their* surfboard = *George and Martha's* surfboard). When they do so, the pronoun and its antecedent agree in **number**; when they don't, you have an agreement problem (see Chapter 27).

Pronouns and their antecedents also must agree in **gender**. That is, a masculine pronoun (*he, him, his*) must refer to a masculine antecedent, and a feminine pronoun (*she, her, hers*) must refer to a feminine antecedent (see Section 29b).

Finally, pronouns and antecedents must agree in **case**, whether objective, subjective, or possessive (see Chapter 28). For example, an antecedent in the possessive case (*Lawrence's* gym) can be replaced only by a pronoun also in the possessive case (*his* gym).

* **agreement, subject and verb.** Verbs and nouns are said to agree in number (see Chapter 22). This means that with a singular subject in the third person (for example, *he, she, it*), a verb in the present tense ordinarily adds an **-s** ending to its base form. With subjects not in the third person singular, the base form of the verb is used.

Third person, singular, present tense:	Barney sits.
	He sits.
	She sits.
First person, singular, present tense:	I sit.
Second person, singular, present tense:	You sit.
First person, plural, present tense:	We sit.
Second person, plural, present tense:	You sit.
Third person, plural, present tense:	They sit.

Most verbs—with the notable exception of *to be*—change their form to show agreement only in third person singular forms (*he, she, it*).

ain't. This word isn't appropriate in academic or professional writing.

all ready/already. Tricky, but not difficult. **All ready**, an adjective phrase, means "fully prepared and set to go." **Already**, an adverb, means "before"or "previously."

The camera was **all ready** for shooting.

Marisa had **already** loaded the film.

all right. **All right** is the only acceptable spelling. **Alright** is not acceptable in standard English, though the misspelling is common in informal and colloquial writing.

allude/elude. Commonly confused. **Allude** means "to refer to" or "to mention indirectly." **Elude** means "to escape."

Soowon laughingly **alluded** to his cat's effort to **elude** the dog.

allude/refer. To **allude** is to mention indirectly; to **refer** is to mention directly or to draw attention to.

> Pledge master Carter **alluded** to secret fraternity traditions and then **referred** the candidates to the day's orientation schedule.

allusion/illusion. These terms are often misused. An **allusion** is an indirect reference. An **illusion** is a false impression or a misleading appearance.

> Professor Frost entertained the **illusion** that everyone understood her **allusion** to *Hamlet.*

a lot. Two words often misspelled as one. **A lot** is considered informal; use **many** or **much** in academic writing.

already. See **all ready/already**.

alright. See **all right**.

among/between. Use **between** with two objects, **among** with three or more.

> Katelyn had to choose **between** Royer and Antonio.
>
> Katelyn had to choose from **among** a dozen actors.

amount/number. Use **amount** for quantities that can be measured but not counted. Use **number** for things that can be counted, but not readily measured: the **amount** of water in the ocean; the **number** of fish in the sea. **Amount of** is followed by a singular noun, and **number of** is followed by a plural noun: an **amount of** *money*; a **number of** *dimes.*

and etc. A redundant expression. Use **etc.** alone or **and so on**. See **etc.**

and/or. A useful form in business and technical writing. But try to avoid it in academic writing. **And/or** is typed with no space before or after the slash (see Section 40d).

anyone/any one. These expressions have different meanings. **Anyone** is a singular pronoun meaning "any person" or "all people." **Any one** is a phrase (usually followed by **of**) meaning "one of a group."

> I doubt that **anyone** will be able to find a solution to **any one** of the equations.

anyways. A nonstandard form. Use **anyway:** *It didn't matter* ***anyway.***

* **appositive.** A word or phrase that stands next to a noun and modifies it by restating or expanding its meaning (see Section 16c-4). Note that appositives ordinarily are surrounded by commas (see Section 36b-2).

Connie Vo, **editor of the paper and a liberal**, was furious when ex-President Clinton gave his only campus interview to Sue Wesley, **chair of the Young Republicans**.

* **articles.** The words **the, a**, and **an** used before a noun. **The** is called a **definite article** because it points to something specific: **the** book, **the** church, **the** criminal. **A** and **an** are **indefinite articles** because they refer to an object more generally: **a** book, **a** church, **a** criminal (see Section 33b).

as being. A wordy expression. You can usually cut **being**.

In most cases, telephone solicitors are regarded **as** ~~being~~ a nuisance.

* **auxiliary verbs.** Verbs, usually some form of *be, do*, or *have*, that combine with other verbs to show various relations of tense, voice, mood, and so on. All the following words in boldface are auxiliary verbs: **has** seen, **will be** talking, **would have been** going, **are** investigating, **did** mention, **should** prefer. Auxiliary verbs are also known as *helping verbs*. See Sections 23a-1 and 32d.

averse/adverse. See **adverse/averse**.

awful. **Awful** is inappropriate as a synonym for **very**.

INAPPROPRIATE	The findings of the two research teams were **awful** close.
BETTER	The findings of the two research teams were **very** close.

awhile/a while. These expressions are not interchangeable, though they both mean "for a short time." **Awhile** is an adverb; **a while** is a noun phrase. After prepositions, always use **a while**.

Winchell stood **awhile** looking at the grass. He decided that it would not have to be cut for **a while**.

bad/badly. **Bad** is an adjective describing what something is like; **badly** is an adverb explaining how something is done.

Stanley's taste in music wasn't **bad**. [adjective modifies **taste**]

Unfortunately, he treated his musicians **badly**. [adverb modifies **treated**]

However, with verbs that explain how something feels, tastes, smells, or looks, use **bad**.

The situation looked **bad**.

I feel **bad**.

For more information, see Section 30c-2.

because of/due to. Careful writers usually prefer **because of,** not **due to,** in many situations.

AWKWARD	The investigation stalled **due to** Officer Bricker's concern for correct procedure.
REVISED	The investigation stalled **because of** Officer Bricker's concern for correct procedure.

Due to is often the better choice when it serves as a **subject complement** after a **linking verb**.

subj. l.v. subj. comp.
The prosecutor's reluctance to bring charges *was* **due to** the political prominence of the Hutton family.

being as/being that. Both of these expressions are wordy and awkward when used in place of **because** or **since**. Use **because** and **since** in formal and academic writing.

INAPPROPRIATE	**Being that** her major was astronomy, Jenny looked forward to the eclipse.
BETTER	**Since** her major was astronomy, Jenny looked forward to the eclipse.

beside/besides. **Beside** is a preposition meaning "next to" or "alongside"; **besides** is a preposition meaning "in addition to" or "other than."

> **Besides** a confession, the detectives had the suspect's fingerprints on a gun found **beside** the body.

Besides can also be an adverb meaning "in addition" or "moreover."

> **Besides**, Kelli actually liked coaching volleyball.

between. See **among/between**.

can/may. Understand the difference between the auxiliary verbs **can** and **may**. (See also **modal auxiliary**.) Use **can** to express an ability; use **may** to express either permission or possibility.

> Charnelle **can** solve differential equations effortlessly.

> You **may** use the answer key to check your solution.

can't hardly. A colloquial expression that is, technically, a double negative. Use **can hardly** instead.

DOUBLE NEGATIVE	I **can't hardly** see the road.
REVISED	I **can hardly** see the road.

censor/censure. As a verb, **censor** means "to cut," "to repress," or "to remove"; **censure** means "to disapprove" and "to condemn."

The editorial board of the newspaper voted to **censor** the article and to **censure** the writer for attempting to publish it.

complement/complementary, compliment/complimentary. These words are not synonyms. **Complement** and **complementary** describe completion or compatibility. **Compliment** and **complimentary** refer to praise or things given away free.

Travis's tan sweater **complemented** his green eyes.

The two parts of the essay were **complementary**, examining the same subject from differing perspectives.

Greta appreciated the teacher's **compliment** on her work.

The dealer featured **complimentary** car washes.

* **conjugation.** The forms of a verb as it appears in all numbers, tenses, voices, and moods. See Chart 32.1.

* **conjunctions, coordinating.** The words *and, or, nor, for, but, yet,* and *so,* used to link words, phrases, and clauses that serve equivalent functions in a sentence. (See Section 16f.) A coordinating conjunction can be used to join two independent clauses or two dependent clauses.

Oscar liked the story, **but** Mary did not.

She said she would come, **yet** she kept delaying her flight.

You can carry your bags, **or** you can check them.

* **conjunctions, correlative.** Paired terms such as *if . . . then, either . . . or, neither . . . nor, whether . . . or, both . . . and,* and *not only . . . but also* that work together as conjunctions to link phrases or clauses within a sentence. The items joined should usually be parallel.

If markets rise, **then** unemployment usually falls.

It doesn't pay **either** to lie **or** to cheat.

* **conjunctions, subordinating.** Words or expressions such as *although, because, if, since, before, after, when, even though, in order that,* and *while* that relate dependent (that is, subordinate) clauses to independent ones. Subordinating conjunctions introduce subordinate clauses. See Section 16g.

subordinate clause

When the show opened, audiences stayed away.

conscience/conscious. **Conscience** is a noun referring to an inner ethical sense; **conscious** is an adjective describing a state of awareness or wakefulness.

The linebacker felt a twinge—likely his **conscience**—after knocking the quarterback **unconscious**.

consensus. This expression is redundant when followed by **of opinion**; **consensus** by itself implies an opinion. Use **consensus** alone. See Section 17c-4.

REDUNDANT	The student senate reached a **consensus of opinion** on the issue of censorship.
REVISED	The student senate reached a **consensus** on the issue of censorship.

* **contraction.** A word shortened by the omission of one or more letters, usually signaled by an apostrophe: cannot—**can't**; you are—**you're**; it is—**it's**. Contractions usually signal a less formal style.

* **coordinating conjunction.** See **conjunctions, coordinating**.

* **correlatives.** See **conjunctions, correlative.**

could of/might of/must of/should of/would of. Incorrect; use **could have, might have, must have, should have,** or **would have**.

couple of. Casual. Avoid it in formal or academic writing.

credible/credulous. **Credible** means "believable"; **credulous** means "willing to believe on slim evidence." See also **incredible/incredulous**.

Officer Bricker found Mr. Hutton's excuse for speeding **credible**.

However, Bricker was a **credulous** police officer, liable to believe any story.

criteria, criterion. **Criteria** is the plural form; **criterion**, the singular.

Instead of a single **criterion**, many **criteria** ought to factor into hiring.

data/datum. In academic writing, use **datum** where the singular is needed, or rewrite the sentence to avoid the singular. (See Chart 22.2.)

SINGULAR	The most intriguing **datum** in the study was the rate of population decline.
PLURAL	In all the **data**, no figure was more intriguing than the rate of population decline.

different from/different than. In formal writing, **different from** is usually preferred to **different than**.

FORMAL	Ike's account was **different from** Nan's.
INFORMAL	Ike's account was **different than** Nan's.

discreet/discrete. **Discreet** means "tactful" or "sensitive to appearances" (*discreet* behavior); **discrete** means "individual" or "separate" (*discrete* objects).

Joel was **discreet** about the money spent on his project.

He had several **discrete** accounts at his disposal.

disinterested/uninterested. **Disinterested** means "neutral" or "uninvolved"; **uninterested** means "not interested" or "bored."

Alyce and Richard sought a **disinterested** party to arbitrate their dispute.

Hector was **uninterested** in the club's management.

don't. Writers sometimes forget the apostrophe in this contraction and others like it: **can't, won't**. See also **contractions.**

due to the fact that. Wordy. Replace it with **because** or **since** whenever you can. See Section 17c.

effect/affect. See **affect/effect**.

elicit/illicit. **Elicit** means to "draw out" or "bring forth"; **illicit** means "illegal" or "prohibited."

The district attorney **elicited** an admission of **illicit** behavior from the CEO.

elude/allude. See **allude/elude**.

eminent/imminent. **Eminent** means "distinguished" and "prominent"; **imminent** means "about to happen."

The arrival of the **eminent** scholar is **imminent**.

enthused. In academic writing, use **enthusiastic** instead.

COLLOQUIAL Sarah Jean was **enthused** about Radiohead's latest album.

REVISED Sarah Jean was **enthusiastic** about Radiohead's latest album.

equally as. Redundant. Use either **equally** or **as** to express a comparison, whichever works in a particular sentence.

REDUNDANT Sue Ellen is **equally as** concerned as Hector about bilingual education.

REVISED Sue Ellen is **as** concerned as Hector about bilingual education.

REVISED Sue Ellen and Hector are **equally** concerned about bilingual education.

etc. This common abbreviation for *et cetera* should be avoided in most academic and formal writing. Instead, use **and so on** or **and so forth**. Never use **and etc.**

everyone/every one. **Everyone** describes a group collectively. **Every one** focuses on the individual elements within a group or collective term.

I doubt that **everyone** will be able to attend **every one** of the sessions.

except/accept. See **accept/except**.

fact that, the. Wordy. You can usually replace the entire expression with **that**.

WORDY Bud was aware of **the fact that** he was in a strange room.

REVISED Bud was aware **that** he was in a strange room.

farther/further. Use **farther** to refer to distances that can be measured. Use **further**, meaning "more" or "additional," when physical distance or separation is not involved.

El Paso is **farther** from Houston than I thought.

The crime warranted **further** investigation.

fewer/less. Use **fewer** with things you can count; use **less** with quantities that must be measured or can be considered as a whole.

We had **fewer** than ten cans of soda and **less** than a gallon of cider.

(Supermarkets get this usage wrong when their express lanes specify "15 items or less.")

flaunt/flout. These words are confused surprisingly often. **Flaunt** means "to show off"; **flout** means "to disregard" or "to show contempt for."

To **flaunt** his wealth, Mr. Lin bought a Van Gogh landscape.

Flouting a gag order, the newspaper published its exposé of corruption in the city council.

fun, funner, funnest. In academic writing, replace **fun** as an adjective with a more formal expression. In all writing, use **more fun** or **most fun** rather than **funner** or **funnest**. (See Section 30h.)

INFORMAL Skiing is a **fun** sport.

FORMAL Skiing is an **enjoyable** sport.

* **gerund.** A verb form used as a noun: *smiling, biking, walking.* (See Section 24a-3.) Most gerunds end in **-ing** and, consequently, look identical to the present participle.

GERUND **Smiling** is good for one's health.

PARTICIPLE A **smiling** critic is dangerous.

The difference is that gerunds function as nouns whereas participles act as modifiers. Gerunds usually appear in the present tense, but they can take other forms.

> **Having been criticized** made Yolanda angry.
> gerund in past tense, passive voice, as subject of sentence
>
> **Being asked** to play an encore was a compliment Otis enjoyed.
> gerund in present tense, passive voice, as subject of sentence

get/got/gotten. The principal parts of this verb are:

PRESENT	PAST	PAST PARTICIPLE
get	got	got, gotten

gotten. Usually sounds more polished than **got** as the past participle, but both forms are acceptable.

> Aretha **has gotten** an *A* in microbiology.
>
> Aretha **has got** an *A* in microbiology.

good and. Informal. Avoid it in academic writing.

INFORMAL	The lake was **good and** cold.
FORMAL	The lake was **icy** cold.

good/well. **Good** is an adjective only; **well** can be either an adjective or an adverb. In these sentences, each word functions as an adjective: Katy is **good**; Katy is **well**.

Good is often mistakenly used as an adverb.

INCORRECT	Juan conducts the orchestra **good**.
CORRECT	Juan conducts the orchestra **well**.

Well is sometimes mistakenly substituted as an adjective for **good**.

INCORRECT	After a bath, the dog smells **well**.
CORRECT	After a bath, the dog smells **good**.
CORRECT	I feel **good**. [Describes a state of mind]
ALSO CORRECT	I feel **well**. [Describes a physical state: not ill.]

hanged, hung. **Hanged** has been the past participle conventionally reserved for executions; **hung** is used on other occasions. The distinction is a nice one, probably worth observing.

> The newspaper editor was **hanged** in effigy.
>
> Portraits of the faculty were **hung** in the student union.

he/she. Using **he/she** (or *his/her* or *s/he*) is a way to avoid a sexist pronoun reference. Many readers find expressions with slashes clumsy and prefer *he or she* and *his or her.* See Sections 29b and 40d.

hisself. A nonstandard form. Use **himself** instead.

hopefully. Some readers object to using the adverb *hopefully* as a sentence modifier. They would consider the following sentence ambiguous and incorrect.

> The government, **hopefully**, will not limit medical procedures for the elderly.

Hopefully, they argue, should be used to mean only "with hope," not "we hope" or it is hoped."

> Traders watched **hopefully** as stock prices improved.

However, English includes many adverbs like *hopefully* that function as sentence modifiers, including words such as *thankfully* and *honestly*. By precedent and general usage, *hopefully* seems entrenched as a sentence modifier.

illicit/elicit. See **elicit/illicit**.

illusion/allusion. See **allusion/illusion**.

imminent/eminent. See **eminent/imminent**.

imply/infer. **Imply** means "to suggest" or "to convey an idea without stating it." **Infer** is what you might do to figure out what someone else has implied: you examine evidence and draw conclusions from it.

> The pilot's voice **implied** that the aircraft was out of danger, but the passengers **inferred** that the landing would not be routine.

incredible/incredulous. **Incredible** means "unbelievable"; **incredulous** means "unwilling to believe" and "doubting." See also **credible/credulous**.

> The press found the governor's explanation for her wealth **incredible**; they were **incredulous** when she attributed her vast holdings to coupon savings.

infer/imply. See **imply/infer**.

* **infinitive.** A verbal that can usually be identified by the word **to** preceding the base form of a verb: *to strive, to find*. Infinitives also take other forms to show various tenses and voices: *to be striving, to have found*. Infinitives can act as nouns, adjectives, adverbs, and absolutes (see Section 24a-1).

INFINITIVE AS NOUN	**To dominate** a grandmaster in chess is not easy. subject of the sentence
INFINITIVE AS ADJECTIVE	Amanda had many posters **to redesign**. modifies the noun *posters*

INFINITIVE AS ADVERB	Mr. Stavros laughed **to forget** his troubles. modifies the verb *laughed*
INFINITIVE AS ABSOLUTE	**To be blunt**, the paper is nonsensical.

* **interjection.** A word that expresses emotion or feeling, but that is not grammatically a part of a sentence. Interjections can be punctuated as exclamations (!) or attached to a sentence with a comma. Interjections include *oh, hey, wow,* and *well.*

irregardless. A nonstandard form. Use **regardless** instead.

irritate/aggravate. See **aggravate/irritate.**

its/it's. Don't confuse these terms. **It's** is a contraction for *it is.* **Its** is a possessive pronoun meaning "belonging to it." See Section 28c for a discussion of this distinction.

judgment/judgement. The British spell this word with two *e*'s. Americans spell it with just one: **judgment.**

kind of. This expression is colloquial when used to mean "rather." Avoid *kind of* in formal writing.

less than. See **fewer than/less than.**

lie/lay. These two verbs cause much trouble and confusion. Here are their parts. (Notice that the past tense of **lie** is the same as the present tense of **lay.**)

PRESENT	PAST	PRESENT PARTICIPLE	PAST PARTICIPLE
lie (to recline)	lay	lying	lain
lay (to place)	laid	laying	laid

It may help you to remember that **to lie** (meaning "to recline") is *intransitive*—that is, it doesn't take an object.

Travis **lies** under the cottonwood tree.

He **lay** there all afternoon.

To lay (meaning "to place" or "to put") is *transitive*—it takes an object.

As we watch, Morgan **lays** a *cookie* on Travis's desk.

Yesterday, she **laid** a *doughnut* on his desk.

like/as. **As, as if**, or **as though** are preferred to *like* when a comparison involves a subject and a verb.

Mr. Butcher is self-disciplined, **as** you would expect a champion weightlifter to be. It looks **as if** he will win the local competition again this year.

Like is acceptable as part of a prepositional phrase.

Lucianne's old Edsel still runs **like** a top.

* **linking verb.** A verb, often a form of *to be,* that connects a subject to a word or phrase that extends or completes its meaning (see **predicate adjective** and **predicate nominative**). Other common linking verbs are *to seem, to appear, to feel,* and *to become.*

Bob King **is** Dean of Liberal Arts.

He **feels** confident.

literally. When you write that something is **literally** true, you mean that it is exactly as you have stated. The following sentence means that Bernice emitted heated water vapor, an unlikely event no matter how angry she was.

Bernice **literally** steamed when Ike ordered her to marry him.

If you want to keep the image (*steamed*), omit **literally**.

Bernice steamed when Ike ordered her to marry him.

lose/loose. **Lose** is a verb, meaning "to misplace," "to be deprived of," or "to be defeated." **Loose** can be either an adjective or a verb. As an adjective, **loose** means "not tight"; as a verb, **loose** means "to let go" or "to release."

The team might **lose** its first game.

The strap on Martin's helmet had worked **loose**.

It **loosened** so much that Martin **lost** his helmet.

majority/plurality. A **majority** is more than half of a group; a **plurality** is the largest part of a group when there is *less than a majority.* In an election, for example, a candidate who wins 50.1 percent of the vote can claim a **majority**. One who wins a race with 40 percent of the vote may claim a **plurality**, but not a majority.

may/can. See **can/may**.

media/medium. **Medium** is the singular of **media**, commonly used to refer to newspapers and magazines, as well as television and radio.

No single **medium** is as powerful as television.

Visual **media** are discussed throughout the textbook.

might of. A nonstandard form. Use **might have** instead.

* **modal auxiliary.** An auxiliary verb that indicates possibility, necessity, permission, desire, capability, and so on. Modal auxiliaries include *can, could, may, might, will, shall, should, ought,* and *must.* See Section 32a.

Hector **can** write. capability

Hector **might** write. possibility

Hector **must** write. necessity

moral, morale. As a noun, **moral** is a lesson; **morale** is a state of mind.

The **moral** of the fable was to avoid temptation.

The **morale** of the team was destroyed by the accident.

must of. Nonstandard. Use **must have** instead.

nice. This adjective usually has little impact when used to mean "pleasant": *It was a **nice** day.* **Nice** can be used effectively to mean "precise" or "fine."

He made a **nice** distinction between the two proposals.

* **noun.** A word that names a person, place, thing, idea, or quality. In sentences, nouns can serve as subjects, objects, complements, appositives, and even modifiers. There are many classes of nouns: **common** and **proper** (see Section 41b-7), **concrete** and **abstract** (see Section 17b-1), **collective** (see Section 22c), and **count** and **noncount** (see Section 33b).

number/amount. See **amount/number**.

off of. A wordy expression. **Off** is enough: *Al drove his Jeep **off** the road.*

O.K./OK/okay. Not the best choice for formal writing. But give the expression respect. It's an internationally recognized expression of approval. OK?

* **participle.** A verb form that is used as a modifier. The present participle ends with **-ing**. For regular verbs, the past participle ends with **-ed**; for irregular verbs, the form of the past participle will vary. See Section 24a for details about forms and uses.

* **parts of speech.** The eight common categories by which words in a sentence are identified according to what they do, how they are formed, where they are placed, and what they mean. These basic categories are **nouns, pronouns, adjectives, verbs, adverbs, prepositions, conjunctions**, and **interjections**.

persecute/prosecute. **Persecute** means "to oppress" or "to torment"; **prosecute** is a legal term meaning "to bring charges or legal proceedings."

Lily felt **persecuted** by criticisms of her political activism.

She threatened to **prosecute** anyone who interfered with her First Amendment rights.

personal/personnel. **Personal** refers to what is private, belonging to an individual. **Personnel** are the people staffing an office or institution.

Drug testing all airline **personnel** might infringe on **personal** freedom.

phenomena/phenomenon. Remember to use **phenomenon** as the singular form.

The **phenomenon** of meteor showers is common in August.

Many other astral **phenomena** are linked to particular seasons.

plurality/majority. See **majority/plurality**.

plus. Don't use **plus** as a conjunction or conjunctive adverb meaning "and," "moreover," "besides," or "in addition to."

* **predicate.** See **verb**.

* **predicate adjective.** An adjective that follows a linking verb and describes the subject.

Barack Obama *was* **popular** in 2009.

I *feel* **uneasy**.

It *is* **cold** today.

* **predicate nominative.** A noun or pronoun that follows a linking verb and restates what the subject is.

Barack Obama *is* the **44th President of the United States**.

Hillary Clinton *became* **Secretary of State** in 2009.

She *was* Obama's **choice** for that job.

prejudice/prejudiced. The noun form of **prejudice** is often used where a verb or adjectival form (**prejudiced**) is required.

WRONG	Joe Kamakura is **prejudice** against vegans.
RIGHT	Joe Kamakura is **prejudice<u>d</u>** against vegans.
WRONG	**Prejudice** people are found in every walk of life.
RIGHT	**Prejudice<u>d</u>** people are found in every walk of life.
COMPARE	**Prejudice** is found in every walk of life.

* **preposition.** A word that links a noun or pronoun to the rest of a sentence. Prepositions point out many kinds of basic relationships: *on, above, to, for, in, out, through, by,* and so on. The combination of a preposition and a noun or pronoun produces a **prepositional phrase**: *on our house, above it, to him, in love, through them, by the garden gate.* (See Section 16c-1.)

principal/principle. **Principal** means "chief" or "most important." It also names the head of an elementary or secondary school (remember "The **principal** is your pal"?). Finally, it can be a sum of money lent or borrowed.

Ike intended to be the **principal** breadwinner of the household.

A **principle**, on the other hand, is a guiding rule or fundamental truth.

Ike declared it was against his **principles** to have his wife work.

proceed to. A wordy and redundant construction when it merely delays the real action of a sentence (see Section 17c-3).

WORDY	We **proceeded to** open the strongbox.
TIGHTER	We **opened** the strongbox.

* **pronoun.** A word that acts like a noun but doesn't name a specific person, place, or thing—*I, you, he, she, it, they, whom, who, what, myself, oneself, this, these, that, all, both, anybody,* and so on. There are many varieties of pronouns: **personal, relative, interrogative, intensive, reflexive, demonstrative, indefinite**, and **reciprocal**. See Chapters 25– 29 and individual glossary entries for details about each type.

real. Often used as a colloquial version of **very**: *I was **real** scared.* This usage is inappropriate in academic writing.

really. An adverb too vague to make much of an impression in many sentences: *It was **really** hot; I am **really** sorry.* Replace **really** with a more precise expression or delete it.

reason is . . . because. This expression is redundant. Use one half of the expression or the other—not both.

REDUNDANT	The **reason** the cat is aggressive is **because** she is protecting her kittens.
REVISED	The **reason** the cat is aggressive is **that** she is protecting her kittens.
REVISED	The cat is aggressive **because** she is protecting her kittens.

refer/allude. See **allude/refer**.

reign/rein. To **reign** means to rule: *Monarchs **reign**.* To **rein** means to pull back: *Juan Bernardo **reined** in his horse.*

set/sit. These two verbs can cause problems. Here are their parts.

PRESENT	PAST	PRESENT PARTICIPLE	PAST PARTICIPLE
set (put down)	set	setting	set
sit (take a seat)	sat	sitting	sat

It may help you to remember that **to sit** (meaning "to take a seat") is *intransitive*—that is, it doesn't take an object. You can't sit *something.*

Haskell **sits** under the cottonwood tree.

He **sat** there all afternoon.

To set (meaning "to place" or "to put") is *transitive*—it takes an object.

Jenny **set** a *plate* on the table.

should of. Mistaken form of **should have.**

sit/set. See **set/sit.**

so. Vague when used as an intensifier, especially when no explanation follows **so**: *Ellen was **so** sad.* Explain how sad she was: *Ellen was **so** sad that she cried.*

* **split infinitive.** An infinitive interrupted by an adverb: *to **boldly** go; to **really** try.* Though correct, split infinitives offend some readers. To alter a split infinitive, simply place the adverb somewhere else in your sentence: *to go **boldly**.* See Section 24c.

stationary/stationery. **Stationary**, an adjective, means "immovable, fixed in place." **Stationery** is a noun meaning "writing material." The words are not interchangeable.

* **subject.** A word or phrase that names what a sentence is about. The simple subject of a sentence is a single word; the complete subject is the simple subject and all its modifiers (see Section 16a).

simple subject
The **captain** of the new squad quit.

complete subject
The captain of the new squad quit.

* **subject complement.** A word or phrase that follows a **linking verb** and completes its meaning. Subject complements can be nouns and pronouns (called **predicate nominatives**) or adjectives (called **predicate adjectives**).

subj. l.v. subj.comp.
Sanjay Sacomdri *is* a **student representative**.

subj. l.v. subj. comp.
The performers *are* **he and she**.

subj. l.v. subj. comp.
The speaker of the house *seems* **unhappy**.

* **subordinating conjunctions.** See **conjunctions, subordinating**.

supposed to. Many writers forget the ***d*** at the end of **suppose** when the word is used with auxiliary verbs: *Calina was **supposed** to call.*

than/then. These words are occasionally confused. **Than** is a conjunction expressing difference or comparison; **then** is an adverb expressing time, sequence, or causation.

If the film is still playing tomorrow, Shannon would rather go **then than** today.

theirselves. A nonstandard form. Use **themselves** instead: *The strikers placed **themselves** in jeopardy.*

then/than. See **than/then**.

thusly. A fussy, nonstandard form. Don't use it. **Thus** is stuffy enough without the *-ly*.

till/until. **Until** is used more often in school and business writing, though the words are usually interchangeable. No apostrophe is used with **till**. You may occasionally see the poetic form **'til**, but don't use it in academic or business writing.

to/too/two. A writer in a hurry can easily put down the preposition **to** when the adverb **too** is intended and vice versa. Homonym errors with **two** are more rare.

toward/towards. **Toward** is preferred, though either form is correct.

try and. An informal expression. In writing, use **try to** instead.

INCORRECT	After its defeat, the soccer team decided to **try and** drown its sorrows.
REVISED	After its defeat, the soccer team decided to **try to** drown its sorrows.

uninterested/disinterested. See **disinterested/uninterested**.

unique. Like other absolute adjectives (see Section 30d), **unique** is a word that logically can't be compared or qualified. Expressions such as *most unique, more unique*, or *very unique* don't make sense. When properly used, **unique** should stand alone.

INCORRECT	Woody Hayes's coaching methods were **very unique**.
REVISED	Woody Hayes's coaching methods were **unique**.

until/till. See **till/until**.

used to. Many writers forget the ***d*** at the end of **use:** *Leroy was **used to** studying after soccer.*

utilize. Many readers prefer the simpler term **use:** *Dr. Bing **used** a scalpel rarely.*

* **verb.** The word or phrase that establishes the action of a sentence or expresses a state of being (see Chapter 23).

verb
The music **played** on.

verb
Turning the volume down **proved** to be difficult.

A verb, along with all its auxiliaries, modifiers, and complements, is called the **predicate** of a sentence.

complete subj. predicate
David's band **would have played throughout the night**.

complete subj. predicate
Turning the volume down on the band **proved to be much more difficult than the neighbors had anticipated it might be**.

* **verbals.** Verb forms that act like nouns, adjectives, or adverbs. The three kinds of verbals are **infinitives, participles**, and **gerunds**. Like verbs, verbals can take objects to form phrases. But verbals are described as nonfinite (that is, "unfinished") verbs because they cannot alone make complete predicates. A complete sentence requires a **finite** verb—that is, a verb that changes form to indicate person, number, and tense. See Chapter 24.

well/good. See **good/well**.

who/whom. Use **who** when the pronoun is a subject; use **whom** when it is an object. See Section 28c.

Who wrote the ticket?

To whom was the ticket given?

with regards to. Drop the **s** in **regards**. The correct expression is **with regard to**.

won't. Writers sometimes forget the apostrophe in this contraction.

would of. Mistaken form of **would have**.

your/you're. Homonyms that often get switched. **You're** is the contraction for *you are*; **your** is a possessive form for the second person pronoun *you*.

You're certain Maxine has been to Iran?

Your certainty on this matter may be important.

Credits

TEXT CREDITS

Abbey, Edward. "Desert Solitaire." New York: McGraw-Hill, 1968.

Angelou, Maya. "Champion of the World" from *I Know Why the Caged Bird Sings.* New York: Random House, 1969.

Angier, Natalie. "Mating for Life" from *The Beauty of the Beastly.* New York: Houghton Mifflin, 1995

Anzaldúa, Gloria. "How to Tame a Wild Tongue" by from *Borderlands/La Frontera: The New Mestiza.* Copyright © 1987, 1999, 2007 by Gloria Anzaldúa. Reprinted by permission of Aunt Lute Books. www.auntlute.com.

Barnett, Rosalind Chait and Caryl Rivers. "The Persistence of Gender Myths in Math." Originally appeared in *Education Week,* October 13, 2004. Reprinted by permission of Rosalind Chait Barnett.

Bauknight, Lee. "Two for the Road."

Bilger, Burkhard. "The Egg Men: How Breakfast Gets Served at the Flamingo Hotel in Las Vegas," from *The New Yorker,* September 5, 2005. Reprinted by permission of author.

Blackwell Synergy. Screenshot of "Scholarly Articles." Reprinted by permission of Wiley-Blackwell.

Bloodworth, Dennis. *The Chinese Looking Glass.* New York: Farrar, Straus & Giroux, 1980.

Boyer, Ernest L. "Creating the New American College." Originally appeared in *The Chronicle of Higher Education,* 1994.

Broache, Anne. "Oh Deer!" Originally published in *Smithsonian,* October, 2005. Copyright © 2009 Smithsonian Institution. Reprinted by permission from Smithsonian Magazine. All rights reserved. Reproduction in any medium is strictly prohibited without permission from Smithsonian Institution. Such permission may be requested from Smithsonian Magazine.

Broder, Eric. Article in *The Cleveland Free Times.*

Brookings Institution. Screenshot of "Getting Real about Gas Prices." Reprinted by permission.

Chesler, Ellen. "Woman of Valor: Margaret Sanger and the Birth Control Movement in America." Copyright © 1992 by Ellen Chesler. Reprinted by permission of Simon & Schuster, Inc.

Churchill, Winston. From a speech to the House of Commons, January 1952.

Codell, Esmé Raji. *Educating Esmé: Diary of a Teacher's First Year.* Copyright © 1999 by Esmé Raji Codell. Reprinted by permission of Algonquin Books of Chapel Hill. All rights reserved.

Cofer, Judith Ortiz. "Silent Dancing: A Partial Remembrance of a Puerto Rican Childhood." Copyright © 1990 by Arte Publico Press – University of Houston. Reprinted by permission of Arte Publico Press – University of Houston.

Costas, Bob. From the Eulogy for Mickey Mantle, August 15, 1995.

Cummings, E. E. "anyone lived in a pretty how town." Copyright © 1940, © 1968, 1991 by the Trustees for the E. E. Cummings Trust, from *Complete Poems: 1904-1962* by E. E. Cummings, edited by George J. Firmage. Used by permission of Liveright Publishing Corporation.

Didion, Joan. "Georgia O'Keeffe" from *The White Album.* New York: Simon & Schuster, 1979.

Ebert, Roger. "Casablanca" from Roger Ebert's web page, Ebert's Great Movies, at www.suntimes.com.

Edge, John T. "I'm Not Leaving Until I Eat This Thing," *Oxford American Magazine*, Issue 19, September/October 1999.

Ellis, Andy. "Stellartone Tonestyler" from *Guitar Player Magazine Online*, January 2005. Reprinted by permission.

Engle, Gary. "What Makes Superman So Darned American?" from *Superman at Fifty: The Persistence of a Legend* by Gary Engle & Dennis Dooley. New Orleans: Octavia Books, 1987.

Farming Futures. "The Carbon Cycle of a Farm" diagram from Farming Futures at www.farmingfutures.org.uk. Reprinted by permission of Farming Futures.

Gould, Stephen Jay. "The Power of Narrative" from *The Urchin in Storm.* New York: W. W. Norton & Company, 1987.

Hamilton, Joan C. "Journey to the Center of the Mind." Reprinted from the April 19, 2004 issue of *Business Week* by special permission. Copyright © 2004 by The McGraw-Hill Companies, Inc.

Hillenbrand, Laura. *Seabiscuit: An American Legend.* New York: Random House, 2001.

Hollandsworth, Skip. "Tyler Hollandsworth" and the Cover from *Texas Monthly*, September 2003. Reprinted by permission of Texas Monthly.

IMPULSE. Screenshot of the Impulse web page at http://impulse.appstate.edu/arch_index.php. Reprinted by permission of IMPULSE.

Isaacson, Walter. *Ben Franklin: An American Life*. New York: Simon & Schuster, 2003.

Johnson, Chuck. "Baker Stands by Heat Comments," *USA Today*, July 7, 2003.

Johnson, Paul. *Intellectuals*. New York: Harper & Row, Inc., 1988.

Johnson, Steven. "Watching TV Makes You Smarter." Originally appeared in *The New York Times Magazine*, April 24, 2005.

Kleine, Ted. "Living the Lansing Dream," *Next: Young American Writers on the New Generation*, edited by Eric Liu. Copyright © 1994 by Eric Liu. Used by permission of the author and W. W. Norton & Company, Inc.

Lapham, Lewis. "Ars longa, vita brevis," *Harper's Magazine*, October 1997.

Lewon, Dennis. "Malaria's Not-So-Magic Bullet," *Escape Magazine*, July 1999. Reprinted by permission of author.

McGrath, Charles. "Not Funnies" from *The New York Times Magazine*, July 11, 2004. Reprinted by permission of The New York Times Syndication Sales Corporation.

McManus, Ray. "Split P Soup Flyer." Reprinted by permission of author.

Moffett, Michael. "How College Students Choose Their Majors" from *Coming of Age in New Jersey*. Piscataway: Rutgers University Press, 1989.

The Nation. February 16, 2009 screen capture of www.thenation.com. Reprinted by permission of *The Nation* magazine. For subscription information, call 1-800-333-8536. Portions of each week's Nation magazine can be accessed at http://www.thenation.com.

Nuland, Sherwin B. "Medical Fads: Bran, Midwives and Leeches," *New York Times*, June 25, 1995.

Olds, Sharon. "The One Girl at the Boy's Party" from *The Dead and The Living*. Copyright © 1987 by Sharon Olds. Used by permission of Alfred A. Knopf, a division of Random House, Inc.

The Onion."Obama's New Fuel Efficiency Plan" from *The Onion*, May 26, 2009, Issue 45-22 from http://www.theonion.com/content/infograph/obamas_new_fuel_efficiency. Copyright © 2009, by ONION, INC. Reprinted with permission of THE ONION.

Patoski, Joe Nick, et al. "Three Cheers for High School Football." *Texas Monthly*, October 1999. Reprinted by permission of Texas Monthly.

Peters, Ralph. "Let 'Em Eat Wurst" from *New York Post Online*, July 13, 2003.

Ravitch, Diane. "Educational Insensitivity." Originally appeared in *The New York Times*, June 5, 2002. Reprinted by permission of author.

Sadker, Myra and David Sadker. *Failing at Fairness: How Our Schools Cheat Girls*. New York: Touchstone Books/Simon & Schuster, 1994.

Santiago, Chiori. "The Fine and Friendly Art of Luis Jimenez," *Smithsonian Magazine*, November 1993. Reprinted by permission of Kathleen Hunt, Trustee and Roberto Santiago.

Schlosser, Eric. *Fast Food Nation: The Dark Side of the All-American Meal.* Copyright © 2001 by Eric Schlosser. Reprinted by permission of Houghton Mifflin Harcourt Publishing Company. All rights reserved.

Schor, Juliet. *The Overworked American: The Unexpected Decline of Leisure.* New York: Basic Books, 1991.

Sigma Tau Delta Newsletter, Spring 2009. Reprinted by permission of the Sigma Tau Delta International English Honor Society.

Stateman, Alison. "Postcards from the Edge," *New York Times*, June 15, 2003.

Stern, Barbara Lang. "Tears Can Be Crucial to Your Physical and Emotional Health." Originally appeared in *Vogue*, June 1979.

Sternberrgh, Adam. "Got Bub All Up in the Hizzle, Yo! If it weren't for rap, our only new words would be "ideate" and "synergy," which first appeared in *The National Post*, March 15, 2003. Reprinted by permission of author.

Stevenson, Seth. "Coffeeholics – A Dunkin Donut Ad for An Addict Nation," *Slate*, April 24, 2006. Reprinted by permission of author and Dunkin' Brands Inc.

Travis, Clay. "ClayNation: Madden Curse doesn't really exist – yet," *Spin on Sports*, October 2, 2006. Reprinted by permission of author.

Turtel, Joel. *Public Schools, Public Menace: How Public Schools Lie to Parents and Betray Our Children, Vol. 1.* Staten Island: Liberty Books, 2005.

University of Texas at Austin. "The Library Catalog Search page." Reprinted by permission of The University of Texas at Austin.

Utne Reader. Screenshot from the Utne Reader home page at http://utne.com. Reprinted by permission of the Utne Reader.

Walzer, Michael. "Feed the Face," *The New Republic*, June 9, 1997. Reprinted by permission of author.

The Weekly Standard. Screenshot of The Weekly Standard web page at http://www.weeklystandard. Reprinted by permission of The Weekly Standard.

West, Cornel. "Race Matters." Boston: Beacon Press, 1993.

Williams, Ted. "Only You Can Postpone Forest Fires," *Sierra*, July/August 1995.

Wright, Richard. *Native Son.* New York: Harper & Brothers, 1940.

Yankelovich, Daniel. "The Work Ethic is Underemployed," *Psychology Today,* May 1982.

Yonke, David. "Threat of War Spurs U.S. Soul-Searching." *The Toledo Blade,* March 1, 2003.

Zinsser, William. *American Places: A Writer's Pilgrimage to 15 of This Country's Most Visited and Cherished Sites.* New York: HarperCollins Publishers, 1992.

PHOTO CREDITS

p. 1: Joel Sartore/National Geographic Image Collection; p. 3 (left): Christy Friend; p. 3 (right): Pearson Education/PH College; p. 3 (bottom): Getty Images; p. 9 (left): Shutterstock; p. 9 (center): Fotosearch.Com, LLC; p. 9 (right): iStockphoto International/Royalty Free; p. 9 (bottom left): David Young-Wolf/PhotoEdit Inc.; p. 9 (bottom center): Spin Magazine; p. 9 (bottom right): David Young-Wolf/PhotoEdit Inc.; p. 16: Ulrike Welsch/ PhotoEdit Inc.; p. 22: AP/Wide World Photos; p. 33 (left): Chuck Savage/ Savage Productions Inc.; p. 33 (right): Getty Images; p. 46 (left): Central Pennsylvania College; p. 46 (center): David Young-Wolff PhotoEdit Inc.; p. 46 (right): Mid-South Community College; p. 54 (left): Library of Congress; p. 54 (right): Corbis; p. 56: General Motors; p. 60: Photofest; p. 75: Chris Johns/National Geographic Image Collection; p. 77 (top): Time Life Pictures/ Getty Images; p. 77 (bottom): Mark Schornak; p. 82 (left): The University of Arizona Press; p. 82 (right): National Institute of Health; p. 94 (right): Peter Macdiarmid/Getty Images News; p. 94 (left): Copyright ©, Pittsburgh Post Gazette, 2009, all rights reserved. Reprinted with permission; p. 108: The Nation; p. 130: Pepsi; p. 132: National Institute of Health; p. 148 (left): Getty Images; p. 155: Christy Friend; p. 156: Christy Friend; p. 158: Mike Simons/ Getty Images; p. 161 (left): Photofest; p. 161 (right): Photofest; p. 167: Photofest; p. 168: The Granger Collection; p. 181: Tim Laman/National Geographic Image Collection; p. 194 (left): Lucasfilm Ltd.; p. 194 (right): Hulton Archive Photos/Getty Images Inc.; p. 215: CORBIS; p. 230: Brendan Smialowski/ Getty Images News; p. 269: George H. H. Huey Photography, Inc.; p. 305: John Eastcott and Yva Momatiuk/National Geographic Image Collection; p. 306: American InkMaker Magazine; p. 347: Photofest; p. 354: John Ruszkiewicz; p. 363: Brad Barket/Getty Images; p. 365: Tim Laman/National Geographic Image Collection; p. 366: Getty Images; p. 381: Corbis; p. 507: Tim Laman/National Geographic Image Collection; p. 554: John Ruszkiewicz; p. 583: Ralph Lee Hopkins/National Geographic Image Collection; p. 585: MarSci: The Premier Journal for undergraduate research in the marine and aquatic sciences; p. 610: “Photo by Sam Jones from Rolling Stone issue dated May 27, 2009 © Rolling Stone LLC 2009. All Rights Reserved. Broadcast by Permission”; p. 641: Anne Keiser/National Geographic Image Collection; p. 653: Christy Friend

Index

A

B

D

E

F

J

K

L

M

N

O

P

Q

R

S

U

V

W

Y

Z

Revision Guide: Editing and Proofreading Symbols

The boldface chapter and section numbers to the right of each symbol and explanation direct you to relevant places in this book.

Symbol	Explanation	Section
abbr	Problem with an **abbr**eviation	42a
adj	Problem with an **adj**ective.	30b–d
adv	Problem with an **adv**erb.	30e–f
agr	Problem with subject-verb or pronoun-antecedent **agr**eement.	22, 27
apos	An **apos**trophe is missing or misused.	25b
art	An **art**icle is misused.	25c, 33b
awk	**Awk**ward. Sentence reads poorly, but problem is difficult to identify.	16f–j, 17a–c
cap	A word needs to be capitalized.	41b
case	A pronoun is in the wrong **case**.	28
coh	A sentence or paragraph lacks **coh**erence.	12a,12b
cs	Sentence contains a **c**omma **s**plice.	35c
div	Word **div**ided in the wrong place.	40c
dm (or dang)	**D**angling **m**odifier. A modifying phrase has nothing to attach itself to.	30a
frag	Sentence **frag**ment.	35a
ital	**Ital**ics needed.	41a
lc	Use a **l**ower**c**ase instead of a capital letter.	41b
mm	A **m**odifier is **m**isplaced.	30a
num	Problem with the use of **num**bers.	42b
p	Error in **p**unctuation.	32 34–38
pass	A **pass**ive verb is used ineffectively.	17a, 23e
pl	**Pl**ural form is faulty.	25a
pron	**Pron**oun is faulty in some way.	26–29
ref	Not clear what a pronoun **ref**ers to.	26
rep	Word or phrase is **rep**eated ineffectively.	17c
run-on (or fs)	A **run-on** sentence or fused sentence.	35d
sexist	A word or phrase is potentially offensive.	15d
sp	A word is mis**sp**elled.	5b
sub	**Sub**ordination is faulty.	16g
trans	A **trans**ition is weak or absent.	14
vb	Problem with **verb** form.	23, 32
w (or wrdy)	A sentence is **w**ordy.	17c
ww	**W**rong **w**ord in this situation.	15
¶	Begin a new paragraph.	12
no ¶	Do not begin a new paragraph.	12
⊙	Insert a period.	34a
^,	Insert a comma.	36a–c 36e
no ^,	No comma needed.	36d
’∨	Insert an apostrophe.	25b
^:	Insert a colon.	37b
^;	Insert a semicolon.	37a
”∨	Insert quotation marks.	38a
//	Make these items parallel.	16h
^	Insert.	
℘	Cut this word or phrase.	
#	Leave a space.	
⌒	Close up a space.	
✕	Problem here; find it.	
∼	Reverse these items.	

Taking Control of Your Writing

This edition features twenty-six "Taking Control" sections offering enhanced coverage of those issues and concerns that will make an immediate difference in your writing. In these sections, you will find helpful explanations and additional examples, as well as boxes that provide candid advice for managing each special topic. All the "Taking Control" sections are listed below, and throughout the book, they are identified by an apple icon in the margin.